ACCA
STUDY TEXT

Professional Paper 10

Accounting and Audit Practice (Accounting)

New in this June 1998 edition

- Thorough, reliable updating of material to 1 June 1998, taking into account the December 1997 exams

- FRS 9, FRS 10 and FRSSE have been incorporated

- List of Key Terms has been expanded

- Many more 'Exam Focus Points' have been added to give you an idea of how we think the Examiner's mind works

FOR DECEMBER 1998 AND JUNE 1999 EXAMS

BPP Publishing
June 1998

First edition 1993
Sixth edition June 1998

ISBN 0 7517 0134 3 (Previous edition 0 7517 0074 6)

British Library Cataloguing-in-Publication Data
A catalogue record for this book is available from the British Library

Published by

BPP Publishing Limited
Aldine House, Aldine Place
London W12 8AW

http://www.bpp.co.uk

Printed in Great Britain by
WM Print Ltd
Frederick Street
Walsall
West Midlands WS2 9NE

We are grateful to the Association of Chartered Certified Accountants for permission to reproduce in this text the syllabus and teaching guide of which the Association holds the copyright.

We are also grateful to the Association of Chartered Certified Accountants for permission to reproduce past examination questions in our Exam Question Bank. The Exam Answer Bank has been prepared by BPP Publishing Limited.

Contents

Page

HOW TO USE THIS STUDY TEXT

Aims of this Study Text

To provide you with the knowledge and understanding, skills and applied techniques required for passing the exam

The Study Text has been written around the ACCA's Official Syllabus and the ACCA's Official 1998-9 Teaching Guide (reproduced below, and cross-referenced to where in the text each topic is covered).

- It is **comprehensive**. We do not omit sections of the syllabus as the examiner is liable to examine any angle of any part of the syllabus - and you do not want to be left high and dry.

- It is **up-to-date as at 1 June 1998**, which means that it fulfils the requirement for the December 1998 exams that students should be up-to-date as at 1 June 1998.

- And it is **on-target** - we do not include any material which is not examinable. You can therefore rely on the BPP Study Text as the stand-alone source of all your information for the exam, without worrying that any of the material is irrelevant.

To allow you to study in the way that best suits your learning style and the time you have available, by following your personal Study Plan (see below)

You may be studying at home on your own until the date of the exam, or you may be attending a full-time course. You may like to (and have time to) read every word, or you may prefer to (or only have time to) skim-read and devote the remainder of your time to question practice. Wherever you fall in the spectrum, you will find the BPP Study Text meets your needs in designing and following your personal Study Plan.

To tie in with the other components of the BPP Effective Study Package to ensure you have the best possible chance of passing the exam

Recommended period of use	Elements of BPP Effective Study Package
3-12 months before exam	**Study Text** Acquisition of knowledge, understanding, skills and applied techniques
1-6 months before exam	**Practice and Revision Kit** Tutorial Questions and helpful checklists of the key points lead you into each area. There are then numerous exam questions to try, graded by topic area, along with realistic suggested solutions prepared by BPP's own authors in the light of the Examiner's Reports. June 1999 examinees will find the 1999 edition of the Kit invaluable for bringing them up-to-date as at 1 December 1998, the cut-off date for the June 1999 examinable material
last minute - 3 months before exam	**Passcards** Short, memorable notes focused on what is most likely to come up in the exam you will be sitting

Settling down to study

By this stage in your career you are probably a very experienced learner and taker of exams. But have you ever thought about *how* you learn? Let's have a quick look at the key elements required for effective learning. You can then identify your learning style and go on to design your own approach to how you are going to study this text - your personal Study Plan.

Key element of learning	Using the BPP Study Text
Motivation	You can rely on the comprehensiveness and technical quality of BPP. You've chosen the right Study Text - so you're in pole position to pass your exam!
Clear objectives and standards	Do you want to be a prizewinner or simply achieve a moderate pass? Decide.
Feedback	Follow through the examples in this text and do the questions and the Quick Quizzes. Evaluate your efforts critically - how are you doing?
Study plan	You need to be honest about your progress to yourself - do not be over-confident, but don't be negative either. Make your Study Plan (see below) and try to stick to it. Focus on the short-term objectives - completing two chapters a night, say - but beware of losing sight of your study objectives
Practice	Use the Quick Quizzes and Chapter Roundups to refresh your memory regularly after you have completed your initial study of each chapter

These introductory pages let you see exactly what you are up against. However you study, you should:

- **read through the syllabus and teaching guide** - this will help you to identify areas you have already covered, perhaps at a lower level of detail, and areas that are totally new to you

- **study the examination paper section**, where we show you the format of the exam (how many and what kind of questions etc) and analyse all the papers set so far under the syllabus.

Key study steps

The following steps are, in our experience, the ideal way to study for professional exams. You can of course adapt it for your particular learning style (see below).

Tackle the chapters in the order you find them in the Study Text. Taking into account your individual learning style, follow these key study steps for each chapter.

Key study steps	Activity
Step 1 *Chapter topic list*	Study the list. Each numbered topic denotes a numbered section in the chapter
Step 2 *Introduction*	Read it through. It is designed to show you *why* the topics in the chapter need to be studied - how they lead on from previous topics, and how they lead into subsequent ones
Step 3 *Knowledge brought forward boxes*	In these we highlight information and techniques that it is assumed you have 'brought forward' with you from your earlier studies. If there are matters which have changed recently due to legislation etc then these topics are explained in full. Do not panic if you do not feel instantly comfortable with the content - it should come back to you as we develop the subject for this paper. If you are really unsure, we advise you to go back to your previous notes
Step 4 *Explanations*	Proceed methodically through the chapter, reading each section thoroughly and making sure you understand. Where a topic has been examined, we state the month and year of examination against the appropriate heading. You should pay particular attention to these topics
Step 5 *Key terms* and *Exam focus points*	• **Key terms** can often earn you *easy marks* if you state them clearly and correctly in an appropriate exam answer (and they are indexed at the back of the text so you can check easily that you are on top of all of them when you come to revise) • **Exam focus points** give you a good idea of how the examiner tends to examine certain topics - and also pinpoint *easy marks*
Step 6 *Note taking*	Take brief notes if you wish, avoiding the temptation to copy out too much
Step 7 *Examples*	Follow each through to its solution very carefully
Step 8 *Case examples*	Study each one, and try if you can to add flesh to them from your own experience - they are designed to show how the topics you are studying come alive (and often come unstuck) in the real world
Step 9 *Questions*	Make a very good attempt at each one
Step 10 *Answers*	Check yours against ours, and make sure you understand any discrepancies
Step 11 *Chapter roundup*	Check through it very carefully, to make sure you have grasped the major points it is highlighting

 BPP Publishing

Key study steps	Activity
Step 12 *Quick quiz*	When you are happy that you have covered the chapter, use the **Quick quiz** to check your recall of the topics covered. The answers are in the paragraphs in the chapter that we refer you to
Step 13 *Examination question(s)*	Either at this point, or later when you are thinking about revising, make a full attempt at the **Examination question(s)** suggested at the very end of the chapter. You can find these at the end of the Study Text, along with the **Answers** so you can see how you did. We highlight for you which ones are introductory, and which are of the full standard you would expect to find in an exam

Developing your personal Study Plan

Preparing a Study Plan (and sticking closely to it) is one of the key elements in learning success.

First you need to be aware of your style of learning. There are four typical learning styles. Consider yourself in the light of the following descriptions. and work out which you fit most closely. You can then plan to follow the key study steps in the sequence suggested.

Learning styles	Characteristics	Sequence of key study steps in the BPP Study Text
Theorist	Seeks to understand principles before applying them in practice	1, 2, 3, 4, 7, 8, 5, 9/10, 11, 12, 13 (6 continuous)
Reflector	Seeks to observe phenomena, thinks about them and then chooses to act	
Activist	Prefers to deal with practical, active problems; does not have much patience with theory	1, 2, 9/10 (read through), 7, 8, 5, 11, 3, 4, 9/10 (full attempt), 12, 13 (6 continuous)
Pragmatist	Prefers to study only if a direct link to practical problems can be seen; not interested in theory for its own sake	9/10 (read through), 2, 5, 7, 8, 11, 1, 3, 4, 9/10 (full attempt), 12, 13 (6 continuous)

Next you should complete the following checklist.

Am I motivated? (a) ⬜

Do I have an objective and a standard that I want to achieve? (b) ⬜

Am I a theorist, a reflector, an activist or a pragmatist? (c) ⬜

How much time do I have available per week, given: (d) ⬜

- the standard I have set myself
- the time I need to set aside later for work on the Practice and Revision Kit and Passcards
- the other exam(s) I am sitting, and (of course)
- practical matters such as work, travel, exercise, sleep and social life?

Now:

- take the time you have available per week for this Study Text (d)   (e)   [   ]
  and multiply it by the number of weeks available to give (e).

- divide (e) by the number of chapters to give (f)   (f)   [   ]

- set about studying each chapter in the time represented by (f), following the key study steps
  in the order suggested by your particular learning style.

This is your personal **Study Plan**.

Short of time?

Whatever your objectives, standards or style, you may find you simply do not have the time available to follow all the key study steps for each chapter, however you adapt them for your particular learning style. If this is the case, follow the Skim Study technique below (the icons in the Study Text will help you to do this).

Skim Study technique

Study the chapters in the order you find them in the Study Text. For each chapter, follow the key study steps 1-3, and then skim-read through step 4. Jump to step 11, and then go back to step 5. Follow through steps 7 and 8, and prepare outline Answers to Questions (steps 9/10). Try the Quick Quiz (step 12), following up any items you can't answer, then do a plan for the Examination Question (step 13), comparing it against our answers. You should probably still follow step 6 (note-taking), although you may decide simply to rely on the BPP Passcards for this.

Moving on...

However you study, when you are ready to embark on the practice and revision phase of the BPP Effective Study Package, you should still refer back to this study text:

- as a source of **reference** (you should find the list of key terms and the index particularly helpful for this)

- as a **refresher** (the Chapter Roundups and Quick Quizzes help you here)

And remember to keep careful hold of this Study Text when you move onto the next level of your exams - you will find it invaluable.

ACCA OFFICIAL SYLLABUS

			Covered in Chapter
1	**The theoretical and regulatory accounting framework**		
(a)	The interpretation and application of the following theories and principles:		5 - 7, 21, 22

    (i)   theories of accounting in relation to the measurement of:
- income
- capital maintenance
- valuation of assets and liabilities

    (ii)   principles of accounting for price level changes

    (iii) accounting conventions

    (iv) the recognition of revenue

    (v)   the recognition of assets and liabilities.

(b)	The objectives of financial statements		1, 7

    (i)   criteria of useful information
    (ii)   usefulness for particular purposes.

(c)	The interpretation and application of all extant SSAPs and FRSs.		9 - 20, 22
(d)	The appreciation of the role of the legal and regulatory framework of accounting.		7

2	**Preparing financial statements**		
(a)	The preparation and presentation of financial statements, under conditions of stable prices, for:		8 - 15

    (i)   partnerships, including conversion of partnership to a limited company

    (ii)   branches

    (iii) limited companies, within the legal and regulatory requirements including the application of all extant SSAPs and FRSs
- profit and loss accounts
- balance sheets
- cash flow statements
- directors' reports.

(b)   Calculation and accounting treatment of:

    (i)   pre-incorporation profits
    (ii)   distributable profits
    (iii) purchase of own shares.   6

2   Preparing financial statements - continued

(c)   Groups of companies   16 - 20

    (i)   explaining statutory and professional requirements relating
        to the preparation for publication of consolidated accounts

    (ii)   accounting for the following organisational situations
- joint ventures
- associated undertakings
- simple groups

    (iii)   evaluating the following alternative group accounting
        methods
- equity accounting
- proportional consolidation
- acquisition accounting
- merger accounting.

3   Analysing and appraising financial and related information   22

(a)   Interpreting and appraising financial statements for indications of
business performance, using inter-firm and inter-temporal
methods.

(b)   Assessing information weaknesses in the financial statements.

4   Communicating to users   1, 3, 22

(a)   Producing reports as specified to meet the needs of internal and
external users, supported by appropriate accounts and financial
statements, which include information on, and where necessary
explanations of:

    (i)   the results of operations and the state of affairs
    (ii)   projected results
    (iii)   accounting policies and practices used
    (iv)   main assumptions on which the reports are based
    (v)   significant departures from accounting standards, concepts
        and conventions
    (vi)   any other material considerations

Covered in
Chapter

5   **Advanced auditing practices and procedures**   *See Note*

(a)   Controlling the audit including advanced aspects of audit
planning, audit programme design and testing, statistical sampling
and sampling methods, evaluation of audit risk and test results.

(b)   Organising and planning complex audit situations including group
audits, joint audits, working with specialists, utilisation of CAATs.

(c)   Reviewing financial statements for their compliance with GAAP.

(d)   Evaluating other critical areas - going concern status, related party
transactions, pending legal action, illegal acts by clients.

(e)   Reviewing the auditor's responsibility for preceding year amounts.

(f)   Reviewing unaudited information included with audited financial
statements.

(g)   Managing the audit client, including compiling and reviewing
information on clients throughout the year.

6   **The audit framework**   *See Note*

(a)   Monitoring and evaluating important developments in

(i)   auditing concepts and principles
(ii)   auditing standards and guidelines
(iii)   auditing methods and techniques
(iv)   Companies Act requirements and case law
(v)   Financial Services Act.

(b)   Monitoring the impact of information systems development on the
audit process including the impact of computers on the auditing
process, monitoring best practice in systems design, operation and
the management of information systems development, and the
resource implications of IT systems.

7   **Current issues and controversies**   *See Note*

(a)   The evaluation of current issues and controversies relating to
auditing, including audit expectations, the regulation of audits.

(b)   The monitoring and evaluation of international issues affecting
auditing including EC developments.

(c)   Monitoring developments in auditing theories and their
implications for the profession.

Note. This Study Text covers Sections 1-4 of the syllabus. Sections 5-7 of the syllabus are
covered in the companion Study Text *Accounting and Audit Practice (Auditing)*.

ACCA OFFICIAL 1998-1999 TEACHING GUIDE

This is the official 1998-1999 Teaching Guide, for the December 1998 and June 1999 exam.

Syllabus reference

Session 1   Review of Basic Concepts

1(a)(b)

- a thorough knowledge of the ASB's *Statement of Principles*
- discuss the characteristics of useful accounting information and financial accounting conventions
- explain the regulatory system of accounting
- discuss the notion of GAAP and a conceptual framework

    Self Study
- revise SSAP 2 included in the Paper 1 syllabus
- prepare the final accounts of a simple business organisation

Session 2   Partnership Conversion to a Limited Liability Company

2(a)

- close off the partnership's books on conversion to a limited company
- open appropriate accounts in the company's records
- prepare final accounts covering the year in which conversion takes place
- describe the implications of partnerships converting to limited liability status (including aspects of legislation, tax and auditing)

Session 3   Branch Accounts

2(a)

- explain the nature of selling branches and the need for controls in the accounting system
- explain the nature of independent branches and the requirements of the accounting system
- prepare the final accounts of a business trading through independent branches
- prepare branch accounts of the combined business, possibly in the form of published financial statements
- explain the audit problems of branches. Note: foreign branches are *not* examinable

    Self Study
- record a set of transactions in the accounts of the head office relating to a selling agency branch

Session 4   Joint Ventures

2(a)(c)(ii)

- explain the following different methods of conducting business in the forms of joint venture:
    jointly controlled operations;
    jointly controlled assets;
    a jointly controlled entity.
- prepare the joint venture accounts for each of the above forms of business
- explain the audit problems of joint ventures

Session 5   Hire Purchase and Leasing

2(a)

- explain and distinguish between credit sale agreements, hire purchase agreements, operating leases and finance leases
- describe the effect in the financial statements of treating a lease either as a finance lease or an operating lease
- record the ledger entries for credit sale, hire purchase, and operating lease
- outline the principles and disclosure provisions of SSAP 21
- record finance leases in the books of the lessor/lessee
- discuss the audit verification of leased assets

Session 6   Recognition of Revenue, Distributable Profits and Purchase/Redemption of Shares

1(a)
2(b)

- outline the principles of revenue recognition and the audit implications thereof
- discuss the rules relating to the distribution of profits
- explain how shares may be redeemed, and record the transactions involving the redemption of shares
- explain the power of companies to purchase their own shares, and record the transactions involving the purchase in the accounting records
- discuss the advantages of companies being able to redeem shares

Session 7   Regulatory Framework

1(a), (d)

- discuss the aims and operating process of the Accounting Standards Board (ASB), Financial Reporting Council (FRC) and Financial Reporting Review Panel (FRRP)
- describe the role of the Urgent Issues Task Force (UITF)
- discuss current perceptions of the ASB and its performance
- discuss the politicisation of the standard setting process
- describe the intended role of the ASB *Statement of Principles*
- explain the significant features of the ASB *Statement of Principles*, and their current status
- evaluate the likely usefulness of the ASB *Statement of Principles*
- outline the principal requirements of UITF Abstracts 4, 5 and 7

Session 8   Preparation of Published Financial Statements (Companies Act Requirements)

2(a)

- explain the legal background to limited companies
- state the requirements of company law regarding the duty to prepare annual accounts and the use of prescribed formats
- describe the content and effect of the main accounting provisions of company law including the accounting rules
- prepare the financial statements of limited companies in accordance with the prescribed formats
- state the criteria for distinguishing small and medium companies and the nature of resulting modifications to the annual financial statements
- discuss other criteria that may be used to identify a small business enterprise and the future impact this may have on the applicability of accounting standards

Session 9   Accounting Standards

1(c)
2(a)

- explain the key elements in SSAP 9 relating to long term contracts including the disclosure requirements
- calculate amounts to be shown in financial statements regarding long term contracts, and the accounting entries thereof
- discuss the audit problems relating to compliance with SSAP 9
- prepare a cash flow statement as described by FRS 1, for an individual company in accordance with FRS 1 (revised)
- appraise the usefulness of, and interpret the information in, a cash flow statement

  Self Study
- revise and review the requirements of the following SSAPs covered at the Paper 1 stage: 9 (except as referred to above), 12, 13, 17, 18

Session 10 Accounting for Taxation

2(a)

- outline the UK system of corporation tax
- explain the relationship between taxation and dividends
- explain ACT and its treatment in the accounts
- record entries relating to corporation tax in the accounting records
- explain the accounting treatment and record the accounting transactions of investment income and unfranked receipts and payments
- explain how an income tax account balance will be dealt with and how ACT may be set off
- apply the rules limiting the recovery of ACT
- apply the disclosure requirements of company law and SSAP 8 in relation to tax

  Self Study
- apply and review the disclosure requirements for VAT under SSAP 5

Session 11 Deferred Taxation

1(c)
2(a)

- demonstrate and explain the effect of timing differences on accounting and taxable profits
- explain the deferral and liability methods of accounting for deferred taxation
- outline the requirements of SSAP 15 and the Companies Act requirements relating to deferred tax
- record entries relating to deferred tax in the accounting records
- discuss the advantages and disadvantages of the methods commonly used for recording deferred taxation
- discuss the problems of SSAP 15 and how it might be improved
- discuss the audit problems associated with SSAP 15

Session 12 Earnings Per Share

1(c)
2(a)

- explain the need for a standard for earnings per share and the problems in determining the earnings of a company
- describe the requirements of FRS 3 regarding the computation of EPS
- explain the implications of FRS 3 for the disclosure of EPS
- calculate the EPS in accordance with SSAP 3 where there have been issues of shares during the year and circumstances that will give rise to a future dilution of the EPS
- explain the significance of the different figures for EPS that a company may disclose
- describe the requirements of SSAP 3 (as revised by FRS 3) regarding EPS

Session 13 Financial Performance

1(c)
2(a)

- discuss the requirements of FRS 3
- explain the problems associated with the definitions of extraordinary items and discontinued activities and the implications for the auditors.
- prepare accounts in accordance with FRS 3
- discuss the usefulness and problems associated with segmental information
- prepare segmental reports in accordance with SSAP 25
- discuss the implications of the above for the auditors
- outline the principal requirements of UITF Abstract 14

Session 14 FRS 4 and FRS 5

1(c)

- explain why FRS 4 and FRS 5 were introduced
- discuss the objectives and principal requirements of FRS 4 and FRS 5
- outline the basic principles underlying the classification of capital instruments
- show how the costs of capital instruments should be dealt with
- show the accounting treatment of debt instruments and share capital, including convertible debt
- explain disclosure requirements of FRS 4
- explain and apply the principles of recognition and derecognition of assets and liabilities as in FRS 5

Session 15 Further Fixed Asset Accounting Including Intangibles

1(c)
2(a)

- describe alternative feasible ways of treating capital-based government grants received
- explain and apply the provision of SSAP 4
- explain why investment properties may need an accounting treatment different from other properties
- explain and apply the SSAP 19 *Accounting for investment properties* requirements for the treatment of investment properties (as amended by FRS 3)
- discuss the validity and legality of SSAP 19
- discuss the way the auditor ensures compliance with the above standards

Session 20 Sundry Accounting Standards

1(c)
2(a)

- explain and distinguish foreign currency conversion and translation
- state the requirements of SSAP 20 regarding the individual company and discuss the validity of their effect on imported earnings
- describe a defined contribution pension scheme and a defined benefit pension scheme
- explain how deficiencies and surpluses of a pension scheme arise, and how they should be treated
- outline and apply the requirements of SSAP 24 *Accounting for pension costs*

Self Study
- discuss the audit implications of the above standards

Session 21 Theoretical Matters

1(a)

- outline the concepts of economic income, entry & exit values, deprival value
- explain the concepts of current purchasing power, and current cost accounting. (Note: detailed calculations based on CCA and CCP are *not* examinable.)
- outline the principles of agency theory and the efficient markets hypothesis
- distinguish between positive and normative accounting concepts
- define economic consequences and discuss its implications for financial reporting

Self Study
- review the methods used to reflect the CPP and CCA methodologies in financial statements

Session 22 Interpretation of Financial Statements

3/4

- calculate useful financial ratios from company or group financial statements
- analyse and discuss the implications of changes in accounting policies and management discretion in the choice of accounting policy
- production of written reports on the position and progress of companies including inter-firm and inter-temporal comparisons
- discuss how comparability may be improved
- discuss how the interpretation of current cost accounts or current purchasing power accounts would differ from the interpretation of historic cost accounts

Please note that the content of reports will draw upon knowledge required in other sessions. This session will concentrate on the preparation of reports and report writing skills.

THE EXAMINATION PAPER

Format of the paper

		Number of marks
Section A:	2 (out of 3) questions on financial accounting	50
Section B:	Compulsory integrated accounting and auditing question	30
	Compulsory auditing question	20
		100

Time allowed: 3 hours

The financial accounting content will account for approximately 65% of the marks and will be examined in Section A and part of Section B. The auditing content will account for the remaining 35% of the marks and will be examined in Section B.

Analysis of pilot paper

The examiner for Paper 10 changed from the June 1997 exam onwards. To reflect the change in style that this caused (although the paper format remained the same), the ACCA produced a pilot paper. The contents are as follows.

Section A (2 out of 3)
1   Published accounts from trial balance
2   Cash flow statement
3   Creative accounting

Section B (compulsory)
4   Audit of group accounts; equity and acquisition methods
5   Audit risk

Analysis of past papers

The analysis below shows the topics which have been examined in the eight sittings of the new syllabus.

December 1997

Section A (2 out of 3)
1   Branch accounts; SSAP 21
2   Fixed assets - SSAPs 4 and 21; FRS 3
3   Revenue recognition; *Statement of Principles*

Section B (compulsory)
4   Consolidated profit and loss account (merger and acquisition accounting); procedures on taking over an audit
5   Audit of newly computerised system; impact of developments in IT on audit

June 1997

Section A (2 out of 3)
1   Consolidated balance sheet; discussion of its usefulness
2   Earnings per share: calculations and disclosure
3   Critical discussion of FRS 3

Section B (compulsory)
4   Report on financial performance and its value to auditors; going concern
5   Non-audit services; weaknesses of audit procedures; liability of auditors

December 1996

Section A (2 out of 3)

1   Consolidated accounts; fair values
2   SSAP 25 segmental report
3   Treatment of goodwill and its effect on realised profits

Section B (compulsory)

4   Redraft foreign accounts under UK standards; principal and other auditors
5   Auditing and the Internet

June 1996

Section A (2 out of 3)

1   Consolidated balance sheet; dividend by subsidiary out of pre-acquisition profits
2   Partnership: conversion to limited company; exemptions from statutory disclosure requirements
3   FRS 3 explanations; effect of transactions on various FRS 3 statements

Section B (compulsory)

4   Long term contracts: accounting and audit aspects
5   Audit risk; cash management confidentiality of client's information

December 1995

Section A (2 out of 3)

1   Redrafting group financial statement to comply with CA 85 and accounting standards
2   Published accounts with branch
3   Agency theory; positive accounting terms, *Statement of Principles*

Section B (compulsory)

4   Audit of group accounts; equity and acquisition methods
5   Audit tests to detect fraud; confidentiality; negligence

June 1995

Section A (2 out of 3)

1   Cash flow statement and notes; advantages of cash flow forecasts
2   Earnings per share calculation: effect on EPS of rights issue; importance of EPS
3   Current cost accounting with ratios

Section B (compulsory)

4   Reconstructing accounts of holding company from consolidated accounts and accounts of subsidiary; controls and audit approach
5   Inherent risk; audit evidence; restrictions of time budgets

December 1994

Section A (2 out of 3)

1   Consolidated P & L account per FRS 3 and CA 1985; group reserves
2   Partnership: new partners P & L a/c and balance sheet; WIP in an audit firm's accounts
3   FRS 5: explanation, discussion; treatment of two items

Section B (compulsory)

4   Private company redeeming shares; use of 'expert systems' in audit work; small company audit
5   New client: risk; ethical problems; opinion shopping; reducing risk of litigation

June 1994

Section A (2 out of 3)

1   Exclusion of subsidiaries from consolidation; consolidated balance sheet; effect of subsidiary's losses

2   Need for accounting standards; criticisms of ASC vs new standard-setting regime; effect of FRS 1 on uniformity

3   Prepare FRS 3 statements; explain effect of closure of subsidiary under FRS 3

Section B (compulsory)

4   Reliance on work of secondary auditor; suitability of stock accounting policies; stock valuation; policy note

5   Computer network: audit risk; control problems with micros; auditor's use of a micro; quality control in an IT environment

Further guidance from the ACCA

The ACCA provides the following further guidance on the examination paper for Paper 10 *Accounting and Audit Practice*.

The objective of the Professional Stage

The main aim of the Professional Stage is to establish evidence of competence to practise as a professional accountant in public practice, public sector or in industry and commerce. This requires candidates to demonstrate not only that they have mastered the range of required knowledge, skills and techniques, but also that they are able to apply them in a managerial context.

By this stage, knowledge has to be fully integrated in the way it is used by professionals with a recognition of how the different subjects contribute to dealing with problems. This stage will present students with problems which test their skills and sensitivity in dealing with new contexts and unforeseen circumstances. In dealing with such situations, students will be expected to tailor situations to previous problems appropriately and in a way which demonstrates their grasp of managerial skills.

Although emphasis will be given to practical issues, students will also be expected to criticise current practice and express views on developments in accounting. They will also be expected to show evidence of the necessary personal qualities and interpersonal skills required of the professional accountant.

Skills to be tested in the Professional Stage

Students should be able to demonstrate the ability to:

- draw on knowledge across all earlier papers studied;
- integrate that knowledge effectively and use it creatively in applying concepts and techniques;
- analyse and interpret data and information and present reasoned conclusions;
- diagnose and formulate appropriate solutions to problems which indicate commercial awareness;
- exercise judgement based on technical, political and commercial factors in developing and evaluating alternatives and in proposing solutions;

- adapt to new systems and circumstances;
- communicate analyses and conclusions effectively and with sensitivity for differing purposes and to contrasting audiences with due emphasis on social expectations.

While the skills identified above will be tested directly by the questions set, in assessing the answers weight will be given to the student's ability to demonstrate a grasp of the following personal skills and attributes:

Interpersonal skills
Tact, sensitivity to political tensions and cultural differences, awareness of social, economic and political pressure, ability to influence.

Management skills
Resource management: people, material, time and money, management of the client, management of change, in particular in technology, and contingency planning.

Personal qualities
Persistence to pursue inquiries and probe responses, integrity, objectivity, independence and public responsibility.

Aim of paper 10

To ensure students have developed a thorough knowledge and understanding of accounting and auditing principles and concepts and can begin to apply this grounding to the situations that they will typically meet at work.

On completion of this paper students should be able to:

- prepare financial statements in a form appropriate for use by various interested parties - partnerships, branches, joint ventures, single and group companies
- appraise the theoretical and regulatory accounting framework, including all extant SSAPs and FRSs
- analyse and interpret financial and related information and produce reports to meet the needs of internal and external users
- understand and implement advanced auditing practice and procedures
- evaluate current issues relating to auditing and the regulation of audits
- demonstrate the skills expected at the Professional Stage

Prerequisite knowledge

Students will be expected to have a thorough understanding of the content of Paper 1 Accounting Framework and Paper 6 Audit Framework.

Paper 10 develops the coverage of financial accounting in Paper 1 by:

- examining the preparation of accounts for partnerships and branches in more complex situations
- introducing further SSAPs and FRSs to be applied in the preparation of accounts for single companies and, in addition, for groups
- introducing recognition and measurement issues involved in accounting
- giving more emphasis to the analysis and interpretation of financial statements

Paper 10 develops the coverage of auditing from Paper 6 by:

- examining advanced audit situations - group audits, joint audits, working with specialists and non-audit engagements
- testing, in more depth, computer auditing issues
- evaluating critical areas - going concern status, audit risk, fraud and error, related party transactions etc
- monitoring and appraising changes to the audit framework
- ethical issues
- managing audit relationships on negotiations with management and other parties

The Teaching Guide has also added the following information as an aid to lecturers and students.

General

The examiner wants to ensure that students understand the basic principles and have a firm footing for Paper 13.

Paper 10 is the last substantive auditing paper, therefore, the examiner will test the more complex areas of auditing as the basic principles will have been covered in Paper 6. Students will not be asked to calculate complicated numbers just for the sake of it. Questions will concentrate on practical and up to date techniques. Students will be required to apply information within a regulatory framework of accounting and auditing.

The examiner will not examine frequently areas which have been examined in a previous paper, however, where such topics are examined a greater depth will be expected. **The main areas of interest will be recent FRSs and those Standards not examined at Paper 1.** Many of the Standards are very detailed, however, at Paper 10 these will be examined at basic/summary level. **Students should be aware of the key elements of the Standards, and why they were introduced.**

Key areas of the syllabus

Accounting

- Concepts of accounting
- Regulatory framework
- Revenue recognition
- Distributable profits

Accounting standards

- Cash Flow (FRS 1)
- Reporting Financial Performance including segmental information (FRS 3 and SSAP 25)
- Capital instruments (FRS 4)
- Reporting the Substance of Transactions (FRS 5)
- Earnings per Share (SSAP 3)
- Accounting for Taxation (SSAP 8 and 15)
- Accounting for Leases and Hire Purchase contracts (SSAP 21)

Group accounting

- Simple groups including Associates and Joint Ventures, the use of acquisition, merger and equity accounting and proportional consolidation simple fair value adjustments (FRS 2, 6, 7 and 9)

Accounting theory

- Interpretation of financial statements

Auditing

- Concepts of auditing
- Statement of Auditing Standards
- Analytical review and audit risk
- Auditing computerised accounting systems
- Group audits, working with another auditor
- Ethical issues
- Audit reports
- Fraud and error

The following areas of the syllabus are not as important although they will be examined occasionally or may form part of a question.

- Accounting Standards that have been examined at Papers 1 and 6: 2, 9, 12, 13, 17 and 18
- Other Accounting Standards: 4, 5, 9 (other than long-term contracts), 19, 20 and 24
- Basic audit principles examined at Paper 6.

Examining approach

The examining approach will be in line with the information given above, ie the Examiner will not set large computational questions for the sake of it. Questions will be in a practical context and students will be required to apply information within the regulatory framework of accounting and auditing. The emphasis of this paper will be on up to date practices in the real world and to ensure that students understand basic principles and have a sound foundation for Paper 13.

The approach of the paper will be:

Questions 1 and 2:   a computation basis often followed by a related written element

Question 3:   a discursive basis with the possibility of some simple calculations for explanatory purposes

Question 4:   a computational element with a mix of accounting and auditing issues

Question 5:   an auditing question, probably based on a case study or scenario format

Articles are regularly published in the *Students' Newsletter* which are relevant to Paper 10. It is important that students read this.

Review of June and December 1997 examinations

Students taking Paper 10 have similar difficulties to those mentioned for students taking Paper 6; poor time management and poor exam technique. Students based in the Far East tend to be very good on the calculations element of the exam paper but weak on the discursive questions. This is an important point because Paper 10 is less concerned with calculations and designed more to test and explore the students' knowledge, understanding of accounting and auditing regulatory framework and their ability to apply it in a given scenario.

Students seem to have particular problems in dealing with case studies, again this is an important issue as, for example, Question 5 of this paper will usually be in a case study format. Many students ignore the facts of the case study and write a general essay on the subject matter of the question, by doing this they fail to gain the marks which have been allocated for practical application of knowledge and format of the answer. Students must be advised to apply their knowledge to the facts of the scenario.

Students should read the articles in the *Students' Newsletter*. Questions on some areas of the syllabus will attract an article from the Examiner to help students in answering the questions on various topics. It is also important that students answer all parts of all the required questions. If students do not do this, they are penalising themselves. Additionally students should realise that markers are instructed to give credit to 'incorrect' answers. It is difficult for students to produce ideal answers therefore credit is given for content, methodology, presentation and other elements of an answer albeit in some ways inaccurate.

December 1997 saw the introduction of the International Stream paper. From this diet onwards all variant papers including the UK paper are based on the International paper. The numbers sitting the 'pure' International paper are, as yet, very low. No doubt these will rise considerably as students progress through the examination stages. There does not appear to have been any significant effect on students performance due to the introduction of the International paper.

Questions and answers

The following replies are from the Examiner in response to questions which have been raised by lecturers since the introduction of the new syllabus.

1   Q   *Where will EDs and SASs appear?*

    A   The Examiner expects candidates to apply SASs in Paper 10 but not to regurgitate them Students should be aware of the main thrust of the EDs listed in the Exam Notes published in the *Students' Newsletter*.

2   Q   *What depth will SSAPs 15 and 21 be examined to?*

    A   SSAPs 15 and 21 will be examined only in terms of their basic concepts.

3   Q   *How is the six month rule implemented?*

    A   Examinable documents for each diet are agreed by committee. At this meeting the six month rule is taken into account.

4   Q   *How deep should the treatment of disposals of subsidiaries be?*

    A   Disposals will only be tested in respect of FRS 3. They will not be tested in group accounting questions.

5   Q   *Where will the audit reporting be examined?*

    A   It is a possible area for Question 5. Candidates would be asked to comment on the audit report not merely to regurgitate its contents.

6   Q   *Which SSAPs and FRSs are examinable in Paper 10?*

    A   All extant SSAPs and FRSs are examinable, however there will be less emphasis on those SSAPs examinable at Paper 1. The Exam Notes published in the *Student's Newsletter* will detail the examinable documents.

7   Q   *Can the Examiner outline the type of numerical question which are likely to be set on FRS 4?*

     A   Questions could be set on the accounting treatment of debt instruments and share capital at a basic level, and/or an allocation of finance costs.

8   Q   *What type of numerical questions is the Examiner likely to ask involving FRS 7?*

     A   Simple fair value calculations in order to determine goodwill and balance sheet values of assets and liabilities.

Part A
The regulatory accounting framework

Chapter 1

REVIEW OF BASIC ACCOUNTING CONCEPTS

Chapter topic list	Syllabus reference
1 Desirable characteristics of financial reports	1(b)
2 The regulatory system of accounting	1(b)
3 GAAP and the conceptual framework of accounting	1(b)
4 Revision: basic accounts	1(b)

Introduction

The syllabus for Paper 10 is very large and varied. But don't worry. Provided you approach your studies logically and leave plenty of extra time you should get through it. You must not skimp on any area of the syllabus, tempting though it is when faced with so much material.

This first chapter is mainly concerned with revision of those concepts and skills covered in your earlier studies.

If you have any difficulties with the exercises in this chapter, you should go back to your earlier study material and revise; doing a few more exercises should help to jog your memory.

We will concentrate on company reports here, although the next few chapters cover unincorporated organisation. We will go back to company reporting in Chapter 8 and subsequent chapters.

1   DESIRABLE CHARACTERISTICS OF FINANCIAL REPORTS

1.1   Financial information, if it is to be useful, should have certain qualities. These qualities were discussed in several documents in the 1970s, notably *The Corporate Report* (issued by the old Accounting Standards Committee). These qualities are listed below. As you can see, they are open to question.

(a)   **Objectivity**. It is not clear to what extent an accounting report can be objective. Some subjective judgements cannot be avoided. The main thing is to make clear where subjective judgement has been used.

(b)   **Comparability**. If one purpose of accounting reports is to enable information users to compare one company's performance against another's, the reports of both companies must be prepared by similar methods. Unless accounting practices are made standard, such comparability is unlikely to occur.

(c)   **Completeness**. *The Corporate Report* suggested that accounting reports should give 'a rounded picture of the economic activities of the reporting entity'. To be complete, information would need to be provided in 'complex rather than simple documents'. There is a reluctance among many organisations to disclose accounting information which is not required by law or other regulation, and 'completeness' does not really exist.

(d) **Consistency**. This principle cannot be pushed too far. If better accounting techniques are developed, old methods of reporting should be changed.

1.2 The disclosure of accounting information is a vexed question which is still the subject of debate within the accountancy profession and Government. There is a strong body of opinion which favours greater disclosure of accounting information, but the common attitude of reporting companies appears to be that disclosure should be kept to a minimum which conforms with the requirements of law or another regulatory body (SSAPs, FRSs and so forth).

Problems of disclosure

1.3 There are several different problems involved in disclosure.

(a) **What accounting concepts should be applied** in arriving at values for profit and capital?

(b) **What accounting policies should be applied** in the valuation of profit and capital?

(c) Do the profit and loss account, balance sheet, and cash flow statement provide sufficient information for the needs of users, or **are additional statements needed?**

(d) **Should more information be included** in the published balance sheets than is shown at the moment, **or in the case of small 'proprietary' companies, would less information be sufficient** for shareholders than for larger company shareholders?

(e) **Should disclosure requirements be enforced** by statute, accounting standards, or Stock Exchange listing requirements?

1.4 These five issues are all discussed at greater length elsewhere in this Study Text. In the remainder of this chapter, we shall consider the general background, and in particular who the users of information are and what type of information and accounting statements they might need. The most useful reference point for this topic is *The Corporate Report*.

The corporate report

KEY TERM

A **corporate report** is a comprehensive package of information which describes an organisation's *economic* activities. It includes the financial statements required by law (profit and loss account and balance sheet) or by another authority (for example, the cash flow statement, which is described in a later chapter). It also includes information in narrative form, such as the chairman's annual report.

1.5 A working party of the Accounting Standards Committee (ASC) produced a discussion paper in 1975 called *The Corporate Report* in which suggestions were made about:

(a) Which types of organisation should be expected to publish regular financial or economic information.

(b) Who the main users of such information should be.

(c) What type of information and reports would best suit these user needs.

1.6 In *The Corporate Report*, a distinction was made between:

(a) The responsibility to make general purpose financial information publicly available (this was called 'public accountability').

(b) The obligation to provide some financial information by law.

(c) Special purpose information provided to particular users for specific needs (for example, a bank might want a company to provide a cash flow forecast and a profit forecast before deciding whether to allow the company an overdraft facility).

1.7 The recommendations of the discussion paper were only concerned with public accountability and general purpose information ((a) above). The report stated:

> 'in our view there is an implicit responsibility to report publicly (whether or not required by law or regulation) incumbent on every economic entity whose size or format renders it significant.'

'Significance' means that the organisation controls sufficient human and material resources that its actions would be noticed by the general community. The organisations concerned would include not only medium to large companies but also Central Government, local authorities, trade associations, co-operative societies, trade unions and charities.

Users

1.8 **Users** of corporate reports were defined as those groups which **have a reasonable right to information** about the reporting entity. These were:

(a) **Shareholders** (existing and potential shareholders)
(b) **Loan creditors**
(c) **Employees**
(d) **Analysts and advisers** (journalists, economists, trade unions, stockbrokers)
(e) **Business contacts** (trade creditors, predator companies, competitors)
(f) The **Government** (including tax officials)
(g) The **public** (taxpayers, ratepayers, consumers, political groups, environmentalists)

1.9 Existing and potential **shareholders** need information about a company to help them decide:

(a) Whether to **buy or sell** the company's shares.
(b) Whether to **subscribe for new shares** in the company when a 'rights issue' is made.
(c) How to **vote at annual general meetings** of the company.

1.10 They are **interested in the level of current and future dividends**, and the likely movements up and down in a share's market price. In addition, existing shareholders will want to know whether management has been running the company efficiently.

1.11 It has often been thought that shareholders' interests are confined to the profit and loss account and balance sheet, and to the 'earnings per share' during each year. *The Corporate Report* suggested that, in addition, shareholders would **want to know that**:

(a) **The company is capable of generating sufficient cash from its internal operations** to cope with inflation and the problems of liquidity.

(b) The company's **future prospects** are good.

(c) The company's **shares compare favourably** with others which are available for purchase by investors.

1.12 **Loan creditors** (or potential loan creditors) have a 'right' to financial information about a company, because they will **want to know that interest repayments on the loan** are **secure**. They are concerned with the risk element of default on these repayments. In addition:

(a) If the loan stock is bought and sold on the stock market, investors need financial information to decide whether to buy or sell at a given price.

(b) If the loan is due for redemption (capital repayment) in the near future, investors will want to know that the company will have sufficient cash to pay off the loan.

(c) If the terms of the loan (known as 'covenants') place certain financial restrictions on the company (for instance, by limiting the debt/equity ratios of the company), the loan creditors will need to know that these terms are being upheld.

1.13 **An organisation has a responsibility for the livelihood of its employees.** Since *The Corporate Report* was published, statutory provisions embodied in the Companies Act 1985 have increased the amount of information about employees which must be disclosed in company accounts. CA 1985 also states (s 309) that directors have a duty to show regard for the interests of the company's employees as well as the interests of its shareholders.

1.14 **Employees need information about the security of employment and future prospects** for jobs in the company **and to help with collective bargaining for wage settlements and terms of employment.** *The Corporate Report* suggested that information for collective bargaining might be obtained more usefully from special purpose reports at site or factory level; nevertheless, general purpose reports might provide information about job security, future prospects, management efficiency, and the ability (or otherwise) of the company to pay higher wages.

1.15 **Analysts and advisers need information which is of interest to their clients or audience.** For example, stockbrokers will want information to advise investors in stocks and shares and credit-rating agencies will want information to advise would-be trade creditors.

1.16 *The Corporate Report* suggested that 'the rights of the **business contact group** to information arise from their existing or potential direct relationship with the reporting entity. For example, suppliers, trade creditors and customers are all likely to place trust in the reporting entity to fulfil an implied or explicit responsibility.'

(a) **Suppliers need to know that a company is able to pay its debts,** and whether the company is likely to be a good long-term customer.

(b) **Customers need to know that the company will be able to continue to deliver goods** in the future, and will not close down.

1.17 **Competitors** will also be interested in information about the company, and there is **mutual benefit to be obtained from the exchange of such information** provided that it does not breach confidentiality. In some industries, formal schemes of Interfirm Comparison (IFC) have been operated. The value of such comparisons is in acting as a **spur to greater efficiency in operations.**

1.18 The general purpose information in a corporate report cannot, however, be specially adapted to the needs of competitors; competitors should usually be satisfied with obtaining whatever information about the company is publicly available.

1.19 Another important business contact group is a **company which is planning a merger or takeover**. These groups have **interests similar to those of investors (shareholders)**. On the other hand, the employees and management of a company subject to a takeover offer will want to know about the past record and management style of the company making the bid.

1.20 The **Government may have an interest in** a company as creditor or customer. In addition, both national and local government will be interested in the:

(a) Current and prospective **contribution of the company to economic well-being and employment** in the area or country.

(b) Ability of the company to pay **taxes**

(c) **Compliance** of the company **with taxation rules and company law**, as verified by independent auditors.

1.21 The Government is in a position to ask for special purpose information (for example, tax returns and the provision of statistics) but might also benefit from more general purpose financial information as provided by a corporate report.

1.22 **Members of the public** may wish to have financial information about a company; in its role as an employer, as a part of the economy, contributing to national wealth and the balance of trade and so on. However, the term 'general public' covers a wide variety of individuals and groups and it would be impossible to provide general purpose accounting information which was specially designed for the needs of the public. However, the public **should have ready access to general purpose information made available to other groups** (shareholders, loan creditors, business contacts).

The objective of corporate reports

1.23 The discussion paper suggested that:

> 'the fundamental objective of corporate reports is to **communicate economic measurements of and information** about the **resources and performance** of the reporting entity useful to those having reasonable rights to such information.'

1.24 Larger organisations, because they are more influential in society, the economy and employment levels, should be expected to provide more information than smaller organisations. In small organisations, employees have easier access to senior managers, directors and even shareholders; therefore formalised information systems are not so necessary. The benefits of the information provided must be expected to justify the costs of collecting it, and in small organisations information costs are proportionately higher in relation to benefits.

1.25 The ASC discussion paper identified the following **criteria of useful information.**

(a) **Relevance**. The information provided should be that which is required to satisfy the needs of users of reports. Such needs will vary as between user groups and over time.

(b) **Comprehensibility**. Too much detail is just as much a defect as too little.

(c) **Reliability**. This will be enhanced in the case of reports which are independently verified.

(d) **Completeness**. 'Reports should present a rounded picture of the economic activities of the reporting entity.'

(e) **Objectivity**. This will be enhanced by the application of standards which are neutral as between competing interests.

(f) **Timeliness**. The usefulness of information is reduced the later it is produced after the time to which it relates and also if the intervals at which it is produced are unreasonably long.

(g) **Comparability**. This involves consistency in the application of accounting concepts and policies.

1.26 The discussion paper also suggested that although some financial reports were already required by law, or Stock Exchange rules, or by the rules of an accounting standard, there are extra reports which could usefully be provided in addition to these.

1.27 Published financial statements which are currently provided (profit and loss account, balance sheet, cash flow statements) have certain **limitations**.

(a) The **emphasis is put on short-term profit**, and consideration of longer-term objectives or non-profit objectives (such as employee welfare) is excluded.

(b) As a result of (a), management concentrates on achieving the best short-term profits to the exclusion of other objectives.

(c) The measurement of a **profit figure is dependent on the choice of accounting policies,** and is not as meaningful as users of the information might like to think.

(d) There is an **implication that the shareholders are the most important users** of the information provided.

Question 1

Quick memory test:

(a)   Who are the users of accounting information? You should be able to think of 7.

(b)   What qualities do they think the information should have? You should be able to think of 7.

Answer

See Paragraphs 1.8 and 1.25.

The ASB's *Statement of Principles*

1.28 The needs of users of accounts were considered more recently by the ASB in formulating its *Statement of Principles*. The *Statement* was issued in November 1995 in exposure draft form.

1.29 The *Statement* is discussed in Chapter 21 of this Study Text, and will mean more to you when you have worked through the intervening chapters.

2   THE REGULATORY SYSTEM OF ACCOUNTING

2.1   **Unincorporated businesses in the UK can usually prepare their financial statements in any form they choose** (subject to the constraints of specific legislation, such as the Financial Services Act 1986 for investment businesses, for example). **However, all companies must comply with the provisions of the Companies Act 1985** in preparing their financial statements and are also with the provisions of Statements of Standard Accounting Practice (**SSAPs**) and Financial Reporting Standards (**FRSs**) which are issued by a body called the Accounting Standards Board.

2.2   In its *Foreword to Accounting Standards* the Accounting Standards Board states that **accounting standards are applicable to all financial statements whose purpose is to give a true and fair view** (explained in Chapter 2). This necessarily includes the financial statements of every company incorporated in the UK.

2.3   The regulatory framework over company accounts is therefore based on several sources.

   (a)   Company law.

   (b)   Accounting standards and other related pronouncements.

   (c)   International accounting standards (and the influence of other national standard setting bodies).

   (d)   The requirements of the Stock Exchange.

Company law

2.4   The Companies Act 1985 (CA 1985) consolidated the bulk of previous company legislation which is relevant to your syllabus. This was substantially amended by the Companies Act 1989 (CA 1989), and all references in this text are to CA 1985 as amended by CA 1989.

The European Union

2.5   Since the United Kingdom became a member of the European Union (EU) it has been obliged to comply with legal requirements decided on by the EU. It does this by enacting UK laws to implement EU directives. For example, the CA 1989 was enacted in part to implement the provisions of the seventh and eighth EU directives, which deal with consolidated accounts and auditors.

> **Exam focus point**
> Although your syllabus does not require you to be an expert on EU procedure, you should be aware that the form and content of company accounts can be influenced by international developments.

Accounting standards

2.6   **Some accounting principles** (such as valuation of assets) **are embodied in legislation, while others** (for example cash flow statements) **are regulated by accounting standards.**

> **KEY TERM**
>
> An **accounting standard** is a rule or set of rules which prescribes the method (or methods) by which accounts should be prepared and presented. These 'working regulations' are issued by a national or international body of the accountancy profession.

2.7 In the UK, such standards were called Statements of Standard Accounting Practice (SSAPs) and were until 31 July 1990 formulated by the Accounting Standards Committee (ASC). SSAPs are gradually being replaced by Financial Reporting Standards (FRSs) produced by the successor to the ASC, the Accounting Standards Board (ASB). The structure of the new standard setting process, which includes the ASB, is discussed below.

2.8 **Accounting standards interact with company law** in several ways.

(a) 'Realised' profits and losses are determined by reference to generally accepted accounting practice, ie SSAPs and FRS 5: s 262 (3).

(b) The accounts must state whether the provisions of accounting standards have been followed or give reasons for, and disclosures of any material departures (see Paragraph 2.18 below): para 36A, Sch 4.

In addition, the Stock Exchange requires listed companies to comply with accounting standards. Failure to comply will also usually lead to the auditors qualifying their report, which the company will want to avoid.

The standard-setting process in the UK

2.9 We have mentioned the previous standard-setting process in the UK, whereby SSAPs were produced by the ASC. In 1987 the Consultative Committee of Accountancy Bodies (CCAB) established a review committee (the Dearing committee) and its report was published in September 1988. Its conclusions were, in essence, that the arrangements then in operation, where 21 unpaid ASC members met for a half-day once a month to discuss new standards, were no longer adequate to produce timely and authoritative pronouncements. On 1 August 1990 the ASC was disbanded and the following regime took its place.

Financial Reporting Council (FRC)

2.10 The FRC was created to cover a wide constituency of interests at a high level. It **guides the standard setting body on policy and sees that its work is properly financed.** It also funds and oversees the Review Panel (see below). It has about 25 members drawn from users, preparers and auditors of accounts.

Accounting Standards Board (ASB)

2.11 **The task of devising accounting standards is now carried out by the ASB,** with a full-time chairman and technical director. A majority of two thirds of the Board is required to approve a new standard. Previously, each new standard had to be approved by the Councils of each of the six CCAB bodies separately before it could be published. The new ASB now issues standards itself on its own authority. The ASB can produce standards more quickly than the ASC and it has the great advantage of legal backing (see below).

Urgent Issues Task Force (UITF)

2.12   An offshoot of the ASB is the UITF, whose function is:

> 'to **tackle urgent matters** not covered by existing standards, and for which, given the urgency, the normal standard-setting process would not be practicable.'
>
> (Sir Ron Dearing)

2.13   The UITF pronouncements, which are called 'abstracts', are intended to come into effect quickly. They therefore tend to become effective within approximately one month of publication date. The UITF has so far issued several abstracts, some of which have been superseded by a new FRSs and Financial Reporting Exposure Drafts (FREDs). The Abstracts close loopholes as soon as they become apparent, triggered frequently by practices in the accounts of companies, thus halting abuses before they become widespread.

2.14   The *Foreword to UITF Abstracts,* issued in February 1994, sets out the authority, scope and application of UITF abstracts. The authority given is that:

> 'The Councils of the CCAB bodies expect their members who assume responsibilities in respect of financial statements to observe UITF Abstracts until they are replaced by accounting standards or otherwise withdrawn by the ASB.'

The scope of and compliance with the abstracts are similar to those associated with accounting standards (accounts which show a true and fair view, non-compliance must be justified and disclosed etc).

Review Panel

2.15   The Review Panel, chaired by a barrister, is **concerned with the examination and questioning of departures from accounting standards by large companies**. It has about 15 members from which smaller panels are formed to tackle cases as they arise. The Review Panel is alerted to most cases for investigation by the results of the new CA 1985 requirement that companies must include in the notes to the accounts a statement that they have been prepared in accordance with applicable accounting standards or, failing that, give details of material departures from those standards, with reasons.

2.16   Although it is expected that most referrals would be resolved by discussion, the Panel (and the Secretary of State for Trade and Industry) **have the power to apply the court for revision of the accounts,** with all costs potentially payable (if the court action is successful) by the company's directors. The auditors may also be disciplined if the audit report on the defective accounts was not qualified with respect to the departure from standards. Revised accounts, whether prepared voluntarily or under duress, will have to be circulated to all persons likely to rely on the previous accounts.

2.17   Because of the Review Panel, listed companies and their auditors are doubtless becoming far more cautious in their attempts to break or bend the rules laid out by both the Companies Act and accounting standards. The actions of the Review Panel against individual companies to date caused no difficulties: most of the companies obeyed the Review Panel dictates without any real argument.

2.18   A summary of the structure of the regulatory framework is shown in the following diagram.

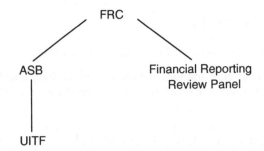

Question 2

Discuss the function of:

(a) the Accounting Standards Board;
(b) the Review Panel;
(c) the Financial Reporting Council;
(d) the Urgent Issues Task Force.

Answer

See Paragraphs 2.9 - 2.18.

International Accounting Standards

2.19   International Accounting Standards (IASs) are produced by the **International Accounting Standards Committee** (IASC). The IASC was set up in 1973 to work for the improvement and harmonisation of financial reporting. **The IASC develops IASs through an international process that involves the world-wide accountancy profession, the preparers and users of financial statements, and national standard setting bodies.**

2.20   The objectives of the IASC are to:

(a)   Formulate and publish in the public interest accounting standards to be observed in the presentation of financial statements and to promote their world-wide acceptance and observance.

(b)   Work generally for the improvement and harmonisation of regulations, accounting standards and procedures relating to the presentation of financial statements.

2.21   The main impact of the IASC on the work of the ASB has involved the IASC's *Framework for the preparation and presentation of financial statements*. The *Framework* was introduced to 'set out the concepts that underlie the preparation and presentation of financial statements for external users'. The ASB has based its own *Statement of Principles* on the IASC's *Framework* (see Section 3). In basic terms, the ASB has adopted the same conceptual approach to financial reporting as the IASC. In its Financial Reporting Standards (FRSs), the ASB states the compliance of the standards with IASs or IAS exposure drafts.

The Stock Exchange

2.22   In the UK there are two different markets on which it is possible for a company to have its securities quoted:

(a)   the Stock Exchange; or

(b)   the Alternative Investment Market (AIM).

2.23   **Shares quoted on the main market, the Stock Exchange, are said to be 'listed'** or to have obtained a 'listing'. In order to receive a listing for its securities, a company must conform with Stock Exchange regulations contained in the Listing Rules or Yellow Book issued by the Council of The Stock Exchange. The company commits itself to certain procedures and standards, including matters concerning the disclosure of accounting information, which are more extensive than the disclosure requirements of the Companies Acts. **The requirements of the AIM are less stringent** than the main Stock Exchange. **It is aimed at new, higher risk or smaller companies.**

2.24   Many requirements of the Yellow Book do not have the backing of law, but the ultimate sanction which can be imposed on a listed company which fails to abide by them is the withdrawal of its securities from the Stock Exchange List: the company's shares would no longer be traded on the market.

3   GAAP AND THE CONCEPTUAL FRAMEWORK OF ACCOUNTING

3.1   The Financial Accounting Standards Board, or FASB (the US standards body), has defined a conceptual framework.

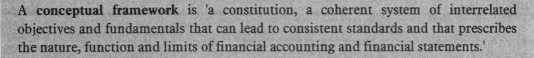

KEY TERM

A **conceptual framework** is 'a constitution, a coherent system of interrelated objectives and fundamentals that can lead to consistent standards and that prescribes the nature, function and limits of financial accounting and financial statements.'

The basic idea is therefore to avoid the 'fire fighting' approach which has characterised the development of SSAPs to date, and instead to develop an underlying philosophy as a basis for consistent accounting principles so that the rationale of each SSAP is structured into the whole framework.

3.2   The ASC stated in a consultative document *Setting Accounting Standards* that whilst an agreed framework of accounting would provide a good basis on which to build accounting standards, it believed that no such framework was currently available and that conclusive results would probably not be rapidly achieved. On the other hand, the FASB began a large-scale project in 1973 to develop such a framework, with immense resources committed to this research: several million dollars have been spent each year since the project began. The FASB's publications on the project already amount to over 3,000 pages (of which statements of concepts and standards amount to some 400 pages).

3.3   A great deal of work on the conceptual framework has been carried out by the International Accounting Standards Committee *Framework for the Preparation and Presentation of Financial Statements*, published in July 1989, and by Professor David Solomons in a 1989 discussion paper addressed to the ASC *Guidelines for Financial Reporting Standards* (the Solomons report).

3.4   The IASC *Framework* is non-mandatory and it deals with the:

(a)   **Objective** of financial statements.

(b)   **Qualitative characteristics** that determine the usefulness of information in financial statements.

(c) **Definition, recognition and measurement** of the elements from which financial statements are constructed.

(d) Concepts of **capital and capital maintenance**.

3.5 The IASC believes that further **international harmonisation** of accounting methods can best be **promoted by focusing on these four topics** since they will then lead to published financial statements that meet the common needs of most users.

3.6 The Solomons report proceeds in a similar way. Chapters deal with:

(a) The purpose of financial reporting.
(b) Financial statements and their elements.
(c) The qualitative characteristics of accounting information.
(d) Recognition and measurement.
(e) The choice of a general purpose accounting model.

3.7 Solomons recognised the unsatisfactory nature of the (then) current 'firefighting' approach to UK standard setting, and produces his own set of guidelines which he argues could yield an explicit statement of agreed financial accounting concepts.

Advantages

3.8 The **advantages arising from using a conceptual framework** may be summarised as follows.

(a) **SSAPs were being developed on a 'patchwork quilt' basis** where a particular accounting problem was recognised by the ASC as having emerged, and resources were then channelled into standardising accounting practice in that area, without regard to whether that particular issue was necessarily the most important issue remaining at that time without standardisation.

(b) As stated above, the development of certain SSAPs (for example SSAP 13) has been subject to considerable political interference from interested parties. Where there is a conflict of interest between user groups on which policies to choose, **policies deriving from a conceptual framework will be less open to criticism that the ASC buckled to external pressure.**

(c) Some SSAPs seem to concentrate on the income statement (profit and loss account), some to concentrate on the valuation of net assets (balance sheet). For instance, SSAP 12 ensures that depreciation is charged on a systematic basis through the profit and loss account to comply with the accruals concept, but the net book value figure in the balance sheet has little meaning. Conversely, SSAP 15 requires the balance sheet provision for deferred tax to be the liability currently envisaged, but the profit and loss charge or credit for deferred tax has no meaning other than representing the balancing figure between a provision brought forward and carried forward in the balance sheet. **An unambiguous definition of 'income' and 'value' would ensure all financial statements have equal usefulness to each user group.**

Disadvantages

3.9 A **counter-argument** to supporters of a conceptual framework might be as follows.

(a) Financial statements are intended for a variety of users, and **it is not certain that a single conceptual framework can be devised which will suit all users.**

(b) Given the diversity of user requirements, there may be a **need for a variety of accounting standards**, each produced for a different purpose (and **with different concepts as a basis**).

(c) It is **not clear that a conceptual framework will make the task of preparing and then implementing standards any easier** than it is now.

> ## IMPORTANT!
>
> The ASB has now focused its attention on developing a conceptual framework, based on both the IASC *Framework* and on the recommendations of the Solomons report. The ASB conceptual framework is encompassed in a *Statement of Principles* published in exposure draft form. The *Statement of Principles* is discussed in detail in Chapter 22. By the time you reach this chapter, you should have a thorough grasp of the problems surrounding asset valuation and profit measurement for various types of transaction, including consolidation which you have not looked at before.

Generally Accepted Accounting Practice (GAAP)

3.10 This term has sprung up in recent years and it **signifies all the rules**, from whatever source, **which govern accounting**. In the UK this is seen primarily as a combination of:

- **Company law** (mainly CA 1985)
- **Accounting standards**
- **Stock exchange requirements**

3.11 Although those sources are the basis for UK GAAP, the concept also includes the effects of non-mandatory sources such as:

(a) **International accounting standards**;
(b) **Statutory requirements in other countries**, particularly the US.

3.12 In the UK, GAAP does not have any statutory or regulatory authority or definition (unlike other countries, such as the US). The term is mentioned rarely in legislation, and only then in fairly limited terms.

3.13 GAAP is in fact a dynamic concept: it **changes constantly as circumstances alter through new legislation, standards *and* practice.** This idea that GAAP is constantly changing is recognised by the ASB in its *Statement of Aims* where it states that it expects to issue new standards and amend old ones in response to:

> 'evolving business practices, new economic developments and deficiencies identified in current practice.'

The emphasis has shifted from 'principles' to 'practice' in UK GAAP.

3.14 The problem of what is 'generally accepted' is not easy to settle, because new practices will obviously not be generally adopted yet. The criteria for a practice being 'generally accepted' will depend on factors such as whether the practice is addressed by UK accounting standards or legislation, their international equivalents, and whether other companies have adopted the practice. Most importantly perhaps, the question should be whether the practice is consistent with the needs of users and the objectives of financial reporting and whether it is consistent with the 'true and fair' concept.

4   REVISION: BASIC ACCOUNTS

4.1   In the next part of this text we move on to the mechanics of preparing financial statements. It would be useful at this point to refresh your memory of the basic accounting you have already studied and these exercises will help you. Make sure that you understand everything before you go on.

Question 3

A friend has bought some shares in a quoted United Kingdom company and has received the latest accounts. There is one page he is having difficulty in understanding.

Briefly, but clearly, answer his questions.

(a)   What is a balance sheet?
(b)   What is an asset?
(c)   What is a liability?
(d)   What is share capital?
(e)   What are reserves?
(f)   Why does the balance sheet balance?
(g)   To what extent does the balance sheet value my investment?

Answer

(a)   A *balance sheet* is a statement of the assets, liabilities and capital of a business as at a stated date. It is laid out to show either total assets as equivalent to total liabilities and capital or net assets as equivalent to capital. Other formats are also possible but the top half (or left hand) total will always equal the bottom half (or right hand) total. Some balance sheets are laid out vertically and others horizontally.

(b)   An *asset* is owned by a business and is expected to be of some future benefit. Its value is determined as the historical cost of producing or obtaining it (unless an attempt is being made to reflect rising prices in the accounts, in which case a replacement cost might be used). Examples of assets are:

   (i)   plant, machinery, land and other long-term or *fixed* assets;

   (ii)   *current* assets such as stocks, cash and debts owed to the business with reasonable assurance of recovery: these are assets which are not intended to be held on a continuing basis in the business.

(c)   A *liability* is an amount owed by a business, other than the amount owed to its proprietors (capital). Examples of liabilities are:

   (i)   amounts owed to the government (VAT or other taxes);
   (ii)   amounts owed to suppliers;
   (iii)   bank overdraft;
   (iv)   long-term loans from banks or investors.

   It is usual to differentiate between 'current' and 'long-term' liabilities. The former fall due within a year of the balance sheet date.

(d)   *Share capital* is the permanent investment in a business by its owners. In the case of limited company, this takes the form of *shares* for which investors subscribe on formation of the company. Each share has a *nominal* (or face) *value* (say £1). In the balance sheet, total issued share capital is shown at its nominal value.

(e)   If a company issues shares for more than their nominal value (at a *premium*) then by law this premium must be recorded separately from the nominal value in a 'share premium account'. This is an example of a reserve. It belongs to the shareholders but cannot be distributed to them, because it is a c*apital* reserve. Other capital reserves include the revaluation reserve, which shows the surpluses arising on revaluation of assets which are still owned by the company.

Share capital and capital reserves are not distributable except on the winding up of the company, as a guarantee to the company's creditors that the company has enough assets to meet its debts. This is necessary because shareholders in limited companies have 'limited liability'; once they have paid the company for their shares they have no further liability to it if it becomes insolvent. The proprietors of other businesses are, by contrast, personally liable for business debts.

Revenue reserves constitute accumulated profits (less losses) made by the company and can be distributed to shareholders as *dividends*. They too belong to the shareholders, and so are a claim on the resources of the company.

(f) Balance sheets do not always balance on the first attempt, as all accountants know. However, once errors are corrected, all balance sheets balance. This is because in double entry bookkeeping every transaction recorded has a dual effect. Assets are always equal to liabilities plus capital and so capital is always equal to assets less liabilities. This makes sense as the owners of the business are entitled to the net assets of the business as representing their capital plus accumulated surpluses (or less accumulated deficit).

(g) The balance sheet is not intended as a statement of a business's worth at a given point in time. This is because, except where some attempt is made to adjust for the effects of rising prices, assets and liabilities are recorded at historical cost and on a prudent basis. For example, if there is any doubt about the recoverability of a debt, then the value in the accounts must be reduced to the likely recoverable amount. In addition, where fixed assets have a finite useful life, their cost is gradually written off to reflect the use being made of them.

Sometimes fixed assets are *revalued* to their market value but this revaluation then goes out of date as few assets are revalued every year.

The balance sheet figure for capital and reserves therefore bears no relationship to the market value of shares. Market values are the product of a large number of factors, including general economic conditions, alternative investment returns (eg interest rates), likely future profits and dividends and, not least, market sentiment.

Question 4

The accountant of Fiddles plc has begun preparing final accounts but the work is not yet complete. At this stage the items included in the trial balance are as follows.

	£'000
Land	100
Buildings	120
Plant and machinery	170
Depreciation provision	120
Share capital	100
Profit and loss balance brought forward	200
Debtors	200
Creditors	110
Stock	190
Operating profit	80
Debentures (16%)	180
Provision for doubtful debts	3
Bank balance (asset)	12
Suspense	1

Notes (i) to (vii) below are to be taken in to account.

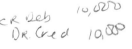

(i) The debtors control account figure, which is used in the trial balance, does not agree with the total of the debtors ledger. A contra of £5,000 has been entered correctly in the individual ledger accounts but has been entered on the wrong side of both control accounts.

A batch total of sales of £12,345 had been entered in the double entry system as £13,345, although the individual ledger accounts entries for these sales were correct. The balance of £4,000 on sales returns account has inadvertently been omitted from the trial balance though correctly entered in the ledger records.

(ii) A standing order of receipt from a regular customer for £2,000, and bank charges of £1,000, have been completely omitted from the records.

(iii) A debtor for £1,000 is to be written off. The provision for doubtful debts balance is to be adjusted to 1% of debtors.

(iv) The opening stock figure had been overstated by £1,000 and the closing stock figure had been understated by £2,000.

(v)   Any remaining balance on suspense account should be treated as purchases if a debit balance and as sales if a credit balance.

(vi)   The debentures were issued three months before the year end. No entries have been made as regards interest.

(vii) A dividend of 10% of share capital is to be proposed.

Required

(a)   Prepare journal entries to cover items in notes (i) to (v) above. You are not to open any new accounts and may use only those accounts included in the trial balance as given.

(b)   Prepare final accounts for internal use in good order within the limits of the available information. For presentation purposes all the items arising from notes (i) to (vii) above should be regarded as material.

Answer

(a)   JOURNAL ENTRIES FOR ADJUSTMENTS

		Debit £	Credit £
(i)	Creditors	10,000	
	Debtors		10,000
	Operating profit	1,000	
	Debtors		1,000
	Operating profit	4,000	
	Suspense		4,000

		Debit £	Credit £
(ii)	Bank	2,000	
	Debtors		2,000
	Operating profit	1,000	
	Bank		1,000
(iii)	Operating profit	1,000	
	Debtors		1,000
	Provision for doubtful debts (W1)	1,140	
	Operating profit		1,140
(iv)	Stocks	2,000	
	Operating profit		2,000
	Profit and loss brought forward	1,000	
	Operating profit		1,000
(v)	Suspense	3,000	
	Operating profit		3,000

(b)   FIDDLES PLC
        BALANCE SHEET

	£	£	£
Fixed assets			
Land and buildings		220,000	
Fixtures and fittings		170,000	
		390,000	
Provision for depreciation		(120,000)	
			270,000
Current assets			
Stock (190 + 2)		192,000	
Debtors (W1)	186,000		
Less provision	(1,860)		
		184,140	
Bank (12 + 2 - 1)		13,000	
		389,140	
Current liabilities			
Creditors (110 - 10)		100,000	
Debenture interest payable		7,200	
Dividends proposed		10,000	
		117,200	

		£
Net current assets		271,940
Debentures		(180,000)
Net assets		361,940
Represented by		
Share capital		100,000
Profit and loss account		261,940
		361,940

FIDDLES PLC
PROFIT AND LOSS ACCOUNT

	£
Operating profit (W2)	80,140
Debenture interest (£180,000 × 16% × 3/12)	(7,200)
	72,940
Dividend	(10,000)
	62,940
Profit and loss account brought forward (200,000 - 1,000)	199,000
Profit and loss account carried forward	261,940

Workings

		£
1	Debtors per opening trial balance	200,000
	Contra	(10,000)
	Miscasting	(1,000)
	Standing order	(2,000)
	Written off	(1,000)
		186,000

	£
Provision b/f	3,000
Provision required	1,860
Journal	1,140

2	*Operating profit*	

	£
Per question	80,000
Wrong batch total	(1,000)
Returns	(4,000)
Bank charges	(1,000)
Bad debt	(1,000)
Bad debt provision	1,140
Stock (2,000 + 1,000)	3,000
Suspense (sales)	3,000
	80,140

Chapter roundup

- At this stage in your studies, you should be confident in your knowledge of:

    o **Double entry bookkeeping**
    o **Basic accounting definitions** (such as those in Question 1 in this chapter)
    o **Simple balance sheet**
    o **Simple profit and loss account**

- If you still feel a little rusty, go back to your old study material (which you should still have!) and practise a few questions.

- The regulatory system of accounting involves several bodies including:

    o The **Financial Reporting Council**
    o The **Review Panel**
    o The **Urgent Issues Task Force**
    o The **Accounting Standards Board**

    You should be able to describe their function.

- You must be able to define a **conceptual framework** and discuss the moves towards a conceptual framework in the UK.

Quick quiz

1   What problems are involved in disclosure in accounts? (see para 1.3)

2   Define a corporate report. (1.4)

3   From which sources does the UK regulatory framework derive? (2.3)

4   What are the responsibilities of the UK statutory authorities to EU directives? (2.5)

5   What is the role of the Review Panel? (2.15)

6   What are the objectives of the International Accounting Standards Committee? (2.20)

7   Define a 'conceptual framework'. (3.1)

Question to try	Level	Marks	Time
1	Introductory	n/a	27 mins

Part B
Preparing financial statements

Chapter 2

PARTNERSHIP ACCOUNTS I

Chapter topic list	Syllabus reference
1 Revision of general principles	2(a)
2 The formation of partnerships by amalgamation	2(a)

Introduction

The basic principles of partnership accounting have been covered in your earlier studies. You should be able to tackle the following topics.

(a)   The Partnership Act 1890
(b)   Partnership capital and appropriation of profits
(c)   Changes in the constitution of a partnership
(d)   Partnership changes during a financial period

Section 1 of this chapter allows you to test your recall with 3 questions. Section 2 covers a more complex aspect of partnerships: amalgamation.

Knowledge brought forward from Paper 1

Partnership is defined by the Partnership Act 1890 as the **relationship which exists** between **persons carrying on a business in common with a view of profit**. In other words, a partnership is an arrangement between two or more individuals in which they undertake to share the risks and rewards of a joint business operation.

It is usual for a partnership to be established formally by means of a **partnership agreement**. However, if individuals act as though they are in partnership even though no written agreement exists, then it will be presumed in law that a partnership does exist and that its terms of agreement are the same as those laid down in the **Partnership Act 1890**.

The partnership agreement is a written agreement in which the terms of the partnership are set out, and in particular the financial arrangements as between partners.

In the absence of a written partnership agreement, the provisions of the Partnership Act 1890 are presumed to apply between the partners. The Act includes the following provisions relating to financial arrangements.

•   Residual profits are shared in equal proportions.

•   There are no partners' salaries.

•   There is no interest on capital invested by partners.

•   If partners advance loans to the business in addition to their agreed capital, they are entitled to interest of 5% per annum on the amount of the loan.

The liability of a partnership to its owners is recorded in two accounts.

•   **Capital account:** records fixed capital of each partner.
•   **Current account:** records each partner's share of profits and losses less any drawings made.

When a new partner is admitted, **goodwill** is brought in in the old profit-sharing ratio and eliminated in the new.

1   REVISION OF GENERAL PRINCIPLES   12/94

1.1   The following exercises are designed to revise your knowledge of these topics. If you experience any difficulties, you should go back and study your Paper 1 material.

Question 1

Scrap, Iron and Ore are partners in a scrap metal business, sharing profits in the ratio 5:3:2 respectively. Their capital and current account balances on 1 January 19X2 were as follows.

	Capital accounts £	Current accounts £
Scrap	24,000	2,000
Iron	18,000	(1,000) Dr
Ore	13,000	1,500

Interest at 10% per annum is given on the fixed capitals, and salaries of £8,000 per annum are credited to Iron and Ore. Expansion of the business was hindered by lack of working capital, so Scrap made a personal loan of £20,000 on 1 July 19X2. The loan was to be repaid in full on 30 June 19X5 and loan interest at the rate of 15% per annum was to be credited to Scrap's account every half year. The partnership profit (before charging loan interest) for the year ended 31 December 19X2 was £63,000 and the partners had made drawings of: Scrap £16,000; Iron £16,500; Ore £19,000, during the year.

Required

Prepare the profit and loss appropriation account, the partners' capital and current accounts and the partnership balance sheet in respect of the year ended 31 December 19X2.

Answer

PROFIT AND LOSS APPROPRIATION ACCOUNT
FOR THE YEAR ENDED 31 DECEMBER 19X2

	£	£
Net profit*		61,500
Interest on capital accounts		
Scrap	2,400	
Iron	1,800	
Ore	1,300	
	5,500	
Salaries		
Iron	8,000	
Ore	8,000	
	16,000	
		21,500
		40,000
Partners' shares of balance		
Scrap (5/10)		20,000
Iron (3/10)		12,000
Ore (2/10)		8,000
		40,000

	£
*Profit per question	63,000
Less loan interest to Scrap (15% × £20,000 × ½)	1,500
Net profit available for appropriation	61,500

PARTNERS' CURRENT ACCOUNTS

	Scrap £	Iron £	Ore £		Scrap £	Iron £	Ore £
Balances b/f		1,000		Balances b/f	2,000		1,500
Drawings (cash)	16,000	16,500	19,000	Loan interest	1,500		
Balances c/d	9,900	4,300		Profit & loss appropri- ation a/c:			
				Interest	2,400	1,800	1,300
				Salary		8,000	8,000
				Balance	20,000	12,000	8,000
				Balance c/d			200
	25,900	21,800	19,000		25,900	21,800	19,000
Balance b/d			200	Balances b/d	9,900	4,300	

BALANCE SHEET AS AT 31 DECEMBER 19X2

	£	£
Total assets less current liabilities (balancing figure)		89,000
Creditor: amount falling due after more than one year Scrap: loan		(20,000)
		69,000
Partners' capital accounts		
Scrap	24,000	
Iron	18,000	
Ore	13,000	
		55,000
Partners' current accounts		
Scrap	9,900	
Iron	4,300	
Ore	(200)	
		14,000
		69,000

Question 2

Owing to staff illnesses, the draft final accounts for the year ended 31 March 19X0 of Messrs Stone, Pebble and Brick, trading in partnership as the Bigtime Building Supply Company, have been prepared by an inexperienced, but keen, clerk. The draft summarised balance sheet as at 31 March 19X0 is as follows.

	£	£
Tangible fixed assets at cost less depreciation to date		45,400
Current assets	32,290	
Less trade creditors	6,390	
		25,900
		71,300

Represented by

	Stone	Pebble	Brick	Total
	£	£	£	£
Capital accounts: at 1 April 19W9	26,000	18,000	16,000	60,000
Current accounts				
Share of net profit for the year ended				
31 March 19X0	12,100	12,100	12,100	= 36,300
Drawings year ended 31 March 19X0	(8,200)	(9,600)	(7,200)	
At 31 March 19X0	3,900	2,500	4,900	11,300
				71,300

The partnership commenced on 1 April 19W9 when each of the partners introduced, as their partnership capital, the net tangible fixed and current assets of their previously separate businesses. However, it has now been discovered that contrary to what was agreed, no adjustments were made in the partnership books for the goodwill of the partners' former businesses now incorporated in the partnership. The agreed valuations of goodwill at 1 April 19W9 are as follows.

	£
Stone's business	30,000
Pebble's business	20,000
Brick's business	16,000

It is agreed that a goodwill account should not be opened in the partnership's books.

It has now been discovered that effect has not been given in the accounts to the following provisions in the partnership agreement effective from 1 January 19X0.

(a)   Stone's capital to be reduced to £20,000 the balance being transferred to a loan account upon which interest at the rate of 11% per annum will be paid on 31 December each year.

(b)   Partners to be credited with interest on their capital account balances at the rate of 5% per annum.

(c)   Brick to be credited with a partner's salary at the rate of £8,500 per annum.

(d)   The balance of the net profit or loss to be shared between Stone, Pebble and Brick in the ratio 5:3:2 respectively.

Notes

1   It can be assumed that the net profit indicated in the draft accounts accrued uniformly throughout the year.

2   It has been agreed between the partners that no adjustments should be made for any partnership goodwill as at 1 January 19X0.

Required

(a)   Prepare the profit and loss appropriation account for the year ended 31 March 19X0.

(b)   Prepare a corrected statement of the partners' capital and current accounts for inclusion in the partnership balance sheet as at 31 March 19X0

Answer

(a)   MESSRS STONE, PEBBLE & BRICK, TRADING AS BIGTIME BUILDING SUPPLY CO
PROFIT AND LOSS APPROPRIATION ACCOUNT
FOR THE YEAR ENDED 31 MARCH 19X0

	Nine months to 31 December 19W9	Three months to 31 March 19X0
	£	£
Net profit (per draft accounts)	27,225	9,075 = 36,300
Interest on loan account (Stone)	-	385
	27,225	8,690

Interest on capital

Stone		250
Pebble		200
Brick		125

Salary: Brick			2,125	
Balance of profit				
Stone	9,075	($^{1}/_{3}$)	2,995	($^{1}/_{2}$)
Pebble	9,075	($^{1}/_{3}$)	1,797	($^{3}/_{10}$)
Brick	9,075	($^{1}/_{3}$)	1,198	($^{3}/_{10}$)
	27,225		8,690	

(b) Corrected statement of partners' capital and current accounts for inclusion in the partnership balance sheet as at 31 March 19X0.

	Stone £	Pebble £	Brick £	Total £
Partners' capital accounts				
At 1 April 19W9	26,000	18,000	16,000	
Goodwill adjustment (see note)	8,000	(2,000)	(6,000)	
Transfer to partner's loan account	(14,000)			
At 31 March 19X0	20,000	16,000	10,000	46,000
Partners' current accounts				
Interest on partners' capital	250	200	125	
Partner's salary			2,125	
Balance of profit				
9 months to 31 December 19W9	9,075	9,075	9,075	
3 months to 31 March 19X0	2,995	1,797	1,198	
Drawings	(8,200)	(9,600)	(7,200)	
At 31 March 19X0	4,120	1,472	5,323	10,915

Note: Goodwill at 1 April 19W9

	Stone £	Pebble £	Brick £	Total £
Valuation of goodwill of former businesses	30,000	20,000	16,000	66,000
Elimination of goodwill	(22,000)	(22,000)	(22,000)	(66,000)
	8,000	(2,000)	(6,000)	-

shared same way as profits.

Question 3

Gear, Brake and Handle commenced business as road hauliers on 1 January 19X5 introducing capital of £20,000, £10,000, £10,000 respectively. They shared profits and losses - Gear 2: Brake 1: Handle 1, and were each entitled to a salary of £6,400 per annum and interest at 10% per annum on their capitals.

On 30 September 19X5, Handle was injured in an accident and decided to retire from the partnership. He agreed to take his partnership car (NBV £3,500) and £3,000 cash in immediate settlement of his entitlement, leaving the balance on loan to the partnership at an interest rate of 12% per annum.

Axle, an employee receiving a salary of £4,000 per annum, was admitted to the partnership on 1 October 19X5 contributing £6,830 cash in respect of his admission. The new partners agreed to share profits in the ratio - Gear 4: Brake 2: Axle 1, to receive salaries of £8,000, £8,000 and £6,000 respectively; and to receive interest on capitals at an increased rate of 12% per annum. Although the book value of assets was agreed to be a fair valuation, partnership goodwill was estimated to be £14,000 but was not to be retained in the accounts.

The draft profit of the partnership for the year ended 31 December 19X5 was £41,000, before charging loan interest and after deducting Axle's salary whilst an employee. Partners' drawings for the year were Gear £7,500; Brake £6,000; Handle £5,700; Axle £2,000.

Prepare the profit and loss appropriation accounts and the partners' capital, current and loan accounts.

Answer

Workings

	£
Profit per question	41,000
Add Axle's salary while employee (9 months)	3,000
	44,000

Assuming that profits are earned evenly over the year:

		£
(a)	Profit for 9 months to 30 September 19X5	33,000
	Less Axle's salary (9 months)	3,000
		30,000
(b)	Profit for 3 months to 31 December 19X5	11,000
	Less loan interest on balance due to Handle	?
		?

Note. The loan interest, and thus the profit available for appropriation for the last three months of the year, cannot be calculated until the entries regarding Handle's retirement have been completed. Therefore the profit and loss appropriation account is prepared in two stages dealing with the nine months first, and then returning to complete the details for the last three months.

PROFIT AND LOSS APPROPRIATION ACCOUNTS
FOR THE YEAR ENDED 31 DECEMBER 19X5

Stage 1		*9 months to 30.9.19X5*	
		£	£
Net profit			30,000
Interest on capital accounts:			
Gear	10% × £20,000 × $^9/_{12}$	1,500	
Brake	10% × £10,000 × $^9/_{12}$	750	
Handle	10% × £10,000 × $^9/_{12}$	750	
			3,000
Salaries			
Gear	£6,400 × $^9/_{12}$	4,800	
Brake	£6,400 × $^9/_{12}$	4,800	
Handle	£6,400 × $^9/_{12}$	4,800	
			14,400
Balance			
Gear	($^2/_4$)	6,300	
Brake	($^1/_4$)	3,150	
Handle	($^1/_4$)	3,150	
			12,600
			30,000

Stage 2		*3 months to 1.12.19X5*	
		£	£
Net profit (£11,000 less 12% × £10,000 × $^3/_{12}$)			10,700
Interest on capital accounts			
Gear	12% × £19,000 × $^3/_{12}$	570	
Brake	12% × £9,500 × $^3/_{12}$	285	
Axle	12% × £4,830 × $^3/_{12}$	145	
			1,000
Salaries			
Gear	£8,000 × $^3/_{12}$	2,000	
Brake	£8,000 × $^3/_{12}$	2,000	
Axle	£6,000 × $^3/_{12}$	1,500	
			5,500
Balance			
Gear	($^4/_7$)	2,400	
Brake	($^2/_7$)	1,200	
Axle	($^1/_7$)	600	
			4,200
			10,700

CAPITAL ACCOUNTS

Stage 1

	Gear £	Brake £	Handle £		Gear £	Brake £	Handle £
Cash			3,000	Capital			
Car			3,500	introduced	20,000	10,000	10,000
Transfer				Goodwill			
to loan a/c			7,000	(2:1:1)	7,000	3,500	3,500
Balances							
c/d	27,000	13,500					
	27,000	13,500	13,500		27,000	13,500	13,500

Stage 2

	Gear £	Brake £	Axle £		Gear £	Brake £	Axle £
				Balances			
Goodwill				b/d	27,000	13,500	
(4:2:1)	8,000	4,000	2,000	Cash			6,830
Balances							
c/d	19,000	9,500	4,830				
	27,000	13,500	6,830		27,000	13,500	6,830
				Balances			
				b/d	19,000	9,500	4,830

CURRENT ACCOUNTS

Stage 1

	Gear £	Brake £	Handle £		Gear £	Brake £	Handle £
Drawings			5,700	Profit:			
Transfer				Interest	1,500	750	750
to loan				Salaries	4,800	4,800	4,800
a/c			3,000				
Balances							
c/d	12,600	8,700		Balance	6,300	3,150	3,150
	12,600	8,700	8,700		12,600	8,700	8,700

Stage 2

	Gear £	Brake £	Axle £		Gear £	Brake £	Axle £
				Balances			
Drawings	7,500	6,000	2,000	b/d	12,600	8,700	
Balances							
c/d	10,070	6,185	245	Profit:			
				Interest	570	285	145
				Salaries	2,000	2,000	1,500
				Balance	2,400	1,200	600
	17,570	12,185	2,245		17,570	12,185	2,245
				Balances			
				b/d	10,070	6,185	245

Stage 1

12% LOAN ACCOUNT - HANDLE

	£		£
Balance c/d	10,000	Transfer from capital a/c	7,000
		Transfer from current a/c	3,000
	10,000		10,000
		Balance b/d	10,000

2 THE FORMATION OF PARTNERSHIPS BY AMALGAMATION

2.1 When two or more businesses decide to combine their operations (to expand their range of operations, achieve some economies of scale etc) the problems of accounting for the **amalgamation** will arise. In respect of partnership accounts **typical problems are concerned with either:**

(a) **two (or more) sole traders amalgamating to form a partnership; or**

(b) **a sole trader amalgamating with an existing partnership; or**

(c) **two partnerships amalgamating to form a new partnership.**

2.2 Whatever the type of amalgamation, the accounting problems are very much the same. As we have already seen, where a partner retires from, or a new partner is admitted to, a partnership, **problems arise in respect of revaluing assets, valuing goodwill, establishing new profit shares, ascertaining new capital introduced,** and so on. All these problems of establishing and evaluating assets which are to be brought in, and liabilities which are to be taken over by the new partnership, are relevant to amalgamations.

Step 1   The old firms' assets and liabilities are **realised by 'sale' to the new firm,** not for cash, but for a share in the capital of the new business, the amount of capital being determined by the value of net assets contributed.

Step 2   A **revaluation account** is used in each of the old firms' existing set of books to account for and apportion to the old partners their share of the profit or loss on revaluation of assets and liabilities. A goodwill account (if necessary) is used to introduce (or increase) the goodwill, and to credit the old partners with their share.

Step 3   Once both firms have **adjusted** their asset, liability and capital accounts to take into account the agreed values, the separate books may be **merged**. The partners' agreed capitals are transferred to the new firm capital accounts and goodwill written off (in new profit sharing ratio) if necessary.

2.3 EXAMPLE: SOLE TRADER AND EXISTING PARTNERSHIP

Ion and Trill were trading as partners sharing profits in the ratio of 3:2 respectively. Nogov was a sole trader in the same line of business. On 1 January 19X1 the two firms were to be merged to form Notrion & Co, the partners sharing profits in the ratio - Nogov 3: Trill 2: Ion 1. The summarised balance sheets of the two firms on 31 December 19X0, were:

BALANCE SHEETS AS AT 31 DECEMBER 19X0

	Iontrill & Co £	Nogov £
Assets		
Freehold property		20,000
Plant etc	12,500	
Debtors	12,000	
Cash	8,000	2,000
	32,500	22,000
Liabilities		
Creditors	(2,500)	
	30,000	22,000
Capital		
Trill	12,000	
Ion	18,000	
Nogov		22,000
	30,000	22,000

The freehold property is to be revalued at £24,000 and the plant at £11,000. Goodwill is agreed at £5,000 for Ion and Trill and £2,500 for Nogov, but is not to appear in the books. All assets and liabilities are taken over by the new firm.

Show the partners' capital accounts in the old and new firms, and the opening balance sheet (in draft form) of Notrion & Co.

2.4 SOLUTION

CAPITAL ACCOUNTS

	Iontrill & Co				Iontrill & Co		
	Ion £	Trill £	Nogov £		Ion £	Trill £	Nogov £
Revaluation				Balances b/f	18,000	12,000	22,000
a/c	900	600		Goodwill a/c	3,000	2,000	2,500
Transfer:				Revaluation			
Notrion & Co	20,100	13,400	28,500	a/c			4,000
	21,000	14,000	28,500		21,000	14,000	28,500

NOTRION & CO - CAPITAL ACCOUNTS

	Nogov £	Trill £	Ion £		Nogov £	Trill £	Ion £
Goodwill							
(3:2:1)	3,750	2,500	1,250	Transfer:			
Balances c/d	24,750	10,900	18,850	old firms	28,500	13,400	20,100
	28,500	13,400	20,100		28,500	13,400	20,100
				Balances b/d	24,750	10,900	18,850

NOTRION & CO
DRAFT OPENING BALANCE SHEET

	£
Assets	
Freehold property	24,000
Plant etc	11,000
Debtors	12,000
Cash	10,000
	57,000
Liabilities	
Creditors	(2,500)
	54,500
Capital	
Nogov	24,750
Trill	10,900
Ion	18,850
	54,500

Further problems in amalgamations

2.5 Certain old firm assets may be sold for cash, while other assets and liabilities may be taken over by the individual partners at agreed valuations. **Care must be taken to ensure that the profits or losses on these 'realisations' are apportioned to the relevant partners.** The journal entries would be:

JOURNAL	Debit	Credit
	£	£
Partner's capital account	X	
Asset account		X
Being transfer of asset to a partner at agreed valuation		
Asset account	X	
Partners' capital accounts: A		X
B		X
Being profit on transfer of asset divided between partners		
in profit sharing ratio.		

An alternative to transferring the profit on transfers directly to the partners' accounts is to transfer it to the revaluation account.

2.6 Where **current accounts** are given in a question they **should be closed off to the partners' capital accounts.** As a new firm is being constituted there is little point in transferring current accounts to the new firm.

2.7 Sometimes, the capitals in the new firm are fixed in profit sharing ratio. This generally requires cash adjustment in the old partnership capital accounts.

2.8   EXAMPLE: TWO PARTNERSHIPS

Arthur and Dent are in partnership as Ardent Co and Ford and Prefect are in partnership as Reford Co. It was mutually agreed that on 1 January 19X8 the partnerships be amalgamated into one firm, Travellers Co. The profit sharing ratios were and are to be:

	Arthur	*Dent*	*Ford*	*Prefect*
Old firms	4	3	3	2
New firm	6	5	4	3

As on 31 December the balance sheets of the firms were as follows.

	Ardent Co £	Reford Co £		Ardent Co £	Reford Co £
Capital accounts			Property	7,400	10,000
Arthur	12,000		Fixtures	1,800	1,400
Dent	10,000		Vehicles	3,000	1,800
Ford		11,300	Stock	8,300	6,600
Prefect		7,400	Investment	800	
Current accounts			Debtors	6,800	5,800
Arthur	3,300		Bank balance	3,400	
Dent	1,000				
Creditors	5,200	6,000			
Bank overdraft		900			
	31,500	25,600		31,500	25,600

The agreement to amalgamate contains the following provisions.

(a) Provision for doubtful debts at the rate of 5% to be made in respect of debtors, and a provision for discount receivable at the rate of $2^{1}/_{2}$ % to be made in respect of creditors.

(b) Travellers & Co to take over the old partnership assets at the following values.

	Ardent Co £	Reford Co £
Property	10,000	
Fixtures	1,600	
Vehicles	2,800	1,300
Stock	8,450	6,390
Goodwill	6,300	4,500

(c) The property and fixtures of Reford Co are not to be taken over by Travellers Co. (These assets were sold for £13,500 cash on 1 January 19X8.)

(d) Dent to take over his firm's investment at a value of £760.

(e) The capital of Travellers Co to be £54,000 and to be contributed by the partners in profit sharing ratios, any adjustments to be made in cash.

You are required to prepare the revaluation accounts, the partners' capital accounts and (in draft form) the opening balance sheet for Travellers Co.

2.9   SOLUTION

ARDENT CO AND REFORD CO
REVALUATION ACCOUNTS

	Ardent Co £	Reford Co £		Ardent Co £	Reford Co £
Fixtures	200		Property	2,600	
Vehicles	200	500	Stock	150	
Stock		210	Creditors	130	150
Debtors	340	290			
Partners' capital a/cs:			Partners' capital a/cs:		
Arthur (4/7)	1,223		Ford (3/5)		510
Dent (3/7)	917		Prefect (2/5)		340
	2,880	1,000		2,880	1,000

CAPITAL ACCOUNTS

| | Ardent Co | | Reford Co | | | Ardent Co | | Reford Co | |
	Arthur	Dent	Ford	Prefect		Arthur	Dent	Ford	Prefect
	£	£	£	£		£	£	£	£
Revaluation a/c			510	340	Balances b/f	12,000	10,000	11,300	7,400
Investment a/c:					Current a/cs	3,300	1,000		
Asset taken					Revaluation				
over		760			a/cs: profit	1,223	917		
Loss on					Goodwill a/cs	3,600	2,700	2,700	1,800
realisation	23	17			Property				
Travellers Co					fixtures a/cs:				
£(54,000					profit on				
in ratio					realisation			1,260	840
6:5:4:3)	18,000	15,000	12,000	9,000	∴ Cash		1,160		
Cash	2,100		2,750	700					
	20,123	15,777	15,260	10,040		20,123	15,777	15,260	10,040
					Transfer:				
					old firms	18,000	15,000	12,000	9,000

TRAVELLERS CO
DRAFT OPENING BALANCE SHEET

	£	£
Fixed assets		
Property		10,000
Fixtures		1,600
Vehicles		4,100
		15,700
Current assets		
Stock	14,840	
Debtors	11,970	
Goodwill	10,800	
Cash (note)	11,610	
	49,220	
Liabilities		
Creditors	(10,920)	
Net current assets		38,300
		54,000
Capital		
Arthur		18,000
Dent		15,000
Ford		12,000
Prefect		9,000
		54,000

Note

CASH ACCOUNT

	Ardent Co	Reford Co		Ardent Co	Reford Co
	£	£		£	£
Balance b/f	3,400		Balance b/f		900
Realisation a/c: sale		13,500	Partners		
Partner: Dent	1,160		Arthur	2,100	
			Ford		2,750
			Prefect		700
			∴ Travellers Co	2,460	9,150
	4,560	13,500		4,560	13,500

£2,460 + £9,150 = £11,610

Question 4

Show how the amalgamation of Ardent Co and Reford Co would appear if a realisation account were used instead of a revaluation account.

Answer

ARDENT CO AND REFORD CO REALISATION ACCOUNTS

	Ardent Co £	Reford Co £		Ardent Co £	Reford Co £
Assets (at book values)			Creditors (at book values)-see note	5,200	6,000
Property	7,400	10,000	Capital a/c-Dent	760	
Fixtures	1,800	1,400	Cash-sale of		
Vehicles	3,000	1,800	property		
Stock	8,300	6,600	& fixtures		13,500
Investment	800		Travellers Co:		
Debtors	6,800	5,800	Assets taken over		
	28,100	25,600	Property	10,000	
Capital accounts**			Fixtures	1,600	
Arthur (4/7)	4,800		Vehicles	2,800	1,300
Dent (3/7)	3,600		Stock	8,450	6,390
Ford (3/5)		3,450	Debtors	6,460	5,510
Prefect (2/5)		2,300	Goodwill*	6,300	4,500
				35,610	17,700
			Less creditors	5,070	5,850
				30,540	11,850
	36,500	31,350		36,500	31,350

Note. It is not strictly correct to show creditors in the realisation account, but it may be expedient to do so in examination problems involving an amalgamation.

* A separate goodwill account could be used if the goodwill had to be written off in the new partnership books.

** The balances and final cash transfers on the partners' capital accounts will be the same as shown in Paragraph 2.12 above. Obviously, the opening balance sheet for the new firm will also be the same.

2.10 **An amalgamation of two (or more) firms may take place in conjunction with the retirement of a partner (or the admission of a new one).** A retiring partner's entitlement is calculated in the usual way, the amount due to him being either:

(a) paid to him by the old firm; or

(b) paid to him personally by his old partners (his share being divided between them in the capital accounts); or

(c)   left on loan with the new firm.

2.11   Generally, **closing adjustments** (usually in cash) between partners are made through the old firms' books (as in example Paragraph 2.12 above), but **occasionally** such adjustments **may have to be made by the partners individually** (**cash transfers between them**), particularly where they need to ensure that their initial capitals in the new firm are in profit sharing ratios.

2.12   In most questions the asset valuations used for the new firm are the same as those used to wind up the old firm. However, if this is not the case, then the problem should be tackled in two steps.

Step 1   Dissolution of the old firm
Step 2   Formation of the new firm

Chapter roundup

- This chapter has revised the general principles of accounting for partnerships.

  o   In general, a profit and loss account may be prepared for a partnership in exactly the same way as for a sole trader.

  o   In the profit and loss appropriation account the net profit is then apportioned between the partners according to the partnership agreement.

- The assets and liabilities of the old firms are **realised** by 'sale' to the new firm, not for cash but for a share in the capital of the new business

- Use a **revaluation a/c** in each of the old firms' books to account for the change in values

- The revaluation a/c balance is then **transferred** to the **existing partners' capital a/cs** in their **PSR**

- Once the old firms have adjusted their books, the separate books may be **merged**

- On amalgamation, certain assets may be sold for cash or taken over by individual partners at agreed valuation; this latter transfer must be treated with care; double entry is:

Debit	Partner's capital a/c	X	
Credit	Asset a/c		X

  Being transfer of asset to partner at agreed valuation

Debit	Asset a/c	X	
Credit	Partners' capital a/c A		X
	B		X

  Being profit on transfer of asset divided between partners in PSR

- Alternatively first transfer profit to revaluation account

Quick quiz

1   Describe the treatment of profits or losses on 'revaluations' of assets in a partnership amalgamation. (see para 2.8)

2   When an amalgamation takes place in conjunction with the retirement of a partner, how is his entitlement calculated and treated? (2.10)

Question to try	Level	Marks	Time
2	Introductory	n/a	36 mins

Chapter 3

PARTNERSHIP ACCOUNTS II

Chapter topic list	Syllabus reference
1 The dissolution of a partnership	2 (a)
2 The conversion of a partnership to a limited company	2 (a)
3 Implications of incorporation	2(a)

Introduction

This chapter introduces more advanced topics related to accounting for partnerships, completing the study of partnership accounts begun in Chapter 2. These are important practical topics, reflecting transactions frequently undertaken.

As in the previous chapter, you should adopt a methodical approach; learning the subject will then be easier.

Remember that, legally, any change in the constitution of a partnership (for example the admission or retirement of a partner) causes the old partnership to dissolve and a new one to be formed. However, it is normally convenient to ignore this fact and treat all accounts on a continuing basis, if the business of the partnership continues.

1   THE DISSOLUTION OF A PARTNERSHIP

Knowledge brought forward from Paper 1

The **sequence of events when the business does not continue** and the partnership ceases to exist is:

Step 1   All assets (except cash) and liabilities are transferred to a realisation account at their book value.

Step 2   Each partner's current account is cleared to his capital account, as the distinction between the two is irrelevant at this stage.

Step 3   As the assets are sold and liabilities are settled, double entry is made between the realisation account and the cash account. Any realisation expenses are debited to the realisation account. If partners take over assets this fact is recorded in their accounts.

Step 4   When all assets are disposed of and all liabilities met, the balance on the realisation account is transferred to the partners' accounts, in their profit sharing ratio. A credit balance on the realisation account represents a profit on dissolution, a debit balance a loss.

Step 5   At this stage the total amount due to the partners should equal the cash balance. The cash is distributed and the partnership is over.

*   If a partner has a debit balance on his account at the end of the dissolution he must make the necessary contribution to the partnership. The case of *Garner v Murray 1904* resulted in the ruling that in the event of the insolvency of a partner, such losses should be shared in the ratio of the last agreed capital balances (ie the capital balances **before** the dissolution begins).

*   Many partnership agreements exclude the rule established in *Garner v Murray*, in which case the deficit must be borne by the other partners in their profit sharing ratio.

1.1   The following exercises are designed to refresh your knowledge of this topic. Should you encounter any difficulties, go back and study your Paper 1 material.

Question 1

Tom, Dick and Harry are in partnership sharing profits and losses in the ratio 2:1:1. The balance sheet of the firm as at 31 May 19X9 was as follows.

BALANCE SHEET OF TOM,. DICK AND HARRY

	£	£		£ Cost	£ Depn	£ Net
Capital accounts			*Fixed assets*			
Tom	40,000		Premises	60,000	-	60,000
Dick	20,000		Plant and equipment	10,000	3,440	6,560
Harry	20,000			70,000	3,440	66,560
		80,000				
Current liabilities			*Current assets*			
Bank overdraft	1,300		Stock	16,000		
Trade creditors	5,500		Debtors	4,240		
		6,800				20,240
		86,800				86,800

On 31 May 19X9 it was agreed to dissolve the partnership and as Dick is continuing in business on his own account he agrees to take over the stock, plant and debtors at valuations of £18,000, £5,500 and £4,100 respectively. He also agrees to acquire the premises at a cost of £105,000 and obtains a mortgage loan of £80,000 which is paid to the partnership. The balance owing by Dick is charged against Tom's capital account as the two parties have agreed that Dick will repay the loan to Tom over a period of three years. Realisation expenses amounting to £1,000 are paid in cash and the creditors of the firm are paid in full.

You are required to record the above transactions in the ledger accounts of the partnership.

Answer

> *Tutorial note.* This topic was examinable for the first time in December 1997. It is not clear yet how difficult questions are going to be.

REALISATION ACCOUNT

19X9		£	*19X9*		£
31 May	Premises	60,000	31 May	Assets taken over by Dick:	
	Plant and equipment	6,560		Stock	18,000
	Stock	16,000		Plant and equipment	5,500
	Debtors	4,240		Debtors	4,100
	Realisation expenses	1,000		Premises	105,000
	Gain on realisation:				
	Tom	22,400			
	Dick	11,200			
	Harry	11,200			
		44,800			
		132,600			132,600

BANK ACCOUNT

	£			£
19X9		*19X9*		
31 May Dick - on account	80,000	31 May Balance		1,300
		Creditors		5,500
		Realisation expenses		1,000
		Tom capital		41,000
		Harry capital		31,200
	80,000			80,000

TOM CAPITAL ACCOUNT

	£			£
19X9		*19X9*		
31 May Loan to Dick	21,400	31 May Balance		40,000
Cash (balance)	41,000	Gain on realisation		22,400
	62,400			62,400

DICK CAPITAL ACCOUNT

	£			£
19X9		*19X9*		
31 May Assets taken over	132,600	31 May Balance		20,000
		Gain on realisation		11,200
		Cash		80,000
		Loan from Tom (bal)		21,400
	132,600			132,600

HARRY CAPITAL ACCOUNT

	£			£
19X9		*19X9*		
31 May Cash	31,200	31 May Balance		20,000
		Gain on realisation		11,200
	31,200			31,200

Question 2

Hop Skip and Jump decide to dissolve their partnership on 1 January 19X2, after an ugly scene at Skip's New Year's Eve party. The balance sheet of the partnership as at 31 December 19X1, was as follows:

	£	£		£	£
Capital accounts			Fixed assets at net		
Hop	21,000		book value		
Skip	21,000		Furniture and fittings		20,000
Jump	10,000		Motor vehicles		16,000
		52,000			36,000
Current accounts			Current assets		
Hop	5,750		Investments	21,000	
Skip	2,450		Debtors	37,000	
Jump	2,500		Balance at bank	3,000	
		10,700			61,000
Loan		15,000			
Creditors		19,300			
		97,000			97,000

The loan was repaid, interest already having been paid up to 31 December 19X1. The furniture and fittings were sold for £18,200 and Jump took over a motor vehicle (which had a net book value of £5,000) at an agreed valuation of £6,000. The other vehicles were sold for £13,450 after repairs had first been carried out on a faulty transit van by the Gloria Monday Service Station, at a cost of £450. Debtors realised only £34,800. Because of large discounts available, creditors were settled for £17,600. The investments realised £22,300. Dissolution expenses, excluding the transit van repair costs, totalled £750. Hop, Skip and Jump share profits and losses in the ratio 2:2:1.

You are required to show the relevant accounts and the final distribution between the partners.

Answer

REALISATION ACCOUNT

	£	£		£
Book values			Book values	
Furniture & fittings		20,000	Loan	15,000
Motor vehicles		16,000	Creditors	19,300
Investments		21,000		
Debtors		37,000	Bank	
Bank			Furniture etc	18,200
Loan repaid		15,000	Motor vehicles	13,450
Creditors		17,600	Debtors	34,800
Repairs		450	Investment	22,300
Expenses		750		
Profit on realisation			Jump (vehicle)	6,000
Hop (2)	500			
Skip (2)	500			
Jump (1)	250			
	1,250			
		129,050		129,050

PARTNERS' ACCOUNTS

	Hop £	Skip £	Jump £		Hop £	Skip £	Jump £
Realisation a/c			6,000	Capital b/d	21,000	21,000	10,000
Cash *	27,250	23,950	6,750	Current b/d	5,750	2,450	2,500
				Realisation a/c	500	500	250
	27,250	23,950	12,750		27,250	23,950	12,750

* Balance due to each partner, and so paid out of the partnership's bank account.

CASH AND BANK

	£		£	£
Balance b/d	3,000	Realisation a/c		
		Loan		15,000
Realisation a/c		Creditors		17,600
Furniture etc	18,200	Repairs		450
Motor vehicles	13,450	Expenses		750
Debtors	34,800			
Investment	22,300	Partners' accounts:		
		Hop	27,250	
		Skip	23,950	
		Jump	6,750	
				57,950
	91,750			91,750

Piecemeal realisation

1.2 It rarely happens in practice that all partnership assets are sold on or about the date set for the dissolution of the firm. Usually the disposal of assets and the payment of creditors takes place over a period of time, and **partners often wish to withdraw some cash as soon as it is available for distribution, rather than wait until all the assets have been sold.**

1.3 In such circumstances **it is important to limit individual withdrawals so that no partner receives more than would be his entitlement should the remaining assets prove to be worthless or impossible to realise.** This is a wise precaution, because if a partner becomes insolvent during the course of the dissolution the other partners do not then have the problem of retrieving funds from his estate.

1.4   As assets are realised the funds must be used as follows.

Step 1   Pay off outside creditors.
Step 2   Repay partners' advances over and above their fixed capital.
Step 3   Pay amounts due to partners on their capital and current accounts.

1.5   A straightforward technique may be adopted to determine the payment due to each partner as and when funds become available for distribution (once liabilities have been paid). A distribution schedule is prepared, commencing with the balances on the partners' accounts. **To find the distributioin payment due**:

(a)   Calculate the **notional loss** which would arise if all the remaining unsold assets were worthless.

(b)   Divide this **maximum potential loss** between the partners in the normal profit and loss sharing ratio.

1.6   The balances show the amount of cash to be paid to each of the partners, and when the payments are made and entered in the partners' accounts, the procedure can be operated (with the new balances) for the next distribution.

1.7   **Should a partner's account become notionally in debit when the maximum potential loss is apportioned to him, the debit balance must be borne by the other partners**. If the partnership agreement excludes *Garner v Murray* the debit balance is divided between the other partners in their respective profit and loss sharing ratios. This ensures that their accounts are brought into the profit sharing ratio as soon as possible during the piecemeal realisation.

Exam focus point
Because piecemeal realisation is specifically excluded from Paper 1 it is a likely candidate for a Paper 10 question.

1.8   EXAMPLE: PIECEMEAL REALISATION WITH GARNER V MURRAY EXCLUDED

Albani, Bernis and Clairvil were in partnership sharing profits in the ratio 3:1:1.

BALANCE SHEET AT DISSOLUTION

	£	£		£
Capital:			Sundry assets	14,000
Albani	8,000		Cash	1,000
Bernis	4,000			
Clairvil	1,000			
		13,000		
Creditors		2,000		
		15,000		15,000

Proceeds of the first four realisations of the assets were:

(a)   £3,000
(b)   £2,000
(c)   £4,000
(d)   £2,500

Assuming the partnership agreement excludes *Garner v Murray*, show the distribution of these sums by means of a distribution schedule, and record the entries in the partners' accounts.

1.9   SOLUTION

After the first realisation cash amounts to £4,000, but since £2,000 must be used to pay the creditors only £2,000 is available for distribution. This £2,000 is deducted from the net assets of £13,000 leaving assets of £11,000 which are treated as valueless. Remember that the total of the partners' accounts finances the net assets of the partnership.

DISTRIBUTION SCHEDULE

	£		Albani £		Bernis £		Clairvil £	Distrib. £
Capitals	13,000		8,000		4,000		1,000	
First realisation								
£(4,000-2,000)	2,000							
Maximum potential loss	11,000	(3/5)	6,600	(1/5)	2,200	(1/5)	2,200	
(divided in profit								
sharing ratio)			1,400		1,800		(1,200)	
C's deficiency is divided								
between A and B in								
profit sharing ratio (3:1)		(3/4)	(900)	(3/4)	(300)		1,200	
∴ *Cash distributed*			500		1,500		–	2,000
Capitals	11,000		7,500		2,500		1,000	
Second realisation	2,000							
Maximum potential loss	9,000	(3/5)	5,400	(1/5)	1,800	(1/5)	1,800	
			2,100		700		(800)	
C's deficiency is divided								
between A and B in								
profit sharing ratio		(3/4)	(600)	(1/4)	(200)		800	
∴*Cash distributed*			1,500		500		–	2,000
Capitals	9,000		6,000		2,000		1,000	
Third realisation	4,000							
Maximum potential loss	5,000	(3/5)	3,000	(1/5)	1,000	(1/5)	1,000	
∴ *Cash distributed*			3,000		1,000		–	4,000
Capitals (now in profit								
sharing ratio)	5,000		3,000		1,000		1,000	
Fourth realisation:								
cash distributed in								
profit sharing ratio	2,500		1,500		500		500	2,500
Capitals (in profit								
sharing ratio)	2,500		1,500		500		500	

PARTNERS' CAPITAL ACCOUNTS

	Albani £	Bernis £	Clairvil £		Albani £	Bernis £	Clairvil £
Cash	500	1,500		Balances b/f	8,000	4,000	1,000
Balances c/d	7,500	2,500	1,000				
	8,000	4,000	1,000		8,000	4,000	1,000
Cash	1,500	500		Balances b/d	7,500	2,500	1,000
Balances c/d	6,000	2,000	1,000				
	7,500	2,500	1,000		7,500	2,500	1,000

	Albani £	Bernis £	Clairvil £		Albani £	Bernis £	Clairvil £
Cash	3,000	1,000		Balances b/d	6,000	2,000	1,000
Balances c/d	3,000	1,000	1,000				
	6,000	2,000	1,000		6,000	2,000	1,000
Cash	1,500	500	500	Balances b/d	3,000	1,000	1,000
Balances c/d	1,500	500	500				
	3,000	1,000	1,000		3,000	1,000	1,000
				Balances b/d	1,500	500	500

1.10 Any further cash arising on realisation of the assets will be divided in profit sharing ratio between the partners.

1.11 If a partnership agreement does not exclude *Garner v Murray,* any debit balances arising on the division of the maximum potential loss between the partners would be charged to the other partners in the ratio of their **last agreed capital balances.**

Question 3

Assume that the Albani, Bernis and Clairvil partnership agreement does *not* exclude *Garner v Murray* and that the given capital balances are the last agreed capital balances. Show the partners' distribution statement and the partners' accounts.

Answer

DISTRIBUTION SCHEDULE

	Total £		Albani £		Bernis £		Clairvil £	Distrib. £
Capitals	13,000		8,000		4,000		1,000	
First realisation	2,000							
Maximum potential loss (divided in profit sharing ratio)	11,000	($^3/_5$)	6,600	($^1/_5$)	2,200	($^1/_5$)	2,200	
			1,400		1,800		(1,200)	
C's deficiency is divided between A and B in last agreed capital ratio (2:1)		($^2/_3$)	(800)	($^1/_3$)	(400)		1,200	
∴ Cash distributed			600		1,400		–	2,000
Capitals	11,000		7,400		2,600		1,000	
Second realisation	2,000							
Maximum potential loss	9,000	($^3/_5$)	5,400	($^1/_5$)	1,800	($^1/_5$)	1,800	
			2,000		800		(800)	
C's deficiency is divided between A and B in last agreed *capital* ratio (2:1)		($^2/_3$)	(534)	($^1/_3$)	(266)		800	
∴ Cash distributed			1,466		534		–	2,000
Capitals	9,000		5,934		2,066		1,000	
Third realisation	4,000							
Maximum potential loss	5,000	($^3/_5$)	3,000	($^1/_5$)	1,000	($^1/_5$)	1,000	
∴ Cash distributed			2,934		1,066		–	4,000
Capitals (now in profit sharing ratio)	5,000		3,000		1,000		1,000	
Fourth realisation: cash distributed in profit sharing ratio	2,500		1,500		500		500	2,500
Capitals (in profit sharing ratio)	2,500		1,500		500		500	

PARTNERS' CAPITAL ACCOUNTS

	Albani £	Bernis £	Clairvil £		Albani £	Bernis £	Clairvil £
Cash	600	1,400		Balances			
Balances				b/f	8,000	4,000	1,000
c/d	7,400	2,600	1,000				
	8,000	4,000	1,000		8,000	4,000	1,000
Cash	1,466	534		Balances			
Balances				b/f	7,400	2,600	1,000
c/d	5,934	2,066	1,000				
	7,400	2,600	1,000		7,400	2,600	1,000
Cash	2,934	1,066		Balances			
Balances				b/d	5,934	2,066	1,000
c/d	3,000	1,000	1,000				
	5,934	2,066	1,000		5,934	2,066	1,000
Cash	1,500	500	500	Balances			
Balances				b/d	3,000	1,000	1,000
c/d	1,500	500	500				
	3,000	1,000	1,000		3,000	1,000	1,000
				Balances			
				b/d	1,500	500	500

2   THE CONVERSION OF A PARTNERSHIP TO A LIMITED COMPANY

6/96

2.1   When a partnership is completely dissolved, its assets are dispersed and it ceases to exist both as a trading and a legal entity. A partnership may, however, be sold to another firm which continues the partnership trading activities but under a different legal umbrella. The new firm may be another partnership, or a sole trader, or as often happens (both in practice and in the examination) a limited company.

2.2   The **acquisition** of the partnership business **may be achieved in one of two ways**.

(a)   **A completely independent limited company taking over the firm for cash consideration.** The partners sell up and, having no further interest in the activities of their old business, close off the partnership books as outlined in the previous chapter.

(b)   **A limited company formed especially for the purpose of acquiring the business of the partnership.** This may occur when a successful partnership (or sole trader) has reached the stage where incorporation is desirable because of:

(i)   The benefits of limited liability.

(ii)   The need to obtain capital through issues of equity (ordinary) shares to outsiders.

(iii)   Possible taxation advantages.

This is the **more common** method.

2.3   **The accounting entries** for the 'sale' of the partnership to the limited company **record**:

(a)   The **cessation of the partnership** and the **realisation of its net assets**.

(b)   The **'purchase' by the newly created company** of the business and net assets of the partnership.

2.4   The sale price, normally referred to as the purchase consideration, is **usually paid** to the partners **in the form of**:

(a)   **shares in the limited company; and/or**

(b)   **debentures in the limited company.**

If the company has already been in existence or has incurred outside borrowings, cash may form part of the purchase consideration, if only to settle any balances due to the partners.

Closing the partnership books

2.5   The accounting procedures usually adopted to close off the partnership books are similar to those on the complete dissolution of a partnership.

Step 1   All assets (except cash) and liabilities are transferred to a realisation account at their book value.

Step 2   Each partner's current account is cleared to his capital account, as the distinction between the two is irrelevant at this stage.

Step 3   If any liabilities are not being taken over by the company, but are settled directly, the entries needed are to credit bank and debit realisation account.

Step 4   If any assets are being taken over by the partners, the agreed values should be credited to the realisation account and debited to the partners' accounts.

Step 5   The purchase consideration to be paid by the company should be credited to the realisation account and debited to a personal account specially opened up for the purchasing company.

Step 6   Close the realisation account by transferring any balance to the partners' accounts in their profit sharing ratios.

Step 7   Close the purchasing company's personal account by crediting it with shares, debentures or cash as appropriate.

Step 8   Close the partners' accounts by debiting them with shares, debentures or cash in the agreed proportions.

2.6   EXAMPLE: CONVERSION TO A LIMITED COMPANY

Macbeth and Hamlet are in partnership selling draughty castles, sharing profits in the ratio 3:2. Their draft balance sheet at 31 December 19X8 is as follows.

	Cost £	Depreciation £	Net £
Fixed assets			
Freehold premises	30,000	–	30,000
Fixtures and fittings	5,000	4,000	1,000
Motor vehicles	4,000	1,000	3,000
	39,000	5,000	34,000
Current assets			
Sundry debtors		20,000	
Cash at bank		600	
		20,600	
Current liabilities			
Sundry creditors		(12,600)	
Net current assets			8,000
			42,000
Creditors - amount falling due after more than one year			
Loan: Macbeth			(16,000)
			26,000

PARTNERSHIP CAPITAL

	£	£
Capital accounts		
Macbeth	20,000	
Hamlet	2,500	
		22,500
Current accounts		
Macbeth	3,000	
Hamlet	500	
		3,500
		26,000

Lear Ltd is incorporated for the purpose of taking over the business. It is to acquire the freehold premises at a valuation of £40,000 and the other assets (with the exception of cash and motor vehicles) at book value. These values are to be introduced into Lear Ltd's books. The current liabilities are also taken over by the new company.

The purchase consideration of £60,000 is to be settled by 20,000 ordinary £1 shares in Lear Ltd and cash of £30,000, obtained by a bank overdraft. Hamlet is to take over both cars at a valuation of £2,500 and the partners have agreed to divide the shares in their profit sharing ratio. Macbeth's loan is to be repaid in cash by the partnership.

Show the ledger account transactions necessary to record the above in the partnership.

2.7   SOLUTION

The order of approach is indicated by reference to the stages outlined in Paragraph 2.5 above.

CAPITAL ACCOUNTS

	Macbeth £	Hamlet £		Macbeth £	Hamlet £
Realisation account			Balance b/f	20,000	2,500
Motor vehicles taken over (d)		2,500	Current accounts (b)	3,000	500
Lear Ltd (h)			Realisation account (f)		
Shares	18,000	12,000	Profit on realisation	12,660	8,440
Bank (h)	17,660		Bank (h)		3,060
	35,660	14,500		35,660	14,500

CURRENT ACCOUNTS

	Macbeth £	Hamlet £		Macbeth £	Hamlet £
Transfer to capital a/c (b)	3,000	500	Balances b/f	3,000	500

REALISATION ACCOUNT

	£	£		£
Assets accounts (a)			Liability accounts (a)	
Freehold premises		30,000	Sundry creditors	12,600
Fixtures and fittings		1,000	Loan: Macbeth	16,000
Sundry debtors		20,000		
Motor vehicles		3,000	Partner's account:	
Bank: Macbeth's			Hamlet (cars taken at	
loan (c)		16,000	valuation)(d)	2,500
Partners' accounts (f)				
Profit on realisation:			Purchase consideration (e)	
Macbeth (3/5)	12,660		Lear	60,000
Hamlet (2/5)	8,440			
		21,100		
		91,100		91,100

LEAR LIMITED

	£		£
Realisation account (e)	60,000	Partners' accounts (g):	
		20,000 shares in Lear Ltd	
		Macbeth (3/5)	18,000
		Hamlet (2/5)	12,000
			30,000
		Bank (g)	30,000
	60,000		60,000

BANK ACCOUNT

	£		£
Balance b/f	600	Loan: Macbeth (c)	16,000
Lear Ltd (g)	30,000	Capital account: Macbeth (h)	17,660
Capital account: Hamlet (h)	*3,060		
	33,660		33,660

*Note that as Hamlet had a net debit balance on his capital account after the allocation of Lear Ltd shares, he must pay this amount in cash. The resulting debit balance on the bank account then equals the credit balance on Macbeth's capital account and this cash is paid over to him in its entirety.

The purchasing company's books

2.8   Having completed all the entries in the partnership books, the company books now have to be considered. Whether or not the company has been newly created for the purpose of acquiring the business of the partnership it will usually be convenient to **record the acquisition by using a purchase of business account.**

2.9   The following entries are made in the purchase of business account.

(a)   **It is credited with the assets to be taken over, individual ledger accounts being debited.** Although the values at which assets are introduced into the new books may often be the same as those found in the old books, there is no general rule that this should be the case. It is important to read the question carefully to ascertain which values are to be used in the company's books.

(b)   **It is debited with the liabilities** in amount and form assumed by the company, **individual ledger accounts being credited.**

(c) **It is debited with the purchase consideration** (same figure as in the closing of the partnership books) **appropriate accounts** (shares, debentures or cash) **being credited**. If shares are valued at greater than nominal value a share premium account must be credited.

2.10 If the purchase consideration exceeds the tangible net assets acquired it will be necessary to balance the purchase of business account by a transfer crediting that account and debiting goodwill. Conversely, a credit balance may be regarded as a capital reserve.

Question 4

Show the purchase of business account in Lear Ltd's ledger, and draft the opening balance sheet of Lear Ltd after completion of the conversion.

Answer

LEAR LIMITED'S BOOKS
PURCHASE OF BUSINESS ACCOUNT

	£	£			£
Creditors 2.9(b)	12,600		Assets 2.9(a)		
Purchase			Freehold premises		40,000
consideration 3.9(c)			Fixtures and fittings		1,000
Bank overdraft	30,000		Debtors		20,000
Share capital	20,000				
Share premium	*10,000		∴ Goodwill (balance:		
		60,000	para 2.10)		11,600
		72,600			72,600

Note. The purchase consideration is £60,000 of which £30,000 is settled in cash. Consequently, the 20,000 £1 ordinary shares must be worth £30,000, thus creating a share premium account.

The opening balance sheet of the new company will show fixed assets of £52,600, current assets (debtors) of £20,000, current liabilities of £42,600, share capital of £20,000 and share premium account of £10,000.

Allocation of profits

2.11 **A problem arises when a partnership converts to a limited company, not on a balance sheet date, but part way through an accounting period.** The partners make no closing entries at all and you are confronted with a trial balance at the end of the year and asked to produce:

(a) A trading and profit and loss account for the year.
(b) Closing entries for the partnership.
(c) The balance sheet of the company at the end of the year.

2.12 **A single column trading account and a two column profit and loss account must be prepared,** both gross profit and expenses being apportioned by time or by any other method indicated. The profit for the first period is credited to the partners' accounts, whilst that for the remaining period is dealt with by the company.

2.13 To **close off** the partnership records all that is necessary is to make appropriate entries in the **partners' capital accounts**:

(a) Credit the partners with their shares of profit.

(b) Debit the partners (and credit share capital etc) with shares and other consideration received.

2.14   To complicate matters further **an interval sometimes emerges between the date of the company's acquisition of the business and its incorporation**. In this case a three column profit and loss account should be prepared and any profit allocated to the company in its pre-incorporation period must be regarded as a capital reserve, or be deducted from goodwill, if this arises.

2.15   EXAMPLE: CONVERSION PART WAY THROUGH AN ACCOUNTING PERIOD

Dorcas and Mopsa are in partnership as butchers, sharing profits equally. They present the following trial balance at the end of their twelve month accounts period to 31 December 19X9.

		Debit	*Credit*
		£	£
Capital:	Dorcas (balance 1.1.19X9)		28,000
	Mopsa (balance 1.1.19X9)		10,000
Sales			165,000
Cost of sales		45,000	
Expenses		48,000	
Freehold property		72,000	
Cash		40,000	
Creditors			2,000
		205,000	205,000

You ascertain that although the partners agreed to convert the business to a company, Shepherds Ltd, as from 1 April 19X9, the company was not incorporated until 1 June 19X9. The consideration for the sale was to be £90,000 in £1 ordinary shares. The shares are to be divided equally between the partners and any adjustments necessary to close the accounts to be made by contributions or withdrawals of cash. Any goodwill arising is to be introduced into the books and any pre-incorporation profit written off against goodwill.

On the assumption that revenue and expenses accrue evenly over time, you are required:

(a)   to produce a trading and profit and loss account, in columnar form, for the year;

(b)   to show closing entries in the partners' capital accounts:

(c)   to produce the draft balance sheet of Shepherds Ltd as at 31 December 19X9.

2.16   SOLUTION

(a)   TRADING AND PROFIT AND LOSS ACCOUNT
FOR THE YEAR ENDED 31 DECEMBER 19X9

		£
Sales		165,000
Cost of sales		45,000
Gross profit		120,000
Dorcas and Mopsa (3/12)	30,000	
Shepherds Ltd (pre inc) (2/12)		20,000
Shepherds Ltd (post inc) (7/12)		70,000
		120,000

	Dorcas & Mopsa 3m to 31.3.X9 £	Shepherds Ltd 2m to 31.5.X9 £	Shepherds Ltd 7m to 31.12.X9 £
Gross profit	30,000	20,000	70,000
Less expenditure (time allocated)	12,000	8,000	28,000
Net profit	8,000	12,000	42,000
Transfers			
Capital accounts: Dorcas	9,000		
Mopsa	9,000		
Goodwill account		12,000	
Profit c/f			42,000
	18,000	12,000	42,000

(b)

PARTNERS' CAPITAL ACCOUNTS

	Dorcas £	Mopsa £		Dorcas £	Mopsa £
Share capital	45,000	45,000	Balances b/f	28,000	10,000
Cash (to balance)	9,000		Profit to 31.3.X9	9,000	9,000
			Goodwill: profit		
			on realisation (W1)	17,000	17,000
			Cash (to balance)		9,000
	54,000	45,000		54,000	45,000

Workings

1   *Profit on realisation*

	£
Partners' capital accounts on 1.1.19X9	
Dorcas	28,000
Mopsa	10,000
	38,000
Profit for period to 31.3.19X9	18,000
Net worth (ie net assets)	56,000
Purchase consideration	
90,000 £1 ordinary shares	90,000
Profit on realisation (divided equally between partners)	34,000

2   *Goodwill account*

The limited company has 'paid' £34,000 more than the value of the net assets of the partnership, at 31.3.19X9, this amount representing goodwill acquired.

GOODWILL ACCOUNT

	£		£
Partners' capital accounts	34,000	Profit and loss account:	
		2 months' pre-incorporation	
		profit	12,000
		Balance c/f	22,000
	34,000		34,000

3   *Cash account*

CASH ACCOUNT

	£		£
Balance b/f	40,000	Dorcas	9,000
Mopsa	9,000	Balance c/f	40,000
	49,000		49,000

(c)   SHEPHERDS LIMITED
      BALANCE SHEET AS AT 31 DECEMBER 19X9

	£	£
Fixed assets		
Goodwill		22,000
Freehold		72,000
		94,000
Current assets		
Cash	40,000	
Current liabilities		
Creditors	2,000	
Net current assets		38,000
		132,000
Capital and reserves		
Share capital		
90,000 £1 ordinary shares (authorised issued and fully paid)		90,000
Profit and loss account		42,000
		132,000

3   IMPLICATIONS OF INCORPORATION

3.1   When a partnership is 'incorporated', **the company formed will be a separate legal entity** with rights and liabilities quite distinct from its owners following *Salomon v Salomon & Co Ltd 1897*.

3.2   The principal advantages and disadvantages of incorporation are:

Advantages	Disadvantages
(a) **Limited liability.** Once each member has paid the full value of his shares to the company, he has no further liability to contribute towards payment of the company's debts (the company's liability, is of course unlimited). In the case of unincorporated businesses, on the other hand, the sole trader or partners will be liable without limit for the debts of the business.	(a) Companies are subject to a vast range of **legal requirements and companies legislation** which do not apply to sole traders and partnerships, resulting in less privacy and additional management and costs.
(b) **Perpetual succession.** The company, as a separate legal entity, exists until it is wound up. Changes in the composition of directors or members will not cause the business or existing contracts to be terminated or the company's status to change.	(b) Limited companies with a turnover of less than £350,000 and a balance sheet total of less than £1.4m **have to be audited,** which is a costly and time-consuming process.
(c) **Transferable interests.** Members' interests may be transferred as a form of property to other persons (subject to any restrictions in the company's constitution).	(c) The **capital and profits** of the business in particular are **subject to stringent rules designed to protect investors** and cannot be withdrawn as easily as from a business operated by a sole trader or partnership.

Advantages	Disadvantages
(d) A company can **borrow money and create a floating charge** in favour of the lender, leaving the company free to continue to deal with its assets until the charge crystallises (which sole traders and partnerships cannot do).	

3.3 **Tax (and National Insurance) considerations will often be a crucial factor** in deciding whether a business should be incorporated. Depending on all the circumstances, incorporation may be more or less attractive from a tax point of view.

Chapter roundup

- Partnerships may be terminated either by **closing down** the business entirely or by **disposing** of the business as a going concern to a **limited company**.

- In either case the key to getting the double entry right is to begin by **closing off asset** and **liability accounts** (except cash) and **transferring** their **balances to a single realisation account**. At this stage, the balances on the realisation account and bank account are matched by the combined balances on the partners' personal accounts.

  - o As **liabilities are settled**, **credit bank** and **debit realisation account**.
  - o As **assets are taken over** by partners or by a limited company at agreed values, **debit personal accounts** and **credit realisation account**.

- **Transfer the balance** on realisation account to the **partners' accounts. Close partners' accounts** by debiting them with cash or shares and debentures in the limited company, or with a mixture.

- In the case of conversion to a limited company, the company's books should only be opened up once the entries to dissolve the partnership are complete.

Quick quiz

1 Describe the sequence of accounting procedures on dissolution of a partnership. (see para 1.1)

2 What is the double entry to record:

(a) the sale of partnership assets for cash? (1.4 (b))
(b) dissolution costs incurred? (1.4 (c))

3 What is the rule in *Garner v Murray*? (1.13)

4 When a partnership's assets are being realised piecemeal, how is the amount available for distribution payment ascertained? (1.19)

5 What entries are made in the purchase of business account in the books of a limited company acquiring a partnership business? (2.9)

6 How should a company account for pre-incorporation profits? (2.14)

7 What are the *disadvantages* of incorporation? (3.2, table)

Question to try	Level	Marks	Time
3	Full exam	20	36 mins
4	Full exam	25	45 mins

Chapter 4

BRANCH ACCOUNTS AND UNINCORPORATED JOINT VENTURES

Chapter topic list	Syllabus reference
1 Why prepare branch accounts?	2(a)(iii)
2 Branch accounts: records in head office books	2(a)(iii)
3 Branch accounts: separate entity	2(a)(iii)
4 Audit problems of branches	2(a)(iii)
5 Unincorporated joint venture accounts	2(a)(ii)

Introduction

Branch accounting is important as a practical topic and, as was the case with partnership accounts, a logical approach will help you to learn the subject and answer examination questions.

The step by step approach given in the exercises is the best way of tackling questions.

Branches are given varying degrees of autonomy by their head office, and the accounting records for the branch may be held at head office or by the branch itself (separate entity).

The principles of branch accounting will help you in later chapters when you look at the treatment of subsidiary companies and the preparation of group accounts.

Joint venture accounts are the final non-company accounting topic that you need to tackle.

1   WHY PREPARE BRANCH ACCOUNTS?

1.1 Where an organisation is increasing in size and/or is intending to diversify its activities, it may find it necessary or advantageous to control operations more precisely by instituting a system of departmental or branch accounting.

> **KEY TERM**
>
> **Branch accounting** means that each department or branch is established as a separate cost and/or accounting centre, the net profit per branch can be found and accumulated to arrive at the profit for the whole business.

1.2 Various types of organisations may operate through branches; for example, banks, building societies, estate agents, accountants, travel agents. However, **examination questions tend to concentrate on retailing businesses such as department stores, or chain stores**. Whatever the business activities may be, the principles outlined below can, with a common sense approach, be used to prepare accounts in any situation.

1.3   Branch accounts may be considered to fall into **two main categories** of accounting problem.

   (a)   Branch accounts **may be prepared to show the performance of both a main trading centre** (the head office) and **subsidiary trading centres** (the branches), **but with all accounting records being maintained by the head office**.

   (b)   'Separate entity' branch accounts are prepared where **branches maintain their own records, which must therefore be combined with head office records in order to prepare accounts for the whole business.**

Exam focus point
If you are revising, go straight to the summaries in Paragraphs 2.4 and 3.20

2   BRANCH ACCOUNTS: RECORDS IN HEAD OFFICE BOOKS

Internal control problems

2.1   When a branch is established, considerable trust is placed in its manager, where stocks are dispatched to his sole control. **Head office can check the manager's honesty and performance and deter him from fraud and outright theft by establishing an internal audit department**, whose staff, amongst other duties, will visit branches to check the records and to count the stock, ensuring that all material differences from the expected value are accounted for.

2.2   It is also the **responsibility of a business's managers to establish an adequate system of internal control so that the business is carried on efficiently and the assets are safeguarded.** One way of doing this is for head office to keep records of stock and other assets sent to the branch and for the branch manager to record sales proceeds in memorandum only, forwarding his sales and stock returns daily, weekly or monthly and banking the sales proceeds intact (probably daily).

2.3   Expenses will probably be paid centrally from head office (except for petty cash items, like staff refreshments). Head office staff can see from the branch returns whether the branch is meeting its sales targets and whether there has been any unusual stock wastage. **Internal and external audit procedures should confirm the accuracy of the branch returns.**

Accounting system when branch stock is transferred at selling price

2.4   The accounts that the **head office must incorporate into its ledger** to deal with the branch include the:

   (a)   **Branch stock (control) account.**
   (b)   **Branch mark-up account.**
   (c)   **Goods sent to branch account.**

   and where necessary the branch:

   (d)   Cash and bank accounts.
   (e)   Debtors accounts (if the branch sells goods on credit as well as for cash).
   (f)   Expense accounts.

2.5   The **branch stock account is maintained at selling price**, being debited with goods sent to branch and credited with sales, returns to head office, shortages or mark-down.

The balance on the branch stock account should always represent the stock of unsold goods at selling price.

2.6   The **branch mark-up account is effectively the trading account for the branch** and is credited with the mark-up, that is, the potential gross profit on the goods held by the branch. Where goods are returned to the head office, or are lost, stolen, destroyed or marked down, the mark-up account must be debited appropriately, the potential gross profit thus being reduced. At the end of the accounting period, the mark-up on unsold goods (future gross profit) is carried down while the balance (profit or loss) is transferred forward to the main profit and loss account.

2.7   As you know, for published accounts it is not permissible to value stocks at selling price, on grounds of prudence. By setting the mark-up on unsold goods against the branch stock balance at the year end, stock is valued at cost.

2.8   The **goods sent to branch account is maintained at cost price** (being credited with goods sent to branch and debited with goods returned to head office) and at the end of the accounting period is closed off to head office purchases (or trading account) in order to reduce the head office cost of sales figure.

> **Exam focus point**
> Separate entity branch accounts have been examined, but branch accounts with records in head office have not yet been examined.

2.9   EXAMPLE: BRANCH ACCOUNTS

Catcher has been trading for a number of years through main premises at Hastings and a branch at Rye. All purchases are made by the head office and goods are 'invoiced' to the branch at the expected selling price, that is, cost plus 25%. The details initially available regarding Catcher's trading are as follows.

	£
Opening stock at branch (at selling price)	12,000
During the year	
Goods sent to branch (at cost)	57,840
Cash sales (including goods marked down during the year)	58,500
Credit sales	9,840
Returns to head office (at cost)	2,000

You are required to open and write up (as far as is possible) the branch stock control account, the branch mark-up account, the goods sent to branch account and the debtors' account in the head office books.

2.10   SOLUTION

In all branch account problems it is of prime importance to establish the price (cost) structure at the very beginning.

	Units
Head office cost	100
Mark-up	25
Selling price	125

The opening stock (balance b/f on the branch stock control account) is at selling price and so the balance b/f on the mark-up account (the anticipated gross profit in respect of the opening stock) must be calculated.

$$\frac{25}{125} \times £12,000 = £2,400$$

2.11   The ledger accounts opened up in the head office books are as follows.

BRANCH STOCK CONTROL ACCOUNT

	£		£
Balance b/f	12,000	Goods returned to head office	2,500
Goods sent to branch	72,300	Cash: sales	58,500
(5/4 × £57,840)		Branch debtors: sales	9,840

BRANCH MARK-UP ACCOUNT

	£		£
Branch stock control account:		Balance b/f	2,400
mark-up on goods returned	500	Branch stock control account	
		mark-up on goods sent to	
		branch (1/4 × £57,840)	14,460

GOODS SENT TO BRANCH ACCOUNT

	£		£
Branch stock control account:		Branch stock control account:	
goods returned to head office,		goods sent to branch, at	
at cost	2,000	cost	57,840

BRANCH DEBTORS ACCOUNT

	£		£
Branch stock control account	9,840		

Summary of double entry and technique

2.12   The following gives the double entry for the usual transactions for this type of branch accounts question.

DEBIT   Branch stock control a/c: selling price
CREDIT   Goods sent to branch a/c: cost
           Mark-up a/c: profit

Being transfers from head office

DEBIT   Cash/debtors: selling price
CREDIT   Branch stock control a/c: selling price

Being sale of stock by branch

DEBIT   Mark-up a/c
CREDIT   Branch stock control a/c

Being mark down in price

DEBIT   Goods sent to branch a/c: cost
           Mark-up a/c: profit
CREDIT   Branch stock control a/c: selling price

Being returns to head office

2.13   Any balance on the branch stock control account represents a loss or gain and is dealt with as follows.

DEBIT   P & L a/c of company: cost
               Mark-up a/c: profit
CREDIT   Branch stock control a/c: selling price

Being loss of goods if head office and branch share the loss

DEBIT   Mark-up a/c: selling price
CREDIT   Branch stock control a/c: selling price

Being loss of goods if branch bears the loss

DEBIT   P & L a/c of company
CREDIT   Branch stock control a/c

Being losses of cash (unrecorded sale)

Question 1

This exercise continues the example started above.

Further details are obtained regarding Catcher's operations at the Rye branch.

During the year	£
Stock lost in burglary (at cost)	4,000
Agreed allowances off selling prices (ie mark-down)	160
Cash received from debtors	8,500
Discount allowed to debtors	100
Bad debts written off	45

The closing stock at the year end (at cost per stocktake) is £6,000 and any stock unaccounted for is to be regarded as normal wastage and pilferage. All goods marked down had been sold during the year.

You are required to complete the branch stock control account, the branch mark-up account, the goods sent to branch account, and the debtors account in the books of head office.

Answer

The journal entries accounting for the above transactions are as follows.

			£	£
(a)	DEBIT	Profit and loss account	4,000	
		Branch mark-up account (25% × £4,000)	1,000	
	CREDIT	Branch stock control account		5,000
		Being the write-off of the abnormal stock loss incurred due to theft (see Paragraph 2.13 below)		

			£	£
(b)	DEBIT	Branch mark-up account	160	
	CREDIT	Branch stock control account		160
		Being the write-down of goods to actual selling price (reducing the potential gross profit)		
(c)	DEBIT	Cash	8,500	
		Profit and loss account: discount allowed	100	
		bad debts written off	45	
	CREDIT	Branch debtors account		8,645
		Being bad debts written off, discount allowed to and cash collected from, branch credit customers		

The ledger accounts can now be written up and closed off.

BRANCH STOCK CONTROL ACCOUNT

	£		£
Balance b/f	12,000	Goods returned to head office	2,500
Goods sent to branch	72,300	Cash: sales	58,500
		Branch debtors: sales	9,840
		Profit & loss and mark-up accounts: burglary	5,000
		Mark-up account: allowance off selling price	160
		∴ Mark-up account: wastage & pilferage (balancing figure)	800
		Balance £(6,000 + 25%) c/d	7,500
	84,300		84,300

BRANCH MARK-UP ACCOUNT

	£		£
Branch stock control account: mark-up on goods returned	500	Balance b/f	2,400
Branch stock control account: burglary	1,000	Branch stock control account: mark-up on goods sent to branch	14,460
Branch stock control account: mark-down	160		
Branch stock control account: wastage and pilferage	800		
∴ Profit & loss account: (balancing figure)	12,900		
Balance (25% × £6,000) c/d	1,500		
	16,860		16,860

GOODS SENT TO BRANCH ACCOUNT

	£		£
Branch stock control account: goods returned to head office at cost	2,000	Branch stock control account: goods sent to branch, at cost	57,840
∴ Head Office purchases (or trading) account	55,840		
	57,840		57,840

BRANCH DEBTORS ACCOUNT

	£		£
Branch stock control account	9,840	Cash	8,500
		Profit & loss account: discount allowed	100
		bad debts written off	45
		Balance c/d	1,195
	9,840		9,840

Further considerations

2.14 Remember that **the branch stock control account must be maintained at selling prices,** the closing stock balance being shown on the balance sheet less the branch mark-up account balance (ie at cost).

(a) Note that the abnormal stock loss of £4,000 is written off to the profit and loss account (or to a ledger account which can be credited with any insurance proceeds received - the balance being written off) instead of being absorbed in the general trading margins.

(b)   The 'normal' wastage and pilfering is charged entirely against the gross profit in the above example, but, if material, the cost of goods lost could be written off in the profit and loss account (as is the abnormal stock loss).

2.15   **Other problems** which may be introduced into such branch account questions include the following.

(a)   **Goods in transit may have been recorded in the books as sent to the branch.** If the closing stock figure (in the branch stock control account) is based on a physical stock take, you must remember to carry down the stock in transit before calculating the 'unknown' balance.

(b)   **Transfers of goods are sometimes made between various branches in the organisation.** Since the head office keeps a full set of ledger accounts for each branch it controls, the transfers can be recorded as if they were, in effect, a return to head office by branch A followed by a despatch to branch B.

(c)   If **goods are purchased locally by the branch** (eg out of takings), they should be entered in the branch stock control account at selling price, the mark-up being credited to the branch mark-up account.

> **Exam focus point**
> Since the **mark-up account** already forms **part of the double entry** accounting system, should an examination question require the preparation of a branch trading account you must remember that such an account is merely memorandum. This memorandum trading account is constructed by extracting relevant figures from the ledger accounts and reconciling the gross profit figure shown in the branch mark-up account.

2.16   EXAMPLE: MEMORANDUM BRANCH TRADING ACCOUNT

MEMORANDUM BRANCH TRADING ACCOUNT

	£	£
Sales: cash		58,500
credit		9,840
		68,340
Cost of sales		
Opening stock *at Cost*	9,600	
Purchases less returns	55,840	
	65,440	
Less closing stock *at Cost*	6,000	
	59,440	
Less cost of goods stolen (Dr P & L a/c)	4,000	
		55,440
Gross profit (as per mark-up account)		12,900

Accounting systems when branch stock is not transferred at selling price

2.17   **Where the head office transfers goods to the branch at cost rather than selling price,** possibly because selling prices cannot be fixed, **the accounts to be maintained in the head office books are:**

(a)   The **branch stock account** (which is effectively a branch trading account used to calculate the branch gross profit).

(b)   The **goods sent to branch account.**

(c) Any other relevant accounts (for example branch debtors account, branch bank account and so on).

2.18 **Where goods are charged out to the branch at cost plus a certain mark-up percentage,** possibly to ensure that at least any overheads are recovered in those circumstances where it is not possible to fix selling prices accurately, the method adopted would normally be the same as that for recording branch stock at selling price. **The principal accounts maintained by the head office are the:**

(a) **Branch stock control account** (maintained at cost plus mark-up).
(b) **Goods sent to branch account.**
(c) **Branch mark-up account.**
(d) **Branch debtors account.**

Normally, as actual selling prices will be greater than cost plus mark-up, a 'surplus' profit (not directly budgeted for) will arise on the branch stock control account. This profit should be credited to the branch mark-up account to arrive at the total branch profit or loss.

3   BRANCH ACCOUNTS: SEPARATE ENTITY   12/95, 12/97

3.1 Where a complete and independent set of records is maintained by the branch (or branches), trading and **profit and loss accounts and balance sheets can be prepared for each branch and the head office.** Accounts for the business as a whole can then be produced by combining the individual accounts.

3.2 In most cases, **the head office** sets up the branch, transfers to it necessary assets and **records the details in its own ledger through a branch current account. The branch,** in opening its ledger, **records the receipt of the assets through a head office current account.** So, from the start of the operation, the branch current account balance in the head office balance sheet is an asset representing the investment in the net worth of the branch. In the branch balance sheet, the credit balance on the head office current account shows the proprietorship, the 'capital' of the branch.

3.3 **Usually, a central buying policy is adopted by organisations** (which thereby may benefit from bulk discounts, standardised product ranges etc) and sales are made to the general public by the branch(es) and, often, the head office. In addition to making normal sales to outsiders the head office transfers goods to the branch(es) either at cost or, more often, at some marked-up price which enables both the head office and the branch to make a profit.

3.4 As the branch becomes fully operational, any **transfers** of goods, cash, other assets or liabilities, expenses recharged and the branch profit or loss, will be **entered in the respective ledgers through the current accounts**.

3.5 The balance (usually debit) in the head office books should equal the balance (usually credit) in the branch books but, in practice, **the accounts will not always agree because of:**

(a) **Errors,** which obviously must be corrected in the appropriate ledger.

(b) **Transit items** (eg goods in transit to the branch, cash in transit to head office), which have been recorded in one set of books but not in the other, at the end of an accounting period. The branch current account balance in the head office books must be reconciled in the head office figure in the branch books.

3.6   EXAMPLE: SEPARATE ENTITY

Small, who had been trading successfully for a number of years from one location, acquired additional freehold premises at a cost of £30,000. On 1 January 19X1 the new branch was opened with Small's friend Parts as manager. The following assets were transferred from the head office to the branch.

	£
The freehold premises	30,000
Fixtures and fittings (original cost £5,000)	4,000
Motor vehicle (original cost £6,000)	4,500
Cash at bank	3,000

The Parts branch, which maintains independent records, installed additional fittings at a cost of £2,000.

During 19X1 the following transactions in respect of the Parts branch were recorded by Small in the head office books.

	£
Goods sent to branch: at cost	40,000
Goods returned by branch: at cost	1,200
Remittances from branch	38,000
Proportion of head office expenses chargeable to the branch	2,800

The transactions recorded by Parts in respect of the head office were:

	£
Goods received from head office: at cost	38,500
Goods returned from branch: at cost	1,200
Remittances to head office	38,800

At the year end goods in transit to the branch were £1,500 and cash in transit to the head office amounted to £800. Show the above transactions in the current accounts in the head office and branch books.

3.7   SOLUTION

As each set of books is maintained independently, goods in transit have not yet been recorded in the branch books and cash in transit has not been recorded in the head office books. To reconcile the current accounts, the chargeable expenses have to be entered by the branch, while the items in transit are carried down as balances in the branch current account in the head office books.

(a)   *Head office books*

BRANCH CURRENT ACCOUNT

	£		£
Freehold premises	30,000	Provisions for depreciation	
Fixtures and fittings	5,000	Fixtures and fittings	1,000
Motor vehicle	6,000	Motor vehicles	1,500
Bank	3,000	Goods returned by branch	1,200
Goods sent to branch	40,000	Bank (remittances)	38,000
Expenses (branch)	2,800	Goods in transit c/d	1,500
		Cash in transit c/d	800
		Balance c/d	42,800
	86,800		86,800

(b) *Branch books*

HEAD OFFICE CURRENT ACCOUNT

	£		£
Provisions for depreciation		Freehold premises	30,000
Fixtures and fittings	1,000	Fixtures and fittings	5,000
Motor vehicles	1,500	Motor vehicles	6,000
Goods returned to head office	1,200	Bank	3,000
Bank (remittances to		Goods received from head	
head office)	38,800	office	38,500
Balance c/d	42,800	Expenses	2,800
	85,300		85,300

Note that the items in transit do not affect the branch records and that the current account balances agree (£42,800) and will 'cancel' each other when a combined balance sheet is produced. The branch will maintain its own fixed asset, accumulated depreciation, sales, expenses and bank accounts, which complete its double entry system.

Provisions for unrealised profits

3.8   In the above examples goods were transferred from the head office to the branch at cost price to the head office. More often, the head office will establish **a mark-up** that **will enable both the head office and branch to make a profit in respect of the transferred goods.**

> **Exam focus point**
> In many examination questions the price structure provides the key to solving and preparing the trading accounts, some items (usually closing stocks) being 'unknown'.

It is vital to ascertain and tabulate the head office and branch mark-ups at the very beginning, for example:

Price structure	Units
Head office cost	100
Head office profit on transfers to the branch	10
Branch cost	110
Branch profit on sales	15
Selling price	125

Armed with this information the gross profits can be calculated and the closing stocks, stock shortages etc, 'discovered' as balancing figures on the trading accounts.

3.9   When preparing the head office trading account, the goods transferred to the branch are shown at branch cost (inclusive of the head office profit). In so far as the branch has sold such goods during the accounting period, the head office can legitimately take credit for the profit made. However, **if the branch closing stock includes goods received (at a profit loaded price) from the head office, or goods are in transit, a provision for the unrealised profit must be made by the head office.**

DEBIT   Head office P&L a/c
CREDIT   Provision for unrealised profit account
*Being the provision for unrealised profit in respect
of the branch closing stock and goods in transit*

3.10 The provision for unrealised profit account is made up, therefore, of two elements, and **in the head office balance sheet:**

(a)   **The provision in respect of branch closing stock is deducted from the branch current account balance.**

(b)   **The provision in respect of goods in transit is deducted from the goods in transit.**

3.11   Remember that, where the organisation has been trading for a number of years, the opening balance sheet (or trial balance) may include a brought forward provision for unrealised profit. As with any 'provision account' entries, you must:

(a)   calculate the required provision at the year end and carry down the new balance in the provision account;

(b)   debit or credit the head office profit and loss account with the difference on the provision account;

(c)   deduct the provision from the appropriate accounts in the head office balance sheet (branch current account or goods in transit).

3.12   **When preparing the combined trading account the closing stock must include goods in transit and must be shown at cost.** As no credit for unrealised profit has been taken in the trading account there is no need to make a provision for unrealised profit in the combined profit and loss account. Note that the balance sheet stock figure is the same as the trading account figure and includes goods in transit.

3.13   As well as receiving goods from the head office, the branch may also make independent purchases on which it can establish its own profit margins. This presents no particular accounting problems, but **care must be taken to exclude directly purchased goods from branch closing stock when calculating the head office provision for unrealised profit.** Naturally, the branch closing stock figure will comprise goods received from head office (at cost to the branch) and directly purchased goods.

> **Exam focus point**
> The branch question in December 1997 included a provision for unrealised profit in the head office accounts.

Lost, obsolete and damaged goods

3.14   Where goods have been **lost**, whether at the head office, or branch, or in transit, it is advisable to **treat the loss as abnormal**.

DEBIT   P&L account
CREDIT   Trading account
Being the cost of goods lost written off in
the appropriate profit and loss accounts

In this way, the standard gross profit percentages on sales can be maintained in the trading accounts, so facilitating the calculation of 'unknown' stock figures etc. Note that the cost of the goods lost is written off and, in the case of goods (from head office) lost at the branch, the cost in the combined accounts (ie cost to the head office) is less than the cost in the branch accounts (ie the cost to the branch).

3.15   Where stock has become **obsolete** and cannot be sold the cost of it **must be written off**. As with lost stock the standard gross profit percentages should be maintained and so:

DEBIT   P&L account
CREDIT   Trading account
Being the cost of obsolete stock written off in the
appropriate profit and loss accounts

In respect of branch obsolete stock (originally received from the head office) the loss in the combined accounts will be less than the loss in the branch accounts (as with goods lost).

3.16   Where stock has to be marked down below cost because of **damage** (or some other reason) the **loss must be recorded in the accounts**.

DEBIT   P&L account
CREDIT   Trading account
Being the mark-down of damaged goods to net
realisable value in the appropriate accounts

By making this entry in the appropriate accounts we ensure that the closing stock figures in the trading accounts include the damaged stock at net realisable value. Note that in respect of a mark-down of goods at the branch (originally received from the head office) the mark-down will be less in the combined accounts than in the branch accounts (the cost of damaged goods to the combined entity being less than the cost to the branch).

3.17   Any **insurance proceeds received** in respect of goods lost, stolen or damaged **should be credited to the profit and loss account** (or deducted from the profit and loss charge in respect of such items).

Preparation of final accounts

3.18   At the end of an accounting period **trial balances** are extracted from the head office and branch ledgers. Using the trial balances accounts may be prepared for:

   (a)   the head office;
   (b)   the branch;
   (c)   the combined firm or company.

3.19   Generally, the trading and profit and loss accounts and balance sheets are produced in columnar form, the head office and branch being treated almost as if they were separate legal entities. The organisation is only regarded as a single concern in the 'combined' columns which are arrived at by totalling appropriate items in the head office and branch columns. In the combined balance sheet the branch current account is replaced by the underlying assets and liabilities.

3.20   **The technique for the preparation of accounts of the head office, branch and combined entity can be summarised as follows.**

   Step 1   Record the cost structure.

   Step 2   Record the question information onto the profit and loss account, balance sheet, current accounts or provision for unrealised profit.

   Step 3   Deal with the notes as follows.

      (a)   Goods in transit: add to head office stock at transfer price (ie including mark-up) and credit the current account.

      (b)   Cash in transit: add to head office cash balance and credit the current account.

(c)   Expenses recharged: adjust the expenses and current account of whichever part of the business has not recorded the item.

(d)   Closing stock: include in head office at cost and in the branch at transfer price.

Step 4   Finish the branch's books and transfer the profit to the head office through the current accounts.

Step 5   Finish the head office's books, dealing with the provision for any unrealised profit.

Step 6   Complete the combined entity remembering that stock includes goods in transit, net of any unrealised profit.

Question 2

As at 31 May 19X8 the following trial balances were struck at the head office and branch of Peray Ltd.

	Head office Debit £	Head office Credit £	Branch Debit £	Branch Credit £
Fixed assets			74,200	
Profit and loss a/c		25,800		
Current accounts	60,500			51,500
Stock at cost or mark-up at 1.6.X7	48,500		15,400	
Purchase/sales	255,000	229,700	148,500	199,700
Expenses	46,900		13,100	
Provision for unrealised profit		1,400		
Goods sent to branch		154,000		
	410,900	410,900	251,200	251,200

Additional information was as follows.

(a)   All goods sold by the branch are supplied from head office at cost plus 10%. At 31.5.X8 goods to the value of £5,500 were in transit to the branch.

(b)   The branch deposited £3,000 on behalf of head office in the bank on 31.5.X8. No record of this transaction had been made in head office books.

(c)   Stocks at 31.5.X8, excluding goods in transit, were as follows.

	£
Head office at cost	54,500
Branch at mark-up	17,600

(d)   Head office has recharged the branch with £500 of expenses. The invoice for which had not reached the branch at 31.5.X8.

Required

Prepare the profit and loss account and balance sheet at 31 May 19X8 for the head office, branch and combined entity.

Answer

PROFIT AND LOSS ACCOUNT FOR THE YEAR ENDED 31 MAY 19X8

	Head office £	Branch £	Combined entity £
Sales	229,700	199,700	429,400
Transfers to branch	154,000		
Opening stock	(48,500)	(15,400)	(62,500)
Purchases	(255,000)		(255,000)
Transfers from head office		(148,500)	
Closing stock	54,500	17,600	75,500
Gross profit	134,700	53,400	187,400
Expenses	(46,900)	(13,100)	(60,500)
Recharge		(500)	
Increase in provision for unrealised profit	(700)		
	87,100	39,800	126,900
Transfers to head office	39,800	(39,800)	-
	126,900	-	126,900

BALANCE SHEET AS AT 31 MAY 19X8

	Head office £	Branch £	Combined entity £
Fixed assets		74,200	74,200
Stock	54,500	17,600	75,500
Goods in transit (5,500 – 500)	5,000		
Cash			3,000
Cash in transit	3,000		
Current account (91,800 – 1,600)	90,200		
Current account		(91,800)	
	152,700	-	152,700
Profit and loss account			
Balance b/f	25,800		25,800
Profit for the period	126,900	-	126,900
	152,700	-	152,700

Workings

1   *Head office books*

CURRENT ACCOUNT WITH BRANCH

	£		£
Balance b/d	60,500	Goods in transit	5,500
		Cash in transit	3,000
Profit	39,800	Balance c/d	91,800
	100,300		100,300

2   *Branch books*

CURRENT ACCOUNT WITH HEAD OFFICE

	£		£
		Balance b/d	51,500
Balance c/d	91,800	Expense recharge	500
		Profit	39,800
	91,800		91,800

3   *Unrealised profit*

PROVISION FOR UNREALISED PROFIT

	£		£
Balance c/d		Balance b/d	1,400
Goods in transit			
(5,500 × 10/110)	500		
Stock at branch			
(17,600 × 10/110)	1,600	To P&L a/c	700
	2,100		2,100

4   AUDIT PROBLEMS OF BRANCHES

4.1   When the auditors are planning their work they must assess the need for visits to branches by audit staff. Normally, only certain **audit procedures** will need to be carried out at branches, namely:

- **Stocktaking**
- **Cash and bank procedures**
- **Petty cash**
- **Wages**
- **Sales testing**

4.2   The auditors must **assess the materiality of the stock** carried at each branch and the level of sales and other transactions carried out there. Some businesses may have branches which have their own accounting functions. In such cases, the auditors will need to carry out almost an entire 'mini-audit', repeating many of the procedures carried out at head office.

4.3   **In businesses with a large number of branches, the auditors may decide that rotational visits are satisfactory**. The auditors would aim to visit all branches, say every three years. Major branches might be visited every year, with smaller branches visited on a rotational basis.

4.4   **Where branches are not visited, but send returns in for the year end accounts, the auditors must review such returns for reasonableness, completeness and accuracy.** The auditors should also review the level of transactions at the branch during the year for reasonableness. Analytical review procedures will be a valuable tool in such cases, to compare branches with each other and with previous years.

5   UNINCORPORATED JOINT VENTURE ACCOUNTS   12/95

5.1   **Two or more persons may decide to enter into a business venture together without wishing to form a formal long-term partnership.** Usually the venturers agree to place limitations on their activities, for example, a joint venture to manufacture and sell 'total eclipse of the sun' souvenirs could be limited by time, while a joint venture to buy and sell a bankrupt's stock (a fairly common occurrence in practice) comes to an end when all the stock has been sold.

5.2   **Joint ventures are often found when each party can contribute in different ways to the venture.** For example, one venturer may provide finance, another purchases or manufactures goods, while a third offers his marketing skills.

5.3   Joint ventures are generally governed by the Partnership Act 1890, but:

(a)   They are **limited by time and/or activity**.

(b)   The venturers usually **carry on their principal businesses** at the same time.

(c)   **Separate books** for the venture are **not** normally maintained.

(d)   The venturers usually agree to a **profit and loss sharing ratio** for the purpose of the venture.

5.4   There are **three methods of accounting for a joint venture:**

(a)   Each joint venturer records his own transactions only.

(b)   One joint venturer records all of the transactions in his books.

(c)   Open up a separate set of books.

Exam focus point

The examiner has stated his intention to examine joint ventures in an 'up to date' way, ie by reference to what is happening in current practice.

Records maintained by each venturer

5.5   **Each venturer incorporates an account for the joint venture into his existing books.** This 'joint venture account' is a personal account maintained by the venturer in the name of his co-venturer(s): for example, Pantagruel may have an account called 'joint venture with Gargantua'. This account would be:

(a)   **debited with anything the venturer puts into the enterprise** (for example cash funds, purchases, expenses paid and so on); and

(b)   **credited with anything the venturer takes out of the enterprise** (for example sales and cash withdrawn, assets withdrawn and so on).

The double entry is completed to the appropriate accounts (for example cash, bills of exchange, purchases, creditors, debtors and so on) in the venturer's ledger.

5.6   Where one venturer is mainly concerned with purchasing or manufacturing goods, while another is responsible for selling them, there must be a movement of goods from one venturer to the other.

(a)   The physical transfer of goods between the venturers is noted in memorandum and is not recorded in the joint venture account: **there is no double entry for the transfer of goods between venturers.**

(b)   **The physical location of goods is irrelevant**; the important point is to record the purchase of goods (or reallocation of existing stock) for the joint venture.

5.7   As the **individual joint venture accounts** only show details of transactions which that particular venturer is responsible for, they **must all be combined in memorandum** (not part of the double entry system) to ascertain the overall profit or loss, and each venturer's share of that profit or loss.

5.8   The memorandum joint venture account is prepared at the end of the venture or, if necessary, at an intermediate stage (such as at the financial year end of a venturer) by each party using information received from the other venturer(s). Provided that all details have been passed on and entered correctly, all the memorandum joint venture accounts must agree.

5.9   **The memorandum joint venture account, in effect a profit and loss account for the venture, enables each venturer to calculate his share of the profit or loss.** This share is then entered in the venturer's own ledger accounts, the double entry being completed between his own profit and loss account and the joint venture account.

5.10   After all this is completed, the balance on each party's joint venture account represents the cash transfer required to close the venture. Naturally in total the debit and credit balances must be equal and are either carried down into the next accounting period or settled by the appropriate bank/cash payment or receipt. The transfer is recorded in the books of each venturer, double entry being completed between the bank/cash account and the joint venture account. Since the transfers are equal and opposite and have no effect on the joint venture profit there is no point in recording them in the memorandum joint venture account.

Summary of procedure and accounting entries

5.11   (a)   The following accounting entries will be made.

   (i)   DEBIT   Joint venture a/c
          CREDIT   Cash
          Venturer makes cash purchase of stock

   (ii)   DEBIT   Cash
          CREDIT   Joint venture a/c
          Venturer makes cash sale

   (iii) DEBIT   Debtors
          CREDIT   Joint venture a/c
          Venturer makes credit sale

   (iv)   DEBIT   Joint venture a/c
          CREDIT   Cash
          Venturer transfers cash to other venturer

   (v)   DEBIT   Purchases/drawings
          CREDIT   Joint venture a/c
          Venturer takes stock out of joint venture

   (vi)   No accounting entry is required for stock transferred between venturers.

(b)   *Profit of the joint venture*

At the end of the venture period, prepare a memorandum account to work out any profit or loss on the venture.

MEMORANDUM JOINT VENTURE

	£		£
Purchases (cash/credit)	X	Sales (cash/credit)	X
Expenses	X		
Balancing figure	X		
	X		X

The balancing figure represents the profit on the venture which is split according to the agreement.

Each venturer records the profit:

DEBIT   Joint venture a/c
CREDIT   P & L a/c

(c)   *Closing the books*

Any remaining balance on the joint venture accounts represents amounts due between the venturers and is settled by a cash transfer between them.

Question 3

Two traders, Gargamelle and Gallet, agreed to undertake a joint venture in low-priced goods, sharing profits in the ratio of 1:3. The venturers kept separate books to record the joint venture transactions which were as follows.

(a)   *Transactions recorded by Gargamelle*

	£
Purchases of goods for cash	200
Expenses incurred	140
Cost of goods appropriated from own stock	200
Cash sales	400
Credit sales	300

(b)   *Transactions recorded by Gallet*   £

	£
Purchases made	600
Expenses incurred	60
Cash sales	800
Unsold stock taken over	100

(c)   At the finalisation of the joint venture, the venturers balanced their accounts with a transfer of cash.

You are required to show in respect of the above transactions:

(a)   the joint venture accounts in the respective venturer's books; and

(b)   a memorandum joint venture account.

Answer

Gargamelle's books

JOINT VENTURE WITH GALLET ACCOUNT

	£		£
Bank: purchases by Gargamelle	200	Bank: sale proceeds received	
Bank: expenses by Gargamelle	140	by Gargamelle	400
Purchases: goods appropriated		Debtors: credit sales by	
from general stock by Gargamelle	200	Gargamelle	300
Profit and loss account: share			
due to Gargamelle *	100 ✓		
Bank: cash paid to			
Gallet to settle (bal)	60		
	700		700

* Profit calculated in the memorandum joint venture account.

Gallet's books

JOINT VENTURE WITH GARGAMELLE ACCOUNT

	£		£
Bank: purchases by Gallet	600	Bank: sale proceeds received	
Bank: expenses by Gallet	60	by Gallet	800
Profit and loss account: share		Asset account: stock taken	
due to Gallet *	300	over by Gallet	100
		Bank: cash received in	
		settlement from Gargamelle (bal)	60
	960		960

* Profit calculated in the memorandum joint venture account.

Each venturer's piece of paper looks like this:

Nobody's books

MEMORANDUM JOINT VENTURE ACCOUNT

	£	£		£
Purchases: in total		1,000	Sales: in total	1,500
Expenses: in total		200	Assets taken over	100
Profit: Gargamelle (¼)	100			
Gallet (¾)	300			
		400		
		1,600		1,600

Total recording by one venturer

5.12 In this case, the venturer opens two accounts:

(a) a **joint venture account,** which records the profit and loss account for the venture; and

(b) a **current account,** which records the debtor/creditor with the other venturer. There will be one account per venturer.

Separate set of books maintained

5.13 A third situation may exist where a bank account is opened for the joint venture.

(a) A separate set of books is maintained.

(b) **The following accounts will be required.**

    (i) Joint venture account (profit and loss account)
    (ii) Joint venture bank account
    (iii) Capital account
    (iv) Any account necessary to complete the double entry.

(c) For items paid through joint venture bank account:

DEBIT   Joint venture account (purchases/expenses)
CREDIT   Joint bank account

(d) For items paid by venturers:

DEBIT   Joint venture account
CREDIT   Capital account (capital put into venture)

> **Exam focus point**
> It is most likely that an examination question will be set based on a situation when records are maintained by both joint venturers.

5.14 In case you have come across joint ventures in practice, it is relevant to point out here that **we have only been discussing unincorporated joint ventures.** Incorporated ie limited company joint venture vehicles must be accounted for under the equity method by each venturer (see FRS 9: chapter 20).

Chapter roundup

- This chapter has described the accounting procedures followed in head office books to record **branch transactions**. These procedures should be applied when the **branch does not itself maintain a ledger**.

- The principal accounts to be maintained by head office are as follows.

  o The **branch stock (control) account** is maintained at **selling price**.
  o The **branch mark-up account** is effectively the **trading account** for the branch.
  o The **goods sent to branch account** is maintained at **cost price**.

- In this chapter we have also looked at the accounting procedures relating to **branches which maintain their own ledger accounting system**.

  o Combine the results of the head office and branch(es).

  o Make adjustments in respect of inter-branch trading.

  o To calculate the necessary adjustments, it is very important to set out the price structure in a working.

- A **joint venture** is an enterprise entered into by two or more persons without the formalities of a long-term partnership agreement.

  o Each venturer records his own transactions in a **joint venture account** within his nominal ledger.

  o At the end of the venture, or at an agreed interim point, a **calculation** is done (in memorandum only) of the **profit or loss** earned.

  o Each venturer **rules off** his joint venture account as appropriate.

  o The joint venture accounts are then **closed** by a transfer of cash or other assets.

Quick quiz

1 What accounts must be opened in head office books to record branch transactions? (see para 2.4)

2 What entries are made in the branch mark-up account? (2.6)

3 At what value are goods shown in the goods sent to branch account? (2.8)

4 What double entry is required if cash takings are stolen from the branch? (2.13)

5 Give two reasons why current accounts in head office and branch books may not agree. (3.5)

6 Describe the accounting treatment of unrealised profits in respect of branch closing stock and goods in transit. (3.9, 3.10)

7 What double entry is required to record the write-off of goods lost in transit from head office to branch? (3.14)

8 What are the differences between a joint venture and a partnership? (5.3)

9 What is the function of a memorandum joint venture account? (5.9)

Question to try	Level	Marks	Time
5	Full exam	20	36 mins

Chapter 5

HIRE PURCHASE AND LEASING

Chapter topic list	Syllabus reference
1 Types of lease and HP agreement	2(a)
2 Lessees	2(a)
3 Lessors	2(a)
4 Post-tax methods of lessor accounting	2(a)
5 Audit verification of leased assets	2(a)

Introduction

Leasing transactions are extremely common so this is an important practical subject. **Lease accounting is regulated by SSAP 21**, which was introduced because of abuses in the use of lease accounting by companies.

These companies effectively 'owned' an asset and 'owed' a debt for its purchase, but showed neither the asset nor the liability on the balance sheet because they were not required to do so. This is called **'off balance sheet finance'**, a term which you will meet again later in this Text.

1   TYPES OF LEASE AND HP AGREEMENT

1.1   Where goods are acquired other than on immediate cash terms, arrangements have to be made in respect of the future payments on those goods. In the simplest case of credit sales, the purchaser is allowed a period of time (say one month) to settle the outstanding amount and the normal accounting procedure in respect of debtors/creditors will be adopted. However, **in recent years there has been considerable growth in hire purchase and leasing agreements.**

1.2   **SSAP 21 Accounting for leases and hire purchase contracts standardises the accounting treatment and disclosure of assets held under lease or hire purchase.**

1.3   In a leasing transaction there is a contract between the lessor and the lessee for the hire of an asset. The lessor retains legal ownership but conveys to the lessee the right to use the asset for an agreed period of time in return for specified rentals. **SSAP 21 recognises two types of lease.**

> **KEY TERMS**
>
> A **finance lease** transfers substantially all the risks and rewards of ownership to the lessee. Although strictly the leased asset remains the property of the lessor, in substance the lessee may be considered to have acquired the asset and to have financed the acquisition by obtaining a loan from the lessor.
>
> An **operating lease** is any lease which is not a finance lease. An operating lease has the character of a rental agreement with the lessor usually being responsible for repairs and maintenance of the asset. Often these are relatively short-term agreements with the same asset being leased, in succession, to different lessees.

1.4 A *finance lease* is very similar in substance to a *hire purchase agreement*. (The difference in law is that under a hire purchase agreement the customer eventually, after paying an agreed number of instalments, becomes entitled to exercise an option to purchase the asset. Under a leasing agreement, ownership remains forever with the lessor.)

1.5 In this chapter the **user** of an asset will often be referred to simply as the **lessee**, and the **supplier** as the **lessor**. You should bear in mind that identical requirements apply in the case of hirers and vendors respectively under hire purchase agreements.

1.6 To expand on the definition above, **a finance lease should be presumed if at the inception of a lease the present value of the minimum lease payments amounts to substantially all (normally 90% or more) of the fair value of the leased asset**.

1.7 The present value should be calculated by using the **interest rate implicit in the lease**.

> **KEY TERMS**
>
> The **minimum lease payments** are the minimum payments over the remaining part of the lease term plus any residual amounts guaranteed by the lessee or by a party related to the lessee.
>
> **Fair value** is the price at which an asset could be exchanged in an arm's length transaction.
>
> The **interest rate implicit in the lease** is the discount rate that, at the inception of a lease, when applied to the amounts which the lessor expects to receive and retain, produces an amount equal to the fair value of the leased asset.
>
> The **lease term** is the period for which the lessee has contracted to lease the asset and any further terms for which the lessee has the option to continue to lease the asset, with or without further payment, which option it is reasonably certain at the inception of the lease that the lessee will exercise.

Accounting for leases: lessees and lessors

1.8 **Operating leases** do not really pose an accounting problem. **Payments by the lessee are charged to the lessee's and credited to the lessor's profit and loss account. The lessor treats the leased asset as a fixed asset and depreciates it in the normal way.**

1.9 For assets held **under finance leases or hire purchase** this accounting treatment would not disclose the reality of the situation. If a lessor leases out an asset on a finance lease, the asset will probably never be seen on his premises or used in his business again. It would be inappropriate for a lessor to record such an asset as a fixed asset. In reality, **what the lessor owns is a stream of cash flows receivable from the lessee. The asset is a debtor rather than a fixed asset.**

1.10 Similarly, a lessee may use a finance lease to fund the 'acquisition' of a major asset which he will then use in his business perhaps for many years. **The substance of the transaction is that the lessee has acquired a fixed asset, and this is reflected in the accounting treatment prescribed by SSAP 21,** even though in law the lessee never becomes the owner of the asset.

> **Exam focus point**
> Questions on leasing could involve a discussion of the reasons for the different accounting treatments of operating and finance leases, from the perspectives of both the lessor and the lessee. Practical questions could involve preparation of the relevant ledger accounts and/or extracts from the financial statements. The December 1997 paper asked candidates to briefly discuss the effect on profits of treating a lease as an operating lease rather than a finance lease.

2   LESSEES   6/95, 12/95, 12/97

Accounting treatment

2.1 In light of the above, **SSAP 21 requires that, when an asset changes hands under a finance lease or HP agreement, lessor and lessee should account for the transaction as though it were a credit sale.** In the lessee's books therefore:

DEBIT   Asset account
CREDIT   Lessor (liability) account

2.2 The amount to be recorded in this way is the capital cost or fair value of the asset. This may be taken as the amount which the lessee might expect to pay for it in a cash transaction.

2.3 A **variant approach** which produces the same net result is to debit the asset account with the fair value, and to debit an interest suspense account with the total amount of interest or finance charges payable under the agreement and to credit a lessor account with the total amount (capital and interest) payable under the agreement. We will see later how this affects the year end accounting entries.

2.4 **The asset should be depreciated over the shorter of:**

(a) the lease term; and
(b) its useful life.

Apportionment of rental payments

2.5 When the lessee makes **a rental payment** it **will comprise two elements.**

(a) **An interest charge on the finance provided by the lessor**. This proportion of each payment is interest payable and interest receivable in the profit and loss accounts of the lessee and lessor respectively.

(b) **A repayment of part of the capital cost of the asset**. In the lessee's books this proportion of each rental payment must be debited to the lessor's account to reduce the outstanding liability. In the lessor's books, it must be credited to the lessee's account to reduce the amount owing (the debit of course is to cash).

2.6 **The accounting problem is to decide what proportion** of each instalment paid by the lessee **represents interest, and what proportion represents a repayment of the capital** advanced by the lessor. There are **three methods** you may encounter:

(a) The **level spread method**.
(b) The **actuarial method**.
(c) The **sum-of-the-digits method**.

Exam focus point
An examination question would always make it clear which method should be used. In theory, the aim is that the profit and loss account finance charge should produce a constant rate of return on outstanding leasing obligations.

2.7 **The level spread method is based on the assumption that finance charges accrue evenly over the term of the lease agreement.** For example, if an asset with a fair value of £3,000 is being 'acquired' on a finance lease for five payments of £700 each, the total interest is £(3,500 – 3,000) = £500. This is assumed to accrue evenly and therefore there is £100 interest comprised in each rental payment, the £600 balance of each instalment being the capital repayment.

The level spread method is quite **unscientific and takes no account of the commercial realities of the transaction.** You should use it in the examination only if you are specifically instructed to or if there is insufficient information to use another method.

2.8 **The actuarial method is the best and most scientific method**. It derives from the commonsense assumption that the **interest charged by a lessor company will equal the rate of return desired by the company, multiplied by the amount of capital it has invested.**

(a) At the beginning of the lease the capital invested is equal to the fair value of the asset (less any initial deposit paid by the lessee).

(b) This amount reduces as each instalment is paid. It follows that the interest accruing is greatest in the early part of the lease term, and gradually reduces as capital is repaid. In this section, we will look at a simple example of the actuarial method.

2.9 **The sum-of-the-digits method** approximates to the actuarial method, splitting the total interest (without reference to a rate of interest) in such a way that the greater proportion falls in the earlier years. The procedure is as follows.

(a) **Assign a digit to each instalment.** The digit 1 should be assigned to the final instalment, 2 to the penultimate instalment and so on.

(b) **Add the digits.** If there are twelve instalments, then the sum of the digits will be 78. For this reason, the sum of the digits method is sometimes called the *rule of 78*.

(c) **Calculate the interest charge included in each instalment**. Do this by multiplying the total interest accruing over the lease term by the fraction:

$$\frac{\text{Digit applicable to the instalment}}{\text{Sum of the digits}}$$

2.10 EXAMPLE: APPORTIONMENT METHODS

On 1 January 19X0 Bacchus Ltd, wine merchants, buys a small bottling and labelling machine from Silenus Limited on hire purchase terms. The cash price of the machine was £7,710 while the HP price was £10,000. The HP agreement required the immediate payment of a £2,000 deposit with the balance being settled in four equal annual instalments commencing on 31 December 19X0. The HP charge of £2,290 represents interest of 15% per annum, calculated on the remaining balance of the liability during each accounting period. Depreciation on the plant is to be provided for at the rate of 20% per annum on a straight line basis assuming a residual value of nil.

You are required to show the breakdown of each instalment between interest and capital, using in turn each of the apportionment methods described above.

2.11 SOLUTION

In this example, enough detail is given to use any of the apportionment methods. In an examination question, you would normally be directed to use one method specifically.

(a) *Level spread method*

The £2,290 interest charges are regarded as accruing evenly over the term of the HP agreement. Each instalment therefore contains £2,290/4 = £572.50 of interest. The break down is then as follows.

	1st instalment £	*2nd instalment* £	*3rd instalment* £	*4th instalment* £
Interest	572.50	572.50	572.50	572.50
Capital repayment (balance)	1,427.50	1,427.50	1,427.50	1,427.50
	2,000.00	2,000.00	2,000.00	2,000.00

(b) *Sum-of-the-digits method*

Each instalment is allocated a digit as follows.

Instalment	*Digit*
1st (19X0)	4
2nd (19X1)	3
3rd (19X2)	2
4th (19X3)	1
	10

The £2,290 interest charges can then be apportioned.

		£
1st instalment	£2,290 × 4/10	916
2nd instalment	£2,290 × 3/10	687
3rd instalment	£2,290 × 2/10	458
4th instalment	£2,290 × 1/10	229
		2,290

The breakdown is then as follows.

	1st instalment £	*2nd instalment* £	*3rd instalment* £	*4th instalment* £
Interest	916	687	458	229
Capital repayment (balance)	1,084	1,313	1,542	1,771
	2,000	2,000	2,000	2,000

(c) *Actuarial method*

Interest is calculated as 15% of the outstanding *capital* balance at the beginning of each year. The outstanding capital balance reduces each year by the capital element comprised in each instalment. The outstanding capital balance at 1 January 19X0 is £5,710 (£7,710 fair value less £2,000 deposit).

	Total £	Capital £	Interest £
Capital balance at 1 Jan 19X0		5,710	
1st instalment			
(interest = £5,710 × 15%)	2,000	1,144	856
Capital balance at 1 Jan 19X1		4,566	
2nd instalment			
(interest = £4,566 × 15%)	2,000	1,315	685
Capital balance at 1 Jan 19X2		3,251	
3rd instalment			
(interest = £3,251 × 15%)	2,000	1,512	488
Capital balance at 1 Jan 19X3		1,739	
4th instalment			
(interest = £1,739 × 15%)	2,000	1,739	261
	8,000		2,290
Capital balance at 1 Jan 19X4		-	

Interest suspense account

2.12   Where an interest suspense account is used (see Paragraph 2.3), the double entry for finance lease/HP instalments is as follows (assuming that the actuarial method is used to record the first instalment payable under the lease in the example above).

(a)   DEBIT   Asset account   £7,710
                     Interest suspense   £2,290
       CREDIT   HP creditor   £10,000
       Being entries required to record acquisition of asset on hire purchase

(b)   DEBIT   Lessor/HP creditor   £2,000
       CREDIT   Bank   £2,000
       Being instalment payment recorded in full

(c)   DEBIT   Interest payable/finance charges (P&L)   £856
       CREDIT   Interest suspense account   £856
       Being year end adjustment to ensure that the year's interest/finance charges are charged to the profit and loss account

2.13   The equivalent entries where a suspense account is not used might be as follows.

(a)   DEBIT   Asset account   £7,710
       CREDIT   HP account   £7,710

(b)   DEBIT   HP creditor   £2,000
       CREDIT   Bank   £2,000

(c)   DEBIT   Interest payable/finance charges (P & L)   £856
       CREDIT   HP creditor   £856

Entry (c) ensures that the interest element is recorded and is an annual adjustment. It is, of course, possible to make the full correct entry as each instalment is paid:

DEBIT   Interest payable/finance charges (P & L)   £856
             Lessor/HP creditor   £1,144
CREDIT   Bank   £2,000

However, in practice in many companies the interest/finance charge calculation is only made annually when preparing published accounts.

2.14 Thus, at the year end, whatever system is used during the year, the balance on the lessor/HP creditor account (where appropriate, less the balance on the interest suspense account) will represent the outstanding capital liability. Future interest/finance charges are not a true liability as the capital could be paid off at any time, thus avoiding these charges.

Repossessions

2.15 Subject to various legal requirements, goods sold on hire purchase (but not credit sale) may be repossessed by the seller **if the hirer fails to maintain his payments.** The ledger accounts in respect of the hire purchase should be closed to **a repossessions account** which **is credited with the value at which the item is brought back into stock and any penalty sums receivable.** Any balance on the repossessions account represents the profit or loss on the repossession.

2.16 EXAMPLE: REPOSSESSIONS

Bacchus, having paid amounts due in 19X0, decided to cease trading in January 19X1. Silenus agreed to cancel the agreement on the payment of a penalty of £1,000 and took the plant into his stock at a value of £4,500. The ledger accounts would be as follows.

HP DEBTORS ACCOUNT

	£		£
Balance b/d	4,566	Repossessions a/c	4,566

REPOSSESSIONS ACCOUNT

	£		£
HP debtors a/c	4,566	Bank: penalty	1,000
P & L a/c: profit on		Purchases:	
repossession	934	Plant taken into stock	
		at valuation *	4,500
	5,500		5,500

* If the question does not give a valuation for the goods repossessed, then they can be taken into stock at the cost element in the outstanding debt:

$$\frac{6,168}{7,710} \times £4,566 = £3,653 \text{ in the above example.}$$

2.17 The total profit Silenus earned from the abortive sale is as follows.

	£
Deposit/instalment received in 19X0	4,000
Penalty received in 19X1	1,000
	5,000
Plant in stock at valuation	4,500
	9,500
Cost of plant T||0 x 20⅟. Depn.	6,168
	3,332

This has been accounted for as follows.

		£
19X0	Gross profit (£1,542) + interest earned (£856)	2,398
19X1	Profit on repossession	934
		3,332

Question 1

Dundas Ltd purchased a machine under a hire purchase agreement on 1 January 19X6. The agreement provided for an immediate payment of £2,000, following by five equal instalments of £3,056, each instalment to be paid on 30 June and 31 December respectively. The cash price of the machine was £10,000. Dundas estimated that it would have a useful economic life of five years, and its residual value would then be £1,000.

In apportioning interest to respective accounting periods, the company uses the 'sum of digits' method.

Required

(a) Write up the following ledger accounts for each of the three years to 31 December 19X6, 19X7 and 19X8 respectively:

(i)   machine hire purchase loan account; and
(ii)   machine hire purchase interest account.

(b) Show the following balance sheet extracts relating to the machine as at 31 December 19X6, 19X7 and 19X8 respectively:

(i)   fixed assets: machine at net book value;

(ii)   creditors: amounts payable within one year - obligation under hire purchase contract; and

(iii) creditors: amounts falling due after more than one year - obligation under hire purchase contract.

Answer

(a)   (i)

MACHINE HIRE PURCHASE LOAN ACCOUNT

19X6		£	19X6		£
1.1	Bank	2,000	1.1	Machine	10,000
30.6	Bank	3,056	1.1	Machine interest	7,280
31.12	Bank	3,056			
31.12	Balance c/d	9,168			
		17,280			17,280
19X7			19X7		
30.6	Bank	3,056	1.1	Balance b/d	9,168
31.12	Bank	3,056			
31.12	Balance c/d	3,056			
		9,168			9,168
19X8			19X8		
30.6	Bank	3,056	1.1	Balance b/d	3,056

(ii)

MACHINE HIRE PURCHASE INTEREST ACCOUNT

19X6		£	19X6		£
1.1	Machine HP		31.12	Profit and loss a/c	4,368
	loan a/c	7,280	31.12	Balance c/d	2,912
		7,280			7,280
19X7			19X7		
1.1	Balance b/d	2,912	31.12	Profit and loss a/c	2,427
			31.12	Balance c/d	485
		2,912			2,912
19X8			19X8		
1.1	Balance b/d	485	31.12	Profit and loss a/c	485

Working

		£
Sum of the digits = 5 + 4 + 3 + 2 + 1 = 15		
(5 half year periods)		

			£
Interest charge 19X6	$= \quad 7{,}280 \times \dfrac{5+4}{15} =$		4,368
Interest charge 19X7	$= \quad 7{,}280 \times \dfrac{3+2}{15} =$		2,427
Interest charge 19X8	$= \quad 7{,}280 \times \dfrac{1}{15} =$		485
			7,280

(b) (i) *Fixed assets: machines at net book value*

		£
At 31.12.X6	Machines at cost	10,000
	Accumulated depreciation	3,600
	Net book value	6,400
At 31.12.X7	Machines at cost	10,000
	Accumulated depreciation	7,200
	Net book value	2,800
At 31.12.X8	Machines at cost	10,000
	Accumulated depreciation	9,000
	Residual value	1,000

Working

		£
Depreciation:	cost	10,000
	residual value	1,000
		9,000
Economic life		2½ years

$$\text{Annual depreciation charge on a straight-line basis} = \frac{£9{,}000}{2\tfrac{1}{2}}$$
$$= £3{,}600 \text{ per year}$$

(ii) *Creditors: amounts payable within one year - obligation under hire purchase contract*

	£
At 31.12.X6	3,685
At 31.12.X7	2,571
At 31.12.X8	-

Workings

		£
31.12.X6	Balance per loan account	9,168
	Less due in 19X8	(3,056)
	Less interest element	(2,427)
		3,685
31.12.X7	Balance per loan account	3,056
	Less interest element	(485)
		2,571

(iii) *Creditors: amounts falling due after more than one year*

	£
At 31.12.X6	2,571
At 31.12.X7	-
At 31.12.X8	-

For working see (b)(ii) above.

Disclosure requirements for lessees

2.18 SSAP 21 requires lessees to disclose the following information.

(a) The **gross amounts of assets held under finance leases* together with the related accumulated depreciation, analysed by class of asset**. This information may be consolidated with the corresponding information for owned assets, and not shown separately. In that case, the net amount of assets held under finance leases* included in the overall total should also be disclosed.

(b) The **amounts of obligations related to finance leases* (net of finance charges allocated to future periods)**. These should be disclosed separately from other obligations and liabilities and should be analysed between amounts payable in the next year, amounts payable in the second to fifth years inclusive from the balance sheet date and the aggregate amounts payable thereafter.

(c) The **aggregate finance charges allocated for the period** in respect of finance leases.*

* Including the equivalent information in respect of hire purchase contracts.

2.19 These disclosure requirements will be illustrated for Bacchus Ltd (above example). We will assume that Bacchus Ltd makes up its accounts to 31 December and uses the actuarial method to apportion finance charges. The company's accounts for the first year of the HP agreement, the year ended 31 December 19X0, would include the information given below.

BALANCE SHEET AS AT 31 DECEMBER 19X0 (EXTRACTS)

	£	£
Fixed assets		
Tangible assets held under hire purchase agreements		
Plant and machinery at cost	7,710	
Less accumulated depreciation (20% × £7,710)	1,542	
		6,168
Creditors: amounts falling due within one year		
Obligations under hire purchase agreements		1,315
Creditors: amounts falling due after more than one year		
Obligations under hire purchase agreements, falling due		
within two to five years £(1,512 + 1,739)		3,251

(Notice that only the outstanding *capital* element is disclosed under creditors. That is what is meant by the phrase 'net of finance charges allocated to future periods' in Paragraph 2.7(b) above.)

PROFIT AND LOSS ACCOUNT
FOR THE YEAR ENDED 31 DECEMBER 19X0

	£
Interest payable and similar charges	
Hire purchase finance charges	856

2.20 As noted above, SSAP 21 requires that **leased assets should be depreciated over the shorter of the lease term and their useful lives; but assets acquired under HP agreements** resembling finance leases **should be depreciated over their useful lives,** because such assets are legally the debtor's property. Bacchus can therefore depreciate the machine over five years, not four years.

2.21   **For operating leases the disclosure is simpler.**

(a)   The **total of operating lease rentals** charged as an expense in the profit and loss account should be disclosed, distinguishing between rentals payable for hire of plant and machinery and other rentals.

(b)   Disclosure should be made of **payments to which the lessee is committed** under operating leases, analysed between those in which the commitment expires:

(i)   **within a year** from the balance sheet date;
(ii)   in the **second to fifth** years inclusive;
(iii) **later than five years** from the balance sheet date.

Commitments in respect of land and buildings should be shown separately from other commitments.

3   LESSORS

Accounting treatment

3.1   In principle, accounting for a finance lease by a **lessor** is a **mirror image of the entries for the lessee**. The asset is recorded in the lessor's books as follows.

DEBIT   Lessee (debtor) account
CREDIT   Sales

3.2   The income derived from the lease is spread over accounting periods so as to give a constant periodic rate of return for the lessor. The complex methods of achieving this are beyond the scope of your syllabus.

FRS 5: SALE AND LEASEBACK TRANSACTIONS

3.3   We will discuss FRS 5 *Reporting the substance of transactions* in Chapter 14. Leases were a common form of off balance sheet finance before SSAP 21 was introduced. Ever since then, businesses have attempted to undertake types of arrangement whereby an asset is 'sold' but in fact the use is still retained.

3.4   **FRS 5 states that where such a transaction is, in effect, a sale and leaseback, no profit should be recognised on entering into the arrangement and no adjustment made to the carrying value of the asset.** As stated in the guidance notes to SSAP 21, **this represents the substance of the transactions,** 'namely the raising of finance secured on an asset that continues to be held and is not disposed of'.

Disclosure requirements for lessors

3.5   SSAP 21 requires lessors to disclose their **net investments in (a) finance leases and (b) hire purchase contracts at each balance sheet date.**

3.6   The accounts of Silenus Ltd (example above) for the year ended 31 December 19X0 would show the information given below.

BALANCE SHEET AS AT 31 DECEMBER 19X0 (EXTRACTS)

	£
Current assets	
Debtors	
Net investment in finance leases (note)	4,566

NOTES TO THE BALANCE SHEET

	£
Net investment in finance leases	
Falling due within one year	1,315
Falling due after more than one year	3,251
	4,566

(The Companies Act 1985 requires amounts included as debtors to be separately disclosed if they fall due more than one year after the balance sheet date.)

3.7   SSAP 21 also requires **disclosure by lessors** of the:

(a) **Gross amounts of assets** held for use **in operating leases**, and the related **accumulated depreciation charges.**

(b) **Policy** adopted for accounting for operating leases and finance leases and, in detail, the policy for accounting for finance lease income.

(c) **Aggregate rentals receivable** in respect of an accounting period in relation to finance leases and operating leases separately.

(d) **Cost of assets acquired,** whether by purchase or finance lease, for the purpose of letting under finance leases.

Question 2

Leisure Services Ltd, Stoke-on-Trent, are electrical wholesalers. On 2 May 19X3, they purchased on credit from TV Suppliers Ltd ten television sets for £1,600. They offered these for sale for cash at £240 each or on hire purchase for a cash deposit of £40 and eight quarterly instalments of £30 each, the first instalment being payable after three months. In the week ended 16 May 19X3 they sold two sets for cash and four on HP terms for which the cash deposits were paid at the time of sale.

On 1 December 19X3 Leisure Services Ltd installed one of their sets permanently on their own premises in a closed circuit television installation to detect theft.

You are required to prepare the necessary accounts (except cash and TV Suppliers Ltd) with dates and narrations in the ledger of Leisure Services Ltd to record the above transactions, balance them and prepare a trading account up to 31 December 19X3.

Note. The amount of HP interest earned in the period, calculated on the sum of the digits method, should be included in the trading account after sales.

Answer

Price structure	£
Cost	160
Gross profit	80
Cash selling price	240
HP interest	40
HP selling price £(40 + (8 × 30))	280

With eight instalments, the sum of the digits is:
$$1 + 2 + ... + 7 + 8 = 36$$

Interest on the first instalment	= 8/36 × £40 = £9
Interest on the second instalment	= 7/36 × £40 = £8
Capital element in first instalment	= £(30 - 9) = £21
Capital element in second instalment	= £(30 - 8) = £22

Ledger accounts

FIXED ASSETS

19X3		£
1 Dec	Purchases - closed circuit TV	160

HP DEBTORS

19X3		£	19X3		£
16 May	Sales (4 × £240)	960	16 May	Bank: deposits	160
			16 Aug	Bank: 1st instalment	
				(4 × £21)	84
			16 Nov	Bank: 2nd instalment	
				(4 × £22)	88
			31 Dec	Balance c/f	628
		960			960

SALES

19X3		£	19X3		£
31 Dec	Trading account	1,440	16 May	HP debtors	960
				Cash (2 × £240)	480
		1,440			1,440

PURCHASES

19X3		£	19X3		£
2 May	Creditors	1,600	1 Dec	Fixed assets	160
			31 Dec	Trading account	1,440
		1,600			1,600

HP INTEREST RECEIVABLE

19X3		£	19X3		£
31 Dec	Trading account	68	16 Aug	Bank: 1st instalment	
				(4 × £9)	36
			16 Nov	Bank: 2nd instalment	
				(4 × £9)	32
		68			68

TRADING ACCOUNT TO 31 DECEMBER 19X3

	£	£
Sales		1,440
HP interest receivable		68
		1,508
Purchases	1,440	
Less closing stock (3 × £160)	480	
Cost of sales		960
Gross profit		548

Note. The inclusion of the HP interest receivable in the trading account is unusual, but is specifically required by the question. It would be more usual to show it as a credit in the profit and loss account.

---

4   POST-TAX METHODS OF LESSOR ACCOUNTING

Exam focus point
Ignore this section if you are in a hurry. It is unlikely to come up.

4.1   Assumptions made so far are that the instalments received from the lessee only go towards payments of interest and repayment of capital. The lessor's business, has, however, other factors which affect the overall investment on the lease. These factors must be taken into account when calculating the allocation of gross earnings. Remember that our aim is to give a constant periodic rate of return on the lessor's net investment in the lease.

4.2   The allocation method of accounting for all the cash flow factors is called the net cash investment. SSAP 21 states that the net cash investment in a lease at a point in time is the amount of funds invested in a lease by a lessor, and comprises the cost of the asset plus or minus the following related payments or receipts.

(a)   Government or other grants receivable towards the purchase or use of the asset (–)

(b)   Rentals received (–)

(c)   Taxation payments (+) and receipts (–), including the effect of capital allowances

(d)   Residual values, if any, at the end of the lease term (–)

(e)   Interest payments (where applicable) (+)

(f)   Interest received on cash surplus (–)

(g)   Profit taken out of the lease (+). (This may be spent on payment of dividends or other costs.)

The net cash investment includes all the effective cash flows relating to the lessor, whereas the net investment does not.

Exam focus point

The examiner has specifically stated in September 1995 that students are not expected to prepare cash flow schedules involving the above detail to determine the net cash investment.

5   AUDIT VERIFICATION OF LEASED ASSETS

5.1   The auditors will verify leases in the lessees books during the audit work on fixed assets. **The main areas of concern will be to identify all leased assets and to ensure that they have been correctly recorded, according to their type.**

5.2   The auditors must examine each lease in turn to discover whether it is an operating or a finance lease. It will not always be easy to judge, and the auditor may have to perform calculations on the lease figures to discover the true situation. All leases should be verified by examining the original lease agreement.

5.3   Once it has been established which leases are finance leases, the auditors will need to check the payments made on each lease and check that the calculations to split the capital and interest elements have been made correctly.

5.4   In the case of operating leases it will only be necessary to verify that payments have been made and the correct charge made in the accounts.

Chapter roundup

- **Finance leases** are like HP contracts. In both cases:
  - Assets acquired should be capitalised
  - Interest element of instalments should be charged against profit.

- **Operating leases** are **rental agreements** and all instalments are charged against profit.

- You must learn (through repeated practice) how to apply the level spread, actuarial and sum-of-the-digits methods of **interest allocation**.

- You must also learn the **disclosure requirements of SSAP 21** for both lessors and lessees.

- You should be aware of the **audit procedures** required in respect of leases.

Quick quiz

1   What two categories of lease are identified in SSAP 21? What are the characteristics of each type? (see para 1.3)

2   Why is it considered inappropriate in certain cases to account for leases according to their legal form? (1.9)

3   What initial accounting entries should be made by a business on acquiring an asset under an HP agreement? (2.1)

4   Describe the mechanics of the sum of the digits method. (2.9)

5   What disclosures are required by SSAP 21 in respect of an asset acquired under a finance lease? (2.18)

6   A lorry with an expected useful life of six years is acquired under a finance lease with a four year term. Over which period should it be depreciated? (2.20)

7   A company leases a photocopier under an operating lease expiring in June 19X2. It also leases office space under an operating lease expiring in January 19X3. In its accounts for the year to 31 December 19X1, how should it disclose its past and future operating lease rentals? (2.21)

8   What are SSAP 21's disclosure requirements in respect of lessor accounting? (3.5-3.7)

9   What work must the auditors carry out in respect of leases? (5.1-5.4)

Question to try	Level	Marks	Time
6	Full exam	20	36 mins

Chapter 6

DISTRIBUTABLE PROFITS AND CAPITAL TRANSACTIONS

Chapter topic list		Syllabus reference
1	Revenue recognition	1(a)
2	Distributable profits	2(b)
3	Redemption of shares	2(b)

Introduction

The topics in this chapter are relevant to all types of accounting transactions, providing a theoretical framework for the topics already covered and for accounting in general.

This chapter also leads on to the legal aspects of financial reporting in the next two chapters. A great deal of the legislation governing distributions and capital transactions is concerned with protection of creditors; the aim is to prevent companies favouring shareholders over creditors.

Exam focus point

This is a long chapter dealing with three topics, two of which rarely seem to get examined. If you are in a hurry, concentrate on Section 2. Skim through the other sections taking note of the highlighted words. Whatever you do, do not spend time on Sections 1 or 3 of this chapter at the expense of the chapters on group accounting and published accounts. One or both of these topics **always** comes up.

1 REVENUE RECOGNITION 12/97

1.1 **Accrual accounting is based on the matching of costs with the revenue they generate.** It is crucially important under this convention that we can establish the point at which revenue may be recognised so that the correct treatment can be applied to the related costs. For example, the costs of producing an item of finished goods should be carried as an asset in the balance sheet until such time as it is sold; they should then be written off as a charge to the trading account. Which of these two treatments should be applied cannot be decided until it is clear at what moment the sale of the item takes place.

1.2 The decision has a direct impact on profit since under the prudence concept it would be unacceptable to recognise the profit on sale until a sale had taken place in accordance with the criteria of revenue recognition.

Point of sale

1.3 **Revenue is generally recognised as earned at the point of sale, because at that point four criteria will generally have been met.**

(a) The product or service has been provided to the buyer.

(b) The buyer has recognised his liability to pay for the goods or services provided. The converse of this is that the seller has recognised that ownership of goods has passed from himself to the buyer.

(c) The buyer has indicated his willingness to hand over cash or other assets in settlement of his liability.

(d) The monetary value of the goods or services has been established.

1.4   At earlier points in the business cycle there will not in general be firm evidence that the above criteria will be met. Until work on a product is complete, there is a risk that some flaw in the manufacturing process will necessitate its writing off; even when the product is complete there is no guarantee that it will find a buyer.

1.5   At later points in the business cycle, for example when cash is received for the sale, the recognition of revenue may occur in a period later than that in which the related costs were charged. Revenue recognition would then depend on fortuitous circumstances, such as the cash flow of a company's debtors, and might fluctuate misleadingly from one period to another.

Times other than point of sale

1.6   However, **occasionally revenue is recognised at other times** than at the completion of a sale.

(a) **Recognition of profit on long-term contract work in progress**. Under SSAP 9 *Stocks and long-term contracts*, credit is taken in the profit and loss account for 'that part of the total profit currently estimated to arise over the duration of the contract which fairly reflects the profit attributable to that part of the work performed at the accounting date'.

(i)   Owing to the length of time taken to complete such contracts, to defer taking profit into account until completion may result in the profit and loss account reflecting not so much a fair view of the activity of the company during the year but rather the results relating to contracts which have been completed by the year end.

(ii) Revenue in this case is recognised when production on, say, a section of the total contract is complete, even though no sale can be made until the whole is complete.

(b) **Sale on hire purchase.** Title to goods provided on hire purchase terms does not pass until the last payment is made, at which point the sale is complete.

(i)   To defer the recognition of revenue until that point, however, would be to distort the nature of the revenue earned.

(ii) The profits of an HP retailer in effect represent the interest charged on finance provided and such interest arises over the course of the HP agreement rather than at its completion. Revenue in this case is recognised when each instalment of cash is received.

1.7   **The determination of whether revenue should be recognised is based partly on the accruals concept, but also on the often conflicting fundamental accounting concept of prudence.** Under the prudence concept revenue and profits are not anticipated and anticipated losses are provided for as soon as they are foreseen (preventing costs being deferred if there is doubt as to their recoverability).

1.8   The question of revenue recognition is obviously closely associated with the definition of realised profits, and this is discussed in the next section.

1.9   **In general terms, under the historical cost system, the following general practice has developed.**

(a)   Revenue from the sale of goods is recognised on the date of delivery to the customer.

(b)   Revenue from services is recognised when the services have been performed and are billable.

(c)   Revenue derived from letting others use the resources of the businesses (for example royalty income, rent and interest) is recognised either as the resources are used or on a time basis.

(d)   Revenue from the sale of assets (other than products of the business) is recognised at the date of the sale.

Problem areas

1.10   The problems with revenue recognition, for businesses and their auditors, is that there are some areas where accounting standards have not (yet) been issued which deal with all types of transaction. We will not go into too much detail here about these situations, but you should be aware of them, and a list is given below (the list is not comprehensive).

(a)   **Receipt of initial fees,** at the beginning of a service, may not have been 'earned' and it is often difficult to determine what they represent.

(b)   **Franchise fees** can be incurred in complex franchise agreements and no standard form of agreement has allowed an accepted accounting practice to develop. Each agreement must be dealt with on its own merits.

(c)   **Advance royalty or licence receipts** would normally be dealt with (under SSAP 2) as deferred income and released to the profit and loss account when earned under the agreement. In some businesses, however, such advances consist of a number of different components which require different accounting treatments, for example in the record industry.

(d)   **Loan arrangement fees** could be recognised in the year the loan is arranged or spread over the life of the loan.

(e)   **Credit card fees** charged by credit card companies on their cardholders might be recognised on receipt or spread over the period that the fee allows the cardholder to use the card.

Exam focus point
A question in December 1997 offered 12 marks for discussing, and giving practical examples of, the points in a given operating cycle where revenue should be recognised.

2   DISTRIBUTABLE PROFITS   6/97

Exam focus point
This is an important section which you must look at.

2.1 A **distribution** is defined by s 263(2) CA 1985 as every description of distribution of a company's assets to members (shareholders) of the company, whether in cash or otherwise, with the exceptions of:

(a) An issue of bonus shares.

(b) The redemption or purchase of the company's own shares out of capital (including the proceeds of a new issue) or out of unrealised profits.

(c) The reduction of share capital by:

(i) reducing the liability on shares in respect of share capital not fully paid up;
(ii) paying off paid-up share capital.

(d) A distribution of assets to shareholders in a winding up of the company.

IMPORTANT!

Companies must not make a distribution except out of profits available for the purpose. These available profits are:

(a) its **accumulated realised profits**, insofar as these have not already been used for an earlier distribution or for 'capitalisation';

(b) **minus its accumulated realised losses**, insofar as these have not already been written off in a reduction or reconstruction scheme.

2.2 Capital profits and revenue profits (if realised) are taken together and capital losses and revenue losses (if realised) are similarly grouped together. *Unrealised profits* cannot be distributed (for example profit on the revaluation of fixed assets); nor must a company apply unrealised profits to pay up debentures or any unpaid amounts on issued shares.

2.3 **Capitalisation of realised profits is the use of profits:**

(a) to issue bonus shares; or
(b) as a transfer to the capital redemption reserve.

2.4 As a point of detail, s 275(2) allows that any **excess depreciation on a revalued fixed asset above the amount of depreciation that would have been charged on its historical cost can be treated as a realised profit for the purpose of distributions.** This is to avoid penalising companies that make an unrealised profit on the revaluation of an asset, and must then charge depreciation on the revalued amount. For example, suppose that a company buys an asset at a cost of £20,000. It has a life of 4 years and a nil residual value. If it is immediately revalued to £30,000, an unrealised profit of £10,000 would be credited to the revaluation reserve. Annual depreciation must be based on the revalued amount, in this case, ¼ of £30,000 or £7,500. This exceeds depreciation which would have been charged on the asset's cost (£5,000 pa) by £2,500 per annum. This £2,500 can be treated as a distributable profit under s 275(2).

2.5 Section 264 imposes **further restrictions on the distributions of public companies**.

IMPORTANT!

A public company cannot make a distribution if at the time:

(a) the amount of its net assets is less than the combined total of its called-up share capital plus its undistributable reserves; or

> (b)   the distribution will reduce the amount of its net assets to below the combined total of its called-up share capital plus its undistributable reserves.

2.6   **'Undistributable reserves' are:**

(a)   The share premium account.

(b)   The capital redemption reserve.

(c)   Any accumulated surplus of unrealised profits over unrealised losses.

(d)   Any other reserve which cannot be distributed, whether by statute, or the company's memorandum or articles of association.

2.7   The key feature of s 264 is that all **accumulated distributable profits, both realised and unrealised, must exceed the accumulated realised and unrealised losses of the company before any distribution can be made**. The difference between the profits and losses is the maximum possible distribution.

2.8   In contrast with s 263, s 264 **includes consideration of unrealised profits and losses,** so that if unrealised losses exceed unrealised profits, the amount of distributions which can be made will be reduced by the amount of the 'deficit'.

2.9   EXAMPLE: PRIVATE COMPANY V PUBLIC COMPANY DISTRIBUTIONS

Huddle Ltd is a private company and Publimco plc is a public limited company. Both companies have a financial year ending on 31 December. On 31 December 19X5, the balance sheets of the companies, by a remarkable coincidence, were identical, as follows.

	Huddle Ltd		*Publimco plc*	
	£'000	£'000	£'000	£'000
Net assets		365		365
Share capital		300		300
Share premium account		60		60
Unrealised losses on asset revaluations		(25)		(25)
Realised profits	50		50	
Realised losses	(20)		(20)	
		30		30
		365		365

What is the maximum distribution that each company can make?

2.10   SOLUTION

(a)   S 263 restricts the distributable profits of Huddle Ltd to £30,000.

(b)   S 264 further restricts the distributable profits of Publimco plc to £30,000 – £25,000 = £5,000 (or alternatively, £365,000 – £300,000 – £60,000 = £5,000. This is the surplus of net assets over share capital plus undistributable reserves, which in this example are represented by the share premium account).

Realised and distributable profits

2.11 Legislation does not define realised profits very clearly. As a **'rule of thumb',** according to the Consultative Committee of Accounting Bodies, **profits in the profit and loss account are realised, while unrealised profits are credited directly to reserves.**

2.12 SSAP 2 *Disclosure of accounting policies* provides a framework for recognising realised profits. If SSAP 2, particularly the prudence concept is followed, profit and loss account profits will be realisable.

Exceptions

2.13 In the case of **sale of revalued fixed assets,** the **unrealised profit on revaluation previously credited to the revaluation reserve** does not pass through the profit and loss account. It is nevertheless to be **regarded as distributable.**

2.14 Where an asset has been revalued, the **increase in depreciation charge** can be treated as a realised profit.

2.15 **Development expenditure** is a realised loss in the year in which it is incurred, except when the costs are capitalised within SSAP 13 guidelines, in which case the costs are amortised as realised losses over a number of years.

2.16 **Provisions** are generally treated as realised losses.

The relevant accounts

2.17 S 270 defines the 'relevant accounts' which should be used to determine the distributable profits. These are the most recent audited annual accounts of the company, prepared in compliance with the Companies Acts. If the accounts are qualified by the auditors, the auditors must state in their report whether they consider that the proposed distribution would contravene the Act.

2.18 **Companies may also base a distribution on interim accounts,** which need not be audited. However, in the case of a public company, such interim accounts must be properly prepared and comply with:

(a) s 228(2) (accounts to give a true and fair view); and
(b) s 238 (directors to sign the company's balance sheet).

A copy of the interim accounts should be delivered to the Registrar.

Investment and insurance companies

2.19 S 265 makes a **special provision for investment companies which are public companies.** Investment companies may make a distribution out of realised revenue profits (insofar as they have not already been utilised or capitalised) less its realised and unrealised revenue losses (insofar as these have not already been written off in a capital reduction or reconstruction) provided that its assets equal at least one and a half times the aggregate amount of its liabilities.

2.20 S 268 refers to insurance companies which have long-term business. Any surplus of assets over liabilities on long-term business which has been properly transferred to the company's profit and loss account should be regarded as a *realised* profit. (This section makes a specific point of clarification, and is therefore relatively minor in importance.)

The duties of directors

2.21 S 309 CA 1985 states that the directors of a company must have regard to the interests of the company's employees in general, as well as to the interests of shareholders. This is a duty which is owed by directors to the company alone.

Question 1

Explain the implications of the following items to profits available for distribution in a public company:

(a) research and development activities;

(b) net deficit on revaluation reserve arising from an overall deficit on the revaluation of fixed assets;

(c) excess depreciation;

(d) goodwill.

Answer

(a) S 263 of the Companies Act 1985 provides that, for the purposes of calculating realised profits, development expenditure carried forward in the balance sheet should be treated as a realised loss. This means that development expenditure may not be regarded as part of net assets.

If, however, there are special circumstances which, in the opinion of the directors, justify the treatment of development expenditure as an asset and not as a loss, then this requirement need not apply. It is generally considered that, if the development expenditure qualifies for treatment as an asset under the provisions of SSAP 13, then it may be treated as an asset and not a loss for the purposes of calculating distributable profits.

(b) A revaluation reserve is a non-distributable reserve because it reflects unrealised profits and losses. A public company cannot make a distribution which reduces its net assets to below the total of called-up share capital and non-distributable reserves. Consequently, any reduction in a revaluation reserve (or an increase in a debit balance) reduces the profits available for distribution.

(c) Excess depreciation is the depreciation on revalued assets in excess of cost. Since excess depreciation is regarded as the realisation (through use) of part of the corresponding revaluation reserve, it is added back to profits available for distribution.

Under FRS10, goodwill must be capitalised and amortised. The annual amount written off is considered a realised loss and reduces distributable profits.

---

3 REDEMPTION OF SHARES   12/94

3.1 **Any limited company is permitted without restriction to cancel unissued shares and in that way to reduce its authorised share capital.** That change does not alter its financial position.

3.2 If a limited company with a share capital wishes to **reduce its issued share capital** (and incidentally its authorised capital of which the issued capital is part) it may do so **provided that:**

(a) it has power to do so in its **articles** of association; and

(b) it passes a **special resolution**; and

(c) it obtains **confirmation** of the reduction **from the court**: s 135.

Requirement (a) is simply a matter of procedure. Articles usually contain the necessary power. If not, the company in general meeting would first pass a special resolution to alter the articles appropriately and then proceed, as the second item on the agenda of the meeting, to pass a special resolution to reduce the capital.

3.3 There are **three basic methods of reducing share capital** specified in s 35(2).

(a) **Extinguish or reduce liability on partly paid shares**. A company may have issued £1 (nominal) shares 75p paid up. The outstanding liability of 25p per share may be eliminated altogether by reducing each share to 75p (nominal) fully paid or some intermediate figure, eg 80p (nominal) 75p paid. Nothing is returned to the shareholders but the company gives up a claim against them for money which it could call up whenever needed.

(b) **Cancel paid up share capital which has been lost or which is no longer represented by available assets**. Suppose that the issued shares are £1 (nominal) fully paid but the net assets now represent a value of only 50p per share. The difference is probably matched by a debit balance on profit and loss account (or provision for fall in value of assets). The company could reduce the nominal value of its £1 shares to 50p (or some intermediate figure) and apply the amount to write off the debit balance or provision wholly or in part. It would then be able to resume payment of dividends out of future profits without being obliged to make good past losses. The resources of the company are not reduced by this procedure of part cancellation of nominal value of shares but it avoids having to rebuild lost capital by retaining profits.

(c) **Pay off part of the paid up share capital out of surplus assets**. The company might repay to shareholders, say, 30p in cash per £1 share by reducing the nominal value of the share to 70p. This reduces the assets of the company by 30p per share.

Role of court in reduction of capital

> **Exam focus point**
> Paragraphs 3.4 - 3.8 are included for completeness, but they are unlikely to be examined as they belong in your Paper 2 studies.

3.4 When application is made to the court for approval of the reduction, its first concern is the effect of the reduction on the company's ability to pay its debts: s 136. If the reduction is by method (a) or (c) the court must, and where method (b) is used the court may, require that creditors shall be invited by advertisement to state their objections (if any) to the reduction to the court unless the court decides to dispense with this procedure.

3.5 In modern practice the company usually persuades the court to dispense with advertising for creditors' objections (which can be commercially damaging to the company if its purpose is misunderstood since it may suggest to creditors that the company is insolvent). Two possible methods are:

(a) Paying off all creditors before application is made to the court; or, if that is not practicable.

(b) Producing to the court a guarantee, perhaps from the company's bank, that its existing debts will be paid in full.

The statutory procedure itself, if it is followed, provides that if a creditor does object his claim shall be met by providing security for his debt or such part of it (if it is in dispute) as the court may decide.

3.6 The court also considers whether, if there is more than one class of share, the reduction is fair in its **effect on different classes of shareholder**. If, for example, the company has both ordinary and preference shares, the holders of the preference shares may be entitled in a winding up to repayment of their capital in priority to any repayment to ordinary shareholders. If that is the position then:

(a) Under method (c) the preference shares must be repaid in full under a reduction of capital before any reduction of ordinary shares is made. For example, the reduction might provide for repayment of £1 per £1 share to the holders of preference shares and then, say, 10p per £1 share (thereby reduced to 90p) for ordinary shareholders.

(b) When method (b) is used (where the reduction reflects a loss which would in winding up diminish the surplus available to ordinary shareholders), the reduction would be made by cancellation of part of the nominal value of the ordinary shares without altering the value of the preference shares, so as to preserve the priority rights of preference shares to whatever assets are available in a winding up.

3.7   If the court is satisfied that the reduction does not prejudice creditors and is fair in its effect on shareholders, it approves the reduction by making an order to that effect. The court has power to require the company to add the words 'and reduced' to its name at the end or to publish the reasons for or information about the reduction: s 137. But neither condition is ever imposed in modern practice.

3.8   A copy of the court order and of a minute, approved by the court, to show the altered share capital is delivered to the registrar who issues a certificate of registration. The reduction then takes effect and, if method (c) is used, the payment to shareholders may then be made: s 138.

Share premium account

3.9   Whenever a company obtains for its shares a consideration in excess of their nominal value, it must transfer the excess to a share premium account. The general rule is that the **share premium account is subject to the same restriction as share capital. However, a bonus issue can be made using the share premium account** (reducing share premium in order to increase issued share capital).

3.10 Following the decision in *Shearer v Bercain 1980,* there is an exemption from the general rules on setting up a share premium account, in certain circumstances where new shares are issued as consideration for the acquisition of shares in another company (see Chapter 19).

3.11 The **other permitted uses of share premium** are to pay:

(a) Capital expenses such as preliminary expenses of forming the company.
(b) Discount on the issue of shares or debentures.
(c) Premium (if any) paid on redemption of debentures: s 130(2).

Private companies (but not public companies) may also use a share premium account in purchasing or redeeming their own shares out of capital.

Redemption or purchase by a company of its own shares

3.12 There is a **general prohibition** (s 143) against any voluntary acquisition by a company of its own shares, but that prohibition is subject to **exceptions**.

3.13 A company may:

(a) Purchase its own shares in compliance with an **order of the court**.

(b) Issue **redeemable shares** and then redeem them.

(c) Purchase its own shares under certain **specified procedures**.

(d) **Forfeit** or accept the surrender of its shares.

These restrictions relate to the **purchase** of shares: there is no objection to accepting a gift.

3.14 The **conditions for the issue and redemption of redeemable shares** are set out in ss 159 to 161.

(a) The articles must give authority for the issue of redeemable shares. Articles do usually provide for it, but if they do not, the articles must be altered before the shares are issued: s 159.

(b) Redeemable shares may only be issued if at the time of issue the company also has issued shares which are not redeemable: a company's capital may not consist entirely of redeemable shares: s 159.

(c) Redeemable shares may only be redeemed if they are fully paid: s 159.

(d) The terms of redemption must provide for payment on redemption: s 159.

(e) The shares may be redeemed out of distributable profits, or the proceeds of a new issue of shares, or capital (if it is a private company) in accordance with the relevant rules: s 160.

(f) Any premium payable on redemption must be provided out of distributable profits subject to an exception described below: s 160.

3.15 The 1948 Act provided regulations which prevented companies from redeeming shares except by transferring a sum equal to the nominal value of shares redeemed from distributable profit reserves to a non-distributable 'capital redemption reserve'. This reduction in distributable reserves is an example of the **capitalisation of profits, where previously distributable profits become undistributable.**

3.16 **The purpose of these regulations was to prevent companies from reducing their share capital investment so as to put creditors of the company at risk.**

3.17 EXAMPLE: CAPITALISATION OF PROFITS

Suppose, for example, that Muffin Ltd had £100,000 of preference shares, redeemable in the very near future at par. A balance sheet of the company is currently as follows.

	£	£
Assets		
Cash	100,000	
Other assets	300,000	
		400,000
Liabilities		
Trade creditors		120,000
Net assets		280,000
Capital and reserves		
Ordinary shares	30,000	
Redeemable preference shares	100,000	
		130,000
Profit and loss account		150,000
		280,000

3.18   Now if Muffin Ltd were able to redeem the preference shares without making any transfer from the profit and loss account to a capital redemption reserve, the effect of the share redemption on the balance sheet would be as follows.

	£
Net assets	
Non-cash assets	300,000
Less trade creditors	120,000
	180,000
Capital and reserves	
Ordinary shares	30,000
Profit and loss account	150,000
	180,000

In this example, the company would still be able to pay dividends out of profits of up to £150,000. If it did, the creditors of the company would be highly vulnerable, financing £120,000 out of a total of £150,000 assets of the company.

3.19   The regulations in the 1948 Act were intended to prevent such extreme situations arising. On redemption of the preference shares, Muffin Ltd would have been required to transfer £100,000 from its profit and loss account to a non-distributable reserve, called at that time a capital redemption reserve fund. The effect of the redemption of shares on the balance sheet would have been:

	£	£
Net assets		
Non-cash assets		300,000
Less trade creditors		120,000
		180,000
Capital and reserves		
Ordinary shares		30,000
Reserves		
Distributable (profit and loss account)	50,000	
Non-distributable (capital redemption reserve fund)	100,000	
		150,000
		180,000

The maximum distributable profits are now £50,000. If Muffin Ltd paid all these as a dividend, there would still be £250,000 of assets left in the company, just over half of which would be financed by non-distributable equity capital.

3.20   When a company redeems some shares, or purchases some of its own shares, they **should be redeemed**:

(a)   **out of distributable profits; or**

(b)   **out of the proceeds of a new issue of shares;**

and if there is any premium on redemption, **the premium must be paid out of distributable profits,** except that if the shares were issued at a premium, then any premium payable on their redemption may be paid out of the proceeds of a new share issue made for the purpose, up to an amount equal to the lesser of:

(a)   the aggregate premiums received on issue of the redeemable shares; and

(b)   the balance on the share premium account (including premium on issue of the new shares).

3.21 EXAMPLE: REDEMPTION OF SHARES

A numerical example might help to clarify this point. Suppose that Jingle Ltd intends to redeem 10,000 shares of £1 each at a premium of 5 pence per share. The redemption must be financed out of:

(a) Distributable profits (10,000 × £1.05 = £10,500).

(b) The proceeds of a new share issue (say, by issuing 10,000 new £1 shares at par). The premium of £500 must be paid out of distributable profits.

(c) Combination of a new share issue and distributable profits.

(d) out of the proceeds of a new share issue where the redeemable shares were issued at a premium. For example, if the redeemable shares had been issued at a premium of 3p per share, then (assuming that the balance on the share premium account after the new share issue was at least £300) £300 of the premium on redemption could be debited to the share premium account and only £200 need be debited to distributable profits.

3.22 (a) Where a company redeems shares or purchases its own shares wholly out of distributable profits, it must transfer to the capital redemption reserve an amount equal to the nominal value of the shares redeemed (s 170 (1)).

In example (a) above the accounting entries would be:

		£	£
DEBIT	Share capital account	10,000	
	Profit and loss account (premium on redemption)	500	
CREDIT	Cash		10,500
DEBIT	Profit and loss account	10,000	
CREDIT	Capital redemption reserve		10,000

(b) Where a company redeems shares or purchases its shares wholly or partly out of the proceeds of a new share issue, it must transfer to the capital redemption reserve an amount by which the nominal value of the shares redeemed exceeds the *aggregate* proceeds from the new issue (ie nominal value of new shares issued plus share premium) (s 170 (2)).

(i) In example (b) the accounting entries would be:

		£	£
DEBIT	Share capital account (redeemed shares)	10,000	
	Profit and loss account (premium)	500	
CREDIT	Cash (redemption of shares)		10,500
DEBIT	Cash (from new issue)	10,000	
CREDIT	Share capital account		10,000

No credit to the capital redemption reserve is necessary because there is no decrease in the creditors' buffer.

(ii) If the redemption in the same example were made by issuing 5,000 new £1 shares at par, and paying £5,500 out of distributable profits:

		£	£
DEBIT	Share capital account (redeemed shares)	10,000	
	Profit and loss account (premium)	500	
CREDIT	Cash (redemption of shares)		10,500
DEBIT	Cash (from new issue)	5,000	
CREDIT	Share capital account		5,000
DEBIT	Profit and loss account	5,000	
CREDIT	Capital redemption reserve		5,000

(iii)   In the example (d) above (assuming a new issue of 10,000 £1 shares at a premium of 8p per share) the accounting entries would be:

		£	£
DEBIT	Cash (from new issue)	10,800	
CREDIT	Share capital account		10,000
	Share premium account		800
DEBIT	Share capital account (redeemed shares)	10,000	
	Share premium account	300	
	Profit and loss account	200	
CREDIT	Cash (redemption of shares)		10,500

No capital redemption reserve is required, as in (i) above. The redemption is financed entirely by a new issue of shares.

Redemption of shares out of capital

3.23   There is one further rule, which is a significant departure from the principle that shares must not be purchased or redeemed in a way which reduces non-distributable equity reserves. This rule applies to private companies only (provided that their articles of association authorise them to do so).

RULE TO LEARN

A private company may redeem or purchase its own shares out of *capital* (ie non-redeemable share capital, capital redemption reserve, share premium account or revaluation reserve) but only on condition that the nominal value of shares redeemed (or purchased):

(a)   exceeds the proceeds of any new share issue to finance the redemption (or purchases); *and also*

(b)   first exhausts the distributable profits of the company entirely.

3.24   In such a situation, a transfer must be made to the capital redemption reserve of the amount by which distributable profits exceed the premium on redemption or purchase. (If the premium on redemption or purchase exceeds the total of distributable profits, the difference must be deducted from non-redeemable share capital, and there will be no capital redemption reserve.)

3.25 EXAMPLE: REDEMPTION OF SHARES OUT OF CAPITAL

Suppose, for example, that Snowflake Ltd has the following capital and reserves.

	£
Fully paid non-redeemable share capital	100,000
Fully paid redeemable share capital	40,000
	140,000
Distributable profits	18,000
	158,000

The redeemable shares are now to be redeemed at a cost of £46,000 (creating a premium of £6,000 on redemption). To partly cover the costs of redemption, a new issue of 25,000 ordinary £1 shares will be made at par.

The **permissible capital payment** under the Companies Act 1985 is:

	£	£
Cost of redemption		46,000
Less: proceeds of new issue	25,000	
distributable profits	18,000	
		43,000
Permissible capital payment		3,000

The distributable profits exceed the premium on redemption by £(18,000 − 6,000) = £12,000. A transfer of £12,000 will be made to the capital redemption reserve, leaving the company's capital and reserves as:

	£
Non-redeemable share capital	100,000
New shares issued	25,000
Capital redemption reserve	12,000
	137,000

The total capital is now £137,000 which is £3,000 less (the capital repayment) than the non-distributable reserves of the company before redemption (£140,000).

3.26 The rules explained above may seem lengthy and difficult to follow. However, you should bear in mind that **the purpose of the regulations is to protect creditors**. If a company pays out money to its shareholders, there may be insufficient 'liquid' funds left within the business to pay its debts. The Companies Act 1985 tries to prevent creditors being 'cheated' out of repayments of the debts owing to them by 'underhand' prior payments to shareholders. (However, a private company is allowed to reduce its non-distributable reserves if it has first of all eliminated all its distributable reserves. This restricts the 'defence' for creditors provided by the Act.)

Commercial reasons for altering capital structure

3.27 These include the following.

- Greater security of finance.
- Better image for third parties.
- A 'neater' balance sheet.
- Borrowing repaid sooner.
- Cost of borrowing reduced.

Question 2

Set out below are the summarised balance sheets of A plc and B Ltd at 30 June 19X5.

	A £'000	B £'000
Capital and reserves		
Called up share capital £1 ordinary shares	300	300
Share premium account	60	60
Profit and loss account	160	20
	520	380
Net assets	520	380

On 1 July 19X5 A plc and B Ltd each purchased 50,000 of their own ordinary shares as follows.

A plc purchased its own shares at 150p each. The shares were originally issued at a premium of 20p. The redemption was partly financed by the issue at par of 5,000 10% redeemable preference shares of £1 each.

B Ltd purchased its own shares out of capital at a price of 80p each.

Required

Prepare the summarised balance sheets of A plc and B Ltd at 1 July 19X5 immediately after the above transactions have been effected.

Answer

Workings for A

	£	£
Cost of redemption (50,000 × £1.50)		75,000
Premium on redemption (50,000 × 50p)		25,000
No premium arises on the new issue.		
Distributable profits		
Profit and loss account before redemption		160,000
Premium on redemption (must come out of distributable profits, no premium on new issue)		(25,000)
		135,000
Remainder of redemption costs	50,000	
Proceeds of new issue 5,000 × £1	(5,000)	
Remainder out of distributable profits		(45,000)
Balance on profit and loss account		90,000
Transfer to capital redemption reserve		
Nominal value of shares redeemed		50,000
Proceeds of new issue		(5,000)
Balance on CRR		45,000

BALANCE SHEET OF A PLC AS AT 1 JULY 19X5

	£'000
Capital and reserves	
Preference shares	5
Ordinary shares	250
Share premium	60
Capital redemption reserve	45
	360
Profit and loss account	90
	450
Net assets	450

Workings for B

	£
Cost of redemption (50,000 × 80p)	40,000
Discount on redemption (50,000 × 20p)	10,000
Cost of redemption	40,000
Distributable profits	(20,000)
Permissible capital payment (PCP)	20,000

Transfer to capital redemption reserve

Nominal value of shares redeemed	50,000
PCP	20,000
Balance on capital redemption reserve	30,000

BALANCE SHEET OF B LIMITED AS AT 1 JULY 19X5

	£'000
Capital and reserves	
Ordinary shares	250
Share premium	60
Capital redemption reserve	30
	340
Net assets	340

Chapter roundup

- **Revenue recognition** is straightforward in most business transactions, but some situations are more complicated. It is necessary to determine the **substance of each transaction, rather than the legal form**.

- You should be able to calculate **maximum distributions available to private and public companies** and to discuss the meaning of distributable and realisable profits.

- You must be able to carry out **simple calculations** showing the amounts to be transferred to the **capital redemption reserve** on purchase or redemption of own shares, how the amount of any **premium** on redemption would be treated, and how much the **permissible capital payment** would be for a private company.

Quick quiz

1   What are the general procedures for recognising revenue under the historical cost system? (see para 1.9)

2   What are the profits statutorily available for distribution? (2.1)

3   What additional restriction is placed on the distributions of public companies? (2.5)

4   What are the 'relevant accounts' for the purposes of determining distributable profits? (2.17)

5   What is the purpose of the rules which require the setting up of a capital redemption reserve? (3.16)

6   When a company redeems or purchases some shares, out of what sources of funds can the shares be redeemed? (3.20)

7   In what circumstances may a private company redeem or purchase its own shares out of capital? (3.23)

Question to try	Level	Marks	Time
7	Full exam	20	36 mins

Chapter 7

THE REGULATORY FRAMEWORK

Chapter topic list	Syllabus reference
1 The Accounting Standards Committee and SSAPs	1(a), (d)
2 The Accounting Standards Board and FRSs	1(a), (d)
3 The Urgent Issues Task Force	1(a), (d)
4 Big GAAP/little GAAP	1(a), (d)

Introduction

The regulatory framework has been briefly described in Chapter 1.

In this chapter, the current financial reporting environment is examined, including the process leading to the creation of Financial Reporting Exposure Drafts (FREDs) and Financial Reporting Standards (FRSs). The role and structure of the major bodies involved in the financial reporting regime are discussed, particularly the Accounting Standards Board (ASB). In Section 4 we look at the question of whether accounting standards are equally applicable to small and large companies.

Both this chapter and Chapter 8 are extremely important. Make sure that you understand and learn their contents before going on to look at individual items and standards in the following chapters.

1   THE ACCOUNTING STANDARDS COMMITTEE AND SSAPS

1.1   We need to discuss briefly the old standard-setting process because some of the standards it produced, the SSAPs, have still not been superseded by FRSs and many are on your syllabus.

1.2   The **ASC** was set up in 1970 as a joint committee of members of the six major accountancy bodies in Britain, the constituent members of the Consultative Committee of Accountancy Bodies (CCAB). Its terms of reference included the production of **SSAPs** after consultation with all interest parties (companies, government, etc). Consultation with these interest groups was not always satisfactory and **some SSAPs** were criticised for being **unrealistic or 'unfair'**.

1.3   Once issued, **SSAPs were intended to apply to all financial accounts which were 'intended to give a true and fair view of the financial position and profit and loss'.** This included overseas companies incorporated in UK group accounts. A standard could, however, specify (ie restrict) the 'scope' of its application. For example, SSAP 3 (on earnings per share) applies only to the audited accounts of listed companies (companies whose shares are listed on the Stock Exchange).

1.4   Although there are some areas where the contents of SSAPs overlap with provisions of company law, standards are detailed working regulations within the framework of government legislation, and **they cover areas in which the law is silent**. The accountancy profession prefers to make its own rules for self-regulation, rather than to have rules imposed by law. In addition, standards are not intended to override exemptions from disclosure which are allowed to special cases of companies by law.

1.5 **The Companies Act 1985 states that a departure from its provisions is permissible if that provision is inconsistent with the true and fair view** (see Chapter 8, Section 3). **This may lead to situations in which a SSAP recommends departure from the legal rules.** For example, SSAP 19 *Accounting for investment properties* sanctions such a departure by stating that investment properties need not be depreciated (see Chapter 9). Other areas of possible conflict between SSAPs and statute will be noted in later chapters.

1.6 **Accounting standards (both SSAPs and FRSs) apply mainly to private bodies rather than the public sector** (although SSAPs which are relevant to accounting in the public sector have been applied by organisations in it). A Public Sector Liaison Committee (PSLC) was set up by the ASB to replace the ASC's Public Sector Liaison Group (PSLG) which has led to the establishment of advisory panels on specific parts of the public sector (including health authority, local authority and university accounting).

1.7 A standard will choose one possible treatment (or perhaps two) from many which are available as the **best practice** to be followed. SSAPs are working regulations for practical application and they have been **developed rather haphazardly without a clear, underlying rationale;** without a conceptual framework, as we saw in Chapter 1.

2   THE ACCOUNTING STANDARDS BOARD AND FRSS   12/95

2.1 The ASB's consultative process leads to the setting of **Financial Reporting Standards** (FRSs). To produce an FRS, first a working Draft for Discussion (DD) is published to get feedback from people closely involved with or with a direct interest in the standard setting process. The DD, as a result of this process, is converted into a Financial Reporting Exposure Draft (FRED). Candidates should be aware of the contents of FRSs published by the ASB (as listed in the CIMA Paper 5 reading list): see below. The ASB publishes other documents as Exposure Drafts, for example chapters of the *Statement of Principles*.

2.2 The standard-setting process can be summarised as follows.

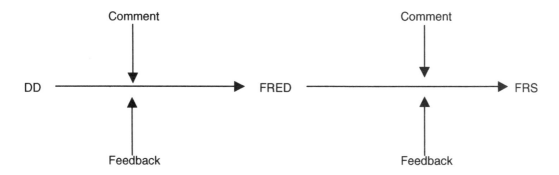

2.3 In July 1991 the ASB published the definitive *Statements of Aims* and, in July 1993, the *Foreword to Accounting Standards*.

Statement of Aims

2.4 The *Statement of Aims* is produced here in full as it is very brief.

'Aims

The aims of the Accounting Standards Board (the Board) are to **establish and improve standards of financial accounting and reporting**, for the benefit of users, preparers and auditors of financial information.

Achieving the aims

The Board intends to achieve its aims by:

1   **Developing principles** to guide it in establishing standards and to provide a framework within which others can exercise judgement in resolving accounting issues.

2   **Issuing new accounting standards**, or amending existing ones, in response to evolving business practices, new economic developments and deficiencies being identified in current practice.

3   **Addressing urgent issues promptly**.

Fundamental guidelines

1   To be objective and to ensure that the **information** resulting from the application of accounting standards **faithfully represents the underlying commercial activity**. Such information should be neutral in the sense that it is free from any form of bias intended to influence users in a particular direction and should not be designed to favour any group of users or preparers.

2   To ensure that accounting standards are **clearly expressed** and supported by a reasoned analysis of the issues.

3   To determine **what should be incorporated in accounting standards** based on research, public consultation and careful deliberation about the usefulness of the resulting information.

4   To ensure that through a process of **regular communication**, accounting standards are produced with due regard to international developments.

5   To ensure that there is **consistency** both from one accounting standard to another and between accounting standards and company law.

6   To issue accounting standards only when the **expected benefits** exceed the perceived costs. The Board recognises that reliable cost/benefit calculations are seldom possible. However, it will always assess the need for standards in terms of the significance and extent of the problem being addressed and will choose the standard which appears to be most effective in cost/benefit terms.

7   To take account of the desire of the financial community for **evolutionary rather than revolutionary change** in the reporting process where this is consistent with the objectives outlined above.'

Foreword to Accounting Standards

2.5   This document, issued in June 1993, is similar in nature to the foreword used by the ASC in relation to SSAPs. The contents are listed briefly here.

    (a)   **Introduction**. This is merely background information about the ASB and the documents it will produce.

    (b)   The **Accounting Standards Board**. Reference is made to the **Statement of Aims**.

    (c)   **Authority**. This section mentions:

        (i)   The legal authority of FRSs in relation to the Act.

        (ii)   Directors' responsibilities to prepare accounts showing a true and fair view.

(iii)   The responsibility of members of CCAB bodies in industry and practice in relation to financial statements (as preparers or auditors).

(iv)   CCAB bodies may investigate non-compliance.

(d)   **Scope and application.** The standards apply to:

(i)   Financial statements of a reporting entity that are intended to give a true and fair view.

(ii)   Group accounts in the UK (and Ireland) including any overseas entities.

(e)   **Compliance with accounting standards.** The following rules and comments are laid down.

(i)   It will normally be necessary to comply with the standards to show a true and fair view.

(ii)   In applying the standards, the user should be guided by their spirit and reasoning.

(iii)   In *rare* cases it may be necessary to depart from a standard to show a true and fair view.

(iv)   Departures should be dealt with objectively according to the 'economic and commercial characteristics of the circumstances'; the departure and its financial effect should be disclosed.

(v)   The Review Panel and the DTI have powers and procedures to investigate departures and to require a restatement through the court.

(f)   **The public sector.** 'The prescription of accounting requirements for the public sector in the United Kingdom is a matter for the Government'.

(g)   **The issue of an FRS.** This section covers the procedures for discussion, consultation and drafting.

(h)   **Accounting standards and the legal framework.** Consistency with UK and EU law is aimed for.

(i)   **International Accounting Standards.** An FRS will contain a section explaining how it relates to the IAS dealing with the same topic. 'The Board supports the IASC in its aims to harmonise international financial reporting'.

(j)   **Early adoption of FREDs.** The contents of FREDs may change before the FRS stage is reached and therefore early adoption is discouraged unless the information is shown as a supplement.

(k)   **Appendix.** A new legal opinion by Mary Arden has been obtained on the true and fair requirement. This opinion endorses the legal force of standards.

> 'Just as a custom which is upheld by the courts may properly be regarded as a source of law, so too, in my view, does an accounting standard which the court holds must be complied with to meet the true and fair requirement become in cases where it is applicable, a source of law in itself in the widest sense of that term.'

2.6   As you can see, the foreword gives the FRSs a context in relation to other standard setting bodies, company law and users and preparers of accounts.

2.7   Note in particular the content of (e) in Paragraph 2.5 above. The spirit of the standards must be followed, but where there is a departure from a standard (to show a true and fair view), this must be disclosed, including full financial effects.

Current accounting standards

2.8 The following standards are extant at the date of writing. The SSAPs which were in force at the date the ASB was formed have been adopted by the Board. They are gradually being superseded by the new Financial Reporting Standards.

UK accounting standards

Issue date

Title

	Foreword to accounting standards	Jun 93
FRS 1	Cash flow statements (revised Oct 96)	Sep 91
FRS 2	Accounting for subsidiary undertakings	July 92
FRS 3	Reporting financial performance	Oct 92
FRS 4	Capital instruments	Dec 93
FRS 5	Reporting the substance of transactions	Apr 94
FRS 6	Acquisitions and mergers	Sep 94
FRS 7	Fair values in acquisition accounting	Sep 94
FRS 8	Related party disclosures	Oct 95
FRS 9	Associates and joint ventures	Nov 97
FRS 10	Goodwill and intangible assets	Dec 98
FRSSE	Financial Reporting Standard for Smaller Entities	Nov 97
SSAP 1	Accounting for associated companies	Apr 82
SSAP 2	Disclosure of accounting policies	Nov 71
SSAP 3	Earnings per share	Aug 74
SSAP 4	Accounting for government grants	Jul 90
SSAP 5	Accounting for value added tax	Apr 74
SSAP 8	The treatment of taxation under the imputation system in the accounts of companies	Dec 77
SSAP 9	Stocks and long-term contracts	Sep 88
SSAP 12	Accounting for depreciation	Jan 87
SSAP 13	Accounting for research and development	Jan 89
SSAP 15	Accounting for deferred tax	May 85
SSAP 17	Accounting for post balance sheet events	Aug 80
SSAP 18	Accounting for contingencies	Aug 80
SSAP 19	Accounting for investment properties	Nov 81
SSAP 20	Foreign currency translation	Apr 83
SSAP 21	Accounting for leases and hire purchase contracts	Aug 84
SSAP 22	Accounting for goodwill	Jul 89
SSAP 24	Accounting for pension costs	May 88
SSAP 25	Segmental reporting	Jun 90

Exam focus point

All these accounting standards are examinable in Paper 10. In the case of newer accounting standards, you may be asked to discuss why such a standard was needed and how the standard was developed. You *must* therefore follow current developments in the field to be able to understand the impact of standards - it is not sufficient to learn their content.

Question

In between now and your examination, make sure you set aside time *every* week or month to read the *Students' Newsletter* and either the *Financial Times, The Economist* or any other equivalent publication. Look for news about the actions of the Accounting Standards Board and the other bodies we have discussed in this chapter and read about the accounts of individual companies as they are discussed in the press.

3   THE URGENT ISSUES TASK FORCE (UITF)

3.1   The UITF is an offshoot of the ASB. Its function is:

> 'to tackle **urgent matters** not covered by existing standards, and for which, given the urgency, the normal standard-setting process would not be practicable.' (Sir Ron Dearing)

3.2   The UITF pronouncements, which are called '**abstracts**', are intended to come into effect quickly. They therefore tend to become effective within approximately one month of publication date. The UITF has so far issued twenty two abstracts. Abstracts 1, 2, 3 and 8 have all been superseded by new FRSs and Financial Reporting Exposure Drafts (FREDs). Only Abstracts 4, 5 and 7 are included in the ACCA's list of examinable documents. These are discussed briefly here and they are mentioned in the relevant parts of this text when necessary.

Abstract 4 Presentation of long-term debtors in current assets

3.3   Where the figure of debtors due after more than one year is material in the context of the total net current assets then it should be **disclosed on the face of the balance sheet**, rather than just by way of a note (as has been the practice in the past where long-term debtors were included in current assets). The figure would be material in relation to net current assets if its non-disclosure on the balance sheet would cause readers to misinterpret the accounts. You should bear this in mind when considering the Companies Acts formats, given in Chapter 8.

Abstract 5 Transfers from current assets to fixed assets

3.4   This abstract requires transfers from current assets to fixed assets to be made **at the lower of cost and net realisable value**. This prevents the practice of transfers being made at a value higher than NRV. This avoids charging the profit and loss account with any diminution in value of what are, in effect, unsold trading assets. Once transferred to fixed assets, the CA 1985 alternative accounting rules could be used to take the debit reflecting the diminution in value to a revaluation reserve. Fixed assets are discussed in Chapter 10, but you should also refer to the Review Panel's ruling on Trafalgar House in Paragraph 1.11 above.

Abstract 7 True and fair override disclosures

3.5   Where the directors depart from provisions of CA 1985 to the extent necessary to give a true and fair view, the Act required that '**particulars of any such departure**, the reasons for it and its effect shall be given in a note to the accounts'. Abstract 7 is discussed in Chapter 8.

Abstract 14 Disclosure of changes in accounting policy

3.6   Where there is a change of accounting policy, companies legislation requires disclosure of particulars, reasons and effect. Abstract 14 deals with the **extent of the disclosure** required. This is covered in Chapter 13

Abstract 15 Disclosure of substantial acquisitions

3.7   This clarifies the threshold for **disclosure of substantial acquisitions** under the Stock Exchange Listing Rules. It is discussed in Chapter 14.

3.8   The UITF is currently considering another topic, marking current asset investments to market.

Foreword to UITF Abstracts

3.9   This foreword was issued in February 1994. It is closely associated with the *Foreword to accounting standards* in its scope and application and users are asked to 'be guided by the spirit and reasoning' behind the abstracts.

3.10 Most importantly, the document sets out the following criteria for compliance with the UITF abstracts.

> 'The Councils of the CCAB bodies expect their members who assume responsibilities in respect of financial statements to **observe UITF Abstracts until they are replaced by accounting standards or otherwise withdrawn** by the ASB.'

3.11 The scope of and compliance with the abstracts are similar to those associated with accounting standards (accounts which show a true and fair view, non-compliance must be justified and disclosed etc).

The effectiveness of the UITF

3.12 There is no doubt that the prompt action of the UITF has **closed many loopholes** as soon as they have become apparent. Some of the abstracts have been triggered by the accounts of individual companies, whereas others reflect concern which has arisen over a period of time. Another aspect of the success of the UITF is the **relative speed** with which the abstracts have been included in new standards, or exposure drafts. In other words, the topics were obviously important enough, not only for the attention of the UITF, but also for the ASB.

3.13 In combination with the Review Panel, the UITF can halt abuses in financial reporting as soon as they occur. This will also act as a preventative measure, causing many companies and their auditors to hesitate before breaking (or even bending) the rules.

4   BIG GAAP/LITTLE GAAP

4.1   Most UK companies are **small companies**. They are generally owned and managed by one person or a family. The owners have invested their own money in the business and there are **no outside shareholders to protect**.

4.2   **Large companies**, by contrast, particularly public limited companies may have shareholders who have invested their money, possibly through a pension fund, with no knowledge whatever of the company. These **shareholders need protection and the regulations for such companies need to be more stringent**.

> ### KEY TERM
>
> It could therefore be argued that company accounts should be of two types: 'simple' ones for small companies with fewer regulations and disclosure requirements and 'complicated' ones for larger companies with extensive and detailed requirements. This is the '**big GAAP/little GAAP**' divide.

4.3   In 1994 a working party of the Consultative Committee of Accountancy Bodies was set up to consider whether small companies should be exempt from most of or all accounting standards. In November 1994 the working party concluded that:

> 'the current form of financial reporting may not best serve the needs of some users. Indeed it could be argued that the application of the full range of present requirements may make some

information less understandable, or even result in a distorted presentation, compared with
figures that users understand.'

4.4   The working party proposed that companies meeting the Companies Act definition of
small (turnover of less than £2.6m, balance sheet total of £1.4m and an average of 50
employees) would be **exempt from all standards, except for certain core ones**, after
taking into account the fact that the accounting regime specified by the Companies Act
lays down most of the fundamental principles necessary to produce accounts which show
a true and fair. The proposed 'core' standards were as follows.

SSAP 4 *Accounting for government grants*
SSAP 9 *Stocks and long-term contracts*
SSAP 13 *Accounting for research and development*
SSAP 17 *Accounting for post balance sheet events*
SSAP 18 *Accounting for contingencies*

4.5   Initially the proposals met with a **frosty reception** by the profession, with the ACCA, for
example, warning that they were 'too radical' and would lead to a 'serious decline in the
quality of financial reporting'. It was suggested that small company accounts might not
show a true and fair view if they do not follow the majority of standards.

4.6   However, in July 1995 it was reported in *Accountancy* that the proposals were beginning
to find favour. Moreover, the Department of Trade and Industry published a
consultation paper *Accounting Simplifications* which addressed the legal aspects of small
company accounts.

Exposure draft FRS for smaller entities

4.7   In December 1995, the debate was significantly accelerated. The working party
published its discussion paper *Designed to fit - a reporting standard for smaller entities*. Then
in December 1996 the ASB published an Exposure Draft of the *Financial Reporting
Standard for Smaller Entities* and this was published in final form in November 1997. It
brings together in one brief document all the accounting guidance which UK small
businesses will require to draw up their financial statements.

4.8   The **FRSSE retains all of the basic principles of accounting standards while
discarding the detailed explanatory notes**. This slims down the volume of accounting
standards dramatically. For example, FRS 4 *Capital instruments* and FRS 5 *Reporting the
substance of transactions* have been reduced to just a couple of paragraphs. The original
standards are very substantial. Disclosure requirements are greatly reduced.

4.9   The FRSSE is applicable to all companies that satisfy the definition of a small company
in companies legislation and is available to other entities that would meet that definition
if they were companies. A company that chooses to comply with the FRSSE is exempt
from all other accounting standards and UITF Abstracts.

4.10   The FRSSE contains in a simplified form the requirements from existing accounting
standards that are relevant to the majority of smaller entities.

4.11   In order to keep the FRSSE as user-friendly as possible some of the requirements in
accounting standards relating to more complex transactions, eg the treatment of
convertible debt in FRS 4 *Capital instruments*, have not been included in the FRSSE, as
they do not affect most smaller entities. Where guidance is needed on a matter not
contained in the FRSSE, regard should be paid to existing practice as set out in the
relevant accounting standards.

Measurement

4.12   The measurement bases in the FRSSE are the same as, or a simplification of, those in existing accounting standards. For example, under the FRSSE a lessee that is a small company could account for the finance charges on a finance lease on a straight-line basis over the life of the lease, rather than, as in SSAP 21, using a constant periodic rate of return.

Detailed requirements

4.13   The main headings of the FRSSE are listed below with explanatory notes, where appropriate, indicating changes from the original standards or other points of significance. (The FRSSE will not be discussed in detail as many of the standards on which it is based are covered elsewhere in this Study Text.)

(a)   **Scope.** The FRSSE is capable of application to smaller **entities** and not just smaller companies. It applies to the companies entitled to the exemptions available in ss 246 and 247 CA 1985 for small companies and which state that they have taken advantage of such exemptions. The FRSSE is also applicable to small groups (as defined by companies legislation) even though there is no statutory requirement for them to prepare consolidated accounts.

(b)   **General.** The financial statements should state that they have been prepared in accordance with the FRSSE.

(c)   **Profit and loss account.** The requirement of FRS 3 *Reporting financial performance* to **analyse the profit and loss account** into continuing, discontinued and acquired operations has been **lifted**.

(d)   **Statement of total recognised gains and losses.** This statement has been **retained**. However, where the only recognised gains and losses are those included in the profit and loss account, no separate statement to that effect is required. This cuts out a large amount of disclosure which, for small companies, was felt to be superfluous. There is no need to show historical cost profits and losses or a reconciliation of movements in shareholders' funds.

(e)   **Foreign currency translation**

(f)   **Taxation**

(g)   **Goodwill**

(h)   **Investment properties**

(i)   **Depreciation**

(j)   **Government grants**

(k)   **Research and development**

(l)   **Short and long-term contracts**

(m)   **Leases.** SSAP 21 *Accounting for leases and hire purchase contracts* is modified such that, for finance leases, charges can normally be spread on a **straight-line basis** and assets and liabilities can normally be recorded at their fair value, rather than the value of the minimum lease payments.

(n)   **Pensions.** There is **no requirement to disclose** the accounting policy for pension scheme contributions, or funding policy, or circumstances where the actuary is an employee or officer of the company.

(o) **Capital instruments.** FRS 4 *Capital instruments* has been **simplified** such that arrangement fees can be charged directly to the profit and loss account rather than spread over the term of the debt where they are not considered significant in amount.

(p) **Contingencies**

(q) **Related parties.** The disclosure requirements for related party transactions in the FRSSE represent a useful dispensation for smaller entities compared with those in FRS 8 *Related party disclosures*. Under FRS 8, related party transactions that are material to the related party, where that related party is an individual, are required to be disclosed in the accounts of the reporting entity even if the transaction is not material to the entity. This is not so for smaller entities adopting the FRSSE, as they need disclose only those related party transactions that are material in relation to the reporting entity.

(r) **Definitions**

Cash flow statement

4.14 Since small entities are already exempt from the requirements of FRS 1 *Cash flow statements* the FRSSE does not include a requirement for a cash flow statement. The ASB nevertheless believes that a cash flow statement is an important aid to the understanding of an entity's financial position and performance and the FRSSE therefore includes a 'voluntary disclosures' section, recommending that smaller entities present a simplified cash flow statement using the indirect method (ie starting with operating profit and reconciling it to the total cash generated (or utilised) in the period).

Small groups

4.15 Small groups are not required by law to prepare consolidated accounts, and therefore in practice not many do so, at least on a statutory basis. The Working Party and the Board, however, agreed with respondents that it would be unfair to those small groups that voluntarily prepare group accounts, if they were not able to take advantage of the provisions in the FRSSE. To import all the necessary requirements from accounting standards and UITF Abstracts into the FRSSE to deal with consolidated accounts would have added substantially to its length and complexity, even though it would have been of interest to only a small percentage of entities. Accordingly, the Working Party and the Board preferred to extend the FRSSE in certain areas and then require small groups adopting the FRSSE to follow those accounting standards and UITF Abstracts that deal with consolidated financial statements. This approach was supported by the majority of respondents to the Exposure Draft commenting on the matter.

4.16 The FRSSE has been described by Barry Johnson (*Certified Accountant*, February 1996) as 'a commendable summary of UK GAAP .... succinct and to the point'. The need for and advantages of such a standard have been indicated above.

4.17 *Criticisms of the FRSSE*

(a) The FRSSE is **unlikely to make it easier or cheaper** to prepare financial statements.

(b) The case in favour of relaxing **measurement** GAAP for smaller companies has not yet been made convincingly. The only exemptions are from disclosure, rather than from measurement. Some argue that this could be achieved more easily by simply stating in the individual FRSs and SSAPs what disclosure requirements apply to all companies and what applies only to large ones.

(c) It is questionable whether accounts prepared under the FRSSE would give a **true and fair view** under company law. The true and fair view requirement applies to all companies, whatever their size.

(d) The present document is **not a 'stand-alone' document**. Users would still need to refer to 'mainstream' standards if they are to prepare financial statements which show a true and fair view.

4.18 However, some commentators back the concept of a financial reporting standard for smaller entities; they feel that the FRSSE provides a satisfactory and workable solution to the problems of smaller entities caused by the increasing complexity of accounting standards.

Future developments

4.19 With the assistance of its advisory committee, the Committee on Accounting for Smaller Entities, the ASB will update and revise the FRSSE periodically to reflect future developments in financial reporting. Any changes to the FRSSE, for example as a result of new accounting standards and UITF Abstracts, will be the subject of public consultation.

4.20 The FRSSE attempts to balance the conflicting views of those who commented on the proposals, ranging from those who believe small companies should be exempt from all accounting standards to those who favour retaining virtually the status quo. Given this divergence of views, the ASB believes that it is particularly important that, going forward, the FRSSE is carefully monitored. It is therefore proposed to review how the FRSSE, as a whole, is working in practice after two full years of effective operation and propose amendments as necessary, in addition to the routine periodic revisions of the FRSSE resulting from new accounting standards and UITF Abstracts.

Exam focus point
As with all topical issues, you should aim to read around the subject. Not all comments on the FRSSE have been favourable.

Small companies and the Companies Act 1985

4.21 Small companies are still required to comply with the normal rules, as set out in the Companies Act 1985 and accounting standards, for measurement. They **no longer need to disclose as much information** in their financial statements as larger companies.

4.22 Despite this, the Companies Act specifically states that the financial statements of smaller companies will still be deemed to give **true and fair view** if they have done nothing more than rely on the exemptions that are available to them. The main reason for this seems to be legal: so that the directors will not be held to be in breach of their statutory duties to prepare proper financial statements. However, it still raises the question of how a specific disclosure can be required in order that the financial statements of one enterprise give a true and fair view, but not required in the case of another.

4.23   Where small companies are subject to audit, their auditors are no longer legally required to state that the financial statements give a true and fair view. It appears that two sets of generally accepted accounting practice are developing. Larger companies will continue to be required to comply with all statutory provisions and accounting standard requirements, while smaller companies will only need to comply with a restricted set of rules.

Chapter roundup

- The aims and operating processes of the **FRC, ASB, FRRP** and **UITF** should all be clear now.

- Most UK companies, are small and it is felt that **accounting standards**, being designed for large companies, are **less relevant to smaller companies**.

- A working party of the CCAB was set up to address this big GAAP/little GAAP problem. It produced the **FRSSE**. Published in final form by the ASB in November 1997, this effectively encapsulates UK GAAP with some simplifications from 'mainstream' accounting standards, notably in respect of FRS 3 and 4.

- The FRSSE contains in a simplified form the requirements from existing accounting standards that are relevant to the majority of smaller entities.

Quick quiz

1   By what process are financial reporting standards developed? (see para 2.1)

2   When is it allowable for financial statements *not* to follow as accounting standard? (2.5(e))

3   Write down the subject matter of UITF Abstracts 4, 5, 7, 14 and 15? (3.3 - 3.7)

4   Why is it felt that a distinction needs to be made between 'big GAAP' and 'little GAAP'? (4.2)

5   Which FRS 3 statement does the proposed FRSSE say may be omitted? (4.9)

Question to try	Level	Marks	Time
8	Full exam	20	36 mins

Chapter 8

COMPANIES ACT REQUIREMENTS AND THE FORMAT OF ACCOUNTS

Chapter topic list	Syllabus reference
1 SSAP 2 Disclosure of accounting policies	2(a)
2 Published accounts	2(a)
3 True and fair view	2(a)
4 The format of the accounts	2(a)
5 Notes to the accounts	2(a)
6 Directors' report	2(a)
7 Auditors' report and chairman's report	2(a)

Introduction

This chapter is as important as Chapter 7 and it may look rather daunting. It lays out the Companies Act formats for the balance sheet and profit and loss account as well as the disclosures required in the notes to the accounts. These are fundamental to the study of financial accounting.

Before we look at the Companies Act, we will refresh your memory of the accounting standard which lays out some of the basic premises upon which accounts are based, SSAP 2. You should be familiar with SSAP 2 from your Paper 1 studies.

This chapter is predominantly concerned with Companies Act requirements, but you should refer back to this chapter when you get to Chapter 14 because of the way FRS 3 has affected the format of published accounts and the notes required.

We will mention the Companies Act requirements for each of the individual items mentioned in the rest of the chapters in this part of the Study Text. You should refer back to this chapter frequently to remind yourself of the position of each item in the accounts.

1   SSAP 2 DISCLOSURE OF ACCOUNTING POLICIES

1.1 You should be familiar with SSAP 2 *Disclosure of accounting policies* from your earlier studies, so a brief summary is given here.

Knowledge brought forward from Paper 1

SSAP 2 Disclosure of accounting policies

SSAP 2 defines three important terms.

- **Fundamental accounting concepts** are the broad basic assumptions which underlie the periodic financial accounts of business enterprises.

- **Accounting bases** are the methods developed for applying fundamental accounting concepts to financial transactions and items, for the purpose of financial accounts; and in particular:

    ° for determining the accounting periods in which revenue and costs should be recognised in the P & L a/c; and

    ° for determining the amounts at which material items should be stated in the B/S.

- **Accounting policies:** a business entity's accounting policies are simply the accounting bases which they have chosen to follow in a situation where there is a choice of accounting bases: eg depreciation of fixed assets.

Fundamental concepts

SSAP deals with the four fundamental concepts.

- The **'going concern' concept:** the enterprise will continue in operational existence for the foreseeable future.

- The **'accruals' concept:** revenue and costs are accrued (that is, recognised as they are earned or incurred, not as money is received or paid).

- The **'consistency' concept:** there is consistency of accounting treatment of like items within each accounting period and from one period to the next.

- The **concept of 'prudence':** revenue and profits are not anticipated, but are recognised by inclusion in the P&L a/c only when realised in the form either of cash or of assets, the ultimate cash realisation of which can be assessed with reasonable certainty

There is always a presumption that these concepts have been observed. If this is not the case, the facts should be explained.

1.2   The CA 1985 and SSAP 2 require the following.

(a)   **Accounting policies should be applied consistently** from one financial year to the next.

(b)   If accounts are prepared on the basis of assumptions which differ in material respects from any of the generally accepted fundamental accounting concepts (principles) the details, **reasons for and the effect of, the departure from the fundamental concepts must be given in a note to the accounts.**

(c)   The **accounting policies** adopted by a company in determining the (material) amounts to be included in the balance sheet and in determining the profit or loss for the year **must be stated by a note to the accounts.**

Exam focus point

For examination purposes, it is useful to give the accounting policy note as the first note to the accounts, making sure that the explanations are clear, fair and as brief as possible.

2   PUBLISHED ACCOUNTS   12/96

2.1   Statutory accounts are part of the price to be paid for the benefits of limited liability. **Limited companies must produce such accounts annually and they must appoint an** independent person to audit and report on them. Once prepared, **a copy** of the accounts **must be sent to the Registrar of Companies,** who maintains a separate file for every company. The Registrar's files may be inspected for a nominal fee by any member of the public. This is why the statutory accounts are often referred to as *published accounts*.

2.2   **It is the responsibility of the company's directors to produce accounts which show a true and fair view of the company's results for the period and its financial position at the end of the period** (see Section 3 of this chapter). The board evidence their approval of the accounts by the signature of one director on the balance sheet. Once this has been done, and the auditors have completed their report, the accounts are laid before the members of the company in general meeting. When the members have adopted the accounts they are sent to the Registrar for filing.

2.3   The requirement that the accounts show a true and fair view is paramount; although statute lays down numerous rules on the information to be included in the published accounts and the format of its presentation, any such rule **may be overridden** if compliance with it would prevent the accounts from showing a true and fair view.

Documents included in the accounts

2.4   The documents which **must be included by law** in the accounts laid before a general meeting of the members are:

(a)   A **profit and loss account** (or an income and expenditure account in the case of a non-trading company).

(b)   A **balance sheet** as at the date to which the profit and loss account is made up.

(c)   A **directors' report.**

(d)   An **auditors' report** addressed to the members (not to the directors) of the company.

2.5   **In addition, FRS 1 requires a cash flow statement** to be given. This statement is discussed in Chapter 14. FRS 3 has also introduced a new statement and notes, covered in Chapter 13. Here we will look at the legally required accounting statements, the profit and loss account and balance sheet.

The accounting reference period

2.6   The Companies Act 1985 contains the following rules about the length of a company's accounting period and the frequency with which it may be altered (ss 223 to 225).

(a)   **Accounts must be prepared for an accounting reference period** (ARP), known as the 'financial year' of the company (whether it is a calendar year or not).

(b)   **The profit and loss account should cover the ARP or a period ending not more than seven days before or after the accounting reference date.** Subsequent accounts should cover the period beginning on the day following the last day covered by the previous profit and loss account, and ending as specified above.

(c)   **The balance sheet should give a true and fair view** of the state of affairs of the company as at the end of the financial year.

(d)   **A company can decide its accounting reference period by giving notice to the Registrar of the date on which the accounting period will end each year.** This date will be the accounting referance date. S 225 makes provisions for the alteration of the accounting reference date.

The laying and delivery of accounts

Exam focus point
You should know paragraphs 2.7 - 2.14 from your Paper 2 studies, so the material is unlikely to come up in the exam.

2.7   S 241 CA 1985 specifies that the directors shall lay before the company in general meeting and also deliver to the Registrar, in respect of each accounting reference period, a copy of every document comprising the accounts for that period. However, the CA 1989 has amended the CA 1985 to allow the members of private companies to elect unanimously to dispense with general meetings. This does *not*, however, exempt the company from providing accounts to members.

2.8   Unlimited companies (with some exceptions) are exempt from the duty to deliver copies of their accounts to the Registrar.

2.9   The **period allowed for laying and delivering accounts** varies, and (s 244):

(a)   For **private companies**, it is **ten months** after the end of the accounting reference period.

(b)   For **other (public etc) companies**, it is **seven** months.

Accounting records

2.10   S 221 requires that every company's **accounting records must**:

(a)   Be sufficient to show and explain the company's transactions.

(b)   Disclose with reasonable accuracy at any time the financial position of the company at that time.

(c)   Enable the directors to ensure that any profit and loss account or balance sheet gives a true and fair view of the company's financial position.

2.11   S 221 also specifies that accounting records **should contain**:

(a)   Day-to-day entries for money received and paid, with an explanation of why the receipts and payments occurred (ie the nature of the transactions).

(b)   A record of the company's assets and liabilities.

(c)   Where the company deals in goods:

(i)   Statements of stocks held at the financial year end.

(ii)   Statements of stocktakings on which the figures in (c)(i) are based.

(iii)   With the exception of goods sold on retail, statements of all goods bought and sold identifying for each item the suppliers or customers.

2.12   S 222 specifies that the **accounting records are to be kept at the registered office** of the company or at such other place as the directors think fit, and they **should be open to inspection at all times by officers of the company.**

2.13   Also in s 222 is a **requirement for companies to preserve their accounting records**:

(a)   **Private** companies, for **3 years**.
(b)   **Other** companies, for **6 years**.

The classification of companies

2.14   **A company is considered to be private unless it is registered as a public company.** A major advantage for a public company is that it can raise new funds from the general public by issuing shares or loan stock; s 81 CA 1985 prohibits a private company from offering shares or debentures to the public.

Related party transactions

2.15   It is generally agreed that separate disclosure of transactions between a company and related parties may be needed if the user of the accounts is to be able to gain a full understanding of the results for the accounting period.

2.16   **Two parties are considered to be related when**:

(a)   one party is able to exercise control or significant influence over the other party; or

(b)   both parties are subject to common control or significant influence from the same source.

For example, companies within the same group will be related parties, or a company and its directors will be related parties.

2.17   The CA 1985 concentrates on requiring disclosure of related party transactions between a company and its directors (or persons 'connected' to directors), including loans and credit transactions.

3   TRUE AND FAIR VIEW

3.1   Section 226 of CA 1985 states that:

> 'the balance sheet shall give a true and fair view of the state of affairs of the company as at the end of the financial year, and the profit and loss account shall give a true and fair view of the profit or loss of the company for the financial year.'

The balance sheet and profit and loss account should also comply with the requirements of the Fourth Schedule (s 226(3) CA 1985).

> **KEY TERM**
>
> 'True and fair view' is not defined. Very roughly it means 'reasonably accurate and not misleading'.

3.2   The term 'true and fair view' is nowhere defined in the Companies Acts, nor in SSAPs or FRSs, which also claim to be authoritative statements on what is a true and fair view. In view of the ASB's policy of reviewing and, if necessary, altering or replacing existing SSAPs and FRSs, a question arises as to whether the concept defined by 'true and fair view' is constant or is changeable over a period of years.

3.3   The ASC received Counsel's opinion on this question. Counsel expressed the opinion that judges, in deciding whether accounts showed a true and fair view, would **look for guidance to the ordinary practices of professional accountants**. A further opinion obtained by the ASB (see Chapter 7 on the *Foreword* to *Accounting Standards*) reinforces this view.

IMPORTANT!

S 226 (5) CA 1985 makes an important statement about the need to give a true and fair view. It states that if, in special circumstances, compliance with any of the Act's provisions would be inconsistent with the requirement to give a true and fair view, then the directors should depart from that provision to the extent necessary to give a true and fair view. This is the **true and fair override.**

3.4   If a balance sheet or profit and loss account drawn up in compliance with these other requirements of the Act would not provide enough information to give a true and fair view, then any necessary additional information must also be given.

3.5   The overriding priority to give a true and fair view **has in the past been treated as an important 'loophole' in the law,** and has been a cause of some argument or debate within the accounting profession. For example, the CA 1985 permits only realised profits to be recognised in the profit and loss account, whereas SSAP 9 requires unrealised profits on long-term contracts to be credited to profit and loss. Such a policy can only be justified by invoking the overriding requirement to show a true and fair view.

3.6   If companies do depart from the other requirements of the Act in order to give a true and fair view, they **must explain the particulars of and reasons for the departure, and its effects on the accounts,** in a note to the accounts. As already noted, the Fourth Schedule also requires a statement in a note to the accounts that the accounts have been prepared in accordance with applicable accounting standards and particulars of any material departure from those standards and the reasons (s 36A Sch 4).

UITF Abstract 7 True and fair override disclosures

3.7   As we saw above, where the directors depart from provisions of CA 1985 to the extent necessary to give a true and fair view, the Act required that 'particulars of any such departure, the reasons for it and its effect shall be given in a note to the accounts'. Abstract 7 seeks to clarify the meaning of that sentence as follows.

(a)   **Particulars of any such departure:** a statement of the treatment which the Act would normally require in the circumstances and a description of the treatment actually adopted.

(b)   **The reasons for it:** a statement as to why the treatment prescribed would not give a true and fair view.

(c)   **Its effect:** a description of how the position shown in the accounts is different as a result of the departure, with quantification if possible, or an explanation of the circumstances.

The disclosures required should either be included in or cross referenced to the note required about compliance with accounting standards, particulars of any material departure from those standards and the reasons for it (Paragraph 36A Sch 4).

4   THE FORMAT OF THE ACCOUNTS

Exam focus point

If you are in a hurry or revising, skip or skim the explanations in Paragraphs 4.1 - 4.8 and go straight to the proformas in Paragraphs 4.8, 4.9 and 5.3.

The form and content of the balance sheet

4.1   The Companies Act 1985 sets out **two formats** for the balance sheet, one **horizontal and the other vertical. Once a company has chosen a format it must adhere to it for subsequent financial years** unless, in the opinion of the directors, there are special reasons for a change. Details of any change and the reason for it must be disclosed by note to the accounts.

4.2   Each item on the balance sheet format is referenced by letters and roman and Arabic numbers. These reference labels do not have to be shown in a company's published accounts but are given in the Act for the guidance of companies and are relevant in identifying the:

(a)   Extent to which information may be combined or disclosed by note (rather than on the face of the accounts).

(b)   Headings and sub-headings which may be adapted or re-arranged to suit the special nature of the company.

(c)   Items which do not need to be disclosed in modified accounts for small and medium-sized companies.

4.3   The following points should be borne in mind.

(a)   Any item preceded by letters or roman numbers **must** be shown on the face of the balance sheet, unless it has a nil value for both the current and the previous year.

(b)   Items preceded by arabic numbers **may** be amalgamated:

(i)   if their individual amounts are not material; or

(ii)   if amalgamation facilitates the assessment of the company's state of affairs (but then the individual items must be disclosed by note).

(c)   Items preceded by arabic numbers **may** be:

(i)   adapted (eg title altered); or
(ii)   re-arranged (in position)

in any case where the special nature of the company's business requires such an alteration.

(d)   Any item required to be shown **may** be shown in greater detail than required by the prescribed format.

(e)   A company's balance sheet (or profit and loss account) **may** include an item not otherwise covered by any of the items listed, except that the following must not be treated as assets in any company's balance sheet:

(i)   Preliminary expenses.
(ii)   Expenses of and commission on any issue of shares or debentures.
(iii)   Costs of research.

4.4   Schedule 4 includes the following notes about the balance sheet format.

(a)   **Concessions, patents, licences, trademarks,** etc (Item B I 2) may only be shown if:

(i)   they were acquired at a purchase cost, and do not consist of goodwill; or
(ii)   they are assets created by the company itself.

(b)   **Goodwill** (Item B I 3) should be included only to the extent that it is purchased goodwill.

(c) **Own shares** (Item B III 7). CA 1985 allows a company to purchase or acquire its own shares.

(d) **Debtors** (Items C II 1 - 6). Any amounts not falling due until after more than one year should be disclosed separately.

(e) **Debenture loans** (Items E1 and H1). Convertible loans should be shown separately from other debenture loans.

(f) **Payments received (in advance) on account** (Items E3 and H3). These should be shown unless they are accounted for as deductions from the value of stocks (as in the case of progress payments for work in progress on long-term contracts).

The form and content of the profit and loss account

4.5   The Companies Act 1985 sets out two **horizontal and** two **vertical formats** for the profit and loss account. The rules applying to the balance sheet formats described above also apply to the profit and loss account.

4.6   The two different formats are distinguished by the way in which expenditure is analysed. Format 1 analyses costs by type of operation or function, whereas Format 2 analyses costs by items of expense.

4.7   The following points should be borne in mind.

(a) Every profit and loss account **must show the company's profit or loss on ordinary activities before taxation,** no matter what format is used nor how much it might be amended to suit the circumstances of a particular case.

(b) Every profit and loss account must also show, as additional items:

(i)   amounts to be **transferred to reserves**, or amounts to be withdrawn from reserves; and

(ii)   the amount of **dividends paid and proposed**.

(c) Amounts representing income may not be set off against items representing expenditure (just as assets and liabilities may not be 'netted off' in the balance sheet).

4.8   Below are proforma balance sheets and profit and loss accounts.

PROFORMA BALANCE SHEET (VERTICAL FORMAT)

				£	£	£
A	CALLED UP SHARE CAPITAL NOT PAID*					X
B	FIXED ASSETS					
	I	Intangible assets				
		1	Development costs	X		
		2	Concessions, patents, licences, trade marks and similar rights and assets	X		
		3	Goodwill	X		
		4	Payments on account	X̲		
					X	
	II	Tangible assets				
		1	Land and buildings	X		
		2	Plant and machinery	X		
		3	Fixtures, fittings, tools and equipment	X		
		4	Payments on account and assets in course of construction	X̲		
					X	
	III	Investments				
		1	Shares in group undertakings †	X		
		2	Loans to group undertakings †	X		
		3	Participating interest †	X		
		4	Loans to undertakings in which the company has a participating interest †	X		
		5	Other investments other than loans	X		
		6	Other loans	X		
		7	Own shares	X̲		
					X̲	
						X̲
C	CURRENT ASSETS					
	I	Stocks				
		1	Raw materials	X		
		2	Work in progress	X		
		3	Finished goods and goods for resale	X		
		4	Payments on account	X̲		
					X	
	II	Debtors				
		1	Trade debtors	X		
		2	Amounts owed by group undertakings †	X		
		3	Amounts owed by undertakings in which the company has a participating interest †	X		
		4	Other debtors	X		
		5	Called up share capital not paid*	X		
		6	Prepayments and accrued income**	X̲		
					X	
	III	Investments				
		1	Shares in group undertakings †	X		
		2	Own shares	X		
		3	Other investments	X̲		
	IV	Cash at bank and in hand		X̲		
					X	
D	PREPAYMENTS AND ACCRUED INCOME**				X	

E   CREDITORS: AMOUNTS FALLING DUE
    WITHIN ONE YEAR

1	Debenture loans	X		
2	Bank loans and overdrafts	X		
3	Payments received on account	X		
4	Trade creditors	X		
5	Bills of exchange payable	X		
6	Amounts owed to group undertakings †	X		
7	Amounts owed to undertakings in which the company has a participating interest †	X		
8	Other creditors including taxation and social security	X		
9	Accruals and deferred income ***	X̲		
			(X̲)	

F	NET CURRENT ASSETS (LIABILITIES)		X
G	TOTAL ASSETS LESS CURRENT LIABILITIES		X

H   CREDITORS: AMOUNTS FALLING DUE
    AFTER MORE THAN ONE YEAR

1	Debenture loans	X		
2	Bank loans and overdrafts	X		
3	Payments received on account	X		
4	Trade creditors	X		
5	Bills of exchange payable	X		
6	Amounts owed to group undertakings †	X		
7	Amounts owed to undertakings in which the company has a participating interest †	X		
8	Other creditors including taxation and social security	X		
9	Accruals and deferred income***	X̲		
			(X)	

I   PROVISIONS FOR LIABILITIES AND CHARGES

1	Pensions and similar obligations †	X		
2	Taxation, including deferred taxation	X		
3	Other provisions	X̲		
			(X)	

J	ACCRUALS AND DEFERRED INCOME ***	(X̲)	
			(X̲)
			X̲

K   CAPITAL AND RESERVES

I	Called up share capital		X	
II	Share premium account		X	
III	Revaluation reserve		X	
IV	Other reserves			
	1 Capital redemption reserve	X		
	2 Reserve for own shares	X		
	3 Reserves provided for by the articles of association	X		
	4 Other reserves	X̲		
			X	
V	Profit and loss account		X̲	
			X̲	

(*), (**), (***). These items may be shown in either of the positions indicated.

4.9   Both vertical formats of the profit and loss account are reproduced below.

PROFORMA PROFIT AND LOSS ACCOUNT: FORMAT 1

		£	£
1	Turnover		X
2	Cost of sales *		(X)
3	Gross profit or loss *		X
4	Distribution costs *	(X)	
5	Administrative expenses *	(X)	
			(X)
			X
6	Other operating income		X
			X
7	Income from shares in group undertakings †	X	
8	Income from shares in undertakings in which the company has a participating interest †	X	
9	Income from other fixed asset investments	X	
10	Other interest receivable and similar income	X	
			X
			X
11	Amounts written off investments	(X)	
12	Interest payable and similar charges	(X)	
			(X)
	Profit or loss on ordinary activities before taxation		X
13	Tax on profit or loss on ordinary activities		(X)
14	Profit or loss on ordinary activities after taxation		X
15	Extraordinary income	X	
16	Extraordinary charges	(X)	
17	Extraordinary profit or loss	X	
18	Tax on extraordinary profit or loss	(X)	
			X
			X
19	Other taxes not shown under the above items		(X)
20	Profit or loss for the financial year		X

* These figures will all include depreciation.

PROFORMA PROFIT AND LOSS ACCOUNT: FORMAT 2

		£	£	£
1	Turnover			X
2	Change in stocks of finished goods and work in progress		(X) or	X
3	Own work capitalised			X
4	Other operating income			X
				X
5	(a) Raw materials and consumables	(X)		
	(b) Other external charges	(X)		
			(X)	
6	Staff costs:			
	(a) wages and salaries	(X)		
	(b) social security costs	(X)		
	(c) other pension costs	(X)		
			(X)	
			(X)	
7	(a) Depreciation and other amounts written off tangible and intangible fixed assets ★★	(X)		
	(b) Exceptional amounts written off current assets	(X)		
			(X)	
8	Other operating charges		(X)	
				(X)
9	Income from shares in group undertakings †		X	
10	Income from shares in undertakings in which the company has a participating interest †		X	
11	Income from other fixed asset investments		X	
12	Other interest receivable and similar income		X	
				X
				X
13	Amounts written off investments		(X)	
14	Interest payable and similar charges		(X)	
				(X)
	Profit or loss on ordinary activities before taxation			X
15	Tax on profit or loss on ordinary activities			(X)
16	Profit or loss on ordinary activities after taxation			X
17	Extraordinary income		X	
18	Extraordinary charges		(X)	
19	Extraordinary profit or loss		X	
20	Tax on extraordinary profit or loss		(X)	
				X
				X
21	Other taxes not shown under the above items			(X)
22	Profit or loss for the financial year			X

★★ This figure will be disclosed by way of a note in Format 1.

Note that because the captions have arabic number references, they do not have to be shown on the face of the profit and loss account but may instead be shown in the notes.

Corresponding amounts for the previous financial year

4.10 Corresponding amounts for the previous financial year **must be given for every item shown in a company's balance sheet or profit and loss account. Where** a corresponding amount for the previous year is **not properly comparable** with an amount disclosed for the current year, **the previous year's amount should be adjusted** (and details of the adjustment given in a note to the accounts).

Some items in more detail

4.11 In the balance sheet, item A and item CII5 are 'called up share capital not paid'. This item is more relevant to other countries in the EU than to Britain (remember that the Fourth Directive applies to all EU countries). However, if at the balance sheet date a company has called up some share capital and not all the called up amounts have been paid, these will be a short-term debt (see Chapter 15 on the issue of shares). This would probably be shown (if material) as item CII5. Item A should not be expected in the accounts of British companies.

4.12 Item BIII7 in the balance sheet, investments in 'own shares', refers to shares which have been bought back by the company, but which have not yet been cancelled.

4.13 '**Turnover**' is defined by the 1985 Act as '**the amounts derived from the provision of goods and services, falling within the company's ordinary activities, after deduction of:**

(a) **Trade discounts.**
(b) **Value added tax.**
(c) **Any other taxes based on the amounts so derived'.**

4.14 '**Cost of sales**' (format 1) is **not defined**, nor are 'distribution costs', nor are 'administrative expenses'. The division of costs between these three categories is based on accepted practice.

4.15 Format 1, unlike Format 2, does not itemise depreciation and wages costs, but:

(a) provisions for depreciation charged in the year; and
(b) wages and salaries, social security costs and other pension costs;

must be disclosed separately in notes to the accounts.

4.16 The Act extends the requirements of FRS 3 about extraordinary profits or losses (see later chapters). The extraordinary profit or loss must be shown as the gross amount, with taxation on it separately disclosed. **Extraordinary items are now extremely rare**.

4.17 The profit and loss account must show profit or loss for the financial year, dividends paid and proposed and transfers to reserves. This means inevitably, that retained profit or loss for the financial year will also be disclosed. There is **no requirement**, however, **to show on the face of the profit and loss account:**

	£
Retained profit for the financial year	X
Profit and loss account brought forward	X
Profit and loss account carried forward	X

However, this well-established practice 'ties together' the information in the profit and loss account with the notes to the balance sheet about movements on reserves and so is often used.

4.18 In itemising staff costs, wages and salaries consist of gross amounts (net pay plus deductions) and social security costs comprise employer's National Insurance contributions.

5 NOTES TO THE ACCOUNTS

5.1 Part III of the Fourth Schedule deals with notes to the balance sheet and profit and loss account. These are sub-divided into:

(a) Disclosure of accounting policies.
(b) Notes to the balance sheet.
(c) Notes to the profit and loss account.

5.2 A note to the accounts must disclose the accounting policies adopted by the company (including the policy used to account for depreciation or the fall in value of assets). This gives statutory backing to the disclosure requirement in SSAP 2. Companies must also now state that all relevant accounting standards have been complied with and if not, what the departures are and the reasons for the departure.

5.3 The following example shows a *pro forma* profit and loss account and balance sheet with the required notes covering your syllabus. These notes are expanded in the subsequent chapters on different accounting standards and disclosures.

STANDARD PLC
PROFIT AND LOSS ACCOUNT FOR THE YEAR ENDED
31 DECEMBER 19X5

	Notes	£'000	£'000
Turnover	2		X
Cost of sales			X
Gross profit			X
Distribution costs			X
Administrative expenses			X
Operating profit	3		X
Income from fixed asset investments			X
			X
Interest payable and similar charges	6		X
Profit on ordinary activities before taxation			X
Tax on profit on ordinary activities	7		X
Profit on ordinary activities after taxation			X
Dividend paid and proposed	8	X	
Transfer to general reserve	19	X	
			X
Retained profit for the financial year			X

STANDARD PLC
BALANCE SHEET AS AT 31 DECEMBER 19X5

	Notes	£'000	£'000
Fixed assets			
Intangible assets	9		X
Tangible assets	10		X
Fixed asset investments	11		X
			X̄
Current assets			
Stocks	12	X	
Debtors	13	X	
Cash at bank and in hand		X	
		X̄	
Creditors: amounts falling due within one year	14	X	
Net current assets			X
Total assets less current liabilities			X̄
Creditors: amounts falling due after more than one year	16		X
Accruals and deferred income	17		X̄
			X̄
Capital and reserves			
Called up share capital	18		X
Share premium account	19		X
Revaluation reserve	19		X
General reserve	19		X
Profit and loss account	19		X
			X̄

Approved by the board on ....

.... Director

The notes on pages XX to XX form part of these accounts.

NOTES TO THE ACCOUNTS

1   **Accounting policies**

(a)   These accounts have been prepared under the historical cost convention of accounting and in accordance with applicable accounting standards.

(b)   Depreciation has been provided on a straight line basis in order to write off the cost of depreciable fixed assets over their estimated useful lives. The rates used are:

Buildings	X%
Plant and machinery	X%
Fixtures and fittings	X%

(c)   Stocks have been valued at the lower of cost and net realisable value.

(d)   Development expenditure relating to specific projects intended for commercial exploitation is carried forward and amortised over the period expected to benefit commencing with the period in which related sales are first made. Expenditure on pure and applied research is written off as incurred.

Notes

(a)   Accounting policies are those followed by the company and used in arriving at the figures shown in the profit and loss accounts and balance sheet.

(b)   CA 1985 requires policies in respect of depreciation and foreign currency translation to be included. Others are required by accounting standards insofar as they apply to the company.

2   Turnover

Turnover represents amounts derived from the provision of goods and services falling within the company's ordinary activities, after deduction of trade discounts, value added tax and any other tax based on the amounts so derived.

	Turnover £'000	Profit before tax £'000
Principal activities		
Electrical components	X	X
Domestic appliances	X	X
	X̄	X̄
Geographical analysis		
UK	X	
America	X	
Europe	X	
	X̄	

Notes

(a)   Directors are to decide on classification and then apply them consistently.

(b)   Geographical analysis must be by destination of sale.

(c)   If the directors believe this disclosure to be seriously prejudicial to the business the information need not be disclosed.

(d)   The profit after tax figures are only required by SSAP 25 (see Chapter 15) for larger companies.

3   Operating profit

Operating profit is stated after charging:

	£'000
Depreciation	X
Amortisation	X
Hire of plant and machinery (SSAP 21: see Chapter 5)	X
Auditors' remuneration	X
Exceptional items	X
Directors' emoluments (see note 4)	X
Staff costs (see note 5)	X
Research and development	X

Notes

Separate totals are required to be disclosed for:

(a)   audit fees and expenses; and
(b)   fees paid to auditors for non-audit work.

This disclosure is not required for small or medium-sized companies.

Question 1

Arco Ltd receives an invoice in respect of the current year from its auditors made up as follows.

	£
Audit of accounts	10,000
Taxation computation and advice	1,500
Travelling expenses: audit	1,100
Consultancy fees charged by another firm of accountants	1,600
	14,200

What figure should be disclosed as auditors' remuneration in the notes to the profit and loss account?

Answer

	£
Audit of accounts	10,000
Expenses	1,100
Taxation computation and advice	1,500
	12,600

The consultancy fees are not received by the auditors.

4   **Directors' emoluments**

New requirements for the disclosure of directors' remuneration were introduced recently by *The Company Accounts (Disclosure of Directors' Emoluments) Regulations 1997* (SI 1997/570). A distinction is made between listed/AIM companies and unlisted companies.

	£'000
Directors	
Aggregate emoluments	X
Gains made on exercise of share options (listed/AIM company only)	X
Amounts receivable (unlisted company: excludes shares) under long-term incentive schemes	X
Company pension contributions	X
Compensation for loss of office	X
Sums paid to third parties for directors' services	X
	X
Highest paid director	
Aggregate emoluments, gains on share options exercised and benefits under long-term incentive schemes (listed/AIM company only)	X
Company pension contributions	X
Accrued pension	X
	X

Notes

(a)   All companies must disclosure aggregate emoluments paid to/receivable by a director in respect of 'qualifying services'.

(b)   **Unlisted companies do not need to disclose:**

(i)   the amount of gains made when directors exercise options, only the number of directors who exercised options; and

(ii)   the net value of any assets that comprise shares, which would otherwise be disclosed in respect of assets received under long-term incentive schemes, but only the number of directors in respect of whose qualifying service shares were receivable under long-term incentive schemes.

(c)   For listed companies, the disclosure requirements for share options do not refer to qualifying services, so gains made on the exercise of shares before appointment must therefore be included.

(d)   Information about the highest paid director only needs to be given if the aggregate of emoluments, gains on exercise of share options, and amounts receivable by the directors under long-term incentive schemes is > £200,000. For unlisted companies, state whether the highest paid direct or exercised any share options and/or received any shares in respect of qualifying services under a long-term incentive scheme.

(e)   The details relating to pensions are beyond the scope of your syllabus.

(f)   **Definitions**

(i) **Emoluments.** Salary, fees, bonuses, expense allowances, money value of other benefits, except share options granted, pension amounts and amounts paid under a long-term incentive scheme. Includes 'golden hellos'.

(ii) **Qualifying services.** Services as a director of a company and services in connection with the management of the company's affairs.

(iii) **Listed company.** A company whose securities have been admitted to the Official List of the Stock Exchange (or AIM).

(iv) **Long-term incentive schemes.** Any agreement or arrangement under which money or other assets become receivable by a director and where one or more of the qualifying candidates relating to service cannot be fulfilled in a single financial year. Bonuses relating to an individual year, termination payments and retirement benefits are excluded.

5 **Employee information**

(a) The **average number of persons** employed during the year was:

By product	
Electrical components	X
Domestic appliances	X
	X
By activity	
Production	X
Selling	X
Administration	X
	X

(b) **Employment costs**

	£'000
Aggregate wages and salaries	X
Social security costs	X
Other pension costs	X
	X

Notes

(a) Classification to be decided by the directors and applied consistently year on year. Must state whether executive directors are included or excluded.

(b) Social security costs are employer's NI.

(c) Other pension costs are contributions by the company to a pension scheme.

(d) **Definitions**

(i) **Staff costs.** Costs incurred in respect of persons employed under contract of service. They include part time employees under contract.

(ii) **Average number**

(1) Ascertain number employed under contracts each week.
(2) Aggregate these numbers.
(3) Divide by the number of months in the period.

Include those persons working wholly or mainly overseas.

Question 2

During a 12 month accounting period, the administration department of Crankie Ltd had the following employees.

(a) 12 worked overseas, of whom 1 returned to work in the UK and 2 resigned after 6 months.

(b) 30 UK employees (including 1 executive director).

(c) 20 part-timers who only worked over the three months' summer season and of whom only 8 were employed under a service contract.

Determine the average number of employees (assuming executive directors are included) to be disclosed for the administration department.

Note. The employee information note may include or exclude executive directors and the company must state which option they have chosen.

Answer

Average number

	No
Overseas (12 − (2 × ½))	11
UK employees	30
Contract part-timers	2
(8 for 3 months, which averages out at 2 per year)	
	43

---

6 Interest payable and similar charges

	£'000
Interest payable on:	
Bank overdrafts and loans	X
Other loans	X
Lease and HP finance charges allocated for the year	X
	X

Note

Similar charges might include arrangement fees for loans.

7 Tax on profits on ordinary activities

	£'000
UK corporation tax (at x% on taxable profit for the year)	X
Tax credit on dividends received	X
Irrecoverable ACT	X
Transfer to/from deferred taxation	X
Under/over provision in prior years	X
Unrelieved overseas taxation	X
	X

Note

The rate of tax must be disclosed (SSAP 8: see Chapter 2).

8 Dividends

			£'000
Preference:	8% paid		X
Ordinary:	interim	3.5p paid	X
	final	7.0p proposed	X
			X

Note

Show for each class of share distinguishing between amounts paid and proposed. Only advisable (and not required) to show amount per share. If the aggregate *proposed* dividend is not shown in the note to the accounts, it must be shown on the face of the P&L a/c.

9 Intangible fixed assets

	Development expenditure £'000
Cost	
At 1 January 19X5	X
Expenditure	X
At 31 December 19X5	X
Amortisation	
At 1 January 19X5	X
Charge for year	X
At 31 December 19X5	X
Net book value at 31 December 19X5	X
Net book value 31 December 19X4	X

Note

The above disclosure should be given for each intangible asset.

10 Tangible fixed assets

		Leasehold land and buildings				
	Freehold land and buildings £'000	*Long leases* £'000	*Short leases* £'000	*Plant and machinery* £'000	*Fixtures and fittings* £'000	*Total* £'000
Cost (or valuation)						
At 1 Jan 19X5	X	X	X	X	X	X
Additions	X	-	X	-	X	X
Revaluation	X	-	-	-	-	X
Disposals	(X)	-	-	(X)	(X)	(X)
At 31 Dec 19X5	X	X	X	X	X	X
Depreciation						
At 1 Jan 19X5	X	X	X	X	X	X
Charge for year	X	X	X	X	X	X
Revaluation	(X)	-	-	-	-	(X)
Disposals	(X)	-	-	(X)	(X)	(X)
At 31 Dec 19X5	X	X	X	X	X	X
Net book value						
At 31 Dec 19X5	X	X	X	X	X	X
At 31 Dec 19X4	X	X	X	X	X	X

Notes

(a) Long leases are ≥ 50 years unexpired at balance sheet date.

(b) Classification by asset type represents arabic numbers from formats.

(c) Motor vehicles (unless material) are usually included within plant and machinery.

(d) Revaluations in the year: state for each asset revalued:

(i) method of valuation;

(ii) date of valuation; and

(iii) the historical cost equivalent of the above information as if the asset had not been revalued.

11 **Fixed asset investments**

	£'000
Shares at cost	
At 1 January 19X5	X
Additions	X
Disposals	(X)
At 31 December 19X5	X

The market value (in aggregate) of the listed investments is £X.

Note

An AIM investment is *not* a listed investment. All stock exchanges of repute allowed. Aggregate market value (ie profits less losses) to be disclosed if material.

12 **Stocks**

	£'000
Raw materials and consumables	X
Work in progress	X
Finished goods	X
	X

The replacement cost of stock is £X higher than its book value.

13 **Debtors**

	£'000
Trade debtors	X
Other debtors	X
Prepayments and accrued income	X
	X

Of this amount £X of recoverable ACT is recoverable after more than one year.

14 **Creditors: amounts falling due within one year**

	£'000
Debenture loans: 8% stock 19X9	X
Bank loans and overdrafts	X
Trade creditors	X
Other creditors including taxation and social security (see note 15)	X
Accruals and deferred income	X
	X

The bank loans and overdraft are secured by a floating charge over the company's assets.

Notes

(a) Give details of security given for all secured creditors.

(b) Include the current portion of instalment creditors here.

15 **Other creditors including taxation and social security**

	£'000
UK corporation tax	X
ACT on dividends	X
	X
Social security	X
Proposed dividend	X
	X

Notes

(a) Liabilities for taxation and social security must be shown separately from other creditors.

(b)   Dividend liabilities to be disclosed separately.

16   Creditors: amounts falling due after more than one year

	£'000
8½% unsecured loan stock 19Y9	X

Notes

(a)   Very long-term creditors:

  (i)   disclose the aggregate amount of debentures and other loans:

    (1)   payable after more than five years;

    (2)   payable by instalments, any of which fall due after more than five years;

  (ii)   for (1) and (2) disclose the terms of repayment and rates of interest.

(b)   Debentures during the year, disclose:

  (i)   class issued;

  (ii)   for each class:

    (1)   amount issued;

    (2)   consideration received.

17   Accruals and deferred income

	£'000
Government grants received	X
Credited to profit and loss account	(X)
	X

Note

Alternative presentation if not included as part of creditors, which saves dividing the accruals or deferred income amount between within and greater than one year.

18   Called up share capital

	£1 ordinary shares £'000	6.2% preference shares £'000
Authorised		
Number	X	X
Value	X	X
Allotted		
Number	X	X
Value	X	X

Notes

(a)   Disclose number and nominal value for each class, both authorised and allotted.

(b)   *Shares issued during the year*, disclose:

  (i)   classes allotted;

  (ii)   for each class:

    (1)   number and aggregate nominal value allotted; and

    (2)   consideration received.

19   **Reserves**

	Share premium £'000	Revaluation £'000	General £'000	Profit and loss £'000
At 1 January 19X5	X	X	X	X
Retained profit for the year	-	-	-	X
Revaluation	-	X	-	-
Transfers	-	-	X	X
At 31 December 1995	X	X	X	X

20   **Contingent liabilities**

Note: governed by SSAP 18 (see Chapter 15).

21   **Post balance sheet events**

Note: governed by SSAP 17 (see Chapter 15).

22   **Capital commitments**

	£'000
Amounts contracted but not provided for	X

Note

This figure is not included in the balance sheet as it is simply a note of future obligations to warn users of likely future capital expenditure.

Question 3

The best way to learn the format and content of published accounts and notes is to practice questions. However, you must start somewhere, so try to learn the above formats, then close this text and write out on a piece of paper:

(a)   a standard layout for a balance sheet and profit and loss account; and

(b)   a list of notes to these accounts which are generally required.

Filing exemptions for small and medium-sized companies

5.4   Small and medium-sized companies are allowed certain 'filing exemptions': **the accounts they lodge with the Registrar of companies, and which are available for public inspection, need not contain all the information which must be published by large companies.**

5.5   This concession allows small and medium-sized companies to reduce the amount of information about themselves available to, say, trading rivals. It **does *not* relieve them of their obligation to prepare full statutory accounts, because all companies,** regardless of their size, **must prepare full accounts for approval by the shareholders.**

5.6   Small and medium-sized companies must therefore balance the expense of preparing two different sets of accounts against the advantage of publishing as little information about themselves as possible. Many such companies may decide that the risk of assisting their competitors is preferable to the expense of preparing accounts twice over, and will therefore not take advantage of the filing exemptions.

5.7   A company qualifies as a **small or medium sized** company in a particular financial year **if**, for that year, **two or more** of the following **conditions are satisfied**.

	Small	Medium
(a) **Turnover** (must be adjusted proportionately in the case of an accounting period greater than or less than 12 months)	≤ £.28m	≤ £11.2m
(b) **Balance sheet total** (total assets before deduction of any liabilities; A-D in the statutory valance sheet format)	≤ £.14m	≤ £5.6m
(c) **Average number of employees**	≤ 50	≤ 250

5.8   **Public companies can never be entitled to the filing exemptions whatever their size;** nor can banking and insurance companies; nor can companies which are authorised persons under the Financial Services Act 1986; nor can members of groups containing any of these exceptions.

5.9   The form and content of the abbreviated accounts are contained in separate schedules of the Act: Schedule 8A for small companies and Schedule 245A for medium-sized companies. **Small companies may file an abbreviated balance sheet** showing only the items which, in the statutory format, are denoted by a letter or Roman number. They are **not required to file either a profit and loss account or a directors' report. No details need be filed of the emoluments of directors. Only limited notes to the accounts are required.**

5.10 **The only exemptions allowed to medium-sized companies are in the profit and loss account. Turnover need not be analysed between a company's different classes of businesses, or its different geographical markets.** The profit and loss account may begin with the figure of gross profit (or loss) by amalgamation of items 1, 2, 3 and 6 in Format 1, or of items 1 to 5 in Format 2.

5.11 If a small or medium-sized company files 'abbreviated accounts' a statement by the directors must appear above the director's signature on the balance sheet. The statement must be that the financial statements have been prepared in accordance with the special provisions of Part VII of the Act relating to small or (as the case may be) medium-sized companies.

5.12 Abbreviated accounts **must be accompanied by a special report** of the company's auditors stating that, in their opinion, the directors are entitled to deliver abbreviated accounts and those accounts are properly prepared. The text of the auditors' report on the full statutory accounts must be included as a part of this special report. A true and fair view is still required, however; if the shorter-form financial statements fail to give a true and fair view because of the use of exemptions, or for any other reason, the auditors should qualify their audit report in the normal way.

Summary financial statements

5.13 CA 1989 amended CA 1985 so that **listed companies need not send all their members their full financial statements but can instead send them summary financial statements** (SFSs). All members who want to receive full financial statements are still entitled to them, however.

5.14   **An SFS must**:

(a)   State that it is only a summary of information in the company's annual accounts and the directors' report.

(b)   Contain a statement by the company's auditors of their opinion as to whether the summary financial statement is consistent with those accounts and that report and complies with the relevant statutory requirements.

(c)   State whether the auditors' report on the annual accounts was unqualified or qualified, and if it was qualified set out the report in full together with any further material needed to understand the qualification.

5.15   SFSs must be derived from the company's annual accounts and the directors' report and the form and content are specified by regulations made by the Secretary of State.

The key figures from the full statements must be included along with the review of the business and future developments shown in the directors' report. Comparative figures must be shown.

6   DIRECTORS' REPORT

6.1   Attached to every balance sheet there must be a directors' report (s 234 CA 1985). (The Companies Act 1985 allows small companies exemption from delivering a copy of the directors' report to the Registrar of companies.) CA 1985 states specifically what information must be included in the directors' report (as well as what must be shown in the accounts themselves or in notes to the accounts as we saw above).

6.2   The directors' report is **largely a narrative report**, but certain figures must be included in it. **The purpose of the report is to give the users of accounts a more complete picture of the state of affairs of the company**. Narrative descriptions should help to 'put flesh on' the skeleton of details provided by the figures of the accounts themselves. However, in practice the directors' report is often a rather dry and uninformative document, perhaps because it must be verified by the company's external auditors, whereas the chairman's report need not be.

6.3   The directors' report is **expected to contain a fair review of the development of the business of the company during that year and of its position at the end of it**. No guidance is given on the form of the review, nor the amount of detail it should go into.

6.4   S 234 CA 1985 also requires the report to **show the** amount, if any, **recommended** for **dividend**.

6.5   Other disclosure requirements are as follows.

(a)   The **principal activities** of the company in the course of the financial year, and any significant changes in those activities during the year.

(b)   Where significant, an estimate should be provided of the **difference between the book value of land held as fixed assets and its realistic market value**.

(c)   **Disabled persons.** Information about the **company's policy** for:

(i)   Giving fair consideration to applications for jobs from disabled persons.

(ii)   Continuing to employ (and train) people who have become disabled whilst employed by the company.

(iii)   Training, career development and promotion of disabled employees.

(Companies with fewer than 250 employees are exempt from (c).)

(d) The names of persons who were **directors** at any time during the financial year.

(e) For those persons who were directors at the year end, the **interests of each** (or of their spouse or infant children) in shares or debentures of the company:

  (i)   at the beginning of the year, or at the date of appointment as director, if this occurred during the year; and

  (ii) at the end of the year.

  If a director has no such interests at either date, this fact must be disclosed. (The information in (e) may be shown as a note to the accounts instead of in the directors' report.)

(f) **Political and charitable contributions made**, if these together exceeded more than £200 in the year, giving:

  (i)   separate totals for political contributions and charitable contributions; and

  (ii) the amount of each separate political contribution exceeding £200, and the name of the recipient.

(g) Particulars of any **important events** affecting the company or any of its subsidiaries which have occurred since the end of the financial year (significant 'post-balance sheet events').

(h) An indication of likely **future developments** in the business of the company and of its subsidiaries.

(i) An indication of the activities (if any) of the company and its subsidiaries in the field of **research and development**.

(j) Particulars of **purchases** (if any) of **its own shares** by the company during the year, including reasons for the purchase.

(k) Particulars of **other acquisitions of its own shares** during the year (perhaps because shares were forfeited or surrendered, or because its shares were acquired by the company's nominee or with its financial assistance).

6.6 Note that the 1985 Act requires details of important post balance sheet events to be explained in the directors' report. The requirements of SSAP 17 (see Chapter 15), which should be considered in conjunction with the 1985 Act, are either for the accounts themselves to be altered, or for the amount of the adjustment to results to be disclosed in a note to the accounts.

6.7 A further requirement relating to the directors' report is contained in the Employment Act 1982. The requirement relates to any company **employing on average more than 250 people each week**. The **directors** of such a company **must state in their report what action** has been **taken** during the financial year **to introduce, maintain or develop arrangements aimed at:**

(a) **Employee information**, providing employees systematically with information on matters of concern to them.

(b) **Employee consultation**, consulting employees or their representatives on a regular basis so that the views of employees can be taken into account in making decisions which are likely to affect their interest.

(c) **Employee involvement**, encouraging the involvement of employees in the company's performance through an employees' share scheme or by some other means.

(d) **Company performance**, achieving common **awareness** on the part of all employees of the financial and economic factors affecting the performance of the company.

6.8 It should be noted that **these provisions do not mean that any such action must be taken, only that if it is taken it must be disclosed** in the directors' report. Moreover, wide discretion is granted to the directors in deciding what needs to be disclosed, since no definition is given of such terms as 'matters of concern to them' or 'decisions which are likely to affect their interests'.

Creditor payment policy

6.9 A recent amendment to CA 1985 requires companies to disclose details of the company's policy on the payment of creditors. This **disclosure requirement applies if:**

(a) **the company was at any time during the year a public company; or**

(b) **the company did not qualify as a small or medium-sized company under s 247 and was at any time within the year a member of a group of which the parent company was a public company.**

6.10 The **directors' report needs to state**, with respect to the financial year immediately following that covered by the report:

(a) Whether in respect of some or all of its suppliers (ie those classified as 'trade creditors') it is the company's policy to follow **any code or standard on payment practice**, and if so, the name of the code or standard, and the place where information about, and copies of, the code or standard can be obtained;

(b) whether in respect of some or all of its suppliers, it is the company's **policy to:**

    (i) **Settle the terms of payment** with those suppliers when agreeing the terms of each transaction.

    (ii) Ensure that those suppliers are **made aware** of the terms of payment.

    (iii) **Abide** by the terms of payment.

(c) **Where** the company's policy is **not as mentioned** in either of the two paragraphs **above**, in respect of some or all of its suppliers, **what its policy is** with respect to the payment of those suppliers.

If the company's policy is different from different suppliers or classes of suppliers, the directors' must identify the suppliers or classes of suppliers to which the different policies apply.

7 AUDITORS' REPORT AND CHAIRMAN'S REPORT

The auditors' report

7.1 **The annual accounts of a limited company must be audited by persons independent of the company.** In practice, this means that the members of the company appoint a firm of Chartered Accountants or Chartered Certified Accountants to investigate the accounts prepared by the company **and report as to whether or not they show a true and fair** view of the company's results for the year and its financial position at the end of the year. **The audit report is governed by auditing regulations.**

7.2 When the auditors have completed their work they must prepare a report explaining the work that they have done and the opinion they have formed. In simple cases they will be able to report that they have carried out their work in accordance with auditing standards and that, in their opinion, the accounts show a true and fair view and are properly prepared in accordance with the Companies Act 1985. This is described as an **unqualified audit report**.

7.3 Sometimes the auditors may disagree with the directors on a point concerned with the accounts. If they are unable to persuade the directors to change the accounts, and if the item at issue is material, it is the auditors' duty to prepare a **qualified report**, setting out the matter(s) on which they disagree with the directors.

7.4 The financial statements to which the auditors refer in their report comprise the:

(a) **Profit and loss account**.
(b) **Balance sheet**.
(c) **Notes to the accounts**.
(d) **Cash flow statement**.

In addition they **must consider whether the information given in the directors' report is consistent with the audited accounts**. If they believes it is not consistent then they must state that fact in their report. Note that the cash flow statement is not mentioned outright.

7.5 The auditors' report is included as a part of the company's published accounts. It is **addressed to the members** of the company (not to the directors).

The chairman's report

7.6 Most large companies include a **chairman's report** in their published financial statements. This is **purely voluntary** as there is no statutory requirement to do so.

7.7 The chairman's report is not governed by any regulations and is often unduly optimistic. Listed companies now include an Operating and Financial Review (OFR) in the annual report: see Chapter 16. This has been introduced to encourage more meaningful analysis.

Question 4

In between now and your examination obtain as many sets of company accounts or annual reports as you can. (You may like to use the Financial Times Free Annual Report Service for this purpose - look at the share price pages of the FT for information.) Read through the whole of each report and compare the format of the accounts and the disclosure of the notes with the contents of this chapter, and with the rest of this Study Text.

Chapter roundup

- This has been a long and detailed chapter but not a conceptually demanding one. You must have a **firm grasp** of its contents before proceeding to the remainder of this second section of the Study Text, in which the statutory and professional requirements of each area of the accounts are discussed in turn.

- You need to learn the *Companies Act formats* and the *notes* required, but remember that the easiest way to do this is to **practise questions**, and read real sets of accounts.

- You will appreciate the *contents* of the auditors' report, the directors' report, the chairman's report if you **read some real annual reports**.

Quick quiz

1   Explain the requirements for the laying and delivery of accounts. (2.7 - 2.9)

2   When are two parties considered 'related'? (2.16)

3   What does CA 1985 say abut a 'true and fair view'? (3.1)

4   Explain the significance of the letters, roman numbers and arabic numbers in the CA 1985 formats. (4.2)

5   How is the turnover of a company defined in the CA 1985? (4.13)

6   Define a small company and a medium-sized company in the context of abbreviated accounts. (5.7, table)

7   List eight disclosures required to be made in the directors' report. (6.4, 6.5)

8   What information must larger companies disclose about their creditor payment policy? (6.10)

9   What documents are comprised in the accounts on which the auditors' report? (7.4)

Question to try	Level	Marks	Time
9	Full exam	25	45 mins

Chapter 9

FIXED ASSETS: TANGIBLE ASSETS

Chapter topic list	Syllabus reference
1 Statutory provisions relating to all fixed assets	1(c), 2(a)
2 SSAP 12 *Accounting for depreciation*	1(c), 2(a)
3 SSAP 19 *Accounting for investment properties*	1(c), 2(a)
4 SSAP 4 *Accounting for government grants*	1(c), 2(a)

Introduction

In Section 1, before we look at individual accounting standards, we will consider the **disclosure requirements** relating to fixed assets laid down by the **Companies Act**. Refer back to Chapter 8 to put these requirements into context. Remember that these provisions apply to *all* fixed assets.

You have already looked at fixed assets and the principles of **depreciation** in your Foundation studies. If you are in any doubt about the possible methods of depreciation you should refer back to your Paper 1 study material. An exercise at the end of Section 2 should serve as a reminder.

The other two standards covered in this chapter are on **investment properties** and **government grants**. These are quite straightforward. Learn their main provisions and make sure that you can carry out the relevant exercises.

1 STATUTORY PROVISIONS RELATING TO ALL FIXED ASSETS 12/97

1.1 The standard balance sheet format of CA 1985 divides fixed assets into three categories:

(a) **Intangible assets** (BI in the CA 1985 format).
(b) **Tangible assets** (BII).
(c) **Investments** (BIII).

1.2 In this chapter we will deal with the general rules of the CA 1985 which relate to *all* fixed assets. Companies Act requirements in regard to fixed assets may be considered under two headings.

(a) **Valuation:** the amounts at which fixed assets should be stated in the balance sheet.

(b) **Disclosure:** the information which should be disclosed in the accounts as to valuation of fixed assets and as to movements on fixed asset accounts during the year.

Valuation of fixed assets

1.3 **Where an asset is purchased, its cost is simply the purchase price plus any expenses incidental to its acquisition.**

1.4   Where an asset is **produced by a company for its own use**, its 'production cost' *must* include the **cost of raw materials, consumables** and other attributable **direct costs** (such as labour). Production cost **may** additionally **include a reasonable proportion of indirect costs**, together with the interest on any capital borrowed to finance production of the asset.

1.5   The '**cost**' of any fixed asset having a limited economic life, whether purchase price or production cost, **must be reduced by provisions for depreciation** calculated to write off the cost, less any residual value, **systematically over the period of the asset's useful life**. This very general requirement is supplemented by the more detailed provisions of SSAP 12 *Accounting for depreciation* which is dealt with in the next section.

1.6   **Provision for a permanent diminution in value of a fixed asset must be made in the profit and loss account and the asset should be disclosed at the reduced amount in the balance sheet.**

1.7   Any such provision should be disclosed on the face of the profit and loss account or by way of note. Where a provision becomes no longer necessary, because the conditions giving rise to it have altered, it should be written back, and again disclosure should be made.

Fixed assets valuation: alternative accounting rules

1.8   Although the Companies Act 1985 maintains historical cost principles as the normal basis for the preparation of accounts, alternative bases allowing for **revaluations** and current cost accounting are permitted provided that:

(a)   The items affected and the basis of valuation are **disclosed** in a note to the accounts;

(b)   The **historical cost** in the current and previous years is **separately disclosed** in the balance sheet or in a note to the accounts. Alternatively, the difference between the revalued amount and historical cost may be disclosed.

KEY TERM

Using the **alternative accounting rules**, the appropriate value of any fixed asset (ie its current cost or market value), rather than its purchase price or production cost, may be included in the balance sheet.

1.9   **Where appropriate, depreciation may be provided on the basis of the new valuation(s),** such depreciation being referred to in the Companies Act 1985 as the 'adjusted amount' of depreciation. For profit and loss account purposes, SSAP 12 (see below) specifically states that depreciation must be charged on the revalued amount and that the *whole* charge must be taken to the profit and loss account.

Revaluation reserve

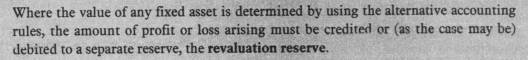

KEY TERM

Where the value of any fixed asset is determined by using the alternative accounting rules, the amount of profit or loss arising must be credited or (as the case may be) debited to a separate reserve, the **revaluation reserve**.

1.10   The calculation of the relevant amounts should be based on the written down values of the assets prior to revaluation. The depreciation charged prior to revaluation should *not* be written back to the profit and loss account (SSAP 12). A recent amendment to CA 1985 also allows any potential deferred tax on a surplus to be taken to the revaluation reserve.

1.11   The revaluation reserve must be **reduced** to the extent that the amounts standing to the credit of the reserves are, in the opinion of the directors of the company, **no longer necessary** for the purposes of the accounting policies adopted by the company. However, an amount may only be **transferred from the reserve to the profit and loss account** if *either*:

(a)   the amount in question was **previously charged** to that account; or

(b)   it represents **realised profit** (for example on disposal of a fixed asset).

The only other transfer possible from the revaluation reserve is on capitalisation, that is, when a bonus issue is made and the resulting debit is taken to the revaluation reserve.

1.12   The amount of a revaluation reserve must be shown under a separate sub-heading in position KIII on the balance sheet. However, the reserve need not necessarily be called a 'revaluation reserve'.

Question 1

Archer Ltd revalued a freehold building on 31 March 19X5 to £300,000. The original purchase cost 10 years ago was £180,000. Archer Ltd depreciates freehold buildings over 40 years.

Show the accounting entries for the revaluation and the depreciation charge for the year ended 31 March 19X6.

Answer

		£	£
(a)	*Revaluation*		
	DEBIT Fixed asset cost (£300,000 - £180,000)	120,000	
	DEBIT Accumulated depreciation (£180,000 ÷ 40 × 10)	45,000	
	CREDIT Revaluation reserve		165,000
(b)	*Depreciation charge*		
	DEBIT Depreciation (£300,000 ÷ 30)	10,000	
	CREDIT Accumulated depreciation		10,000

Fixed assets: disclosure

1.13 **Notes to the accounts must show, for each class of fixed assets, an analysis of the movements on both costs and depreciation provisions.** Refer back to the note on fixed assets in Chapter 8.

1.14 **Where** any fixed assets of a company (other than listed investments) are **included** in the accounts **at an alternative accounting valuation, the following information must also be given:**

(a) The years (so far as they are known to the directors) in which the assets were severally valued and the several values.

(b) In the case of assets that have been valued during the financial period, the names of the persons who valued them or particulars of their qualifications for doing so and (whichever is stated) the bases of valuation used by them.

1.15 A note to the accounts must classify land and buildings under the headings of:

(a) **Freehold property**.

(b) **Leasehold property**, distinguishing between:

(i) Long leaseholds, in which the unexpired term of the lease at the balance sheet date is not less than 50 years.

(ii) Short leaseholds which are all leaseholds other than long leaseholds.

2   SSAP 12 ACCOUNTING FOR DEPRECIATION   12/97

2.1 As noted earlier, the **Companies Act 1985 requires that all fixed assets having a limited economic life should be depreciated**. SSAP 12 gives a useful discussion of the purpose of depreciation and supplements the statutory requirements in important respects. Note, however, that **SSAP 12 does not apply to:**

(a) **Investment properties** (SSAP 19 - see below)

(b) **Goodwill** (FRS 10 - see Chapter 10).

(c) **Development costs** (SSAP 13 - see Chapter 10).

(d) **Investments** (fixed or current), which can be said to vary in value rather than depreciate.

(e) **Freehold land** (per SSAP 12 itself - depreciation is not normally required).

(f) Assets so **well maintained** or with an infinite economic life so that depreciation is unnecessary (rare cases).

Knowledge brought forward from Paper 1

SSAP 12 Accounting for depreciation

Definition

- Depreciation is the measure of the wearing out, consumption or other reduction in the useful economic life of a fixed asset, whether arising from use, effluxion of time or obsolescence through technology and market changes.

Accounting treatment

- Depreciation should be allocated so as to charge a fair proportion of the cost/valuation less residual value of the asset to each accounting period expected to benefit from its use (matching concept).

- Consider:
    - the carrying value of the asset (cost of acquisition/production or up-to-date valuation);
    - the length of useful economic life to the present owner;
    - the estimated residual value based on prices on acquisition/revaluation;
    - the method used should be that which is most appropriate to the type of asset.

- An asset's **useful life** may be:
    - pre-determined, as in leaseholds;
    - directly governed by extraction or consumption (mine or quarry);
    - dependant on the extent of use (motor car);
    - reduced by economic or technological obsolescence.

- **Revision of useful life**:
    - normally write off the NBV over the revised remaining useful life;
    - except, if future results would be materially distorted, recognise the cumulative effect in the current year (FRS 3).

- **Permanent diminution in value**: the NBV will not be recoverable in full: write down immediately to estimated recoverable amount, which is the lower of:
    - net realisable value;
    - the amount recoverable from further use.

- **Change in method of depreciation**: write off the net book amount over remaining useful life, using the new method.

- **Depreciation charge**
    - P&L a/c: based on the value in the B/S
    - No charge is taken directly to reserves
    - No supplementary depreciation is charged in the P&L a/c
    - No write back of any depreciation charged prior to revaluation
    - Freehold land does not usually require depreciation
    - Buildings should be depreciated

- **Disposals of revalued assets accounted for according to FRS 3**
    - the profit/loss represents the sales proceeds less the carrying amount; and
    - the revaluation surplus is transferred to the P&L a/c (as realised profits).

Disclosure

- For each major class of asset disclose:
    - the depreciation method;
    - the useful economic lives or depreciation rates;
    - the total depreciation charge for the period; and
    - the gross amount of depreciable assets and related accumulated depreciation.

Knowledge brought forward from Paper 1 (continued)

- In the year of change/revaluation disclose:

    ° the effect of any change in the method of depreciation; and
    ° the effect of any revaluation,

    on the depreciation charge for the year, if material; if there is a change in method, also give the reason for the change.

- There are **various methods of depreciation**.

    ° Straight line method   ° Revaluation   ° Annuity (actuarial) method
    ° Reducing balance method ° Sum of digits method ° Outside investments
    ° Machine hour method

Exam focus point

In December 1997, candidates had to calculate a revised depreciation charge after correcting for an error on disposal and after accounting for leased assets.

Question 2

ABC Ltd prepares accounts to 31 December each year. On 1 January 19X4 it had the following balances on its fixed asset accounts.

	Debit	Credit
	£	£
Motor vehicles at cost	15,000	
Plant and equipment at cost	24,000	
Motor vehicles: depreciation		9,000
Plant and equipment: depreciation		10,500

During the year to 31 December 19X4 the following transactions took place.

(a) Purchased a new machine on 1 February at a cost of £7,500.

(b) Installed office equipment in its office building on 14 March at a cost of £11,500.

(c) Sold equipment on 1 April for £2,000. It had originally been purchased on 1 January 19X0 for £5,600.

(d) Sold a motor vehicle on 31 July for £3,400 which had been purchased on 1 August 19X1 for £9,400 including £100 road tax and £300 warranty against mechanical defects for two years.

(e) Purchased a motor vehicle on 1 August for £10,000 including £500 delivery, £100 road tax and £400 extended warranty against mechanical defects for three years.

(f) Carried out major repairs to some equipment on 1 October costing £15,000. This included a new motor costing £5,000 which increased the efficiency of the equipment by 200%.

The company provides a full year's depreciation on fixed assets at the end of each year using the following methods and rates.

Motor vehicles	25% per annum, reducing balance
Plant and equipment	20% per annum, straight line

Required

(a) Record the transactions numbered (a) to (f) above in the ledger accounts of ABC Ltd and provide depreciation as appropriate for the year ended 31 December 19X4.

(b) Show an extract from the profit and loss account for the year ended 31 December 19X4 in respect of the above transactions.

Answer

(a)

PLANT AND EQUIPMENT ACCOUNT

		£			£
1.1.X4	Balance b/d	24,000	1.4.X4	Plant disposal	5,600
1.2.X4	Cash	7,500			
14.3.X4	Cash	11,500			
1.10.X4	Cash	5,000	31.12.X4	Balance c/d	42,400
		48,000			48,000
1.1.X5	Balance b/d	42,400			

MOTOR VEHICLE ACCOUNT

		£			£
1.1.X4	Balance b/d	15,000	31.7.X4	Motor vehicle disposal	9,000
1.8.X4	Cash	9,500	31.12.X4	Balance c/d	15,500
		24,500			24,500
1.1.X5	Balance b/d	15,500			

PLANT AND EQUIPMENT: PROVISION FOR DEPRECIATION

		£			£
1.1.X4	Plant disposal	4,480	1.4.X4	Balance b/d	10,500
31.12.X4	Balance c/d	14,500	31.12.X4	P & L	8,480
		18,980			18,980
			1.1.X5	Balance b/d	14,500

MOTOR VEHICLES: PROVISION FOR DEPRECIATION

		£			£
31.7.X4	Vehicle disposal	5,203	1.1.X4	Balance b/d	9,000
31.12.X4	Balance c/d	6,723	1.12.X4	P & L	2,926
		11,926			11,926
				Balance b/d	6,723

PLANT AND EQUIPMENT: DISPOSALS

		£			£
1.1.X4	Plant & equipm't	5,600	1.4.X4	Depreciation	4,480
31.12.X4	P & L	880	1.4.X4	Cash	2,000
		6,480			6,480

MOTOR VEHICLES: DISPOSALS

		£			£
31.7.X4	Motor vehicles	9,000	31.7.X4	Depreciation	5,203
			31.7.X4	Cash	3,400
			31.12.X4	P & L	397
		9,000			9,000

MOTOR VEHICLE EXPENSES

		£			£
1.1.X4	Balance b/d	58	31.12.X4	P & L	156
1.8.X4	Cash	500	31.12.X4	Balance c/d	402
		558			558

REPAIRS AND MAINTENANCE

		£			£
1.10.X4	Cash	10,000	31.12.X4	P & L	10,000

(b)   PROFIT AND LOSS ACCOUNT (EXTRACT) - YEAR ENDED 31 DECEMBER 19X4

	£
Depreciation	11,406
Profit on disposal of assets	(483)
	10,923
Repairs and maintenance	10,000
Motor vehicle expenses	156

3   SSAP 19 ACCOUNTING FOR INVESTMENT PROPERTIES

3.1   The introduction of SSAP 12, with its requirement that all fixed assets including freehold buildings (though excluding freehold land) should be depreciated, caused a stir amongst property investment companies who feared that their reported profits would be severely reduced. The lobby was sufficiently strong to result in the publication of a separate standard for such properties.

Definition of investment properties

3.2   SSAP 19 defines an investment property as follows.

> **KEY TERM**
>
> '.... An **investment property** is an interest in land and/or buildings:
>
> (a)   in respect of which construction work and development have been completed; and
>
> (b)   which is held for its investment potential, any rental income being negotiated at arm's length.
>
> '....The following are exceptions from the definition:
>
> (a)   a property which is owned and occupied by a company for its own purposes is not an investment property;
>
> (b)   a property let to and occupied by another group company is not an investment property for the purposes of its own accounts or the group accounts.'

Accounting treatment of investment properties

3.3   **The provisions of SSAP 19 are based on the principle that the item of prime importance is the current value of the investment properties and changes in their current value,** rather than a calculation of systematic annual depreciation.

3.4   This leads to the following **accounting treatment.**

> '.... Investment properties **should not be subject to periodic charges for depreciation** on the basis set out in SSAP 12, except for properties held on lease which should be depreciated on the basis set out in SSAP 12 at least over the period when the unexpired term is 20 years or less.
>
> Investment properties **should be included in the balance sheet at their open market value.'**

3.5   The explanatory note to the standard suggests that the valuation need not be made by a qualified independent valuer, except that in cases where a major enterprise holds a substantial portfolio of investment properties, then an external valuation ought to be made at least once every five years.

3.6 The name of the valuer or his qualifications must be disclosed together with the basis of valuation used. If a person making a valuation is an employee or officer of the company or group which owns the property this fact should be disclosed.

3.7 Changes in the value of an investment property should not be taken to the profit and loss account. In other words a company cannot claim profit on the unrealised gains of such properties. The **revaluation should be disclosed as a movement on an investment revaluation reserve** (IRR).

3.8 The investment revaluation reserve should be disclosed prominently in the accounts. Investment properties can be owned by ordinary trading companies as well as property investment companies, and if the assets of a company consist wholly or mainly of investment properties, this fact should also be disclosed.

3.9 Further points to note about SSAP 19 are as follows.

(a) It is recognised in SSAP 19 that exemption from depreciation for investment property is **contrary** to the depreciation rules in the **Companies Act 1985**. This departure is considered permissible because the Act states that compliance with the rules is a subordinate requirement to the **'overriding purpose of giving a true and fair view'**. A note should disclose the non-compliance with the Act (see UITF Abstract 7 in Chapter 7).

(b) SSAP 19 **does not apply to immaterial items**.

(c) **'Prominent display'** should be given to investment properties and the IRR in the financial statements.

Disposals

3.10 **SSAP 19 does not deal with the problem of accounting for the disposal of investment properties. However, FRS 3** *Reporting financial performance* **states the following** in relation to the disposal of any revalued fixed assets.

(a) The profit or loss on disposal of an asset should be accounted for as the difference between the sale proceeds and the net carrying amount.

(b) Any revaluation surplus remaining is now realised, so FRS 3 requires this to be transferred to the profit and loss reserve.

Diminution in value: Amendment to SSAP 19

3.11 Until recently, under SSAP 19, any deficit on the IRR had to be taken to the profit and loss account. In other words, where the value of one or more investment property fell so far that the total IRR was insufficient to cover the deficit, then the excess was taken to the profit and loss account. SSAP 19 has now been amended as follows.

(a) **Any diminution in value which is considered permanent should be charged to the profit and loss account.**

(b) **Where diminution is temporary, a temporary IRR deficit is allowed.**

Question 3

Compare the accounting treatment of land and buildings as laid down by SSAP 12 with the accounting treatment of investment properties as laid down by SSAP 19 and explain why a building owned for its investment potential should be accounted for differently from one which is occupied by its owners.

Answer

SSAP 12 requires that all fixed assets should be depreciated, including freehold buildings. The only exception to this is freehold land which need only be depreciated if it is subject to depletion, for example, quarries or mines.

Where a property is revalued, depreciation should be charged so as to write off the new valuation over the estimated remaining useful life of the building.

SSAP 19, by contrast, recognises that there is a conceptual difference between *investment properties* and other fixed assets. Such properties are not depreciated and are carried in the balance sheet at open market value, re-assessed every year. An external valuation should be made at least once every five years.

Changes in the value of an investment property should not be taken to the profit and loss account. In other words, a company cannot claim profit on the unrealised gains on revaluation of such properties. The revaluation should be disclosed as a movement on an 'investment revaluation reserve'. Should this reserve show a debit balance (a loss) the full amount of the balance should be removed by charging it to the profit and loss account.

SSAP 19 acknowledges that there is a difference between investment properties and other fixed assets, including non-investment properties. Investment properties are held 'not for consumption in the business operations but as investments, the disposal of which would not materially affect any manufacturing or trading operations of the enterprise'.

It follows from this that the item of prime importance is the current value of the investment properties and changes in their current value rather than a calculation of systematic annual depreciation should be reported.

4   SSAP 4 ACCOUNTING FOR GOVERNMENT GRANTS   12/97

4.1   One further aspect of accounting for fixed assets concerns the accounting treatment of government grants which may be available to assist in the purchase of assets.

Capital and revenue grants

4.2   In the UK, the government provides grants to companies which invest in assisted areas (say development areas or special development areas). These grants may be:

(a)   **revenue grants** to cover some of the costs of certain categories of revenue expenditure; or

(b)   **capital grants,** which are cash grants to cover a proportion of the costs of certain items of capital expenditure (for example buildings, plant and machinery).

Companies receiving such grants must account for them. No particular problem arises in respect of revenue grants as they can be credited to revenue in the same period in which the revenue expenditure to which they relate is charged. However, capital grants may be treated in a number of ways.

Problems with capital grants

4.3   On receipt, should a company **credit the full amount** of the capital grant **to either:**

(a)   the **profit and loss account; or**

(b) a **non-distributable reserve** (for example a Government grant reserve permanently maintained in the balance sheet)?

In the first case there is an immediate effect on earnings and in the second there is none, and in both cases the concept of matching costs and revenues is not applied. The grant, like the depreciation cost of fixed assets, applies to the full life of the assets and so should be spread over that period of time.

4.4 **SSAP 4 states that grants relating to fixed assets should be credited to revenue over the expected useful life of the assets and this can be done in one of two ways:**

(a) **By reducing the acquisition cost of the fixed asset** by the amount of the grant, and providing depreciation on the reduced amount;

(b) By **treating** the amount of the grant **as a deferred credit and transferring a portion of it to revenue** annually.

4.5 EXAMPLE: ACCOUNTING FOR GOVERNMENT GRANTS

A company receives a 20% grant towards the cost of a new item of machinery, which cost £100,000. The machinery has an expected life of four years and a nil residual value. The expected profits of the company, before accounting for depreciation on the new machine or the grant, amount to £50,000 per annum in each year of the machinery's life.

The results of the company for the four years of the plant's life would be as follows.

(a) *Reducing the cost of the asset*

	Year 1 £	Year 2 £	Year 3 £	Year 4 £	Total £
Profits					
Profit before depreciation	50,000	50,000	50,000	50,000	200,000
Depreciation*	20,000	20,000	20,000	20,000	80,000
Profit	30,000	30,000	30,000	30,000	120,000

*The depreciation charge on a straight line basis, for each year, is ¼ of £(100,000 − 20,000) = £20,000.

Balance sheet at year end (extract)

	£	£	£	£
Fixed asset at cost	80,000	80,000	80,000	80,000
Depreciation	20,000	40,000	60,000	80,000
Net book value	60,000	40,000	20,000	-

(b) *Treating the grant as a deferred credit*

	Year 1 £	Year 2 £	Year 3 £	Year 4 £	Total £
Profits					
Profit before grant & dep'n	50,000	50,000	50,000	50,000	200,000
Depreciation	(25,000)	(25,000)	(25,000)	(25,000)	(100,000)
Grant	5,000	5,000	5,000	5,000	20,000
Profit	30,000	30,000	30,000	30,000	120,000

Balance sheet at year end (extract)

Fixed asset at cost	100,000	100,000	100,000	100,000
Depreciation	(25,000)	(50,000)	(75,000)	(100,000)
Net book value	75,000	50,000	25,000	-
Deferred income				
Government grant				
deferred credit	15,000	10,000	5,000	-

4.6 **The annual profits under both methods are the same, and both methods apply the matching concept in arriving at the profit figure.** Reducing the cost of the asset is simpler since, by reducing the depreciation charge, the amount of the grant is automatically credited to revenue over the life of the asset. However, the **deferred credit method has the advantage of recording fixed assets at their actual cost, which allows for comparability and is independent of government policy.** In addition, the **former method** may be **in conflict with the Companies Act 1985** in that the asset would no longer be carried at its purchase price or production cost.

4.7 The application of SSAP 4 is limited to grants made for the purchase of fixed assets in the UK and the Republic of Ireland and permits the use of either of the methods described above. However, because of the possible legal problem with the 'netting' method, the **deferred credit method is to be preferred.**

4.8 Where the second method is used then **the amount of the deferred credit, if material, should be shown separately in the balance sheet**. SSAP 4 states that it should not be shown as part of the shareholders' funds and it is suggested that the amount should appear under the heading of 'Accruals and deferred income' in the balance sheet.

4.9 The SSAP requires the **disclosure of the accounting policy** adopted for government grants **and** also requires disclosure of:

(a) The **effect** of government grants on the **company's profits** in the period and/or on its financial position generally.

(b) Any **potential liability** to repay grants.

(c) The nature of **government aid other than grants** which has materially affected profits in the period and an estimate of the effects, where possible.

4.10 A grant may be awarded to assist the financing of a project as a whole, where both capital and revenue expenditure are combined. In such cases the accounting treatment should be to match the grant with the relative proportions of revenue and capital expenditure incurred in the total project cost. For example, if two thirds of a project's costs are capital in nature and one third is revenue in nature, then any grant awarded against the whole project cost should be treated as one-third revenue-based and two thirds capital-based.

Exam focus point
An optimal question in the December 1997 paper included a government grant towards fixed assets which had to be accounted for.

Question 4

Greko plc is to receive a relocation grant of 30% of total expenses incurred. In 19X8 the company incurred the following costs associated with the relocation.

	£'000
Capital cost of factory	2,000
Training costs	200
Removal/relocation costs	300
	2,500

Required

Show the treatment of the government grant for 19X8.

Answer

	£'000
Grant received = 30% × 2,500 =	750
Capital expenditure	2,000
Revenue expenditure	500
	2,500

$$\text{Revenue grant} = \frac{500}{2,500} \times 750 = \qquad 150$$

$$\text{Capital grant} = \frac{2,000}{2,500} \times 750 = \qquad 600$$

	750

		£'000	£'000
DEBIT	Cash	750	
CREDIT	P&L account		150
CREDIT	Deferred income		600

4.11 Section summary

The following accounting treatments apply.

(a) *Revenue-based grants*

DEBIT	Cash
CREDIT	P & L account

in the period in which the revenue expenditure to which the grant relates is charged.

(b) *Capital-based grants*

DEBIT	Cash
CREDIT	Accruals and deferred income

when the grant is received.

DEBIT	Accruals and deferred income
CREDIT	P & L account

over the useful life of the related fixed asset.

4.12 Disclosure will be as follows.

(a) *Balance sheet: deferred income note*

	£
Balance at 1.1.19X0	X
Grants received during year	X
Transferred to profit and loss account	(X)
Balance at 31.12.19X0	X

(b) *Profit and loss account*: credit under 'other operating income'.

Exam focus point

A full question on intangible fixed assets might combine two or even all three of the standards covered here, but according to the Teaching Guide would not be set just on any one standard.

Chapter roundup

- A number of accounting regulations on the valuation and disclosure of fixed assets are contained in the **Companies Act 1985**.

- In the case of tangible fixed assets, these regulations are supplemented by the provisions of **SSAP 12** on depreciation, SSAP 19 on investment properties and SSAP 4 on the accounting treatment of government grants.

- **SSAP 19** conflicts with the statutory requirement to depreciate all fixed assets with a limited economic life, by stating that **investment properties need not ordinarily** be **depreciated**. Companies taking advantage of this provision will need to justify their departure from statute as being necessary to provide a true and fair view.

- Remember that Section 1 of this chapter lists the **statutory requirements** applying to **all fixed assets**, including the intangible assets and investments dealt with in the next chapter.

- You should now go back to Chapter 8 and consider how the accounting treatments and disclosure requirements of these three standards fit in to the published accounts formats and notes and the CA 1985 requirements.

Quick quiz

1   What elements of expenditure are included in the production cost of a fixed asset? (see para 1.4)

2   What disclosures are required when a fixed asset is valued according to the alternative valuation rules? (1.8)

3   In what circumstances may an amount be transferred from the revaluation reserve to the credit of the profit and loss account? (1.11)

4   Define 'depreciation'. (Knowledge brought forward)

5   What accounting treatment is required if the estimated useful life of a fixed asset is revised? (Knowledge brought forward)

6   Give the SSAP 19 definition of investment properties. (3.2)

7   State the accounting treatment required by SSAP 19 for investment properties. (3.4)

8   What is the required accounting treatment in respect of government grants? (4.4)

Question to try	Level	Marks	Time
10	Full exam	25	45 mins

Chapter 10

FIXED ASSETS: INTANGIBLE ASSETS AND INVESTMENTS

Chapter topic list	Syllabus reference
1 Intangible assets: the requirements of the Companies Act 1985	1(c), 2(a)
2 SSAP 13 *Accounting for research and development*	1(c), 2(a)
3 Goodwill: introduction	1(c), 2(a)
4 FRS 10 *Goodwill and intangible assets*	1(c), 2(a)
5 Investments	1(c), 2(a)

Introduction

We will look at intangible assets in this chapter, the main categories of which are R & D costs and goodwill.

Accounting for research and development according to SSAP 13 is relatively straightforward, and has been covered in your Paper 1 studies.

Our discussion on goodwill is closely connected with the later chapters on group accounts. When you reach these chapters you should refer back to the discussion here on goodwill.

The treatment of investments is addressed only briefly here, again because the topic is closely related to group accounts, covered in Chapters 16 to 19.

1 INTANGIBLE ASSETS: THE REQUIREMENTS OF THE COMPANIES ACT 1985

1.1 The **statutory balance sheet** format lists the following intangible fixed assets (item BI in the format).

(a) **Development costs**
(b) **Concessions, patents, licences, trade marks** and similar rights and assets
(c) **Goodwill**
(d) **Payments on account**

1.2 With regard to **concessions, patents, licences, trade marks etc** the Companies Act states that such items **should only be treated, and disclosed, as assets if they were either:**

(a) **acquired for valuable consideration**; or
(b) **created by the company itself.**

1.3 With regard to **development costs,** the Act states that such costs **may only be treated as an asset** in the balance sheet (rather than being written off immediately) in 'special circumstances'. The Act does not define these circumstances and this is a case where a SSAP goes further than statute. SSAP 13 (see below) lays down strict criteria for determining when such expenditure may be treated as an asset. The Act merely states that, if it is so treated, the following disclosures must be made by way of note:

(a)   The period over which the amount of the costs originally capitalised is being or is to be written off.

(b)   the reasons for capitalising the development costs.

1.4   With regard to goodwill, the Act implicitly makes a **distinction between inherent goodwill and purchased goodwill.** The distinction will be explained when we come to look at FRS 10 *Goodwill and intangible assets*, but for now it is enough to say that **the Act does not permit inherent goodwill to be included as an asset** in the balance sheet. The difficulties of valuing such goodwill are in any case so great that very few companies have ever carried it in their balance sheets. However, several listed companies have capitalised brands which were developed in-house.

1.5   **Purchased goodwill may be treated as an asset in the balance sheet.** If it is so treated (rather than being written off immediately), it must be written off systematically over a period chosen by the directors. The period chosen must not exceed the useful economic life of the goodwill. Disclosure should be made of the period chosen and of the reasons for choosing that period.

1.6   **This statutory requirement to amortise any goodwill capitalised does not extend to goodwill arising on consolidation.** Even so, companies have to amortise consolidation goodwill to comply with the stricter requirements of FRS 10. You should note that FRS 10 is stricter than CA 19085 in the case of goodwill on acquisition, as we will see below.

2   SSAP 13 ACCOUNTING FOR RESEARCH AND DEVELOPMENT   12/94

2.1   In many companies, especially those which produce food, or 'scientific' products such as medicines, or 'high technology' products, the expenditure on research and development (R & D) is considerable. **When R & D is a large item of cost, its accounting treatment may have a significant influence on the profits of a business and its balance sheet valuation.**

Exam focus point

Although SSAP 13 might feature in a small way, as it did in December 1994 as part of a consolidation question, it is very unlikely to form a major question. This is because it was in Paper 1 and the examiner has said so in the Teaching Guide.

Knowledge brought forward from Paper 1

SSAP 13 Accounting research and development

Definitions

- **Pure/basic research** is experimental/theoretical work with no commercial end in view and no practical application.

- **Applied research** is original investigation directed towards a specific practical aim/objective.

- **Development** is the use of scientific/technical knowledge in order to produce new/substantially improved materials, devices, processes etc.

Accounting treatment

- **Pure and applied research** should be written off as incurred.

- **Development expenditure** should be written off in year of expenditure, *except* in certain circumstances when it *may* be deferred to future periods.

    S   Separately defined project
    E   Expenditure separately identifiable
    C   Commercially viable
    T   Technically feasible
    O   Overall profit expected
    R   Resources exist to complete the project

- Show deferred development costs as an intangible asset amortised from the beginning of commercial production, systematically by reference to sales, etc.

- Deferred costs should be reviewed annually; where the above criteria no longer apply, write off the cost immediately.

- Development expenditure previously written off can be reinstated if the uncertainties which led to it being written off no longer apply.

- R & D fixed assets should be capitalised and written off over their estimated economic lives.

- Deferral of costs should be applied consistently to all projects.

- SSAP 13 does not apply to:

    ° fixed assets used for R&D (except amortisation);
    ° the cost of locating mineral deposits in extractive industries; and
    ° expenditure where there is a firm contract for reimbursement.

Disclosure

- R & D activities should be disclosed in the directors' report.

- Private companies outside groups which include a plc are exempt from disclosing R & D expenditures (except amortisation) if they would meet the criteria for a medium-sized company × 10.

- *Disclose:*

    ° movements on deferred development expenditure;

    ° R & D charged to the P & L a/c analysed between current year expenditure and amortisation; and

    ° an accounting policy note.

2.2   The importance of R & D disclosure was emphasised in another survey of what users really needed in financial statements. UK institutional investors said the top requirement was future prospects and plans (84%). R & D is seen to form a crucial quantitative element of prospects and plans. When specifically asked about R & D, 64% of UK investors said the data was very, or extremely, important to them. Unfortunately, the top companies analysed failed dismally to provide the information required. There is a wide variety of treatment and information given on R & D and improvements are required in the reporting of R & D.

Question 1

In connection with SSAP 13 Accounting for research and development:

(a)   define 'applied research' and 'development';

(b)   explain why it is considered necessary to distinguish between applied research and development expenditure and how this distinction affects the accounting treatment;

(c)   state whether the following items are included within the SSAP 13 definition of research and development, and give your reasons:

    (i)   market research;
    (ii)   testing of pre-production prototypes;
    (iii)   operational research;
    (iv)   testing in search of process alternatives.

Answer

(a)   *Applied research* expenditure is expenditure on original investigations which are carried out in order to gain new scientific or technical knowledge, but which also have a specific practical aim or objective. An example might be research into a disease with the intention of finding a cure or a vaccine.

Development expenditure is expenditure on the application of existing scientific or technical knowledge in order to produce new or substantially improved materials, devices, products, processes, systems or services prior to the commencement of commercial production. The costs of developing a prototype would be development expenditure.

(b)   SSAP 13 considers that:

'pure and applied research can be regarded as part of a continuing operation required to maintain a company's business and its competitive position. In general, no one particular period rather than any other will be expected to benefit and therefore it is appropriate that these costs should be written off as they are incurred.'

This is in accordance with the matching concept which requires that revenue and costs are 'matched with one another *so far as their relationship can be established or justifiably assumed'* (SSAP 2 paragraph 14) and also with the prudence concept.

This has the affect that applied research costs must be written off as incurred but development expenditure can be deferred (that is, capitalised as an intangible asset) and amortised over the life of the product, service, process or system developed. This treatment is only permissible if the project meets certain criteria designed to ensure that deferral is prudent.

(c)   (i)   Market research is not normally considered to be research and development activity. It is specifically excluded in the SSAP. This is presumably because it does not depart from routine activity and it does not contain an appreciable element of innovation.

    (ii)   Testing of prototypes is included in SSAP 13's list of activities normally to be considered as research and development. A prototype must be constructed and tested before full-scale production can be risked and so it is an essential stage in the development process.

    (iii)   'Operational research not tied to a specific research and development activity' is an activity which SSAP 13 considers should not normally be included in research and development. 'Operational research' is presumably used here to denote the branch of applied mathematics which includes techniques such as linear programming and network analysis. The implication is that routine use of such techniques (to improve production efficiency, for example) does not fall within SSAP 13's jurisdiction, in spite of the use of the word 'research'.

(iv) 'Testing in search for, or evaluation of, product, service or process alternatives' is considered to be research and development work by SSAP 13. It would fall within the definition of applied research.

Question 2

Fredericks plc incurs the following expenditure in years 19X1-19X5.

	Research £'000	Development £'000
19X1	40	65
19X2	45	70
19X3	49	-
19X4	41	-
19X5	43	-

You are told that Fredericks plc capitalises development expenditure when appropriate. The item developed in 19X1 and 19X2 goes on sale on 1 January 19X3 and it will be three years from then until any competitor is expected to have a similar product on the market.

Required

Show the profit and loss account and balance sheet extracts for all five years.

Answer

PROFIT AND LOSS ACCOUNT (EXTRACTS)

	19X1 £'000	19X2 £'000	19X3 £'000	19X4 £'000	19X5 £'000
Research expenditure	40	45	49	41	43
Amortisation of development costs	-	-	40	40	40

BALANCE SHEET (EXTRACT)

	19X1 £'000	19X2 £'000	19X3 £'000	19X4 £'000	19X5 £'000
Intangible fixed assets					
Development costs	65	135	135	135	135
Amortisation	-	-	(45)	(90)	(135)
Net book value	65	135	90	45	-

Audit implications

2.3 **The auditors must check that any development expenditure which is to be deferred meets the requirements** defined in the standard.

(a) The criteria of a **clearly defined project and separately identifiable expenditure** will be easy to establish.

(b) As to the outcome of the project in question, the auditors must examine **feasibility** studies and so forth to determine the project's viability, and perhaps consult technical experts.

(c) To check whether **all costs** will be **exceeded by revenue**, future cash flows should be examined.

(d) The **resources of the company to complete the project** can only be determined by reviewing the overall situation of the company on a going concern basis.

2.4 **In future years the auditors should review the situation again to ensure that the criteria are still met**. The auditors should also check that amortisation is charged on a systematic basis, beginning when the product in question comes into commercial production.

2.5 Research (and development) expenditure which is written off to the profit and loss account must be checked for accuracy, validity and completeness.

3 GOODWILL: INTRODUCTION 6/94, 12/94, 6/95, 12/95, 12/96

3.1 By definition, goodwill is an asset which cannot be realised separately from the business as a whole.

KEY TERM

Goodwill is the difference between the aggregate fair value of the net assets of a business and the value of the business as a whole.

3.2 There are many factors which may explain why goodwill arises. Examples are a skilled management team, good labour relations and a strategic location. These factors are intangible and it is difficult to place a money value on them. **Until recently, it was not usual to show goodwill as an asset in the balance sheet; any amount at which it was valued was considered to be arbitrary and subject to fluctuations.**

Inherent goodwill and purchased goodwill

Exam focus point

Because FRS 10 *Goodwill and intangible assets* has only recently been published, this topic is ripe for examination.

3.3 It is generally agreed that goodwill of a kind exists in every business. However, the only time when **goodwill is valued and may be disclosed as an asset in the balance sheet** is **when one business acquires another as a going concern.** This is because there is then a positive indication available of the value of goodwill acquired. This is **known as purchased goodwill. Goodwill which is presumed to exist, but which has not been evidenced in a purchases transaction, is called non purchased or inherent goodwill.**

Suggested treatments for purchased goodwill

3.4 **Non-purchased goodwill never appears** in financial statements. However, in relation to **purchased goodwill** a **wide variety of accounting treatments** have been used in the past. They can be summarised as follows.

(a) **Retain goodwill** as an asset in the balance sheet indefinitely unless a permanent reduction in its value becomes evident.

(b) Show goodwill as an **asset** but **amortise** it over its estimated useful life or over an arbitrary but specified maximum or minimum period.

(c) **Write off the entire amount** against:

    (i) income; or
    (ii) reserves;

    at the time of acquisition.

(d) Show goodwill as a continuing and separately identifiable **deduction from shareholders' funds** (the 'dangling debit' method).

Arguments for amortisation

3.5   The principal arguments for amortisation are as follows.

(a)   Goodwill is an asset which at the date of acquisition **has a definite value** to the business.

(b)   This asset is a measure of the extent to which the earnings of the purchased business will exceed those which could be expected from the use of its identifiable assets. Consequently, it should be amortised so as to **match costs against income** (the accruals concept). This is one of the views adopted by FRS 10 *Goodwill and intangible assets*.

Arguments for immediate write-off

3.6   The arguments for write-off are as follows.

(a)   (i)   Writing off purchased goodwill immediately would be **consistent with the treatment of inherent goodwill.**

(ii)   Alternatively, the purchased goodwill becomes **indistinguishable from the total goodwill** of the merged enterprise and should therefore be written off.

(iii) Goodwill might be treated as an asset, but too much uncertainty exists over its value and economic life, therefore **prudence** dictates that it should be written off.

(b)   (i)   Goodwill is **not an asset** as such and therefore to show it as an asset would be misleading.

(ii)   Both inherent and purchased goodwill would be **excluded** (**consistency**, as in (c) above).

(iii) Analysts may treat goodwill as they like if it is not amortised.

SSAP 22 treatment

3.7   SSAP 22 *Accounting for goodwill,* the forerunner of FRS 10, allowed a choice of two methods of accounting for purchased goodwill.

(a)   Purchased goodwill **could be eliminated immediately by write-off against reserves,** (against retained reserves brought forward, not as a charge in the current year's profit and loss account). This was regarded as the normal accounting treatment (adopted by over 95% of UK companies). Goodwill would then never appear in the balance sheet.

(b)   Goodwill **could be carried as an intangible fixed asset** in the balance sheet, but if so it **had to be amortised** over its estimated useful life. It was not permissible to carry goodwill indefinitely at its original cost.

3.8   SSAP 22 specifically **prohibited any accounting entries in respect of non-purchased (inherent) goodwill.** In this, and in the accounting treatment it prescribes for purchased goodwill, the standard conformed to the statutory requirements on goodwill contained in the CA 1985.

3.9   One difference between the standard and statute mentioned above relates to goodwill arising on consolidation (the goodwill arising when one limited company acquires a controlling interest in another limited company: see the later chapters of this Study Text on group accounts). According to SSAP 22, such goodwill had to be treated in the same way as any other purchased goodwill; CA 1985 is more permissive and allows goodwill arising on consolidation to be carried in the balance sheet indefinitely at its original cost.

Negative goodwill

3.10   Negative goodwill arises when the price paid for a business is less than the fair value of the separable net assets acquired, for example, if the vendor needed cash quickly and was forced to sell at a bargain price.

3.11   **SSAP 22 required negative goodwill to be accounted for as a credit to unrealised reserves.**

The goodwill controversy

3.12   The treatment of goodwill and intangible assets has always been controversial and there is a wide range of practice in different countries worldwide. As well as the treatment of goodwill itself, **there have been problems in the past with the recognition of values for brands and similar intangibles.** When purchased externally, some objective value could be attached to such assets, but internally generated brands were also recognised by some companies, where no such objective valuation criterion was available.

3.13   The old ASC only got as far as an exposure draft. The ASB had to tackle such an important issue early on, but it took two discussion/working papers and a series of public meetings for the board to reach the stage of producing an exposure draft and finally an FRS.

3.14   The two main questions are as follows.

(a)   **Should intangible assets, such as brands, be recognised separately from goodwill?**

(b)   **Which accounting treatment for goodwill should be adopted?**

3.15   The ASB seems to have overcome the first problem by deciding that there are circumstances where purchased intangible assets can be shown separately, but that in any case the **treatment of both intangibles and goodwill should be the same.** This means that the overall effect will be the same whether intangible assets are shown separately or whether they are subsumed in goodwill.

3.16   As far as the second question is concerned, **the ASB seems never to have entertained the idea of allowing non-purchased goodwill (or intangibles) to be recognised. An earlier discussion paper laid out the possible treatments for purchased goodwill, as follows.**

Asset-based methods	Treatment of purchased goodwill
1 Capitalisation and predetermined life amortisation	Capitalise then amortise over a predetermined finite life subject to a maximum of eg 20 years. Its amortised carrying value is assessed each year for recoverability.
2 Capitalisation and annual review	Capitalise, then amortise through the application of systematic annual review procedures to estimate the required annual amortisation charges. There may be years when the annual amortisation charge is zero.
3 Combination of 1 and 2 above	1 would be the method to use for most acquisitions, but 2 should be used in special and limited circumstances where it is believed that the goodwill has an economic life of greater than twenty years.
Elimination methods	**Treatment of purchased goodwill**
4 Immediate write-off reserve	Eliminate against reserves immediately on acquisition.
5 Separate write-off reserve	Transfer to a separate goodwill write-off reserve immediately on acquisition.
6 Variant of 5: Separate write-off reserve with recoverability assessment	Transfer to a separate goodwill write-off reserve immediately on acquisition. The balance in this reserve is assessed for recoverability at each year-end. Losses reducing the recoverable amount below the balance in the write-off reserve are charged to the P&L account.

3.17 This provides a succinct summary of the different treatments desired by different people. The ASB, very sensibly, recognised that it was impossible to obtain agreement from *all* interested parties on the treatment of goodwill because of the **conceptual difficulties** surrounding the issue.

Criticisms of SSAP 22

3.18 SSAP 22 was criticised for a number of reasons.

(a) It **permitted a choice** of accounting treatment.

(b) The **preferred treatment** (immediate write off), used most of the time:

(i) **gave the impression that the acquirer's net worth had been depleted** or even eliminated; and

(ii) **caused the financial statements to overstate the rates of return achieved on acquired investments.**

(c) This equity depletion **encouraged companies to reduce purchased goodwill by separately valuing brands and similar intangible assets as identifiable assets on the balance sheet.** Such assets are similar in nature to goodwill and yet their accounting treatment in such circumstances was very different.

(d) **Inconsistencies existed in the manner in which the elimination of goodwill against reserves was presented** (deduction from the profit and loss account, separate goodwill reserve etc).

(e)   SSAP 22's preferred treatment was **not accepted internationally**.

FRED 12 *Goodwill and intangible assets*

3.19   It became clear from the ASB's consultations that there was no conceptually perfect answer. The ASB concluded that the most important aspects were as follows.

- The accounting method chosen should avoid arbitrary attempts to reduce goodwill by separately valuing brands
- It should hold management accountable for amounts invested in purchased goodwill

3.20   An approach that requires the capitalisation of purchased goodwill and intangible assets, and write-down only if their values have not been maintained, aims to achieve this. The ASB set up public hearings to discuss this approach, using a combination of amortisation for short-life assets and impairment reviews for longer-life assets, before publishing it in FRED 12 *Goodwill and intangible assets* in June 1996. With the majority support of the commentators, **FRED 12 has now become FRS 10.**

4   FRS 10 GOODWILL AND INTANGIBLE ASSETS

Exam focus point
If you are in a hurry or revising, so straight to the summary at the end of this section.

4.1   FRS 10 *Goodwill and intangible assets* was published in December 1997. It is **effective for accounting periods ending on 23 December 1998 or later.**

4.2   The FRS applies to **all financial statements** except those entities applying the Financial Reporting Standard for Smaller Entities which do not prepare consolidated accounts.

4.3   The requirements of the FRS **apply to all intangible assets except those specifically addressed by another accounting standard,** eg SSAP 13. Oil and gas exploration and development costs are also exempt.

4.4   Although it is framed around the purchase of a subsidiary undertaking, it also applies to the acquisition of unincorporated entities.

Objective

4.5   The objective stated by the FRS is to ensure that:

- **capitalised goodwill and intangible assets are charged in the P&L account** as far as possible **in the periods in which they are depleted; and**
- **sufficient information is disclosed** in the financial statements to enable users **to determine the impact of goodwill and intangible assets on the financial position and performance of the reporting entity.**

Definitions

4.6   The FRS introduces a variety of new definitions, some of which relate to terms used above.

> **KEY TERMS**
>
> - **Class of intangible assets**: a group of intangible assets that have similar nature or function in the business of the entity.
>
> - **Identifiable assets and liabilities**: the assets and liabilities of an entity that are capable of being disposed of or settled separately, without disposing of a business of the entity.
>
> - **Purchased goodwill**: the difference between the fair value of the consideration paid for an acquired entity and the aggregate of the fair values of that entity's identifiable assets and liabilities. Positive goodwill arises when the fair value of the consideration paid exceeds the aggregate fair values of the identifiable assets and liabilities. Negative goodwill arises when the aggregate fair values of the identifiable assets and liabilities of the entity exceed the fair value of the consideration paid.
>
> - **Residual value**: the net realisable value of an asset at the end of its useful economic life. Residual values are based on prices at the date of acquisition (or revaluation) of the asset and do not take account of expected future price changes.
>
> - **Useful economic life:** the useful economic life of an intangible asset is the period over which the entity expects to derive economic benefit from that asset. The useful economic life of purchased goodwill is the period over which the value of the underlying business is expected to exceed the values of its identifiable net assets.   *(FRS 10)*

4.7   FRS 10 also includes definitions of the following terms, which are also defined in FRED 15 and are given in Chapter 2.

- Impairment
- Intangible assets
- Net realisable value
- Readily ascertainable market value
- Recoverable amount
- Value in use

Purchased goodwill is also defined by FRED 15, but the definition given here is fuller.

Initial recognition

Goodwill

4.8   **Positive purchased goodwill should be capitalised and classified as an asset on the balance sheet.**

4.9   **Internally generated goodwill should not be capitalised.** This requirement is the same as in the old SSAP 22.

Intangible assets

4.10 An intangible asset **purchased separately** from a business should be **capitalised at cost**.

4.11 Where an intangible asset is acquired **as part of the acquisition of a business** the treatment depends on whether its value can be measured reliably on its initial recognition.

    (a) If its value **can be measured reliably,** it should initially be **recorded at its fair value.** (The fair value should not create or increase any negative goodwill arising on the acquisition unless the asset has a readily ascertainable market value.)

Question 3

What should fair value be based on according to FRS 7 *Fair values in acquisition accounting*? You should know this from your Paper 10 studies.

Answer

Replacement cost - normally market value.

    (b) If the value of the asset **cannot be measured reliably,** the intangible asset must be **subsumed within the amount of the purchase price attributed to goodwill.**

Non-purchased intangibles

4.12 FRS 10 states that companies may **capitalise non-purchased** ('internally-developed') **intangibles** but **only to the extent that they have a 'readily ascertainable market value'.** This is an important definition that **means that:**

- **the asset must be a member of a group of homogenous assets** (ie they are all of the same kind), which are equivalent in all material respects; and

- **there is an active market for that group of assets,** evidenced by frequent transactions.

4.13 Examples given by the FRS of intangibles that may meet these conditions include certain operating licences, franchises and quotas. The FRS goes on to say that intangibles such as brands and publishing titles are not equivalent in all material aspects - in fact they are all unique - and so do not have readily ascertainable market values. They are therefore not examples of non-purchased intangibles that can be capitalised.

Approach to amortisation and impairment

4.14 The approach of the FRS to amortisation reflects the wish to charge goodwill to the profit and loss account only to the extent that the carrying value of the goodwill is not supported by the current value of the goodwill within the acquired business.

4.15 The approach is based on a combination of:

- Amortising over a limited period on a systematic basis; and
- An annual impairment review.

4.16 The first task is to decide whether or not the goodwill or intangible has a limited useful economic life.

Assets with a limited useful economic life

Amortisation

4.17   The FRS states that, where goodwill and intangible assets are regarded as having **limited useful economic lives** they should be **amortised on a systematic basis over those lives**.

4.18   The standard gives little guidance on how to predict an asset's useful economic life, which can be very difficult for goodwill and intangibles as it is impossible to see them actually wearing out. It dose, however, give examples of relevant considerations, which include certain economic and legal factors relating to the asset. An intangible may, for example, be linked to a product with a specific lifespan, or there may be time periods attached to legal rights (eg patents).

4.19   **There is a rebuttable presumption that the useful economic lives of purchased goodwill and intangible assets are limited to periods of 20 years or less**. This presumption may be rebutted and a useful economic life regarded as a longer period or indefinite only if:

(a)   the durability of the acquired business or intangible asset can be demonstrated and justifies estimating the useful economic life to exceed 20 years; and

(b)   the goodwill or intangible asset is capable of continued measurement (so that annual impairment reviews will be feasible).

Question 4

The circumstances where an indefinite useful economic life longer than 20 years may be legitimately presumed are limited. What factors determine the durability of goodwill?

Answer

FRS 10 mentions the following.

(a)   The nature of the business
(b)   The stability of the industry in which the acquired business operates
(c)   Typical lifespans of the products to which the goodwill attaches
(d)   The extent to which the acquisition overcomes market entry barriers that will continue to exist
(e)   The expected future impact of competition on the business

4.20   Uncertainty about the length of the useful economic life is not a good reason for choosing one that is unrealistically short or for adopting a 20 year useful economic life by default.

4.21   In amortising an intangible asset, a residual value may be assigned to that asset only if such residual value can be measured reliably. No residual value may be assigned to goodwill. In practice, the residual value of an intangible asset is often insignificant.

4.22   The method of amortisation should be chosen to reflect the expected pattern of depletion of the goodwill or intangible asset. A **straight-line method should be chosen unless another method can be demonstrated to be more appropriate**.

4.23   Whatever the **useful economic life** chosen, the company should be able to justify it. It **should be reviewed annually and revised if appropriate**.

Impairment review

4.24   In addition to the amortisation, the asset should have an **impairment review** (see below) **after the first year** to ensure that its performance was as expected.

4.25   If this review shows that results are as predicted, **no other review is required unless events or changes in the future indicate that the value of the goodwill or intangible may not be recoverable**.

4.26   If the review shows that the post-acquisition performance is poorer than anticipated, a full review is required in accordance with the FRS on impairment of fixed assets (at present only in FRED form: FRED 15 *Impairment of fixed assets and goodwill*).

4.27   Goodwill and intangible assets that are amortised over a period **exceeding 20 years** from the date of acquisition should be **reviewed for impairment at the end of each reporting period**.

Assets with an indefinite useful economic life

No amortisation

4.28   Where goodwill and intangible assets are regarded as having **indefinite useful economic lives**, they **should not be amortised**.

4.29   'Indefinite' is not the same as 'infinite', it means merely that no limit can be fixed for it.

IMPORTANT!

If the option not to amortise is taken, this constitutes a departure form the Companies Act and will need to be justified by invoking the **true and fair override**.

Impairment review

4.30   Goodwill and intangible assets that are **not amortised** (because their useful economic life is deemed to be indefinite) should be **reviewed for impairment at the end of each reporting period**.

4.31   If an impairment loss is recognised, the revised carrying value, if being amortised, should be amortised over the current estimate of the remaining useful economic life.

4.32   If goodwill arising on consolidation is found to be impaired, the carrying amount of the investment held in the accounts of the parent undertaking should also be reviewed for impairment.

4.33   **The emphasis on impairment reviews is a key feature of the new FRS**. The ASB believes that a formal requirement to monitor the value of acquired goodwill and intangible assets using standardised methods and to report any losses in the financial statements will enhance the quality of the information provided to users of financial statements.

Reversal of impairment

4.34   Normally, once an impairment review has identified a loss, this cannot be restored at a later date. However, **if the loss was caused by an *external* event that later reversed in a**

way that was not foreseen, the original impairment loss may be restored. An example of this might be: if a direct competitor came on to the market, leading to an impairment loss, and then the competitor did not survive or produced a different product from the one originally envisaged.

Revaluation

4.35 **Goodwill may not be revalued, except** in the circumstances described above, ie the **reversal of an impairment**. If an intangible asset has a readily ascertainable market value, it may be revalued to its market value.

4.36 Future amortisation should always be made on the revalued amount, just like depreciation for a revalued tangible fixed asset.

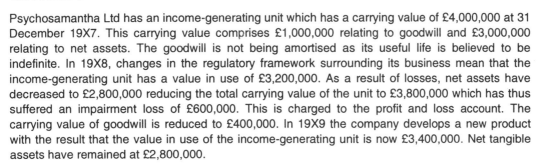

Question 5

Psychosamantha Ltd has an income-generating unit which has a carrying value of £4,000,000 at 31 December 19X7. This carrying value comprises £1,000,000 relating to goodwill and £3,000,000 relating to net assets. The goodwill is not being amortised as its useful life is believed to be indefinite. In 19X8, changes in the regulatory framework surrounding its business mean that the income-generating unit has a value in use of £3,200,000. As a result of losses, net assets have decreased to £2,800,000 reducing the total carrying value of the unit to £3,800,000 which has thus suffered an impairment loss of £600,000. This is charged to the profit and loss account. The carrying value of goodwill is reduced to £400,000. In 19X9 the company develops a new product with the result that the value in use of the income-generating unit is now £3,400,000. Net tangible assets have remained at £2,800,000.

Can all or any of the impairment loss be reversed?

Answer

No. Despite the value in use of the business unit now being £3,400,000 compared to its carrying value of £3,200,000, it is not possible to reverse £200,000 of the prior year's impairment loss of £600,000 since the reason for the increase in value of the business unit (the launch of the new product) is not the same as the reason for the original impairment loss (the change in the regulatory environment in which the business operates).

Negative goodwill

4.37 As mentioned earlier, negative goodwill arises when the fair value of the net assets acquired is more than the fair value of the consideration. In other words, the investor has got a bargain.

4.38 FRS 10 states that **the investee's assets should be checked for impairment and the liabilities checked for understatement to ensure that the negative goodwill is justified.** If indeed any negative goodwill remains after these tests, it needs to be disclosed consistently with positive goodwill.

4.39 Rather than being shown on the bottom half of the balance sheet as a capital reserve - as was required by SSAP 22 - **it is now disclosed in the intangible fixed assets category, directly under positive goodwill, ie as a 'negative asset'.** A sub-total of the net amount of positive and negative goodwill should be shown on the face of the balance sheet.

4.40 This presentation may seem a little odd. However, the ASB argues that negative goodwill does not meet the definition of a liability under the *Statement of Principles* and that this treatment is consistent with that of positive goodwill.

4.41 Negative goodwill should be **recognised in the profit and loss account in the periods when the non-monetary assets acquired are depreciated or sold.**

4.42 There are two important points to note.

(a) It would be strange for the investor to pay less than its fair value for the monetary items acquired. The value of cash, for example, is pretty universal. It is more **likely that the negative goodwill represents a shortfall in the value of the non-monetary items.**

(b) The **benefit** of the 'bargain' of getting these non-monetary items at less than fair value **will only be realised when the non-monetary items themselves are realised.**

Therefore it makes sense to credit the negative goodwill to the profit and loss account only when the non-monetary assets themselves are realised, and this is when they are either depreciated or sold.

Question 6

Brookie plc acquired its investment in Stenders Ltd in the year ended 31 December 19X8. The goodwill on acquisition was calculated as follows.

	£'000	£'000
Cost of investment		200
Fair value of net assets acquired		
Fixed assets	350	
Stock	50	
Net monetary assets	100	
		(500)
Negative goodwill		(300)

Required

Calculate the amount relating to negative goodwill as reflected in the profit and loss account and balance sheet for the year ended 31 December 19X8.

Answer

Amortisation in the profit and loss account for 19X8

Non-monetary assets recognised through the profit and loss account for the year ended 31 December 19X8:

	£'000
Stock	50
Depreciation (£350,000 ÷ 7)	50
	100
Total non-monetary assets at acquisition	400
Proportion recognised this year	¼

This means that a credit of £25,000 (£100,000 × ¼) of the negative goodwill will be charged to the profit and loss account for the year ended 31.12.X8. The remaining £75,000 will be carried in the balance sheet as a deduction from positive goodwill as part of intangible fixed assets.

Over the next six years (the remaining useful life of the non-monetary assets originally purchased), it will be released into the profit and loss account (£12,500 a year).

Disclosures

4.43 FRS 10 requires various disclosures relating to the following.

• Recognition and measurement
• Amortisation of positive goodwill and intangible assets

- Revaluation
- Negative goodwill
- Impairment (as in FRED 15, discussed in Chapter 2).

4.44 The **disclosure requirements are the same as for any other fixed asset,** including the table showing a reconciliation of movements during the year, for every category of intangible assets (including goodwill), details of revaluations, accounting policies and details of amortisation charged.

4.45 Significant **additional disclosure** requirements include requirements to explain:

- The **bases of valuation** of intangible assets

- The **grounds for believing a useful economic life to exceed 20 years** or to be indefinite

- The **treatment adopted of negative goodwill**

Transitional arrangements

4.46 **FRS 10 represents a radical change in accounting for goodwill and intangible assets in the United Kingdom.** As a consequence, the transitional arrangements within the standard are especially important. The standard only deals with the accounting adjustments for the most common types of transitional situations. These are summarised in the table below.

FRS 10: Transitional arrangements

Circumstances		Options		Method
(a)	Goodwill previously eliminated against reserves	1	Leave eliminated against reserves until business disposed of	If necessary, transfer from separate write-off reserve to another reserve. Deduct from profit on any future disposal
		2	Capitalise at cost less amortisation or impairment attributed to previous periods. Amortise thereafter where appropriate	Make prior year adjustment
(b)	Internally developed assets that do not meet new recognition criteria		Write off	Make prior year adjustment
(c)	Revalued purchased intangible assets	1	If asset has a readily ascertainable market value, update value	Report value change as current year gain or loss
		2	If asset does not have a readily ascertainable market value, restate at cost less amortisation or impairment attributed to previous periods	Make prior year adjustment

Note. It would appear that these transitional options will only be available in the accounting period in which FRS 10 is implemented.

Criticisms of FRS 10

4.47   **The new rules will mean significant changes to the accounts of many companies.** Over 95% of companies in the UK adopted the 'immediate write off' treatment permitted under SSAP 22. Some commentators have suggested that some deals will not be done because of the new, tougher rules. This is probably an exaggeration, but it is certainly possible that the new standard will not be popular.

4.48   More seriously, criticisms have been made by the firm Ernst & Young of the thinking behind the standard. The main criticisms are as follows.

(a)   **FRS 10 still allows a choice of accounting treatments.** Companies can follow a regime that permits the goodwill to be carried as a permanent asset. This may allow some spurious assets to remain indefinitely in the balance sheet, potentially providing fuel for criticism of the profession in the next wave of accounting scandal.

(b)   **The impairment review,** if it is to be based on FRED 15, applies 'labyrinthine methodologies to very soft members'. In other words, it **is subjective,** not least in determining how the business is to be segmented. Forecasting cashflows is also problematic.

(c)   **The importance of negative goodwill has been underestimated.** It is more likely to arise now that FRS 7 bans reorganisation provisions, thus raising the value of the net assets acquired.

(d)   **The treatment of negative goodwill is 'strange'.** It is a 'dangling credit' in the balance sheet and the profit and loss account treatment simply mirrors that required for depreciation without regard to the fact that this is a **credit** to the profit and loss account.

4.49 Section summary

- Purchased goodwill and intangible assets will both be capitalised as assets in the balance sheet. The option for goodwill of immediate write off to reserves, by-passing the profit and loss account, will no longer be available as it was under SSAP 22.

- Where goodwill and intangible assets have limited lives they will be amortised to the profit and loss account over their expected lives.

- Amortisation will not be required for assets that can be justified as having indefinite lives. They need to be written down only if their values drop below those in the balance sheet.

- There is a general presumption that the lives of goodwill and intangible assets will be no more than 20 years. A longer or indefinite life may be assigned only if the durability of the asset can be demonstrated and if it is possible to remeasure its value each year to identify any reduction.

- Impairment reviews must be performed annually where lives of more than 20 years are chosen. For lives of less than 20 years, they are required only in the year after acquisition, and in other years if there is some indication that the asset's value might have fallen below its recorded value.

5   INVESTMENTS

5.1   The last category of fixed assets we need to consider is investments. Not all investments, however, are held by a company for the long term and it will be convenient to **deal with fixed asset investments and current asset investments together.**

> **KEY TERM**
>
> An **investment** can be defined as an asset that generates economic benefits in the form of distributions and/or appreciation in value.

5.2   Investments intended to be retained by a company on a continuing basis (for use in the company's activities) should be treated as fixed assets, while any other investments should be taken to be current assets.

5.3   The categories into which investments should be grouped and separately disclosed are given in the pro-forma balance sheet shown in Chapter 29 under sections BIII and CIII.

Fixed asset investments

5.4   The provisions relating to fixed assets in general, which were given in the previous chapter, embrace investments which are held as fixed assets. But investments will not normally have a limited economic life, so that **the requirement of systematic depreciation does not apply.** Fixed asset investments will therefore be carried at cost less provisions for permanent diminutions in value with revaluations taken to a revaluation reserve

5.5   The **alternative accounting** rules allow the following bases of valuation, other than cost, for fixed asset investments:

(a)   **market value:** if this is higher than the stock exchange value, the latter should also be disclosed; or

(b)   **directors' valuation.**

As always when advantage is taken of the alternative accounting rules, disclosure must be made of the items affected, the basis of valuation adopted and the comparable amounts determined according to the historical cost convention.

Current asset investments

5.6   Current asset investments which are **readily marketable** investments should be shown at **current market value**, with increases or decreases in value taken to the profit and loss account.

5.7   **Other current asset investments** should be shown, in accordance with the prudence concept, at the **lower of purchase price and net realisable value.**

Listed vs unlisted

5.8   Investments, whether fixed assets or current assets, must be split between those listed on a recognised stock exchange and those which are unlisted. Shares dealt with on the Alternative Investment Market (AIM), are *not* 'listed', but they are 'quoted'. The amount of income from listed investments need not be shown in the profit and loss account, according to a recent amendment to CA 1985.

5.9   If the aggregate market value of investments listed on a recognised stock exchange differs from their carrying value in the balance sheet, the market value should be disclosed.

Chapter roundup

- This chapter has set out the **statutory accounting requirements** relating to intangible fixed assets and investments. These requirements are supplemented in the case of development costs by SSAP 13 and in the case of goodwill by FRS 10.

- **SSAP 13** is a standard which is generally accepted and well understood. You should ensure that you are very familiar with its provisions. Don't forget to learn the disclosure requirements.

- The treatment of **goodwill and intangibles,** on the other hand, is a controversial and complex area. You must ensure that you can discuss the current thinking on the nature of fixed assets, intangible assets and goodwill and that you can discuss all the possible treatments of positive and negative goodwill in accounts and the arguments on brand accounting. You should be familiar with, and be able to explain, the ASB's requirements as set out in FRS 10 *Goodwill and intangible asset.*

- Go back now to Chapter 8 and consider how the accounting treatments and disclosure requirements discussed in this chapter fit in with the **published accounts formats and notes**.

Quick quiz

1   In what circumstances may concessions, patents etc be treated as assets in a company's accounts? (see para 1.2)

2   What are the statutory disclosure requirements in relation to deferred development costs? (1.3)

3   In what circumstances does SSAP 13 permit the capitalisation of development costs? (Knowledge brought forward)

4   What are the disclosure requirements of SSAP 13 in relation to deferred development costs? (Knowledge brought forward)

5   Bob buys Elba's business for £28,000. The business assets are a car valued at £6,000, stocks valued at £15,000 and debtors of £4,000. How much is goodwill valued at? (3.1)

6   State four accounting methods which have been used for purchased goodwill in the past. (3.4)

7   Summarise the methods which have been identified by the ASB for dealing with goodwill. (3.16)

8   What are the main criticisms of SSAP 22? (3.18)

9   What is the normal treatment prescribed by FRS 10 for positive purchased goodwill? (4.8)

10   The useful economic life of goodwill or intangible assets is always 20 years or less. True or false? (4.19)

11   When must an impairment review be carried out? (4.24 - 4.27)

12   How should negative goodwill be shown in the balance sheet? (4.39)

13   What methods of valuing fixed asset investments are permitted under the alternative accounting rules? (5.5)

Question to try	Level	Marks	Time
11	Full exam	30	54 mins

Chapter 11

STOCKS AND WORK IN PROGRESS

Chapter topic list	Syllabus reference
1 Stocks and short-term work in progress	1(c), 2(a)
2 Long-term contract work in progress	1(c), 2(a)
3 Audit implications	1(c), 2(a)

Introduction

You have encountered stocks and stock valuation in your Foundation studies. Stock valuation has a direct impact on a company's gross profit and it is usually a material item in any company's accounts. This is therefore an important subject area. If you have any doubts about accounting for stocks and methods of stock valuation you would be advised to go back to your Paper 1 study material and revise this topic.

Section 1 of this chapter goes over some of this ground again, concentrating on the effect of SSAP 9. Section 2 goes on to discuss a new area, long-term contract work in progress. You should find this topic fairly logical as long as you work through the examples and exercise carefully.

In Section 3 we consider the audit implications for an area which is almost always important in any audit.

1   STOCKS AND SHORT-TERM WORK IN PROGRESS   6/94

1.1 In most businesses the value put on stock is an important factor in the determination of profit. Stock valuation is, however, a highly subjective exercise and consequently there is a wide variety of different methods used in practice.

1.2 The Companies Act 1985 regulations and SSAP 9 *Stocks and long-term contracts* requirements were developed to achieve greater uniformity in the valuation methods used and in the disclosure in financial statements prepared under the historical cost convention.

1.3 **SSAP 9 defines stocks and work in progress as:**

   (a)   Goods or other assets purchased for resale.
   (b)   Consumable stores.
   (c)   Raw materials and components purchased for incorporation into products for sale.
   (d)   Products and services in intermediate stages of completion.
   (e)   Long-term contract balances.
   (f)   Finished goods.

1.4 In published accounts, the Companies Act 1985 requires that these stock categories should be grouped and disclosed under the following headings:

(a) Raw materials and consumables ((c) and (b) above).

(b) Work in progress ((d) and (e) above).

(c) Finished goods and goods for resale ((f) and (a) above).

(d) Payments on account (presumably intended to cover the case of a company which has paid for stock items but not yet received them into stock).

1.5 **A distinction is also made in SSAP 9 between:**

(a) stocks and work in progress other than long-term contract work in progress; and

(b) long-term contract work in progress.

We will look at long-term contracts later in the chapter. Stocks and short-term work in progress are revised briefly here.

Knowledge brought forward from Paper 1

SSAP 9 Stock and long-term contracts (Stock and short-term WIP)

Under the matching concept costs must be allocated between the cost of goods sold (matched against current revenues) and closing stock (matched against future revenues).

- Stock should be valued at the **lower of cost and net realisable value** (NRV).

- **Costs** should include those incurred in the **normal course of business** in bringing a product or service to its **present location and condition**.

- Costs include direct costs (labour, materials), production overheads and other attributable overheads. Exclude all 'abnormal' overheads, eg exceptional spoilage.

- CA 1985 also allows the inclusion of interest payable on capital borrowed to finance the production of the asset (allowed by SSAP 9 under 'other attributable overheads').

- **NRV is the actual or estimated selling price less further costs to be incurred in marketing, selling and distribution.**

- The method used in allocating costs to stock should produce the fairest approximation to the expenditure incurred.

- Methods include (per CA 1985): average cost, base stock, current cost, FIFO, LIFO, replacement cost, standard cost, unit cost; however, base stock and LIFO are not allowed under SSAP 9.

- The principle situation where NRV will be less than cost will be where:

  ° there have been increases in the costs or falls in selling price;
  ° physical deterioration of stock has occurred;
  ° products have become obsolescent;
  ° the company has decided to make and sell a product at a loss;
  ° there are errors in production or purchasing.

1.6 The following question is a very simple reminder of how FIFO and LIFO operate.

Question 1

A retailer commenced business on 1 January 19X5, with a capital of £500. He decided to specialise in a single product line and by the end of June 19X5, his purchases and sales of this product were as follows.

	Purchases		Sales	
	Units	Unit price	Units	Unit price
		£		£
January	30	5.00	20	7.00
February	-	-	5	7.20
April	40	6.00	25	8.00
May	25	6.50	30	8.50
June	20	7.00	20	9.00
	115		100	

Required

(a) Ascertain the retailer's gross profit for the period assuming that:

    (i)   stock is valued using FIFO;
    (ii)   stock is valued using LIFO.

(b) Assuming that all purchases and sales are made for cash and that there are no other transactions for the period, draw up balance sheets as at 30 June 19X5, showing:

    (i)   stock valued on a FIFO basis;
    (ii)   stock valued on a LIFO basis.

Comment briefly on the significance of these balance sheets.

Answer

(a) (i)   *LIFO basis*

	SALES			COST OF SALES		
	Unit	Unit price	Total	Unit	Unit price	Total
		£	£		£	£
January	20	7.00	140.00	20	5.00	100.00
February	5	7.20	36.00	5	5.00	25.00
April	25	8.00	200.00	25	6.00	150.00
May	30	8.50	255.00	25	6.50	162.50
				5	6.00	30.00
June	20	9.00	180.00	20	7.00	140.00
	100		811.00	100		607.50
Closing stock				10	6.00	60
				5	5.00	25
				15		85

	£
Sales	811.00
Less cost of sales	607.50
Gross profit	203.50

  (ii) *FIFO basis*

	£	£
Sales		811.00
Purchases	692.50	
Less closing stock (15 @ £7.00)	105.00	
		587.50
		223.50

(b)   BALANCE SHEETS AS AT 30 JUNE 19X5

	(i) LIFO basis £	(ii) FIFO basis £
Original capital	500.00	500.00
Profit	203.50	223.50
	703.50	723.50
Stock	85.00	105.00
Cash	618.50	618.50
	703.50	723.50

In a time of rising prices LIFO (which uses the most current costs) will tend to give a more realistic measure of profit, but results in an outdated stock valuation being disclosed in the balance sheet.

2   LONG-TERM CONTRACT WORK IN PROGRESS   6/96

2.1   The most controversial aspect of SSAP 9 is its regulation concerning the valuation of work in progress for incomplete long-term contracts.

> **KEY TERM**
>
> A **long-term contract** is defined as: 'a contract entered into for the design, manufacture or construction of a single substantial asset or the provision of a service (or of a combination of assets or services which together constitute a single project) where the time taken substantially to complete the contract is such that the contract activity falls into different accounting periods.'

Usually long-term contracts will exceed one year in duration, **although a particularly large contract whose activity straddles a balance sheet date should still be accounted for as a long-term contract even if it will last in total less than a year.** This is to ensure that the accounts for both accounting periods involved will still give a true and fair view of the activities of the company.

> **Exam focus point**
> If you are revising, go to the summary of accounting treatment in Paragraph 2.14.

2.2   It is the following regulation which causes the greatest controversy around the standard.

> 'Separate consideration needs to be given to long-term contracts. Owing to the length of time taken to complete such contracts, to defer recording turnover and taking profit into account until completion may result in the profit and loss account reflecting not so much a fair view of the results of the activity of the company during the year but rather the results relating to contracts that have been completed in the year. It is therefore appropriate to take credit for ascertainable turnover and profit while contracts are in progress ....'

Some companies might prefer to value work in progress on long-term contracts at cost, and to defer taking any profit on the contract into the profit and loss account until the contract had been completed. This policy may be considered prudent, and has the further advantage that since profits would be deferred, tax liabilities might also be deferred.

2.3 EXAMPLE: LONG-TERM CONTRACTS

A numerical example might help to illustrate the problem. Suppose that a contract is started on 1 January 19X5, with an estimated completion date of 31 December 19X6. In the first year, to 31 December 19X5:

(a) costs incurred amounted to £600,000;

(b) half the work on the contract was completed;

(c) the final contract price is £1,500,000;

(d) certificates of work completed have been issued, to the value of £750,000. (*Note.* It is usual, in a long-term contract, for a qualified person such as an architect or engineer to inspect the work completed, and if it is satisfactory, to issue certificates. This will then be the notification to the customer that progress payments are now due to the contractor. Progress payments are commonly the amount of valuation on the work certificates issued, minus a precautionary retention of 10%.);

(e) it is estimated with reasonable certainty that further costs to completion in 19X6 will be £600,000.

What is the contract profit in 19X5, and what entries would be made for the contract at 31 December 19X5 if:

(a) profits are deferred until the completion of the contract;

(b) a proportion of the estimated turnover and profit is credited to the profit and loss account in 19X5?

2.4 SOLUTION

(a) If profits were deferred until the completion of the contract in 19X6, the turnover and profit recognised on the contract in 19X5 would be nil, and the value of work in progress on 31 December 19X5 would be £600,000. SSAP 9 takes the view that this policy is unreasonable, because in 19X6, the total profit of £300,000 would be recorded. Since the contract revenues are earned throughout 19X5 and 19X6, a profit of nil in 19X5 and £300,000 in 19X6 would be contrary to the matching concept of accounting.

(b) It is fairer to recognise turnover and profit throughout the duration of the contract.

As at 31 December 19X5 turnover of £750,000 should be matched with cost of sales of £600,000 in the profit and loss account, leaving an attributable profit for 19X5 of £150,000.

The only balance sheet entry as at 31 December 19X5 is a debtor of £750,000 recognising that the company is owed this amount for work done to date. No balance remains for stock, the whole £600,000 having been recognised in cost of sales.

Definitions

2.5 SSAP 9 gives some other important definitions, as well as that of long-term contracts themselves given above.

KEY TERMS

'**Attributable profit.** That part of the total profit currently estimated to arise over the duration of the contract, after allowing for estimated remedial and maintenance costs and increases in costs so far as not recoverable under the terms of the contract, that fairly reflects the profit attributable to that part of the work performed at the accounting date. (There can be no attributable profit until the profitable outcome of the contract can be assessed with reasonable certainty.)

Foreseeable losses. Losses which are currently estimated to arise over the duration of the contract (after allowing for estimated remedial and maintenance costs and increases in costs so far as not recoverable under the terms of the contract). This estimate is required irrespective of:

(a) where or not work has yet commenced on such contracts;
(b) the proportion of work carried out at the accounting date;
(c) the amount of profits expected to arise on other contracts.

Payments on account. All amounts received and receivable at the accounting date in respect of contracts in progress.'

Rules for calculating turnover and profit to be taken

2.6   The SSAP 9 rules for calculating the turnover and profit to be taken on incomplete long-term contracts follow directly from the definitions given above.

(a) **Turnover and profit must reflect the proportion of the work carried out at the accounting date** (and allow for any known inequalities in profitability in the various stages of a contract).

(b) **Where the outcome of a contract cannot be foreseen with reasonable certainty,** so that the expected profit cannot be reasonably assessed, **it is prudent not to take up any profit.** (This will be especially appropriate in the case of long-term contracts in their early stages.) However, 'in such circumstances, if no loss is expected it may be appropriate to show as turnover a proportion of the total contract value using a zero estimate of profit' (SSAP 9).

(c) **If there is an expected loss on a contract, provision must be made for the whole of the loss as soon as it is foreseen** (so none of the loss should be deferred). This has the effect of reducing the value of WIP to its net realisable value. For example, if a contract is 75% complete, and:

(i)   costs incurred to date are £300,000
(ii)   further costs to completion are expected to be £100,000
(iii) the contract price is £360,000

in addition to a suitable proportion of costs incurred, then the full expected loss of £40,000 should be charged against profit in the current period.

2.7   Note the following.

(a) The **estimated future costs must take into account estimated costs of rectification and guarantee work** and any possible increases in wages, prices of raw materials etc, so far as these are not recoverable from the customer under the terms of the contract.

(b) **Interest payable** for finance etc **must be excluded from costs unless specifically attributable to the contract.**

2.8 An appropriate proportion of the estimated total turnover and profit may then be taken into account which might be calculated by using the formulae:

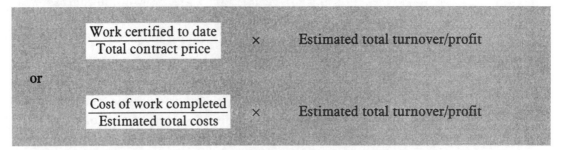

$$\frac{\text{Work certified to date}}{\text{Total contract price}} \times \text{Estimated total turnover/profit}$$

or

$$\frac{\text{Cost of work completed}}{\text{Estimated total costs}} \times \text{Estimated total turnover/profit}$$

The profit so calculated is called the **attributable profit**.

2.9 Some companies feel that it is more prudent to take credit for profit only in respect of the cash which has been received from the customer. The profit attributable to the accounting period may be reduced in proportion to the cash received:

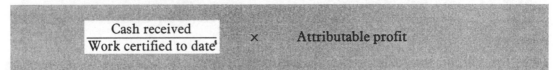

$$\frac{\text{Cash received}}{\text{Work certified to date}} \times \text{Attributable profit}$$

In fact, this final result may be arrived at directly by using the formula:

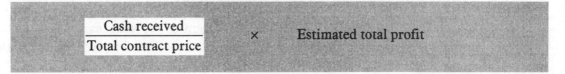

$$\frac{\text{Cash received}}{\text{Total contract price}} \times \text{Estimated total profit}$$

2.10 The amount of turnover and profit on a long-term contract to be recognised in an accounting period is found by the calculation:

	£
Cumulative turnover/attributable profit	X
Less any turnover/attributable profit taken into account in previous years	X
Turnover/profit to be recognised in current period	X

2.11 It is accepted that **estimates of total profit may change from one year to another, and so attributable profits have to be recalculated at the end of each period.** Remember that at an early stage in the contract, in order to show a true and fair view of activity in the period, an appropriate proportion of turnover should be recorded in the profit and loss account but, on grounds of prudence, no profit should be recorded until the overall result of the contract is more certain.

2.12 In valuing long-term WIP and the other disclosures required under SSAP 9, an organised approach is essential. The following suggested method breaks the process down into **five logical steps.**

Step 1 Compare the contract value and the total costs expected to be incurred on the contract. If a loss is foreseen (that is, if the costs to date plus estimated costs to completion exceed the contract value) then it must be charged against profits. If a loss has already been charged in previous years, then only the difference between the loss as previously and currently estimated need be charged (or credited).

Step 2 Using the percentage completed to date (or other formula given in the question), calculate turnover attributable to the contract for the period (for example percentage complete × total contract value, less of course, turnover taken in previous periods).

Step 3 Calculate the cost of sales on the contract for the period.

	£
Total contract costs × percentage complete (or follow instructions in question)	X
Less any costs charged in previous periods	(X)
	X
Add foreseeable losses in full (not previously charged)	X
Cost of sales on contract for the period	X

Step 4 Deduct the cost of sales for the period as calculated above (including any foreseeable loss) from work in progress at cost up to the total balance on the account. If the cost of sales transfer exceeds this balance, then show the excess as a provision for liabilities and charges or as an accrual.

Step 5 Calculate **cumulative** turnover on the contract (the total turnover recorded in respect of the contract in the profit and loss accounts of all accounting periods since the inception of the contract). Compare this with total progress payments to date.

(a) If turnover exceeds payments on account, an 'amount recoverable on contracts' is established and separately disclosed within debtors.

(b) If payments on account exceed cumulative turnover then the excess is:

(i)   first deducted from any remaining balance on work in progress;

(ii) any balance is disclosed within creditors.

Double entry

2.13 The accounting double entry for a long-term contract is as follows.

(a) *During the year*

(i)   DEBIT   Contract account (WIP)
      CREDIT   Cash/creditors

      Being costs incurred

(ii) DEBIT   Trade debtors
      CREDIT   Debtors: amounts recoverable on contracts

      Being progress payments invoiced

(iii) DEBIT   Bank
      CREDIT   Trade debtors

      Being cash received

(b) *At year end*

(i)   DEBIT   Debtors: amounts recoverable on contracts
      CREDIT   Turnover (P&L)

      Being turnover recognised

(ii) DEBIT   Cost of sales (P&L)

CREDIT   Contract account

Being costs matched against turnover

(iii)   DEBIT   Provisions on long-term contracts (P&L)
          CREDIT   Provision for future losses (B/S)

Being a provision for future losses

Summary of accounting treatment

2.14   The following summarises the accounting treatment for long-term contracts - **make sure that you understand it.**

Profit and loss account

(a)   **Turnover and costs**

(i)   Turnover and associated costs should be recorded in the profit and loss account 'as contract activity progresses'.

(ii)   Include an 'appropriate proportion of total contract value as turnover' in the profit and loss account.

(iii)   The costs incurred in reaching that stage of completion are matched with this turnover, resulting in the reporting of results which can be attributed to the proportion of work completed.

(iv)   Turnover is the 'value of work carried out to date'.

(b)   **Attributable profit**

(i)   It must reflect the proportion of work carried out.

(ii)   It should take into account any known inequalities in profitability in the various stages of a contract.

Balance sheet

(a)   **Stocks**

	£
Costs to date	X
Less transfer to profit and loss a/c	(X)
	X
Less foreseeable losses	(X)
	X
Less payments on account in excess of turnover	(X)
WIP	X

(b)   **Debtors**

	£
Cumulative turnover recognised	X
Less payments on account	(X)
Amount recoverable on contracts	X

(c)   **Creditors**. Where payments on account exceed both cumulative turnover and net WIP the excess should be included in creditors under 'payments on account'.

(d)   **Provisions**. To the extent foreseeable future losses exceed WIP, the losses should be provided.

Question 2

The main business of Santolina Ltd is construction contracts. At the end of September 19X3 there are two uncompleted contracts on the books, details of which are as follows.

CONTRACT	A	B
Date commenced	1.9.X3	1.4.X1
Expected completed date	23.12.X3	23.12.X3
	£	£
Final contract price	70,000	290,000
Costs to 30.9.X3	21,000	210,450
Value of work certified to 30.9.X3	20,000	230,000
Progress payments invoiced to 30.9.X3	20,000	210,000
Cash received to 30.9.X3	18,000	194,000
Estimated costs to completion at 30.9.X3	41,000	20,600

Required

Prepare calculations showing the amounts to be included in the balance sheet at 30 September 19X3 in respect of the above contracts.

Answer

Contract A is a short-term contract and will be included in the balance sheet as work in progress at cost less amounts received and receivable £(21,000 − 20,000) ie £1,000.

Contract B is a long-term contract and will be included in the balance sheet at cost plus attributable profit less amounts received and receivable.

The estimated final profit is:

	£
Final contract price	290,000
Less: cost to date	(210,450)
estimated future costs	(20,600)
	58,950

The attributable profit is found as follows.

$$\text{Estimated final profit} \times \frac{\text{Work certified}}{\text{Total contract work}} \times \frac{\text{Cash received}}{\text{Invoiced amounts}}$$

$$£58,950 \times \frac{230,000}{290,000} \times \frac{194,000}{210,000}$$

Attributable profit = £43,191

Long-term contract work in progress

CONTRACT B

	£
Costs to date	210,450
Attributable profit	43,191
Anticipated loss	-
	253,641
Progress payments received and receivable	210,000
	43,641

Profitable and loss-making contracts

2.15 Students sometimes find accounting for long-term contracts quite confusing, particularly where contracts are loss-making. We can look at the differences between profitable and loss-making contracts in more depth.

Profitable contracts

2.16 PROFIT AND LOSS ACCOUNT (EXTRACT)

	£
Turnover	X
Cost of sales	(X)
Attributable profit	X̲

2.17 BALANCE SHEET (EXTRACT)

	£
Current assets	
Stock: long-term contracts	
Costs to date	X
Less P&L a/c cost of sales	(X)
Less excess payments on account	(X)
	X̲
Debtors: amounts recoverable on contracts	£
Sales value of work: turnover	X
Less progress payments invoiced	(X)
	X̲
Debtors: trade debtors	£
Progress payments invoiced less cash received	X̲
Current liabilities	£

Payments on account (when payments received in excess of turnover which cannot be offset against stock balance) — X̲

Loss-making contracts

2.18 PROFIT AND LOSS ACCOUNT (EXTRACT)

	£
Turnover	X
Cost of sales	(X)
	(X)
Provision for loss (balancing figure to give)	(X)
Total foreseeable loss	(X)

2.19 BALANCE SHEET (EXTRACT)

	£
Current assets	
Stock: long-term contracts	
Costs incurred	X
Less cost of sales	(X)
Less provision for loss	(X)
Less negative debtors balance	(X)
Positive/nil balance	X̲
Debtors: amounts recoverable on contracts	£
Sales value of work	X
Less progress payments invoiced	(X)
Positive/nil balance	X̲
Debtors: trade debtors	£
Progress payments invoiced less cash received	X̲

Current liabilities	£
Payments on account	
Negative debtor balance not relieved against stock	X̲
Provision for liabilities and charges	£
Provision for loss not offset against stock balance	X̲

Exam focus point
A question is more likely to be set on long-term contracts than on stock or short term WIP, simply because stock and short term WIP were covered in depth for Paper 1.

2.20 The following comprehensive question should make things clearer.

Question 3

Haggrun plc has two contracts in progress, the details of which are as follows.

	Happy (profitable)	*Grumpy (loss-making)*
	£'000	£'000
Total contract price	300	300
Costs incurred to date	90	150
Estimated costs to completion	135	225
Progress payments invoiced and received	116	116

Required

Show extracts from the profit and loss account and the balance sheet for each contract, assuming they are both:

(a)   40% complete; and
(b)   36% complete.

Answer

(a)   *Happy contract*

    (i)   *40% complete*

        £'000

        Profit and loss account

	£'000
Turnover (40% × 300)	120
Cost of sales (40% × 225)	90
Gross profit	30̲

        Balance sheet

Debtors (120 – 116)	4̲
WIP (90 – 90)	-̲

    (ii)   *36% complete*

        £'000

        Profit and loss account

Turnover (36% × 300)	108
Cost of sales (36% × 225)	81
Gross profit	27̲

        Balance sheet

Debtors (108 – 116 = –8)	-̲
WIP (90 – 81 – 8*) =	1̲

* Set off excess payments on account against WIP.

(b)   *Grumpy contract*

    (i)   *40% complete*

      Working

	£'000	£'000
Total contract price		300
Less: costs to date	150	
estimated costs to completion	225	
		375
Foreseeable loss		(75)

Profit and loss account	£'000
Turnover (40% × 300)	120
Cost of sales (40% × 375)	(150)
	(30)
Provision for future losses (bal fig)	(45)
Gross loss	(75)

Balance sheet	£'000
Debtors (120 – 116)	4
WIP (150 – 150)	-
Provision for future losses	(45)

    (ii)   *36% complete*

	£'000
Profit and loss account	
Turnover (36% × 300)	108
Cost of sales (36% × 375)	(135)
	(27)
Provision for future losses (balancing figure)	(48)
Gross loss	(75)

Balance sheet	
Debtors (108 – 116 = –8)	-
WIP (150 – 135 – 48* = –33)	-
Creditors: payments on account	8
Provisions: provisions for future losses	33

    * Set off provision for losses before excess payments on account.

3   AUDIT IMPLICATIONS   6/94

3.1   **The auditors' work in relation to SSAP 9 will concern stock valuation and disclosure.**

    (a)   The auditors will determine the correct valuation of stock by comparing cost and net realisable value.

    (b)   Cost will be checked by examining purchase invoices, while NRV will be checked by examining sales invoices immediately after the year end.

    (c)   Disclosure in the accounts must be checked, including the accounting policy note.

3.2   **The following audit substantive procedure would be relevant for long term contracts.**

    (a)   Ensure that the **classification** of contracts into long and short-term is in accordance with the revised SSAP 9 and consistently applied.

    (b)   For each material long-term contract summarise:

- **Type** of contract
- Contract **price**
- **Terms** of payment and progress payments
- **Cancellation** terms and penalties
- **Cost increase** provisions
- **Insurance** requirements
- **Equipment and materials** supplied
- **Renegotiation** provisions
- **Retentions**

(c) Obtain/prepare **summary** of contract work in progress, showing costs to date, valuation to date, progress payments applied for and received, costs to complete, contract price (including agreed variations), expected profit margin and so on.

(d) **Verify cost figures** with contract cost records.

(e) **Check basis and calculation of overhead additions**; verify that:

    (i) the calculation is based on actual expenditure (or else close estimates) and on actual levels of activity;

    (ii) the elements of expenses included are appropriate and consistent from year to year.

(f) Check that any **contingencies and allowances** are reasonable.

(g) Check the **basis of allocating** WIP to profit and loss account. Verify that:

    (i) profit is recognised on long-term contracts only where it may be foreseen with reasonable certainty;

    (ii) losses are taken as soon as they are foreseen;

    (iii) the appropriate fraction of WIP is being allocated to profit and loss in each case.

(h) Verify that the **treatment of progress payments** is correct. Check that:

    (i) cumulative payments on account are being compared with cumulative turnover on a contract basis to calculate the amount recoverable;

    (ii) amounts recoverable on long-term contracts are classified as debtors;

    (iii) any excess of payments on account over turnover are correctly treated, in the first place by deduction from any long-term contract balances included in work in progress.

Chapter roundup

- The **Companies Act 1985** requires that the balance sheet should show stocks (CI) sub-divided as follows.

  Stocks
  Raw materials and consumables
  Work in progress
  Finished goods and goods for resale
  Payments on account (of purchases)

- Stocks must be valued at the **lower of cost and net realisable value**.

  - **NRV** is selling price less all costs to completion and less selling costs.

  - **Cost** comprises cost of purchase and costs of conversion. You must learn the definitions of these terms.

  - **FIFO and weighted average costing** are the most widely accepted means of valuing stock in accordance with both CA 1985 and SSAP 9.

- The rules for calculating accounting entries on **long-term contracts** can be summarised as follows.

  - Turnover taken on long-term contracts should be debited to 'Amounts recoverable on contracts' (and credited to the profit and loss account).

  - The amount at which long-term contract work in progress is stated in accounts should be cost, less cost of sales to date, including any foreseeable losses.

  - Progress payments received and receivable should first be credited to 'Amounts recoverable on contracts' and then to any remaining balance on work in progress.

  - Any remaining balance of progress payments should be disclosed within creditors.

- At this stage of your studies the most difficult aspect of SSAP 9 to be mastered is the **valuation and disclosure of long-term contracts**.

- You must be able both to calculate all the balances to be included in accounts and to discuss the reasons for SSAP 9's provisions, along with alternative possibilities.

Quick quiz

1   What categories of stock are identified in the statutory accounts formats of CA 1985? (see para 1.4)

2   What is the general rule of stock valuation? (Knowledge brought forward)

3   Define a long-term contract. (2.1)

4   What are the rules for calculating turnover and profit to be taken on long-term contracts? (2.8)

5   Outline the five steps to be taken when valuing long-term contracts. (2.12)

6   Summarise the accounting treatment of long-term contracts. (2.14)

Question to try	Level	Marks	Time
12	Full exam	30	54 mins

Chapter 12

TAXATION IN COMPANY ACCOUNTS

Chapter topic list	Syllabus reference
1 Corporation tax and advance corporation tax (ACT)	1(c), 2(a)
2 Income tax	1(c), 2(a)
3 Proposed dividends	1(c), 2(a)
4 Surplus ACT	1(c), 2(a)
5 SSAP 5 *Accounting for value added tax*	1(c), 2(a)
6 SSAP 15 *Accounting for deferred tax*	1(c), 2(a)
7 Taxation in company accounts	1(c), 2(a)
8 Disclosure requirements	1(c), 2(a)

Introduction

Students often seem to have problems with taxation in examinations, so you should read and work through this chapter very carefully. There are plenty of exercises here - make sure that you attempt each one yourself without referring to the solution immediately.

Some of the topics discussed in this chapter are more straightforward than others. Accounting for VAT is particularly easy and you should be relatively familiar with the workings of the tax. Do not overlook the SSAP 5 requirements.

In relation to corporation tax and dividends you must be able to calculate the relevant tax figures *and* know how they should be disclosed in the accounts according to SSAP 8.

Deferred taxation is probably the most difficult topic in this chapter. Concentrate on trying to understand the logic behind the tax and the reasons why the SSAP 15 approach has been adopted.

1   CORPORATION TAX AND ADVANCE CORPORATION TAX (ACT) 12/95

1.1   Companies are required to pay **corporation tax** on their taxable profits. The **taxable profits** of a company are essentially its **net profit before dividends, adjusted for certain items where the tax treatment differs from the accounts treatment.**

1.2   The **rate** at which companies are charged to corporation tax **depends on the level of** their **profits**. Companies with small profits currently (1998) pay corporation tax at a rate of 21%; other companies currently pay at a rate of 31%.

1.3   The amount of tax to which a company is assessed on its profit for an accounting period is called its tax liability for that period. Under the current system of pay and file (set to change in 1999), a company must generally pay its tax liability nine months after the end of the relevant accounting period and file accounts and tax computations with the Inland Revenue within one year. However, **if a company pays dividends during an accounting period it may be required to make an advance payment of corporation tax.** The balance of tax due (known as the mainstream liability) would then be payable at the normal time.

1.4   In the past, the amount of any advance payment of corporation tax depended on the level of dividend paid and the prevailing income tax rate. However, the ACT fraction (which is applied to the dividend) is now $^{20}/_{80}$ or $^1/_4$ (rather than $^{23}/_{77}$) in spite of the fact that the income tax basic rate is still 23% (although there is a 20% band).

1.5   SIMPLE EXAMPLE: ACT

Suppose a company in the middle of its accounting period pays out a cash dividend of £8,000 to its shareholders. The company will be required to pay £2,000 ($^1/_4 \times$ £8,000) in ACT to the Inland Revenue. When the tax liability for the period is eventually computed, the company will be given credit for the £2,000 already paid in the period and the mainstream liability will be reduced accordingly.

DEBIT   ACT recoverable
CREDIT   ACT payable

When the dividend is paid

DEBIT   ACT payable
CREDIT   Cash

When ACT is paid

1.6   A shareholder receiving a dividend of, say, £200 cash is deemed by the Inland Revenue to have received a gross dividend of £250 from which income tax of £50 ($^1/_4 \times$ £200) has been deducted. In other words, **the ACT paid by the company is imputed as a tax credit to the shareholder. This feature gives the name imputation system to the UK system of corporation tax.**

1.7   For purposes of collecting ACT, the Inland Revenue establishes four **quarterly return periods**, ending on 31 March, 30 June, 30 September and 31 December. A company whose accounting period does not coincide with any of those dates will have a fifth return period ending on its balance sheet date. **ACT is payable 14 days after the end of the relevant return period.**

1.8   A company A Ltd may own shares in another company B Ltd and receive dividends on those shares. B Ltd will account for ACT due on dividends paid; the proportion of such ACT which relates to A Ltd's share of the dividends may be set off by A Ltd against any ACT due on its own dividends. For example, suppose that A Ltd receives a dividend of £100 from its shares in B Ltd. B Ltd will pay to the Inland Revenue £25 of ACT in respect of the dividend paid to A Ltd. If A Ltd now pays a dividend of £6,000, the ACT of £1,500 ($^1/_4 \times$ £6,000) which would normally be payable is reduced by the £25 tax credit on the dividend received from B Ltd. A Ltd's payment of ACT will therefore be £1,475.

1.9   EXAMPLE: ACT AND MAINSTREAM CORPORATION TAX

Cadis Ltd supplies the following information.

	£
Year to 30 June 19X0	
Dividend received (net) (no dividend paid)	10,000
Year to 30 June 19X1	
Trading profits	100,000
Dividend received (net)	20,000
Dividend paid for the year (net)	35,000

Assuming that the rate of corporation tax is 33% and ACT $^1/_4$, calculate the mainstream corporation tax liability for the year to 30 June 19X1.

1.10	£	£	£
Corporation tax: 33% × £100,000			33,000
ACT payable 1/4 × £35,000		8,750	
Less tax credits on dividends received			
b/f 1/4 × £10,000 =	2,500		
1/4 × £20,000 =	5,000		
		7,500	
			1,250
Mainstream corporation tax liability			31,750

Notice that the profit and loss account charge will be £33,000 and this will not coincide with the final balance sheet liability to tax (£31,750). This is an inevitable feature of the imputation system of taxation.

Terminology

1.11   Dividend payments are made from taxed profits. **Gross dividend payments are called franked payments**. A company which receives a dividend of £300, say, from another company is said to have either:

(a)   **dividend income** (or dividends receivable) of £300; or

(b)   **franked investment income** (FII) of £375 (£300 cash plus the imputed tax credit of $^1/_4$× £300 = £75).

> **Exam focus point**
> The term **franked investment income** therefore **refers to the gross amount of the dividend.**
> If a question refers to dividends actually received, it means the net amount of the dividend
> which must be grossed up if the figure of FII is required. When dividend payments are
> expressed as a percentage (for example 'a 50% final dividend on the ordinary shares'), this
> refers to the cash actually paid.

2   INCOME TAX

2.1   A company pays corporation tax, not income tax. However, **when a company pays certain expenses such as debenture interest, it must deduct income tax at a specified rate and pay this to the Revenue**; the company is thus a collector of taxes. The recipient receives the net income (ie he or she has suffered tax deducted at source). For debenture interest, the income tax rate applied is 20%.

2.2 For example, a company pays debenture interest of £100,000.

		£	£
DEBIT	Profit and loss account	100,000	
CREDIT	Debenture holder		80,000
	Inland revenue control		20,000

2.3 When a company **receives** such interest net of basic rate income tax, it is not liable for the tax that it has paid. If a company received £80,000 in debenture interest, the entry to 'gross up' the interest is would be as follows.

		£	£
DEBIT	Inland Revenue control (£80,000 × 20/80)	20,000	
CREDIT	Interest received		20,000

With the tax credit

2.4 **Gross debenture interest received is treated as taxable profit for corporation tax and gross debenture interest paid is treated as a tax allowable expense**. The company may reclaim the tax 'paid' on debenture interest received in the following order.

(a) Set off income tax suffered against income tax payable to the Revenue.
(b) Set the excess against the year's mainstream corporation tax liability (no limit).
(c) Reclaim a refund from the Revenue.

Exam focus point

The examiner has said that, in an exam question, he would give detailed instructions in the unlikely event any grossing up of this sort was required. If a question involved debenture interest receivable, then the examiner would normally assume that all figures were gross and any tax recoverable had already been offset against tax collected from interest payable.

2.5 The following straightforward question demonstrates both grossing up and offset.

Question 1

Flounders Ltd presents the following information for the year to 31 March 19X1.

	£
Trading profit (equal to taxable trading profit)	700,000
Debenture interest received (gross)	30,000
Debenture interest paid (gross)	20,000
Dividend paid (net)	20,000

Assuming that the rate of corporation tax is 33%, the rate of income tax on debenture interest is 20%, and the ACT fraction $^1/_4$ calculate the mainstream corporation tax liability for the year to 31 March 19X1 and show the ledger accounts recording this information.

Answer

(a)

	£
Trading profit	700,000
Debenture interest received	30,000
	730,000
Debenture interest paid	20,000
Taxable profit	710,000

	£	£
Corporation tax at 33%		234,300
Less: ACT ¼ × £20,000	5,000	
income tax 20% × £(30,000 – 20,000)	2,000	
		7,000
Mainstream corporation tax liability		227,300

(b)

DEBENTURE INTEREST RECEIVED ACCOUNT

	£		£
Profit and loss account	30,000	Bank account	24,000
		Income tax account	6,000
	30,000		30,000

DEBENTURE INTEREST PAID ACCOUNTS

	£		£
Bank account	16,000	Profit and loss account	20,000
Income tax account	4,000		
	20,000		20,000

DIVIDENDS PAID ACCOUNT

	£		£
Bank account	20,000	Profit and loss account	20,000

PROFIT AND LOSS ACCOUNT

	£		£
Debenture interest paid	20,000	Trading profit	700,000
Corporation tax	234,300	Debenture interest received	30,000
Dividends paid	20,000		
Balance c/f	455,700		
	730,000		730,000

INCOME TAX ACCOUNT

	£		£
Debenture interest received account	6,000	Debenture interest paid account	4,000
		Corporation tax	2,000
	6,000		6,000

ACT ACCOUNT

	£		£
Bank	5,000	Corporation tax account	5,000

CORPORATION TAX ACCOUNT

	£		£
ACT account	5,000	Profit and loss account	234,300
Income tax account	2,000		
Balance c/f	227,300		
	234,300		234,300

3   PROPOSED DIVIDENDS

3.1   The **ACT available for set off against corporation tax is that on dividends actually paid during an accounting period.** The **ACT on a proposed dividend will be recovered** (in most cases) **by set off against the corporation tax for the following accounting period** (the one in which the dividend will be paid). Since this corporation tax will not be paid until over a year after the end of the current period, **when a proposed dividend is provided for in the profit and loss account there arises:**

(a)   a **current liability** for the ACT payable in the next financial accounting period (on the proposed dividend actually paid in that period); and

(b)   a **deferred (or long-term) asset** in respect of the ACT recoverable after more than one year.

In other words:

DEBIT   ACT recoverable (>1 year)
CREDIT   ACT payable (< 1 year)

> **IMPORTANT!**
>
> In published accounts questions, the ACT on proposed dividends should be shown both under current liabilities and under current assets.

3.2   **It will be necessary to disclose by note that the amount included under current assets is receivable after more than one year.** No ledger accounting entries are required. (Later in this chapter we will look at deferred taxation; companies with a provision for deferred taxation in their accounts may adopt a different treatment in respect of the deferred ACT asset.)

4   SURPLUS ACT

4.1   **ACT paid is not necessarily recoverable in full against current corporation tax because the maximum set off is 20% of taxable profits** (including capital gains).

4.2   EXAMPLE: SURPLUS ACT

Drayda Ltd has trading income of £118,000, capital gains of £12,000 and pays a dividend of £110,000. Assuming corporation tax at 33% and ACT at $^1/_4$, calculate the mainstream corporation tax liability and show the ACT account.

4.3   SOLUTION

	£	£
(a)		
Corporation tax at 33% on £130,000		42,900
ACT paid 1/4 × £110,000	27,500	
Limited to 20% × £130,000	26,000	26,000
Surplus ACT	1,500	
Mainstream liability		16,900

(b)

	ACT ACCOUNT		
	£		£
Bank	27,500	Corporation tax	26,000
		Balance c/d	1,500
	27,500		27,500

Treatment of surplus ACT

4.4 The surplus ACT (the £1,500 debit balance in the above example) may be treated in several different ways.

(a) It can be **carried forward indefinitely and set against corporation tax on future profits.** This 'deferred asset' is usually debited to the deferred taxation account (see later) but may sometimes be disclosed in the balance sheet (or by note) under the heading of current assets. The logic for setting it against deferred tax is that both items represent tax payable or repayable after more than one year but whose recovery/payment dates are not fixed but depend on future events.

(b) It can be **carried back and set against the corporation tax liability of the preceding six years** (subject to the limitation described above). For balance sheet purposes this amount may be deducted from the corporation tax payable in respect of previous years, or, if such liabilities have been paid at balance sheet date, included in current assets.

(c) It **must**, however, **be written off** (as part of the tax charge) **if its recovery is uncertain** (this is the only time ACT appears in the profit and loss account). ACT is normally treated as irrecoverable unless it appears that it will be recovered in the next accounting period. An explanation should be included in the note detailing the total taxation charge. ACT on proposed dividends will also be deemed irrecoverable and should be written off.

> **Exam focus point**
> ACT will be abolished with effect from 1 July 1999. Special arrangements (shadow ACT) will come into force to ensure that companies carrying forward surplus ACT will not lose out. Although these new rules are beyond the scope of your syllabus, there is never any harm in letting the examiner know (briefly) that your knowledge is up-to-date.

5 SSAP 5 ACCOUNTING FOR VALUE ADDED TAX

5.1 **VAT is a tax on the supply of goods and services.** The tax authority responsible for collecting VAT is HM Customs & Excise. **Tax is collected at each transfer point in the chain from prime producer to final consumer.** Eventually, the consumer bears the tax in full and any tax paid earlier in the chain can be recovered by the trader who paid it.

5.2 EXAMPLE: VAT

A manufacturing company, A Ltd, purchases raw materials at a cost of £1,000 plus VAT at 17½%. From the raw materials A Ltd makes finished products which it sells to a retail outlet, B Ltd, for £1,600 plus VAT. B Ltd sells the products to customers at a total price of £2,000 plus VAT. How much VAT is paid to Customs & Excise at each stage in the chain?

5.3   SOLUTION

	Value of goods sold £	VAT at 17½% £
Supplier of raw materials	1,000	175
Value added by A Ltd	600	105
Sale to B Ltd	1,600	280
Value added by B Ltd	400	70
Sales to 'consumers'	2,000	350

How is VAT collected?

5.4   Although it is the final consumer who eventually bears the full tax of £350, the sum is **collected and paid over to Customs & Excise by the traders who make up the chain.** Each trader must assume that his customer is the final consumer and must collect and pay over VAT at the appropriate rate on the full sales value of the goods sold. He is entitled to reclaim VAT paid on his own purchases (inputs) and so makes a net payment to Customs & Excise equal to the tax on value added by himself.

5.5   In the example above, the supplier of raw materials collects from A Ltd VAT of £175, all of which he pays over to Customs & Excise. When A Ltd sells goods to B Ltd VAT is charged at the rate of 17½% on £1,600 = £280. Only £105, however, is paid by A Ltd to Customs & Excise because the company is entitled to deduct VAT of £175 suffered on its own purchases. Similarly, B Ltd must charge its customers £350 in VAT but need only pay over the net amount of £70 after deducting the £280 VAT suffered on its purchase from A Ltd.

Registered and non-registered persons

5.6   **Traders whose sales (outputs) are below a certain minimum need not register for VAT.** Such traders neither charge VAT on their outputs nor are entitled to reclaim VAT on their inputs. They are in the same position as a final consumer.

5.7   **All outputs of registered traders are either taxable or exempt.** Traders carrying on exempt activities (such as banks) cannot charge VAT on their outputs and consequently cannot reclaim VAT paid on their inputs.

5.8   Taxable outputs are chargeable at one of **two rates:**

(a)   **zero per cent (zero-rated items);**
(b)   **17½% (standard-rated items).**

Customs & Excise publish lists of supplies falling into each category. **Persons carrying on taxable activities** (even activities taxable at zero per cent) **are entitled to reclaim VAT paid on their inputs.**

5.9   Some traders carry on a **mixture of taxable and exempt activities.** Such traders need to apportion the VAT suffered on inputs and **can only reclaim the proportion relating to taxable outputs.**

Accounting for VAT

5.10   As a general principle the treatment of VAT in the accounts of a trader should reflect his role as a collector of the tax and **VAT should not be included in income or in expenditure whether of a capital or of a revenue nature.**

Irrecoverable VAT

5.11   Where the **trader bears the VAT** himself, as in the following cases, this should be reflected in the accounts.

(a)   **Persons not registered** for VAT will suffer VAT on inputs. This will effectively increase the cost of their consumable materials and their fixed assets and must be so reflected, ie shown **inclusive of VAT.**

(b)   **Registered persons** who also carry on **exempted** activities will have a residue of VAT which falls directly on them. In this situation the costs to which this residue applies will be inflated by the **irrecoverable VAT**.

(c)   **Non-deductible inputs will be borne** by all traders (examples are tax on cars bought which are not for resale, entertaining expenses and provision of domestic accommodation for a company's directors).

> **Exam focus point**
> Where VAT is not recoverable it must be regarded as an inherent part of the cost of the items purchased and included in the P&L charge or balance sheet as appropriate.

Further points

5.12   **VAT is charged on the price net of any discount** and this general principle is carried to the extent that where a cash discount is offered, VAT is charged on the net amount **even where the discount is not taken up.**

5.13   Most VAT registered persons are obliged to record VAT when a supply is received or made (effectively when a credit sales invoice is raised or a purchase invoice recorded). This has the effect that **the net VAT liability has on occasion to be paid to Customs & Excise before all output tax has been paid by customers**. If a debt is subsequently written off, the VAT element may not be recovered from Customs & Excise for six months from the date of sale, even if the customer becomes insolvent.

5.14   **Some small businesses can join the cash accounting scheme whereby VAT is only paid to Customs & Excise after it is received from customers**. This delays recovery of input tax but improves cash flow overall, although it may involve extra record keeping. Bad debt relief is automatic under this scheme since if VAT is not paid by the customer it is not due to Customs & Excise.

Question 2

Mussel Ltd is preparing accounts for the year ended 31 May 19X9. Included in its balance sheet as at 31 May 19X8 was a balance for VAT recoverable of £15,000.

Its summary profit and loss account for the year is as follows.

	£'000
Sales (all standard rated)	500
Purchases (all standard rated)	120
Gross profit	380
Expenses	280
Operating profit	100
Interest receivable	20
Profit before tax	120

Note: expenses	£000
Wages and salaries	200
Entertainment expenditure	10
Other (all standard rated)	70
	280

Payments of £5,000, £15,000 and £20,000 have been made in the year and a repayment of £12,000 was received. What is the balance for VAT in the balance sheet as at 31 May 19X9? Assume a 17.5% standard rate of VAT.

Answer

MUSSEL LIMITED: VAT ACCOUNT

	£		£
Balance b/d	15,000	Sales (£500,000 × 17.5%)	87,500
Purchases (£120,000 × 17.5%)	21,000	Bank	12,000
Expenses (£70,000 × 17.5%)	12,250		
Bank	40,000		
Balance c/d	11,250		
	99,500		99,500

Requirements of SSAP 5

5.15 SSAP 5 requires the following accounting rules to be followed.

(a) **Turnover** shown in the profit and loss account should **exclude VAT** on taxable outputs. If gross turnover must be shown then the VAT in that figure must also be shown as a deduction in arriving at the turnover exclusive of VAT.

(b) **Irrecoverable VAT** allocated to fixed assets and other items separately disclosed should be **included in their cost** where material and practical.

(c) The **net amount due to (or from) Customs & Excise** should be **included in the total for creditors** (or **debtors**), and need not be separately disclosed.

5.16 Note that the CA 1985 also requires disclosure of the cost of sales figure in the published accounts. This amount should exclude VAT on taxable inputs.

6   SSAP 15 ACCOUNTING FOR DEFERRED TAX   12/95

6.1 This section may seem quite complicated. Do not worry about the numbers too much, but remember that you must be able to **explain** the purpose of the deferred tax balance.

6.2 Accounting profits form the basis for computing **taxable profits,** on which the corporation tax liability for the year is calculated; however **accounting profits and taxable profits are different.** There are **two reasons for the differences.**

(a) **Permanent differences.** These occur when certain items of revenue or expense are excluded from the computation of taxable profits (for example, entertainment expenses are not normally allowable for tax purposes).

(b) **Originating timing differences**. These occur when items of revenue or expense are included in both accounting profits and taxable profits, but not for the same accounting period. For example, an expense which is allowable as a deduction in arriving at taxable profits for 19X7 might not be included in the financial accounts until 19X8 or later. In the long run, the total taxable profits and total accounting profits will be the same (except for permanent differences) so that:

> 'timing differences originate in one period and are capable of reversal in one or more subsequent periods.'

6.3 **Deferred tax is the tax attributable to timing differences. Deferred tax applies the matching concept to taxation, in an attempt to produce less distorted results.** Income recorded in a period is matched with the related tax charge, even though that income may be taxed in a different period, ie deferred tax provides for future tax liabilities.

6.4 **SSAP 15 identifies the main categories in which timing differences can occur.**

(a) **Short-term timing differences**. These arise because taxable profits are calculated on a receipts and payments basis, whereas accounting profits are calculated on an accruals basis. **Examples** of short-term timing differences **include**:

(i) **Deferred development expenditure** is chargeable to the accounting profits of future years, but is allowable for tax purposes in the year in which it is incurred.

(ii) **General provisions for bad debts** in the financial accounts are not allowable for tax purposes until they crystallise into specific bad debts.

Short-term timing differences are usually reversed in the next accounting period.

(b) **Accelerated capital allowances**. When new assets are purchased, capital allowances may be available against taxable profits which exceed the amount of depreciation chargeable on the assets in the financial accounts for the year of purchase. In the past, companies have been allowed to claim capital allowances of up to 100% in the year of acquiring an asset. Capital allowances are nowadays awarded much less generously and this will no longer be such a major source of timing differences. However, for the sake of simplicity, a first year allowance of 100% is assumed in the example given below.

(c) **Revaluation surpluses** on fixed assets for which a taxation charge does not arise until the fixed assets are eventually realised. (Note that the deferred tax associated with such surpluses can now be taken to the revaluation reserve, according to a recent CA 1985 amendment.)

(d) **Surpluses on disposals** of fixed assets which are subject to rollover relief.

Accelerated capital allowances

6.5 An example of accelerated capital allowances will be used to explain the concept of deferred taxation. Suppose that a company began trading on 1 January 19X4. It purchased a fixed asset on that date at a cost of £150,000. A 100% first year capital allowance was available on the asset, which has an estimated life of 3 years and a nil residual value. Straight line depreciation is used in the financial accounts. The profits of the company for each of the subsequent 3 years were £200,000 before depreciation and taxation. Corporation tax was 30% of taxable profits in each year.

6.6 The profits for each year might be calculated as follows.

		Year to 31 December		
	19X4	*19X5*	*19X6*	*Total*
	£	£	£	£
Profit before depreciation	200,000	200,000	200,000	600,000
Depreciation	50,000	50,000	50,000	150,000
Profit before tax	150,000	150,000	150,000	450,000
Taxation (30%)				135,000
30% of £(200,000 – 150,000)	15,000			
30% of £200,000		60,000	60,000	
Profit after tax	135,000	90,000	90,000	315,000

6.7 The profit after tax in each year is based in this example on the **'taxes payable'
principle; the tax charged against the accounting profits is the estimated tax payable
on the profits for the year.** This method suffers from the important drawback, which
should be apparent from the example, that because capital allowances are claimed all at
once, the profit in the first year is much higher than the profit in either of the
subsequent years. It is argued that such a method of reporting would give a misleadingly
'uneven' view of profitability.

6.8 Indeed, if it is accepted that taxation on income is an expense, the accruals concept
requires that taxes should be matched against the revenue and expenditure to which they
are related. In our example, the accruals concept would suggest that the taxation relief
should be spread over the life of the asset.

	19X4	*19X5*	*19X6*
	£	£	£
Capital allowance	150,000		
Depreciation	50,000	50,000	50,000
Timing difference	* 100,000	** (50,000)	** (50,000)

* This is an **originating** timing difference
** These are known as **reversing** timing differences.

6.9 As stated above, deferred taxation is the taxation charge on the *originating* timing
differences.

(a) If the capital allowance in the year **exceeds** the amount of depreciation on the asset
(as in 19X4) the tax charge on the originating timing difference should be:

(i) Debited against profit.
(ii) Credited to a deferred taxation account.

(b) If the capital allowance is **less** than the depreciation charge, an appropriate reverse
entry should be made:

(i) Debit the deferred taxation account.
(ii) Credit the profit and loss account.

	19X4	*19X5*	*19X6*
	£	£	£
Profit before tax	150,000	150,000	150,000
Corporation tax payable	15,000	60,000	60,000
	135,000	90,000	90,000
Transfer to deferred tax a/c (30% of £100,000)	(30,000)		
Transfer from deferred tax a/c (30% of £50,000)		15,000	15,000
Profit after tax	105,000	105,000	105,000

The reported profit in each year is the same, which in the circumstances of our example,
gives a more satisfactory figure for the annual profit after tax.

Basis of provision

6.10   **A comprehensive tax allocation system** would be one in which **deferred taxation is computed for every instance of timing differences**. For various reasons a comprehensive system of accounting for deferred tax was rejected in favour of a selective system in SSAP 15.

6.11   At the opposite pole to comprehensive allocation is the **nil provision** or **flow-through approach**. This is based on the principle that only the tax payable in respect of a period should be charged in that period. **No provision for deferred tax would** therefore **be made**.

6.12   **SSAP 15 rejects both these approaches** because of what it calls a crucial disadvantage.

> 'They can lead to a purely arithmetical approach, in which certainty of calculation is given precedence over a reasoned assessment of what the tax effects of transactions will actually be.'

6.13   **The standard therefore prescribes a middle course, called partial provision**, which will be described shortly. In addition, the standard **requires the use of the liability method**, ie use of the rate of tax ruling in the year in which the deferred tax is credited.

Advance corporation tax (ACT) and the deferred tax account

6.14   One other point about the deferred tax account concerns ACT payable on dividends. In the UK, when a company pays a dividend to shareholders, it must also pay ACT to the government. For example, if a company pays a dividend of £100,000 and the rate of ACT is $^{20}/_{80}$, £25,000 will become payable at once to the government. When the company eventually pays its 'mainstream' corporation tax on profits for the year, the ACT will usually be 'recoverable', ie it will be deducted from the 'mainstream' tax payment.

6.15   A timing difference can occur whereby the ACT payable cannot be recovered out of the corporation tax liability of the current year, but instead must be carried forward and recovered out of the corporation tax liability of the next year. Subject to certain limitations, the **recoverable ACT can be set off against the (credit) balance on the deferred tax account** (SSAP 8 makes this point although it is also referred to in SSAP 15).

(a)   Thus, if a dividend of £100,000 is payable and there is an ACT liability of £25,000 which will be recoverable out of the tax liability for the following year, the accounting entries would be:

CREDIT	ACT payable	£25,000
DEBIT	Deferred tax account	£25,000

(b)   When the ACT is paid to the government:

DEBIT	ACT payable	£25,000
CREDIT	Cash	£25,000

(c)   When the ACT is eventually recovered out of the corporation tax liability for the next year:

CREDIT	Deferred tax account	£25,000
DEBIT	Corporation tax account	£25,000

Provisions of SSAP 15

6.16   **The statement of the partial provision method is contained in the standard.**

IMPORTANT!

'Tax deferred or accelerated by the effect of timing differences should be accounted for to the extent that it is possible that a liability or asset will crystallise. Tax deferred or accelerated by the effect of timing differences should not be accounted for to the extent that it is probable that a liability or asset will not crystallise.': SSAP 15

6.17 **The probability that a liability or asset will crystallise should be assessed by the directors on the basis of reasonable assumptions**. They should take into account all relevant information available up to the date on which they approve the financial statements, and also their intentions for the future. Ideally, financial projections of future plans should be made for a number (undefined) of years ahead. The directors' judgement should be exercised with prudence.

6.18 All categories of timing differences should be considered together and the balance carried forward on the deferred tax account should represent their anticipated net tax effect. If the balance on the deferred tax account is a liability, it may be appropriate to offset against it any ACT recoverable out of the corporation tax liability on the income of future periods.

6.19 For example, any ACT payable on dividends proposed but unpaid by the balance sheet date will not be recoverable against the current year's tax liability, but may be recoverable against a corporation tax liability expected to arise in the following year. Such ACT would appear in the balance sheet as a current liability and as a debit in the deferred tax account, if any.

6.20 **Debit balances on the deferred tax account should *not* normally be carried forward as assets.**

Exam focus point

So far questions on deferred tax for Paper 10 have been fairly straightforward. It has been tested as part of a larger question rather than a question in its own right.

Audit problems associated with SSAP 15

6.21 **Deferred taxation is a difficult area for the auditors.** In particular, in the case of partial provision, the auditors must determine whether management's forecasts for the relevant period of assessment are reasonable and support the partial provision. The forecasts that the auditors may be concerned with include profit and cash flow, capital expenditure and disposals, and depreciation charges on allowable capital expenditure.

6.22 The following **procedures** are suggested.

(a) **Obtain or prepare analysis of movements** in the nominal ledger tax accounts, **current and deferred, for the period:** and

　　(i)　Test for mathematical accuracy.

　　(ii)　Compare amounts paid during the current period to copies of assessments and cash book.

　　(iii)　Compare refunds received to correspondence with the Inland Revenue.

(b) **Verify, or prepare, the computation of the corporation tax charge:**

    (i)   Verify calculations of non-allowable expenses, and other adjustments.

    (ii)   Verify fixed asset additions and disposals with fixed asset movements schedule and check calculation of capital allowances.

(c) **Identify timing differences** at year-end.

(d) **Check provision** for deferred tax is made at the corporation tax rate at the year end on all timing differences less losses and ACT, except to the extent that it is probable that a liability will not crystallise.

(e) **Assess the justification for non-provision** of part (or all) of the taxation deferred, by references to forecasts and projections for a sufficient period of years in the circumstances, in respect of cashflow, capital expenditure and disposals.

    (i)   Consider the reliability of forecasts made in previous years.

    (ii)   Consider the likelihood of management bias in forecasting.

    (iii)   Test the reasonableness of forecasts in the light of economic forecasts, industry trends, company trends.

    (iv)   Perform sensitivity analysis on forecasts if there are doubts about reliability in order to establish materiality of possible misstatements.

    (v)   Test check calculations and the resulting amount of tax provided and unprovided.

(f) (i)   **Check that deferred tax on asset revaluations above cost is provided where disposal is intended** (and rollover relief is not available) out of the revaluation surplus.

    (ii)   If asset revaluation is not incorporated in the accounts, **check that the note** (or directors' report) **indicates the tax effect** (if any) **which would arise** if the asset were realised at the stated value.

(g) **Confirm** that the amount of any **unprovided deferred tax** in respect of the period is **disclosed in the notes,** analysed into its main components.

(h) **Prepare a reconciliation of the tax charge in the profit and loss account** (this is an overall check that accounts profits have been brought into tax, whether current or deferred).

(i) **Check that profit and loss, balance sheet and notes classification and disclosure of taxation is fairly presented.**

7   TAXATION IN COMPANY ACCOUNTS

7.1   We have now looked at the 'ingredients' of taxation in company accounts. There are two aspects to be learned:

(a) Taxation on profits in the profit and loss account.
(b) Taxation payments due, shown as a liability in the balance sheet.

Taxation in the profit and loss account

7.2   The tax on profit on ordinary activities is calculated by **aggregating**:

(a) **corporation tax** on taxable profits;

(b) **tax credits on dividends received** as franked investment income;

(c) **transfers to or from deferred taxation**;

(d) any **under provision or overprovision** of corporation tax on profits of previous years;

(e) any **surplus ACT written off** (see earlier section).

7.3 Corporation tax and deferred tax have already been explained but the treatment of franked investment income is rather unusual and should be noted carefully. When a company receives a dividend from another company, its cash income is the net dividend on the shares it holds. **In the profit and loss account**, however:

(a) the **income from investments must be shown as the gross dividend** (net dividend plus tax credit); and

(b) **taxation on profits will include** the **tax credit on the dividends received.**

7.4 The result of including the gross dividend as income and the tax credit as part of the tax charge will be that the net income is the net dividend received. (*Note.* The company receiving the dividend does not pay corporation tax on this income because corporation tax has already been charged once on the profits of the company which pays the dividend.)

7.5 When corporation tax on profits is calculated for the profit and loss account, **the calculation is only an estimate of what the company thinks its tax liability will be. In subsequent dealings with the Inland Revenue, a different corporation tax charge might eventually be agreed.**

7.6 The difference between the estimated tax on profits for one year and the actual tax charge finally agreed for the year is made as an adjustment to taxation on profits in the following year, **resulting in the disclosure of either an underprovision or an overprovision of tax.**

Question 3

In the accounting year to 31 December 19X3, Ben Nevis Ltd made an operating profit before investment income and taxation of £110,000. Income from dividends was £15,000 (that is, without the associated tax credit).

Corporation tax on the operating profit has been estimated as £45,000.

In the previous year (19X2) corporation tax on 19X2 profits had been estimated as £38,000 but it was subsequently agreed at £40,500 with the Inland Revenue.

A transfer to the deferred taxation account of £16,000 will be made in 19X3.

An interim dividend of £20,000 was paid in June 19X3 and a final dividend of £30,000 is proposed.

Advance corporation tax is $^1/_4$ of net dividend.

Required

(a) Calculate the tax on profits for 19X3 for disclosure in the accounts.

(b) Calculate the amount of ACT paid in the accounting period and the amount of mainstream corporation tax payable on 30 September 19X4.

Answer

(a)

	£
Corporation tax on profits	45,000
Tax credit attributable to dividends received (¼ × £15,000)	3,750
Deferred taxation	16,000
Underprovision of tax in previous year £(40,500 – 38,000)	2,500
Tax on profits for 19X3	67,250

(b)   £

ACT on the interim dividend (¼ of £20,000)	5,000
Less tax credit on dividends received (see (a))	3,750
ACT paid in the accounting period	1,250
Tax payable on 19X3 profits	45,000
Less ACT paid	1,250
Mainstream corporation tax liability	43,750

Remember that ACT payable on proposed dividends can not be offset against the current year's tax liability.

Taxation in the balance sheet

7.7 It should already be apparent from the previous examples that the corporation tax charge in the profit and loss account will not be the same as corporation tax liabilities in the balance sheet.

7.8 In the balance sheet, there are several items which we might expect to find.

(a) **Income tax may be payable** in respect of (say) interest payments paid in the last accounting return period of the year, or accrued.

(b) If a dividend is proposed, then there should be a **liability for ACT**. Until the dividend is paid, ACT will not be paid and it remains a current liability until then.

(c) If no corporation tax is payable (or very little), then there might be an **income tax recoverable asset** disclosed in current assets (income tax is normally recovered by offset against the tax liability for the year).

(d) There will usually be a **liability for mainstream corporation tax**, possibly including the amounts due in respect of previous years but not yet paid.

(e) We may also find a **liability on the deferred taxation account**. Deferred taxation is shown under 'provisions for liabilities and charges' in the balance sheet.

(f) **Deferred taxation might be reduced by the amount of any surplus ACT**. If there is no deferred tax balance, then surplus ACT thought to be recoverable will be shown as a deferred asset.

7.9 For example, suppose that Eiger Ltd has a credit balance of £80,000 on its deferred taxation account. The company proposes a final dividend of £40,000 on which ACT of £10,000 will be payable. Corporation tax on profits for the next year is forecast as £50,000. In the company's balance sheet:

(a) there will be a current tax liability of £10,000 for ACT; but
(b) the deferred tax account will be reduced by £10,000 to £70,000.

7.10 When the dividend is paid the ACT will be paid.

(a) The deferred taxation account will then be *increased* by the amount of ACT. In our example the deferred taxation account will be restored to £80,000.

(b) The liability for mainstream corporation tax will be *reduced* by the ACT paid. In our example, the corporation tax liability will be reduced by £10,000 to £40,000. (This reduction is only made, however, when the ACT has been paid. Until then, ACT payable is a deduction from deferred taxation, not from mainstream corporation tax.)

Question 4

For the year ended 31 July 19X4 Matterhorn Ltd made taxable trading profits of £1,200,000 on which corporation tax is payable at 33%.

(a) In January 19X4 the company paid an interim dividend of £25,000. In the same month, it received a net dividend of £5,000 on some shares it holds in Mont Blanc Ltd.

(b) A final dividend of £30,000 has been proposed.

(c) A transfer of £20,000 will be made to the deferred taxation account. The balance on this account was £100,000 before making any adjustments for items listed in this paragraph.

(d) The estimated tax on profits for the year ended 31 July 19X3 was £80,000, but tax has now been agreed with the Inland Revenue at £84,000 and fully paid.

(e) Mainstream corporation tax on profits for the year to 31 July 19X4 is payable on 1 May 19X5.

(f) In the year to 31 July 19X4 the company made a capital gain of £60,000 on the sale of some property. This gain is taxable at a rate of 33%.

Required

(a) Calculate the tax charge for the year to 31 July 19X4.
(b) Calculate the tax liabilities in the balance sheet of Matterhorn as at 31 July 19X4.

Note. ACT should be taken as ¼ of net dividend.

Answer

(a)   *Tax charge for the year*

		£
(i)	Tax on trading profits (33% of £1,200,000)	396,000
	Tax on capital gain	19,800
	Tax credit associated with dividends received (¼ of £5,000)	1,250
	Deferred taxation	20,000
		437,050
	Underprovision of taxation in previous years £(84,000 − 80,000)	4,000
	Tax charge on ordinary activities	441,050

(ii)   *Note.* The profit and loss account will show the following.

	£	£
Operating profit (assumed here to be the same as taxable profits)		1,200,000
Profit from sale of asset (exceptional)		60,000
Income from investments (100/80 × £5,000)		6,250
Profit on ordinary activities before taxation		1,266,250
Tax on profit on ordinary activities		441,050
Profit on ordinary activities after taxation		825,200
Dividends: interim paid	25,000	
final proposed	30,000	
		55,000
Retained profits for the year		770,200

(b)   *Taxation in the balance sheet*

	£
ACT already paid in the year	
ACT on interim dividend (¼ × £25,000)	6,250
Less tax credit on dividends received (¼ × £5,000)	(1,250)
ACT paid	5,000
ACT payable on the (final) proposed dividend is (¼ × £30,000)	7,500

This is both a current liability and a deduction from deferred taxation.

	£
Deferred taxation	
Balance brought forward	100,000
Transferred from profit and loss account	20,000
	120,000
Less ACT payable on proposed dividend	(7,500)
Deferred taxation in the balance sheet	112,500

The mainstream corporation tax liability is as follows.

Payable on 1 May 19X5	£
Tax on ordinary profits (33% of £1,200,000)	396,000
Tax on capital gain (33% of £60,000)	19,800
	415,800
Less ACT already paid on profits of current year	
(interim dividend)	(5,000)
Due on 1 May 19X5	410,800

Summary	£
Creditors: amounts falling due within one year	
ACT on proposed dividend	7,500
Mainstream corporation tax, payable on 1 May 19X5	410,800
	418,300
Provisions for liabilities and charges	
Deferred taxation	112,500

Note. It may be helpful to show the journal entries for these items.

			£	£
(a)	DEBIT	Tax charge (profit and loss account)	441,050	
	CREDIT	Corporation tax creditor		*419,800
		Investment income		1,250
		Deferred tax		20,000

* This account will show a debit balance of £4,000 until the underprovision is recorded, since payment has already been made: (396,000 + 19,800 + 4,000).

				£	£
(b)	(i)	DEBIT	Bank	5,000	
		CREDIT	Investment income		5,000
		DEBIT	ACT recoverable	5,000	
		CREDIT	Bank		5,000

These entries are made during the year.

				£	£
	(ii)	DEBIT Corporation tax creditor		5,000	
		CREDIT	ACT recoverable		5,000
		DEBIT	ACT recoverable (to be netted off against deferred tax in the balance sheet)	7,500	
		CREDIT	ACT payable		7,500

These entries are made at the year end.

8   DISCLOSURE REQUIREMENTS

8.1   The CA 1985 requires that the 'tax on profit or loss on ordinary activities' is disclosed on the face of the profit and loss account or in a note to the accounts. In addition, the notes to the profit and loss account must state:

(a)   the basis on which the charge for UK corporation tax and UK income tax is computed; and

(b)   the amounts of the charge for:

(i)   UK corporation tax (showing separately the amount, if greater, of UK corporation tax before any double taxation relief);

    (ii) UK income tax;

    (iii) non-UK taxation on profits, income and capital gains.

  (*Note.* The same details must be given, if relevant, in respect of the 'tax on extraordinary profit or loss'.)

SSAP 8

8.2 SSAP 8 *The treatment of taxation under the imputation system in the accounts of companies* supplements and extends these provisions requiring that a company's *profit and loss account* should disclose separately (if material):

 (a) the **amount of the UK corporation** tax specifying:

    (i) the **charge for corporation tax** on the income of the year (stating the rate used to make the provision);

    (ii) **transfers** to or from the **deferred taxation** account;

    (iii) tax **attributable to franked investment** income (tax credit on dividends received);

    (iv) **irrecoverable ACT**;

    (v) the **relief for overseas taxation**;

 (b) the **total overseas taxation** relieved and unrelieved.

8.3 SSAP 8 also requires that in respect of the **profit and loss account**:

 (a) **dividends paid (and proposed)** should be included as an appropriation at the actual amount of cash paid (the dividend **excluding the tax credit**);

 (b) **dividends received** should be included at the amount of **cash received plus the related tax credit**;

 (c) **taxed receipts and payments** should be included at the **gross amounts** (including the income tax deducted at source).

SSAP 15

8.4 SSAP 15 requires that **deferred** tax relating to the ordinary activities of the enterprise should be **shown separately** as a part of the tax on profit or loss on ordinary activities, either on the face of the profit and loss account, or by note.

8.5 The amount of any **unprovided deferred tax** in respect of the period and the total amount of any unprovided deferred tax, **should be disclosed by note,** analysed into its major components.

8.6 **Adjustments** to deferred tax arising from changes in tax rates and tax allowances should normally be **disclosed separately** as part of the tax charge for the period.

8.7 The **deferred tax balance,** and its major components, should be **disclosed in the balance sheet or notes**. Transfers to and from deferred tax should be disclosed in a note.

8.8 Where amounts of deferred tax arise which relate to **movements on reserves** (for example resulting from the expected disposal of revalued assets) the **amounts transferred to or from deferred tax should be shown separately** as part of such movements.

CA 1985

8.9 Finally, the **Companies Act 1985 requires certain disclosures in respect of deferred tax.**

(a) Deferred tax should be shown **in the balance sheet under the heading 'provisions for liabilities and charges'** and in the category of provision for 'taxation, including deferred taxation'. The amount of any provision for taxation other than deferred taxation must be disclosed. The provision for taxation is different from tax liabilities which are shown as creditors in the balance sheet.

(b) **Movements on reserves and provisions** must be disclosed, including provisions for deferred tax:

    (i) the amount of the provision at the beginning of the year and the end of the year;

    (ii) the amounts transferred to or from the provision during the year;

    (iii) the source/application of any amount so transferred.

(c) Information must be disclosed about any **contingent liability** not provided for in the accounts **(such as deferred tax not provided for) and its legal nature**. It is understood that deferred tax not provided for is a contingent liability within the terms of the Act.

(d) The **basis on which the charge for UK tax is computed** has to be stated. Particulars are required of any special circumstances affecting the tax liability for the financial year or succeeding financial years.

Chapter roundup

- The **SSAP 8 disclosure requirements** relating to company taxation are very **detailed** and **must be learned**. The best way is to practise on past exam questions.

- You must, however, be able to discuss the **reasons** for recording dividends payable net of ACT and dividends receivable gross; the possible treatments of ACT recoverable in the accounts and the treatment of unfranked receipts and payments and income tax balances.

- **SSAP 15** lays down complex provisions on calculating **deferred** tax.

    ○ It is essential that you can **explain** the **deferred tax balance** and account for transfers to and from it.

    ○ It is unlikely that complicated numerical questions will be set in the exam so concentrate on **understanding** deferred tax.

- You must also be able to prepare the **notes to the accounts** on tax for publication. This means mastering the disclosure requirements of SSAP 8, SSAP 15 and the CA 1985.

- Finally, do not forget to revise the provisions of **SSAP 5** on accounting for **VAT**.

Quick quiz

1   What is the current general rule for the due date of payment of corporation tax? (see para 1.3)

2   What is a franked payment? (1.11)

3   In what ways may a company recover the income tax suffered on taxed receipts? (2.4)

4   How should the ACT payable on a proposed dividend be disclosed in the balance sheet? (3.1)

5   How is the maximum set-off of ACT calculated? (4.1)

6   What are the possible accounting treatments of surplus ACT? (4.4)

7   What is the SSAP 5 requirement relating to the disclosure of turnover in company accounts? (5.15)

8   Distinguish between permanent differences and timing differences in relation to deferred taxation. (6.2) List the four main categories of timing differences. (6.4)

9   What are the components of the profit and loss figure for 'tax on profit on ordinary activities'? (7.2)

10 How is franked investment income disclosed in the profit and loss account? (7.3)

11 What are the disclosure requirements of the Companies Act 1985 in relation to taxation? (8.1, 8.9)

12 What are the disclosure requirements of SSAP 8? (8.2, 8.3)

Question to try	Level	Marks	Time
13	Full exam	20	36 mins

Chapter 13

EARNINGS PER SHARE AND REPORTING FINANCIAL PERFORMANCE

Chapter topic list	Syllabus reference
1 Earnings per share (EPS)	1(c), 2(a)
2 FRS 3 *Reporting financial performance*	1(c), 2(a)
3 Substance over form	1(c), 2(a)
4 Off balance sheet finance	1(c), 2(a)

Introduction

Section 1 of this chapter involves the description of EPS, the mechanics of its calculation and the disclosure required by SSAP 3. EPS is an important indicator of a company's performance.

FRS 3 *Reporting financial performance* introduced radical changes to the format of the profit and loss account and the associated notes to the accounts. Of major importance are the definitions of extraordinary and exceptional items and prior year adjustments. You may be asked to produce a statement of total recognised gains and losses.

Remember that you will appreciate the contents of this chapter far more if you obtain and examine some company reports (those of *public companies* are required in this case).

1   EARNINGS PER SHARE (EPS)   6/95, 6/97

1.1   **Earnings per share** (EPS) is widely used by investors as a measure of a company's performance and **is of particular importance in:**

     (a)   **comparing the results** of a company **over a period of time;**

     (b)   **comparing the performance** of one company's equity shares **against** the performance of **another company's equity,** and also against the returns obtainable from loan stock and other forms of investment.

Exam focus point

The purpose of any earnings yardstick is to achieve as far as possible clarity of meaning, comparability between one company and another, one year and another, and attributability of profits to the equity shares. SSAP 3 *Earnings per share* (as amended by FRS 3 *Reporting financial performance*) goes some way to ensuring that all these aims are achieved.

1.2   SSAP 3 (as amended by FRS 3) defines earnings per share as follows.

> **KEY TERM**
>
> **Earnings per share** is 'the profit in pence attributable to each equity share, based on the (consolidated) profit of the period after tax, minority interests, extraordinary items and preference dividends, divided by the number of equity shares in issue (and ranking for dividend in respect of the period).'

1.3   It is worthwhile to note that:

(a)   **The extent to which earnings are distributed to shareholders** (ie any **dividend** on ordinary shares) **is irrelevant.**

(b)   The **EPS for the previous accounting period must also be calculated and shown.**

(c)   **FRS 3 amended the old definition of earnings which excluded extraordinary items.**

1.4   The effect of a company's capital structure can best be appreciated by trying the following exercise.

Question 1

Flame plc a company with a called up and paid up capital of 100,000 ordinary shares of £1 each, manufactures gas appliances. During its financial year to 31 December the company had to pay £50,000 compensation and costs arising from an uninsured claim for personal injuries suffered by a customer while on the company premises. Sharkies plc, a trading company with a called and paid up capital of £160,000 comprising ordinary shares of 50p each; and 20,000 10% preference shares of £1 each, suffered a bad debt of £50,000 during an equivalent accounting period.

The gross profit of both companies (excluding the above items) was £200,000. Flame plc declared a dividend of 42p per share while Sharkies plc paid the required preference dividend and declared an ordinary dividend of 12½p per share. Assuming a corporation tax rate of 33% on the given figures show the effect of the losses incurred on the results and EPS of each company.

Note. Treat the compensation costs as extraordinary and the bad debt as exceptional. The extraordinary item would not be allowed under FRS 3 but it illustrates here that extraordinary items do not affect EPS.

Answer

TRADING RESULTS		Flame plc		Sharkies plc
	£	£	£	£
Gross profit		200,000		200,000
Less exceptional item		-		50,000
Profit on ordinary activities		200,000		150,000
Tax on profit on ordinary activities (33%)		66,000		49,500
Profit on ordinary activities after tax		134,000		100,500
Extraordinary charges	50,000			
Tax on extraordinary charges	(16,500)			
		33,500		-
Profit for the financial year		100,500		100,500
Less dividends				
Preference		-	2,000	
Ordinary	42,000		40,000	
		42,000		42,000
		58,500		58,500

EARNINGS PER SHARE

$$\frac{100,500}{100,000} = 100.5\text{p} \qquad \frac{98,500 \; ^*}{320,000} = 30.8\text{p}$$

*(£100,500 − £2,000 preference div = £98,500)

1.5 Notice in the above exercise that each company has the same basic profit for the year, the same basic tax charge for the year and pays the same amount of dividend. The **difference in their earnings per share is due to:**

(a) a **different capital structure** (Sharkies plc has preference shares, the dividends on which must be deducted from earnings);

(b) the **different numbers of ordinary shares.**

Alternative EPS

1.6 **FRS 3 allows disclosure of any alternative EPS figures, but for any such figure:**

(a) **It should be presented no more prominently** than the SSAP 3 basic EPS.

(b) **It should be applied consistently over time.**

(c) **Its significance should be explained prominently.**

(d) **It should be reconciled to the basic EPS**, with each adjustment shown and quantified.

Net basis and nil basis of calculating EPS

1.7 Under the UK 'imputation' system of company taxation, when a company pays a dividend it must also pay advance corporation tax (ACT) to the government. This ACT will usually be recoverable later against the 'mainstream' corporation tax payment on the company's annual profits. However, there may be occasions where the company has wholly or partially irrecoverable ACT.

1.8 This may confuse the comparison between one company's earnings and another's and SSAP 3 identifies the irrecoverable ACT as a 'variable' element in the taxation charge. (SSAP 3 also identified another variable element, overseas taxation unrelieved as a result of dividend policy. Changes in tax law since then mean that this is no longer a variable element.)

1.9 There are, therefore, alternative bases for calculating earnings:

KEY TERMS

(a) Under the **net basis** earnings are calculated by deducting the 'actual' taxation charge (including the variable taxation elements).

(b) Under the **nil basis** earnings are calculated by deducting the constant taxation elements (excluding the variable elements).

The nil basis provides a better comparison between the earnings of companies with different dividend policies. However, for a company with no irrecoverable ACT there will be no variable element in the taxation charge and the nil and net bases will give the same figure. SSAP 3 requires disclosure on the net basis.

Effect on EPS of changes in capital structure

1.10 The calculation of EPS can become rather more complex when the number of shares in issue changes during the course of an accounting period. You should remember that **a major reason for calculating an EPS is to compare the current year's performance against previous years.**

1.11 **If there is a change in the number of shares issued,** we might expect total earnings to change as well. This is only reasonable to expect, since if new shares are issued to raise extra capital, we should expect the capital so raised to generate extra profits and earnings. **Adjustments are** therefore **required to the EPS calculations to make sure that the current year's performance (allowing for extra shares in issue, extra capital employed and returns on that extra capital) is compared fairly with the previous year.** There are three situations in particular to consider a:

(a) **new issue** of shares during the current year at full market price;
(b) **rights issue** of shares during the year (ie at below current market price);
(c) **bonus issue** of shares during the year.

1.12 If a **new issue of shares** at full market price is made during the course of the year, the extra profits earned from the capital raised will only apply to that part of the year from the time that the share issue was made. It would therefore be unreasonable to calculate the EPS using the total number of shares in issue. Instead **a weighted average total of shares should be used.**

1.13 EXAMPLE: EARNINGS PER SHARE WITH A NEW ISSUE

On 30 September 19X2, Boffin plc made an issue at full market price of 1,000,000 ordinary shares. The company's accounting year runs from 1 January to 31 December. Relevant information for 19X1 and 19X2 is as follows:

	19X2	*19X1*
Shares in issue as at 31 December	9,000,000	8,000,000
Profits after tax and preference dividend	£3,300,000	£3,280,000

Calculate the EPS for 19X2 and the corresponding figure for 19X1.

1.14 SOLUTION

	19X2	*19X1*
Weighted average number of shares		
9 months × 8 million	6,000,000	
3 months × 9 million	2,250,000	
	8,250,000	8,000,000
Earnings	£3,300,000	£3,280,000
EPS	40 pence	41 pence

In spite of the increase in total earnings by £20,000 in 19X2, the EPS is not as good as in 19X1, because there was extra capital employed for the final 3 months of 19X2.

1.15 A **rights issue** of shares is an issue of new shares to existing shareholders at a price below the current market value. The offer of new shares is made on the basis of x new shares for every y shares currently held; eg a 1 for 3 rights issue is an offer of 1 new share at the offer price for every 3 shares currently held.

1.16   To arrive at figures for EPS when a rights issue is made, we **need to calculate first of all the theoretical ex-rights price.** This is a weighted average value per share, and is perhaps explained most easily with a numerical example.

1.17   Suppose that Egghead plc has 10,000,000 shares in issue. It is now proposed to make a 1 for 4 rights issue at a price of £3 per share. The market value of existing shares on the final day before the issue is made is £3.50 (this is the 'cum rights' value). What is the theoretical ex-rights price per share?

	£
Before issue 4 shares, value £3.50 each	14.00
Rights issue 1 share, value £3	3.00
Theoretical value of 5 shares	17.00

$$\text{Theoretical ex-rights price} = \frac{£17.00}{5} = £3.40 \text{ per share}$$

1.18   The procedures for calculating the EPS for the current year and a corresponding figure for the previous year are now as follows:

(a)   The **EPS for corresponding previous period** should be multiplied by the following fraction.

> **FORMULA TO LEARN**
>
> $$\frac{\text{Theoretical ex-rights price}}{\text{Market price on last day of quotation (cum rights)}}$$

(b)   To obtain the **EPS for the current year** you should:

(i)   multiply the number of shares before the rights issue by the fraction of the year before the date of issue and by the following fraction.

> **FORMULA TO LEARN**
>
> $$\frac{\text{Market price on last day of quotation cum rights}}{\text{Theoretical ex-rights price}}$$

(ii)   multiply the number of shares after the rights issue by the fraction of the year after the date of issue and add to the figure arrived in (i).

The total earnings should then be divided by the total number of shares so calculated.

1.19   EXAMPLE: EARNINGS PER SHARE WITH A RIGHTS ISSUE

Brains plc had 100,000 shares in issue, but then makes a 1 for 5 rights issue on 1 October 19X2 at a price of £1. The market value on the last day of quotation cum rights was £1.60.

Calculate the EPS for 19X2 and the corresponding figure for 19X1 given total earnings of £50,000 in 19X2 and £40,000 in 19X1.

1.20 SOLUTION

Calculation of theoretical ex-rights price:

	£
Before issue 5 shares, value × £1.60	8.00
Rights issue 1 share, value × £1.00	1.00
Theoretical value of 6 shares	9.00

Theoretical ex-rights price $= \dfrac{£9}{6} = £1.50$

1.21 EPS for 19X1

EPS as calculated before taking into account the rights issue = 40p (£40,000 divided by 100,000 shares).

$\text{EPS} = \dfrac{1.50}{1.60} \times 40p = 37\frac{1}{2}p$

(Remember: this is the corresponding value for 19X1 which will be shown in the P & L account for Brains plc at the end of 19X2.)

1.22 *EPS for 19X2*

Number of shares before the rights issue was 100,000. 20,000 shares were issued.

Stage 1:	100,000	×	$^{9}/_{12}$	×	$\dfrac{1.60}{1.50}$	=	80,000
Stage 2:	120,000	×	$^{3}/_{12}$	=			30,000
							110,000

$\text{EPS} = \dfrac{£50,000}{110,000} = 45\frac{1}{2}p$

The figure for total earnings is the actual earnings for the year.

1.23

A bonus issue is a capitalisation of reserves and will have no effect on the earnings capacity of the company because no new capital is raised. The earnings per share for the accounting period in which the issue is made and for the corresponding period should be adjusted to take into consideration the new issue.

1.24 EXAMPLE: EARNINGS PER SHARE WITH A BONUS ISSUE

Greymatter plc had 400,000 shares in issue, until on 30 September 19X2 it made a bonus issue of 100,000 shares. Calculate the EPS for 19X2 and the corresponding figure for 19X1 if total earnings were £80,000 in 19X2 and £75,000 in 19X1. The company's accounting year runs from 1 January to 31 December.

1.25 SOLUTION

	Year 2	*Year 1*
Earnings	£80,000	£75,000
Shares at 1 January	400,000	400,000
Bonus issue	100,000	100,000
	500,000 shares	500,000 shares
EPS	16p	15p

The number of shares for 19X1 must also be adjusted if the figures for EPS are to remain comparable.

Question 2

The draft profit and loss account of Pilum plc for the year ended 31 December 19X4 is set out below.

DRAFT PROFIT AND LOSS ACCOUNT
FOR YEAR ENDED 31 DECEMBER 19X4

	£	£
Profit before tax and extraordinary items		2,530,000
Less taxation		
Corporation tax	1,058,000	
Under provision for 19X3	23,000	
Irrecoverable advance corporation tax	69,000	
		1,150,000
		1,380,000
Extraordinary loss	207,000	
Tax on extraordinary loss	92,000	
		115,000
		1,265,000
Transfer to reserves	115,000	
Dividends		
Paid preference interim dividend	138,000	
Paid ordinary interim dividend	184,000	
Proposed preference final dividend	138,000	
Proposed ordinary final dividend	230,000	
		805,000
Retained profit		460,000

On 1 January 19X4 the issued share capital of Pilum plc was 4,600,000 6% preference shares of £1 each and 4,140,000 ordinary shares of £1 each.

Required

Calculate the earnings per share (on basic and fully diluted basis) in respect of the year ended 31 December 19X4 for each of the following circumstances. (Each of the five circumstances (a) to (e) is to be dealt with separately).

(a)   On the basis that there was no change in the issued share capital of the company during the year ended 31 December 19X4.

(b)   On the basis that the company made a bonus issue on 1 October 19X4 of one ordinary share for every four shares in issue at 30 September 19X4.

(c)   On the basis that the company made a rights issue of £1 ordinary shares on 1 October 19X4 in the proportion of 1 for every 5 shares held, at a price of £1.20. The middle market price for the shares on the last day of quotation cum rights was £1.80 per share.

(d)   On the basis that the company made no new issue of shares during the year ended 31 December 19X4 but on that date it had in issue £1,150,000 10% convertible loan stock 19X8 - 19Y1. This loan stock will be convertible into ordinary £1 shares as follows.

19X8	90 £1 shares for £100 nominal value loan stock
19X9	85 £1 shares for £100 nominal value loan stock
19Y0	80 £1 shares for £100 nominal value loan stock
19Y1	75 £1 shares for £100 nominal value loan stock

(e)   On the basis that the company made no issues of shares during the year ended 31 December 19X4 but on that date there were outstanding options to purchase 460,000 ordinary £1 shares at £1.70 per share.

Assume where appropriate that:

(i)   corporation tax rate is 50%;
(ii)   the quotation for 2½% Consolidated Stock was £25.

Answer

(a)

	Earnings	
	Net basis	Nil basis
	£	£
Profit before tax	2,530,000	2,530,000
Less taxation	1,127,000	1,058,000
Profit after tax	1,403,000	1,472,000
Less: preference dividends	276,000	276,000
extraordinary items	115,000	115,000
Earnings	1,012,000	1,081,000
Earnings per share =	1,012,000	1,081,000
	4,140,000	4,140,000
	= 24.4p	= 22.1p

(b) Shares in issue at 31 December 19X4
      4,140,000 + 4,140,000/4 = 5,175,000

	Net basis	Nil basis
∴ EPS =	1,012,000	1,081,000
	5,175,000	5,175,000
	= 19.6p	= 20.9p

(c) The first step is to calculate the theoretical ex-rights price. Consider the holder of 5 shares.

	No.	£
Before rights issue	5	9.00
Rights issue	1	1.20
After rights issue	6	10.20

The theoretical ex-rights price is therefore £10.20/6 = £1.70.

The number of shares in issue before the rights issue must be multiplied by the fraction:

$$\frac{\text{Market price on last day of quotation cum rights}}{\text{theoretical ex - rights price}} = \frac{£1.80}{£1.70}$$

Number of shares in issue during the year

	Proportion of year	Shares in issue	Fraction	Total
1 1.X4 - 30.9.X4	$^9/_{12}$ ×	4,140,000	× 1.8/1.7	3,287,647
1.10.X4 - 31.12.X4	$^3/_{12}$ ×	4,968,000		1,242,000
				4,529,647

EPS on net basis $= \dfrac{1,012,000}{4,529,647} = 22.3p$

EPS on nil basis $= \dfrac{1,081,000}{4,529,647} = 23.9p$

(d) The maximum number of shares into which the loan stock could be converted is 90% × 1,150,000 = 1,035,000. The calculation of fully diluted EPS should be based on the assumption that such a conversion actually took place on 1 January 19X4. Shares in issue during the year would then have numbered (4,140,000 + 1,035,000) = 5,175,000 and revised earnings would be as follows.

	£	Net basis £	Nil basis £
Earnings from (a) above		1,012,000	1,081,000
Interest saved by conversion	115,000		
Less attributable taxation	57,500		
		57,500	57,500
		1,069,500	1,138,500
∴ EPS =		1,069,500	1,138,500
		5,175,000	5,175,000
		= 20.7p	= 22.0p

(e) EPS in this case must be calculated on these assumptions.

    (i) All the options had been exercised on 1 January 19X4. The number of shares in issue throughout the year would then have been (4,140,000 + 460,000) = 4,600,000.

    (ii) The proceeds on exercise of the options (460,000 × £1.70) = £782,000 had been invested on 1 January 19X4 in 2½% consolidated stock. At a price of £25 for £100 nominal value of stock, a nominal amount of £782,000 × 100/25 = £3,128,000 could have been purchased.

Revised earnings would be as follows.

	£	Net basis £	Nil basis £
Earnings from (a) above		1,012,000	1,081,000
Notional interest on consolidated			
stock (2½% × £3,128,000)	78,200		
Less attributable taxation	39,100		
		39,100	39,100
		1,051,100	1,120,100
∴ EPS =		1,051,100	1,120,100
		4,600,000	4,600,000
		= 22.85p	= 24.35p

Fully diluted earnings per share

1.26 At the end of an accounting period, a company may have in issue some **securities which do not (at present) have any 'claim' to a share of equity earnings, but may give rise to such a claim in the future**. These securities **include:**

(a) a **separate class of equity shares** which at present is not entitled to any dividend, but will be entitled after some future date;

(b) **convertible loan stock** or **convertible preference shares** which give their holders the right at some future date to exchange their securities for ordinary shares of the company, at a pre-determined conversion rate.

1.27 In such circumstances, the future number of shares ranking for dividend might increase, which in turn results in a fall in the EPS. In other words, **a future increase in the number of equity shares will cause a dilution or 'watering down' of equity**, and **it is possible to calculate a fully diluted earnings per share** (ie the EPS that would have been obtained during the financial period if the dilution had already taken place). This will **indicate to investors the possible effects of a future dilution.**

1.28 EXAMPLE: FULLY DILUTED EPS

If, in addition to the 100,000 £1 ordinary shares Flame plc (Exercise 1 above) also had in issue £40,000 15% Convertible Loan Stock which is convertible in 2 years time at the rate of 4 ordinary shares for every £5 of stock, the fully diluted EPS would be calculated as follows.

(a) EPS (as above)   100.5p

(b) The additional equity on conversion of the loan stock will be:

        40,000 × 4/5 =   32,000 shares

(c) Flame plc will save interest payments of £6,000 but this increase in profits will be taxed. Hence the earnings figure may be recalculated:

	£
Gross profit £(200,000 + 6,000)	206,000
Tax on ordinary activities (33%)	67,980
Profit on ordinary activities after taxation	138,020
Less net extraordinary item	33,500 104,520

(d) Fully diluted EPS = $\dfrac{104,520}{132,000}$ = 79.2p

(e) The dilution in earnings would be 100.5p – 79.2p = 21.3p per share

Question 3

Ardent plc has 5,000,000 ordinary shares of 25 pence each in issue, and also had in issue:

(a) £1,000,000 of 14% convertible loan stock, convertible in three years' time at the rate of 2 shares per £10 of stock;

(b) £2,000,000 of 10% convertible loan stock, convertible in one year's time at the rate of 3 shares per £5 of stock.

The total earnings in 19X4 were £1,750,000.

The rate of corporation tax is 35%.

Required

Calculate the EPS and fully diluted EPS.

Answer

(a) EPS = $\dfrac{£1,750,000}{5\ \text{million}}$ = 35 pence

(b) On dilution, the (maximum) number of shares in issue would be:

	Shares
Current	5,000,000
On conversion of 14% stock	200,000
On conversion of 10% stock	1,200,000
	6,400,000

	£	£
Current earnings		1,750,000
Add interest saved (140,000 + 200,000)	340,000	
Less tax thereon at 35%	119,000	
		221,000
Revised earnings		1,971,000

Fully diluted EPS = $\dfrac{£1,971,000}{6.4\ \text{million}}$ = 30.8p

Disclosure requirements of SSAP 3 Earnings per share

1.29 SSAP 3 **applies to companies having a listing** on a recognised stock exchange for any class of equity. The requirements of the standard are:

(a) In a company's audited accounts, the **EPS** (calculated on **net basis**) should be shown **on the face of the profit and loss account**, both **for the period under review and** for the **corresponding previous period**. It is also desirable that EPS on the **nil distribution basis should be shown where materially different** from that on the net basis.

(b) The **basis of calculating EPS should be disclosed,** either in the profit and loss account or in a note thereto. In particular the amount of earnings and the number of equity shares used in the calculation should be shown.

(c) The **fully diluted EPS and the basis of calculation should also be shown if the dilution is material**. (*Note*. Dilution amounting to **5% or more** of the basic EPS is regarded as material for this purpose.) Fully diluted EPS should be given equal prominence with the basic EPS wherever both are disclosed.

(d) In accordance with FRS 3 *Reporting financial performance*, where a reporting entity wishes to present an **additional earnings per share** calculated on another level of earnings the additional indicator should be presented on a consistent basis over time and, wherever disclosed, **reconciled to the amount required by the FRS**. Such a reconciliation should list the items for which an adjustment is being made and disclose their individual effect on the calculation. **The earnings per share required by the FRS should be at least as prominent as any additional version presented** and the **reason for calculating the additional version should be explained.**

Significance of earnings per share

1.30   Earnings per share (EPS) is **one of the most frequently quoted statistics in financial analysis**. Because of the widespread use of the price earnings (P/E) ratio **as a yardstick for investment decisions**, it became increasingly important.

1.31   It seems that reported and forecast EPS **can, through the P/E ratio, have a significant effect on a company's share** price. Thus, a share price might fall if it looks as if EPS is going to be low. This is not very rational, as EPS can depend on many, often subjective, assumptions used in preparing a historical statement, namely the profit and loss account. It does not necessarily bear any relation to the value of a company, and of its shares. Nevertheless, the market is sensitive to EPS.

1.32   EPS has also **served as a means of assessing the stewardship and management role performed by company directors and managers**. Remuneration packages might be linked to EPS growth, thereby increasing the pressure on management to improve EPS. The danger of this, however, is that management effort goes into distorting results to produce a favourable EPS.

1.33   The **ASB believed that undue emphasis was being placed on EPS**, and that this led to simplistic interpretations of financial performance. Consequently, in issuing FRS 3 *Reporting financial performance*, the ASB attempted to de-emphasise EPS by requiring it to be calculated after extraordinary items. Because of this, and other changes, EPS is now very volatile and, arguably less useful for analysis; many companies are providing additional EPS figures, prepared on what they see as a more meaningful basis.

Exam focus point

EPS has featured twice so far. Explanation and critical assessment might be required as well as calculation.

2   **FRS 3 REPORTING FINANCIAL PERFORMANCE**
                                    6/94, 12/94, 12/95, 6/96, 6/97, 12/97

Exam focus point

As you can see, this is an extremely popular exam topic. Make sure that you familiarise yourself fully with the contents of this standard.

2.1   FRS 3 represents an attempt by the ASB to improve the quality of financial information provided to shareholders. In particular it was **an attempt to move away from the high profile of the earnings per share**. The main elements of the FRS are as follows.

(a)   New structure of the profit and loss account
(b)   Extraordinary items
(c)   Statement of total recognised gains and losses
(d)   Other new disclosures
(e)   Earnings per share

2.2   FRS 3 replaced SSAP 6 *Extraordinary items and prior year adjustments*, changing definitions and creating a substantial impact on the reported results of the company.

Exceptional and extraordinary items

2.3   A company may experience events or undertake transactions which are 'out of the ordinary', ie they are not the same as what the company normally does.

2.4   FRS 3 lays down the rules for dealing with 'out of the ordinary' items in the P & L account and restricts the way companies can manipulate these figures.

Exceptional items

KEY TERM

FRS 3 defines **exceptional items** as: 'Material items which derive from events or transactions that fall within the ordinary activities of the reporting entity and which individually or, if of a similar type, in aggregate, need to be disclosed by virtue of their *size or incidence* if the financial statements are to give a true and fair view.'

2.5   The definition of **ordinary activities** is important.

'Any activities which are undertaken by a reporting entity as **part of its business** and such related activities in which the reporting entity engages in furtherance of, incidental to, or arising from these activities. Ordinary activities include the effects on the reporting entity of any event in the various environments in which it operates including the political, regulatory, economic and geographical environments irrespective of the frequency or unusual nature of the event.'

2.6   There are **two** types of exceptional items and their accounting treatment is as follows.

(a)   Firstly there are **three categories of exceptional items which must be shown separately on the face of the profit and loss account** after operating profit and before interest and allocated appropriately to discontinued and continued activities.

(i)   **Profit or loss on the sale or termination** of an operation

(ii)   **Costs of a fundamental reorganisation** or restructuring that has a material effect on the nature and focus of the reporting entity's operations

(iii)   **Profit or loss on disposal of fixed assets**

For both items (i) and (iii) profit and losses may not be offset within categories.

(b)   **All other items should be allocated to the appropriate statutory format heading** and attributed to continuing or discounted operations as appropriate. If the item is sufficiently material that it is needed to show a true and fair view it must be disclosed on the face of the profit and loss account.

2.7   In both (a) and (b) an adequate description must be given in the notes to the accounts to enable its nature to be understood.

2.8   FRS 3 does not give examples of the type of transaction which is likely to be treated as exceptional. However, its predecessor on the subject, SSAP 6, gave a useful list of examples of items which if of a sufficient size might normally be treated as exceptional.

(a)   Abnormal charges for bad debts and write-offs of stock and work in progress.
(b)   Abnormal provisions for losses on long-term contracts.
(c)   Settlement of insurance claims.

Extraordinary items

2.9   Under SSAP 6 and SSAP 3 (on earnings per share) the term extraordinary item was one of great significance. However, **the ASB publicly stated that it does not envisage such items appearing on a company's profit and loss account after the introduction of FRS 3.** Its decline in importance has been achieved by tightening of the definition of an extraordinary item.

> **KEY TERM**
>
> **Extraordinary items** are defined as material items possessing a high degree of abnormality which arise from events or transactions that fall outside the ordinary activities of the reporting entity and which are not expected to recur.

2.10   Extraordinary items should be shown on the face of profit and loss account before dividends and other minority interests (for group accounts). Tax and minority interest in the extraordinary item should be shown separately. A description of the extraordinary items should be given in the notes to the accounts.

Structure of the profit and loss account

2.11   **All statutory headings from turnover to operating profit must be subdivided between that arising from continuing operations and that arising from discontinued operations.** In addition, turnover and operating profit must be further analysed between that from existing and that from newly acquired operations.

2.12   **Only figures for turnover and operating profit need be shown on the face of the P & L account;** all additional information regarding costs may be relegated to a note.

PROFIT AND LOSS EXAMPLE 1

	1993 £m	1993 £m	1992 as restated £m
Turnover			
Continuing operations	550		500
Acquisitions	50		
	600		
Discontinued operations	175		190
		775	690
Cost of sales		(620)	(555)
Gross profit		155	135
Net operating expenses		(104)	(83)
Operating profit			
Continuing operations	50		40
Acquisitions	6		
	56		
Discontinued operations	(15)		12
Less 1992 provision	10		
		51	52
Profit on sale of properties in continuing operations		9	6
Provision for loss on operations to be discontinued			(30)
Loss on disposal of discontinued operations	(17)		
Less 1992 provision	20		
		3	
Profit on ordinary activities before interest		63	28
Interest payable		(18)	(15)
Profit on ordinary activities before taxation		45	13
Tax on profit on ordinary activities		(14)	(4)
Profit on ordinary activities after taxation		31	9
Minority interests		(2)	(2)
Profit before extraordinary items		29	7
Extraordinary items - included only to show positioning		-	-
Profit for the financial year		29	7
Dividends		(8)	(1)
Retained profit for the financial year		21	6
Earnings per share		39p	10p
Adjustments (to be itemised and an adequate description to be given)		Xp	Xp
Adjusted earnings per share		Yp	Yp

Note. Reason for calculating the adjusted earnings per share to be given.

PROFIT AND LOSS ACCOUNT EXAMPLE 2 (to operating profit line)

	Continuing operations 1993 £m	Acquisitions 1993 £m	Discontinued of operations 1993 £m	Total 1993 £m	Total 1992 as restated £m
Turnover	550	50	175	775	690
Cost of sales	(415)	(40)	(165)	(620)	(555)
Gross profit	135	10	10	155	135
Net operating expenses	(85)	(4)	(25)	(114)	(83)
Less 1992 provision			10	10	—
Operating profit	50	6	(5)	51	52
Profit on sale of properties	9			9	6
Provision for loss on operations to be discontinued					(30)
Loss on disposal of the discontinued operations			(17)	(17)	
Less 1992 provision			20	20	
Profit on ordinary activities before interest	59	6	(2)	63	28

Thereafter example 2 is the same as example 1.

NOTES TO THE FINANCIAL STATEMENTS

Note required in respect of profit and loss account example 1

	1993			1992 (as restated)		
	Continuing £m	Discontinued £m	Total £m	Continuing £m	Discontinued £m	Total £m
Cost of sales	455	165	620	385	170	555
Net operating expenses						
Distribution costs	56	13	69	46	5	51
Administrative expenses	41	12	53	34	3	37
Other operating income	(8)	0	(8)	(5)	0	(5)
	89	25	114	75	8	83
Less 1992 provision	0	(10)	(10)			
	89	15	104			

The total figures for continuing operations in 1993 include the following amounts relating to acquisitions: cost of sales £40 million and net operating expenses £4 million (namely distribution costs £3 million, administrative expenses £3 million and other operating income £2 million).

Note required in respect of profit and loss account example 2

	1993			1992 (as restated)		
	Continuing £m	Discontinued £m	Total £m	Continuing £m	Discontinued £m	Total £m
Turnover				500	190	690
Cost of sales				385	170	555
Net operating expenses						
Distribution costs	56	13	69	46	5·	51
Administrative expenses	41	12	53	34	3	37
Other operating income	(8)	0	(8)	(5)	0	(5)
	89	25	114	75	8	83
Operating profit				40	12	52

The total figure of net operating expenses for continuing operations in 1993 includes £4 million in respect of acquisitions (namely distribution costs £3 million, administrative expenses £3 million and other operating income £2 million).

Discontinued operations

2.13 A **discontinued operation** is one which **meets all of the following conditions.**

(a) The sale or termination must have been **completed** before the earlier of 3 months after the year end or the date the financial statements are approved. (Terminations not completed by this date may be disclosed in the notes.)

(b) Former activity must have **ceased permanently**.

(c) The sale or termination has a **material effect** on the nature and focus of the entity's operations and represents a material reduction in its operating facilities resulting either from:

(i) its withdrawal from a particular market (class of business or geographical); or from

(ii) a material reduction in turnover in its continuing markets.

(d) The assets, liabilities, results of operations and activities are **clearly distinguishable**, physically, operationally and for financial reporting purposes.

Accounting for the discontinuation

2.14 (a) **Results**

The results of the discontinued operation up to the date of sale or termination or the balance sheet date should be shown **under each of the relevant profit and loss account headings**.

(b) **Profit/loss on discontinuation**

The profit or loss on discontinuation or costs of discontinuation should be **disclosed separately** as an exceptional item after operating profit and before interest.

(c) **Comparative figures**

Figures for the previous year **must be adjusted for** any **activities** which have become **discontinued in the current year**.

Exam focus point

In the December 1997 paper, 7 marks were available for advising directors, in line with FRS 3 requirements, on the correct treatment of the disposal of a division.

Acquisitions

2.15 Acquisitions include **most holdings acquired by a group** (beyond the scope of your syllabus), **as well as unincorporated businesses purchased**. However, start-ups are not acquisitions.

Question 4

B&C plc's profit and loss account for the year ended 31 December 19X2, with comparatives, is as follows.

	19X2	19X1
	£'000	£'000
Turnover	200,000	180,000
Cost of sales	(60,000)	(80,000)
Gross profit	140,000	100,000
Distribution costs	(25,000)	(20,000)
Administration expenses	(50,000)	(45,000)
Operating profit	65,000	35,000

During the year the company sold a material business operation with all activities ceasing on 14 February 19X3. The loss on the sale of the operation amounted to £2.2m. The results of the operation for 19X1 and 19X2 were as follows.

	19X2	19X1
	£'000	£'000
Turnover	22,000	26,000
Profit/(loss)	(7,000)	(6,000)

In addition, the company acquired a business which contributed £7m to turnover and an operating profit of £1.5m.

Required

Prepare the profit and loss account and related notes for the year ended 31 December 19X2 complying with the requirements of FRS 3 as far as possible.

Answer

	19X2 £'000	£'000	19X1 £'000	£'000
Turnover				
Continuing operations				
(200 – 22 – 7)/(180 – 26)		171.0		154
Acquisitions		7.0		-
		178.0		154
Discontinued		22.0		26
		200.0		180
Cost of sales		(60.0)		(80)
Gross profit		140.0		100
Distribution costs		(25.0)		(20)
Administration expenses (50 – 2.2)		(47.8)		(45)
Operating profit				
Continuing operations* (bal)	72.7		41	
Acquisitions	1.5		-	
	74.2		41	
Discontinued	(7.0)		(6)	
		67.2		35
Exceptional item		(2.2)		-
		65.0		35

* ie 65.0 + 2.2 + 7.0 – 1.5 = 72.7; 35 + 6 = 41

Note to the profit and loss account

	19X2			19X1 (as restated)		
	Continuing £'000	Discontinued £'000	Total £'000	Continuing £'000	Discontinued £'000	Total £'000
Cost of sales	X	X	60.0	X	X	80
Net operating expenses						
Distribution costs	X	X	25.0	X	X	20
Administration expenses	X	X	47.8	X	X	45
	X	X	72.8	X	X	65

FRS 3 statements and notes

2.16   FRS 3 introduced a new statement and a variety of new notes to expand the information required in published accounts which we saw in Chapter 8.

Statement of total recognised gains and losses

2.17   This is required by FRS 3 to be presented with the same prominence as the P & L account, balance sheet and cash flow statement, ie as a **primary statement**.

2.18   The statement will include all gains and losses occurring during the period and so would typically include the following.

	£
Profit for the year (per the profit and loss account)	X
Items taken directly to reserves (not goodwill written off to reserves)	
Surplus on revaluation of fixed assets	X
Surplus/deficit on revaluation of investment properties	X
Total recognised gains and losses for the year	X
Prior period adjustments (see later)	(X)
Total gains and losses recognised since last annual report	X

2.19 At a glance, it seems that all this new statement does is to reconcile the opening and closing net assets of a business. This is, however, not so since FRS 3 requires that **transactions with shareholders are to be excluded**, ie:

(a) dividends paid and proposed; and

(b) share issues and redemptions;

since these transactions do not represent either gains or losses.

2.20 In the case of goodwill, which is capitalised and amortised under FRS 10, the amortisation charge will appear indirectly (as part of the results for the year) in the statement.

2.21 **Where the profit or loss for the year is the only recognised gain or loss**, a **statement to that effect should be given** immediately below the profit and loss account.

Realised and distributable profits

2.22 At this point it may be worth pointing out that just because gains and losses are 'recognised' in this statement, they are, **not necessarily 'realised'** (described below', or **'distributable'**, ie as a dividend. Realised and distributable profits were covered in an earlier chapter.

Reconciliation of movements in shareholders' funds

2.23 This reconciliation is required by FRS 3 to be included in the notes to the accounts. What the statement aims to do is to **pull together financial performance** of the entity as is reflected in:

(a) The profit and loss account.

(b) Other movements in shareholders' funds as determined by the statement of total recognised gains and losses.

(c) All other changes in shareholders funds not recognised in either of the above such as goodwill immediately written off to reserves.

2.24 The typical contents of the reconciliation would be as follows.

	£
Profit for the financial year	X
* Dividends	(X)
	X
Other recognised gains and losses (per statement of total recognised gains and losses)	X
* New share capital	(X)
Net addition to shareholders' funds	X
Opening shareholders' funds	X
Closing shareholders' funds	X

* Items not appearing in the statement of recognised gains and losses

Question 5

Extracts from Z Ltd's profit and loss account for the year ended 31 December 19X1 were as follows.

	£'000
Profit after tax	512
Dividend	(120)
Retained profit	392

During the year the following important events took place.

(a)   Assets were revalued upward by £110,000.

(b)   £300,000 share capital was issued during the year.

(c)   Certain stock items were written down by £45,000.

(d)   Opening shareholders' funds at 1 January 19X1 were £3,100,000.

Show how the events for the year would be shown in the statement of recognised gains and losses and the reconciliation of movements in shareholders funds.

Answer

STATEMENT OF RECOGNISED GAINS AND LOSSES

	£'000
Profit after tax	512
Asset revaluation	110
	622

RECONCILIATION OF MOVEMENTS IN SHAREHOLDERS' FUNDS

	£'000
Profit after tax	512
Dividend	(120)
	392
Other recognised gains and losses (622 – 512)	110
New share capital	300
Net addition to shareholders' funds	802
Opening shareholders' funds	3,100
Closing shareholders' funds	3,902

Note of historical cost profits and losses

2.25   If a company has adopted any of the alternative accounting rules as regards revaluation of assets then the reported profit figure per the profit and loss account may deviate from the historical cost profit figure. If this deviation is material then the financial statements must include a reconciliation statement after the statement of recognised gains and losses or the profit and loss account. The profit figure to be reconciled is profit before tax; however, the retained profit for the year must also be restated.

2.26 Note that **FRS 3 requires the profit or loss on the disposal of a revalued asset to be calculated by reference to the difference between proceeds and the net carrying amount** (revalued figure less depreciation). The profit or loss based on historical cost will appear in the note of historical cost profits.

Question 6

A Ltd reported a profit before tax of £162,000 for the year ended 31 December 19X1. During the year the following transactions in fixed assets took place.

(a) An asset with a book value of £40,000 was revalued to £75,000. The remaining useful life is estimated to be five years.

(b) An asset (with a five year useful life at the date of revaluation) was revalued by £20,000 (book value £30,000) was sold one year after revaluation for £48,000.

Show the reconciliation or profit to historical cost profit for the year ended 31 December 19X1.

Answer

RECONCILIATION OF PROFIT TO HISTORICAL COST PROFIT
FOR THE YEAR ENDED 31 DECEMBER 19X1

	£'000
Reported profit on ordinary activities before taxation	162
Realisation of property revaluation gains	20
Difference between historical cost depreciation charge and the actual depreciation charge of the year calculated on the revalued amount (75,000 - 40,000)/5	7
	189

Prior period adjustments

2.27 When the financial statements of a company are compiled, certain items (eg accruals, provisions) represent best estimates at a point in time. Further evidence received in the following year may suggest that previous estimates were incorrect. In most cases the 'error' will not be significant in size and so as a result the difference should be dealt with in the current year's accounts.

2.28 There are **two situations where a prior period adjustment is necessary:**

(a) **fundamental errors** - evidence is found to suggest last year's accounts were wrong; and

(b) a **change in accounting policy**.

2.29 **The following accounting treatment should be used.**

(a) Restate prior year profit and loss account and balance sheet.

(b) Restate opening reserves balance.

(c) Include the adjustment in the reconciliation of movements in shareholders' funds.

(d) Include a note at the foot of the statement of total recognised gains and losses of the current period.

2.30   Prior period adjustments are therefore defined by FRS 3 as follows.

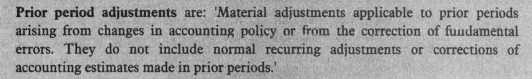

KEY TERM

Prior period adjustments are: 'Material adjustments applicable to prior periods arising from changes in accounting policy or from the correction of fundamental errors. They do not include normal recurring adjustments or corrections of accounting estimates made in prior periods.'

2.31   A **fundamental error** is an error which is **so significant that the truth and fairness of the financial statements is not achieved.**

2.32   A **change in accounting policy requires a prior period adjustment based on the fundamental accounting concept of consistency.** For users of the financial statements to make meaningful comparisons of a company's results it is important that the current year's and the last year's comparatives are prepared on the same basis. Therefore if for any reason a company changes its accounting policy they must go back and represent last year's accounts on the same basis.

2.33   Reasons for a change in accounting policy, then, are:

(a)   to show a **truer and fairer view**; or

(b)   introduction of, or change to, **standards or legislation.**

Question 7

Wick Ltd was established on 1 January 19X0. In the first three years' accounts deferred development expenditure was carried forward as an asset in the balance sheet. During 19X3 the directors decided that for the current and future years, all development expenditure should be written off as it is incurred. This decision has not resulted from any change in the expected outcome of development projects on hand, but rather from a desire to favour the prudence concept. The following information is available.

(a)   Movements on the deferred development account.

Year	Deferred development expenditure incurred during year	Transfer from deferred development expenditure account to P & L account
	£'000	£'000
19X0	525	-
19X1	780	215
19X2	995	360

(b)   The 19X2 accounts showed the following.

	£'000
Retained reserves b/f	2,955
Retained profit for the year	1,825
Retained profits carried forward	4,780

(c)   The retained profit for 19X3 after charging the actual development expenditure for the year was £2,030,000.

Required

Show how the change in accounting policy should be reflected in the statement of reserves in the company's 19X3 accounts.

Ignore taxation.

Answer

If the new accounting policy had been adopted since the company was incorporated, the additional profit and loss account charges for development expenditure would have been:

	£'000
19X0	525
19X1 (780 – 215)	565
	1,090
19X2 (995 – 360)	635
	1,725

This means that the reserves brought forward at 1 January 19X3 would have been £1,725,000 less than the reported figure of £4,780,000; while the reserves brought forward at 1 January 19X2 would have been £1,090,000 less than the reported figure of £2,955,000.

The statement of reserves in Wick Ltd's 19X3 accounts should, therefore, appear as follows.

STATEMENT OF RESERVES (EXTRACT)

		Comparative (previous year) figures	
	19X3	19X2	
	£'000	£'000	
Retained profits at the beginning of year			
Previously reported	4,780	2,955	
Prior year adjustment (note 1)	1,725	1,090	
Restated	3,055	1,865	
Retained profits for the year	2,030	1,190	(note 2)
Retained profits at the end of the year	5,085	3,055	

Notes

1   The accounts should include a note explaining the reasons for and consequences of the changes in accounting policy. (See above workings for 19X3 and 19X2.)

2   The retained profit shown for 19X2 is after charging the additional development expenditure of £635,000.

UITF Abstract 14 *Disclosure of changes in accounting policy*

2.34   This Abstract clarifies an aspect of the statutory disclosure requirements that has caused some uncertainty as to its meaning. **When there is a change of accounting policy companies legislation requires disclosure of particulars, reasons and effect.** The issue concerns the extent of the disclosure necessary to give the 'effect' of the change. The UITF has received legal advice that an **indication of the effect on the current year's figures** is required. This is in addition to the effect on the results for the **preceding** period, which is a disclosure requirement of FRS 3 *Reporting financial performance.* As this is a clarification of the law this consensus should be adopted as soon as practicable.

2.35   There has also been some debate about the extent of the disclosure necessary to cover the 'reasons' for the change. In this connection **FRS 3 states that 'a change in accounting may ... be made only if it can be justified on the grounds that the new policy is preferable to the one it replaces because it will give a fairer presentation of the result and of the financial position of a reporting entity'.** This, together with the requirements in companies legislation for 'special reasons', is a stringent test and directors of companies contemplating a possible change of policy should ensure that the reasons for any change are compelling.

2.36   The issue of a **new accounting standard** requiring a change **would constitute sufficient reason,** since accounts prepared adopting a policy no longer permitted by a new standard would normally not give a true and fair view. On the other hand, where the existing policy continues to be acceptable, either because the relevant standard permits a choice or because, in the absence of a relevant standard, both policies are generally accepted, it would not be in accordance with the legislation or FRS 3 if a change was made from one such alternative policy to another unless the reasons for the change were compelling, in that the new policy provided better information for users of the accounts.

2.37 UITF 7 (see Chapter 7) elaborates on the requirement to state 'reasons' and in the context of a change of accounting policy this would imply a statement as to why the continuation of the previous accounting policy would not be appropriate.

2.38 Where the change of accounting policy was imposed on the company, for example by a new accounting standard, a simple statement to this effect will normally suffice. However, where a change has been made from one generally accepted policy to another, in the absence of a new accounting standard or other similar requirement, the reasons justifying the change need to be clearly and fully disclosed.

Potential problems with FRS 3

2.39 FRS 3 was designed to put an end to various abuses, for example extraordinary items. The latter have now been outlawed. As Sir David Tweedie, Chairman of the ASB, put it:

> **'If the Martians landed and destroyed a company's factory, that could be treated as an extraordinary item.'**

2.40 Other aspects of FRS 3 have remained problematic. Two aspects may be highlighted.

Discontinued operations

2.41 **Companies may** take advantage of the requirement to analyse operations into continuing and discontinued and **use the analysis to hide 'bad news'**. A discontinued operation is likely to be a poor performer so it is in the company's interests to remove it from the rest of the results.

2.42 **Auditors must consider very carefully whether the FRS 3 criteria for classification of an operation as continuing or discontinued have been met.** The following should be singled out for close consideration.

(a) Have sales and costs relating to the discontinued activity been identified? The directors may wish to include sales in continuing operations if possible and costs in discontinued operation if possible.

(b) Provisions for profits or (more likely) losses on discontinuance must be considered carefully, as there is scope for manipulation.

Lack of consensus

2.43 FRS 3 was the first manifestation of the ASB's **balance sheet approach** to income recognition as outlined in the Board's draft *Statement of Principles* (discussed in Chapter 22). This was highlighted through the introduction into UK GAAP of an additional primary statement of financial performance - the statement of total recognised gains and losses - which focuses on changes in wealth as the means of performance measurement, rather than traditional historical cost profit and loss.

2.44   **Concern has been expressed that the ASB seems to be entrenching into an accounting standard a conceptual approach** which has not been the subject of due process, has no general agreement and which is still only at an early stage of development and discussion. In fact, one of the most crucial chapters of the ASB's framework - that dealing with measurement - had not even been issued in draft form by the time FRS 3 was issued.

3   SUBSTANCE OVER FORM

3.1   The phrase '**substance over form**' is described in IAS 1 *Disclosure of accounting policies* as follows.

> 'Transactions and other events should be accounted for and presented in accordance with their substance and financial reality and not merely with their legal form.'

3.2   This is a very important concept and, although it was not used by the ASC, it **has been used to determine accounting treatment in financial statements through accounting standards and so prevent off balance sheet transactions**. The following paragraphs give examples of where the principle of substance over form is enforced, particularly in accounting standards.

SSAP 21 *Accounting for leases and hire purchase* contracts

3.3   In SSAP 21, as we saw in the previous chapter, there is an explicit requirement that if the lessor transfers substantially all the risks and rewards of ownership to the lessee then, even though the legal title has not passed, the item being leased should be shown as an asset in the balance sheet of the lessee and the amount due to the lessor should be shown as a liability.

FRS 8 *Related party disclosures*

3.4   FRS 8 requires financial statements to disclose fully material transactions undertaken with a related party by the reporting entity, regardless of any price charged.

SSAP 9 *Stocks and long-term contracts*

3.5   In SSAP 9 there is a requirement to account for attributable profits on long-term contracts under the accruals convention. However, there may be a problem with realisation, since it is arguable whether we should account for profit which, although attributable to the work done, may not have yet been invoiced to the customer. It is argued that the convention of substance over form is applied to justify ignoring the strict legal position.

FRS 2 *Accounting for subsidiary undertakings*

3.6   This is perhaps the most important area of off balance sheet finance which has been prevented by the application of the substance over form concept.

3.7 The use of quasi-subsidiaries was very common in the 1980s. A **quasi-subsidiary** is defined by FRS 5: in effect it **is a vehicle which does not fulfil the definition of a subsidiary, but it operates just like a subsidiary.**

3.8 The main off balance sheet transactions involving quasi-subsidiaries were as follows.

(a) **Sale of assets**. The sale of assets to a quasi-subsidiary was carried out to remove the associated borrowings from the balance sheet and so reduce gearing; or perhaps so that the company could credit a profit in such a transaction. The asset could then be rented back to the vendor company under an operating lease (no capitalisation required by the lessee).

(b) **Purchase of companies or assets**. One reason for such a purchase through a quasi-subsidiary is if the acquired entity is expected to make losses in the near future. Post-acquisition losses can be avoided by postponing the date of acquisition to the date the holding company acquires the purchase from the quasi-subsidiary.

(c) **Business activities conducted outside the group**. Such a subsidiary might have been excluded through a quasi-subsidiary or not consolidated under the 'dissimilar activities' requirement in SSAP 1. Exclusion from consolidation might be undertaken because the activities are high risk and have high gearing.

3.9 CA 1989 introduced a new definition of a subsidiary based on *control* rather than just ownership rights and this definition (along with other related matters) was incorporated into FRS 2, thus substantially reducing the effectiveness of this method of off-balance sheet finance.

Creative accounting

3.10 Creative accounting, the **manipulation of figures for a desired result**, takes many forms. Off balance sheet finance is a major type of creative accounting and it probably has the most serious implications. Before we look at some of the other types of creative accounting, we should consider some important points.

3.11 Firstly, **it is very rare for a company, its directors or employees to manipulate results for the purpose of fraud. The major consideration is usually the effect the results will have on the share price of the company**. If the share price falls, the company becomes vulnerable to takeover.

3.12 Analysts, brokers and economists, whose opinions affect the stock markets, are often perceived as having an outlook which is both short-term and superficial. Consequently, **companies will attempt to produce the results the market expects or wants**. The companies will aim for steady progress in a few key numbers and ratios and they will aim to meet the market's stated expectation.

3.13 Another point to consider, particularly when you approach this topic in an examination, is that the **number of methods** available for creative accounting and the determination and imagination of those who wish to perpetrate such acts are **endless**. It has been seen in the past that, wherever an accounting standard or law closes a loophole, another one is found. This has produced a change of approach in regulators and standard setters, towards general principles rather than detailed rules.

3.14   Let us now examine some examples of creative accounting, the reaction of the standard setters and possible actions in the future which may halt or change such practices. Remember that this list is not comprehensive and that the frequency and materiality of the use of each method will vary a great deal. Remember also that we have already covered several methods in our examination of off balance sheet finance.

Income recognition and cut-off

3.15   **Manipulation of cut-off is relatively straightforward.** A company may issue invoices before the year end and inflate sales for the year when in fact they have not received firm orders for the goods. Income recognition can be manipulated in a variety of ways.

3.16   One example is where a company sells software under contract. The sales contracts will only be realised in full over a period of time, but the company might recognise the full sales value of the contract once it has been secured, even though some payments from clients will fall due over several years. This is clearly imprudent, but the company might justify it by pointing to the irrevocable nature of the contract. But what if a customer should go in to liquidation? No income would be forthcoming from the contract under such circumstances.

Reserves

3.17   **Reserves are often used to manipulate figures, avoiding any impact on the profit and loss account.** This occurs particularly in situations where an accounting standard allows a choice of treatments.

3.18   For example, foreign exchange losses or gains on foreign subsidiaries should be taken as a movement on reserves. If a company states that a foreign currency loan in its books was taken out as a hedge against the investment in the foreign subsidiary, then any losses or gains on that loan can also be taken to reserves and offset against the foreign exchange impact of the investment in the subsidiary. Substantial foreign exchange movements through reserves occurred in the Polly Peck accounts before its collapse.

Revaluations

3.19   **The optional nature of the revaluation of fixed assets leaves such practices open to manipulation.** The choice of whether to revalue can have a significant impact on a company's balance sheet. Companies which carried out such revaluations would expect to suffer a much higher depreciation charge as a result. However, many companies charged depreciation in the profit and loss account based on the historical cost only. The rest of the depreciation charge (on the excess of the revalued amount over cost) was transferred to reserves and offset against the revaluation reserve.

3.20   Again, this is an abuse of the use of reserves and it was outlawed by the revised SSAP 12. Companies must now charge depreciation on the revalued amount and pass the whole charge through the profit and loss account.

Exam focus point
'Creative accounting' is not mentioned in your syllabus or Teaching Guide, but the examiner put it in the pilot paper.

Other creative accounting techniques

3.21 The examples given above are some of the major 'abuses' in accounting over recent years. A few more are mentioned here and you should aim to think up as many examples of each as you can. You may also know of other creative accounting techniques which we have not mentioned here.

(a) **Window dressing.** This is where transactions are passed through the books at the year end to make figures look better, but in fact they have not taken place and are often reversed after the year end. An example is where cheques are written to creditors, entered in the cash book, but not sent out until well after the year end.

(b) **Taxation.** It has been known for some companies to decide how much they want to pay in taxes for the year and state their profits accordingly! Although the relationship between taxable profits and accounting profits is not straightforward, there is a direct effect on the accounts.

(c) **Change of accounting policies.** This tends to be a last resort because companies which change accounting policies know they will not be able to do so again for some time. The effect in the year of change can be substantial and prime candidates for such treatment are depreciation, stock valuation, changes from current cost to historical cost (practised frequently by privatised public utilities) and foreign currency losses.

(d) **Manipulation of accruals, prepayments and contingencies.** These figures can often be very subjective, particularly contingencies. In the case of impending legal action, for example, a contingent liability is difficult to estimate, the case may be far off and the solicitors cannot give any indication of likely success, or failure. In such cases companies will often only disclose the possibility of such a liability, even though the eventual costs may be substantial.

Question 8

Creative accounting, off balance sheet finance and related matters (in particular how ratio analysis can be used to discover these practices) often come up in articles in, for example, the *Financial Times* and *The Economist*. Find a library, preferably a good technical library, which can provide you with copies of back issues of such newspapers or journals and look for articles on creative accounting. In particular, you might look for the following.

(a) An article on Atlantic Computers by Andrew Jack in the *Financial Times* on 28 July 1994.

(b) A series of articles in the weekend *Financial Times* on 9/10 March 1996 and 16/17 March 1996 by Gillian O'Connor on creative accounting.

4   OFF BALANCE SHEET FINANCE   12/94

> ### KEY TERM
>
> **Off balance sheet finance** has been described as 'the funding or refinancing of a company's operations in such a way that, under legal requirements and existing accounting conventions, some or all of the finance may not be shown on its balance sheet.'

4.1   **Off balance sheet transactions' is the term used for transactions which meet the above objective.** These transactions may involve the removal of assets from the balance sheet, as well as liabilities, and they are likely to have a significant impact on the profit and loss account.

The off balance sheet finance problem

4.2   The result of the use of increasingly sophisticated off balance sheet finance transactions is a situation where the users of financial statements do not have a proper or clear view of the state of the company's affairs. The disclosures required by company law and current accounting standards do not provide sufficient rules for disclosure of off balance sheet finance transactions and so very little of the true nature of the transaction is exposed.

4.3   Whatever the purpose of such transactions, insufficient disclosure creates a problem. This problem has been debated over the years by the accountancy profession and other interested parties and some progress has been made (see the later sections of this chapter).

4.4   The incidence of company collapses over the last few years has risen due to the recession and a great many of these have revealed much higher borrowings than originally thought, because part of the borrowing was off balance sheet.

4.5   **The main argument used for disallowing off balance sheet finance is that the true substance of the transactions should be shown, not merely the legal form,** particularly when it is exacerbated by poor disclosure.

ASB initiatives

4.6   Although the ASB wanted to give the old exposure draft on this subject priority in its work programme, there were problems. A general problem was how to ensure that any new standard was consistent with the *Statement of Principles*. There was also a specific problem with securitisation because of opposition from the banking industry. All these aspects are discussed below.

4.7   Two chapters of the *Statement of Principles* affect the question of off balance sheet finance: *The elements of financial statements* and *The recognition of items in financial statements*. Both these chapters are currently in draft form.

4.8   The definitions are as follows.

KEY TERMS

(a) **Assets** are defined as 'rights or other access to future economic benefits controlled by an entity as a result of past transactions or events'.

(b) **Liabilities** are defined as 'an entity's obligations to transfer economic benefits as a result of past transactions or events'.

4.9 This chapter also lays out the **criteria for recognition** and derecognition of assets and liabilities.

(a) An item should be recognised in financial statements if:

(i) The item meets the definition of an element of financial statements (such as an asset or a liability).

(ii) There is enough evidence that the change in assets or liabilities inherent in the item has occurred (including evidence that a future inflow or outflow of benefit will occur).

(iii) The item can be measured in monetary terms with sufficient reliability.

(b) An item should cease to be recognised as an asset or liability if:

(i) The item no longer meets the definition of the relevant element of financial statements; or

(ii) there is no longer enough evidence that the enterprise has access to future economic benefits or an obligation to transfer economic benefits.

FRS 5 Reporting the substance of transactions

4.10 After many years' work on the subject of off balance sheet finance (some of it detailed above), the ASB has finally published FRS 5 *Reporting the substance of transactions*. It is a daunting document, running to well over 100 pages, although the standard section itself is relatively short.

Scope and exclusions

4.11 **FRS 5 applies to all entities whose accounts are intended to give a true and fair view, with no exemptions for any particular type or size of companies. However, it excludes a number of transactions from its scope,** unless they are part of a larger series of transactions that is within the scope of the standard. These exclusions are:

(a) **Forward contracts and futures** (such as those for foreign currencies or commodities).

(b) **Foreign exchange and interest rate swaps.**

(c) contracts where a net amount will be paid or received based on the movement in a price or an index (sometimes referred to as '**contracts for differences**').

(d) **Expenditure commitments** (such as purchase commitments) and orders placed, until the earlier of delivery or payment.

(e) **Employment contracts.**

Relationship to other standards

4.12   The interaction of FRS 5 with other standards and statutory requirements is also an important issue; **whichever rules are the more specific should be applied**. Leasing provides a good example (as we will see in the next chapter): straightforward leases which fall squarely within the terms of SSAP 21 should continue to be accounted for without any need to refer to FRS 5, but where their terms are more complex, or the lease is only one element in a larger series of transactions, then FRS 5 comes into play.

4.13   In addition, the standard requires that its general principle of substance over form should apply to the application of other existing rules.

Exam focus point

A full question on FRS 5, covering both knowledge and application could be set, as in December 1994.

Application notes

4.14   FRS 5 deals with certain specific aspects of off balance sheet finance in detailed **application notes**. The topics covered are:

(a)   **Consignment stock.**
(b)   **Sale and repurchase agreements**.
(c)   **Factoring of debts.**
(d)   **Securitised assets.**
(e)   **Loan transfers**.

4.15   The application notes explain how to apply the standard to the particular transactions which they describe, and also contain specific disclosure requirements in relation to those transactions. The application notes are not exhaustive and they do not override the general principles of the standard itself, but they are regarded as authoritative insofar as they assist in interpreting it. The notes are discussed in more detail in the next section.

Basic principles

4.16   **FRS 5's fundamental principle is that the substance of an entity's transactions should be reflected in its accounts**. The key considerations are whether a transaction has given rise to new assets and liabilities, and whether it has changed any existing assets and liabilities. Definitions of assets and liabilities and rules for their recognition and derecognition are discussed below.

4.17   Sometimes there will be a series of connected transactions to be evaluated, not just a single transaction. It is necessary to identify and account for the substance of the series of transactions as a whole, rather than addressing each transaction individually.

Definitions of assets and liabilities

4.18   According to the standard:

'**Assets** are rights or other access to future economic benefits controlled by an entity as a result of past transactions or events.'

'**Liabilities** are an entity's obligations to transfer economic benefits as a result of past transactions or events.'

4.19   The standard goes on to say that identification of who has the risks relating to an asset will generally indicate who has the benefits and hence who has the asset. It also says that if an entity is in certain circumstances unable to avoid an outflow of benefits, this will provide evidence that it has a liability. The various risks and benefits relating to particular assets and liabilities are discussed in the application notes.

Recognition

4.20   The next key question is deciding **when** something which satisfies the definition of an asset or liability has to be recognised in the balance. sheet. The standard seeks to answer this by saying that:

> 'where a transaction results in an item that meets the definition of an asset or liability, that item should be recognised in the balance sheet if:
>
> (a)   there is sufficient evidence of the existence of the item (including, where appropriate, evidence that a future inflow or outflow of benefit will occur), and
>
> (b)   the item can be measured at a monetary amount with sufficient reliability.'

Derecognition

4.21   As the name suggests, derecognition is the opposite of recognition. It **concerns the question of when to remove from the balance sheet the assets and liabilities which have previously been recognised.** FRS 5 addresses this issue only in relation to assets, not liabilities, and its rules are designed to determine one of three outcomes, discussed below: complete derecognition, no derecognition, and the in-between case, partial derecognition.

4.22   **The issue of derecognition is perhaps one of the most common aspects of off balance sheet transactions; has an asset been sold or has it been used to secure borrowings?** The concept of partial derecognition is a new addition to FRS 5 and attempts to deal with the in-between situation of where sufficient benefits and risks have been transferred to warrant at least some derecognition of an asset.

Complete derecognition

4.23   **In the simplest case, where a transaction results in the transfer to another party of all the significant benefits and risks relating to an asset, the entire asset should cease to be recognised.** In this context, the word 'significant' is explained further: it should not be judged in relation to all the conceivable benefits and risks that could exist, but only in relation to those that are likely to occur in practice. This means that the importance of the risk retained must be assessed in relation to the magnitude of the total realistic risk which exists.

No derecognition

4.24   At the other end of the spectrum, **where a transaction results in no significant change to the benefits or to the risks relating to the asset in question, no sale can be recorded and the entire asset should continue to be recognised.** Retaining *either* the benefits or the risks is sufficient to keep the asset on the balance sheet. This means that the elimination of risk by financing the asset on a non-recourse basis will not remove it from the balance sheet; it would be necessary to dispose of the upside as well in order to justify recording a sale. (A further possible treatment, the special case of a 'linked presentation', is discussed below.)

4.25 The standard says that **any transaction that is 'in substance a financing' will not qualify for derecognition**; the item will therefore stay on the balance sheet, and the finance will be introduced as a liability.

Partial derecognition

4.26 As can be seen, the above criteria are relatively restrictive. The standard therefore goes on to deal with circumstances where, although not all significant benefits and risks have been transferred, the transaction is more than a mere financing and has transferred enough of the benefits and risks to warrant at least some derecognition of the asset. It addresses three such cases.

(a) **Where an asset has been subdivided**

Where an identifiable part of an asset is separated and sold off, with the remainder being retained, the asset should be split and a partial sale recorded. Examples include the sale of a proportionate part of a loan receivable, where all future receipts are shared equally between the parties, or the stripping of interest payments from the principal of a loan instrument.

(b) **Where an item is sold for less than its full life**

This exception arises where the seller retains a residual value risk by offering to buy the asset back at a predetermined price at a later stage in the asset's life. Such an arrangement is sometimes offered in relation to commercial vehicles, aircraft, and so on. The standard says that in such cases the original asset will have been replaced by a residual interest in the asset together with a liability for its obligation to pay the repurchase price.

(c) **Where an item is transferred for its full life but some risk or benefit is retained**

This may arise, for example, where a company gives a warranty or residual value guarantee in relation to the product being sold. Under the standard, this does not preclude the recording of the sale so long as the exposure under the warranty or guarantee can be assessed and provided for if necessary. Companies may also sometimes retain the possibility of an upward adjustment to the sale price of an asset based on its future performance, for example, when a business is sold subject to an earn-out clause, but again this should not preclude the recognition of the sale.

4.27 In all of these cases of partial disposals, the amount of the initial profit or loss may be uncertain. **FRS 5 says that the normal rules of prudence should be applied, but also that the uncertainty should be disclosed if it could have a material effect on the accounts.**

Linked presentation

4.28 The exposure draft, FRED 4, introduced the concept of a 'linked presentation' and this has been carried through into FRS 5. This requires **non-recourse finance** to be **shown on the face of the balance sheet as a deduction from the asset to which it relates** (rather than in the liabilities section of the balance sheet), provided certain stringent criteria are met. This is really a question of how, rather than whether, to show the asset and liability in the balance sheet, so it is not the same as derecognition of these items, although there are some similarities in the result.

4.29 The standard says the linked presentation should be used when an asset is financed in such a way that:

(a)   the finance will be repaid only from proceeds generated by the specific item it finances (or by transfer of the item itself) and there is no possibility whatsoever of a claim on the entity being established other than against funds generated by that item (or against the item itself); and

(b)   there is no provision whereby the entity may either keep the item on repayment of the finance or reacquire it at any time.

There are also several more specific conditions which elaborate on these principles.

Offset

4.30   FRS 5 makes it clear that **assets and liabilities which qualify for recognition should be accounted for individually, rather than netted off**. Offset is allowed by the standard only where the debit and credit balances are not really separate assets and liabilities, for example where there are amounts due to and from the same third party and there is a legal right of set-off. The key consideration is whether the entity can enforce a right of set-off so that there is no possibility of having to pay the creditor balance without recovering the debtor amount.

4.31   The detailed criteria which **permit offset** are set out in FRS 5:

(a)   The **parties owe each other determinable monetary amounts**, denominated either in the same currency or in different but freely convertible currencies.

(b)   The **reporting entity has the ability to insist on a net settlement**, which can be enforced in all situations of default by the other party.

(c)   The **reporting entity's ability to insist on a net settlement is assured beyond doubt**. This means that the debit balance must be receivable no later than the credit balance requires to be paid, otherwise the entity could be required to pay the other party and later find that it was unable to obtain payment itself. It also means that the ability to insist on a net settlement would survive the insolvency of the other party (which may require detailed examination in group situations).

Consolidation of other entities

4.32   The Companies Act definition of a 'subsidiary undertaking' means that the consolidation of other entities is based largely on *de facto* control. However, FRS 5 takes the view that this is not conclusive in determining which entities are to be included in consolidated accounts. It envisages that there will be occasions where the need to give a true and fair view will require the inclusion of '**quasi subsidiaries**'. FRS 5 defines a quasi subsidiary in these terms.

KEY TERM

'A **quasi subsidiary** of a reporting entity is a company, trust, partnership or other vehicle that, though not fulfilling the definition of a subsidiary, is directly or indirectly controlled by the reporting entity and gives rise to benefits for that entity that are in substance no different from those that would arise were the vehicle a subsidiary.'

4.33   The **key feature of this definition is control, which means the ability to direct the vehicle's financial and operating policies with a view to gaining economic benefit from its activities**. Control is also indicated by the ability to prevent others from exercising those policies or from enjoying the benefits of the vehicle's net assets. A 'deadlock' 50:50 joint venture will still be off balance sheet for both parties, provided the two parties concerned are genuine equals in terms of both their ability to control the venture and their interests in its underlying assets.

4.34   FRS 5 requires that when quasi subsidiaries are included in consolidated accounts, the fact of their inclusion should be disclosed, together with a summary of their own financial statements.

Disclosure

4.35   FRS 5 has a general requirement to **disclose transactions in sufficient detail to enable the reader to understand their commercial effect,** whether or not they have given rise to the recognition of assets and liabilities. This means that where transactions or schemes give rise to assets and liabilities which are *not* recognised in the accounts, disclosure of their nature and effects still has to be considered in order to ensure that the accounts give a true and fair view.

4.36   A second general principle is that an **explanation** should be given **where there are any assets or liabilities whose nature is different from that which the reader might expect** of assets or liabilities appearing in the accounts under that description. The standard also calls for specific disclosures in relation to the use of the linked presentation, the inclusion of quasi subsidiaries in the accounts, and the various transactions dealt with in the application notes.

Common forms of off balance sheet finance

4.37   The application notes attached to FRS 5 are intended to clarify and develop the methods of applying the proposed standard to the particular transactions which they describe and to provide guidance on how to interpret it in relation to other similar transactions. These transactions are the more common types.

Consignment stock

4.38   Consignment stock is an arrangement where stock is **held by one party** (say a distributor) but is **owned by another party** (for example a manufacturer or a finance company). Consignment stock is common in the motor trade and is similar to goods sold on a 'sale or return' basis.

4.39   **To identify the correct treatment, it is necessary to identify the point at which the distributor acquired the benefits of the asset** (the stock) **rather than the point at which legal title was acquired.** If the manufacturer has the right to require the return of the stock, and if that right is likely to be exercised, then the stock is not an asset of the dealer. If the dealer is rarely required to return the stock, then this part of the transaction will have little commercial effect in practice and should be ignored for accounting purposes. The potential liability would need to be disclosed in the accounts.

Sale and leaseback transactions

4.40   These are arrangements under which the company sells an asset to another person on terms that allow the company to repurchase the assets in certain circumstances. **The key question is whether the transaction is a straightforward sale, or whether it is, in effect, a secured loan.** It is necessary to look at the arrangement to determine who has the rights to the economic benefits that the asset generates, and the terms on which the asset is to be repurchased.

4.41 If the seller has the right to the benefits of the use of the asset, and the repurchase terms are such that the repurchase is likely to take place, the transaction should be accounted for as a loan.

Factoring of debts

4.42 Where debts are factored, the original creditor sells the debts to the factor. The sales price may be fixed at the outset or may be adjusted later. It is also common for the factor to offer a credit facility that allows the seller to draw upon a proportion of the amounts owed.

4.43 In order to determine the correct accounting treatment it is **necessary to consider whether the benefit of the debts has been passed on to the factor, or whether the factor is, in effect, providing a loan on the security of the debtors.** If the seller has to pay interest on the difference between the amounts advanced to him and the amounts that the factor has received, and if the seller bears the risks of non-payment by the debtor, then the indications would be that the transaction is, in effect, a loan. Depending on the circumstances, either a linked presentation or separate presentation may be appropriate.

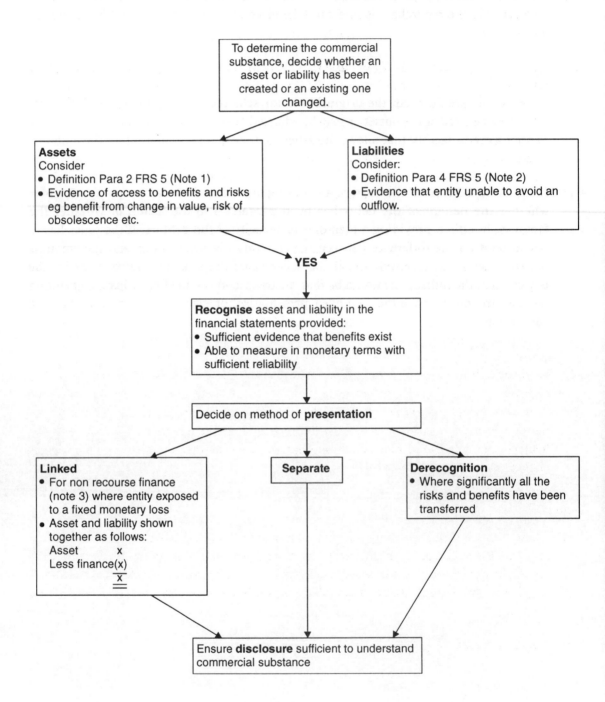

To determine the commercial substance, decide whether an asset or liability has been created or an existing one changed.

Assets
Consider
- Definition Para 2 FRS 5 (Note 1)
- Evidence of access to benefits and risks eg benefit from change in value, risk of obsolescence etc.

Liabilities
Consider:
- Definition Para 4 FRS 5 (Note 2)
- Evidence that entity unable to avoid an outflow.

YES

Recognise asset and liability in the financial statements provided:
- Sufficient evidence that benefits exist
- Able to measure in monetary terms with sufficient reliability

Decide on method of **presentation**

Linked
- For non recourse finance (note 3) where entity exposed to a fixed monetary loss
- Asset and liability shown together as follows:
Asset   x
Less finance(x)
               x̲

Separate

Derecognition
- Where significantly all the risks and benefits have been transferred

Ensure **disclosure** sufficient to understand commercial substance

Securitised assets

4.44 Securitisation is **very common in the financial services industry,** and the **assets** that are **most commonly securitised are mortgages and credit card accounts,** although hire purchase loans, trade debts and even property and stocks are sometimes securitised. Blocks of assets are thus financed, rather than the company's general business.

4.45 The **normal procedure is for the assets to be transferred by the person who held them (the originator) to a special purpose company (the issuer) in exchange for cash.** The issuer will use the proceeds of an issue of debentures or loan notes to pay for the assets. The shares in the issuer are usually held by a third party so that it does not need to be consolidated. The issuer will usually have a very small share capital, and so most of the risk will be borne by the people who lent it the money through the debentures to pay for the assets. For this reason there is usually some form of insurance taken out on the assets to give some security for the lenders.

4.46 **If the originator has retained significant benefits or risks** (say in the event of non-payment) **then the assets should continue to be shown on the originator's balance sheet and the money it received should be shown as a loan creditor.** If the requirements for linked presentation are satisfied, then the two items may be disclosed together on the balance sheet with the loan being subtracted from the asset. If these requirements are not met, then the asset and the liability should be shown under the appropriate headings.

4.47 **Derecognition is only appropriate where the originator has not retained any significant benefits.** In determining this it is necessary to consider whether the originator has access to the benefits of the securitised assets or exposure to their inherent risks, and whether the originator has a liability to repay the proceeds of the debenture or loan note issue. If derecognition is appropriate, then neither the asset nor the loan is shown on the originator's balance sheet.

Loan transfers

4.48 These are arrangements where a loan is transferred to a transferee from an original lender. This will usually be done by the assignment of rights and obligations by the lender, or the creation of a new agreement between the borrower and the transferee. The **same principles apply to loan transfers as apply to debt factoring and securitised assets.**

4.49 The diagram on the previous page will serve as a useful summary.

Chapter roundup

- You must learn:

  o the difference between the **net** and the **nil bases** of calculating **EPS**;
  o the effect on EPS of: a new issue of shares; a rights issue; a bonus issue;
  o how to calculate **fully diluted EPS**;
  o the **disclosure** requirements of SSAP 3.

  The only way to do this is by repeated question practice.

- FRS 3 *Reporting financial performance* has introduced radical **changes to the profit and loss** account of large and medium sized companies.

- You must know the **FRS 3 definitions** of:

  o **extraordinary items**;
  o **exceptional items**;
  o **prior year adjustments**;
  o **discontinued operations**;
  o **total recognised gains and losses**.

- You must know the format of the **statement of total recognised gains and losses** and understand its contents.

- Transactions must be accounted for according to their **substance**, **not** just their legal **form.**

- There are a number of **'creative accounting'** techniques, the purpose of which is to manipulate figures for a desired result.

- The subject of **off balance sheet finance** is complex and difficult to understand. In practice, off balance sheet finance schemes are often very sophisticated and they are beyond the range of this syllabus.

- Make sure that you have memorised the definitions for **assets and liabilities** and the **criteria** for their **recognition** and **derecognition** given in FRS 5 *Reporting the substance of transactions.*

- You also need to understand the methods of presentation described in FRS 5, particularly **offset** and **linked presentation.**

Quick quiz

1   Define earnings per share. (see para 1.2)

2   Distinguish between the net basis and the nil basis of calculating EPS. Which basis is prescribed by SSAP 3? (1.9)

3   Following a rights issue, what is the fraction by which the EPS for the corresponding previous period should be multiplied? (1.18)

4   What is 'fully diluted EPS'? (1.27)

5   Summarise the disclosure requirements of SSAP 3. (1.29)

6   How does FRS 3 define ordinary activities? (2.5)

7   Which exceptional items must be shown on the face of the P & L account? (2.6)

8   What accounting treatments are presented by FRS 3 for exceptional items? (2.6)

9   Define extraordinary items. (2.9)

10 What components of financial performance should be shown on the face of the profit and loss account according to FRS 3? (2.12)

11 What conditions must be satisfied for a sold or terminated operation to be classified as discontinued? (2.13(c)).

12 What is shown in the statement of total recognised gains and losses? (2.18)

13 What is the accounting treatment of prior period adjustments? (2.29)

14 What is meant by 'substance over form'? (3.1)

14 How are assets and liabilities defined in the *Statement of Principles*? (4.8)

15 Describe 'linked presentation' and 'offset' as set out in FRS 5. (4.29, 4.31)

16 What topics does FRS 5 discuss in the application notes? (4.39 - 4.49)

Question to try	Level	Marks	Time
14	Full exam	25	45 mins

Chapter 14

CASH FLOW STATEMENTS

Chapter topic list		Syllabus reference
1	FRS 1 Cash flow statements	1(c), 2(a)
2	Preparing a cash flow statement	1(c), 2(a)
3	Interpretation of cash flow statements	1(c), 2(a)
4	Cash flow forecasts	1(c), 2(a)

Introduction

You have already covered basic cash flow accounting in your Foundation studies. Here, the study of cash flow statement revolves around FRS 1, which governs the content and disclosure of cash flow statements in company accounts.

FRS 1 was the first standard produced by the Accounting Standards Board and it was revised in October 1996.

This chapter adopts a systematic approach to the preparation of cash flow statements in examinations; you should learn this method and you will then be equipped for any problems in the exam itself.

The third section in the chapter looks at the information which is provided by cash flow statements and how it should be analysed. Finally we look at cash flow forecasts.

1 FRS 1 CASH FLOW STATEMENTS   6/94, 6/95

1.1 It has been argued that 'profit' does not always give a useful or meaningful picture of a company's operations. **Readers of a company's financial statements might even be misled by a reported profit figure**.

(a) Shareholders might believe that if a company makes a profit after tax of, say, £100,000 then this is the amount which it could afford to **pay as a dividend**. Unless the company has **sufficient cash** available to stay in business and also to pay a dividend, the shareholders' expectations would be wrong.

(b) Employees might believe that if a company makes profits, it can afford to **pay higher wages** next year. This opinion may not be correct: the ability to pay wages depends on the **availability of cash**.

(c) Survival of a business entity depends not so much on profits as on its **ability to pay its debts when they fall due**. Such payments might include 'profit and loss' items such as material purchases, wages, interest and taxation etc, but also capital payments for new fixed assets and the repayment of loan capital when this falls due (for example on the redemption of debentures).

1.2 From these examples, it may be apparent that a company's performance and prospects depend not so much on the 'profits' earned in a period, but more realistically on liquidity or **cash flows**.

1.3   The great advantage of a cash flow statement is that it is unambiguous and provides information which is additional to that provided in the rest of the accounts. It also describes to the cash flows of an organisation by activity and not by balance sheet classification.

FRS 1 *Cash flow statements* (revised)

1.4   **FRS 1 sets out the structure of a cash flow statement and it also sets the minimum level of disclosure.** In October 1996 the ASB issued a revised version of FRS 1 *Cash flow statements*. The revision of FRS 1 was part of a normal process of revision, but it also responded to various criticisms of the original FRS 1. Although cash flow statements were found to be useful, some shortcomings were perceived, which we will discuss in Section 3.

> **Exam focus point**
> You only need to learn the revised version of the standard. Examination questions are likely to be computational, but some discussion and interpretation may be required.

Objective

1.5   The FRS begins with the following statement.

'The objective of this FRS is to ensure that reporting entities falling within its scope:

(a)   report their cash generation and cash absorption for a period by highlighting the significant components of cash flow in a way that facilitates comparison of the cash flow performance of different businesses; and

(b)   provide information that assists in the assessment of their liquidity, solvency and financial adaptability.'

Scope

1.6   The FRS applies to all financial statements intended to give a true and fair view of the financial position and profit or loss (or income and expenditure), except those of various exempt bodies in group accounts situations or where the content of the financial statement is governed by other statutes or regulatory regimes. In addition, **small entities are excluded** as defined by companies legislation.

Format of the cash flow statement

1.7   An example is given of the format of a cash flow statement for a single company and this is reproduced below.

1.8   A cash flow statement should list its cash flows for the period classified under the following **standard headings**.

> ## STANDARD HEADINGS
>
> (a) Operating activities (using either the direct or indirect method)
> (b) Returns on investments and servicing of finance
> (c) Taxation
> (d) Capital expenditure and financial investment
> (e) Acquisitions and disposals
> (f) Equity dividends paid
> (g) Management of liquid resources
> (h) Financing

The last two headings can be shown in a single section provided a subtotal is given for each heading. Acquisitions and disposals are not on your syllabus; the heading is included here for completeness.

1.9 Individual categories of inflows and outflows under the standard headings should be disclosed separately either in the cash flow statements or in a note to it unless they are allowed to be shown net. Cash inflows and outflows may be shown net if they relate to the management of liquid resources or financing and the inflows and outflows either:

(a) relate in substance to a single financing transaction (unlikely to be a concern in Paper 10); or

(b) are due to short maturities and high turnover occurring from rollover or reissue (for example, short-term deposits).

The requirement to show cash inflows and outflows separately does not apply to cash flows relating to operating activities.

1.10 Each cash flow should be classified according to the substance of the transaction giving rise to it.

Links to other primary statements

1.11 Because the information given by a cash flow statement is best appreciated in the context of the information given by the other primary statements, the FRS requires **two reconciliations**, between:

(a) **operating profit and the net cash flow from operating activities**; and
(b) the **movement in cash in the period and the movement in net debt.**

Neither reconciliation forms part of the cash flow statement but each may be given either adjoining the statement or in a separate note.

1.12 The **movement in net debt** should identify the following components and reconcile these to the opening and closing balance sheet amount:

(a) The **cash flows** of the entity.
(b) **Other non-cash changes**.
(c) The recognition of **changes in market value** and **exchange rate movements**.

Definitions

1.13   The FRS includes the following **important definitions** (only those of direct concern to your syllabus are included here). Note particularly the definitions of cash and liquid resources.

(a)   An **active market** is a market of sufficient depth to absorb the investment held without a significant effect on the price. (This definition affects the definition of liquid resources below.)

(b)   **Cash** is cash in hand and deposits repayable on demand with any qualifying financial institution, less overdrafts from any qualifying financial institution repayable on demand. Deposits are repayable on demand if they can be withdrawn at any time without notice and without penalty or if a maturity or period of notice of not more than 24 hours or one working day has been agreed. Cash includes cash in hand and deposit denominated in foreign currencies.

(c)   **Cash flow** is an increase or decrease in an amount of cash.

(d)   **Liquid resources** are current asset investments held as readily disposable stores of value. A readily disposable investment is one that:

(i)   is disposable by the reporting entity without curtailing or disrupting its business; and

(ii)   is either:

(1)   readily convertible into known amounts of cash at or close to its carrying amount, or

(2)   traded in an active market.

(e)   **Net debt** is the borrowings of the reporting entity less cash and liquid resources. Where cash and liquid resources exceed the borrowings of the entity reference should be to 'net funds' rather than to 'net debt'.

(f)   **Overdraft** is a borrowing facility repayable on demand that is used by drawing on a current account with a qualifying financial institution.

Classification of cash flows by standard heading

1.14   The FRS looks at each of the cash flow categories in turn.

> **Exam focus point**
> If you are in a hurry or revising skim through these definitions, taking in the highlighted words and go straight to the example in paragraph 1.39.

Operating activities

1.15   Cash flows from operating activities are in general the **cash effects of transactions** and other events **relating to operating or trading activities**, normally shown in the profit and loss account in arriving at operating profit. They include cash flows in respect of operating items relating to provisions, whether or not the provision was included in operating profit.

1.16   A **reconciliation** between the operating profit reported in the profit and loss account and the net cash flow from operating activities should be given **either adjoining the cash flow statement or as a note**. The reconciliation is not part of the cash flow statement: if adjoining the cash flow statement, it should be clearly labelled and kept separate. The reconciliation should disclose separately the movements in stocks, debtors and creditors related to operating activities and other differences between cash flows and profits.

Returns on investments and servicing of finance

1.17 These are **receipts resulting from the ownership of an investment and payments to providers of finance and non-equity shareholders** (eg the holders of preference shares).

1.18 **Cash inflows** from returns on investments and servicing of finance include:

(a) **Interest received**, including any related tax recovered.
(b) **Dividends received**, net of any tax credits.

1.19 **Cash outflows** from returns on investments and servicing of finance include:

(a) **Interest paid** (even if capitalised), including any tax deducted and paid to the relevant tax authority.

(b) Cash flows that are treated as **finance costs** (this will include issue costs on debt and non-equity share capital).

(c) The **interest element of finance lease rental** payments.

(d) **Dividends paid on non-equity shares** of the entity.

Taxation

1.20 These are cash flows to or from taxation authorities in respect of the reporting entity's revenue and capital profits. VAT and other sales taxes are discussed later.

(a) Taxation cash **inflows** include **cash receipts** from the relevant tax authority of tax rebates, claims or returns of overpayments.

(b) Taxation cash **outflows** include **cash payments** to the relevant tax authority of tax, including payments of advance corporation tax.

Capital expenditure and financial investment

1.21 These **cash flows** are those **related to the acquisition or disposal of any fixed asset** other than one required to be classified under 'acquisitions and disposals' (discussed below), **and any current asset investment** not included in liquid resources (also dealt with below). If no cash flows relating to financial investment fall to be included under this heading the caption may be reduced to 'capital expenditure'.

1.22 The **cash inflows** here include:

(a) **receipts from sales or disposals** of property, plant or equipment; and
(b) **receipts from the repayment of** the reporting entity's **loans** to other entities.

1.23 **Cash outflows** in this category include:

(a) **payments to acquire property**, plant or equipment; and
(b) **loans made** by the reporting entity.

Acquisitions and disposals

1.24 These cash flows are related to the acquisition or disposal of any trade or business, or of an investment in an entity that is either an associate, a joint venture, or a subsidiary undertaking (these group matters are beyond the scope of your syllabus).

(a) Cash **inflows** here include **receipts from sales of trades or businesses**.
(b) Cash **outflows** here include **payments to acquire trades or businesses**.

Equity dividends paid

1.25 The cash outflows are **dividends paid on** the reporting entity's **equity shares**, excluding any advance corporation tax.

Management of liquid resources

1.26 This section should include cash flows in respect of liquid resources as defined above. Each entity should explain what it includes as liquid resources and any changes in its policy. The cash flows in this section can be shown in a single section with those under 'financing' provided that separate subtotals for each are given.

1.27 **Cash inflows** include:

(a) **withdrawals from short-term deposits** not qualifying as cash; and

(b) inflows from **disposal or redemption** of any other investments held as liquid resources.

1.28 **Cash outflows** include:

(a) **payments into short-term deposits** not qualifying as cash; and
(b) outflows to **acquire any other investments** held as liquid resources.

Financing

1.29 Financing cash flows comprise receipts or repayments of principal from or to external providers of finance. The cash flows in this section can be shown in a single section with those under 'management of liquid resources' provided that separate subtotals for each are given.

1.30 Financing **cash inflows** include receipts **from issuing**:

(a) **Shares** or other equity instruments.

(b) **Debentures,** loans and from other long-term and short-term borrowings (other than overdrafts).

1.31 Financing cash **outflows** include:

(a) **Repayments of amounts borrowed** (other than overdrafts).
(b) The **capital element of finance lease rental** payments.
(c) Payments to **reacquire or redeem the entity's shares**.
(d) Payments of **expenses or commission on any issue of equity shares**.

Exceptional and extraordinary items and cash flows

1.32 Where cash flows relate to items that are classified as exceptional or extraordinary in the profit and loss account they **should be shown under the appropriate standard headings according to the nature of each item**. The cash flows relating to exceptional or extraordinary items should be identified in the cash flow statement or a note to it and the relationship between the cash flows and the originating exceptional or extraordinary item should be explained.

1.33   **Where cash flows are exceptional because of their size of incidence** but are not related to items that are treated as exceptional or extraordinary in the profit and loss account, **sufficient disclosure should be given to explain their cause and nature.**

Value added tax and other taxes

1.34   **Cash flows should be shown net of any attributable value added tax or other sale tax unless the tax is irrecoverable by the reporting entity.** The net movement on the amount payable to, or receivable from the taxing authority should be allocated to cash flows from operating activities unless a different treatment is more appropriate in the particular circumstances concerned. Where restrictions apply to the recoverability of such taxes, the irrecoverable amount should be allocated to those expenditures affected by the restrictions. If this is impracticable, the irrecoverable tax should be included under the most appropriate standard heading.

1.35   **Taxation cash flows other than those** in respect of the reporting entity's revenue and capital profits and value added tax, or other sales tax, **should be included within the cash flow statement** under the same standard heading as the cash flow that gave rise to the taxation cash flow, unless a different treatment is more appropriate in the particular circumstances concerned.

Material non-cash transactions

1.36   Material transactions not resulting in movements of cash of the reporting entity **should be disclosed in the notes** to the cash flow statement if disclosure is necessary for an understanding of the underlying transactions.

Comparative figures

1.37   Comparative figures **should be given for all items in the cash flow statement** and such notes thereto as are required by the FRS with the exception of the note to the statement that analyses changes in the balance sheet amount making up net debt.

Effective date

1.38   The revised FRS is effective for financial statements with accounting periods ending on or after 23 March 1997 although earlier adoption is encouraged.

1.39   EXAMPLE: SINGLE COMPANY

The following example is provided by the standard for a single company.

XYZ LIMITED
CASH FLOW STATEMENT FOR THE YEAR ENDED 31 DECEMBER 1996

Reconciliation of operating profit to net cash inflow from operating activities

	£'000
Operating profit	6,022
Depreciation charges	899
Increase in stocks	(194)
Increase in debtors	(72)
Increase in creditors	234
Net cash inflow from operating activities	6,899

CASH FLOW STATEMENT

	£'000
Net cash inflow from operating activities	6,889
Returns on investments and servicing of finance (note 1)	2,999
Taxation	(2,922)
Capital expenditure (note 1)	(1,525)
	5,441
Equity dividends paid	(2,417)
	3,024
Management of liquid resources (note 1)	(450)
Financing (note 1)	57
Increase in cash	2,631

Reconciliation of net cash flow to movement in net debt (note 2)

	£'000	£'000
Increase in cash in the period	2,631	
Cash to repurchase debenture	149	
Cash used to increase liquid resources	450	
Change in net debt*		3,230
Net debt at 1.1.96		(2,903)
Net funds at 31.12.96		327

*In this example all change in net debt are cash flows.

The reconciliation of operating profit to net cash flows from operating activities can be shown in a note.

NOTES TO THE CASH FLOW STATEMENT

1 *Gross cash flows*

	£'000	£'000
Returns on investments and servicing of finance		
Interest received	3,011	
Interest paid	(12)	
		2,999
Capital expenditure		
Payments to acquire intangible fixed assets	(71)	
Payments to acquire tangible fixed assets	(1,496)	
Receipts from sales of tangible fixed assets	42	
		(1,525)
Management of liquid resources		
Purchase of treasury bills	(650)	
Sale of treasury bills	200	
		(450)
Financing		
Issue of ordinary share capital	211	
Repurchase of debenture loan	(149)	
Expenses paid in connection with share issues	(5)	
		57

Note. These gross cash flows can be shown on the face of the cash flow statement, but it may sometimes be neater to show them as a note like this.

2   *Analysis of changes in net debt*

	As at 1 Jan 1996 £'000	Cash flows £'000	Other changes £'000	At 31 Dec 1996 £'000
Cash in hand, at bank	42	847		889
Overdrafts	(1,784)	1,784		
		2,631		
Debt due within 1 year	(149)	149	(230)	(230)
Debt due after 1 year	(1,262)		230	(1,032)
Current asset investments	250	450		700
Total	(2,903)	3,230	-	327

Question 1

Close the book for a moment and jot down the format of the cash flow statement.

---

2   PREPARING A CASH FLOW STATEMENT   6/94, 6/95

Exam focus point

In essence, preparing a cash flow statement is very straightforward. You should therefore simply learn the format given above and apply the steps noted in the example below. Note that the following items are treated in a way that might seem confusing, but the treatment is logical if you think in terms of **cash**.

2.1   (a)   **Increase in stock** is treated as **negative** (in brackets). This is because it represents a cash **outflow**; cash is being spent on stock.

      (b)   An **increase in debtors** would be treated as **negative** for the same reasons; more debtors means less cash.

      (c)   By contrast an **increase in creditors** is **positive** because cash is being retained and not used to pay off creditors. There is therefore more of it.

2.2   EXAMPLE: PREPARATION OF A CASH FLOW STATEMENT

Kane Ltd's profit and loss account for the year ended 31 December 19X2 and balance sheets at 31 December 19X1 and 31 December 19X2 were as follows.

KANE LIMITED
PROFIT AND LOSS ACCOUNT FOR THE YEAR ENDED 31 DECEMBER 19X2

	£'000	£'000
Sales		720
Raw materials consumed	70	
Staff costs	94	
Depreciation	118	
Loss on disposal	18	
		300
Operating profit		420
Interest payable		28
Profit before tax		392
Taxation		124
		268
Dividend		72
Profit retained for year		196
Balance brought forward		490
		686

KANE LIMITED
BALANCE SHEETS AS AT 31 DECEMBER

	19X2		19X1	
	£'000	£'000	£'000	£'000
Fixed assets				
Cost		1,596		1,560
Depreciation		318		224
		1,278		1,336
Current assets				
Stock	24		20	
Trade debtors	66		50	
Recoverable ACT	10		8	
Bank	48		56	
	148		134	
Current liabilities				
Trade creditors	12		6	
Taxation	102		86	
Proposed dividend	30		24	
	144		116	
Working capital		4		18
		1,282		1,354
Long-term liabilities				
Long-term loans		200		500
		1,082		854
Share capital		360		340
Share premium		36		24
Profit and loss		686		490
		1,082		854

During the year, the company paid £90,000 for a new piece of machinery.

Required

Prepare a cash flow statement for Kane Ltd for the year ended 31 December 19X2 in accordance with the requirements of FRS 1 (revised).

2.3 SOLUTION

Step 1 Set out the proforma cash flow statement with all the headings required by FRS 1 (revised). You should leave plenty of space. Ideally, use three or more sheets of paper, one for the main statement, one for the notes (particularly if you have a separate note for the gross cash flows) and one for your workings. It is obviously essential to know the formats very well.

Step 2 Complete the reconciliation of operating profit to net cash inflow as far as possible. When preparing the statement from balance sheets, you will usually have to calculate such items as depreciation, loss on sale of fixed assets and profit for the year (see Step 4).

Step 3 Calculate the figures for tax paid, dividends paid, purchase or sale of fixed assets, issue of shares and repayment of loans if these are not already given to you (as they may be). Note that you may not be given the tax charge in the profit loss account. You will then have to assume that the tax paid in the year is last year's year-end provision and calculate the charge as the balancing figure.

Step 4 If you are not given the profit figure, open up a working for the profit and loss account. Using the opening and closing balances, the taxation charge and dividends paid and proposed, you will be able to calculate profit for the year as the balancing figure to put in the statement.

Step 5 Complete note 1, the gross cash flows. Alternatively this information may go straight into the statement.

Step 6 You will now be able to complete the statement by slotting in the figures given or calculated.

Step 7 Complete note 2 the analysis of changes in net debt.

KANE LIMITED
CASH FLOW STATEMENT FOR THE YEAR ENDED 31 DECEMBER 19X2

Reconciliation of operating profit to net cash inflow

	£'000
Operating profit	420
Depreciation charges	118
Loss on sale of tangible fixed assets	18
Increase in stocks	(4)
Increase in debtors	(16)
Increase in creditors	6
Net cash inflow from operating activities	542

CASH FLOW STATEMENT

	£'000	£'000
Net cash flows from operating activities		542
Returns on investment and servicing of finance		
Interest paid		(28)
Taxation		
Corporation tax paid (including ACT) (W1)		(110)
Capital expenditure		
Payments to acquire tangible fixed assets	(90)	
Receipts from sales of tangible fixed assets	12	
Net cash outflow from capital expenditure		(78)
		326
Equity dividends paid (72 – 30 + 24)		(66)
		260
Financing		
Issues of share capital (360 + 36 – 340 – 24)	32	
Long-term loans repaid (500 – 200)	(300)	
Net cash outflow from financing		(268)
Decrease in cash		(8)

NOTES TO THE CASH FLOW STATEMENT

Analysis of changes in net debt

	At 1 Jan 19X2	*Cash flows*	*At 31 Dec 19X2*
	£'000	£'000	£'000
Cash in hand, at bank	56	(8)	48
Debt due after 1 year	(500)	300	(200)
Total	(444)	292	(152)

Workings

1   *Corporation tax paid (including ACT)*

	£'000
Opening CT payable	86
ACT recoverable	(8)
Charge for year	124
Net CT payable at 31.12.X2 (102 – 10)	(92)
Paid	110

2   *Fixed asset disposals*

COST

	£'000			£'000
At 1.1.X2	1,560	At 31.12.X2		1,596
Purchases	90	Disposals		54
	1,650			1,650

ACCUMULATED DEPRECIATION

	£'000			£'000
At 31.1.X2	318	At 1.1.X2		224
Depreciation on disposals	24	Charge for year		118
	342			342

	£'000
NBV of disposals	30
Net loss reported	(18)
Proceeds of disposals	12

Alternative methods

2.4 **FRS 1 allows two possible layouts** for cash flow statement in respect of operating activities:

    (a) the **indirect method,** which is the one we have used so far; or

    (b) the **direct method.**

2.5 Under the **direct method** the operating element of the cash flow statement should be shown as follows.

	£'000
Operating activities	
Cash received from customers	X
Cash payments to suppliers	(X)
Cash paid to and on behalf of employees	(X)
Other cash payments	(X)
Net cash flow from operating activities	X

2.6 Points to note are as follows.

    (a) The **reconciliation** of operating profits and cash flows is **still required** (by note).

    (b) **Cash received from customers** represents cash flows received during the accounting period in respect of sales.

    (c) **Cash payments to suppliers** represents cash flows made during the accounting period in respect of goods and services.

    (d) **Cash payments to and on behalf of employees** represents amounts paid to employees including the associated tax and national insurance. It will, therefore, comprise gross salaries, employer's National Insurance and any other benefits (eg pension contributions).

2.7 **The direct method is, in effect, an analysis of the cash book.** This information does not appear directly in the rest of the financial statements and so many companies might find it difficult to collect the information. Problems might include the need to reanalyse the cash book, to collate results from different cash sources and so on. The indirect method may be easier as it draws on figures which can be obtained from the financial statements fairly easily.

Question 2

The summarised accounts of Rene plc for the year ended 31 December 19X8 are as follows.

RENE PLC
BALANCE SHEET AS AT 31 DECEMBER 19X8

	£'000	*19X8* £'000	£'000	*19X7* £'000
Fixed assets				
Tangible assets		628		514
Current assets				
Stocks	214		210	
Debtors	168		147	
Cash	7		-	
	389		357	
Creditors: amounts falling due within one year				
Trade creditors	136		121	
Tax payable	39		28	
Dividends payable	18		16	
Overdraft	-		14	
	193		179	
Net current assets		196		178
Total assets less current liabilities		824		692
Creditors: amounts falling due after more than one year				
10% debentures		(80)		(50)
		744		642
Capital and reserves				
Share capital (£1 ords)		250		200
Share premium account		70		60
Revaluation reserve		110		100
Profit and loss account		314		282
		744		642

RENE PLC
PROFIT AND LOSS ACCOUNT
FOR THE YEAR ENDED 31 DECEMBER 19X8

	£'000
Sales	600
Cost of sales	(319)
Gross profit	281
Other expenses (including depreciation of £42,000)	(194)
Profit before tax	87
Tax	(31)
Profit after tax	56
Dividends	(24)
Retained profit for the year	32

You are additionally informed that there have been no disposals of fixed assets during the year. New debentures were issued on 1 January 19X8. Wages for the year amounted to £86,000.

Required

Produce a cash flow statement using the direct method suitable for inclusion in the financial statements, as per FRS 1 (revised 1996).

Answer

RENE PLC
CASH FLOW STATEMENT
FOR THE YEAR ENDED 31 DECEMBER 19X8

	£'000	£'000
Operating activities		
Cash received from customers (W1)	579	
Cash payments to suppliers (W2)	(366)	
Cash payments to and on behalf of employees	(86)	
		127
Returns on investments and servicing of finance		
Interest paid		(8)
Taxation		
UK corporation tax paid (W5)		(20)
Capital expenditure		
Purchase of tangible fixed assets (W6)	(146)	
Net cash outflow from capital expenditure		(146)
		(47)
Equity dividends paid (W4)		(22)
Financing		
Issue of share capital	60	
Issue of debentures	30	
Net cash inflow from financing		90
Increase in cash		21

NOTES TO THE CASHFLOW STATEMENT

1   *Reconciliation of operating profit to net cash inflow from operating activities*

	£'000
Operating profit (87 + 8)	95
Depreciation	42
Increase in stock	(4)
Increase in debtors	(21)
Increase in creditors	15
	127

2   *Reconciliation of net cash flow to movement in net debt*

	£'000
Net cash inflow for the period	21
Cash received from debenture issue	(30)
Change in net debt	(9)
Net debt at 1 January 19X8	(64)
Net debt at 31 December 19X8	(73)

3   *Analysis of changes in net debt*

	At 1 January 19X8 £'000	Cash flows £'000	At 31 December 19X8 £'000
Cash at bank	-	7	7
Overdrafts	(14)	14	-
		21	
Debt due after 1 year	(50)	(30)	(80)
Total	(64)	(9)	(73)

Workings

1   *Cash received from customers*

DEBTORS CONTROL ACCOUNT

	£'000		£'000
B/f	147	Cash received (bal)	579
Sales	600	C/f	168
	747		747

2   *Cash paid to suppliers*

CREDITORS CONTROL ACCOUNT

	£'000		£'000
Cash paid (bal)	366	B/f	121
C/f	136	Purchases (W3)	381
	502		502

3   *Purchases*

	£'000
Cost of sales	319
Opening stock	(210)
Closing stock	214
Expenses (194 – 42 – 86 – 8 debenture interest)	58
	381

4   *Dividends*

DIVIDENDS

	£'000		£'000
∴ Dividends paid	22	Balance b/f	16
Balance c/f	18	Dividend for year	24
	40		40

5   *Taxation*

TAXATION

	£'000		£'000
∴ Tax paid	20	Balance b/f	28
Balance c/f	39	Charge for year	31
	59		59

6   *Purchase of fixed assets*

	£'000
Opening fixed assets	514
Less depreciation	(42)
Add revaluation (110 – 100)	10
	482
Closing fixed assets	628
Difference = additions	146

3   INTERPRETATION OF CASH FLOW STATEMENTS

3.1   FRS 1 *Cash flow statements* was introduced on the basis that it would provide better, more comprehensive and more useful information than its predecessor standard. So what kind of information does the cash flow statement, along with its notes, provide?

3.2   Some of the **main areas where FRS 1 should provide information not found elsewhere in the accounts are as follows.**

(a)   The **relationships between profit and cash** can be seen clearly and analysed accordingly.

(b)   **Management of liquid resources** is highlighted, giving a better picture of the liquidity of the company.

(c) **Financing inflows and outflows must be shown, rather than simply passed through reserves**.

3.3 One of the most important things to realise at this point is that, as the ASB is always keen to emphasise, it is wrong to try to assess the health or predict the death of a reporting entity solely on the basis of a single indicator. When analysing cash flow data, the **comparison should not just be between cash flows and profit, but also between cash flows over a period of time** (say three to five years).

3.4 Cash is not synonymous with profit on an annual basis, but you should also remember that the 'behaviour' of profit and cash flows will be very different. **Profit is smoothed out** through accruals, prepayments, provisions and other accounting conventions. This does not apply to cash, so the **cash flow figures are likely to be 'lumpy' in comparison**. You must distinguish between this 'lumpiness' and the trends which will appear over time.

3.5 The **relationship between profit and cash flows will vary constantly**. Note that healthy companies do not always have reported profits exceeding operating cash flows. Similarly, unhealthy companies can have operating cash flows well in excess of reported profit. The value of comparing them is in determining the extent to which earned profits are being converted into the necessary cash flows.

3.6 **Profit is not as important as the extent to which a company can convert its profits into cash on a continuing basis.** This process should be judged over a period longer than one year. The cash flows should be compared with profits over the same periods to decide how successfully the reporting entity has converted earnings into cash.

3.7 Cash flow figures should also be considered in terms of their specific relationships with each other over time. A form of **'cash flow gearing' can** be determined by comparing operating cash flows and financing flows, particularly borrowing, to **establish the extent of dependence of the reporting entity on external funding.**

3.8 **Other relationships** can be examined.

(a) Operating cash flows and investment flows can be related to match cash recovery from investment to investment.

(b) Investment can be compared to distribution to indicate the proportion of total cash outflow designated specifically to investor return and reinstatement.

(c) A comparison of tax outflow to operating cash flow minus investment flow will establish a 'cash basis tax rate'.

3.9 The 'ratios' mentioned above can be monitored inter- and intra-firm and the analyses can be undertaken in monetary, general price-level adjusted, or percentage terms.

The advantages of cash flow accounting   6/96

3.10 The advantages of cash flow accounting are as follows.

(a) Survival in business depends on the **ability to generate** cash. Cash flow accounting directs attention towards this critical issue.

(b) Cash flow is **more comprehensive** than 'profit' which is dependent on accounting conventions and concepts.

(c) **Creditors** (long and short-term) **are more interested in an entity's ability to repay them than in its profitability**. Whereas 'profits' might indicate that cash is likely to be available, cash flow accounting is more direct with its message.

(d) Cash flow reporting provides a **better means of comparing the results** of different companies than traditional profit reporting.

(e) Cash flow reporting **satisfies the needs of all users** better.

   (i) For **management**, it provides the sort of information on which decisions should be taken: (in management accounting, 'relevant costs' to a decision are future cash flows); traditional profit accounting does not help with decision-making.

   (ii) For **shareholders and auditors**, cash flow accounting can provide a satisfactory basis for stewardship accounting.

   (iii) As described previously, the information needs of **creditors and employees** will be better served by cash flow accounting.

(f) Cash flow forecasts are **easier to prepare**, as well as more useful, than profit forecasts.

(g) They can in some respects be **audited more easily** than accounts based on the accruals concept.

(h) The accruals concept is confusing, and cash flows are **more easily understood**.

(i) Cash flow accounting should be both retrospective, and also include a forecast for the future. This is of **great information value** to all users of accounting information.

(j) **Forecasts** can subsequently be **monitored** by the publication of variance statements which compare actual cash flows against the forecast.

Question 3

Can you think of some possible disadvantages of cash flow accounting?

Answer

The main disadvantages of cash accounting are essentially the advantages of accruals accounting (proper matching of related items). There is also the practical problem that few businesses keep historical cash flow information in the form needed to prepare a historical cash flow statement and so extra record keeping is likely to be necessary.

Why FRS 1 was revised

3.11 We mentioned at the beginning of this chapter that FRS 1 was revised, at least in part, because of certain criticisms. We will look at these briefly.

3.12 **The original FRS 1 included 'cash equivalents' with cash.** Cash equivalents were highly liquid investments with a maturity date of less than three months from the date of acquisitions (netted off against similar advances from banks). The inclusion of cash equivalents was criticised because it did not reflect the way in which businesses were managed: in particular, the requirement that to be a cash equivalent an investment had to be within three months of maturity was **considered unrealistic. In the revised FRS, only cash in hand and deposits repayable on demand, less overdrafts, are included in 'cash'.**

3.13 To distinguish the management of assets similar to cash (which previously might have been classed as 'cash equivalents') from other investment decisions, the revised FRS has a section dealing separately with the cash flows arising from the management of liquid resources.

3.14 The **new note** required by FRS 1 (revised) **reconciling movement in net debt** gives **additional information** on company performance, solvency and financial adaptability.

4   CASH FLOW FORECASTS   6/95

Exam focus point
Cash flow forecasts are not mentioned in the Syllabus or Teaching Guide for Paper 10. However, a question in the June 1995 paper did ask for a discussion of the advantages of cash flow forecasting, so a brief treatment will be given here.

The purpose of forecasts

4.1 Many businesses fail because of cash flow problems. Cash forecasting is vital to ensure that sufficient funds will be available when they are needed at an acceptable cost. Forecasts **provide an early warning of liquidity problems, by estimating:**

    (a) **How much cash is required.**
    (b) **When it is required.**
    (c) **How long it is required for.**
    (d) **Whether it will be available** from anticipated sources.

4.2 The timing of cash flows, as well as the amount, is important because a company must know when it might need to borrow and for how long, not just what amount of funding could be required.

4.3 This liquidity information is **of help to creditors and investors as well as to management,** as it assists them in assessing the ability of the company to pay its way. Banks have increasingly insisted that customers provide cash forecasts (or a business plan that includes a cash forecast) as a precondition of lending. A newly-established company wishing to open a bank account will also normally be asked to supply a business plan. The cash and sales forecasts will also allow the bank to monitor the progress of the new company, and control its lending more effectively.

Types of forecast

4.4 There are two broad types of cash forecast.

    (a) Cash flow based forecasts (or cash budgets) in **receipts and payments format.**
    (b) Balance sheet and **financial statement based forecasts.**

Receipts and payments

4.5 Cash flow based forecasts (receipts and payments) are **forecasts of the amount and timing of cash receipts and payments,** net cash flows and changes in cash balances, for each time period covered by the forecast. Cash flow based forecasts include cash budgets up to a year or so ahead and short-term forecasts of just a few days.

4.6 Forecasting **should have a logical structure based on:**

(a) **identification** of component cash flows, each component having its own characteristics; and

(b) **assumptions** about the timing and pattern of cash flows.

4.7 The **advantages** of preparing cash flow forecasts in receipt and payments format, which involves forecasting the cash position for a number of individual items, are these.

(a) They are based on the **timings** which might be **identified in the operating cycle**.

(b) They are **straightforward** to prepare.

(c) They **clearly identify the distinction between operational and other cash flows**. Each type of cash flow might have different implications for management.

(d) **Temporary surpluses or deficiencies** within a budget period **are picked up**, as the timing of receipts and payments can be taken into account.

(e) They are likely to be **relevant** to movements in and out of the firm's bank account (subject to clearance delay, see below).

(f) They can **identify any long term trends** in the declining cash balances.

4.8 **However, they do not indicate overall changes in the firm's working capital** such as debtors, creditors or stocks, of which cash is a part. A bias in one figure can, if projected, render further figures unhelpful and wrong. After all, a company's operational cash flows are intimately connected with its levels of stocks, debtors and creditors.

Balance sheet

4.9 A balance sheet based forecast is **an estimate of the company's balance sheet at a future date.** It is used to identify either the cash surplus or the funding shortfall in the company's balance sheet at the forecast date.

(a) **It is not an estimate of cash inflows and outflows**. A number of sequential forecasts can be produced, for example a forecast of the balance sheet at the end of each year for the next five years.

(b) The balance sheet **is produced for management accounting purposes** and so not for external publication or statutory financial reporting.

Uses and limitations of balance sheet-based forecasts

4.10 Balance sheet-based forecasts have two main **uses**:

(a) as **longer-term (strategic) estimates,** to assess the scale of funding requirements or cash surpluses the company expects over time;

(b) **to act as a check on the realism of cash flow-based forecasts**. The estimated balance sheet should be roughly consistent with the net cash change in the cash budget, after allowing for approximations in the balance sheet forecast assumptions.

4.11 Balance sheet-based forecasts have several **limitations**.

(a) Their **practical value is restricted to long-term forecasts and checking the reliability of cash budgets**. Unlike cash budgets, they have no operational or control use.

(b) They will be of **limited accuracy**, given the range of assumptions that must be used and the long timescale of the estimate.

(c)   They are **difficult to construct for a multinational group,** especially when several currencies are involved.

Disadvantages of published cash flow forecasts

4.12   Many believe that companies should publish cash flow forecasts. However, published cash flow forecasts have certain disadvantages, which are as follows.

(a)   The **information** contained in them **may be manipulated** by unscrupulous managers wishing to show a favourable impression.

(b)   They are **only as good as the assumptions on which they are based**. Clearly there is an element of subjectivity and uncertainty involved in preparing them. However, users of cash flow forecasts should be aware of their limitations.

(c)   Cash flow forecasts are **very difficult to audit,** because they are **based on subjective prediction**. However, auditors can assess the accounting principles adopted and the consistency with which they are applied.

(d)   It is possible that **competitors could make use of the information** disclosed in a cash flow forecast, although if they were compulsory for all companies no single company would benefit from this advantage.

Chapter roundup

- **Cash flow statements** were made compulsory for companies because it was recognised that accounting profit is not the only indicator of a company's performance. FRS 1 *Cash flow statements* was revised in October 1996.

- Cash flow statements concentrate on the **sources** and **uses of cash** and are a useful indicator of a company's **liquidity** and **solvency**.

- You need to learn the **format** of the statement; setting out the format is an essential first stage in preparing the statement but it will only really sink in with more question practice.

- Remember the **step-by-step preparation** procedure and use it for all the questions you practise.

- Cash flow statements provide **useful information** about a company which is not provided elsewhere in the accounts.

- Note that you may be expected to **analyse** or **interpret** a cash flow statement.

- Cash flow forecasts are of two main types
  - Cash budgets in **receipts and payments** form
  - Balance sheet and **financial statements based** forecasts.

Quick quiz

1 What are the aims of a cash flow statement? (see para 1.5)

2 What are the standard headings required by FRS 1 (revised) to be included in a cash flow statement? (1.8)

3 What are the two reconciliations required by FRS 1 (revised)? (1.11)

4 Define cash according to FRS 1 (revised). (1.13(b))

5 Define 'liquid resources'. (1.13(d))

6 How does the direct method differ from the indirect method? (2.5, 2.7)

7 What are the advantages of cash flow accounting? (3.10)

8 What are the disadvantages of published cash flow forecasts? (4.12)

Question to try	Level	Marks	Time
15	Full exam	25	45 mins

Chapter 15

MISCELLANEOUS DISCLOSURES AND ACCOUNTING STANDARDS

Chapter topic list	Syllabus reference
1 SSAP 17 and SSAP 18	1(c), 2(a)
2 Creditors	1(c), 2(a)
3 Provisions and reserves	1(c), 2(a)
4 Called up share capital and FRS 4 *Capital instruments*	1(c), 2(a)
5 SSAP 25 *Segmental reporting*	1(c), 2(a)
6 SSAP 20 *Foreign currency translation*	1(c), 2(a)
7 SSAP 24 *Accounting for pension costs*	1(c), 2(a)

Introduction

These topics are lumped together, under the title 'miscellaneous disclosures' but they are all very important, so don't skip over this chapter.

In particular, SSAPs 17 and 18 are very important as they can affect many items in the accounts. Students sometimes get them confused with each other, so make sure you learn all the relevant definitions and understand the standard accounting treatment. You should remember these standards from your Foundation studies.

There are various disclosures relating to creditors, provisions and reserves, and share capital which it is convenient to mention here. The profit and loss disclosures are additional to the FRS 3 disclosures mentioned in the last chapter.

SSAP 25 is a straightforward standard - learn the definitions and formats.

SSAPs 20 and 24 are quite complicated, but here we simply cover the important definitions, requirements and disclosures of each standard.

1   SSAP 17 AND SSAP 18

1.1   SSAP 17 and SSAP 18 should be familiar to you from your Paper 1 studies. The most important aspects are highlighted in the summary below.

Exam focus point
The examiner has said that it is unlikely that a whole question would be based on these standards.

Knowledge brought forward from Paper 1

SSAP 17 Accounting for post balance sheet events

- *Post balance sheet event (PBSEs)* are events, both favourable and unfavourable, which occur between the B/S date and the date on which the financial statements are approved by the board of directors.

- *Adjusting events* are PBSEs which provide additional evidence of conditions existing at the B/S date, and therefore need to be incorporated into the financial statements.

- *Non-adjusting events* are PBSEs which concern conditions which did *not* exist at the B/S date.

- *Window dressing* is the arranging of transactions, the substance of which is primarily to alter the appearance of the B/S: it is *not* falsification of accounts. SSAP 17 does allow window dressing but *disclosure* should be made of such transactions

SSAP 18 Accounting for contingencies

- *Contingency is* a condition which exists at the B/S date, where the outcome will be confirmed only on the occurrence or non-occurrence of one or more uncertain future events.

- *Accounting treatment*

Expected outcome	*Contingent loss/liability*	*Contingent gain/asset*
Reasonably certain	Provide	Accrue
Probable	Provide	Disclose
'Possible'	Disclose	-
Remote	-	-

- *Disclosure*
  - ° The nature of the contingency.
  - ° The uncertainties expected to affect the ultimate outcome.
  - ° A prudent estimate of the financial effect if possible.

1.2   The **audit implications** of SSAP 17 are complex and lengthy and are therefore covered in detail in the companion Paper 10 *Auditing* Study Text. As regards SSAP 18, the auditors should search for any possible contingencies and the following sources should be examined.

(a)   Correspondence with customers and suppliers.

(b)   Correspondence with legal advisers.

(c)   Insurance documents.

(d)   Bank letter (to check whether the company has guaranteed any loans, for example to subsidiary companies).

(e)   Product warranties or guarantees.

(f)   Pension fund status.

The audit implications of SSAP 18 are also covered in more detail in the companion Paper 10 *Auditing* Study Text.

Question 1

In dealing with the annual accounts of three companies, the following information is available.

(a) At the balance sheet date Builditt Ltd has an overseas contract at cost, net of progress payments, of £2.6 million. Total work in progress is £13.7 million. Progress payments on the overseas contract are £1 million in arrears. Before the accounts are finalised there is a change of regime in the foreign country and the company suspended work on the contract. There is no export credit guarantee in force.

(b) Welditt Ltd has a contract to build an oil pipeline in the Middle East for a North American company. Part of the pipeline has been handed over. During unusual weather conditions, the pipeline has been damaged and this has resulted in considerable financial loss to the North American company. The latter company has indicated that it will take out civil actions in both the British and American courts claiming $16 million.

Welditt Ltd has obtained Counsel's opinion that any case to be heard in the British courts will fail. Counsel is unable to give an opinion on the outcome of the case if heard in America until he has sight of the claimant's case. At the date the accounts were approved by the directors no case had been filed or legal proceedings commenced in either country.

(c) Clampitt Ltd specialises in design and construction of roller coasters. During 19X3 it completed eight roller coasters and commenced work on a further seven. During the final commissioning checks on the first completed roller coaster, a stress fracture was discovered in a major structural girder. The cost of replacing the girders in all roller coasters is estimated to be £1.9 million. All fifteen customers have been advised that the replacements will be carried out immediately at no cost to themselves and they have accepted that satisfactory completion of the work is the only redress they will seek.

The manufacturer of the girders, a substantial quoted company, has accepted liability and agreed to meet all costs incurred by Clampitt Ltd.

You are required to discuss how Builditt Ltd, Welditt Ltd and Clampitt Ltd should deal with the above matters in their accounts.

Answer

(a) *Builditt Ltd*

There are two aspects to consider in respect of the overseas contract of Builditt Ltd. Firstly, Builditt Ltd is currently carrying assets totalling £3.6 million in its accounts and it is necessary to consider whether there is reasonable certainty as to the recovery of the assets. These assets comprise £2.6 million work in progress and a debtor of £1 million in respect of progress payments in arrears.

The recovery of work in progress is dependent upon the successful completion of the contract and the receipt of all contract monies due. In view of the suspension of work on the contract and the change of regime in the foreign country, there would appear to be some doubts about the completion of the contract and therefore, prudently, the work in progress should be written down to nil. With respect to the debtor for progress payments there must also be doubts about its recovery, particularly in the light of work on the contract being suspended. Thus, prudently, provision should also be made in respect of the debtor. These write downs may need to be disclosed by way of note to the profit and loss account as exceptional. This will depend on their materiality.

Secondly, it is necessary to consider whether any additional provision is required in respect of the contract due to possible penalty clauses arising from delays in completion or possible non-completion of the contract. It seems unlikely that such a provision would be required since it appears that the customer was not complying with the terms of the contract (since progress payments were in arrears) and this was partially the cause of the suspension of work on the contract.

In view of the uncertainties surrounding the outcome of the contract, disclosure should be made in a note to the accounts in accordance with SSAP 18. The disclosure would refer to the recovery of the work in progress and debtor if it was felt probable (but not reasonably certain) that recovery would be achieved. The disclosure would also refer to possible further provisions in respect of penalty clauses unless these were considered to be remote contingencies. In both cases the disclosure should state the nature of the contingency, the uncertainties surrounding the ultimate outcome and a prudent estimate of the financial effect.

(*Note*. The above discussion is based on the assumption that the foreign regime is hostile and that work on the contract will not recommence.)

(b)   *Welditt Ltd*

On the evidence currently available, it seems unlikely that the claim by the North American company will succeed although there is obviously still some uncertainty about the situation in the American courts. In view of the above, it would not be appropriate to provide for the £16 million claim in the accounts although consideration should be given as to whether any provision in respect of legal fees in defending the action should be made.

Since there is a possibility that the claim will succeed, disclosure should be made as a note to the accounts stating the nature of the contingency, the uncertainties surrounding the ultimate outcome and a prudent estimate of the financial effect.

(c)   *Clampitt Ltd*

In respect of the eight completed roller coasters, full provision should be made in the accounts of Clampitt Ltd for the costs of replacing the girders. In respect of the further seven that are still under construction, consideration should be given as to whether to write down work in progress to reflect the additional rectification costs. However, in view of the recovery of the costs from the girder manufacturer it seems unlikely that such a write down would be necessary on the grounds of prudence.

In respect of any provision for rectification work made, a corresponding debtor should be recognised in respect of the amount recoverable from the girder manufacturer to the extent that recovery is regarded as reasonably certain. From the information given, it appears that there is reasonable certainty as regards the recoverability from the manufacturer.

2   CREDITORS

2.1   If any liabilities included under creditors have been **secured,** the amounts secured and the nature of the security must be **stated.**

2.2   Any amounts included which are **payable** (or repayable) **more than five years** after the balance sheet date must be **specified,** together with the terms of payment or repayment and the rate of any interest payable.

2.3   The amount of any **proposed dividend** should be stated. Details of any arrears of dividends on cumulative preference shares must also be given.

2.4   Where **debentures** have been issued during the year, **details of the issue** (including the reasons why it was made) should be given in a note.

3   PROVISIONS AND RESERVES

3.1   As defined in the CA 1985, **provisions for liabilities and charges** are amounts retained to provide for any liability or loss which is either likely to be incurred or certain to be incurred, but uncertain as to amount or as to the date on which it will crystallise.

3.2   Where a reserve or provision is disclosed as a separate item in a company's balance sheet or in a note, any movements on the account during the year should be specified. The amount of any **provisions for taxation other than deferred taxation must be stated and details must be given of any pension commitments.**

3.3   The pro-forma balance sheet requires that any **share premium account** (KII) **and** any **revaluation reserve** (KIII) be **shown separately.** Any other reserves built up by a company should be disclosed under the appropriate headings (or amalgamated if not material) with the profit and loss account balance (KV) being shown separately.

4   CALLED UP SHARE CAPITAL AND FRS 4 CAPITAL INSTRUMENTS

12/95

4.1   The amount of **allotted share capital and** the amount of **called up share capital** which has been paid up must be **shown separately**.

4.2   The following information must be given by note with respect to a company's share capital:

(a)   the authorised share capital; and

(b)   where shares of more than one class have been allotted, the number and aggregate nominal value of shares of each class allotted.

4.3   In the case of any part of the allotted share capital that consists of **redeemable shares,** the **following information must be given**:

(a)   The earliest and latest **dates** on which the company has power to redeem those shares.

(b)   Whether the shares **must be redeemed** in any event **or** are liable to be redeemed **at the option of the company.**

(c)   Whether any (and if so, what) **premium** is payable on redemption.

4.4   **If** the company has **allotted** any shares **during the financial year**, the **following information must be given:**

(a)   The **reason** for making the allotment.

(b)   The **classes** of shares allotted.

(c)   As respects each class of shares, the **number** allotted, their **aggregate nominal value**, and the **consideration received by** the company for the allotment.

FRS 4 capital instruments

12/97

4.5   The ASB issued FRS 4 *Capital instruments* in December 1993.

> **KEY TERM**
>
> **Capital instruments** are instruments which are issued to raise finance. There are many different types. Common ones include bank loans, corporate bonds, convertible debt, ordinary shares, preference shares and options and warrants to subscribe for shares.

4.6   FRS 4 addresses how issuers should account for capital instruments. The standard covers all capital instruments except leases, options or warrants granted under employee share schemes and equity shares issues in a business combination accounted for as a merger.

4.7   The standard **applies to all financial statements** intended to give a true and fair view of a reporting entity's financial position and profit or loss (or income and expenditure). No exemptions have been given on the grounds of size, ownership or industry. Comparative figures may require restatement where the effect on prior years is material.

Distinguishing between debt and equity

4.8   One of the key users' ratios is the gearing ratio, ie the measure of the proportion of debt to equity. In order for this measure to be meaningful there must be consistency in the allocation of financial instruments between these two categories.

4.9   **Capital instruments should be included in one of three categories in the balance sheet: liabilities, shareholders' funds or minority interests.** The rules for distinguishing between debt and equity are based on the accounting model being developed in the ASB's *Statement of Principles*. They require:

   (a)   a company's **shares** to remain **in shareholders' funds**;

   (b)   capital instruments to be reported as **liabilities if they contain an 'obligation to transfer economic benefits'**; and

   (c)   capital instruments to be reported as **shareholders' funds if they do not contain an 'obligation to transfer economic benefits'.**

KEY TERM

An 'obligation to transfer economic benefits' means any requirement to make cash payments or transfer other kinds of property even if the requirement is only contingent.

4.10   Some capital instruments have **features of both debt and equity**. The common example of such **'hybrid' instruments** is convertible debt, which is economically equivalent to conventional debt plus a warrant to acquire shares in the future.

4.11   If the individual components of such instruments are physically separable, the FRS requires that they should be accounted for separately. Where the components are inseparable, the instrument should be accounted for as a single instrument. Thus, for example, a convertible bond should not be notionally 'split' into debt and an option to acquire shares.

4.12   The rule for determining whether a capital instrument is a liability is widely drawn. Convertible debt instruments are liabilities.

4.13   The effect of applying these criteria is that **the classification of capital instruments will be consistent with their substance, rather than their legal form**.

Disclosure: general

4.14   A fundamental part of FRS 4's approach on hybrid instruments and other less conventional forms of finance is to require issuers to make **considerable disclosure** about them.

4.15   In order to distinguish shares with debt characteristics from other share capital, the FRS contains a definition of a **'non-equity' shares**. Broadly speaking, these are shares that **contain preferential rights to participate in the company's profits or assets** (for example preference shares) or are redeemable.

4.16   The main new disclosure requirement is the analysis of the following items in the balance sheet.

Item	*Analysed between*	
Shareholders' funds	Equity interests	Non-equity interests
Minority interests in subsidiaries	Equity interests in subsidiaries	Non-equity interests in subsidiaries
Liabilities	Convertible liabilities	Non-convertible liabilities

4.17 Such analysis is usually to be given on the face of the balance sheet. Dividends to shareholders and the minority interests' share of the results for the year should be analysed similarly in the profit and loss account. Considerable disclosure is also required about the rights and terms of each class of non-equity share and convertible debt.

4.18 The overall effect is to provide the users of financial statements with quite a **detailed analysis of shareholders' funds** showing the amounts pertaining to each separate class of share and a summary of the rights of the holders.

Exam focus point

The distinction between equity and non-equity interest has been tested as part of a published accounts question. You may also be required to analyse and explain, as on the pilot paper.

Question 2

A company issues a convertible instrument which does not pay a coupon and is mandatorily convertible into shares of the issuer after 3 years. The holder is compensated through the conversion rights attached to the instrument. Although it is mandatorily convertible, the holders will rank as creditors in the event of insolvency of the issuer.

How should the instrument be classified?

Answer

Under FRS 4, this instrument should be classified in shareholders' funds as there is no 'obligation to transfer economic benefits'. Hence, this will be accounted for like a 'fully-paid' warrant. Its impact will be to dilute shareholders' interests in the future.

(Source: *Capital Instruments: A Guide to FRS 4, Ernst & Young*)

Accounting for debt instruments

4.19 **Debt should be recorded in the balance sheet at the fair value of the consideration received less costs incurred directly in connection with the issue of the instrument.** Such issue costs are narrowly defined and sometimes have to be written off immediately, but otherwise are spread over the life of the debt.

4.20 **The carrying amount of debt should be increased by the finance cost** in respect of the reporting period **and reduced by payments made in respect of the debt** in that period.

KEY TERM

The **finance cost** of debt is the difference between the total payments required to be made and the initial carrying value of the debt (that is the interest cost or the dividends plus any premium payable on redemption or other payments).

4.21 This **should be charged to the profit and loss account over the term of the instrument at a constant rate of interest on the outstanding amount of the debt**. The effective rate of interest implicit in the debt instrument will be required for that purpose.

4.22 Note that under s 130 CA 1985 discounts on the issue of debentures may be taken against the share premium account. This would be shown as a transfer in reserves.

> **Exam focus point**
>
> The December 1997 paper offered 5 marks for calculating profit and loss account and balance sheet amounts in respect of the issue of new loan stock.
>
> In order to calculate correctly the deductible finance cost for the P&L account, candidates had to know that only direct costs are deductible and that apportioned administration costs are not.
>
> Candidates were instructed to use the straight line basis for calculating annual costs.

Question 3

On 1 January 19X4, an entity issued a fixed rate debt instrument and received £900,000. Interest is payable annually in arrears at a rate of 5% on the stated principal amount of £1,000,000. The instrument has a 5 year term and the stated principal will be repaid at maturity. Issue costs of £50,000 were incurred.

State the disclosure of the instrument in the profit and loss account and the balance sheet for each year of the term.

Answer

The net proceeds of this issue are £850,000. The finance cost of this instrument is £400,000, being the difference between the total future payments (ie £1,250,000, see column (a) below) and the net proceeds from the issue.

The effective rate of interest implicit in this instrument is the discount rate which equates the present value of future cash flows to the net proceeds received. This is calculated as 8.84% by applying the NPV formula (use interpolation).

The interest charge for the year (column (b) below) is calculated by applying this rate to the carrying value of the debt in the balance sheet during the year.

	(a) Cash flows £'000	(b) Interest charge £'000	(c) Carrying value in the balance sheet £'000
At January 19X4	(850)		850.0
At 31 December 19X4	50	75.1	875.1
At 31 December 19X5	50	77.4	902.5
At 31 December 19X6	50	79.8	932.3
At 31 December 19X7	50	82.4	964.7
At 31 December 19X8	1,050	85.3	-
Total	400	400.0	

(Source: *Capital Instruments: A Guide to FRS 4*, Ernst & Young)

4.23 **If debt is repurchased or settled before its maturity, any gains or losses should be recognised immediately** in the profit and loss account.

4.24 In comparison with the Companies Act requirements, a more detailed analysis of maturity of debt is needed as shown below. This should be derived by reference to the earliest date on which the lender could require repayment. The FRS requires committed facilities which satisfy strict conditions to be considered when determining such dates.

These conditions will affect some existing practices - for example, commercial paper can no longer be shown as long-term debt.

Convertible debt

4.25 FRS 4 requires that **conversion of debt should not be anticipated** but rather reported in liabilities with the finance cost calculated on the assumption that the debt will never be converted. When the debt is converted, the amount of consideration recognised in respect of shares should be the amount of the liability for the debt at the date of conversion.

Disclosure: debt

4.26 (a) **Maturity of debt.** The financial statements or notes should include an analysis of the maturity of debt showing amount falling due:

   (i) In one year or less, or on demand.
   (ii) Between one and two years.
   (iii) Between two and five years.
   (iv) In five years or more.

   The maturity of the debt should be determined by reference to the earliest date on which the lender can demand repayment.

   (b) **Convertible debt should be stated separately** from other liabilities. Details given must include:

   (i) The date of redemption.
   (ii) The amount payable on redemption.
   (iii) The number and class of shares into which the debt may be converted.
   (iv) The period in which the conversion may take place.
   (v) Whether conversion is at the option of the issuer or holder.

Repurchase of own debt

4.27 **Any profits or losses arising on the repurchase of debt should be recognised in the year of repurchase.**

Accounting for shares

4.28 **Share issues should be recorded at the fair value of the consideration received less issue costs.** Issue costs should be written off directly to reserves and should not be reported in the statement of total recognised gains and losses, ie those relating directly to the issue of the instrument should be accounted for as a reduction in the proceeds of a capital instrument.

Question 4

A company issues 100 £1 ordinary shares at par. Issue costs of £2 are incurred.

State how this transaction should be recorded and disclosed.

Answer

If there is a share premium account in existence, the share issue may be recorded by increasing share capital by £100 and setting off the issue costs against share premium account. In the analysis of total shareholders' funds, the equity interests will have increased by £98.

If there is no share premium account, share capital will be increased by £100 but the issue costs would be deducted from another reserve (usually profit and loss account reserve) subject to the provisions of the company's articles. Prior to FRS 4, companies in this situation had to charge the issue costs to the profit and loss account. The equity interest within shareholders' funds also increases by £98 in this case.

(Source: *Capital Instruments: A Guide to FRS 4*, Ernst & Young)

4.29 As stated above, under FRS 4 **the balance sheet should show the amount of shareholders' funds attributable to equity interests and the amount attributable to non-equity interests.**

4.30 The **finance cost of non-equity** shares should be **calculated on the same basis as for debt instruments. Dividends in respect of non-equity shares** have to be accounted for **on an accruals basis.** The only exception is where there are insufficient distributable profits and the dividend rights are non-cumulative. Arrears of preference dividends must therefore be provided for rather than simply disclosed.

Warrants

4.31 **Warrants should be included in shareholders' funds at the net proceeds of the issue.** If the warrant lapses unexercised, the amount paid for it becomes a gain and should be taken to the statement of total recognised gains and losses. If the warrant is exercised, the shares issued should be recorded at the aggregate of the net proceeds received when the warrant was issued and the fair value of the consideration received on exercise less issue costs of the shares.

Scrip dividends

4.32 If shares are issued in lieu of dividends, the value of the shares issued, being equal to the value of the dividend payable, should be reflected in the P & L account as an **appropriation of profit.**

Disclosure: shares

4.33 These disclosures should be made.

    (a) Analysis of shares between **equity and non-equity** interests.

    (b) The **rights** of each class of shares should be **summarised** detailing:

        (i) The rights to **dividends.**

        (ii) The dates at which shares are **redeemable** and the amounts payable in respect of redemption.

        (iii) Their **priority and amounts receivable on a winding up.**

        (iv) Their **voting rights.**

    (c) Where warrants or convertible debt are in issue that may require the company to issue shares of a class not currently in issue the details in (b) above must be given.

    (d) The **aggregate dividends** for each class of shares should be disclosed.

Minority interests

4.34 In consolidated financial statements, shares of subsidiary companies which are not owned by the group are accounted for as minority interests. There is one exception to this rule. In some situations (for example where the parent or another group company has guaranteed their dividends or redemption), such shares become liabilities from the perspective of the group and therefore have to be reported as such on consolidation.

Exam focus point

FRS 4 is technically extremely complex. It is unlikely that you would be asked to perform any very difficult calculations, and you should therefore concentrate on the reasons why FRS 4 was considered necessary. You should be able to discuss the main provisions of the standard.

4.35 Generally speaking, FRS 4 was issued to stop companies treating debt as equity and vice versa, on legal form rather than the substance of the transactions. It also forces companies to recognise finance costs.

5   SSAP 25 SEGMENTAL REPORTING   12/96

5.1   SSAP 25 *Segmental reporting* was introduced in June 1990 and builds on the CA 1985 requirements to provide limited segmental analyses.

(a)   Where a company has **two or more classes of business, it must show in a note** the amount of **turnover and operating profit attributable to each class** of business; and

(b)   where a company operates in **more than one geographical market**, it **must show** in a note the amount of **turnover attributable to each market**.

Any or all of these analyses can be omitted on grounds of commercial sensitivity, but the directors must then state that these analyses would have been published but for these considerations.

5.2   SSAP 25 **applies only to** any entity which:

(a)   Is a **public company** or has a public limited company as a subsidiary undertaking; or

(b)   is a **banking or insurance company or group** or

(c)   **exceeds the criteria, multiplied in each case by 10,** for defining a **medium-sized company** under s 248 of the Companies Act 1985, as amended from time to time by statutory instrument. (The criteria for defining a medium-sized company are given in Chapter 8.)

5.3   The standard adds:

'However, a subsidiary that is not a public limited company or a banking or insurance company need not comply with these provisions if its parent provides segmental information in compliance with this accounting standard.

All entities are encouraged to apply the provisions of this accounting standard in all financial statements intended to give a true and fair view of the financial position and profit or loss.

Where, in the opinion of the directors, the disclosure of any information required by this accounting standard would be seriously prejudicial to the interests of the reporting entity, that information need not be disclosed; but the fact that any such information has not been disclosed must be stated.'

5.4   **SSAP 25 extends the Companies Act requirements** on analysis of turnover and profits as follows:

(a)   the **result** as well as turnover **must be disclosed for all segments;**

(b) 'result' for these purposes is profit or loss before tax, minority interests and extraordinary items;

(c) **each segment's net assets should be disclosed** (so that return on capital employed can be calculated);

(d) **segmental turnover must be analysed between sales to customers outside the group and inter-segment sales/transfers** (where material).

Like the CA 1985, SSAP 25 requires analysis by two types of segment, class of business and geographical market.

KEY TERM

The SSAP defines a **class of business** as: 'a distinguishable component of an entity that provides a separate product or service or a separate group of related products or services.'

5.5   Factors to take into account in making this distinction are the nature of the products or services and production processes, markets distribution channels, organisation of activities and legislative framework relating to any part of the business.

5.6   SSAP 25 requires that turnover should be analysed by **geographical market** in two different ways, explained as follows.

KEY TERMS

'A **geographical segment** is a geographical area comprising an individual country or a group of countries in which an entity operates, or to which it supplies products or services.

A **geographical analysis** should help the user of the financial statements to assess the extent to which an entity's operations are subject to factors such as the following:

(a)   expansionist or restrictive economic climates;
(b)   stable or unstable political regimes;
(c)   exchange control regulations;
(d)   exchange rate fluctuations.

5.7   The SSAP amplifies those statements as follows.

'The factors listed above apply both to the geographical locations of the entity's operations and to the geographical locations of its markets. The user of the financial statements gains a fuller understanding of the entity's exposure to these factors if turnover is disclosed according to both location of operations and location of markets. For the purposes of this accounting standard, origin of turnover is the geographical area from which products or services are supplied to a third party or another segment. Destination of turnover is the geographical area to which goods or services are supplied. Because disclosure relating to segment results and net assets will generally be based on location of operations, an analysis of turnover on the same basis will enable the user to match turnover, result and net assets on a consistent basis, and to relate all three to the perceived risks and opportunities of the segments. For these reasons this accounting standard requires the disclosure of sales by origin, but reporting entities should also disclose turnover by destination unless there is no material difference between the two. If there is no material difference, a statement to that effect is required.'

5.8   Identifying segments could be difficult and the SSAP suggests as a **rule of thumb that a segment should normally be regarded as material if its third party turnover is ≥ 10%**

of the entity's total third party turnover or its profit is ≥ 10% of the combined results of all segments in profit (or its loss is ≥ 10% of the combined results of all loss making segments) or its net assets are ≥ 10% of total net assets of the entity. The aim is to inform users of the accounts about activities earning a different rate of return from the rest of the business; or subject to different degrees of risk; or experiencing different growth rates; or with different potential for future development.

5.9 Reproduced below is the example given by SSAP 25 in its Appendix. Notice how the segmental results are reconciled to the entity's reported profit before taxation. This is a requirement of the SSAP. The example shows a segmental analysis based on a consolidated profit and loss account. However, SSAP 25 also applies to companies which do not need to prepare group accounts.

5.10 It is quite common for larger companies to operate through divisions or branches, and each of these could qualify as a segment, depending on the circumstances in each case. In both groups of companies and divisionalised single entity companies, there is frequently considerable trade between divisions.

Exam focus point
It is worth memorising this format. The only question set so far on SSAP 25 was very straightforward indeed.

Notes on the example

5.11 (a) **Common costs should be treated in the way that the directors deem most appropriate** in pursuance of the objectives of segmental reporting. For internal accounting purposes, some companies routinely apportion common costs between divisions, segments and so on and others do not; the same considerations prompting that decision should be applied to segmental reporting.

(b) **For companies in the financial sector it would normally be more sensible to include the net interest income or expense as part of the segment's operating results.** In the majority of cases non-interest bearing operating assets less non-interest bearing liabilities would be the most appropriate measure of capital employed; however, if interest is included in the segment results, then the relevant interest-bearing assets and liabilities should be included in calculating capital employed.

Arguments against reporting by segment

5.12 Those who argue against this form of disclosure generally emphasise the practical problems, which **include**:

(a) **Identifying segments** for reporting purposes.

(b) **Allocating common income** and costs among the different segments.

(c) **Reporting inter-segment transactions**.

(d) Providing information in such a way as to **eliminate misunderstanding** by investors.

(e) **Avoiding any potential damage** that may be done to the reporting entity by disclosing information about individual segments.

CLASSES OF BUSINESS

	Industry A		*Industry B*		*Other Industries*		*Group*	
	19X2 £'000	*19X1* £'000	*19X2* £'000	*19X1* £'000	*19X2* £'000	*19X1* £'000	*19X2* £'000	*19X1* £'000
Turnover								
Total sales	33,000	30,000	42,000	38,000	26,000	23,000	101,000	91,000
Inter-segment sales	(4,000)	-	-	-	(12,000)	(14,000)	(16,000)	(14,000)
Sales to third parties	29,000	30,000	42,000	38,000	14,000	9,000	85,000	77,000
Profit before taxation								
Segment profit	3,000	2,500	4,500	4,000	1,800	1,500	9,300	8,000
Common costs							300	300
Operating profit							9,000	7,700
Net interest							(400)	(500)
							8,600	7,200
Group share of the profit before taxation of associated undertakings	1,000	1,000	1,400	1,200	-	-	2,400	2,200
Group profit before taxation							11,000	9,400
Net assets								
Segment net assets	17,600	15,000	24,000	25,000	19,400	19,000	61,000	59,000
Unallocated assets*							3,000	3,000
							64,000	62,000
Group share of the net assets of associated undertakings	10,200	8,000	8,800	9,000	-	-	19,000	17,000
Total net assets							83,000	79,000

* Unallocated assets consist of assets at the group's head office in London amounting to £2.4 million (1989: £2.5 million) and at the group's regional office in Hong Kong amounting to £0.6 million (1989: 0.5 million).

GEOGRAPHICAL SEGMENTS

	United Kingdom		North America		Far East		Other		Group	
	19X2 £'000	19X1 £'000	19X2 £'000	19X1 £'000	19X2 £'000	19X1 £'000	19X2 £'000	19X1 £'000	19X2 £'000	19X1 £'000
Turnover										
Turnover by destination										
Sales to third parties	34,000	31,000	16,000	14,500	25,000	23,000	10,000	8,500	85,000	77,000
Turnover by origin										
Total sales	38,000	34,000	29,000	27,500	23,000	23,000	12,000	10,500	102,000	95,000
Inter-segment sales	-	-	(8,000)	(9,000)	(9,000)	(9,000)	-	-	(17,000)	(18,000)
Sales to third parties	38,000	34,000	21,000	18,500	14,000	14,000	12,000	10,500	85,000	77,000
Profit before taxation										
Segment profit	4,000	2,900	2,500	2,300	1,800	1,900	1,000	900	9,300	8,000
Common costs									300	300
Operating profit									9,000	7,700
Net interest									(400)	(500)
									8,600	7,200
Group share of the profit before taxation of associated undertakings	950	1,000	1,450	1,200	-	-	-	-	2,400	2,200
Group profit before taxation									11,000	9,400
Net assets										
Segment net assets	16,000	15,000	25,000	26,000	16,000	15,000	4,000	3,000	61,000	59,000
Unallocated assets*									3,000	3,000
									64,000	62,000
Group share of the net assets of associated undertakings	8,500	7,000	10,500	10,000	-	-	-	-	19,000	17,000
Total net assets									83,000	79,000

* Unallocated assets consist of assets at the group's head office in London amounting to £2.4 million (1989: £2.5 million) and at the group's regional office in Hong Kong amounting to £0.6 million (1989: 0.5 million).

Question 5

The Multitrade Group has three divisions (all based in the UK), A. B and C. Details of their turnover, results and net assets are given below.

	£'000
Division A	
Sales to B	304,928
Other UK sales	57,223
Middle East export sales	406,082
Pacific fringe export sales	77,838
	846,071
Division B	
Sales to C	31,034
Export sales to Europe	195,915
	226,949
Division C	
Export sales to North America	127,003

	Division A £'000	Division B £'000	Division C £'0000
Operational profit/(loss) before tax	162,367	18,754	(8,303)
Re-allocated costs from			
Hear office	48,362	24,181	24,181
Interest costs	3,459	6,042	527

	Head office £'000			
Fixed assets	49,071	200,921	41,612	113,076
Net current assets	47,800	121,832	39,044	92,338
Long-term liabilities	28,636	16,959	6,295	120,841
Deferred taxation	1,024	24,671	9,013	4,028

Required

Prepare a segmental report in accordance with SSAP 25 for publication in Multitrade's group.

Answer

Ignoring comparative figures, Multitrade plc's segmental report would look like this.

CLASSES OF BUSINESS

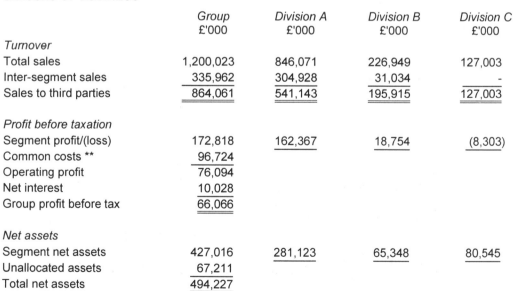

	Group £'000	Division A £'000	Division B £'000	Division C £'000
Turnover				
Total sales	1,200,023	846,071	226,949	127,003
Inter-segment sales	335,962	304,928	31,034	-
Sales to third parties	864,061	541,143	195,915	127,003
Profit before taxation				
Segment profit/(loss)	172,818	162,367	18,754	(8,303)
Common costs **	96,724			
Operating profit	76,094			
Net interest	10,028			
Group profit before tax	66,066			
Net assets				
Segment net assets	427,016	281,123	65,348	80,545
Unallocated assets	67,211			
Total net assets	494,227			

GEOGRAPHICAL SEGMENTS

	Group	United Kingdom	Middle East	Pacific fringe	Europe	North America
Turnover						
Turnover by destination ***						
Sales to third parties	64,061	57,223	406,082	77,838	195,915	127,003

*   Turnover, profit, net interest and net assets should be the same as those shown in the consolidated accounts.

**   Common costs and unallocated assets are those items in the consolidated accounts which cannot reasonably be allocated to any one segment nor does the group wish to apportion them between segments. An example of a common cost is the cost of maintaining the holding company share register, and an example of an unallocated asset might be the head office building.

***   Turnover by destination must be disclosed in accordance with the Companies Act 1985. If Multitrade's divisions were not all in the UK, then another analysis would be required by SSAP 25 on the same lines as that shown for classes of business but analysed between the geographical origins of turnover.

Audit implications

5.13   The auditors will check whether the **disclosure requirements** of SSAP 25 have been followed. The client will probably produce a schedule showing how the segmental figures have been derived. The auditors will need to trace the figures back to the audited accounts of each company in the group.

5.14   It may be that the company finds it **impossible to allocate all transactions exactly**. Where this is the case, results will be **apportioned as an estimated basis**. The auditors must check that this apportionment is applied consistently from year to year, or that any change is justified.

6   SSAP 20 FOREIGN CURRENCY TRANSLATION

6.1   At this point in your studies we will look at the basic aspects of foreign currency translation. This will lay the foundation for your later studies, which will involve foreign exchange translation in consolidation. **This is a topic of great practical importance as many companies, from large multi-nationals to the smallest of companies, will buy and sell goods overseas.** In this section we will consider how a single company deals with foreign currency translation.

6.2   If a company trades overseas, it will buy or sell assets in foreign currencies; for example, a British company might buy materials from the United States, and pay for them in US dollars, and then sell its finished goods in West Germany, receiving payment in German marks, or perhaps in some other currency. If the company owes money in a foreign currency at the end of the accounting year, or holds assets which were bought in a foreign currency, those liabilities or assets must be translated into £ sterling, in order to be shown in the books of account.

6.3   A company might have a subsidiary abroad, and the subsidiary will trade in its own local currency. The subsidiary will keep books of account and prepare its annual accounts in its own currency. However, at the year end, the UK holding company must consolidate the results of the overseas subsidiary into its group accounts, so that somehow, the assets and liabilities and the **annual profits of the subsidiary must be translated from the foreign currency into £ sterling.**

6.4   If foreign currency exchange rates remained constant, there would be no accounting problem. As you will be aware, however, foreign exchange rates are continually changing; and it is not inconceivable for example, that the rate of exchange between the US dollar and the pound might be $8.40 to £1 at the start of the accounting year, and $8.05 to £1 at the end of the year (in this example, a 25% increase in the relative strength of the dollar).

6.5   There are **two distinct types of foreign currency transaction, conversion and translation.**

Conversion gains and losses

6.6   **Conversion is the process of exchanging amounts of one foreign currency for another.** For example, suppose a company buys a large consignment of goods from a supplier in Germany. The order is placed on 1 May and the agreed price is 124,250 Deutschmarks. At the time of delivery the rate of foreign exchange was 3.50 DM to £1. The UK company would record the creditor in its books as follows.

DEBIT	Stores account (124,250 ÷ 3.5)	£35,500	
CREDIT	Creditors' account		£35,500

6.7   When the UK company comes to pay the supplier, it needs to obtain some foreign currency. By this time, however, if the rate of exchange has altered to 3.55DM to £1, the cost of raising 124,250 DM would be (÷ 3.55) £35,000. The company would need to spend only £35,000 to settle a debt for stocks 'costing' £35,500. Since it would be administratively difficult to alter the value of the stocks in the company's books of account, it is more appropriate to record a profit on conversion of £500.

DEBIT	Creditors' account	£35,500	
CREDIT	Cash		£35,000
	Profit on conversion		£500

Profits (or losses) on conversion would be included in the profit and loss account for the year in which conversion (whether payment or receipt) takes place.

6.8   Suppose that another UK company sells goods to a French company, and it is agreed that payment should be made in French francs at a price of 116,000 francs. We will further assume that the exchange rate at the time of sale is 10.75 Fr to £1, but when the debt is eventually paid, the rate has altered to 10.8 Fr to £1. The company would record the sale as follows.

DEBIT	Debtor account (116,000 ÷ 10.75)	£10,800	
CREDIT	Sales account		£10,800

6.9   When the 116,000 francs are paid, the UK company will convert them into pounds, to obtain (÷ 10.8) £10,750. In this example, there has been a loss on conversion of £50 which will be written off to the profit and loss account:

CREDIT	Debtor account		£10,800
DEBIT	Cash	£10,750	
	Loss on conversion	£50	

6.10   **There are no accounting difficulties concerned with foreign currency conversion gains or losses, and the procedures described above are uncontroversial.**

Translation

6.11   Foreign currency translation, as distinct from conversion, does not involve the act of exchanging one currency for another. **Translation is required at the end of an accounting period when a company still holds assets or liabilities in its balance sheet which were obtained or incurred in a foreign currency.**

6.12   These assets or liabilities might consist of:

(a)   An individual UK company holding individual assets or liabilities originating in a foreign currency 'deal'.

(b)   An individual UK company with a separate branch of the business operating abroad which keeps its own books of account in the local currency.

(c)   A UK company which wishes to consolidate the results of a foreign subsidiary.

6.13   There has been **great uncertainty about the method which should be used**:

(a)   To translate the value of assets and liabilities from a foreign currency into £ for the year end balance sheet.

(b)   To translate the profits reported by an independent foreign branch or foreign subsidiary into £ for the annual profit and loss account.

6.14   Suppose, for example, that a Belgian subsidiary purchases a piece of property for 2,100,000 Belgian francs on 31 December in year 1. The rate of exchange at this time was 70 BFr to £1. During year 2, the subsidiary charged depreciation on the building of 16,800 Francs, so that at 31 December year 2, the subsidiary recorded the asset as follows.

	BFr
Property at cost	2,100,000
Less accumulated depreciation	16,800
Net book value	2,083,200

At this date, the rate of exchange has changed to 60 BFr to £1.

6.15   The UK holding company must translate the asset's value into £s, but there is a **choice of exchange rates**:

(a)   should the rate of exchange for translation be the rate which existed at the date of purchase, which would give a net book value of 2,083,200 ÷ 70 = £29,760? or

(b)   should the rate of exchange for translation be the rate existing at the end of year 2 (the closing rate of 60Fr to £1)? This would give a net book value of £34,720.

6.16   Similarly, should depreciation be charged in the consolidated profit and loss account at the rate of 70 Francs to £1 (the historical rate), 60 Francs to £1 (the closing rate), or at an average rate for the year (say, 64 Francs to £1)?

6.17   In the accounting debate as to which method of translating foreign currencies was most appropriate, the major problems focused on the consolidation of the results of foreign subsidiaries, and **two 'rival' methods emerged**:

(a)   The **temporal** (or 'historical') **method**.
(b)   The **closing rate method,** or closing rate/net investment method.

It is beyond the range of your syllabus to discuss these methods here. You will encounter the consolidation of foreign subsidiaries in your later studies.

Requirements of SSAP 20

6.18   We are now in a position to consider the requirements of SSAP 20 *Foreign currency translation* (issued in 1983) on accounting for foreign currency translation. SSAP 20 makes a distinction between accounting procedures by an individual company, and the accounting procedures for consolidation in group accounts.

The individual company stage

6.19   These rules relate to a UK company which buys or sells abroad in a foreign currency, or raises foreign currency loans abroad, and enters the transactions in its own books of account (in £ sterling).

(a) **During an accounting period**, if a company buys or sells goods or services which are denominated in a foreign currency, **the result of each transaction should be entered in the company's books in sterling, using the exchange rate in operation on the date the transaction occurred**. Minor adjustments to this rule are:

(i)   If exchange rates do not fluctuate significantly in the period, an **average rate** for the period may be used.

(ii)   If a transaction is **negotiated at a fixed rate** of exchange (eg if a company sells goods abroad for US$12,000 at a fixed rate of $8.20 to £1) then this fixed rate should be used for the translation.

(iii) If a company takes out **forward exchange cover** to purchase or sell the foreign currency (from or to its bank) the rate of exchange in the forward exchange contract should be used. For example, if a company buys goods costing $24,000 from a supplier in the USA, and arranges payment by means of a term bill of exchange which will mature in 3 months' time, the company can enter into a forward exchange contract with its bank to buy $24,000 in 3 months' time at a specified rate of exchange. This rate of exchange should then be used for translating the cost of the goods into sterling.

(b) Once **non-monetary assets** (fixed assets and stocks and also equity investments) have been translated into sterling in the company's books, they will remain valued at that sterling amount (subject to depreciation, loss of value etc) and **no subsequent re-translation** of the assets **should normally be needed.**

(c) At the balance sheet date, there might be **monetary assets and liabilities** (debtors, creditors, loans, cash in a foreign currency account etc) and these **should be translated into sterling at the exchange rate ruling at the balance sheet date** (unless fixed price contracts or forward exchange contracts have been arranged for the assets or liabilities, in which case the rate of exchange in the respective contract should be used).

RULES TO LEARN

The rules for an individual company are as follows.

(a)   Fixed assets and stocks: translate at actual rate on date of transaction.

(b)   Monetary assets and liabilities: translate at closing rate.

(c)   Profit and loss account:

   (i)   depreciation: based on rate at date of initial asset purchase;

   (ii)   sales and direct cost of sales: based on actual rates or an average rate for the year.

6.20   **SSAP 20 states that, for the individual company stage, exchange gains or losses should be recognised as part of the profit or loss for the year.** It bases its recommendations on the fact that they reflect cash flows (gains or losses) to the company. Exchange gains or losses arising on settled transactions in the context of an individual company's operations have already been reflected in cash flows, since a change in the exchange rate increases or decreases the local currency equivalent of amounts paid or received in cash settlement.

6.21   Similarly, it is reasonably certain that exchange gains or losses on unsettled short-term monetary items will soon be reflected in cash flows. Therefore, it is normally appropriate, because of the cash flow effects, to recognise such gains and losses as part of the profit or loss for the year; they should be included in profit or loss from ordinary activities unless they arise from events which themselves would fall to be treated as extraordinary items, in which case they should be included as part of such items'.

6.22   **SSAP 20 also takes the view that it is appropriate to state long-term assets and liabilities at the closing rate in the balance sheet, and that any exchange gains** or losses **on these items should also be reported in the profit and loss account.**

'However, it is necessary to consider on the grounds of prudence whether the amount of (any) gain ... to be recognised in the profit and loss account should be restricted in exceptional cases where there are doubts as to the convertibility or marketability of the currency in question.'

For example, it would not be prudent to report a large exchange gain on a loan in roubles, if roubles are not easily sold and convertible into sterling on the foreign exchange markets.

6.23   In the individual company's books, foreign currency translation should be done according to the same method, no matter whether the company is dealing with an overseas subsidiary, a fellow-subsidiary or a third party.

Case examples

Some examples might illustrate these individual company regulations.

(a)   Bulldog Ltd, a UK company, buys some machinery for use in the UK from a Swedish company for 19,000 Krona in May 19X4. At this date the rate of exchange is, say, 9.5 Krona to £1. Bulldog Ltd would translate the cost of the asset into £ at this rate, ie £200. There will be no further translations, and no exchange differences will arise. (There may be a subsequent gain or loss on conversion when the asset is paid for, but this is a separate matter.)

(b)   Bulldog Ltd purchases goods from an Italian company for 11 million lire in October 19X4 when the rate of exchange is 2,200 lire to £1. At the end of Bulldog's accounting year, the debt had not yet been paid and the exchange rate had changed to 2,000 lire to £1 (say). The cost of the purchase would be recorded as £5,000. In the December balance sheet, the creditor would be recorded as £5,500. The exchange loss on translation would be charged in the profit and loss account from ordinary operations for the year.

(c)   Bulldog Ltd borrowed $5,500,000 from a bank in the USA on 1 March 19X5. The loan was converted into sterling when the rate of exchange was $8.1 to £1, and £5,000,000 would therefore be recorded in the books of Bulldog as a liability on the loan. At the end of the year, the loan was still outstanding, and the exchange rate had changed to $8.05 to £1. It would be shown in the balance sheet at £5,238,095, and there would be an exchange loss of £238,095 for the accounting year. This should be reported in the profit and loss account for the year as a part of ordinary operations (although disclosed, perhaps, as an exceptional item according to FRS 3).

Disclosure

6.24   The **disclosure requirements of SSAP 20 are that:**

(a)   companies (or groups of companies) should disclose the **net amount** of exchange gains and losses on foreign currency borrowings less deposits, distinguishing between:

(i)   the amount offset in reserves; and

(ii)   the net amount charged or credited to the profit and loss account

(b)   companies (or groups) should disclose the **net movement on reserves** arising from exchange differences.

Requirements of the Companies Act 1985

6.25   The Companies Act 1985 includes certain disclosure requirements affecting foreign exchange translation.

(a)   When a company's accounts (balance sheet or P & L account) include sums which were originally denominated in a foreign currency, the basis on which those sums have been translated must be stated. In other words, the **accounts must disclose whether temporal rates, closing rates or average rates have been used.**

(b)   **Exchange gains or losses** reported in the profit and loss account will be **included under**:

(i)   Other operating income or

(ii)   Other operating charges (if they arise from trading transactions) or

(iii)   Other interest receivable and similar income or

(iv)   Interest payable and similar charges (if they arise from arrangements which may be considered as financing).

However, exchange gains or losses arising from extraordinary events should be included as extraordinary items in the P & L account.

(c)   In the balance sheet, the Act requires **disclosure about movements on any reserves:**

(i)   The amount of the reserve at the start of the year.

(ii)   The amount of the reserve at the balance sheet date.

(iii)   Any amounts transferred to or from the reserve during the year.

(iv)   The source and application of any amounts so transferred.

In other words, disclosure of exchange gains or losses as movements on reserves is required by the 1985 Act.

6.26 **A possible conflict between statute and SSAP 20 arises in the case of long-term monetary items. SSAP 20 says that gains and losses on the translation of such items should be reported in the profit and loss account.**

6.27 **The courts have ruled in the past that the process of translation is not equivalent to realisation and translation gains do not count as realised profits.** The Companies Act 1985 allows only realised profits to be reported in the profit and loss account, so that compliance with SSAP 20 may result in a breach of the Companies Act. Companies following the recommendations of SSAP 20 will presumably **justify** the breach **by invoking the true and fair override.**

Question 6

White Cliffs Ltd, whose year end is 31 December, buys some goods from Mid West Inc of the USA on 30 September. The invoice value is $40,000 and is due for settlement in equal instalments on 30 November and 31 January. The exchange rate moved as follows.

	$ = £1
30 September	8.60
30 November	8.80
31 December	8.90
31 January	8.85

Required

State the accounting entries in the books of White Cliffs Ltd.

Answer

The purchase will be recorded in the books of White Cliffs Ltd using the rate of exchange ruling on 30 September.

| DEBIT | Purchases | £25,000 | |
| CREDIT | Trade creditors | | £25,000 |

Being the sterling cost of goods purchased for $40,000 ($40,000 ÷ $8.60/£1)

On 30 November, White Cliffs must pay $20,000. This will cost $20,000 ÷ $8.80/£1 = £11,111 and the company has therefore made an exchange gain of £12,500 - £11,111 = £1,389.

DEBIT	Trade creditors	£12,500	
CREDIT	Exchange gains: P & L account		£1,389
	Cash		£11,111

On 31 December, the balance sheet date, the outstanding liability will be recalculated using the rate applicable to that date: $20,000 ÷ $8.90/£1 = £10,526. A further exchange gain of £1,974 has been made and will be recorded as follows.

| DEBIT | Trade creditors | £1,974 | |
| CREDIT | Exchange gains: P & L account | | £1,974 |

The total exchange gain of £3,363 will be included in the operating profit for the year ending 31 December.

On 31 January, White Cliffs must pay the second instalment of $20,000. This will cost them £10,811 ($20,000 ÷ $8.85/£1).

DEBIT	Trade creditors	£10,526	
	Exchange losses: P & L account	£285	
CREDIT	Cash		£10,811

Audit implications

6.28   The auditors will be concerned that all transactions carried out in a foreign currency have been correctly recorded in the books of the company. Any profits or losses on conversion must be correctly recorded in the profit and loss account for the period.

6.29   In order to check such transactions, the auditors will probably select a sample of them (if there are a great many) and they will check that the **calculations made for conversion are correct and that they have been properly recorded.** The auditors will also check that the conversion rate used matches the rate ruling at the date of conversion. This can be found from issues of the *Financial Times* for the day after the relevant date (it gives the rate for the previous day).

6.30   The auditors will check the **date** of and **vouch for the receipt or payment of foreign exchange monies.** They can then go on to check that any profit or loss on conversion has been correctly calculated.

7   SSAP 24 ACCOUNTING FOR PENSION COSTS

7.1   An increasing number of companies are providing a pension as part of their employees' remuneration package. In view of this trend, it is important to standardise the way in which pension costs are recognised, measured and disclosed in the accounts of sponsoring companies.

7.2   Before looking at the ASC's approach in SSAP 24 in detail it is necessary to understand the difference between a 'defined contribution' pension scheme and a 'defined benefit' scheme.

> **KEY TERMS**
>
> (a)   Under a **defined contribution scheme,** the employer will normally discharge his obligation by making agreed contributions to a pension scheme. The amount of pension ultimately payable to the employee is not guaranteed: it depends on the investment earnings of the funds contributed. Under this kind of scheme the cost to the employer is easily measured. It is simply the amount of the contributions payable in the period.
>
> (b)   Under a **defined benefit scheme** the eventual benefit payable to the employee is a predetermined amount, usually depending on the employee's salary immediately prior to retirement. In these circumstances it is impossible to be sure in advance that the regular contributions will generate a fund sufficient to provide the benefits. The employer may be obliged for legal reasons, or in the interest of maintaining good employee relations, to make good any deficiency in funding. This means that the cost to the company is uncertain.

7.3   From the employer's point of view, a pension is part of the cost of obtaining an employee's services. **The accounting objective is** therefore **that the employer should recognise the cost of providing a pension over the period during which he derives benefit from the employee's services.** SSAP 24 deals with the method by which the allocation of this cost should be achieved. The standard is mainly concerned with defined benefit schemes because, as already mentioned, the cost of defined contribution schemes is easily established.

7.4   **It is common with defined benefit schemes to make use of actuarial calculations to** determine the pension cost to be charged each year. Most pension schemes undergo a formal actuarial valuation every three years, in which the actuary confirms that the present and future expected contribution levels are at least sufficient to provide for payment of the promised benefits. From his valuation, the actuary will **recommend a funding plan** to be followed by the company to enable future expected benefits to be paid.

7.5   The usual funding plan is a level contribution rate ie a fixed proportion of each employee's pensionable pay is transferred to the pension scheme. In each case it is up to the accountant to confirm whether the actuary's funding plan is a satisfactory basis for allocating the pension costs to meet the accounting objective.

7.6   **SSAP 24** does not attempt to specify a particular actuarial valuation method from the many in use, but it does require that the **method selected should recognise the effect of future increases in earnings and in pensions where the employer has an expressed or implied commitment.** The method selected **should be used consistently and disclosed.** In the very exceptional cases where there is a change of method the fact should be disclosed and the effect quantified.

Regular pension costs and variations from regular costs

7.7   SSAP 24 analyses the total cost of pensions in a year into two elements:

(a) the **regular cost,** which is the consistent ongoing cost recognised under the actuarial method used; and

(b) **variations from regular costs.** These may arise from revisions in the actuarial estimates of an employer's ultimate obligation; or from the retroactive effects of changes in assumptions, actuarial method, benefits or conditions for membership; or from increases to pensions currently being paid which have not previously been provided for.

7.8   The **regular cost** of pensions is adequately **measured,** in normal circumstances, **by a stable contribution rate** specified by an actuary and expressed as a percentage of pensionable earnings.

7.9   **Variations from regular costs** should normally be **allocated over the expected average remaining service lives of employees** in the scheme, **unless prudence dictates** that a **shorter period** should be used. If a significant change in the normal level of contributions occurs because contributions are adjusted to eliminate the surplus or deficiency resulting from a significant reduction in the number of employees in the scheme, then a contribution holiday should be spread over its duration and a deficit recognised in full at once.

Disclosure requirements: general

7.10   Sufficient information should be disclosed to give the user of the financial statements a broad understanding of the significance of the pension arrangements.

Disclosure requirements: defined contribution schemes

7.11   (a)   The **nature** of the scheme (defined contribution).

      (b)   **Accounting policy.**

    (c) **Pension cost charge** for the period.

    (d) Any **outstanding or prepaid contributions** at the balance sheet date.

Illustration of disclosure for a defined contribution scheme in SSAP 24

7.12 'The company operates a defined contribution pension scheme. The assets of the scheme are held separately from those of the company in an independently administered fund. The pension cost charge represents contributions payable by the company to the fund and amounted to £500,000 (19X4 £450,000). Contributions totalling £25,000 (19X4 £15,000) were payable to the fund at the year end and are included in creditors.'

Disclosure requirements: defined benefit scheme

7.13 (a) The **nature** of the scheme (**defined benefit**).

    (b) Whether scheme is **funded or unfunded**.

    (c) **Accounting policy** (and if different, funding policy).

    (d) Whether pension cost and liability (or asset) are assessed in accordance with the advice of a professionally **qualified actuary** and if so disclose:

        (i) Date of most recent **formal actuarial valuation** or later review used for this purpose.

        (ii) If the actuary is an **employee or officer** of the company or group.

    (e) The **pension cost charge** for the period together with explanations of significant changes from the previous period.

    (f) **Provisions or prepayments** (difference between costs recognised and funding amounts).

    (g) Amount of **deficiency on a current funding level basis**. Indicate action, if any, being taken to deal with deficiency in the current and future financial statements.

    (h) Outline of **results of most recent formal actuarial valuation** or later review of funding of scheme on an ongoing basis. Disclose:

        (i) Actuarial method used and a brief description of the main actuarial assumptions.

        (ii) Market value of scheme assets at the date of their valuation or review.

        (iii) Level of funding expressed in percentage terms.

        (iv) Comments on any material actuarial surplus or deficiency indicated by (iii) above.

    (i) Expected **effects** on financial statements of **commitments to make additional payments** over a limited number of years.

    (j) Accounting treatment of a **refund** (which is subject to deduction of tax) where a credit appears in the financial statements in relation to it.

    (k) Details of expected **effects on future costs** of any **material changes** in the group's and/or company's arrangements.

Question 7

What information should be disclosed as part of a formal actuarial valuation, on an ongoing basis, of a defined benefit pension scheme?

Answer

The formal actuarial valuation, on an ongoing basis, of a defined benefit scheme should include the following information.

(a)   the actuarial method used and a brief description of the main actuarial assumptions;
(b)   the market value of scheme assets at the date of their valuation or review;
(c)   the level of funding expressed in percentage terms;
(d)   comments on any material actuarial surplus or deficiency indicated by (c) above.

Discussion

7.14   **SSAP 24 is orientated towards the profit and loss account rather than the balance sheet and seeks to even out the impact of pension contributions on earnings**. As such, the asset or liability recorded in the balance sheet is a balancing figure, the cumulative difference between the P & L charge and the amount paid. It may be either a prepayment or an accrual, depending on whether contributions are in advance or arrears of 'cost' in P & L terms.

7.15   The balance can also be analysed as the combination of two figures:

(a)   the most recently reported actuarial surplus or deficiency in the fund (as adjusted for subsequent contributions and regular costs); and

(b)   the cumulative amount of unamortised variations awaiting recognition in the profit and loss account.

7.16   **The standard's requirements on measurement are inevitably subjective** because no single actuarial process is required and because actuarial calculations are sometimes subjective. The standard's principal effect in achieving comparability between companies will result from its extensive disclosure requirements.

7.17   It has been commented that the standard has the effect of breaking down the distinction between pension fund and employer. This is not strictly correct; the standard is simply recognising the effect the current status of the fund has on the employer's obligation to contribute to it. However, the subjectivity involved in this process is certainly **open to manipulation**, and this has attracted adverse comment.

7.18   A final point to mention is that the application of SSAP 24 **may result in timing differences and so will affect deferred tax calculations.**

Audit implications

7.19   The **audit risks** associated with pension costs in the accounts of the employer company **can be high as the figures are likely to be material**. However, pension schemes must be audited and, as the pension costs and figures in the employer company's accounts will be based on the pension scheme accounts, some of the audit risk can be reduced.

7.20   The **relationship between the auditors of the company and the auditors of the pension scheme will be similar to that between the 'principal' and 'other' auditors in a group situation**. It will often be the case that the same auditors are responsible for the company and the pension fund, and then such difficulties will not arise. Where the auditors are different, then the company auditors should ask the company's and trustee's permission to approach the pension scheme auditors. Assuming permission is given, the company auditors can obtain any necessary information on the pension scheme audit.

7.21 The company auditors should **consider** the:

(a) **Terms** of the pension scheme auditors' engagement and any limitation placed on their work.

(b) **Standard of work** of the pension scheme auditors and the nature and extent of their auditing examination.

(c) **Independence** of the pension scheme auditors.

7.22 Even if satisfactory information is received, the company auditors should perform various **substantive procedures**.

(a) **Vouch payments** to the pension fund (usually as part of payroll testing).

(b) **Review signed actuary's report** and ensure that it agrees with the pension scheme accounts.

(c) **Check all calculations** for SSAP 24 accounting for pension costs. Ensure all disclosure requirements have been made according to SSAP 24 and CA 1985.

(d) Obtain **confirmation of the actuarial valuation** direct from the actuary.

7.23 If the pension figures in the company accounts are significant, and if unsatisfactory replies are received from the pension scheme auditors, then the company auditors should consider reperforming all or part of the pension scheme audit.

7.24 Note that, in the company audit report, the company auditors **may not mention the pension scheme auditors, nor any other specialist involved, such as the actuary. The opinion must be only his own.**

7.25 A 'worst case' situation for the company auditors in relation to pension costs **is probably where the value of the fund is depleted either by fraud or by mismanagement.** The company will probably become liable for the shortfall and a substantial liability may become due. This was the situation in the Robert Maxwell and Mirror Group Newspaper affair, where misappropriation from the pension fund had to be made good by the company.

7.26 Obviously, failure to provide for such a liability means that the company accounts do not show a true and fair view. On the other hand, where the company's auditors have performed all the proper and necessary work to determine whether the pension figures show a true and fair view, then they will normally have defence.

Chapter roundup

- SSAP 17 amplifies the CA 1985 requirement to take account of **post balance sheet** liabilities and losses.

  ○ It distinguishes between adjusting and non-adjusting events and gives examples.

  ○ It also requires disclosure of window dressing transactions.

  ○ Where an otherwise non-adjusting event indicates that the going concern concept is no longer appropriate, then the accounts may have to be restated on a break-up basis.

  ○ You should be able to define and discuss all these terms and apply them to practical examples.

- SSAP 18 defines a **contingency** and requires different treatments for contingent gains and losses.

  ○ You must learn the definition and required treatments and be able to discuss why losses and gains are treated differently.

  ○ You must also be able to give examples of each. You must also be able to explain the difference between the CA 1985's requirements and those of SSAP 18.

- FRS 4 *Capital instruments* is a complex standard. It has been issued to halt abuses in the accounting for **debt and equity**.

- SSAP 25 is primarily a **disclosure statements** concerned to improve the quality of information provided by published accounts.

- You must be able to prepare a **segmental analysis** and if necessary to use the results to help with interpretation of the accounts, as well as to discuss the **advantages and limitations** of segmental reporting.

- At this stage in your studies you need only be concerned with conversion of **foreign currency** in a **single company**.

- You should know the rules in **SSAP 20** and CA 1985 relating to **foreign currency exchange** gains and losses.

- **SSAP 24** is a complicated standard, but at this stage you should know the **disclosure requirements** and the **general purpose** of the standard.

- The other disclosure requirements covered in this chapter are uncontroversial but it is essential to have a good knowledge of these requirements when preparing or discussing published accounts.

Quick quiz

1   Define post balance sheet events. (see knowledge brought forward)

2   Define 'contingency'. (see knowledge brought forward)

3   What are the statutory disclosure requirements in respect of reserves? (3.2, 3.3)

4   What information must be disclosed in relation to a company's share capital? (4.2)

5   How should debt and equity be distinguished under FRS 4? (4.9)

6   How should hybrid instruments be disclosed according to FRS 4? (4.17)

7   How should the finance costs of debt be allocated under FRS 4? (4.20)

8   What companies fall within the scope of SSAP 25? (5.2)

9   What is SSAP 25's rule of thumb as to what constitutes a material segment for disclosure purposes? (5.8)

10 How should common costs be allocated in segmental accounts? (5.11)

11 Distinguish between the conversion and the translation of foreign currencies. (6.6, 6.11)

12 Distinguish between a defined contribution scheme and a defined benefit scheme. (7.2)

13 Over what period of time does SSAP 24 require that variations from regular costs be allocated? (7.9)

Question to try	Level	Marks	Time
16	Full exam	25	45 mins

Chapter 16

CONSTITUTION OF A GROUP

Chapter topic list	Syllabus reference
1 Definitions	2(c)
2 Exclusion of subsidiary undertakings from group accounts	2(c)
3 Exemption from the requirement to prepare group accounts	2(c)
4 Content of group accounts	2(c)
5 Group structure	2(c)
6 FRS 8 *Related party disclosures*	2(c)

Introduction

This is the first time you have faced group accounts and consolidation. It is an extremely important area of your Paper 10 syllabus as **you are almost certain to face a large compulsory consolidation question in the examination.**

The key to consolidation questions in the examination is to adopt a logical approach and to practise as many questions as possible beforehand.

In this chapter we will look at the major definitions in consolidation and the relevant statutory requirements and accounting standards. These matters are fundamental to your comprehension of group accounts, so make sure you can understand them and then learn them.

Section 6 considers a less directly connected topic: FRS 8 *Related party disclosures*.

The next two chapters deal with the basic techniques of consolidation, and then we move on to more complex aspects in the following chapters.

In all these chapters, make sure that you work through each example and question properly.

1   DEFINITIONS

1.1   There are many reasons for businesses to operate as groups; for the goodwill associated with the names of the subsidiaries, for tax or legal purposes and so forth. Company law requires that the results of a group should be presented as a whole. Unfortunately, it is not possible simply to add all the results together and this chapter and those following will teach you how to **consolidate** all the results of companies within a group.

1.2   **In traditional accounting terminology, a group of companies consists of a holding company (or parent company) and one or more subsidiary companies which are controlled by the holding company.** The CA 1989 widened this definition. (The Act amended the CA 1985 and references below are to the amended sections.) As a result, FRS 2 *Accounting for subsidiary undertakings* was published in July 1992 by the ASB, incorporating the CA 1989 changes.

Exam focus point
If you are revising, go straight to the summary at the end of this section.

1.3 There are **two definitions of a group in company law. One** uses the terms 'holding company' and 'subsidiary' and applies **for general purposes. The other** is wider and applies **only for accounting purposes.** It **uses the terms 'parent undertaking' and 'subsidiary undertaking'**. The purpose of this widening of the group for accounting purposes was to curb the practice of structuring a group in such a way that not all companies or ventures within it had to be consolidated. This is an example of off balance sheet financing and has been used extensively to make consolidated accounts look better than is actually justified (see Chapter 13).

1.4 We are only really interested in the accounting definitions of parent and subsidiary undertaking here: they automatically include 'holding companies' and 'subsidiaries' under the general definition.

Parent and subsidiary undertakings: definition

1.5 FRS 2 states that an undertaking is the **parent undertaking** of another undertaking (**a subsidiary undertaking**) if any of the following apply.

PARENT UNDERTAKING

(a) It holds a **majority of the voting rights** in the undertaking.

(b) It **is a member of the undertaking and has the right to appoint or remove directors** holding a majority of the voting rights at meetings of the board on all, or substantially all, matters.

(c) **It has the right to exercise a dominant influence over the undertaking:**

   (i) by virtue of provisions contained in the undertaking's memorandum or articles; or

   (ii) by virtue of a control contract (in writing, authorised by the memorandum or articles of the controlled undertaking, permitted by law).

(d) **It is a member of the undertaking and controls alone,** under an agreement with other shareholders or members, **a majority of the voting rights in the undertaking.**

(e) It **has a participating interest in the undertaking** and:

   (i) it actually exercises a dominant influence over the undertaking; or
   (ii) it and the undertaking are managed on a unified basis.

(f) A parent undertaking is **also treated as the parent undertaking of the subsidiary undertakings of its subsidiary undertakings.**

1.6 This replaced the previous criterion of owning a majority of equity with one of holding a majority of voting rights. **Also, the board is considered to be controlled if the holding company has the right to appoint directors with a majority of the voting rights on the board** (not just to appoint a simple majority of the directors, regardless of their voting rights).

Exam focus point

The above definition is extremely important and you may be asked to apply it to a given situation in an exam. It depends in turn, however, on the definition of various terms which are included in Paragraph 1.6.

Participating interest

KEY TERM

FRS 2 states that a **participating interest is an interest held by an undertaking in the shares of another undertaking which it holds on a long-term basis for the purpose of securing a contribution to its activities by the exercise of control or influence** arising from or related to that interest.

(a) A holding of **20% or more** of the shares of an undertaking is **presumed** to be a participating interest unless the contrary is shown.

(b) An interest in shares includes an interest which is convertible into an interest in shares, and includes an option to acquire shares or any interest which is convertible into shares.

(c) An interest held on behalf of an undertaking shall be treated as held by that undertaking (ie all group holdings must be aggregated to determine if a subsidiary exists).

1.7 A 'participating interest', like an investment in a 'subsidiary undertaking', **need not be in a company**, because an 'undertaking' means:

(a) a body corporate; or

(b) a partnership; or

(c) an unincorporated association carrying on a trade or business, with or without a view to profit.

1.8 **'Shares'** therefore **means**:

(a) **allotted** shares; **or**

(b) for undertakings without share capital, **the right to share in the capital and profits and the corresponding liability to meet losses and debts on winding up.**

Dominant influence

KEY TERM

FRS 2 defines **dominant influence** as influence that can be exercised to achieve the operating and financial policies desired by the holder of the influence, notwithstanding the rights or influence of any other party.

1.9 The standard then distinguishes between the two different situations involving dominant influence.

(a) In the context of Paragraph 1.6(c) above, **the right to exercise a dominant influence** means that the holder has **a right to give directions** with respect to the operating and financial policies of another undertaking with which its directors are obliged to comply, whether or not they are for the benefit of that undertaking.

(b) **The actual exercise of dominant influence** is the exercise of an influence that achieves the result that the operating and financial policies of the undertaking influenced are set in accordance with the wishes of the holder of the influence and for the holder's benefit whether or not those wishes are explicit. The actual exercise of dominant influence is identified by its effect in practice rather than by the way in which it is exercised.

1.10 There are four other important definitions.

> (a) **Control** is the ability of an undertaking to direct the financial and operating policies of another undertaking with a view to gaining economic benefits from its activities.
>
> (b) An **interest held on a long-term basis** is an interest which is held other than exclusively with a view to subsequent resale.
>
> (c) An **interest held exclusively with a view to subsequent resale** is either:
>
> (i) an interest for which a purchaser has been identified or is being sought, and which is reasonably expected to be disposed of within approximately one year of its date of acquisition; or
>
> (ii) an interest that was acquired as a result of the enforcement of a security, unless the interest has become part of the continuing activities of the group or the holder acts as if it intends the interest to become so.
>
> (d) **Managed on a unified basis:** two or more undertakings are managed on a unified basis if the whole of the operations of the undertakings are integrated and they are managed as a single unit. Unified management does not arise solely because one undertaking manages another.

Other definitions from the standard will be introduced where relevant over the next few chapters.

The requirement to consolidate

1.11 FRS 2 requires a parent undertaking to prepare consolidated financial statements for its group unless it uses one of the exemptions available in the standard (see Section 2).

> **KEY TERM**
>
> **Consolidation** is defined as: 'The process of adjusting and combining financial information from the individual financial statements of a parent undertaking and its subsidiary undertaking to prepare consolidated financial statements that present financial information for the group as a single economic entity.'

Associated undertakings

1.12   Another important definition, which applies only for the purposes of preparing group accounts, is that of an 'associated undertaking'. This is not defined by FRS 2, but as CA 1985 (and FRS 9: see Chapter 20).

> ### KEY TERM
>
> 'An **"associated undertaking"** means an undertaking in which an undertaking included in the consolidation has a participating interest and over whose operating and financial policy it exercises a significant influence, and which is not:
>
> (a)   a subsidiary undertaking of the parent company; or
> (b)   a joint venture'. (s 20(1) Sch 4A, CA 1985)
>
> 'Where an undertaking holds 20% or more of the voting rights in another undertaking, it shall be presumed to exercise such an influence over it unless the contrary is shown.'
>
> (s 20(2) Sch 4A, CA 1985)

1.13   The importance of this definition is that **parent companies are required by law to use equity accounting to account for holdings in 'associated undertakings'.** However, holdings in 'associated companies' (FRS 9 definition: see Chapter 20) are **already accounted for in this way to comply with the SSAP.**

1.14   **Participating interests,** on the other hand, which are not in 'associated undertakings' **have to be disclosed separately from other investments but do not have to be accounted for by the equity method.** Participating interests must be disclosed both in group accounts and in individual company accounts. If you refer back to the statutory accounts formats in Chapter 8, you will see the captions in both the balance sheet and the profit and loss account which refer to 'participating interests'.

1.15   However, in **group accounts** these formats must be amended if necessary as follows.

(a)   Income from interests in associated undertakings   X
       Income from other participating interests   X

       should replace the captions at 8 (format 1) and 10 (format 2) 'Income from participating interests' in the profit and loss account.

(b)   Interests in associated undertakings   X
       Other participating interests   X

       should replace item BIII 3 'Participating interests' in the balance sheet.

1.16   An undertaking **S is a subsidiary undertaking of H if:**

(a)   H is a member of S and *either* holds or **controls > 50% of the voting rights** *or* controls the board; *OR*

(b)   S is a **subsidiary** of H (ie S is a sub-subsidiary); *OR*

(c)   H has the right to exercise a **dominant influence** over S (laid down in the memorandum or articles or a control contract); *OR*

(d)   H has a **participating interest** in S **and** either **actually** exercises a **dominant influence** over S *or* H and S are managed on a unified basis.

∴ **Special treatment: consolidate**

1.17 An undertaking A is an **associated undertaking** of H if:

(a) H and/or one or more of its subsidiary undertakings have a **participating interest** in A and **either** hold more than **20%** of the voting rights **or** can otherwise be demonstrated to exercise a **significant** influence over A's operating and financial policy; *AND*

(b) A is not a subsidiary undertaking of H nor is it a joint venture.

∴ **Special treatment: equity accounting**

1.18 An investment in an undertaking P is a **participating interest** of H if:

(a) the H group owns **more than 20%** of P's share capital; *OR*

(b) the H group has a shareholding or equivalent interest in P **for the long term** and for the purpose of securing a contribution to its activities.

∴ **Special treatment: separate disclosure**

> **Exam focus point**
> A question on the pilot paper required you to determine, on the basis of control, whether an investment was a subsidiary or not.

2   EXCLUSION OF SUBSIDIARY UNDERTAKINGS FROM GROUP ACCOUNTS   6/94

2.1 S 229 CA 1985 (as amended by the CA 1989) provides that a **subsidiary may be omitted** from the consolidated accounts of a group **if:**

(a) in the opinion of the directors, its inclusion 'is **not material** for the purpose of giving a true and fair view; but two or more undertakings may be excluded only if they are not material taken together'; or

(b) there are **severe long-term restrictions** in exercising the parent company's rights eg civil war in the country of an overseas subsidiary; or

(c) the holding is **exclusively for resale**; or

(d) the information cannot be obtained 'without **disproportionate expense** or undue delay'

2.2 If in the opinion of the directors, a subsidiary undertaking's consolidation is undesirable because the **business of the holding company and subsidiary are so different that they cannot reasonably be treated as a single undertaking, then that undertaking** *must* **be excluded.**

> 'This .... does not apply merely because some of the undertakings are industrial, some commercial and some provide services, or because they carry on industrial or commercial activities involving different products or provide different services.'

2.3 FRS 2 states that a **subsidiary must be excluded** from consolidation if:

(a) **Severe long-term restrictions are substantially hindering the exercise of the parent's rights** over the subsidiary's assets or management.

(b) The group's interest in the subsidiary undertaking is **held exclusively with a view to subsequent resale and** the subsidiary has **not been consolidated previously.**

(c) The subsidiary undertaking's **activities are so different** from those of other undertakings to be included in the consolidation **that its inclusion would be incompatible with the obligation to give a true and fair view.**

The FRS requires the circumstances in which subsidiary undertakings are to be excluded from consolidation to be interpreted **strictly**.

2.4 Where a subsidiary is excluded from group accounts, FRS 2 lays down supplementary provisions on the disclosures and accounting treatment required.

2.5 Where a subsidiary is excluded on grounds of **dissimilar activities** (which should be exceptional), the group accounts should **include separate financial statements for that subsidiary including:**

(a) A note of the **holding company's interest**.

(b) Details of **intra-group balances**.

(c) The **nature of its transactions** with the rest of the group.

(d) A **reconciliation of the subsidiary's results** (as shown separately) with the value in the consolidated accounts for the 'group's investment in the subsidiary'.

In the consolidated accounts, the excluded subsidiary **should be accounted for by the equity method** of accounting (as though it were an associated company). This is explained in Chapter 14 on accounting for associated companies.

2.6 Subsidiary undertakings **excluded** from consolidation **because of severe long-term restrictions** are to be **treated as fixed asset investments**. They are to be included at their carrying amount when the restrictions came into force, and no further accruals are to be made for profits or losses of those subsidiary undertakings, unless the parent undertaking still exercises significant influence. In the latter case they are to be treated as associated undertakings.

2.7 The following information should be **disclosed** in the group accounts:

(a) Its **net assets**.

(b) Its **profit or loss** for the period.

(c) Any amounts included in the **consolidated profit and loss account** in respect of:

    (i)   **Dividends received** by the holding company from the subsidiary.

    (ii)   **Writing down the value of the investment**.

2.8 If control is temporary (the investment is **held purely for resale**), the temporary investment **should be included under current assets** in the consolidated balance sheet at the lower of cost and net realisable value.

2.9 In all cases given above, FRS 2 states that the consolidated accounts should show:

(a) The **reasons** for exclusion.
(b) The **names** of subsidiaries excluded.
(c) The **premium or discount on acquisition** not written off.
(d) **Anything else required** by the Companies Acts.

2.10 The CA 1985 requires that when consolidated group accounts are not prepared, or if any subsidiaries are excluded from the group accounts (for any of the reasons given above), **a note to the accounts should be given:**

(a) to explain the reasons why the subsidiaries are not dealt with in group accounts;

(b) to disclose any auditors' qualifications in the accounts of the excluded subsidiaries.

A note to the (holding) company's accounts (or the consolidated accounts, if any) should also state, for subsidiaries which are not consolidated in group accounts, the aggregate value of the total investment of the holding company in the subsidiaries, by way of the 'equity method' of valuation.

2.11 Section summary

The following table summaries the rules relating to exclusion of a subsidiary.

Reason	Accounting treatment
• Severe long-term restrictions hindering exercise of parent's rights	B/S: equity method up to date of severe restrictions less amounts written off if permanent fall in value
	P&L a/c: dividends received only
• Held exclusively for subsequent resale; has never been consolidated	Current asset at the lower of cost and net realisable value
• Dissimilar activities	Equity method (see Chapter 20)

3 EXEMPTION FROM THE REQUIREMENT TO PREPARE GROUP ACCOUNTS

3.1   The CA 1989 introduced a completely new provision exempting some groups from preparing consolidated accounts. There are two grounds.

(a) **Smaller groups** can claim exemptions on grounds of size (see below).

(b) **Parent companies** (*except* for listed companies) **whose immediate parent is established in an EU member country** need not prepare consolidated accounts. The accounts must give the name and country of incorporation of the parent and state the fact of the exemption. In addition, a copy of the audited consolidated accounts of the parent must be filed with the UK company's accounts. Minority shareholders can, however, require that consolidated accounts are prepared.

FRS 2 adds that exemption may be gained if all of the parent's subsidiary undertakings gain exemption under s 229 CA 1985 (see Paragraph 2.1).

3.2   The **exemption** from preparing consolidated accounts is **not available to:**

(a) Public companies.

(b) Banking and insurance companies.

(c) Authorised persons under the Financial Services Act 1986.

(d) Companies belonging to a group containing a member of the above classes of undertaking.

3.3 Any two of the following **size criteria** for small and medium-sized groups must be met.

	Small	Medium-sized
Aggregate turnover	≤ £2.8 million net/ £3.36 million gross	≤ £11.2 million net/ £13.44 million gross
Aggregate gross assets	≤ £1.4 million net/ £1.68 million gross	≤ £5.6 million net/ £6.72 million gross
Aggregate number of employees (average monthly)	≤ 50	≤ 250

3.4 The aggregates can be calculated either before (gross) or after (net) consolidation adjustments for intra-group sales, unrealised profit on stock and so on (see following chapters). The qualifying conditions **must be met**:

(a) **in the case of the parent's first financial year, in that year; and**
(b) **in the case of any subsequent financial year, in that year and the preceding year.**

If the qualifying conditions were met in the preceding year but not in the current year, the exemption can be claimed. If, in the subsequent year, the conditions are met again, the exemption can still be claimed, but if they are not met, then the exemption is lost until the conditions are again met for the second of two successive years.

3.5 When the exemption is claimed, but the auditors believe that the company is not entitled to it, then they must state in their report that the company is in their opinion not entitled to the exemption and this report must be attached to the individual accounts of the company (ie no report is required when the company *is* entitled to the exemption).

4 CONTENT OF GROUP ACCOUNTS

4.1 The information contained in the individual accounts of a holding company and each of its subsidiaries does not give a picture of the group's activities as those of a single entity. To do this, a separate set of accounts can be prepared from the individual accounts. *Note*. **Remember that a group has no separate (legal) existence, except for accounting purposes.**

4.2 There is more than one way of amalgamating the information in the individual accounts into a set of group accounts, but the most common way (and now the legally required way) is to prepare consolidated accounts. **Consolidated accounts are one form of group accounts which combines the information contained in the separate accounts of a holding company and its subsidiaries as if they were the accounts of a single entity.** 'Group accounts' and 'consolidated accounts' are often used synonymously, and now that UK law *requires* group accounts to be consolidated accounts, this tendency will no doubt increase.

4.3 In simple terms a set of consolidated accounts is prepared by **adding together** the assets and liabilities of the holding company and each subsidiary. The **whole of the assets and liabilities of each company** are included, **even though some subsidiaries may be only partly owned.** The 'capital and reserves' side of the balance sheet will indicate how much of the net assets are attributable to the group and how much to outside investors in partly owned subsidiaries. These **outside investors** are known as **minority interests**.

4.4 The CA 1985 requires that group accounts should be prepared whenever a company:

(a) is a parent company at the end of its financial year; and

(b) is not itself a wholly owned subsidiary of a company incorporated in Great Britain.

4.5 Most parent companies present their own individual accounts and their group accounts in a single **package**. The package typically comprises a:

(a) **Parent company balance sheet**, which will include 'investments in subsidiary undertakings' as an asset.

(b) **Consolidated balance sheet.**

(c) **Consolidated profit and loss** account.

(d) **Consolidated cash flow statement.**

It is not necessary to publish a parent company profit and loss account (s 230 CA 1985), provided the consolidated profit and loss account contains a note stating the profit or loss for the financial year dealt with in the accounts of the parent company and the fact that the statutory exemption is being relied on.

Exam focus point
If you are in a hurry skim or skip the rest of Section 4.

Co-terminous accounting periods

4.6 S 223 (5) CA 1985 requires that the directors of the holding company **should ensure that the financial year of each of the subsidiaries in the group shall coincide with the financial year of the holding company.** This is to prevent any possible 'window dressing' (although financial years need not coincide if the directors hold the opinion that there are reasons against it).

4.7 If the financial year end of a subsidiary does not coincide with the financial year of the holding company, the appropriate results to include in the group accounts for the subsidiary will be those for its year ending before the year end of the holding company; or if this ended more than three months previously, from interim accounts prepared as at the holding company's year end (s 2(2) Sch 4A CA 1985). These two provisions are included in FRS 2.

4.8 Additionally, FRS 2 requires that a note to the group accounts should disclose the:

(a) Reasons why the directors consider that coinciding dates are not appropriate.

(b) Name(s) of the subsidiary(ies) concerned.

(c) Accounting date and length of the accounting period of each relevant subsidiary.

Disclosure of subsidiaries

4.9 The CA 1985 requires that a parent company disclose, by note:

(a) The name of each subsidiary undertaking.

(b) Its country of incorporation (or, if unincorporated, address of principal place of business).

(c) The identity and proportion of the nominal value of each class of shares held (distinguishing between direct and indirect holdings).

(d) The reason for treating a subsidiary undertaking as such *unless* a majority of the voting rights are held and the proportion is the same as that of shares held.

FRS 2 confirms these provisions and also requires that the nature of each subsidiary's business should be indicated.

(*Note.* A subsidiary company must show, in its own accounts, its ultimate holding company's name and country of incorporation.)

Further provisions of FRS 2

4.10 FRS 2 also requires the following.

(a) **Uniform accounting policies should be applied by all companies in the group,** or if this is not done, appropriate adjustments should be made in the consolidated accounts to achieve uniformity. (If, in exceptional cases, such adjustments are impractical, the different accounting policies used, the effect of the difference on the results and net assets, and the reason for the different treatment should all be disclosed). This is also required by the CA 1985.

(b) **Where there are material additions to the group there should be disclosure of the extent to which the results of the group are affected by profits and losses** of subsidiaries brought in for the first time. This is also now required by the CA 1985.

(c) **Outside or minority interests in the share capital and reserves of companies consolidated should be disclosed separately in the consolidated balance sheet** (also required by the CA 1985). Debit balances should be shown only if there is a binding obligation on minority shareholders to make good any losses. Similarly, the profits and losses of such companies attributable to outside interests should be shown separately in the consolidated profit and loss account after arriving at group profit or loss after tax but before extraordinary items. Minority interests in extraordinary items should be deducted from the relevant amounts.

(d) Changes in membership of a group occur on the date control passes, whether by a transaction or other event. **Changes in the membership of the group during the period should be disclosed.**

(e) When a subsidiary undertaking is acquired the FRS requires its **identifiable assets and liabilities to be brought into the consolidation at their fair values at the date that undertaking becomes a subsidiary** undertaking, even if the acquisition has been made in stages. When a group increases its interest in an undertaking that is already its subsidiary undertaking, the identifiable assets and liabilities of that subsidiary undertaking should be calculated by reference to that fair value. This revaluation is not required if the difference between fair values and carrying amounts of the identifiable assets and liabilities attributable to the increase in stake is not material.

(f) The effect of consolidating the parent and its subsidiary undertakings may be that aggregation obscures useful information about the different undertakings and activities included in the consolidated financial statements. Parent undertakings are encouraged to give **segmental analysis to provide** readers of consolidated financial statements with **useful information on the different risks and rewards, growth and prospects of the different parts of the group.** The specification of such analysis, however, falls outside the scope of the FRS.

Further provisions of the Companies Act 1985

4.11 For each material acquisition in the period, in addition to the above disclosures, a note must state:

(a) The composition and **fair value** of the consideration given.

(b) The name of the undertaking (of the parent undertaking in the case of a newly acquired group).

(c) Whether acquisition or merger accounting has been used (see Chapter 20).

4.12 If **acquisition accounting** was used, a table of the book values and *fair values* as at acquisition of each class of assets and liabilities of the undertaking or group acquired is to be given, including a statement of the amount of any goodwill or negative consolidation difference arising and an explanation of any significant adjustments made.

4.13 If **merger accounting** is used, then an explanation is to be given of any significant adjustments made together with a statement of adjustments to consolidated reserves.

4.14 For each **material disposal** in the period, the name of the subsidiary must be disclosed, along with the FRS 2 requirements (see Section 2).

4.15 Finally, the CA 1985 requirement to disclose cumulative goodwill written off has been amended recently to exclude goodwill written off through the profit and loss account. Consequently, only the **cumulative goodwill that has been written off direct to reserves** in the current year or past years need now be disclosed. Note that negative goodwill does not require disclosure.

5   GROUP STRUCTURE

5.1 With the difficulties of definition and disclosure dealt with, let us now look at group structures. The simplest are those in which a holding company has only a direct interest in the shares of its subsidiary companies. For example:

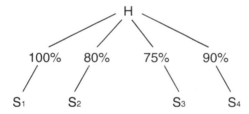

S_1 Ltd is a wholly owned subsidiary of H Ltd. S_2 Ltd, S_3 Ltd and S_4 Ltd are partly owned subsidiaries; a proportion of the shares in these companies is held by outside investors.

5.2 Often a holding company will have indirect holdings in its subsidiary companies. This can lead to more complex group structures.

(a)

H Ltd owns 51% of the equity shares in S Ltd, which is therefore its subsidiary. S Ltd in its turn owns 51% of the equity shares in SS Ltd. SS Ltd is therefore a subsidiary of S Ltd and consequently a subsidiary of H Ltd. SS Ltd would describe S Ltd as its **parent** (or holding) company and H Ltd as its **ultimate parent** (or holding) company.

Note that although H Ltd can control the assets and business of SS Ltd by virtue of the chain of control, its interest in the assets of SS Ltd is only 26%. This can be seen by considering a dividend of £100 paid by SS Ltd: as a 51% shareholder, S Ltd would receive £51; H Ltd would have an interest in 51% of this £51 = £26.01.

(b)

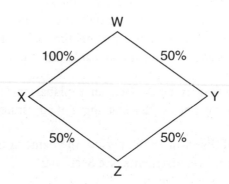

W Ltd owns 100% of the equity of X Ltd and 50% of the equity of Y Ltd. X Ltd and Y Ltd each own 50% of the equity of Z Ltd. Assume that:

(i)   W Ltd does not control the composition of Y Ltd's board; and

(ii)   W Ltd does not hold or control more than 50% of the *voting rights* in Y Ltd; and

(iii)   W Ltd does not have the right to exercise a dominant influence over Y Ltd by virtue of its memorandum, articles or a control contract; and

(iv)   W Ltd and Y Ltd are not managed on a unified basis; and

(v)   W Ltd does not actually exercise a dominant influence over Y Ltd; and

(vi)   none of the above apply to either X Ltd's or Y Ltd's holdings in Z Ltd.

In other words, because W Ltd is not in co-operation with the holder(s) of the other 50% of the shares in Y Ltd, neither Y nor Z can be considered subsidiaries.

In that case:

(i)   X Ltd is a subsidiary of W Ltd;

(ii)   Y Ltd is not a subsidiary of W Ltd;

(iii)   Z Ltd is not a subsidiary of either X Ltd or Y Ltd. Consequently, it is not a subsidiary of W Ltd.

If Z Ltd pays a dividend of £100, X Ltd and Y Ltd will each receive £50. The interest of W Ltd in this dividend is as follows.

	£
Through X Ltd (100% × £50)	50
Through Y Ltd (50% × £50)	25
	75

Although W Ltd has an interest in 75% of Z Ltd's assets, Z Ltd is not a subsidiary of W Ltd.

(c)

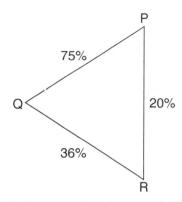

Q Ltd is a subsidiary of P Ltd. P Ltd therefore has indirect control over 36% of R Limited's equity. P Ltd also has direct control over 20% of R Limited's equity. R Ltd is therefore a subsidiary of P Ltd, although P Limited's interest in R Limited's assets is only 20% + (75% × 36%) = 47%.

Examples (b) and (c) illustrate an important point in company law: in deciding whether a company A holds more than 50% of the equity (or equivalent) of an undertaking B it is necessary to aggregate:

(i)   shares (or equivalent) in B held directly by A; and

(ii)   shares (or equivalent) in B held by undertakings which are subsidiaries of A.

Question 1

During the time until your examination you should obtain as many sets of the published accounts of top quoted companies as possible. Examine the accounting policies in relation to subsidiary and associated companies and consider how these policies are shown in the accounting and consolidation treatment. Consider the effect of any disposals during the year. Also, look at all the disclosures made relating to fair values, goodwill etc and match them to the disclosure requirements outlined in this chapter and in subsequent chapters on FRSs 6 and 7.

Alternatively (or additionally) you should attempt to obtain such information from the financial press.

---

6   FRS 8 RELATED PARTY DISCLOSURES

6.1   The ASB has produced its most recent FRS on related parties. FRS 8 *Related party disclosures* makes it clear why a standard was required on this subject.

'In the absence of information to the contrary, it is assumed that a reporting entity has independent discretionary power over its resources and transactions and pursues its activities independently of the interests of its individual owners, managers and others. Transactions are presumed to have been undertaken on an arm's length basis, ie on terms such as could have obtained in a transaction with an external party, in which each side bargained knowledgeably and freely, unaffected by any relationship between them.

These assumptions may not be justified when related party relationships exist, because the requisite conditions for competitive, free market dealings may not be present. Whilst the parties may endeavour to achieve arm's length bargaining the very nature of the relationship may preclude this occurring.'

6.2   FRS 8 can be summarised as follows.

(a)   FRS 8 *Related party disclosures* requires the **disclosure** of:

(i)   **information on related party transactions**; and

(ii) the **name of the party controlling** the reporting entity and, if different, that of the ultimate controlling party whether or not any transactions between the reporting entity and those parties have taken place.

Aggregated disclosures are allowed subject to certain restrictions.

Related parties are defined below.

(b) **No disclosure** is required in consolidated financial statements of **intragroup transactions** and balances eliminated on consolidation. A parent undertaking is not required to provide related party disclosures in its own financial statements when those statements are presented with consolidated financial statements of its group.

(c) Disclosure is not required in the financial statements of **subsidiary undertakings**, 90% or more of whose voting rights are controlled within the group, of transactions with entities that are part of the group or investees of the group qualifying as related parties provided that the consolidated financial statements in which that subsidiary is included are publicly available.

FRS 8 is not long and the more detailed requirements are as follows.

Objective

6.3 The objective of FRS 8 is to ensure that financial statements contain the disclosures necessary to draw attention to the possibility that the reported financial position and results may have been affected by the existence of related parties and by material transactions with them. In other words, this is a standard which **is primarily concerned with disclosure**.

6.4 The definitions given in FRS 8 are fundamental to the effect of the standard.

DEFINITIONS

(a) **Close family** are those family members, or members of the same household, who may be expected to influence, or be influenced by, that person in their dealings with the reporting entity.

(b) **Control** means the ability of an undertaking to direct the financial and operating policies of another undertaking with a view to gaining economic benefits from its activities.

(c) **Key management** are those persons in senior positions having authority or responsibility for directing or controlling the major activities and resources of the reporting entity.

(d) **Persons acting in concert** comprise persons who, pursuant to an agreement or understanding (whether formal or informal), actively co-operative, whether through the ownership by any of them of shares in an undertaking or otherwise, to exercise control or influence over that undertaking.

6.5 The most important definitions are of *related parties* and *related party transactions*.

'Related parties

(a) Two or more parties are related parties when at any time during the financial period:

(i) one party has **direct or indirect control** of the other party; or

(ii) the parties are **subject to common control** from the same source; or

(iii)   one party has **influence over the financial and operating policies** of the other party to an extent that that other party might be inhibited from pursuing at all times its own separate interests; or

(iv)   the parties, in entering a transaction, are subject to **influence from the same source** to such an extent that one of the parties to the transaction has subordinated its own separate interests.

(b)   For the avoidance of doubt, the following are **related parties** of the reporting entity:

(i)   its ultimate and intermediate **parent undertakings**, subsidiary undertakings, and fellow subsidiary undertakings;

(ii)   its **associates and joint ventures**;

(iii)   the **investor or venturer** in respect of which the reporting entity is an associate or a joint venture;

(iv)   **directors*** of the reporting entity and the directors of its ultimate and intermediate parent undertakings; and

(v)   pension funds for the benefit of employees of the reporting entity or of any entity that is a related party of the reporting entity;

[* Directors include shadow directors, which are defined in companies legislation as persons in accordance with whose directions or instructions the directors of the company are accustomed to act.]

(c)   and the following are **presumed to be related parties** of the reporting entity unless it can be demonstrated that neither party has influenced the financial and operating policies of the other in such a way as to inhibit the pursuit of separate interests:

(i)   the **key management** of the reporting entity and the key management of its parent undertakings or undertakings;

(ii)   a person owning or able to exercise control over **20 per cent or more of the voting rights** of the reporting entity, whether directly or through nominees;

(iii)   each person **acting in concert** in such a way as to be able to exercise control or influence [in terms of part (a)(iii) of the definition of related party transitions, above] over the reporting entity; and

(iv)   an entity managing or managed by the reporting entity under a **management contract**.

(d)   Additionally, because of their relationship with certain parties that are, or are presumed to be, related parties of the reporting entity, the following are also presumed to be related parties of the reporting entity:

(i)   **members of the close family** of any individual falling under parties mentioned in (a) - (c) above; and

(ii)   partnerships, companies, trusts or other **entities** in which any individual or member of the close family in (a) - (c) above has a **controlling interest**.

Sub-paragraphs (b), (c) and (d) are not intended to be an exhaustive list of related parties.

Related party transaction
The transfer of assets or liabilities or the performance of services by, or for a related party irrespective of whether a price is charged.'

6.6   The most important point is in paragraph (a) of the definition of related parties because it defines in **general terms** what related party transactions are; the succeeding paragraphs of definition only add **some specifics**.

Scope

6.7   FRS 8 applies to all financial statements that are intended to give a true and fair view but it **excludes some transactions**; it does *not* require disclosure:

(a) In consolidated financial statements, of any transactions or balances between **group entities** that have been **eliminated on consolidation**.

(b) In a **parent's own financial statements** when those statements are presented together with its consolidated financial statements.

(c) In the financial statements of **subsidiary undertakings**, 90% per cent or more of whose voting rights are controlled within the group, of transactions with entities that are part of the group or investees of the group qualifying as related parties, provided that the consolidated financial statements in which that subsidiary is included are publicly available.

(d) Of **pension contributions** paid to a pension fund.

(e) Of **emoluments** in respect of services as an **employee** of the reporting entity.

Reporting entities taking advantage of the exemption in (c) above are required to state that fact.

6.8 Further types of transaction are also excluded as the FRS does not require disclosure of the relationship and transactions between the reporting entity and the parties listed in (a) to (d) below simply as a result of their role as:

(a) **providers of finance** in the course of their business in that regard
(b) **utility companies**
(c) **government departments** and their sponsored bodies,

even though they may circumscribe the freedom of action of an entity or participate in its decision-making process; and

(d) a customer, supplier, franchiser, distributor or general agent with whom an entity transacts a significant volume of business.

6.9 **FRS 8 then states the disclosures it requires, under two headings:**

(a) **disclosure of control**; and
(b) **disclosure of transactions and balances**.

Disclosure of control

6.10 When the reporting entity is controlled by another party, there should be disclosure of the related party relationship and the name of that party and, if different, that of the ultimate controlling party. If the controlling party or ultimate controlling party of the reporting entity is not known, that fact should be disclosed. This information should be disclosed **irrespective of whether any transactions have taken place** between the controlling parties and the reporting entity.

Disclosure of transactions and balances

6.11 Financial statements should **disclose material transactions** undertaken by the reporting entity with a related party. Disclosure should be made **irrespective of whether a price is charged**. The disclosure should include:

(a) The **names** of the transacting parties.

(b) A description of the **relationship** between the parties.

(c) A description of the **transactions**.

(d) The **amounts** involved.

(e) **Any other elements** of the transactions necessary for an understanding of the financial statements.

(f) The **amounts due** to or from related parties **at the balance sheet** date and provisions for doubtful debts due from such parties at that date.

(g) **Amounts written off** in the period in respect of debts due to or from related parties.

Transactions with related parties may be disclosed on an aggregated basis (aggregation of similar transactions by type of related party) unless disclosure of an individual transaction, or connected transactions, is necessary for an understanding of the impact of the transactions on the financial statements of the reporting entity or is required by law.

6.12 Further points of interest are made in the explanatory notes, particularly those on applying the definition of 'related party' given above.

(a) **Common control** is deemed to exist when **both parties are subject to control from boards having a controlling nucleus of directors in common.**

(b) The difference between control and influence is that **control brings with it the ability to cause the controlled party to subordinate its separate interests whereas the outcome of the exercise of influence is less certain.** Two related parties of a third entity are not necessarily related parties of each other.

6.13 Examples of such a situation of 'influence' rather than 'control' are given:

(a) Where two companies are associates of the same investor.

(b) When one party is subject to control and another party is subject to influence from the same source.

(c) Where two parties have a director in common.

In these cases the two parties would not normally be treated as related parties.

Disclosable related party transactions

6.14 The explanatory notes also give examples of related party transactions which would require disclosure:

(a) Purchases or sales of goods (finished or unfinished).
(b) Purchases or sales of property and other assets.
(c) Rendering or receiving of services.
(d) Agency arrangements
(e) Leasing arrangements.
(f) Transfer of research and development.
(g) Licence agreements.
(h) Provision of finance (including loans and equity contributions in cash or in kind).
(i) Guarantees and the provision of collateral security.
(j) Management contracts.

6.15 The *materiality* of related party transactions is also an important question because **only material related party transactions must be disclosed.** You should be familiar with the general definition of materiality, that transactions are material when disclosure might reasonably be expected to influence decisions made by the users of general purpose financial statements. In the case of related party transactions, materiality:

'is to be judged, not only in terms of their significance to the reporting entity, but also in relation to the other related party when that party is:

(a)   a director, key manager or other individual in a position to influence, or accountable for stewardship of, the reporting entity; or

(b)   a member of the close family of any individual mentioned in (a) above; or

(c)   an entity controlled by any individual mentioned in (a) or (b) above.'

Question 2

Which transactions are *excluded* by FRS 8?

Answer

See Paragraphs 6.7 and 6.8.

Current CA 1985 and Stock Exchange requirements

6.16   Some types of related party transactions are covered by existing statutory or Stock Exchange requirements, such as the provisions of the Companies Act 1985 covering transactions by directors and connected persons and 'Class IV' circulars which listed companies are required to send to shareholders when an acquisition or disposal of assets is made from or to a director, substantial shareholder or associate.

Chapter roundup

- This chapter has explained the concept of a **group** and introduced several important definitions.

- The principal **regulations** governing the preparation of group accounts have been explained. Many of these are hard to understand and you should re-read this chapter after you have completed your study of this section of the text.

- A number of possible **group structures** have been illustrated to show that a company may hold an interest in the net assets of another company which exceeds 50%, without conferring control of the other company. The converse is also true.

- **FRS 8** is primarily a **disclosure statement**. It is concerned to improve the quality of information provided by published accounts and also to strengthen their stewardship role.

Quick quiz

1   What is the FRS 2 definition of a 'subsidiary'? (see para 1.5)

2   What is a 'participating interest'? (1.7)

3   What is a 'dominant influence'? (1.9)

4   How must investments in associated undertakings be treated in a parent company's own accounts? (1.13)

5   Under what circumstances *may* subsidiary undertakings be excluded under the CA 1985? (2.1) When *must* an undertaking be excluded? (2.3)

6   How should a subsidiary excluded on the grounds of temporary control be accounted for in the consolidated balance sheet? (2.8)

7   What are the size criteria for exemption from preparing group accounts under the CA 1985? (3.3)

8   What is the profit which a parent company must disclose if it wishes to claim exemption under s 230 CA 1985 from publishing its own profit and loss account? (4.5)

9   What must be disclosed in the notes to the consolidated accounts in respect of all newly acquired subsidiary undertakings (if material to the group)? (4.10(b), 4.11) What extra disclosures are required depending on the consolidation method adopted? (4.12, 4.13)

10 Summarise the requirements of FRS 8 (6.2)

11 How does FRS 8 define related parties? (6.5 (a))

12 Which parties are *deemed* to be related parties of the reporting entity? (6.5 (b)-(d))

13 What are the disclosure requirements of FRS 8? (6.10, 6.11)

Question to try	Level	Marks	Time
17	Full exam	20	36 mins

Chapter 17

CONSOLIDATED BALANCE SHEET: BASIC PRINCIPLES

Introduction

This chapter introduces the *basic procedures* required in consolidation and gives a formal step plan for carrying out a balance sheet consolidation. This step procedure should be useful to you as a starting guide for answering any question, but remember that you cannot rely on it to answer the question for you.

Each question must be approached and answered on its own merits. Examiners often put small extra or different problems in because, as they are always reminding students, it is not possible to 'rote-learn' consolidation.

The method of consolidation shown here uses schedules for workings (reserves, minority interests etc) rather than the ledger accounts used in some other texts. This is because we believe that ledger accounts lead students to 'learn' the consolidation journals without thinking about what they are doing - always a dangerous practice in consolidation questions.

There are plenty of questions in this chapter - work through *all* of them carefully.

1 CANCELLATION AND PART CANCELLATION

1.1 The preparation of a consolidated balance sheet, in a very simple form, consists of two procedures.

(a) Take the individual accounts of the holding company and each subsidiary and **cancel out items which appear as an asset in one company and a liability in another.**

(b) **Add together all the uncancelled assets** and liabilities throughout the group.

1.2 **Items requiring cancellation** may include the following.

(a) The asset **'shares in subsidiary companies'** which appears in the parent company's accounts will be matched with the liability 'share capital' in the subsidiaries' accounts.

(b)   There may be **inter-company trading** within the group. For example, S Ltd may sell goods to H Ltd. H Ltd would then be a debtor in the accounts of S Ltd, while S Ltd would be a creditor in the accounts of H Ltd.

1.3   EXAMPLE: CANCELLATION

H Ltd regularly sells goods to its one subsidiary company, S Ltd. The balance sheets of the two companies on 31 December 19X6 are given below.

H LIMITED
BALANCE SHEET AS AT 31 DECEMBER 19X6

		£	£	£
Fixed assets				
Tangible assets				35,000
40,000 £1 shares in S Ltd at cost				40,000
				75,000
Current assets				
Stocks			16,000	
Debtors:	S Ltd	2,000		
	Other	6,000		
			8,000	
Cash at bank			1,000	
			25,000	
Current liabilities				
Creditors			14,000	
				11,000
				86,000
Capital and reserves				
70,000 £1 ordinary shares				70,000
Reserves				16,000
				86,000

S LIMITED
BALANCE SHEET AS AT 31 DECEMBER 19X6

	£	£	£
Fixed assets			
Tangible assets			45,000
Current assets			
Stocks		12,000	
Debtors		9,000	
		21,000	
Current liabilities			
Bank overdraft		3,000	
Creditors: H Ltd	2,000		
Other	2,000		
		4,000	
		7,000	
			14,000
			59,000
Capital and reserves			
40,000 £1 ordinary shares			40,000
Reserves			19,000
			59,000

Prepare the consolidated balance sheet of H Ltd.

1.4   SOLUTION

The cancelling items are:

(a)   H Ltd's asset 'investment in shares of S Ltd' (£40,000) cancels with S Ltd's liability 'share capital' (£40,000);

(b)   H Ltd's asset 'debtors: S Ltd' (£2,000) cancels with S Ltd's liability 'creditors: H Ltd' (£2,000).

The remaining assets and liabilities are added together to produce the following consolidated balance sheet.

H LIMITED
CONSOLIDATED BALANCE SHEET AS AT 31 DECEMBER 19X6

	£	£
Fixed assets		
Tangible assets		80,000
Current assets		
Stocks	28,000	
Debtors	15,000	
Cash at bank	1,000	
	44,000	
Current liabilities		
Bank overdraft	3,000	
Creditors	16,000	
	19,000	
		25,000
		105,000
Capital and reserves		
70,000 £1 ordinary shares		70,000
Reserves		35,000
		105,000

Notes on the example

1.5   (a)   H Ltd's bank balance is not netted off with S Ltd's bank overdraft. To offset one against the other would be less informative and would conflict with the statutory principle that assets and liabilities should not be netted off.

(b)   The share capital in the consolidated balance sheet is the share capital of the parent company alone. This must *always* be the case, no matter how complex the consolidation, because the share capital of subsidiary companies must *always* be a wholly cancelling item.

Part cancellation

1.6   **An item may appear in the balance sheets of a parent company and its subsidiary, but not at the same amounts.**

(a)   **The parent company may have acquired shares in the subsidiary at a price greater or less than their nominal value**. The asset will appear in the parent company's accounts at cost, while the liability will appear in the subsidiary's accounts at nominal value. **This raises the issue of goodwill**, which is dealt with later in this chapter.

(b)   Even if the parent company acquired shares at nominal value, it **may not have acquired all the shares of the subsidiary** (so the subsidiary may be only partly owned). This **raises the issue of minority interests,** which are also dealt with later in this chapter.

(c) The inter-company trading balances may be out of step because of **goods or cash in transit.**

(d) One company may have **issued loan stock of which a proportion only is taken up** by the other company.

1.7 The following example illustrates the techniques needed to deal with the second two items. The procedure is to **cancel as far as possible. The remaining uncancelled amounts will appear in the consolidated balance sheet.**

(a) Uncancelled loan stock will appear as a liability of the group.

(b) Uncancelled balances on inter-company accounts represent goods or cash in transit, which will appear in the consolidated balance sheet.

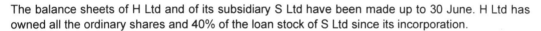

Question 1

The balance sheets of H Ltd and of its subsidiary S Ltd have been made up to 30 June. H Ltd has owned all the ordinary shares and 40% of the loan stock of S Ltd since its incorporation.

H LIMITED
BALANCE SHEET AS AT 30 JUNE

	£	£
Fixed assets		
Tangible assets		120,000
Investment in S Ltd, at cost		
80,000 ordinary shares of £1 each		80,000
£20,000 of 12% loan stock in S Ltd		20,000
		220,000
Current assets		
Stocks	50,000	
Debtors	40,000	
Current account with S Ltd	18,000	
Cash	4,000	
	112,000	
Creditors: amounts falling due within one year		
Creditors	47,000	
Taxation	15,000	
	62,000	
Net current assets		50,000
		270,000
Creditors: amounts falling due after more than one year		
10% loan stock		75,000
		195,000
Capital and reserves		
Ordinary shares of £1 each, fully paid		100,000
Reserves		95,000
		195,000

S LIMITED
BALANCE SHEET AS AT 30 JUNE

	£	£
Tangible fixed assets		100,000
Current assets		
Stocks	60,000	
Debtors	30,000	
Cash	6,000	
	96,000	
Creditors: amounts falling due within one year		
Creditors	16,000	
Taxation	10,000	
Current account with H Ltd	12,000	
	38,000	
		58,000
		158,000
Creditors: amounts falling due after more than one year		
12% Loan stock		50,000
		108,000
Capital and reserves		
80,000 ordinary shares of £1 each, fully paid		80,000
Reserves		28,000
		108,000

The difference on current account arises because of goods in transit. Prepare the consolidated balance sheet of H Ltd.

Answer

H LIMITED
CONSOLIDATED BALANCE SHEET AS AT 30 JUNE

	£	£
Tangible fixed assets		220,000
Current assets		
Stocks	110,000	
Goods in transit	6,000	
Debtors	70,000	
Cash	10,000	
	196,000	
Creditors: amounts falling due within one year		
Creditors	63,000	
Taxation	25,000	
	88,000	
		108,000
		328,000
Creditors: amounts falling due after more than one year		
10% loan stock	75,000	
12% loan stock	30,000	
		105,000
		223,000
Capital and reserves		
Ordinary shares of £1 each, fully paid		100,000
Reserves		123,000
		223,000

Note especially how:

(a)   the uncancelled loan stock in S Ltd becomes a liability of the group;

(b)   the goods in transit is the difference between the current accounts (£18,000 – £12,000).

2   MINORITY INTERESTS

2.1   It was mentioned earlier that the total assets and liabilities of subsidiary companies are included in the consolidated balance sheet, even in the case of subsidiaries which are only partly owned. A proportion of the net assets of such subsidiaries in fact belongs to investors from outside the group (minority interests).

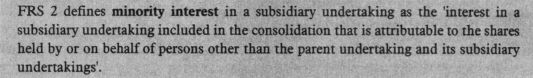

> **KEY TERM**
>
> FRS 2 defines **minority interest** in a subsidiary undertaking as the 'interest in a subsidiary undertaking included in the consolidation that is attributable to the shares held by or on behalf of persons other than the parent undertaking and its subsidiary undertakings'.

In the consolidated balance sheet it is necessary to distinguish this proportion from those assets attributable to the group and financed by shareholders' funds.

2.2   The net assets of a company are financed by share capital and reserves. The consolidation procedure for dealing with partly owned subsidiaries is to **calculate the proportion of ordinary shares, preference shares and reserves attributable to minority interests.**

2.3   EXAMPLE: MINORITY INTERESTS

H Ltd has owned 75% of the share capital of S Ltd since the date of S Ltd's incorporation. Their latest balance sheets are given below.

H LIMITED - BALANCE SHEET

	£
Fixed assets	
Tangible assets	50,000
30,000 £1 ordinary shares in S Ltd at cost	30,000
	80,000
Net current assets	25,000
	105,000
Capital and reserves	
80,000 £1 ordinary shares	80,000
Reserves	25,000
	105,000

S LIMITED
BALANCE SHEET

	£
Tangible fixed assets	35,000
Net current assets	15,000
	50,000
Capital and reserves	
40,000 £1 ordinary shares	40,000
Reserves	10,000
	50,000

Prepare the consolidated balance sheet.

2.4   SOLUTION

All of S Ltd's net assets are consolidated despite the fact that the company is only 75% owned. The amount of net assets attributable to minority interests is calculated as follows.

	£
Minority share of share capital (25% × £40,000)	10,000
Minority share of reserves (25% × £10,000)	2,500
	12,500

Of S Ltd's share capital of £40,000, £10,000 is included in the figure for minority interest, while £30,000 is cancelled with H Ltd's asset 'investment in S Limited'.

The consolidated balance sheet can now be prepared.

H GROUP
CONSOLIDATED BALANCE SHEET

	£
Tangible fixed assets	85,000
Net current assets	40,000
	125,000
Share capital	80,000
Reserves £(25,000 + (75% × 10,000))	32,500
Shareholders' funds	112,500
Minority interest	12,500
	125,000

2.5   In this example we have shown minority interest on the 'capital and reserves' side of the balance sheet to illustrate how some of S Ltd's net assets are financed by shareholders' funds, while some are financed by outside investors. You may see minority interest as a deduction from the other side of the balance sheet. The second half of the balance sheet will then consist entirely of shareholders' funds. The Companies Act 1985 permits either of the above presentations, but **FRS 4 seems to require the disclosure shown above.**

Exam focus point

In more complicated examples the following technique is recommended for dealing with minority interests.

Step 1   Cancel common items in the draft balance sheets. If there is a minority interest, the subsidiary company's share capital will be a partly cancelled item. Ascertain the proportion of ordinary shares and the proportion (possibly different) of preference shares held by the minority.

Step 2   Produce a working for the minority interest. Add in the amounts of preference and ordinary share capital calculated in step 1: this completes the cancellation of the subsidiary's share capital.

Add also the minority's share of each reserve in the subsidiary company. Reserves belong to equity shareholders; the proportion attributable to minority interests therefore depends on their percentage holding of *ordinary* shares.

Step 3   Produce a separate working for each reserve (capital, revenue etc) found in the subsidiary company's balance sheet. The initial balances on these accounts will be taken straight from the draft balance sheets of the parent and subsidiary company.2.6

Step 4   The closing balances in these workings can be entered directly onto the consolidated balance sheet.

Question 2

Set out below are the draft balance sheets of H Ltd and its subsidiary S Ltd. You are required to prepare the consolidated balance sheet.

H LIMITED

	£	£
Fixed assets		
Tangible assets		31,000
Investment in S Ltd		
12,000 £1 ordinary shares at cost	12,000	
4,000 £1 preference shares at cost	4,000	
£4,000 10% debentures at cost	4,000	
		20,000
		51,000
Net current assets		11,000
		62,000
Capital and reserves		
Ordinary shares of £1 each		40,000
Revenue reserve		22,000
		62,000

S LIMITED

	£
Tangible fixed assets	34,000
Net current assets	22,000
	56,000
Long-term liability	
10% debentures	10,000
	46,000
Capital and reserves	
Ordinary shares of £1 each	20,000
Preference shares of £1 each	16,000
Capital reserve	6,000
Revenue reserve	4,000
	46,000

Answer

Partly cancelling items are the components of H Ltd's investment in S Ltd, ie ordinary shares, preference shares and loan stock. Minorities have an interest in 75% (12,000/16,000) of S Ltd's preference shares and 40% (8,000/20,000) of S Ltd's equity, including reserves.

You should now product workings for minority interests, capital reserve and revenue reserve as follows.

Workings

1   *Minority interests*

		£
Ordinary share capital (40% of 20,000)		8,000
Reserves:	capital (40% × 6,000)	2,400
	revenue (40% × 4,000)	1,600
		12,000
Preference share capital (75% × 16,000)		12,000
		24,000

2   *Capital reserve*

	£
H Ltd	-
Share of S Ltd's capital reserve (60% × 6,000)	3,600
	3,600

3   *Revenue reserve*

	£
H Ltd	22,000
Share of S Ltd's revenue reserves (60% × 4,000)	2,400
	24,400

The results of the workings are now used to construct the consolidated balance sheet (CBS).

H GROUP
CONSOLIDATED BALANCE SHEET

	£
Tangible fixed assets	65,000
Net current assets	33,000
	98,000
Long-term liability	
10% debentures	6,000
	92,000
Capital and reserves	
Ordinary shares of £1 each	40,000
Capital reserve	3,600
Revenue reserve	24,400
Shareholders' funds	68,000
Minority interests	24,000
	92,000

Notes

(a) S Ltd is a subsidiary of H Ltd because H Ltd owns 60% of its equity capital. It is unimportant how little of the preference share capital is owned by H Ltd.

(b) As always, the share capital in the consolidated balance sheet is that of the parent company alone. The share capital in S Ltd's balance sheet was partly cancelled against the investment shown in H Ltd's balance sheet, while the uncancelled portion was credited to minority interest.

(c) The figure for minority interest comprises the interest of outside investors in the share capital and reserves of the subsidiary. The uncancelled portion of S Ltd's loan stock is not shown as part of minority interest but is disclosed separately as a liability of the group.

3   DIVIDENDS PAYABLE BY A SUBSIDIARY

3.1   When a subsidiary company pays a dividend during the year the accounting treatment is not difficult. Suppose S Ltd, a 60% subsidiary of H Ltd, pays a dividend of £1,000 on the last day of its accounting period. Its total reserves before paying the dividend stood at £5,000.

(a) £400 of the dividend is paid to minority shareholders. The cash leaves the group and will not appear anywhere in the consolidated balance sheet.

(b) The holding company receives £600 of the dividend, debiting cash and crediting profit and loss account.

(c) The remaining balance of reserves in S Ltd's balance sheet (£4,000) will be consolidated in the normal way. The group's share (60% × £4,000 = £2,400) will be included in group reserves in the balance sheet; the minority share (40% × £4,000 = £1,600) is credited to the minority interest account.

3.2   More care is needed when dealing with **proposed dividends** not yet paid by a subsidiary. The **first step** must be to **ensure that the draft accounts of both subsidiary and parent company are up-to-date and reflect the proposed dividend.**

Exam focus point

A question may state that both companies have accrued for the proposed dividend; alternatively you may be presented with draft balance sheets in which one or other company, or possibly both companies, have omitted to make the necessary entries.

3.3   If neither company has accrued for the proposed dividend you will need to make appropriate adjustments to the draft balance sheets.

(a)   If the subsidiary has not yet accrued for the proposed dividend, the adjustment is:

DEBIT	Revenue reserves
CREDIT	Dividends payable

with the full amount of the dividend payable in the subsidiary's books, whether it is due to the parent company or to minority shareholders.

(b)   If the parent company has not yet accrued for its share of the proposed dividend, the adjustment is:

DEBIT	Debtors (dividend receivable)
CREDIT	Revenue reserves

with the *parent company's share* of the dividend receivable in the parent's books.

3.4   **On consolidation, the dividend payable in S Ltd's accounts will cancel with the dividend receivable in H Ltd's accounts.** If S Ltd is a wholly owned subsidiary, there will be complete cancellation; if S Ltd is only partly owned, there will be only part cancellation. The uncancelled portion will be the amount of dividend payable to minority shareholders and this will appear in the consolidated balance sheet as a current liability.

3.5   **When preparing the workings for reserves and minority interest, the relevant reserves figures for both companies are the figures** *after* **adjusting for the proposed dividend.**

3.6   EXAMPLE: DIVIDENDS

Set out below are the draft balance sheets of Hug Ltd and its subsidiary Bug Ltd. Hug Ltd has not yet taken account of the dividend proposed by Bug Ltd.

You are required to prepare the consolidated balance sheet.

HUG LIMITED

	£	£
Fixed assets		
Tangible assets		1,350
Investment in Bug Ltd: 1,500 shares at cost		1,500
		2,850
Current assets	700	
Current liabilities		
Creditors	400	
		300
		3,150
		£
Capital and reserves		
Ordinary shares of £1 each		1,000
Revenue reserves		2,150
		3,150

BUG LIMITED

	£	£
Tangible fixed assets		2,500
Current assets	900	
Current liabilities		
Creditors	200	
Proposed dividend	200	
		500
		3,000
Capital and reserves		
Ordinary shares of £1 each		2,000
Revenue reserves		1,000
		3,000

3.7   SOLUTION

The first step is to bring Hug Ltd's balance sheet up to date by accruing for its share of the dividend receivable from Bug Ltd. Hug Ltd owns 75% (1,500/2,000) of the shares in Bug Ltd. Its share of the proposed dividend is therefore 75% × £200 = £150. Hug Ltd's draft balance sheet should be adjusted as follows.

DEBIT	Debtors: dividend receivable	£150	
CREDIT	Revenue reserves		£150

3.8   Next deal with cancellation. There are two part-cancelling items, the shares of Bug Ltd and the dividend receivable/payable.

3.9   The workings may now be produced. Notice how the relevant reserves figures are the figures after adjusting for the proposed dividend. Because Bug Ltd's accounts are up-to-date, and reflect the proposed figure, the correct reserves figure (£1,000) can be taken straight from the draft balance sheet. In the case of Hug Ltd, it is the adjusted reserves figure (£2,150 + £150 = £2,300) which is used.

Workings

1   *Minority interests*

	£
Share capital (25% × 2,000)	500
Revenue reserves (25% × 1,000)	250
	750

2   *Revenue reserves*

	£
Hug Ltd (as adjusted)	2,300
Share of Bug Ltd's revenue reserves (1,000 × 75%)	750
	3,050

HUG GROUP
CONSOLIDATED BALANCE SHEET

	£	£
Tangible fixed assets		3,850
Current assets	1,600	
Current liabilities		
Creditors	600	
Minority proposed dividend	50	
		950
		4,800

Capital and reserves	£
Ordinary shares of £1 each	1,000
Revenue reserves	3,050
Shareholders' funds	4,050
Minority interests	750
	4,800

3.10 If there is a proposed *preference dividend* payable by the subsidiary the same procedure should be applied. Again, the first step is to bring both companies' balance sheets up to date, and again the workings accounts will deal with reserves figures *after* adjusting for the proposed dividends.

3.11 EXAMPLE: PROPOSED PREFERENCE DIVIDEND

Set out below are the draft balance sheets of H Ltd and S Ltd. Neither company has yet provided for any dividend, but you should now provide for:

(a) the preference dividend of S Ltd;
(b) a proposed ordinary dividend of 10% by S Ltd;
(c) a proposed ordinary dividend of 20% by H Ltd.

You are required to prepare the consolidated balance sheet.

H LIMITED

	£	£
Fixed assets		
Tangible assets		72,000
Investment in S Ltd		
30,000 £1 ordinary shares at cost	30,000	
6,000 £1 7% preference shares at cost	6,000	
		36,000
		108,000
Current assets	73,000	
Current liabilities	21,000	
		52,000
		160,000
Capital and reserves		
Ordinary shares of £1 each		100,000
Revenue reserves		60,000
		160,000

S LIMITED

	£	£
Tangible fixed assets		40,000
Current assets	51,700	
Current liabilities	19,000	
		32,700
		72,700
Capital and reserves		
Ordinary shares of £1 each		40,000
7% preference shares of £1 each		10,000
		50,000
Revenue reserves		22,700
		72,700

3.12 SOLUTION

The draft balance sheet of S Ltd must be adjusted by the following entries.

DEBIT	Revenue reserves	£4,700	
CREDIT	Proposed dividends		
	Preference (7% × £10,000)		£700
	Ordinary (10% × £40,000)		£4,000

The adjusted balance on S Ltd's revenue reserves is now £(22,700 – 4,700)=£18,000.

H Ltd's share in these dividends is:

	£
Preference (60%)	420
Ordinary (75%)	3,000
	3,420

H Ltd's balance sheet must therefore be adjusted as follows.

DEBIT	Debtors: dividends receivable	£3,420	
CREDIT	Revenue reserves		£3,420

A further adjustment to H Ltd's balance sheet is necessary in respect of the company's own proposed dividend of 20% × £100,000 = £20,000.

DEBIT	Revenue reserves	£20,000	
CREDIT	Proposed dividend		£20,000

The adjusted balance on H Ltd's revenue reserve is now £(60,000 + 3,420 – 20,000) = £43,420.

3.13 After S Ltd's share capital and the dividends payable/receivable have been part-cancelled, the workings can be drawn up.

Workings

1   *Minority interests*

	£
Ordinary share capital (25% × 40,000)	10,000
Revenue reserves (25% × 18,000)	4,500
	14,500
Preference share capital (40% × 10,000)	4,000
	18,500

2   *Revenue reserves*

	£
H Ltd's (adjusted balance)	43,420
Share of S Ltd's revenue reserve (75% × 18,000)	13,500
	56,920

H LIMITED CONSOLIDATED BALANCE SHEET

	£	£
Tangible fixed assets		112,000
Current assets	124,700	
Current liabilities		
Sundry	40,000	
Proposed dividend	20,000	
Minority proposed dividend (25% × £4,000) + (40% × £700)	1,280	
		63,420
		175,420

Capital and reserves

Ordinary shares of £1 each	100,000
Revenue reserves	56,920
Shareholders' funds	156,920
Minority interests	18,500
	175,420

4   GOODWILL ARISING ON CONSOLIDATION

4.1   In the examples we have looked at so far the cost of shares acquired by the parent company has always been equal to the nominal value of those shares. This is seldom the case in practice and we must now consider some more complicated examples. To begin with, **we will examine the entries made by the parent company in its own balance sheet when it acquires shares.**

4.2   When a company H Ltd wishes to **purchase shares** in a company S Ltd it must pay the previous owners of those shares. The most obvious form of payment would be in **cash**. Suppose H Ltd purchases all 40,000 £1 shares in S Ltd and pays £60,000 cash to the previous shareholders in consideration. The entries in H Ltd's books would be:

DEBIT	Investment in S Ltd at cost	£60,000	
CREDIT	Bank		£60,000

4.3   However, the previous shareholders might be prepared to accept some other form of consideration. For example, they might accept an agreed number of **shares** in H Ltd. H Ltd would then issue new shares in the agreed number and allot them to the former shareholders of S Ltd. This kind of deal might be attractive to H Ltd since it avoids the need for a heavy cash outlay. The former shareholders of S Ltd would retain an indirect interest in that company's profitability via their new holding in its parent company.

4.4   Continuing the example, suppose the shareholders of S Ltd agreed to accept one £1 ordinary share in H Ltd for every two £1 ordinary shares in S Ltd. H Ltd would then need to issue and allot 20,000 new £1 shares. How would this transaction be recorded in the books of H Ltd?

4.5   The simplest method would be as follows.

DEBIT	Investment in S Ltd	£20,000	
CREDIT	Share capital		£20,000

However, if the 40,000 £1 shares acquired in S Ltd are thought to have a value of £60,000 this would be misleading. The former shareholders of S Ltd have presumably agreed to accept 20,000 shares in H Ltd because they consider each of those shares to have a value of £3. This view of the matter suggests the following method of recording the transaction in H Ltd's books.

DEBIT	Investment in S Ltd	£60,000	
CREDIT	Share capital		£20,000
	Share premium account		£40,000

The second method is the one which the Companies Act 1985 requires should normally be used in preparing consolidated accounts.

4.6   The amount which H Ltd records in its books as the cost of its investment in S Ltd may be more or less than the book value of the assets it acquires. Suppose that S Ltd in the previous example has nil reserves, so that its share capital of £40,000 is balanced by net assets with a book value of £40,000. For simplicity, assume that the book value of S Ltd's assets is the same as their market or fair value.

4.7 Now when the directors of H Ltd agree to pay £60,000 for a 100% investment in S Ltd they must believe that, in addition to its tangible assets of £40,000, S Ltd must also have intangible assets worth £20,000. This amount of £20,000 paid over and above the value of the tangible assets acquired is called **goodwill arising on consolidation** (sometimes **premium on acquisition**).

4.8 Following the normal cancellation procedure the £40,000 share capital in S Ltd's balance sheet could be cancelled against £40,000 of the 'investment in S Limited' in the balance sheet of H Ltd. This would leave a £20,000 debit uncancelled in the parent company's accounts and this £20,000 would appear in the consolidated balance sheet under the caption 'Intangible fixed assets. Goodwill arising on consolidation' (although see below for FRS 10's requirements on this type of goodwill).

Goodwill and pre-acquisition profits

4.9 Up to now we have assumed that S Ltd had nil reserves when its shares were purchased by H Ltd. Assuming instead that S Ltd had earned profits of £8,000 in the period before acquisition, its balance sheet just before the purchase would look as follows.

	£
Net tangible assets	48,000
Share capital	40,000
Reserves	8,000
	48,000

4.10 If H Ltd now purchases all the shares in S Ltd it will acquire net tangible assets worth £48,000 at a cost of £60,000. Clearly in this case S Ltd's intangible assets (goodwill) are being valued at £12,000. It should be apparent that **any reserves earned by the subsidiary prior to its acquisition by the parent company must be incorporated in the cancellation process so as to arrive at a figure for goodwill arising on consolidation.** In other words, not only S Ltd's share capital, but also its pre-acquisition reserves, must be cancelled against the asset 'investment in S Ltd' in the accounts of the parent company. The uncancelled balance of £12,000 appears in the consolidated balance sheet.

4.11 The consequence of this is that any pre-acquisition reserves of a subsidiary company are not aggregated with the parent company's reserves in the consolidated balance sheet. **The figure of consolidated reserves comprises the reserves of the parent company plus the post-acquisition reserves only of subsidiary companies. The post-acquisition reserves are simply reserves at the consolidation date less reserves at acquisition.**

4.12 EXAMPLE: GOODWILL AND PRE-ACQUISITION PROFITS

Sing Ltd acquired the ordinary shares of Wing Ltd on 31 March when the draft balance sheets of each company were as follows.

SING LIMITED
BALANCE SHEET AS AT 31 MARCH

	£
Fixed assets	
Investment in 50,000 shares of Wing Ltd at cost	80,000
Net current assets	40,000
	120,000
Capital and reserves	
Ordinary shares	75,000
Revenue reserves	45,000
	120,000

WING LIMITED
BALANCE SHEET AS AT 31 MARCH

	£
Net current assets	60,000
Share capital and reserves	
50,000 ordinary shares of £1 each	50,000
Revenue reserves	10,000
	60,000

Prepare the consolidated balance sheet as at 31 March.

4.13 SOLUTION

The technique to adopt here is to produce a new working: 'Goodwill'. A proforma working is set out below.

Goodwill	£	£
Cost of investment		X
Share of net assets acquired as represented by:		
Ordinary share capital	X	
Share premium	X	
Reserves on acquisition	X	
Group share	a%	(X)
		X
b% preference shares		(X)
Goodwill		X

4.14 Applying this to our example the working will look like this.

	£	£
Cost of investment		80,000
Share of net assets acquired as represented by:		
Ordinary share capital	50,000	
Revenue reserves on acquisition	10,000	
	60,000	
Group share 100%		60,000
Goodwill		20,000

SING LIMITED
CONSOLIDATED BALANCE SHEET AS AT 31 MARCH

	£
Fixed assets	
Goodwill arising on consolidation	20,000
Net current assets	100,000
	120,000
Capital and reserves	
Ordinary shares	75,000
Revenue reserves	45,000
	120,000

SSAP 22 *Accounting for goodwill*

4.15 Goodwill arising on consolidation is one form of **purchased goodwill**, and is therefore governed by FRS 10. As explained in an earlier chapter FRS 10 requires that purchased goodwill should be capitalised and classified as an asset on the balance sheet. It is then eliminated from the accounts by **amortisation** through the profit and loss account.

4.16 **A consolidation adjustment** will be required each year as follows.

DEBIT	Consolidated P&L account
CREDIT	Provision for amortisation of goodwill

The **unamortised portion** will be included in the consolidated balance sheet under **fixed assets**.

4.17 Goodwill arising on consolidation is the difference between the cost of an acquisition and the value of the subsidiary's net assets acquired. This difference can be **negative**: the aggregate of the fair values of the separable net assets acquired may exceed what the holding company paid for them. This 'negative goodwill', also sometimes called 'discount arising on consolidation', is required by FRS 10 to be disclosed in the intangible fixed assets category, directly under positive goodwill, ie as a 'negative asset'

5   A TECHNIQUE OF CONSOLIDATION   6/94, 6/95, 6/96, 12/96, 6/97

5.1 We have now looked at the topics of cancellation, minority interests and goodwill arising on consolidation. It is time to set out an approach to be used in tackling consolidated balance sheets. The approach we recommend consists of five stages.

Stage 1 Update the draft balance sheets of subsidiaries and parent company to take account of any proposed dividends not yet accrued for.

Stage 2 Agree inter-company current accounts by adjusting for items in transit.

Stage 3 Cancel items common to both balance sheets.

Stage 4 Produce working for minority interests as shown in Paragraph 2.4.

Stage 5 Produce a goodwill working as shown in Paragraph 4.13 above. Then produce a working for capital and revenue reserves.

5.2 You should now attempt to apply this technique to the following question.

Question 3

The draft balance sheets of Ping Ltd and Pong Ltd on 30 June 19X4 were as follows.

PING LIMITED
BALANCE SHEET AS AT 30 JUNE 19X4

	£	£
Fixed assets		
Tangible assets	50,000	
20,000 ordinary shares in Pong Ltd at cost	30,000	
		80,000
Current assets		
Stock	3,000	
Debtors (including £4,000 dividend proposed by Pong Ltd)	20,000	
Cash	2,000	
	25,000	
Creditors: amounts falling due within one year		
Owed to Pong Ltd	8,000	
Trade creditors	10,000	
	18,000	
Net current assets		7,000
		87,000
Capital and reserves		
Ordinary shares of £1 each		45,000
Capital reserves		12,000
Revenue reserves		30,000
		87,000

PONG LIMITED
BALANCE SHEET AS AT 30 JUNE 19X4

	£	£
Tangible fixed assets		40,000
Current assets		
Stock	8,000	
Owed by Ping Ltd	10,000	
Debtors	7,000	
	25,000	
Creditors: amounts falling due within one year		
Trade creditors	7,000	
Proposed dividends	5,000	
	12,000	
Net current assets		13,000
		53,000
		£
Capital and reserves		
Ordinary shares of £1 each		25,000
Capital reserves		5,000
Revenue reserves		23,000
		53,000

Ping Ltd acquired its investment in Pong Ltd on 1 July 19X1 when the revenue reserves of Pong Ltd stood at £6,000. There have been no changes in the share capital or capital reserves of Pong Ltd since that date. At 30 June 19X4 Pong Ltd had invoiced Ping Ltd for goods to the value of £2,000 which had not been received by Ping Ltd.

Goodwill is deemed to have an indefinite useful life and is therefore to remain in the balance sheet.

Prepare the consolidated balance sheet of Ping Ltd as at 30 June 19X4.

Answer

Stage 1. Ensure parent company and subsidiary balance sheets have correctly taken account of the proposed dividends.

Ping Ltd has £4,000 included in debtors for its share (80%) of Pong Ltd's proposed dividend, so there is no adjustment to make. Similarly, Pong Ltd has correctly accounted for its dividend payable.

Stage 2. Agree current accounts.

Ping Ltd has stock in transit of £2,000 making its total stock £3,000 + £2,000 = £5,000 and its liability to Pong Ltd £8,000 + £2,000 = £10,000.

Stage 3. Cancel common items: these are the current accounts between the two companies of £10,000 each and the dividends payable by Pong to Ping. This leaves a creditor for the dividend owed to the minority in Pong.

Stage 4. Calculate the minority interest.

Minority interest

	£
Ordinary share capital (20% × 25,000)	5,000
Capital reserves (20% × 5,000)	1,000
Revenue reserves (20% × 23,000)	4,600
	10,600

Note. In this particular case, where there are no preference shares or adjustments to Pong Ltd's revenue reserves, the minority interest figure may simply be calculated as 20% of Pong Ltd's net assets, ie 20% × £53,000. Because, however, such adjustments and complications often arise, it is a good idea to get into the habit of producing the working as shown.

Stage 5. Calculate goodwill and reserves.

Goodwill

	£	£
Cost of investment		30,000
Share of assets acquired as represented by:		
Ordinary share capital	25,000	
Capital reserves on acquisition	5,000	
Revenue reserves on acquisition	6,000	
	36,000	
Group share 80%		28,800
Goodwill		1,200

Consolidated capital reserves

	£
Ping Ltd	12,000
Share of Pong Ltd's post acquisition capital reserve	-
	12,000

Consolidated revenue reserves

	£
Ping Ltd	30,000
Share of Pong Ltd's post acquisition	
revenue reserves: 80%(23,000 - 6,000)*	13,600
	43,600

*Note. Post acquisition reserves of Pong Ltd are simply reserves now less reserves at acquisition. The consolidated balance sheet may now be written out.

PING LIMITED
CONSOLIDATED BALANCE SHEET AS AT 30 JUNE 19X4

	£	£
Fixed assets		
Intangible fixed assets: goodwill		1,200
Tangible assets (£50,000 + £40,000)		90,000
		91,200
Current assets		
Stocks (£5,000 + £8,000)	13,000	
Debtors (£16,000 + £7,000)	23,000	
Cash	2,000	
	38,000	
Creditors: amounts falling due within one year		
Trade creditors (£10,000 + £7,000)	17,000	
Minority dividends	1,000	
	18,000	
Net current assets		20,000
		111,200
Capital and reserves		
Ordinary shares of £1 each		45,000
Capital reserves		12,000
Revenue reserves		43,600
Shareholders' funds		100,600
Minority interests		10,600
		111,200

Exam focus point

A consolidated balance sheet will come up as regularly as clockwork. There will nearly always be an adjustment for inter-company trading.

6   INTER-COMPANY TRADING   6/94, 6/95, 6/96, 12/96, 6/97

6.1   We have already come across cases where one company in a group engages in trading with another group company. Any debtor/creditor balances outstanding between the companies are cancelled on consolidation. No further problem arises if all such intra-group transactions are undertaken at cost, without any mark-up for profit.

6.2   However, each company in a group is a separate trading entity and may wish to treat other group companies in the same way as any other customer. In this case, a company (say A Ltd) may buy goods at one price and sell them at a higher price to another group company (B Ltd). The accounts of A Ltd will quite properly include the profit earned on sales to B Ltd; and similarly B Ltd's balance sheet will include stocks at their cost to B Ltd at the amount at which they were purchased from A Ltd.

6.3   This gives rise to **two problems.**

(a)   Although A Ltd makes a profit as soon as it sells goods to B Ltd, the group does not make a sale or achieve a profit until an outside customer buys the goods from B Ltd.

(b)   Any purchases from A Ltd which remain unsold by B Ltd at the year end will be included in B Ltd's stock. Their balance sheet value will be their cost to B Ltd, which is not the same as their cost to the group.

6.4   The objective of consolidated accounts is to present the financial position of several connected companies as that of a single entity, the group. This means that **in a consolidated balance sheet the only profits recognised should be those earned by the group** in providing goods or services to outsiders; and similarly, stock in the consolidated balance sheet should be valued at cost to the group.

6.5   Suppose that a holding company H Ltd buys goods for £1,600 and sells them to a wholly owned subsidiary S Ltd for £2,000. The goods are in S Ltd's stock at the year end and appear in S Ltd's balance sheet at £2,000. In this case, H Ltd will record a profit of £400 in its individual accounts, but from the group's point of view the figures are:

Cost	£1,600
External sales	nil
Closing stock at cost	£1,600
Profit/loss	nil

6.6   If we add together the figures for retained reserves and stock in the individual balance sheets of H Ltd and S Ltd the resulting figures for consolidated reserves and consolidated stock will each be overstated by £400. A **consolidation adjustment** is therefore necessary as follows.

DEBIT   **Group reserves**
CREDIT   **Group stock (balance sheet)**

with the amount of profit unrealised by the group.

Question 4

H Ltd acquired all the shares in S Ltd when the reserves of S Ltd stood at £10,000. Draft balance sheets for each company are as follows.

	H Ltd		S Ltd	
	£	£	£	£
Fixed assets				
Tangible assets		80,000		40,000
Investment in S Ltd at cost		46,000		
		126,000		
Current assets	40,000		30,000	
Current liabilities	21,000		18,000	
		19,000		12,000
		145,000		52,000
Capital and reserves				
Ordinary shares of £1 each		100,000		30,000
Reserves		45,000		22,000
		145,000		52,000

During the year S Ltd sold goods to H Ltd for £50,000, the profit to S Ltd being 20% of selling price. At the balance sheet date, £15,000 of these goods remained unsold in the stocks of H Ltd. At the same date, H Ltd owed S Ltd £12,000 for goods bought and this debt is included in the creditors of H Ltd and the debtors of S Ltd.

Note. Goodwill is deemed to have an indefinite useful life and is therefore to remain in the balance sheet.

Required

Prepare a draft consolidated balance sheet for H Ltd.

Answer

1   *Goodwill*

	£	£
Cost of investment		46,000
Share of net assets acquired as represented by		
Share capital	30,000	
Reserves	10,000	
	40,000	
Group share (100%)		40,000
Goodwill		6,000

2   *Reserves*

	£
H Ltd	45,000
Share of S Ltd's post acquisition retained reserves	
£(22,000 − 10,000)	12,000
	57,000
Stock: unrealised profit (20% × £15,000)	3,000
Group reserves	54,000

H LIMITED
CONSOLIDATED BALANCE SHEET

	£	£
Intangible fixed assets: goodwill		6,000
Tangible fixed assets		120,000
		126,000
Current assets (W1)	55,000	
Current liabilities (W2)	27,000	
		28,000
		154,000
Capital and reserves		
Ordinary shares of £1 each		100,000
Reserves		54,000
		154,000

Workings

1   *Current assets*

	£	£
In H Ltd's balance sheet		40,000
In S Ltd's balance sheet	30,000	
Less S Ltd's current account with H Ltd cancelled	12,000	
		18,000
		58,000
Less unrealised profit excluded from stock valuation		3,000
		55,000

2   *Current liabilities*

	£
In H Ltd's balance sheet	21,000
Less H Ltd's current account with S Ltd cancelled	12,000
	9,000
In S Ltd's balance sheet	18,000
	27,000

Minority interests in unrealised inter-company profits

6.7   **A further problem occurs where a subsidiary company which is not wholly owned is involved in inter-company trading within the group.** If a subsidiary S Ltd is 75%

owned and sells goods to the holding company for £16,000 cost plus £4,000 profit, ie for £20,000 and if these stocks are unsold by H Ltd at the balance sheet date, the 'unrealised' profit of £4,000 earned by S Ltd and charged to H Ltd will be partly owned by the minority interest of S Ltd. As far as the minority interest of S Ltd is concerned, their share (25% of £4,000) amounting to £1,000 of profit on the sale of goods would appear to have been fully realised. It is only the group that has not yet made a profit on the sale.

6.8   **There are three different possibilities as regards the treatment of these inter-company profits.** Remove:

(a)   Only the group's share of the profit loading.

(b)   The whole profit loading, charging the minority with their proportion.

(c)   The whole of the profit without charging the minority (to reduce group reserves by the whole profit loading).

6.9   **The method most commonly used until recently was the most prudent one, (c).**

| DEBIT | Profit and loss account of group |) | with profit loading |
| CREDIT | Asset account |) | |

However, the ASB in its *Interim statement on consolidated accounts* has stated that the minority should be charged or credited with its share of all consolidation adjustments where the adjustment is made in respect of partly owned subsidiaries' profits. If the parent company has made the unrealised profit or loss, then the minority interest is not affected.

6.10   The double entry is therefore as follows.

> **ENTRIES TO LEARN**
>
> | DEBIT | Group reserves |
> | DEBIT | Minority interest |
> | CREDIT | Group stock (balance sheet) |

6.11   EXAMPLE: MINORITY INTERESTS AND INTER-COMPANY PROFITS

H Ltd has owned 75% of the shares of S Ltd since the incorporation of that company. During the year to 31 December 19X2, S Ltd sold goods costing £16,000 to H Ltd at a price of £20,000 and these goods were still unsold by H Ltd at the end of the year. Draft balance sheets of each company at 31 December 19X2 were as follows.

	H Limited		S Limited	
Fixed assets	£	£	£	£
Tangible assets		125,000		120,000
Investment: 75,000 shares in S Ltd at cost		75,000		-
		200,000		120,000
Current assets				
Stocks	50,000		48,000	
Trade debtors	20,000		16,000	
	70,000		64,000	
Creditors	40,000		24,000	
		30,000		40,000
		230,000		160,000
Capital and reserves				
Ordinary shares of £1 each fully paid		80,000		100,000
Reserves		150,000		60,000
		230,000		160,000

Required

Prepare the draft consolidated balance sheet of H Ltd.

6.12 SOLUTION

The profit earned by S Ltd but unrealised by the group is £4,000 of which £3,000 (75%) is attributable to the group and £1,000 (25%) to the minority.

Remove the whole of the profit loading, charging the minority with their proportion; this is the treatment used here, as required by the ASB.

Reserves	£
H Ltd	150,000
Share of S Ltd's post-acquisition retained reserves	
£(60,000 − 4,000) × 75%	42,000
	192,000

Minority interest	£
Share capital (25% × £100,000)	25,000
Reserves £(60,000 − 4,000) × 25%	14,000
	39,000

H LIMITED
CONSOLIDATED BALANCE SHEET AS AT 31 DECEMBER 19X2

	£	£
Tangible fixed assets		245,000
Current assets		
Stocks £(50,000 + 48,000 − 4,000)	94,000	
Trade debtors	36,000	
	130,000	
Creditors	64,000	
Net current assets		66,000
		311,000
Capital and reserves		
Ordinary shares of £1 each		80,000
Reserves		192,000
Shareholders' funds		272,000
Minority interest		39,000
		311,000

7   INTER-COMPANY SALES OF FIXED ASSETS   6/94, 6/95

7.1   As well as engaging in trading activities with each other, **group companies may on occasion wish to transfer fixed assets. In their individual accounts the companies concerned will treat the transfer just like a sale between unconnected parties:** the selling company will record a profit or loss on sale; while the purchasing company will record the asset at the amount paid to acquire it, and will use that amount as the basis for calculating depreciation.

7.2   **On consolidation, the usual 'group entity' principle applies.** The consolidated balance sheet must show assets at their cost to the group, and any depreciation charged must be based on that cost. **Two consolidation adjustments** will usually be needed to achieve this.

(a)   An **adjustment to alter reserves and fixed assets cost so as to remove any element of unrealised profit or loss.** This is similar to the adjustment required in respect of unrealised profit in stock.

(b)   An **adjustment to alter reserves and accumulated depreciation** is made so that consolidated depreciation is based on the asset's cost to the group.

7.3   **The double entry is as follows.**

(a)   *Sale by holding company*

DEBIT   Group reserves
CREDIT   Fixed assets

with the profit on disposal.

DEBIT   Fixed assets
CREDIT   Group reserves (H's share)
CREDIT   Minority interest (MI's share)

with the additional depreciation.

(b)   *Sale by subsidiary*

DEBIT   Group reserves (H's share)
DEBIT   Minority interest (MI's share)
CREDIT   Fixed assets

with the profit on disposal.

DEBIT   Fixed assets
CREDIT   Group reserves

with the additional depreciation.

7.4   EXAMPLE: INTER-COMPANY SALE OF FIXED ASSETS

H Ltd owns 60% of S Ltd and on 1 January 19X1 S Ltd sells plant costing £10,000 to H Ltd for £12,500. The companies make up accounts to 31 December 19X1 and the balances on their revenue reserves at that date are:

H Ltd after charging depreciation of 10% on plant	£27,000
S Ltd including profit on sale of plant	£18,000

Required

Show the revenue reserves account.

7.5 SOLUTION

Revenue reserves

	£
H Ltd	27,000
Share of S Ltd's post-acquisition retained reserves	
£(18,000 – 2,500) × 60%	9,300
Depreciation on plant (10% × £2,500)	250
	36,550

Notes

1   The minority interest in the revenue reserves of S Ltd 40% × £(18,000 – 2,500) = £6,200.

2   The asset is written down to cost and depreciation on the 'profit' element is removed. The group profit and loss account for the year is thus reduced by a net ((£2,500 × 60%) – £250) = £1,250.

8   SUMMARY: CONSOLIDATED BALANCE SHEET

Purpose	To show the net assets which H controls and the ownership of those assets.
Net assets	Always 100% H plus 100% S providing H holds a majority of voting rights.
Share capital	H only.
Reason	Simply reporting to the holding company's shareholders in another form.
Reserves	100% H plus group share of post-acquisition retained reserves of S less consolidation adjustments.
Reason	To show the extent to which the group actually owns net assets included in the top half of the balance sheet.
Minority interest	MI share of S's consolidated net assets.
Reason	To show the extent to which other parties own net assets that are under the control of the holding company.

Chapter roundup

- This chapter has covered the mechanics of preparing simple **consolidated balance sheets**. In particular, procedures have been described for dealing with
  - Cancellation
  - Calculation of minority interests
  - Calculation of goodwill arising on consolidation

- A five-stage drill has been described and exemplified in a comprehensive example.

- The stages are as follows.
  - Update the draft balance sheets to take account of proposed dividends not accrued for
  - Agree intercompany current accounts by adjusting for items in transit
  - Cancel items common to both balance sheets
  - Minority interests
  - Goodwill

- We have examined the consolidation adjustments necessary when group companies trade **with or sell fixed assets to each** other.
  - The guiding principle is that the consolidated balance sheet must show assets at their cost to the group.
  - Any profit arising on intra-group transactions must be eliminated from the group accounts unless and until it is realised by a sale outside the group.

- It is important that you have a clear understanding of the material in this chapter before you move on to more complicated aspects of consolidation.

Quick quiz

1 What are the components making up the figure of minority interest in a consolidated balance sheet? (see para 2.2)

2 What adjustment is necessary before consolidation in cases where a holding company has not accrued for dividends receivable from a subsidiary? (3.3)

3 What is 'goodwill arising on consolidation'? (4.6, 4.7) How is it calculated? (4.10)

4 How should 'negative goodwill' be disclosed in the consolidated balance sheet? (4.18)

5 What consolidation problems arise when trading takes place between two companies within the same group? (6.3)

6 What is the basic principle of consolidation that determines the accounting treatment of inter-company trading? (6.4)

7 What are the three possible methods of accounting for minority interests in unrealised inter-company profits? (6.8)

8 What two consolidation adjustments are necessary to account for fixed assets transferred between two companies within the same group? (7.2)

To get you started, the question recommended is rather easier than you could expect in an exam

Question to try	Level	Marks	Time
18	Introductory	n/a	36 mins

Chapter 18

ACQUISITION OF SUBSIDIARIES

Chapter topic list	Syllabus reference
1 Acquisition of a subsidiary during its accounting period	2(c)
2 Dividends and pre-acquisition profits	2(c)
3 FRS 7 *Fair values in acquisition accounting*	2(c)

Introduction

This chapter deals with the problems associated with the consolidation of a subsidiary acquired during the accounting period (a fairly common occurrence).

You will not understand the rest of the chapters on consolidation, particularly Chapters 14 and 17, unless you grasp the principles laid out in this chapter. You should pay particular attention to the determination of pre- and post-acquisition profits and the effect of dividends in Section 2.

The major topic of merger accounting vs acquisition accounting is covered in Chapter 19, along with the consolidated profit and loss account and accounting for associated undertakings.

You should note the interaction of FRS 7 with FRS 2 *Accounting for subsidiary undertakings* (Chapter 16) and FRS 6 *Acquisitions and mergers* (Chapter 19).

1 ACQUISITION OF A SUBSIDIARY DURING ITS ACCOUNTING PERIOD 12/96, 12/97

1.1 When a holding company acquires a subsidiary **during its accounting period the only** accounting **entries will be those recording the cost of acquisition in the holding company's books.** As we have already seen, **at the end of the accounting year** it will be necessary to **prepare consolidated accounts**.

1.2 The subsidiary company's accounts to be consolidated will show the subsidiary's profit or loss for the whole year. **For consolidation** purposes, however, it will be necessary to **distinguish between:**

(a) **profits earned before acquisition;** and
(b) **profits earned after acquisition.**

1.3 In practice, a subsidiary company's profit may not accrue evenly over the year; for example, the subsidiary might be engaged in a trade, such as toy sales, with marked seasonal fluctuations. Nevertheless, statute permits the **assumption** to be made **that profits accrue evenly** whenever it is impracticable to arrive at an accurate split of pre- and post-acquisition profits.

1.4 Once the amount of pre-acquisition profit has been established the appropriate consolidation workings (goodwill, reserves) can be produced.

1.5 Bear in mind that **in calculating minority interests the distinction between pre- and post-acquisition profits is irrelevant.** The minority shareholders are simply credited with their share of the subsidiary's total reserves at the balance sheet date.

1.6 It is worthwhile to summarise what happens on consolidation to the reserves figures extracted from a subsidiary's balance sheet. Suppose the accounts of S Ltd, a 60% subsidiary of H Ltd, show reserves of £20,000 at the balance sheet date, of which £14,000 were earned prior to acquisition. The figure of £20,000 will appear in the consolidated balance sheet as follows.

	£
Minority interests working: their share of total reserves at balance sheet date (40% × £20,000)	8,000
Goodwill working: group share of pre-acquisition profits (60% × £14,000)	8,400
Consolidated reserves working: group share of post-acquisition profits (60% × £6,000)	3,600
	20,000

Question 1

Hinge Ltd acquired 80% of the ordinary shares of Singe Ltd on 1 April 19X5. On 31 December 19X4 Singe Ltd's accounts showed a share premium account of £4,000 and revenue reserves of £15,000. The balance sheets of the two companies at 31 December 19X5 are set out below. Neither company has paid or proposed any dividends during the year.

You are required to prepare the consolidated balance sheet of Hinge Ltd at 31 December 19X5.

Note. Goodwill is to be amortised over 25 years. A full year's amortisation is charged in the year of acquisition.

HINGE LIMITED
BALANCE SHEET AS AT 31 DECEMBER 19X5

	£
Fixed assets	
Tangible assets	32,000
16,000 ordinary shares of 50p each in Singe Ltd	50,000
	82,000
Net current assets	65,000
	147,000
Capital and reserves	
Ordinary shares of £1 each	100,000
Share premium account	7,000
Revenue reserves	40,000
	147,000

SINGE LIMITED
BALANCE SHEET AS AT 31 DECEMBER 19X5

	£
Tangible fixed assets	30,000
Net current assets	23,000
	53,000
Capital and reserves	
20,000 ordinary shares of 50p each	10,000
Share premium account	4,000
Revenue reserves	39,000
	53,000

Answer

Singe Ltd has made a profit of £24,000 (£39,000 − £15,000) for the year. In the absence of any direction to the contrary, this should be assumed to have arisen evenly over the year; £6,000 in the three months to 31 March and £18,000 in the nine months after acquisition. The company's pre-acquisition revenue reserves are therefore as follows.

	£
Balance at 31 December 19X4	15,000
Profit for three months to 31 March 19X5	6,000
Pre-acquisition revenue reserves	21,000

The balance of £4,000 on share premium account is all pre-acquisition.

The consolidation workings can now be drawn up.

1   *Minority interest*

	£
Ordinary share capital (20% × £10,000)	2,000
Revenue reserves (20% × £39,000) (pre-acquisition)	7,800
Share premium (20% × £4,000)	800
	10,600

2   *Goodwill*

	£	£
Cost of investment		50,000
Share of net assets acquired represented by		
Ordinary share capital	10,000	
Revenue reserves (pre-acquisition)	21,000	
Share premium	4,000	
	35,000	
Group share (80%)		28,000
Goodwill		22,000

3   *Revenue reserves*

	£
Hinge Ltd	40,000
Share of Singe Ltd's post acquisition retained reserves	
£(39,000 − 21,000) × 80%	14,400
	54,400
Less: goodwill amortised on consolidation (22,000 ÷ 25)	(880)
	53,520

4   *Share premium account*

	£
Hinge Ltd	7,000
Share of Singe Ltd's post acquisition retained reserve	-
	7,000

HINGE LIMITED
CONSOLIDATED BALANCE SHEET AS AT 31 DECEMBER 19X5

	£
Intangible fixed assets: goodwill	21,120
Tangible fixed assets	62,000
Net current assets	88,000
	171,120
Capital and reserves	
Ordinary shares of £1 each	100,000
Reserves	
Share premium account	7,000
Revenue reserves	53,520
Shareholders' funds	160,520
Minority interest	10,600
	171,120

1.7   EXAMPLE: PRE-ACQUISITION LOSSES OF A SUBSIDIARY

As an illustration of the entries arising when a subsidiary has pre-acquisition *losses*, suppose H Ltd acquired all 50,000 £1 ordinary shares in S Ltd for £20,000 on 1 January 19X1 when there was a debit balance of £35,000 on S Ltd's revenue reserves. In the years 19X1 to 19X4 S Ltd makes profits of £40,000 in total, leaving a credit balance of £5,000 on revenue reserves at 31 December 19X4. H Ltd's reserves at the same date are £70,000. Any goodwill is deemed to have an indefinite useful life and should be held in the balance sheet.

1.8   The consolidation workings would appear as follows.

1   *Goodwill*

	£	£
Cost of investment		20,000
Share of net assets acquired as represented by		
Ordinary share capital	50,000	
Revenue reserves	(35,000)	
	15,000	
Group share (100%)		15,000
Goodwill		5,000

2   *Revenue reserve*

	£
H Ltd	70,000
Share of S Ltd's post-acquisition retained reserves	40,000
Group reserves	110,000

2   DIVIDENDS AND PRE-ACQUISITION PROFITS

2.1   **A further problem in consolidation occurs when a subsidiary pays out a dividend soon after acquisition.** The holding company, as a member of the subsidiary, is entitled to its share of the dividends paid but it is necessary to decide whether or not these dividends come out of the pre-acquisition profits of the subsidiary.

2.2   **If the dividends come from post-acquisition profits** there is no problem. **The holding company simply credits the relevant amount to its own profit and loss account**, as with any other dividend income. The double entry is **quite different**, however, **if the dividend is paid from pre-acquisition profits**, being as follows.

DEBIT   Cash
CREDIT Investment in subsidiary

The holding company's balance sheet would then disclose the investment as 'Investment in subsidiary at cost less amounts written down'.

2.3   It is **very important that you are clear about the reason for this**. Consider the following balance sheets of S_1 Ltd and S_2 Ltd as at 31 March 19X4.

	S_1 Ltd £	S_2 Ltd £
Current assets	30,000	30,000
Current liabilities	10,000	10,000
Ordinary shareholders' funds	20,000	20,000

Both companies have goodwill, not reflected in the books, valued at £5,000 and are identical in every respect, except that the current liabilities of S_1 Ltd are trade creditors while the current liabilities of S_2 Ltd are a proposed ordinary dividend.

2.4 H_1 Ltd, a prospective purchaser of S_1 Ltd, is willing to pay £25,000 for 100% of S_1, including goodwill. H_2 Ltd, a prospective purchaser of S_2 Ltd, will clearly be willing to pay £35,000 for the acquisition of that company in the knowledge that £10,000 of the cost will immediately be 'refunded' by way of dividend.

2.5   Assume that the two purchases are completed on 31 March 19X4 and on 1 April 19X4 S_1 Ltd and S_2 Ltd pay off their current liabilities as appropriate. H_1 and H_2 will then own identical investments, each consisting of £20,000 of current assets plus £5,000 of goodwill, and it is clearly appropriate that the investment figures in their own balance sheets should be identical. This will be the case if H_2 Ltd sets off the £10,000 dividend receivable against the £35,000 cost of the acquisition, disclosing the investment in S_2 at a net cost of £25,000.

2.6   The point to grasp is that H_2 Ltd cannot credit the dividend to profit because no profit has been made. The correct way of looking at it is to say that H_2 Ltd was willing to pay 'over the odds' for its investment in the presumption that a part of its cost would immediately be repaid. When the dividend is paid, this presumption must be pursued to its conclusion by treating the dividend as a reduction of the cost of the investment.

2.7   **This accounting treatment** used to be a legal requirement but is not *required* by the CA 1985 (or any current SSAP or FRS). However, it **must be considered best practice.**

2.8   **EXAMPLE: DIVIDENDS AND PRE-ACQUISITION PROFITS**

Hip Ltd acquired 8,000 of the 10,000 £1 ordinary shares of Sip Ltd on 1 January 19X5 for £25,000. Sip Ltd's balance sheet at 31 December 19X4 showed a proposed ordinary dividend of £4,000 and retained reserves of £12,000. The balance sheets of the two companies at 31 December 19X5 are given below.

HIP LIMITED
BALANCE SHEET AS AT 31 DECEMBER 19X5

	£
Fixed assets	
Tangible assets	35,000
Investment in Sip Ltd at cost less	
amounts written down	21,800
	56,800
Net current assets	27,000
	83,800
Capital and reserves	
Ordinary shares of £1 each	50,000
Retained reserves	33,800
	83,800

SIP LIMITED
BALANCE SHEET AS AT 31 DECEMBER 19X5

	£
Tangible fixed assets	14,500
Net current assets	12,500
	27,000
Capital and reserves	
Ordinary shares of £1 each	10,000
Retained reserves	17,000
	27,000

Required

Prepare the consolidated balance sheet of Hip Ltd at 31 December 19X5.

Note. Goodwill is deemed to have a useful life of 10 years and is therefore to be amortised over that period.

2.9 SOLUTION

During the year Sip Ltd has paid the £4,000 proposed dividend in its 19X4 balance sheet. Hip Ltd's share (80% × £4,000 = £3,200) has been correctly credited by that company to its 'investment in Sip Ltd' account. That account appears in the books of Hip Ltd as follows.

INVESTMENT IN SIP LIMITED

	£		£
Bank: purchase of 8,000		Bank: dividend received from	
£1 ordinary shares	25,000	pre-acquisition profits	3,200
		Balance c/f	21,800
	25,000		25,000

If Hip Ltd had incorrectly credited the pre-acquisition dividend to its own profit and loss account, it would have been necessary to make the following adjustments in Hip Ltd's accounts before proceeding to the consolidation.

DEBIT	Retained reserves	£3,200	
CREDIT	Investment in Sip Ltd		£3,200

This procedure is sometimes necessary in examination questions.

The consolidation workings can be drawn up as follows.

1   *Minority interest*

	£
Share capital (20% × £10,000)	2,000
Reserves (20% × £17,000)	3,400
	5,400

2   *Goodwill*

	£	£
Cost of investment		25,000
Less share of pre-acquisition dividend (80% × £4,000)		3,200
		21,800
Share of net assets acquired as represented by		
Ordinary share capital	10,000	
Reserves	12,000	
	22,000	
Group share (80%)		17,600
Goodwill		4,200

3   *Reserves*

	£
Hip Ltd	33,800
Share of Sip Ltd's post acquisition retained reserves	
£(17,000 – 12,000) × 80%	4,000
	37,800
Goodwill amortised on consolidation (4,200 × 1/10)	(420)
	37,380

HIP LIMITED
CONSOLIDATED BALANCE SHEET AS AT 31 DECEMBER 19X5

	£
Intangible fixed assets	3,780
Tangible fixed assets	49,500
Net current assets	39,500
	92,780
Capital and reserves	
Ordinary shares of £1 each	50,000
Retained reserves	37,380
Shareholders' funds	87,380
Minority interest	5,400
	92,780

2.10   The example above included an ordinary dividend paid from pre-acquisition profits. The treatment would be exactly the same if a **preference dividend** had been paid from pre-acquisition profits. Any share of such a preference dividend received by the holding company would be credited not to profit and loss account, but to the investment in subsidiary account.

Is the dividend paid from pre-acquisition profits?

2.11   We need next to consider how it is decided whether a dividend is paid from pre-acquisition profits. In the example above there was no difficulty: Hip Ltd acquired shares in Sip Ltd on the first day of an accounting period and the dividend was in respect of the previous accounting period. Clearly, the dividend was paid from profits earned in the period before acquisition.

2.12   **The position is less straightforward if shares are acquired during the subsidiary's accounting period.** An example will illustrate the point.

2.13   EXAMPLE: ACQUISITION DURING SUBSIDIARY'S ACCOUNTING PERIOD

H Ltd and S Ltd each make up their accounts to 31 December. H Ltd buys 80,000 of the 100,000 £1 ordinary shares of S Ltd for £175,000 on 1 October 19X1. S Ltd's revenue reserves (after deducting proposed dividends) stood at £50,000 on 31 December 19X0. S Ltd's profits after tax for the year to 31 December 19X1 were £20,000. In January 19X2 S Ltd declared a first and final dividend for 19X1 of £10,000. At 31 December 19X1, H Ltd's reserves stood at £110,000; this does not include any adjustment for dividends receivable from S Ltd.

Required

Prepare consolidation workings for revenue reserves, minority interest and cost of control as at 31 December 19X1.

2.14   SOLUTION

The problem is to decide how much of the dividend paid by S Ltd comes from pre-acquisition profits. There are several possible ways of doing this but the method we recommend is based on time-apportionment. The 19X1 dividend eventually declared by S Ltd is deemed to have accrued evenly over the year.

Note. Of the £8,000 dividend receivable by H Ltd, £6,000 is deemed to have come from pre-acquisition profits and is credited to 'Investment in S Ltd'. £2,000 comes from post-acquisition profits and is added to reserves.

1   *Minority interest*

	£
Share capital (20% × £100,000)	20,000
Revenue reserves (20% × £60,000)	12,000
	32,000

The minority also has an interest (£2,000) in the proposed dividend payable by S Ltd. This will appear as a current liability in the consolidated balance sheet.

2   *Goodwill*

	£	£
Cost of investment		175,000
Less pre-acquisition dividend		
£10,000 × $^9/_{12}$ × 80%		6,000
		169,000
Share of net assets acquired as		
represented by		
Ordinary share capital	100,000	
Revenue reserves		
£(50,000 + 15,000 − 7,500)	57,500	
	157,500	
Group share (80%)		126,000
Goodwill		43,000

3   *Revenue reserves*

	£
H Ltd	110,000
Dividend receivable	2,000
	112,000
Share of S Ltd's post acquisition	
retained reserves £(60,000 − 57,500) × 80%	2,000
Group reserves	114,000

2.15   It has been argued by some that the question as to whether a dividend from a subsidiary to the holding company is available for onward distribution by the holding company depends on whether receipt of the dividend can be regarded as giving rise to a **realised profit** in the financial statements of the holding company and not simply whether it derives from the pre- or post-acquisition profits of the subsidiary.

2.16   In other words if the subsidiary **recovers in value** after the distribution, the **loss in value is temporary** and need not be deducted from the cost of the investment (only permanent diminutions should be provided).

2.17   Where the investment is carried at fair value, however, it is likely that a dividend which represents a return of pre-acquisition profits would give rise to a **diminution in the value** of investment and thus should be applied in reducing the cost (carrying value) of that investment.

2.18   If this **diminution is not permanent,** this treatment is **not mandatory**. Thus companies could distribute all the subsidiary's pre-acquisition profits as long as the subsidiary could replace them in the future.

2.19   This practice may be legal but it offends good accounting practice. The pre-acquisition dividend is a return of the purchase price and it seems right to deduct it from the cost of the investment.

3   FRS 7 FAIR VALUES IN ACQUISITION ACCOUNTING   12/96

3.1   FRS 10 *Goodwill and intangible assets* **defines goodwill as the difference between the purchase consideration paid by the acquiring company and the aggregate of the 'fair values' of the identifiable assets and liabilities acquired.** The balance sheet of a subsidiary company at the date it is acquired may not be a guide to the fair value of its net assets. For example, the market value of a freehold building may have risen greatly since it was acquired, but it may appear in the balance sheet at historical cost less accumulated depreciation.

Fair value adjustment calculations

3.2   Until now we have calculated goodwill as the difference between the cost of the investment and the **book value** of net assets acquired by the group. If this calculation is to comply with the definition in FRS 10 we **must ensure that the book value of the subsidiary's net assets is the same as their fair value.**

3.3   There are **two possible ways** of achieving this.

(a)   **The subsidiary company might incorporate any necessary revaluations in its own books of account.** In this case, we can proceed directly to the consolidation, taking asset values and reserves figures straight from the subsidiary company's balance sheet.

(b)   **The revaluations may be made as a consolidation adjustment without being incorporated in the subsidiary company's books.** In this case, we must make the necessary adjustments to the subsidiary's balance sheet as a working. Only then can we proceed to the consolidation.

Note. Remember that when depreciating assets are revalued there may be a corresponding alteration in the amount of depreciation charged and accumulated.

3.4   EXAMPLE: FAIR VALUE ADJUSTMENTS

H Ltd acquired 75% of the ordinary shares of S Ltd on 1 September 19X5. At that date the fair value of S Ltd's fixed assets was £23,000 greater than their net book value, and the balance of retained profits was £21,000. The balance sheets of both companies at 31 August 19X6 are given below. S Ltd has not incorporated any revaluation in its books of account.

H LIMITED
BALANCE SHEET AS AT 31 AUGUST 19X6

	£
Fixed assets	
Tangible assets	63,000
Investment in S Ltd at cost	51,000
	114,000
Net current assets	62,000
	176,000
Capital and reserves	
Ordinary shares of £1 each	80,000
Retained profits	96,000
	176,000

S LIMITED
BALANCE SHEET AS AT 31 AUGUST 19X6

	£
Tangible fixed assets	28,000
Net current assets	33,000
	61,000
Capital and reserves	
Ordinary shares of £1 each	20,000
Retained profits	41,000
	61,000

If S Ltd had revalued its fixed assets at 1 September 19X5, an addition of £3,000 would have been made to the depreciation charged in the profit and loss account for 19X5/X6.

Required

Prepare H Ltd's consolidated balance sheet as at 31 August 19X6.

Note: goodwill is deemed to have a useful life of 5 years and is to be amortised over that period.

3.5   SOLUTION

S Ltd has not incorporated the revaluation in its draft balance sheet. Before beginning the consolidation workings we must therefore adjust the company's balance of profits at the date of acquisition and at the balance sheet date.

S Ltd adjusted balance of retained profits

	£	£
Balance per accounts at 1 September 19X5		21,000
Consolidation adjustment: revaluation surplus		23,000
∴ Pre-acquisition profits for consolidation purposes		44,000
Profit for year ended 31 August 19X6		
Per draft accounts £(41,000 – 21,000)	20,000	
Consolidation adjustment: increase in depreciation charge	(3,000)	
		17,000
Adjusted balance of retained profits at 31 August 19X6		61,000

In the consolidated balance sheet, S Ltd's fixed assets will appear at their revalued amount: £(28,000 + 23,000 – 3,000) = £48,000. The consolidation workings can now be drawn up.

1   *Minority interest*

	£
Share capital (25% × £20,000)	5,000
Revenue reserves (25% × £61,000)	15,250
	20,250

2   *Goodwill*

	£	£
Cost of investment		51,000
Share of net assets acquired as represented by		
Ordinary share capital	20,000	
Revenue reserves		
£(21,000 + 23,000)	44,000	
	64,000	
Group share (75%)		48,000
Goodwill		3,000

3   *Revenue reserves*

	£
H Ltd	96,000
Share of S Ltd's post acquisition retained reserves	
£(41,000 − 21,000 − 3,000) × 75%	12,750
Goodwill amortised on consolidation	(600)
Group reserves	108,150

H LIMITED CONSOLIDATED BALANCE SHEET AS AT 31 AUGUST 19X6

	£
Intangible fixed assets: goodwill	2,400
Tangible fixed assets £(63,000 + 48,000)	111,000
Net current assets	95,000
	208,400
Capital and reserves	
Ordinary shares of £1 each	80,000
Retained profits	108,150
Shareholders' funds	188,150
Minority interest	20,250
	208,400

Question 2

An asset is recorded in S Ltd's books at its historical cost of £4,000. On 1 January 19X1 P Ltd bought 80% of S Ltd's equity. Its directors attributed a fair value of £3,000 to the asset as at that date. It had been depreciated for two years out of an expected life of four years on the straight line basis. There was no expected residual value. On 30 June 19X1 the asset was sold for £2,600. What is the profit or loss on disposal of this asset to be recorded in S Ltd's accounts and in P Ltd's consolidated accounts for the year ended 31 December 19X1?

Answer

S Ltd: NPV at disposal (at historical cost) = £4,000 × 1½/4 = £1,500

∴ Profit on disposal = £1,100 (depreciation charge for the year = £500)

P Ltd: NPV at disposal (at fair value) = £3,000 × 1½/2 = £2,250

∴ Profit on disposal for consolidation = £350 (depreciation for the year = £750). The minority would be credited with 20% of both items as part of the one line entry in the profit and loss account.

FRS 7 *Fair values in acquisition accounting*

3.6   FRS 7 and FRS 6 *Acquisitions and mergers* were published together in September 1994 in order to reform both acquisition and merger accounting practices. Merger accounting and FRS 6 are both discussed in Chapter 19.

> **IMPORTANT!**
>
> The basic principles stated by FRS 7 are that:
>
> (a) **all identifiable assets and liabilities** should be **recognised** which are in existence **at the date of acquisition**; and
>
> (b) such recognised assets and liabilities should be **measured at fair values** which reflect the conditions existing at the date of acquisition.
>
> Fair values should not reflect either the acquirer's intentions or events subsequent to the acquisition.

3.7 In addition any **changes** to the acquired assets and liabilities, and the resulting gains and losses, that arise **after control** of the acquired entity has passed to the acquirer should be reported as part of the **post-acquisition profits** of the group.

3.8 FRS 7 also sets out specific rules on how fair values should be determined for the main categories of asset and liability. The underlying principle remains that **fair values should reflect the price at which an asset or liability could be exchanged in an arm's length transaction.** For long-term monetary assets and liabilities, fair values may be derived by discounting.

3.9 The standard also describes how the value attributed to the consideration given for the acquisition should be determined, and the acquisition expenses that may be included as part of the cost.

Definitions

3.10 The following definitions are given by FRS 7. They are self explanatory except for the highlighted terms.

   (a) Acquisition
   (b) Business combination
   (c) Date of acquisition
   (d) **Fair value**
   (e) Identifiable assets and liabilities
   (f) **Recoverable amount**
   (g) **Value in use**

> **KEY TERMS**
>
> (a) In particular note the definition of **fair value**.
>
>   'The amount at which an asset or liability could be exchanged in an arm's length transaction between informed and willing parties, other than in a forced or liquidation sale.'
>
> (b) **Recoverable amount** is the greater of the net realisable value of an asset and, when appropriate, the amount recoverable from its further use.
>
> (c) **Value in use** is the present value of the future cash flows obtainable as a result of an asset's continued use, including those resulting from the ultimate disposal of the asset.

Scope

3.11 FRS 7 applies to all financial statements that are intended to give a true and fair view. Although the FRS is framed in terms of the acquisition of a subsidiary undertaking by a parent company that prepares consolidated financial statements, it **also applies where an individual company entity acquires a business other than a subsidiary undertaking**. This last point means that companies cannot avoid the provisions of FRS 7 when taking over an unincorporated entity or joint venture vehicle.

Determining the fair values of identifiable assets and liabilities acquired

3.12 Most importantly, the FRS lists those **items which do not affect fair values** at the date of acquisition, and **which are therefore to be treated as post-acquisition items:**

(a) Changes resulting from the **acquirer's intentions or future actions.**

(b) **Impairments** or other changes, resulting from events subsequent to the acquisition.

(c) **Provisions or accruals for future operating losses** or for reorganisation and integration costs expected to be incurred as a result of the acquisition, whether they relate to the acquired entity or to the acquirer.

Assessing fair value of major categories

3.13 In general terms, fair values should be determined in accordance with the acquirer's accounting policies for similar assets and liabilities. The standard does, however, go on to describe how the major categories of assets and liabilities should be assessed for fair values.

(a) **Tangible assets: fair value based on:**

    (i) **market value**, if similar assets are sold on the open market; or
    (ii) **depreciated replacement cost**, reflecting normal business practice.

    However, **fair value ≤ replacement cost.**

(b) **Intangible assets**, where recognised: **fair value should be based on replacement costs,** which will normally be estimated market value.

(c) **Stocks and work in progress**

    (i) For stocks which are replaced by purchasing in a **ready market** (commodities, dealing stock etc), the fair value is **market value**.

    (ii) For other stocks, with **no ready market** (most manufacturing stocks), fair value is represented by the **current cost** to the acquired company of reproducing the stocks.

(d) **Quoted investments:** value at **market price**, adjusted where necessary for unusual price fluctuations or the size of the holding.

(e) **Monetary assets and liabilities:** fair values should take into account the **amounts expected to be received or paid** and their timing. Reference should be made to market prices (where available) or to the current price if acquiring similar assets or entering into similar obligations, or to the discounted present value.

(f) **Contingencies: reasonable estimates** of the expected outcome may be used.

(g) **Pensions and other post-retirement benefits: the fair value of a deficiency, a surplus** (to the extent it is expected to be realised) or accrued obligation should be **recognised** as an asset/liability of the acquiring group. Any changes on acquisition should be treated as post-acquisition items.

(h) **Deferred taxation:** deferred tax assets and liabilities should be considered **in terms of the whole group**. The benefit to the group of any tax losses attributable to an acquired entity should be valued according to SSAP 15.

Business sold or held with a view to subsequent resale

3.14   The fair value exercise for such an entity, 'sold as a single unit, within approximately one year of acquisition', should be carried out on the basis of a **single asset investment**.

> 'Its fair value should be based on the **net proceeds of the sale, adjusted for the fair value of any assets or liabilities transferred** into or out of the business, unless such adjusted net proceeds are demonstrably different from the fair value at the date of acquisition as a result of a post-acquisition event.'

Any relevant part of the business can be treated in this way if it is separately identifiable, ie it does not have to be a separate subsidiary undertaking.

3.15   Where the first financial statements after the date of acquisition come for approval, but the business has not been sold, the above treatment can still be applied if:

(a)   a purchaser has been identified or is being sought; *and*
(b)   the disposal is expected to occur within one year of the date of acquisition.

3.16   The interest (or its assets) should be shown in current assets. On determination of the sales price, the original estimate of fair value should be adjusted to reflect the actual sales proceeds.

Investigation period and goodwill adjustments

3.17   FRS 7 states that:

> 'The recognition and measurement of assets and liabilities acquired should be completed, if possible, by the date on which the first post-acquisition financial statements of the acquirer are approved by the directors.'

Where this has not been possible, provisional valuations should be made, amended if necessary in the next financial statements with a corresponding adjustment to goodwill. Such adjustments should be incorporated into the financial statements in the full year following acquisition. After that, any adjustments (except for the correction of fundamental errors by prior year adjustment) should be recognised as profits or losses as they are identified.

Determining the fair value of purchase consideration

3.18   The cost of acquisition is the amount of cash paid and the fair value of other purchase consideration given by the acquirer, together with the expenses of the acquisition. Where a subsidiary undertaking is acquired in stages, the cost of acquisition is the total of the costs of the interests acquired, determined as at the date of each transaction.

3.19   The main likely components of purchase consideration are as follows.

(a)   *Ordinary shares*

(i)   **Quoted shares** should be valued at **market price** on the date of acquisition.

(ii)   Where there is **no suitable market,** estimate the value using:

(1)   the value of **similar quoted securities;** *or*
(2)   the **present value of the future cash** flows of the instrument used; *or*
(3)   any **cash alternative** which was offered.

(b) **Other securities:** the value should be based on similar principles to those given in (a).

(c) **Cash or monetary amounts:** value at the **amount paid or payable**.

(d) **Non-monetary assets:** value at **market price**, estimated realisable value, independent valuation or based on other available evidence.

(e) **Deferred consideration: discount** the amounts calculated on the above principles (in (a) to (d)). An appropriate discount rate is that which the acquirer could obtain for a similar borrowing.

(f) **Contingent consideration:** use the **probable** amount. When the actual amount is known, it should be recorded in the financial statements and goodwill adjusted accordingly.

Exam focus point

Valuing the purchase consideration has been tested, but not for many marks.

3.20 **Acquisition cost** (the fees and expenses mentioned above) should be **included in the cost of the investment**. Internal costs and the costs of issuing capital instruments should *not* be capitalised, according to the provisions of FRS 4, ie they must be written off to the profit and loss account.

Summary and assessment

3.21 **The most important effect of FRS 7 is the ban it imposes on making provisions for future trading losses** of acquired companies and the costs of any related rationalisation or reorganisation, unless outgoing management had already incurred those liabilities. This is a controversial area, demonstrated by the dissenting view of one member of the ASB.

3.22 **Some commentators argued that the ASB's approach ignores the commercial reality of the transaction** by treating as an expense the costs of reorganisation that the acquirer regards as part of the capital cost of the acquisition; and that within defined limits a provision for planned post-acquisition expenditure should be permitted to be included in the net assets acquired.

Case example

The Hundred Group of finance directors gave an example. If you buy a house for, say £100,000 that you know needs £50,000 spent on it to bring it into good condition and make it equivalent to a property that sells for £150,000, then you would treat the £50,000 renovation expense as part of the cost of the house and not as part of ordinary outgoings. The group states that FRS 7 goes beyond standards set in other countries, including the US. It also recommends that abuses in this area should be dealt with by tightening existing accounting standards and through 'proper policing' by external auditors (the standard is seen to undermine the professional judgement of the auditor) and 'not by distorting accounting concepts'.

3.23 The ASB rejected this view, saying that an intention to incur revenue expenditure subsequent to the acquisition could not properly be regarded as a liability of the acquired business at the date of acquisition.

> 'Acquisition accounting should reflect the business that is acquired as it stands at the date of acquisition and ought not to take account of the changes that an acquirer might intend to

make subsequently. Nor could the ASB accept the proposition that some of the inadequacies of the present system could be met by better disclosure. In the ASB's view deficient accounting cannot be put right by disclosure alone.'

3.24   This is still an open area of debate and you should keep track of the arguments in the financial and accountancy press.

Question 3

Tyzo plc prepares accounts to 31 December. On 1 September 19X7 Tyzo plc acquired 6 million £1 shares in Kono plc at £2.00 per share. The purchase was financed by an additional issue of loan stock at an interest rate of 10%. At that date Kono plc produced the following interim financial statements.

	£m		£m
Tangible fixed assets (note 1)	16.0	Trade creditors	3.2
Stocks (note 2)	4.0	Taxation	0.6
Debtors	2.9	Bank overdraft	3.9
Cash in hand	1.2	Long-term loans (note 6)	4.0
		Share capital (£1 shares)	8.0
		Profit and loss account	4.4
	24.1		24.1

Notes

1   The following information relates to the tangible fixed assets of Kono plc at 1 September 19X7.

	£m
Gross replacement cost	28.4
Net replacement cost	16.6
Economic value	18.0
Net realisable value	8.0

The fixed assets of Kono plc at 1 September 19X7 had a total purchase cost to Kono plc of £27.0 million. They were all being depreciated at 25% per annum pro rata on that cost. This policy is also appropriate for the consolidated financial statements of Tyzo plc. No fixed assets of Kono plc which were included in the interim financial statements drawn up as at 1 September 19X7 were disposed of by Kono plc prior to 31 December 19X7. No fixed asset was fully depreciated by 31 December 19X7.

2   The stocks of Kono plc which were shown in the interim financial statements at cost to Kono plc of £4 million would have cost £4.2 million to replace at 1 September 19X7 and had an estimated net realisable value at that date of £4.8 million. Of the stock of Kono plc in hand at 1 September 19X7, goods costing Kono plc £3.0 million were sold for £3.6 million between 1 September 19X7 and 31 December 19X7.

3   The long-term loan of Kono plc carries a rate of interest of 10% per annum, payable on 31 August annually in arrears. The loan is redeemable at par on 31 August 2001. The interest cost is representative of current market rates. The accrued interest payable by Kono plc at 31 December 19X7 is included in the trade creditors of Kono plc at that date.

4   On 1 September 19X7 Tyzo plc took a decision to rationalise the group so as to integrate Kono plc. The costs of the rationalisation (which were to be borne by Tyzo plc) were estimated to total £3.0 million and the process was due to start on 1 March 19X8. No provision for these costs has been made in any of the financial statements given above.

Required

Compute the goodwill on consolidation of Kono plc that will be included in the consolidated financial statements of the Tyzo plc group for the year ended 31 December 19X7, explaining your treatment of the items mentioned above. You should refer to the provisions of relevant accounting standards.

Answer

Goodwill on consolidation of Kono Ltd

	£m	£m
Consideration (£2.00 × 6m)		12.0
Group share of fair value of net assets acquired		
Share capital	8.0	
Pre acquisition reserves	4.4	
Fair value adjustments		
Tangible fixed assets (16.6 – 16.0)	0.6	
Stocks (4.2 – 4.0)	0.2	
	13.2	
Group share	75%	9.9
Goodwill		2.1

Notes on treatment

(a) It is assumed that the market value (ie fair value) of the loan stock issued to fund the purchase of the shares in Kono plc is equal to the price of £12.0m. FRS 2 *Accounting for subsidiary undertakings* requires goodwill to be calculated by comparing the fair value of the consideration given with the fair value of the separable net assets of the acquired business or company.

(b) Share capital and pre-acquisition profits represent the book value of the net assets of Kono plc at the date of acquisition. Adjustments are then required to this book value in order to give the fair value of the net assets at the date of acquisition. For short-term monetary items, fair value is their carrying value on acquisition.

(c) FRS 7 *Fair values in acquisition accounting* states that the fair value of tangible fixed assets should be determined by market value or, if information on a market price is not available (as is the case here), then by reference to depreciated replacement cost, reflecting normal business practice. The net replacement cost (ie £16.6m) represents the gross replacement cost less depreciation based on that amount, and so further adjustment for extra depreciation is unnecessary.

(d) FRS 7 also states that stocks which cannot be replaced by purchasing in a ready market (eg commodities) should be valued at current cost to the acquired company of reproducing the stocks. In this case that amount is £4.2m.

(e) The fair value of the loan is the present value of the total amount payable, ie on maturity and in interest. If the quoted interest rate was used as a discount factor, this would give the current par value.

(f) The rationalisation costs must be reported in post-acquisition results under FRS 7 *Fair values in acquisition accounting*, so no adjustment is required in the goodwill calculation.

Chapter roundup

- In this chapter we have looked at certain problems involved in distinguishing between **pre-acquisition** and **post-acquisition profits** of subsidiary companies.

- When a subsidiary is acquired **during its accounting period**, its **pre-acquisition profits** will include a **proportion of its total profits** for the accounting period.

- In the absence of information to the contrary, the profits earned during the period may be assumed to have **accrued evenly** and should be allocated accordingly.

- **Dividends** paid by a subsidiary to its parent company may only be **credited to the parent's profit and loss account** to the extent that they are paid from **post-acquisition profits**.

- **Dividends** received by the holding company **from pre-acquisition profits** should be credited to 'investment in subsidiary' account and treated as **reducing the cost of the shares** acquired.

- **Goodwill arising on consolidation** is the difference between the purchase consideration and the fair value of net assets acquired.

- **Goodwill** should be calculated **after revaluing** the subsidiary company's assets.

- If the subsidiary does not incorporate the revaluation in its own accounts, it should be done as a **consolidation adjustment**.

- The accounting requirements and disclosures of the **fair value exercise** are covered by **FRS 7**, which is controversial as it outlaws the use of provisions for future losses and for reorganisation costs on acquisition of a subsidiary.

Quick quiz

1   A holding company can assume that, for a subsidiary acquired during its accounting period, profits accrue evenly during the year. True or false? (see para 1.3)

2   What entries are made in the consolidated workings accounts to record the pre-acquisition losses of a subsidiary? (1.8)

3   What entries are made in the holding company's accounts to record a dividend received from a subsidiary's pre-acquisition profits? (2.2)

4   Describe the requirement of FRS 10 in relation to the revaluation of a subsidiary company's assets. (3.2)

5   How may this requirement be achieved in practice? (3.3)

6   What are the basic principles in determining the fair value of identifiable assets and liabilities? (3.6)

7   How is 'fair value' defined by FRS 7? (3.10, *Glossary*)

8   Which items does FRS 7 state *must* be treated as post-acquisition? (3.12)

9   How should businesses which are held for resale be treated in the fair value exercise? (3.14)

10 For how long can fair values be adjusted after acquisition? (3.17)

Question to try	Level	Marks	Time
19	Full exam	25	45 mins

Chapter 19

PROFIT AND LOSS ACCOUNT; MERGERS

Chapter topic list	Syllabus reference
1 The consolidated profit and loss account	2(c)
2 FRS 6 *Acquisitions and mergers*	2(c)
3 FRS 6 disclosures	2(c)
4 Further practical issues	2(c)

Introduction

Generally speaking, the preparation of the consolidated profit and loss account is more straightforward than the preparation of the consolidated balance sheet. Complications do arise, however, usually in the form of inter-company transactions and accounting for pre-acquisition profits.

The consolidated profit and loss account will appear again in Chapter 20 where we consider the treatment of associated companies and joint ventures.

Merger accounting is a very contentious area at the moment. The standard, FRS 6, has drawn criticism for its approach and it is likely to remain controversial for some time. In the future, the use of merger accounting (for 'true' mergers) could be very rare.

The distinction between merger accounting and merger relief is an important one. Make sure you can accurately describe both concepts.

1 THE CONSOLIDATED PROFIT AND LOSS ACCOUNT

12/94, 6/95, 12/96

1.1 As always, the source of the consolidated statement is the individual accounts of the separate companies in the group. **It is customary in practice to prepare a working paper** (known as a **consolidation schedule**) **on which the individual profit and loss accounts are set out side by side and totalled to form the basis of the consolidated profit and loss account.**

Exam focus point

In an examination it is very much quicker not to do this. Use workings to show the calculation of complex figures such as the minority interest and show the derivation of others on the face of the profit and loss account, as shown in our examples.

1.2   CONSOLIDATED PROFIT AND LOSS ACCOUNT: SIMPLE EXAMPLE

H Ltd acquired 75% of the ordinary shares of S Ltd on that company's incorporation in 19X3. The summarised profit and loss accounts of the two companies for the year ending 31 December 19X6 are set out below.

	H Ltd	S Ltd
	£	£
Turnover	75,000	38,000
Cost of sales	30,000	20,000
Gross profit	45,000	18,000
Administrative expenses	14,000	8,000
Profit before taxation	31,000	10,000
Taxation	10,000	2,000
Retained profit for the year	21,000	8,000
Retained profits brought forward	87,000	17,000
Retained profits carried forward	108,000	25,000

Required

Prepare the consolidated profit and loss account.

1.3   SOLUTION

H LIMITED
CONSOLIDATED PROFIT AND LOSS ACCOUNT
FOR THE YEAR ENDED 31 DECEMBER 19X6

	£
Turnover (75 + 38)	113,000
Cost of sales (30 + 20)	50,000
Gross profit	63,000
Administrative expenses (14 + 8)	22,000
Profit before taxation	41,000
Taxation (10 + 2)	12,000
Profit after taxation	29,000
Minority interest (25% × £8,000)	2,000
Group retained profit for the year	27,000
Retained profits brought forward	
(group share only: 87 + (17 × 75%))	99,750
Retained profits carried forward	126,750

1.4   **Notice how the minority interest is dealt with.**

(a)   **Down to the line 'profit after taxation' the whole of S Ltd's results is included without reference to group share or minority share. A one-line adjustment is then inserted to deduct the minority's share of S Ltd's profit after taxation.**

(b)   **The minority's share (£4,250) of S Ltd's retained profits brought forward is excluded.** This means that the carried forward figure of £126,750 is the figure which would appear in the balance sheet for group retained reserves.

1.5   This last point may be clearer if we revert to our balance sheet technique and construct the working for group reserves.

Group reserves

	£
H Ltd	108,000
Share of S Ltd's PARR★ (75% × £25,000)	18,750
	126,750

The minority share of S Ltd's reserves comprises the minority interest in the £17,000 profits brought forward plus the minority interest (£2,000) in £8,000 retained profits for the year. (*Note*. PARR = Post acquisition retained reserves.)

1.6 Notice that a consolidated profit and loss account links up with a consolidated balance sheet exactly as in the case of an individual company's accounts: the figure of retained profits carried forward at the bottom of the profit and loss account appears as the figure for retained profits in the balance sheet.

1.7 We will now look at the **complications introduced by inter-company trading, inter-company dividends and pre-acquisition profits in the subsidiary.**

INTER-COMPANY TRADING

1.8 Like the consolidated balance sheet, the consolidated profit and loss account should deal with the results of the group as those of a single entity. When one company in a group sells goods to another an identical amount is added to the turnover of the first company and to the cost of sales of the second. Yet as far as the entity's dealings with outsiders are concerned no sale has taken place.

The consolidated figures for turnover and cost of sales should represent sales to, and purchases from, outsiders. An adjustment is therefore necessary to reduce the turnover and cost of sales figures by the value of inter-company sales during the year.

1.9 We have also seen in an earlier chapter that any **unrealised profits on inter-company trading should be excluded** from the figure of group profits. This will occur whenever goods sold at a profit within the group remain in the stock of the purchasing company at the year end. The best way to deal with this is to **calculate the unrealised profit** on **unsold stocks at the year end and reduce consolidated gross profit by this amount.** Cost of sales will be the balancing figure

1.10 EXAMPLE: INTER-COMPANY TRADING

Suppose in our earlier example that S Ltd had recorded sales of £5,000 to H Ltd during 19X6. S Ltd had purchased these goods from outside suppliers at a cost of £3,000. One half of the goods remained in H Ltd's stock at 31 December 19X6.

1.11 SOLUTION

The consolidated profit and loss account for the year ended 31 December 19X6 would now be as follows.

	Group
	£
Turnover (75 + 38 − 5)	108,000
Cost of sales (balancing figure)	46,000
Gross profit (45 + 18 − 1*)	62,000
Administrative expenses	(22,000)
Profit before taxation	40,000
Taxation	(12,000)
	28,000
Minority interest (25% × (£8,000 − £1,000*))	1,750
Group retained profit for the year	26,250
Retained profits brought forward	99,750
Retained profits carried forward	126,000

*Provision for unrealised profit: ½ × (£5,000 − £3,000)

A provision will be made for the unrealised profit against the stock figure in the consolidated balance sheet, as explained in Chapter 18.

Inter-company dividends

1.12 In our example so far we have assumed that S Ltd retains all of its after-tax profit. It may be, however, that S Ltd distributes some of its profits as dividends. As before, the minority interest in the subsidiary's profit should be calculated immediately after the figure of after-tax profit. For this purpose, **no account need be taken of how much of the minority interest is to be distributed by S Ltd as dividend.**

1.13 A complication may arise **if the subsidiary** has preference shares and **wishes to pay a preference dividend as well** as an ordinary dividend. In such a case **great care is needed in calculating the minority interest in S Ltd's after-tax profit.**

1.14 EXAMPLE: INTER-COMPANY DIVIDENDS

Sam Ltd's capital consists of 10,000 6% £1 preference shares and 10,000 £1 ordinary shares. On 1 January 19X3, the date of Sam Ltd's incorporation, Ham Ltd acquired 3,000 of the preference shares and 7,500 of the ordinary shares. The profit and loss accounts of the two companies for the year ended 31 December 19X6 are set out below.

	Ham Ltd £	Sam Ltd £
Turnover	200,000	98,000
Cost of sales	90,000	40,000
Gross profit	110,000	58,000
Administrative expenses	35,000	19,000
Profit before tax	75,000	39,000
Taxation	23,000	18,000
Profit after tax	52,000	21,000
Dividends proposed: preference	-	600
ordinary	14,000	2,000
Retained profit for the year	38,000	18,400
Retained profits brought forward	79,000	23,000
	117,000	41,400

Ham Ltd has not yet accounted for its share of the dividends receivable from Sam Ltd.

Prepare Ham Ltd's consolidated profit and loss account.

1.15 SOLUTION

To calculate the minority interest in Sam Ltd's after-tax profit it is necessary to remember that the first £600 of such profits goes to pay the preference dividend. The balance of after-tax profits belongs to the equity shareholders. The calculation is as follows.

	Total £		Minority share £
Profits earned for preference shareholders	600	(70%)	420
Balance earned for equity shareholders	20,400	(25%)	5,100
Total profits after tax	21,000		5,520

It is irrelevant how much of this is distributed to the minority as dividends: the whole £5,520 must be deducted in arriving at the figure for group profit. The dividends receivable by Ham Ltd, calculated below would cancel with the dividends payable by Sam Ltd to its holding company.

	£
Preference dividend (30% × £600)	180
Ordinary dividend (75% × £2,000)	1,500
	1,680

1.16   HAM LIMITED
CONSOLIDATED PROFIT AND LOSS ACCOUNT
FOR THE YEAR ENDED 31 DECEMBER 19X5

	Group £
Turnover (200 + 98)	298,000
Cost of sales (90 + 40)	130,000
Gross profit	168,000
Administrative expenses (35 + 19)	54,000
Profit before tax	114,000
Taxation (23 + 18)	41,000
Profit after tax	73,000
Minority interest (as above)	5,520
Group profit for the year	67,480
Dividend proposed (parent company only)	14,000
Retained profit for the year	53,480
Retained profits brought forward	
(group share only: 79 + (23 × 75%))	96,250
Retained profits carried forward	149,730

Pre-acquisition profits

1.17   As explained above, the figure for retained profits at the bottom of the consolidated profit and loss account must be the same as the figure for retained profits in the consolidated balance sheet. We have seen in previous chapters that **retained profits in the consolidated balance sheet comprise:**

(a)   **the whole of the parent company's retained profits; plus**

(b)   a proportion of the subsidiary company's retained profits. The proportion is **the group's share of post-acquisition retained profits in the subsidiary.** From the total retained profits of the subsidiary we must therefore exclude both the minority's share of total retained profits and the group's share of pre-acquisition retained profits.

1.18   **A similar procedure is necessary in the consolidated profit and loss account** if it is to link up with the consolidated balance sheet. Previous examples have shown how the minority share of profits is excluded in the profit and loss account: their share of profits for the year is deducted from profit after tax; while the figure for profits brought forward in the consolidation schedule includes only the group's proportion of the subsidiary's profits.

1.19   In the same way, when considering examples which include pre-acquisition profits in a subsidiary, the figure for profits brought forward should include only the group's share of the post-acquisition retained profits. If the subsidiary is acquired *during* the accounting year, it is therefore necessary to apportion its profit for the year between pre-acquisition and post-acquisition elements. There are two approaches which may be used for this in the consolidated profit and loss account: the whole-year method and the part-year method.

1.20   With the **whole-year method, the whole of the subsidiary's turnover, cost of sales and so on is included and a deduction is then made lower down to exclude the profit accruing prior to acquisition.**

1.21   With the **part-year method, the entire profit and loss account of the subsidiary is split between pre-acquisition and post-acquisition proportions**. Only the post-acquisition figures are included in the profit and loss account. **This method is more usual** than the whole-year method and is the one which will be used in this Study Text.

Question 1

H Ltd acquired 60% of the equity of S Ltd on 1 April 19X5. The profit and loss accounts of the two companies for the year ended 31 December 19X5 are set out below.

	H Ltd £	S Ltd £	S Ltd ($^9/_{12}$) £
Turnover	170,000	80,000	60,000
Cost of sales	65,000	36,000	27,000
Gross profit	105,000	44,000	33,000
Administrative expenses	43,000	12,000	9,000
Profit before tax	62,000	32,000	24,000
Taxation	23,000	8,000	6,000
Profit after tax	39,000	24,000	18,000
Dividends (paid 31 December)	12,000	6,000	
Retained profit for the year	27,000	18,000	
Retained profits brought forward	81,000	40,000	
Retained profits carried forward	108,000	58,000	

H Ltd has not yet accounted for the dividends received from S Ltd.

Prepare the consolidated profit and loss account.

Answer

The shares in S Ltd were acquired three months into the year. Only the post-acquisition proportion (9/12ths) of S Ltd's P & L account is included in the consolidated profit and loss account. This is shown above for convenience.

H LIMITED CONSOLIDATED PROFIT AND LOSS ACCOUNT
FOR THE YEAR ENDED 31 DECEMBER 19X5

	£
Turnover (170 + 60)	230,000
Cost of sales (65 + 27)	92,000
Gross profit	138,000
Administrative expenses (43 + 9)	52,000
Profit before tax	86,000
Taxation (23 + 6)	29,000
Profit after tax	57,000
Minority interest (40% × £18,000)	7,200
Group profit for the year	49,800
Dividends (H Ltd only)	12,000
Retained profit for the year	37,800
Retained profits brought forward*	81,000
Retained profits carried forward	118,800

* All of S Ltd's profits brought forward are pre-acquisition.

Disclosure requirements

1.22 S 230 CA 1985 allows a parent company to dispense with the need to publish its own individual profit and loss account.

(a) Companies taking advantage of this dispensation are obliged to state in their consolidated profit and loss account how much of the group's profit for the financial year is dealt with in the parent company's own profit and loss account.

(b) For internal purposes, of course, it will still be necessary to prepare the parent company's profit and loss account and the profit or loss shown there is the figure to be shown in the note to the group accounts.

(c) This is a point which has been clarified by the CA 1989. In the example above, H Ltd should disclose its own profit after adjustment for its share of the S Ltd dividend (from post-acquisition profits - remember that the pre-acquisition element should be credited to the cost of H's investment in S Ltd).

1.23 Where there are **extraordinary items** (now very rare) in the profit and loss account of a group company the **group share only** of such items should be included, after minority interest and the adjustment for inter-company dividends but before dividends payable by the parent company.

1.24 If you are required to prepare a consolidated profit and loss account in statutory form, you may need to disclose a figure for **directors' emoluments**. The figure should represent the emoluments of **parent company directors only**, whether those emoluments are paid by the parent company or by subsidiary companies. The emoluments of directors of subsidiary companies should be excluded, unless they are also directors of the parent company.

1.25 The movement of reserves statement may be required to show a transfer from the profit and loss account to other reserves. Where this transfer occurs in a subsidiary, only the group's (post-acquisition) share of the transfer will be recorded in the movement of reserves statement. Any minority interest or pre-acquisition profits would be excluded.

MOVEMENT OF RESERVES

	£
Profit and loss account brought forward	X
Add retained profit for the year	X
	X
Less transfer to reserves (all of parent company transfers plus the group share of transfers in a subsidiary)	(X)
Profit and loss account carried forward	X

Question 2

The following information relates to the Brodick group of companies for the year to 30 April 19X7.

	Brodick plc £'000	Lamlash Ltd £'000	Corrie Ltd £'000
Turnover	1,100	500	130
Cost of sales	630	300	70
Gross profit	470	200	60
Administrative expenses	105	150	20
Dividend from Lamlash Ltd	24	-	-
Dividend from Corrie Ltd	6	-	-
Profit before tax	395	50	40
Taxation	65	10	20
Profit after tax	330	40	20
Interim dividend	50	10	-
Proposed dividend	150	20	10
Retained profit for the year	130	10	10
Retained profits brought forward	460	106	30
Retained profits carried forward	590	116	40

Additional information

(a) The issued share capital of the group was as follows.

>   Brodick plc : 5,000,000 ordinary shares of £1 each.
>   Lamlash Ltd : 1,000,000 ordinary shares of £1 each.
>   Corrie Ltd : 400,000 ordinary shares of £1 each.

(b) Brodick plc purchased 80% of the issued share capital of Lamlash Ltd in 19X0. At that time, the retained profits of Lamlash amounted to £56,000.

(c) Brodick plc purchased 60% of the issued share capital of Corrie Ltd in 19X4. At that time, the retained profits of Corrie amounted to £20,000.

(d) Brodick plc recognises dividends proposed by other group companies in its profit and loss account.

Required

Insofar as the information permits, prepare the Brodick group of companies' consolidated profit and loss account for the year to 30 April 19X7 in accordance with the Companies Act 1985 and related statements of accounting practice.

Note. Notes to the profit and loss account are not required but you should append a statement showing the make up of the 'retained profits carried forward', and your workings should be submitted.

Answer

You are not asked for notes, but you should know that Brodick would have to state in the notes that it had taken advantage of the provisions of s 230 CA and was not publishing its own profit and loss account. It would then show its own profit for the year, which the Act now states clearly should be the profit shown in its own books (in this case, including dividends received and receivable from Lamlash and Corrie). Brodrick's profit for the financial year is £330,000, as shown in the question. An analysis of reserves would also be given as a note to the balance sheet, showing movements on both company and consolidated reserves.

CONSOLIDATED PROFIT AND LOSS ACCOUNT
FOR THE YEAR TO 30 APRIL 19X7

	£'000
Turnover (1,100 + 500 + 130)	1,730
Cost of sales (630 + 300 + 70)	1,000
Gross profit	730
Administrative expenses (105 + 150 + 20)	275
Profit on ordinary activities before taxation	455
Tax on profit on ordinary activities (65 + 10 + 20)	95
Profit on ordinary activities after taxation	360
Minority interests (W1)	16
Profit for the financial year	344
Dividends paid and proposed (parent only)	200
Retained profit for the year	144
Retained profit brought forward 1 May 19X6 (W2)	506
Retained profit carried forward 30 April 19X7	650

Workings

1   *Minority interests*

	£
In Lamlash (20% × profit after tax)	8,000
In Corrie (40% × profit after tax)	8,000
	16,000

2   *Retained profits brought forward*

	£
Brodick plc	460,000
Group share of post-acquisition retained profits brought forward	
Lamlash 80% × £(106,000 - 56,000)	40,000
Corrie 60% × £(30,000 - 20,000)	60,000
	506,000

1.26 Section summary

The table below summaries the main points about the consolidated profit and loss account.

Summary: consolidated P & L account

Purpose	To show the results of the group for an accounting period as if it were a single entity.
Turnover to profit after tax	100% H + 100% S (excluding dividend receivable from subsidiary and adjustments for inter-company transactions).
Reason	To show the results of the group which were controlled by the holding company.
Inter-company sales *Unrealised profit on inter-company sales*	Strip out inter-company activity from both turnover and cost sales. (a) *Goods sold by H Ltd.* Increase cost of sales by unrealised profit. (b) *Goods sold by S Ltd.* Increase cost of sales by full amount of unrealised profit and decrease minority interest by their share of unrealised profit.
Depreciation	If the value of S Ltd's fixed assets have been subjected to a fair value uplift then any additional depreciation must be charged in the consolidated profit and loss account. The minority interest will need to be adjusted for their share.
Transfer of fixed assets	Expenses must be increased by any profit on the transfer and reduced by any additional depreciation arising from the increased carrying value of the asset.

Minority interests
 	
 Reason
	S's profit after tax (PAT) X
	 Less: * unrealised profit (X)
	        * profit on disposal of fixed assets (X)
	        additional depreciation following FV uplift (X)
	 Add: ** additional depreciation following
	         disposal of fixed assets $\frac{X}{X}$
	
	 MI% X
	
	 * Only applicable if sales of goods and fixed assets made by subsidiary.
	
	 ** Only applicable if sale of fixed assets made by holding company.
	
	 To show the extent to which profits generated through H's control are in fact owned by other parties.

Dividends *Reason*	H's only. S's dividend is due (a) to H; and (b) to MI. H has taken in its share by including the results of S in the consolidated P & L a/c. The MI have taken their share by being given a proportion of S's PAT. Remember: PAT = dividends + retained profit.
Retained reserves	As per the balance sheet calculations.

2 FRS 6 ACQUISITIONS AND MERGERS   12/97

2.1   FRS 6 *Acquisitions and mergers* (superseding SSAP 23 *Accounting for acquisitions and mergers*) deals with the accounting treatment of business combinations which arise when one or more companies become subsidiaries of another company. Two different methods of accounting for such combinations have evolved in practice.

(a) **Acquisition accounting is the traditional method of accounting for business combinations** and is the method which has been described in the previous chapters of this section. A company acquires shares in another company (or companies) and either pays for them in cash or issues its own shares or loan stock in exchange for them. If much of the purchase price is paid in cash, there may be a significant outflow of assets from the group.

(b) **Merger accounting is a method which has become popular more recently.** It is a method of preparing consolidated accounts which may be regarded as appropriate in cases where a business combination is brought about without any significant outflow of funds from the group. This might happen, for example, where one company acquires shares in another company and issues its own shares as consideration for the purchase, rather than paying cash.

2.2 You should be clear in your mind that the term merger accounting refers to a method of preparing consolidated accounts. FRS 6 hardly mentions the problems of how to account for share acquisitions in the individual accounts of the acquiring company. This is a problem to which statutory provisions are relevant; we will discuss it later in this chapter.

Problem with acquisition method

2.3 The **main problem** with using the acquisition method **concerns the effect on the holding company's distributable profits**. Suppose that H Ltd acquires all the shares of S Ltd on day 1 and on day 2 S Ltd pays a dividend equal to the entire amount of its distributable profits. Using the conventional techniques of acquisition accounting described in earlier chapters, H Ltd would not credit the dividend received to its own profit and loss account, so as to increase its own distributable profits; instead, the dividend would be applied to reduce the cost of the investment in S Ltd. The profits available for distribution to members of H Ltd would be unchanged from what they were before the combination.

2.4 If the shares in S Ltd were purchased for cash, this might seem reasonable: cash has been paid out as well as received and so net assets have not increased. The amount of profits available to distribute to the original shareholders of H Ltd remains unchanged, being the distributable profits shown in H Ltd's own individual accounts. On this assumption, conventional acquisition accounting seems to achieve a fair result.

2.5 But what happens if the shareholders in S Ltd are **not bought out for cash**? This would be the case if H Ltd paid for the shares in S Ltd by, say, an issue of new shares in H Ltd. This would mean that members of S Ltd would exchange their shares in that company for a share of the newly-formed group. The **number of shareholders** of H Ltd would now be greatly **increased**. But using acquisition accounting there would be **no corresponding increase in the distributable profits** of H Ltd.

2.6 This **result can be avoided if merger accounting principles are used**. We will come later to the detailed criteria of the Companies Act 1985 and FRS 6, but broadly speaking a **business combination may be accounted for as a merger if payment for the shares acquired is by means of a share exchange; if payment is by cash, conventional acquisition accounting must be used.** An example will illustrate the differences between the two methods. We will show a combination where the purchase consideration is satisfied by means of a share exchange.

2.7 EXAMPLE: ACQUISITION V MERGER ACCOUNTING

John Smith and Fred Jones run electrical wholesaling businesses of identical size. Both businesses are incorporated as limited liability companies, the shareholders of which are Smith, Jones and their respective wives.

In 19X1, Smith and Jones decide to combine their businesses and for this purpose they form a new company Smith and Jones Ltd. It is agreed that the new company will acquire all of the shares of John Smith Ltd and Fred Jones Ltd, the consideration in each case being the issue of equal numbers of shares in the new company. The balance sheets of John Smith Ltd and Fred Jones Ltd as at 31 December 19X1 are set out below.

	John Smith Ltd	*Fred Jones Ltd*
	£'000	£'000
Net assets	100	100
Share capital	20	20
Profit and loss account	80	80
	100	100

The fair value of each business is considered to be £160,000.

2.8 SOLUTION

Using normal acquisition accounting principles, the balance sheet of Smith and Jones Ltd after the share transfers will be as follows.

	Smith and Jones Ltd
	£'000
Investment in John Smith Ltd	160
Investment in Fred Jones Ltd	160
	320
Share capital	40
Share premium	280
	320

The balance on the share premium account is the difference between the nominal value of the shares issued and the value of the assets acquired.

Assuming that the net assets of John Smith Ltd and Fred Jones Ltd are already stated at their fair value, the difference between the book value of the assets (£100,000 in each case) and the fair value of the business (£160,000 in each case) will be goodwill.

The consolidated balance sheet at the date of transfer will therefore be as follows.

	£'000
Goodwill arising on consolidation	120
Net assets	200
	320
Share capital	40
Share premium	280
	320

2.9 From the above, it can be seen that **the new company will have no distributable reserves at the date of the transfer.** Smith and Jones may well consider that this situation is highly unsatisfactory, as from their point of view there is no real change of ownership, merely a pooling of interests. Furthermore there has been no change in the underlying net assets, even though their balance sheet values have increased.

2.10   **It is in the kind of situation outlined above that merger accounting may be appropriate.** In merger accounting, the emphasis is on the continuity of the amalgamated businesses.

> **Exam focus point**
>
> The single most important feature of **merger accounting** is that when a holding company issues shares in consideration for the transfer to it of shares in another company, the shares issued are accounted for at their **nominal value only**. (Under **acquisition accounting** the shares must be accounted for at their **market value**.)

2.11   The other features of merger accounting are demonstrated in the example below.

If we apply merger accounting in the above example, the entry in the books of Smith and Jones Ltd will be:

		£'000	£'000
DEBIT	Investment in John Smith Ltd	20	
	Investment in Fred Jones Ltd	20	
CREDIT	Share capital		40

The investment in the subsidiaries is therefore recorded as the nominal value of the consideration given.

2.12   Under the merger method, the balance sheet of Smith and Jones Ltd would be:

	Smith & Jones Ltd
	£'000
Investment in John Smith Ltd	20
Investment in Fred Jones Ltd	20
	40
Share capital	40

Consolidation would involve cancellation of the 'investment in subsidiary' with the subsidiary's share capital and aggregation of the net assets. The resulting consolidated balance sheet would be:

	£'000
Net assets	200
Share capital	40
Profit and loss account	160
	200

2.13   A **comparison** of the merger balance sheet with the acquisition balance sheet will demonstrate the following features of merger accounting.

(a)   Assets can be recorded at their previous values, as there is no obligation to record them at fair value.

(b)   No share premium account will arise in the books of the holding company, as shares issued are recorded at their nominal value only.

(c)   A premium on acquisition will never arise under merger accounting.

(d)   Previously distributable reserves of the individual companies may remain distributable as there is no enforced freezing of pre-acquisition reserves.

(e)   It is simpler than acquisition accounting.

2.14 Point (a) above means that **a ROCE based on a merger balance sheet is usually higher than one based on an acquisition balance sheet.** This, together with point (d), has contributed greatly to the popularity enjoyed by merger accounting with US companies.

Exam focus point
If you are in a hurry or revising, go straight to paragraph 2.23.

2.15 In the UK, merger accounting was not introduced until the Companies Act 1985 removed the barrier imposed by the old s 56 CA 1948. This stated that when a company issued shares for a premium, a sum equal to the value of the premium should be transferred to a share premium account. This provision made merger accounting, in effect, illegal.

2.16 This illegality was emphasised by a legal case *Shearer v Bercain Ltd 1980*. In this case, as well as forcing the creation of a share premium account, the court held that pre-acquisition profits were not available for distribution as dividends to the shareholders of the holding company (under Sch 8, CA 1948).

2.17 The CA 1985 offers relief from creation of a share premium where the issuing company has secured at least 90% of all classes of equity shares in another company in pursuance of an arrangement providing for the allotment of equity shares in the issuing company in consideration for the issue or transfer to the issuing company of equity shares in the other company, or the cancellation of any such shares not held by the issuing company (s 131 CA 1985). This opened the door to merger accounting in the UK. The relief given was fairly wide and this was on the understanding that the accounting profession would produce a more restrictive standard on merger accounting soon after the CA 1981.

2.18 Before we look at FRS 6, which was published in September 1994, let us briefly examine the Companies Act requirements for merger accounting and the requirements of the old standard, which FRS 6 replaced, SSAP 23 *Accounting for acquisitions and mergers*.

Companies Act 1985 and SSAP 23

2.19 **CA 1985 lays down the following conditions for accounting for acquisition as a merger** (s 10 Sch 4A CA 1985).

(a) **At least 90%** of the nominal value of the 'relevant shares'* in the undertaking acquired must be held by the group.

(b) This must be achieved as a result of an arrangement providing for the **issue of equity shares** by the parent company (or one or more of its subsidiaries).

(c) The **fair value** of any consideration other than equity shares **must not exceed 10% of the nominal value** of the equity shares issued.

(d) Adoption of the merger method **must accord with generally accepted accounting principles** or standards.

*'Relevant shares' are 'those carrying unrestricted rights to participate both in distributions and in the assets of the undertaking upon liquidation': usually these will be equity shares.

2.20 These requirements were very similar to those in the old SSAP 23.

2.21 If any or all of these conditions were not met, the business combination was an acquisition and the principles of acquisition accounting, as stated in FRS 2, had to be applied. Even if all the conditions were met, SSAP 23 only said that merger accounting principles *may* be used. The investing company could still choose to use acquisition accounting.

2.22 If a business combination met all the criteria of SSAP 23 (and CA 1985), and if the holding company elected to use the merger method on consolidation, the **consequences** were as follows.

(a) It is **not necessary to adjust the carrying values** of the assets and liabilities of the subsidiary **to fair value** either in its own books or as a consolidation adjustment.

(b) Even if the subsidiary were acquired during the accounting period its **profit or loss should be included for the entire period, without any adjustment in respect of the part year preceding the merger**. Corresponding amounts should be presented as if the companies had been combined throughout the previous period and at the previous balance sheet date.

(c) The **difference between the carrying value** of the investment in the subsidiary **and the nominal value** of the shares acquired **should be treated as an addition to or deduction from reserves.**

In fact, these consequences - the mechanics of merger accounting - still apply, **only the conditions for merger accounting and related disclosure have been changed by FRS 6.**

2.23 You should be clear that the CA 1985 requirements still exist. However, **FRS 6 has tightened the requirements for merger accounting by concentrating on the spirit of the transaction**, rather than on mechanical aspects, such as levels of shareholding.

Criticisms of SSAP 23 on merger accounting

2.24 It was considered necessary to replace SSAP 23 because of the following criticisms.

(a) **Creation of instant earnings** by combining the results of the companies in both the year of merger and the corresponding year figures. This is no real criticism when a genuine merging of interests takes place as the same shareholders have interests in the same earnings both before and after the merger.

(b) **Creation of instant distributable reserves.** Again, this criticism is not valid as the same shareholders have the same access to the same reserves both before and after the merger.

(c) **Assets understated** as no fair value exercise is undertaken. However, this was the situation before the merger as well and there is no reason why a revaluation should not take place anyway.

(d) **Holding company profitability.** Dividends paid by the acquired company out of pre-acquisition profits could be credited to the holding company's profit and loss account, distorting profitability. These dividends, however, will be eliminated on consolidation and disclosure of such dividends by way of a note could clarify the situation.

(e) **Exceptional gains** can arise by selling off assets or investments owned by one of the combining companies. Any profit was mostly accrued pre merger as the assets were brought into the accounts at historic cost, and thus the operating profit of the group is distorted, particularly as FRS 3 would presumably treat such events as exceptional, where previously they would be treated as extraordinary.

2.25   The general criticism of the existing standard given by the ASB is:

> 'Inappropriate use of merger accounting to **enhance the acquiring group's earnings by including the results of the acquired company for the whole of the year** rather than just from the date of acquisition.'

2.26   The ASB saw FRS 6 as a remedy to this problem.

> 'FRS 6 restricts the use of merger accounting to very rare cases of mergers that cannot properly be viewed as the takeover of one company by another; all other business combinations must be accounted for by using acquisition accounting.'

> 'FRS 6 sets out disclosure requirements, for both acquisitions and mergers, to ensure that full explanation of the effect of the combination is disclosed in the financial statements. It also encourages further voluntary disclosure of the acquirer's intended expenditure on the acquired business.'

2.27   Let us now look at FRS 6 in more detail.

FRS 6 *Acquisitions and mergers*

2.28   In general terms **FRS 6 aims to prevent the use of merger accounting for anything other than 'true' mergers, where a partnership is formed, on an equal footing.** Where there is an identifiable 'acquirer', then acquisition accounting *must* be used.

Objective

2.29   The objective of FRS 6 is as follows.

> 'The objective of this FRS is to ensure that **merger accounting is used only for those business combinations that are not**, in substance, the **acquisition** of one entity by another **but** the formation of a new reporting entity as a substantially **equal partnership** where no party is dominant; to ensure the use of acquisition accounting for all other business combinations; and to ensure that in either case the financial statements provide relevant information concerning the effect of the combination.'

Definitions

2.30   The definitions given by the standard are as follows. Note that several definitions are repeated in FRS 7, which we looked at in Chapter 18.

'Acquisition
A business combination that is not a merger.

Business combination
The bringing together of separate entities into one economic entity as a result of one entity uniting with, or obtaining control over the net assets and operations of, another.

Equity shares
Shares other than non-equity shares.

Group reconstruction
Any of the following arrangements:

(a)   the transfer of a shareholding in a subsidiary undertaking from one group company to another;

(b)   the addition of a new parent company to a group;

(c)   the transfer of shares in one or more subsidiary undertakings of a group to a new company that is not a group company but whose shareholders are the same as those of the group's parent;

(d)   the combination into a group of two or more companies that before the combination had the same shareholders.

KEY TERM

Merger. A business combination that results in the creation of a new reporting entity formed from the combining parties, in which the shareholders of the combining entities come together in a partnership for the mutual sharing of the risks and benefits of the combined entity, and in which no party to the combination in substance obtains control over any other, or is otherwise seen to be dominant, whether by virtue of the proportion of its shareholders' rights in the combined entity, the influence of its directors or otherwise.

Non-equity shares
Shares possessing any of the following characteristics:

(a) any of the rights of the shares to receive payments (whether in respect of dividends, in respect of redemptions or otherwise) are for a limited amount that is not calculated by reference to the company's assets or profits or the dividends on any class of equity share;

(b) any of the rights to participate in a surplus in a winding up are limited to a specific amount that is not calculated by reference to the company's assets or profits and such limitation had a commercial effect in practice at the time the shares were issued or, if later, at the time the limitation was introduced.

(c) the shares are redeemable, either according to their terms or because the holder, or any party other than the issuer, can require their redemption.'

Scope

2.31 FRS 6 applies to:

'**all financial statements** that are intended to give a true and fair view of a reporting entity's financial position and profit or loss (or income and expenditure) for a period. Although the FRS is framed in terms of an entity becoming a subsidiary undertaking of a parent company that prepares consolidated financial statements, it also applies where an individual company or other reporting entity combines with a business other than a subsidiary undertaking.'

Use of merger accounting

Exam focus point
Merger accounting should be used when:

(a) the use of merger accounting is not prohibited by companies legislation; and
(b) the five specific criteria for a merger laid out in FRS 6 are satisfied by the combination.

2.32 The criteria for determining whether the definition of a merger is met are as follows. (Note that convertible share or loan stock should be regarded as equity to the extent that it is converted into equity *as a result of the business combination.*)

Criterion 1   Neither party is portrayed, by either its management or any other party, as either acquirer or acquired.

Criterion 2   All parties take part in setting up a management structure and selecting personnel for the combined entity on the basis of consensus rather than purely by exercise of voting rights.

Criterion 3   The relative sizes of the parties are not so disparate that one party dominates the combined entity by virtue of its relative size.

Criterion 4   A substantial part of the consideration for equity shareholdings in each party will comprise equity shares; conversely, non-equity shares or equity shares with reduced voting rights will comprise only an 'immaterial' part of the consideration. This criterion also covers existing shareholdings.

> 'Where one of the combining entities has, within the period of two years before the combination acquired shares in another of the combining entities, the consideration for this acquisition should be taken into account in determining whether this criterion has been met.'

Note that this criterion states in general terms what is laid out in the Companies Act 1985 in terms of specific shareholdings.

Criterion 5   No equity shareholders of any of the combining entities retains any material interest in the future performance of only part of the combined equity.

2.33   Note that, for the purpose of Criterion 4, the consideration should *not* include:

'(a)   an interest in a peripheral part of the business of the entity in which they were shareholders and which does not form part of the combined entity; or

(b)   the proceeds of the sale of such a business, or loan stock representing such proceeds.

A peripheral part of the business is one that can be disposed of without having a material effect on the nature and focus of the entity's operations.'

Group reconstructions, new parents etc

2.34   Despite the strict criteria which must be met before merger accounting can be used, FRS 6 does allow the use of merger accounting in various **other**, slightly unusual **situations**.

(a)   In **group reconstructions**, provided:

(i)   the use of merger accounting is not prohibited by companies legislation;

(ii)   the ultimate shareholders remain the same, and the rights of each such shareholders, relative to the others, are unchanged; and

(iii)   no minority's interest in the net assets of the group is altered by the transfer.

(b)   In **a combination effected by using a new parent company**, where a direct combination of the parties concerned would have met the FRS 6 criteria for merger accounting. If there *is* an 'acquirer', then the acquirer and new parent should first be combined using merger accounting, then other parties combined using acquisition accounting.

(c)   In **various structures of business combination** the FRS should be applied to other transactions which achieve the same results.

Merger accounting

2.35   The main accounting provisions of the merger method are listed by the FRS as follows.

(a)   **No fair value exercise** is required, but appropriate **adjustments to achieve uniformity of accounting policies** should be made.

(b)   In the group accounts in the year of merger, **results** should be shown **as if the entities had always been combined**, in both that year and the previous year as shown in the corresponding figures.

(c) **Differences** between the nominal value of the shares issued plus the fair value of any other consideration given, and the nominal value of any shares received in exchange should be **shown as a movement on other reserves** in the consolidated financial statements.

(d) Any **existing balance on the new subsidiary's share premium account** or capital redemption reserve should be **shown as a movement on other reserves**. The transactions in (c) and (d) should be shown in the reconciliation of movements in shareholders' funds.

(e) **Merger expenses** should be **charged to the profit and loss account** of the combined entity at the date of the merger (ie *not* as a movement on reserves) in accordance with FRS 3.

2.36 These provisions contrast directly with the requirements of acquisition accounting as we saw earlier.

3 FRS 6 DISCLOSURES

3.1 The disclosure requirements of FRS 6 are lengthy and substantial, but we will try to summarise them here.

Exam focus point
In December 1997, 4 marks were available to using merger accounting to prepare consolidated reserves

Acquisitions and mergers

3.2 The following information should be disclosed for both acquisitions and mergers **in the accounts of the acquirer** or issuing entity, for each combination in the period:

(a) The **names** of the combining entities (other than the reporting entity).
(b) Whether the combination has been accounted for as an **acquisitions or a merger**.
(c) The **date** of the combination.

Mergers

3.3 For each business combination (except group reconstructions) **in the accounts of the combined entity**:

(a) An **analysis** of the principal components of the **current year's profit and loss account and statement of total recognised gains and losses into:**

   (i) **Amounts relating to the merged entity for the period after the date of the merger.**

   (ii) For each party to the merger, amounts relating to that party **for the period up to the date of the merger.**

(b) An analysis between the parties to the merger of the principal components of the profit and loss account and statement of total recognised gains and losses **for the previous financial year**.

(c) The **composition and fair value of the consideration** given by the issuing company and its subsidiary undertakings.

(d) The **aggregate book value of the net assets** of each party to the merger at the **date of the merger.**

(e) The **nature and amount of significant accounting adjustments** made to the net assets of any party to the merger to achieve consistency of accounting policies and an explanation of any other significant adjustments made to the net assets of any party to the merger as a consequence of the merger.

(f) A statement of the **adjustments to consolidated reserves** resulting from the merger.

3.4 In the case of (a) and (b), at a *minimum* disclosure should be made of turnover, operating profit and exceptional items, split between continuing operations, discontinued operations and acquisitions; profit before taxation; taxation and minority interests; and extraordinary items.

Acquisitions

3.5 In relation to the consideration:

'The composition and fair value of the consideration given by the acquiring company and its subsidiary undertakings should be disclosed. The nature of any deferred or contingent purchase consideration should be stated, including, for contingent consideration, the range of possible outcomes and the principal factors that affect the outcome.'

3.6 We have already discussed the disclosure requirements relating to fair values and goodwill in Chapter 11 when we were looking at goodwill. This is a good opportunity for you to go back to that chapter, look at the disclosure requirements, and consider how FRS 6 interacts with FRS 10.

3.7 FRS 6 also interacts with FRS 3:

'As required by FRS 3, in the period of acquisition the post-acquisition results of the acquired entity should be shown as a component of continuing operations in the profit and loss account, other than those that are also discontinued in the same period; and where an acquisition has a material impact on a major business segment this should be disclosed and explained.'

You should go back to the section in Chapter 13 on FRS 3 and consider the impact FRS 6 has.

3.8 If it is not possible to determine the post-acquisition results to the end of the period of acquisition, an indication of the entity's contribution to turnover and operating results should be given; if not, the reason should be explained.

3.9 Also in relation to FRS 3:

'Any exceptional profit or loss in periods following the acquisition that is determined using the fair values recognised on acquisition should be disclosed in accordance with the requirements of FRS 3, and identified as relating to the acquisition.'

3.10 The FRS then makes it very clear that any **costs incurred post-acquisition** for **reorganising, restructuring and integrating the acquisition should be shown in the profit and loss account of that period (ie post acquisition).** Such costs are described as those that:

'(a) would not have been incurred had the acquisition not taken place; and

(b) relate to a project identified and controlled by management as part of a reorganisation or integration programme set up at the time of acquisition or as a direct consequence of an immediate post-acquisition review.'

In other words, such costs **cannot be treated as movements on reserves.**

3.11 The FRS also lays out disclosure requirements for movements on provisions and accruals made in relation to the acquisition, which should be:

'disclosed and analysed between the amounts used for the specific purpose for which they were created and the amounts released unused.'

3.12 The cash flow impact of the acquisition should be disclosed according to FRS 1 *Cash flow statements* (see Chapter 14).

3.13 Finally, for a material acquisition:

'the profit after taxation and minority interests of the acquired entity should be given for:

(a) the period from the beginning of the acquired entity's financial year to the date of acquisition, giving the date on which this period began; and

(b) its previous financial year.

Substantial acquisitions

3.14 Extra information should be disclosed for 'substantial acquisitions', which are defined as each business combination accounted for by using acquisition accounting where:

(a) For listed companies, the combination is a Class I or Super Class I transaction under the Stock Exchange Listing Rules (see below).

(b) For other entities, either:

(i) the net assets or operating profits of the acquired entity exceed 15% of those of the acquiring entity; or

(ii) the fair value of the consideration given exceeds 15% of the net assets of the acquiring entity.

and should also be made in other exceptional cases where an acquisition is of such significance that the disclosure is necessary in order to give a true and fair view.

3.15 The **extra information** requiring disclosure is a **summarised profit and loss account, and statement of total recognised gains and losses** of the acquired entity from the beginning of the period to the date of acquisition. The **profit after tax and minority interests for the acquired entity's previous financial year** should also be disclosed.

UITF Abstract 15 *Disclosure of substantial acquisitions*

3.16 In relation to Paragraph 3.13 (a) above, in August 1995 the Stock Exchange revised its Listing Rules and they no longer refer to Class 1 transactions.

3.17 The Stock Exchange Listing Rules classify transactions by assessing their size relative to that of the company proposing to make the transaction. It does this by ascertaining whether any of a number of ratios (eg the net assets of the target to the net assets of the offeror) exceeds a given percentage. Class 1 transactions used to be those where the percentage exceeded 15%. Super Class 1 are those where the percentage exceeds 25%. FRS 6 uses the 15% criterion for non-listed entities.

3.18 The UITF reached a consensus that, in order to retain the ASB's original intentions for FRS 6, the reference to Class 1 transactions should be interpreted as meaning those transactions in which any of the ratios set out in the London Stock Exchange Listing Rules defining Super Class 1 transactions exceeds 15%.

Exam focus point

FRS 6 and FRS 7 (which was published at the same time) represent a major revision of the principles and practices of merger and acquisition accounting. They are controversial and arguments are likely to be carried on in the financial and accountancy press for some time. You *must* go back to Chapters 16 and 18 to tie in the disclosure and other requirements of FRS 6 to FRS 2 *Accounting for subsidiary undertakings* and FRS 7 *Fair values in acquisition accounting*. **These three standards are interrelated and you should be able to discuss the relationships between them.**

Question 5

List the criteria for merger accounting given by FRS 6.

Answer

See Paragraph 2.33.

3.19 EXAMPLE: DISCLOSURE OF REORGANISATION COSTS

In an appendix at the end of the standard, the ASB lays out an illustrative example of the disclosure of reorganisation and integration costs. The explanatory part of the standard suggests that management may wish to include these in the notes to the financial statements. The example given below is optional; the best method will depend on individual circumstances.

COSTS OF REORGANISING AND INTEGRATING ACQUISITIONS

	Acquisition of European business (note (a)) £	Other acquisitions £	Total £
Announced but not charged as at the previous year	-	25	25
Announced in relation to acquisitions during the year	170	-	170
Adjustments to previous year's estimates	-	(5)	(5)
	170	20	190
Charged in the year:			
Operating profit	55	12	67
Elsewhere	65	-	65
	120	12	132
Announced but still to be charged at 31 December 1995	50	8	58

Note (a): Acquisition of European business

	£	£
Cost of acquisition		400
Reorganisation and integration expenditure announced		
Fundamental restructuring		
Withdrawal from existing US business and		
related redundancies	65	
Other items (to be charged to operating profit)		
Other redundancy costs	75	
Re branding and redesign costs	30	
Announced reorganisation and integration costs		
as shown in above table		170
Total investment		570

In addition to the £120 million expenditure shown in the above table, reorganisation and integration costs charged during the year include £30 million in respect of write-downs to fixed assets consequent on the closure of XYZ plant.

4   FURTHER PRACTICAL ISSUES

4.1   The Smith and Jones example in paragraph 2.7 above involved a share for share exchange where the nominal value of the shares issued was equal to the nominal value of the shares acquired. Where this is not the case, or where there is additional consideration in some form other than equity shares, the basic method needs some modification.

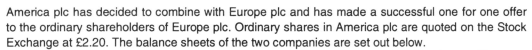

Question 6

America plc has decided to combine with Europe plc and has made a successful one for one offer to the ordinary shareholders of Europe plc. Ordinary shares in America plc are quoted on the Stock Exchange at £2.20. The balance sheets of the two companies are set out below.

	America plc £	Europe plc £
Fixed assets	2,800	2,400
Net current assets	1,400	800
	4,200	3,200
Ordinary shares of £1 each	3,000	2,000
Reserves (realised)	1,200	1,200
	4,200	3,200

Required

Prepare a consolidated balance sheet on a merger basis for America plc:

(a)   using the information given above;

(b)   assuming that the offer had been 3 shares in America plc for every 2 shares in Europe plc;

(c)   assuming that the offer had been 1 share in America plc for every 2 shares in Europe plc;

(d)   assuming that America plc had paid 25p per share for Europe plc as well as giving a one for one share exchange.

Answer

The investment in Europe plc shown in the accounts of America plc will be as follows.

Under (a)	£2,000
Under (b)	£3,000
Under (c)	£1,000
Under (d) (£2,000 + £500)	£2,500

CONSOLIDATED BALANCE SHEETS

	(a)	(b)	(c)	(d)
	£	£	£	£
Fixed assets	5,200	5,200	5,200	5,200
Net current assets	2,200	2,200	2,200	1,700
	7,400	7,400	7,400	6,900
Ordinary shares of £1 each	5,000	6,000	4,000	5,000
Unrealised reserve	-	-	1,000	-
Realised reserves	2,400	1,400	2,400	1,900
	7,400	7,400	7,400	6,900

The balance sheet in (a) shows no change in the total realised reserves. This is because the nominal value of the shares acquired exactly matches the nominal value of the shares issued.

The balance sheet in (b) reflects the fact that America plc has issued 3,000 shares, whose nominal value is £1,000 more than the nominal value of the shares taken over. The difference is deducted from realised reserves, since the group has no unrealised reserves.

The balance sheet in (c) includes an unrealised reserve, created because the nominal value of the shares issued is £1,000 less than the nominal value of the shares acquired.

The (d) balance sheet shows net current assets reduced by £500, the amount of cash paid. The difference between America's investment in subsidiary (£2,500) and the nominal value of the shares acquired (£2,000) is again deducted from realised reserves on consolidation.

4.2 It should be obvious from the above that the **total net assets figure never changes** (unless part of the consideration is cash). **Under merger accounting consolidated reserves become in effect a balancing figure.**

Profit and loss account

4.3 Interest in merger accounting generally focuses on the balance sheet. The **profit and loss account aspect** is really **extremely simple**: it involves **aggregation** of the individual company's figures, with **normal consolidation adjustments but no attempt to distinguish between pre- and post-merger profits in the year of merger**. All comparatives are restated as though the companies had always been merged. Note the FRS 3 effects in Section 2.

Minority interest

4.4 Any minority interest (which will never exceed ten per cent under CA 1985, and under FRS 6 will be *very* rare) **is accounted for in the usual way**, namely:

(a) The minority interest in the subsidiary's shareholders' funds is a deferred liability.

(b) Their share of any proposed dividend is a current liability.

(c) Their share of the subsidiary's profits after tax is deducted in the consolidated profit and loss account.

Merger relief

4.5 Although this section of the text is concerned with group accounts it is worthwhile to consider here the way in which a holding company records a share acquisition in its own individual accounts. We are mainly concerned with s 131 CA 1985.

4.6 S 131 CA 1985 provides that **no share premium** account need be created **on an issue of shares provided that:**

(a) **the shares are issued as part of an arrangement to acquire shares in another company**; and

(b) **the investing company, after the issue, has managed to secure at least 90% of the equity shares in the other company.** Any shares held by the investing company prior to the new issue may be counted towards the 90% but the relief under s 131 will *only* apply to the shares issued as part of the arrangement.

4.7 The exemption granted by s 131 is often referred to as **merger relief.** This is not the same as merger accounting. You should be clear in your mind that the statutory provisions relate to the recording of a share issue in the **individual accounts** of an investing company **not consolidated accounts.**

4.8 A company taking advantage of merger relief has **a choice of accounting methods when recording the share issue for purposes of its own** (not its consolidated) accounts. Assuming an issue of shares with a nominal value of £50,000 and a market value of £220,000, the choices are as follows.

(a) DEBIT Investment in subsidiary   £50,000
    CREDIT Ordinary share capital   £50,000

This method has the disadvantage that it disguises the true value of the investment acquired. The individual balance sheet will be misleading.

(b) DEBIT Investment in subsidiary   £220,000
    CREDIT Ordinary share capital   £50,000
            Share premium account   £170,000

This is a most unlikely option in practice. To show a more realistic balance sheet, the company foregoes the relief available under s 131 and creates an unwelcome share premium account.

(c) DEBIT Investment in subsidiary   £220,000
    CREDIT Ordinary share capital   £50,000
            Merger reserve   £170,000

This is perhaps the most likely choice. To record the investment at its 'true' cost, the company shows the share issue at its market value by setting up a reserve account; but the restrictions attaching to a share premium account are avoided by labelling the reserve a 'merger reserve'.

4.9 The method chosen from these three options will not affect the decision on the method of consolidation to be adopted. That decision must be taken in the light of the CA 1985 and FRS 6 criteria.

Question 7

You are given the following information.

(a) On 30 June 19X7 Stepney plc obtained acceptance by 100% of the ordinary shareholders of Brennan plc of its offer of one new ordinary share in Stepney plc for every one ordinary share in Brennan plc. The offer was also declared unconditional on 30 June 19X7 and arrangements were made for the share exchange to take place within the next few days. On 30 June 19X7 the ordinary shares of Stepney plc had a market value of £8.50 each. The newly-formed group became known as the Stepney Group plc.

(b) It may be assumed that profits before extraordinary items of both companies accrue evenly over the year. The extraordinary charge in the accounts of Stepney plc relates to an event occurring in March 19X7.

(c) Stepney plc uses the average cost method of stock valuation while Brennan plc has used the FIFO method in preparing its 19X7 financial statements. The directors of the new group have agreed to standardise accounting practice by using average cost throughout the group. This change would have affected Brennan plc's stock values as shown below.

Stock values (Brennan plc)	FIFO basis £'000	Average cost basis £'000
Stock (31 December 19X6)	2,748	2,528
Stock (31 December 19X7)	3,826	3,014

(d) SUMMARISED BALANCE SHEETS AT 31 DECEMBER 19X7

	Stepney plc £'000	Brennan plc £'000
Fixed assets	61,376	24,299
Investment in Brennan plc	2,000	-
Current assets	22,685	8,623
	86,061	32,922
Current liabilities	12,472	5,461
Ordinary share capital	15,000 *	1,000 **
Retained profits	58,589	26,461
	86,061	32,922

* called-up share capital in ordinary shares of £1.00 each
** called-up share capital in ordinary shares of £0.50 each.

(e) SUMMARISED PROFIT AND LOSS ACCOUNTS
FOR THE YEAR ENDED 31 DECEMBER 19X7

	Stepney plc £'000	Brennan plc £'000
Turnover	41,456	15,396
Cost of sales	18,221	5,492
Gross profit	23,235	9,904
Administration expenses	2,694	1,063
Selling and distribution costs	4,143	1,824
Profit on ordinary activities before taxation	16,398	7,017
Taxation	5,240	2,076
Profit on ordinary activities after taxation	11,158	4,941
Extraordinary items less taxation	2,616	-
	8,542	4,941
Dividend	2,000	-
Retained profit for year	6,542	4,941
Retained profits at 1 January 19X7	52,047	21,520
Retained profits at 31 December 19X7	58,589	26,461

You are required to prepare, on a merger accounting basis, the consolidated balance sheet at 31 December 19X7 and the consolidated profit and loss account for the year ended 31 December 19X7 of the Stepney Group plc. Assume that the merger requirements of FRS 6 have been met.

Answer

STEPNEY PLC
CONSOLIDATED BALANCE SHEET AS AT 31 DECEMBER 19X7

	£'000	£'000
Fixed assets		85,675
Current assets (W1)	30,496	
Current liabilities	17,933	
Net current assets		12,563
Total assets less current liabilities		98,238
Capital and reserves		
Share capital		15,000
Profit and loss account		83,238
		98,238

CONSOLIDATED PROFIT AND LOSS ACCOUNT
FOR THE YEAR ENDED 31 DECEMBER 19X7

	£'000	£'000
Turnover		56,852
Cost of sales (W3)		24,305
Gross profit		32,547
Distribution costs		5,967
Administrative expenses		3,757
Profit on ordinary activities before taxation		22,823
Tax on profit on ordinary activities		7,316
Profit on ordinary activities after taxation		15,507
Extraordinary losses		2,616
Profit for the financial year		12,891
Dividend		2,000
		10,891
Merger adjustment (W2)		(1,000)
Retained profit for the financial year		9,891
Retained profits brought forward		
As previously reported (52,047 + 21,520)	73,567	
Prior year adjustment (2,748 - 2,528)	(220)	
As restated		73,347
Retained profits carried forward		83,238

Workings

1   *Current assets*

	£'000	£'000
Stepney		22,685
Brennan		8,623
		31,308
Adjustment in respect of Brennan's closing stock		
FIFO cost	3,826	
Average cost	3,014	
		(812)
		30,496

2   *Merger adjustment*

	£'000
Nominal value of shares issued by Stepney	2,000
Nominal value of shares acquired by Stepney	1,000
Difference to be deducted from group reserves	1,000

3   *Cost of sales*

	£'000	£'000
Stepney		18,221
Brennan		
Unadjusted	5,492	
Adjustment in respect of stock valuation		
(3,826 - 3,014) - (2,748 - 2,528)	592	
		6,084
		24,305

Chapter roundup

- This chapter has explained how to prepare a **consolidated profit and loss account** by combining the profit and loss accounts of each group company.

- **Adjustments** must be made:

  o to reduce turnover by the amount of any **intra-group trading**, and to deduct from consolidated gross profit any unrealised profit on stocks thus acquired which are held at the year end. Cost of sales will be the balancing figure;

  o to reduce stock values by the amount of any **unrealised profit** on intra-group trading;

  o to calculate the **minority interest** in subsidiary companies' results for the year;

  o to account for **intra-group dividends**;

  o to **eliminate pre-acquisition** profits.

- **Merger accounting** is a very topical issue. Make sure you know the **criteria** for merger accounting under **FRS 6** and CA 1985 and that you can discuss the differences in approach and the criticisms of merger accounting.

- Make sure also that you can clearly **differentiate acquisitions from mergers** and that you can prepare accounts using both acquisition and merger accounting.

- You should also be able to explain s 131 CA 1985 (**merger relief**) and distinguish it *clearly* from merger accounting.

- FRS 6 represents a major step in **restricting** the practice of businesses who use merger accounting in non-merger situations and therefore distort the true picture of their affairs. The controversy surrounding the standard is bound to continue for some time.

Quick quiz

1   Describe the preparation of a consolidated profit and loss account in its simplest form. (see para 1.1)

2   At what stage in the consolidated profit and loss account does the figure for minority interests appear? (1.4)

3   What adjustments are made to the consolidated profit and loss account in respect of inter-company trading? (1.8)

4   What dispensation is granted to a parent company by s 230 CA 1985? (1.22)

5   Describe the make-up of the figure for directors' emoluments in a consolidated profit and loss account. (1.24)

6   When can a business combination be treated as a merger under CA 1985? (2.19)

7   What were the main criticisms of merger accounting? (2.24)

8   How does FRS 6 define a merger? (2.30)

9   When should merger accounting be used? (2.32)

10   List the five criteria for merger accounting given by FRS 6. (2.33)

11   When can merger accounting be used in a group reconstruction? (2.34)

12   List the disclosure requirements for each business combination in a merger. (3.2)

13   What is a substantial acquisition? (3.13)

14   How is a minority dealt with in merger accounting? (4.4)

15   Which section of CA 1985 deals with merger relief? (4.5) and what is it? (4.8)

Question to try	Level	Marks	Time
20	Full exam	25	45 mins

Chapter 20

ASSOCIATES AND JOINT VENTURES

Chapter topic list	Syllabus reference
1 Background	2(c)
2 FRS 9 *Associates and joint ventures*	2(c)
3 Associates	2(c)
4 Incorporated joint ventures and joint arrangements	2(c)
5 Disclosures for associates and joint ventures	2(c)

Introduction

Some investments which do not satisfy the criteria for classification as subsidiaries may nevertheless be much more than trade investments. The most important of these are associates and joint ventures which are the subject of this chapter and of one of the ASB's recent standards FRS 9 *Associates and joint ventures.*

1   BACKGROUND

1.1   In the 1960s it became increasingly common for companies to trade through companies in which a **substantial but not a controlling interest** was held. Traditionally such companies were accounted for in the same way as trade investments. In other words the income from associated companies was only included in the investing company's accounts to the extent of the dividends received and receivable up to its balance sheet date. However, it was felt that this treatment did not reflect the reality of the investment, not least because the investor could in many cases influence the investee's dividend policy. The need thus arose for an **intermediate form of accounting for those investments which lie between full subsidiary and trade investment status**.

Equity accounting, Companies Act 1985 and SSAP 1

1.2   The intermediate form of accounting developed for this purpose is known as **equity accounting.** The full, up-to-date (FRS 9) definition of equity accounting will be given later in this chapter. For now, think of it as follows.

> ### KEY TERM
>
> **Equity accounting** is a modified form of consolidation of the results and assets of the investee where the investor has exercise significant influence but not control. Rather than full, line by line consolidation, it involves incorporating the investor's share of the profit/loss and assets of the investee **in one line** in the investor's profit and loss account and balance sheet.

1.3   Equity accounting was first recognised in UK accounting literature in SSAP 1 *Accounting for associated companies*. **Parent companies are also required by law to use equity accounting to account for holdings in associated undertakings, defined as follows.**

> **KEY TERM**
>
> 'An "**associated undertaking**" means an undertaking in which an undertaking included in the consolidation has a participating interest and over whose operating and financial policy it exercises a significant influence, and which is not:
>
> (a)   a subsidiary undertaking of the parent company; or
>
> (b)   a joint venture'. (s 20(1) Sch 4A, CA 1985)
>
> 'Where an undertaking holds 20% or more of the voting rights in another undertaking, it shall be presumed to exercise such an influence over it unless the contrary is shown.'
>
> (s 20(2) Sch 4A, CA 1985)

1.4   **Participating interests** which are not in associated undertakings have to be disclosed separately from other investments but do not have to be accounted for by the equity method.

1.5   **Holdings in associated companies** (only one form of undertaking) **already had to be equity accounted in order to comply with SSAP 1.**

1.6   SSAP 1 *Accounting for associated companies* required that X Ltd should adopt equity accounting principles if its investment in Y Ltd was such that Y Ltd had the status of an associated company. SSAP 1 said that Y Ltd would be considered as an associated company if X Ltd was able to exercise significant influence over its financial and operating policy decisions (including dividend policy). If X Ltd held **20% or more** of Y Ltd's equity shares it was to be **assumed that significant influence was present** and consequently Y Ltd would be regarded as an associate company. But the key point was the presence or absence of significant influence: the 20% criterion was only a guideline.

1.7   When applying the 20% test, holdings of the holding company and subsidiaries were aggregated but holdings via another associated company were excluded.

1.8   For practical purposes, the CA 85 and SSAP 1 definitions had the same effect. Both **SSAP 1 and the CA 85 require the use of equity accounting for associates in consolidated accounts but do not permit it in the parent's accounts.** Instead the holding is treated as an investment and disclosed as a participating interest.

Revision and criticisms of SSAP 1

1.9   SSAP 1 was first issued in 1971 and revised in 1982. The ASB decided to carry out a full review of SSAP 1 for the following reasons.

(a)   The SSAP **did not deal with** identifying or accounting for **joint ventures.**

(b)   The SSAP encouraged but **did not require additional disclosures** where significant interests were included by equity accounting. There was little evidence of additional disclosures being made.

(c)   The **definition** of associated company **was interpreted too literally,** being applied to the form of a reporting entity's interests (eg 20% or more) rather than the substance.

1.10   In March 1996 the ASB issued FRED 11 *Associates and joint ventures* containing proposals developed in the light of comments on its earlier Discussion Paper (July 1994) to revise SSAP 1. The proposals in FRED 11 were generally well received and were carried forward with some modification into FRS 9 *Associates and joint ventures*.

2   FRS 9 ASSOCIATES AND JOINT VENTURES

2.1   FRS 9 *Associates and joint ventures* was issued in November 1997. It sets out the definition and accounting treatments for associates and joint ventures, two types of interests that a reporting entity may have in other entities. The FRS also deals with joint arrangements that are not entities. The definitions and treatments prescribed have been developed to be consistent with the Accounting Standards Board's approach to accounting for subsidiaries (dealt with in FRS 2 *Accounting for subsidiary undertakings*). The requirements are consistent with companies legislation.

Objective

2.2   The objective of FRS 9 is **to reflect the effect on an investor's financial position and performance of** its interest in two special kinds of investments - **associates and joint ventures**. The investor is partly accountable for the activities of these investments because of the closeness of its involvement.

(a)   It is closely involved in **associates** as a result of its **participating interest** and **significant influence**.

(b)   Its close involvement with **joint ventures** arises as a result of its **long-term interest** and **joint control**.

2.3   The FRS **also deals with joint arrangements that do not qualify as associates or joint ventures because they are not entities.**

Scope

2.4   The FRS applies to all financial statements intending to give a true and fair view. It is **not yet required for those smaller entities adopting the Financial Reporting Standard for Smaller Entities** and preparing consolidated financial statements. However, it is envisaged that a future revision to the FRSSE will require such entities to adopt the FRS. The FRS is effective in respect of financial statements of accounting periods ending on or after 23 June 1998.

Exam focus point

- At this stage, read through the summary and example **for overview only**. Do not expect to understand everything you read.

- **At the end of the chapter**, when you have worked through the detailed sections on associates and joint ventures, **come back to this section to put it in context.**

- When you come to **revise**, look at this section as it contains a clear summary of the requirements of the FRS.

Summary

2.5   The table below, taken from the FRS, describes the **different sorts of interest that a reporting entity may have in other entities or arrangements**. The sections marked with an asterisk (*) are covered by the FRS. The defining relationships described in the table form the basis for the definitions used in the FRS.

Entity/ arrangement	*Nature of relationship*	*Description of the defining relationship - the full definitions are given in the FRS*
Subsidiary	Investor controls its investee	Control is the ability of an entity to direct the operating and financial policies of another entity with a view to gaining economic benefits from its activities. To have control an entity must have both: (a) the ability to deploy the economic resources of the investee or to direct it; and (b) the ability to ensure that any resulting benefits accrue to itself (with corresponding exposure to losses) and to restrict the access of others to those benefits.
* Joint arrangement that is not an entity	Entities participate in an arrangement to carry on part of their own trades or businesses	A joint arrangement, whether or not subject to joint control, does not constitute an entity unless it carries on a trade or business of its own.
* Joint venture	Investor holds a long-term interest and shares control under a contractual arrangement	The joint venture agreement can override the rights normally conferred by ownership interests with the effect that: • acting together, the venturers can control the venture and there are procedures for such joint action • each venturer has (implicitly or explicitly) a veto over strategic policy decisions. There is usually a procedure for settling disputes between venturers and, possibly, for terminating the joint venture.
* Associate	Investor holds a participating interest and exercises significant influence	The investor has a long-term interest and is actively involved, and influential, in the direction of its investee through its participation in policy decisions covering the aspects of policy relevant to the investor, including decisions on strategic issues such as: (i) the expansion or contraction of the business, participation in other entities or changes in products, markets and activities of its investee; and (ii) determining the balance between dividend and reinvestment.
Simple investment		The investor's interest does not quality the investee as an associate, a joint venture or a subsidiary because the investor has limited influence or its interest is not long-term.

2.6   The table below, also taken from the FRS, sets out the **treatments in consolidated financial statements** for the different interests that a reporting entity may have in other entities and for joint arrangements that are not entities - the sections marked with an asterisk (*) are covered by the FRS.

Type of investment	Treatment in consolidated financial statements
Subsidiaries	The investor should consolidate the assets, liabilities, results and cash flows of its subsidiaries.
* Joint arrangements that are not entities	Each party should account for its own share of the assets, liabilities and cash flows in the joint arrangement, measured according to the terms of that arrangement, for example pro rata to their respective interests.
Joint ventures	The venturer should use the gross equity method showing in addition to the amounts included under the equity method, on the face on the balance sheet, the venturer's share of the gross assets and liabilities of its joint ventures, and, in the profit and loss account, the venturer's share of their turnover distinguished from that of the group. Where the venturer conducts a major part of its business through joint ventures, it may show fuller information provided all amounts are distinguished from those of the group.
Associates	The investor should include its associates in its consolidated financial statements using the equity method. In the investor's consolidated profit and loss account the investor's share of its associates' operating results should be included immediately after group operating results. From the level of profit before tax, the investor's share of the relevant amounts for associates should be included within the amounts for the group. In the consolidated statement of total recognised gains and losses the investor's share of the total recognised gains and losses of its associates should be included, shown separately under each heading, if material. In the balance sheet the investor's share of the net assets of its associates should be included and separately disclosed. The cash flow statement should include the cash flows between the investor and its associates. Goodwill arising on the investor's acquisition of its associates, less any amortisation or write-down, should be included in the carrying amount for the associates but should be disclosed separately. In the profit and loss account the amortisation or write-down of such goodwill should be separately disclosed as part of the investor's share of its associates' results.
Simple investments	The investor includes its interests as investments at either cost or valuation.

2.7   EXAMPLE: CONSOLIDATED FINANCIAL STATEMENTS

The following example of consolidated financial statements is taken from Appendix IV of FRS 9. Study it for an overview and come back to it when you have finished the chapter.

2.8   The format is illustrative only. The amounts shown for 'Associates' and 'joint ventures' are subdivisions of the item for which the statutory prescribed heading is 'Income from interests in associated undertakings'. The subdivisions may be shown in a note rather than on the face of the profit and loss account.

CONSOLIDATED PROFIT AND LOSS ACCOUNT

	£m	£m
Turnover: group and share of joint ventures	320	
Less: share of joint ventures' turnover	(120)	
Group turnover		200
Cost of sales		(120)
Gross profit		80
Administrative expenses		(40)
Group operating profit		40
Share of operating profit in		
Joint ventures	30	
Associates	24	
		54
		94
Interest receivable (group)		6
Interest payable		
Group	(26)	
Joint ventures	(10)	
Associates	(12)	
		(48)
Profit on ordinary activities before tax		52
Tax on profit on ordinary activities ★		(12)
Profit on ordinary activities after tax		40
Minority interests		(6)
Profit on ordinary activities after taxation and minority interest		34
Equity dividends		(10)
Retained profit for group and its share of associates and joint ventures		24

★Tax relates to the following:	Parent and subsidiaries	(5)
	Joint ventures	(5)
	Associates	(2)

CONSOLIDATED BALANCE SHEET

	£m	£m	£m
Fixed assets			
Tangible assets		480	
Investments			
Investments in joint ventures:			
Share of gross assets	130		
Share of gross liabilities	(80)		
		50	
Investments in associates		20	
			550
Current assets			
Stock		15	
Debtors		75	
Cash at bank and in hand		10	
		100	
Creditors (due within one year)		(50)	
Net current assets			50
Total assets less current liabilities			600
Creditors (due after more than one year)			(250)
Provisions for liabilities and charges			(10)
Equity minority interest			(40)
			300
Capital and reserves			
Called up share capital			50
Share premium account			150
Profit and loss account			100
Shareholders' funds (all equity)			300

Notes

In the example, there is no individual associate or joint venture that accounts for more than 25 per cent of any of the following for the investor group (excluding any amount for associates and joint ventures).

- Gross assets
- Gross liabilities
- Turnover
- Operating results (on a three-year average)

Additional disclosures for joint ventures (which in aggregate exceed the 15 per cent threshold)

	£m	£m
Share of assets		
Share of fixed assets	100	
Share of current assets	30	
		130
Share of liabilities		
Liabilities due within one year or less	(10)	
Liabilities due after more than one year	(70)	
		(80)
Share of net assets		50

Additional disclosures for associates (which in aggregate exceed the 15 per cent threshold)

	£m	£m
Share of turnover of associates		90
Share of assets		
Share of fixed assets	4	
Share of current assets	28	
		32
Share of liabilities		
Liabilities due within one year or less	(3)	
Liabilities due after more than one year	(9)	
		(12)
Share of net assets		20

3   ASSOCIATES

3.1   Associated undertakings **should be included** by an entity **in its consolidated financial statements using the equity method. In the investor's individual statements,** the interest in associates is **shown as a fixed asset investment,** at cost (less any amounts written off) or valuation.

3.2   The most important definitions relate to the **identification** of associates.

> **KEY TERMS**
>
> - **Associate:** an entity (other than a subsidiary) in which another entity (the investor) has a participating interest and over whose operating and financial policies the investor exercises a significant influence.
>
> - **Control** the ability of an entity to direct the operating and financial policies of another entity with a view to gaining economic benefits from its activities.
>
> - **Entity:** a body corporate, a partnership or an unincorporated association carrying on a trade or business with or without a view to profit.   *(FRS 9)*

Participating interest

3.3   FRS 9 defines 'participating interest' in the same way as FRS 2.

> **KEY TERM**
>
> **Participating interest:** an interest held in the shares of another entity on a long-term basis for the purpose of securing a contribution to the investor's activities by the exercise of control or influence arising from or related to that interest.   *(FRS 9)*

3.4   The investor's interest must be **beneficial,** the benefits linked to the exercise of significant influence. An interest convertible to an interest in shares and an option to acquire shares also qualify.

3.5   A participating interest is a **continuing relationship** and the interest does not cease only because the investor sells its interest in the associate.

Long-term interest

3.6   This definition relates to a participating interest.

> **KEY TERM**
>
> **Interest held on a long-term basis:** an interest that is held other than exclusively with a view to subsequent resale. An interest held exclusively with a view to subsequent resale is:
>
> - an interest for which a purchaser has been identified or is being sought, and which is reasonably expected to be disposed or within approximately one year of its date of acquisition; or
>
> - an interest that was acquired as a result of the enforcement of a security, unless the interest has become part of the continuing activities of the group or the holder acts as if it intends the interest to become so.   *(FRS 9)*

3.7   This definition is extremely important and it tightens the definition in SSAP 1.

> **KEY TERM**
>
> **Exercise of significant influence:** the exercise of a degree of influence by an investor over the operating and financial policies of its investee that results in the following conditions being fulfilled.
>
> (a)   The investor is actively involved and is influential in the direction of its investee through its participation in policy decisions covering all aspects of policy relevant to the investor, including decisions on strategic issues such as:
>
>   (i)   the expansion or contraction of the business, participation in other entities, changes in products, markets and activities of its investee; and
>
>   (ii)   determining the balance between dividend and reinvestment.
>
> (b)   Over time, the investee generally implements policies that are consistent with the strategy of the investor and avoids implementing policies that are contrary to the investor's interests.   *(FRS 9)*

3.8   Significant influence is **usually wielded through nomination to the board of directors,** although it may be achieved in other ways. It presupposes an agreement (formal or informal) between the investor and investee.

3.9   **The 20% rule given in SSAP 1 is followed here,** so that a holding of 20% or more of the voting rights suggests (but does not guarantee) that the investor exercises significant influence. At 20% the presumption of the exercise of significant influence can be rebutted if the criteria above are not fulfilled. The holdings of both parent and subsidiaries in the entity should be taken into account.

Accounting for associates

3.10   Following FRS 9, a reporting entity that prepares **consolidated financial statements** should include its associates in those statements using the **equity method in all the primary statements.** In the investor's **individual financial statements**, its interests in associates should be treated as **fixed asset investments** and shown either **at cost less any amounts written off or at valuation.**

3.11   The equity method is discussed here in more detail with regard to each of the primary statements.

Consolidated profit and loss account

3.12   FRS 9 stipulates the following.

     (a)   The investor's **share of its associates' operating results** should be **included immediately after group operating result** (but after the investor's share of the results of its joint ventures, if any).

     (b)   Any **amortisation** or write-down **of goodwill** arising on acquiring the associates should be **charged** at this point **and disclosed.**

     (c)   The **investor's share of any exceptional items** included after operating profit (paragraph 20 of FRS 3) or of interest should be **shown separately** from the amounts for the group.

     (d)   **At and below the level of profit before tax,** the **investor's share** of the relevant amounts for associates should be **included within the amounts for the group,** although for items **below this level,** such as taxation, the **amounts relating to associates should be disclosed.**

     (e)   Where it is helpful to give an indication of the size of the business as a whole, a total combining the investor's share of its associates' turnover with **group turnover may be shown as a memorandum item** in the profit and loss account **but** the investor's share of its **associates' turnover should be clearly distinguished** from group turnover.

     (f)   Similarly, the **segmental analysis of turnover and operating profit** (if given) should clearly **distinguish between** that of the **group and** that of **associates.**

Consolidated balance sheet

3.13   FRS 9 requires the following.

     (a)   The investor's **consolidated balance sheet should include as a fixed asset investment the investor's share of the net assets of its associates** shown as a separate item.

(b) **Goodwill** arising on the investor's acquisition of its associates, less any amortisation or write-down, should be **included in the carrying amount for the associates but should be disclosed separately**.

Consolidated cash flow statement

3.14 Cash flow statements are covered in Chapter 19. FRS 9 amends the revised version of FRS 1 to reflect the following.

(a) The consolidated cash flow statement should include **dividends received from associates as a separate item** between operating activities and returns on investments and servicing of finance.

(b) Any other cash flows between the investor and its associates should be included under the appropriate cash flow heading for the activity giving rise to the cash flow. None of the other cash flows of the associates should be included.

Consolidated statement of total recognised gains and losses

3.15 The statement of total recognised gains and losses is discussed in Chapter 10 which deals with FRS 3. FRS 9 requires the **investor's share of the total recognised gains and losses of its associates to be included**. If the amounts included are material they should be shown separately under each heading, either in the statement or in a note that is referred to in the statement.

3.16 EXAMPLE: ASSOCIATED COMPANY IN INVESTOR'S OWN ACCOUNTS

H Ltd, a company with subsidiaries, acquires 25,000 of the 100,000 £1 ordinary shares in A Ltd for £60,000 on 1 January 19X0. A Ltd meets the FRS 9 definitions of an associate. In the year to 31 December 19X0, A Ltd earns profits after tax of £24,000, from which it declares a dividend of £6,000.

How will A Ltd's results be accounted for in the individual and consolidated accounts of H Ltd for the year ended 31 December 19X0?

3.17 SOLUTION

In the individual accounts of H Ltd, the investment will be recorded on 1 January 19X0 at cost. Unless there is a permanent diminution in the value of the investment, this amount will remain in the individual balance sheet of H Ltd permanently. The only entry in H Ltd's individual profit and loss account will be to record dividends received. For the year ended 31 December 19X0, H Ltd will:

DEBIT	Cash	£1,500	
CREDIT	Income from shares in associated companies		£1,500

Consolidated profit and loss account

3.18 A consolidation schedule may be used to prepare the consolidated profit and loss account of a group with associates. The treatment of the associate's profits in the following example should be studied carefully.

3.19 EXAMPLE: ASSOCIATE COMPANY IN CONSOLIDATED ACCOUNTS

The following consolidation schedule relates to the H Ltd group, consisting of the holding company, an 80% owned subsidiary (S Ltd) and an associate (A Ltd) in which the group has a 30% interest.

CONSOLIDATION SCHEDULE

	Group £'000	H Ltd £'000	S Ltd £'000		A Ltd £'000
Turnover	1,400	600	800		300
Cost of sales	770	370	400		120
Gross profit	630	230	400		180
Distribution costs and administrative expenses (including depreciation, directors' emoluments etc)	290	110	180		80
Group operating profit	340	120	220		100
Share of operating profit in associate	30	-	-	30%	30
	370	120	220		30
Interest receivable (group)	30	30	-		-
	400	150	220		30
Interest payable (group)	(20)	-	(20)		-
Profit on ordinary activities before tax	380	150	200		30
Taxation					
H Ltd	(150)	(60)	(90)		
Associate	(12)	-	-		(12)
Profit after taxation	218	90	110		18
Minority interest	(22)		(22)		
	196	90	88		18
Inter-company dividends	-	20	(18)		(2)
Group profit	196	110	70		16
Dividends paid and proposed	(45)	(45)	-		-
Retained profits for the financial year	151	65	70		16
Retained profits brought forward	45	30	10		5
Retained profits carried forward	196	95	80		21

Notes

(a) **Group turnover, group gross profit and costs** such as depreciation etc **exclude** the turnover, gross profit and costs etc of **associates**.

(b) The **group share of the associate's operating profit is credited** to the group profit and loss account (here, 30% of £100,000 = £30,000). If the associated company has been acquired during the year, it would be necessary to deduct the pre-acquisition profits.

(c) **Taxation** consists of:

   (i)   Taxation **on the holding company and subsidiaries in total.**

   (ii) Only the **group's share of the tax charge of the associated company**; A Ltd tax would be £40,000, so that the group share is £40,000 × 30% = £12,000.

(d) The **minority interest will only ever apply to subsidiary companies.**

(e) **Inter-company dividends** from subsidiaries and associated companies **should all be recorded**.

(f) **Dividends** paid and proposed **relate to the holding company only.**

Pro-forma consolidated profit and loss account

3.20   The following is a **suggested layout** (using the figures given in the illustration above) for a profit and loss account for a company having subsidiaries as well as associates. It follows the FRS 9 example given in Section 2 of this chapter.

	£'000	£'000
Turnover		1,400
Cost of sales		770
Gross profit		630
Distribution costs and administrative expenses		290
Group operating profit		340
Share of operating profit in associate		30
		370
Interest and similar income receivable (group)		30
		400
Interest payable and similar charges (group)		(20)
Profit on ordinary activities before tax		380
Tax on profit on ordinary activities★		162
Profit after taxation		218
Minority interest (in the current year post tax profits of subsidiary)		(22)
Profit for the financial year attributable to the group		196
(of which £111,000 has been dealt with in the accounts of the holding company)		196
Dividends (of the holding company)		
Paid	20	
Proposed	25	
		45
		151
Earnings per share		Xp
Retained profits for the year		£'000
Holding company		66
Subsidiary		70
Associated company		15
		151
★Tax relates to the following:		
Parent and subsidiaries	150	
Associate	12	

Question 1

'When a subsidiary pays a dividend out of pre-acquisition profits there are different ways of treating the dividend in the accounts of the holding company.'

Discuss.

Answer

Generally, a dividend paid out of pre-acquisition profits should be applied to reduce the cost of the investments in the balance sheet of the holding company. It should not be treated as realised profit.

The thinking behind this is that the holding company cannot credit the dividend to profit because no profit has been made. The holding company was willing to pay 'over the odds' for its investment in the presumption that part of its cost would be immediately re-paid. When the dividend is paid, this presumption must be pursued to its conclusion by treating the dividend as a reduction of the cost of investment or a return of capital.

However, this accounting treatment is no longer a legal requirement, and it is possible to argue that, provided the investment will eventually recover the value that has been removed from it by the distribution, then it is unnecessary to write it down and the dividend to the holding company may be distributed. This implies that, provided the level of profits made by the subsidiary is to be maintained, those profits may be distributed by the holding company.

According to FRS 6 *Acquisitions and mergers,* a dividend must be applied to reduce the carrying value of the investment in a subsidiary only to the extent that this is necessary to provide for any diminution in value. Any other amount is realised profit in the hands of the parent company.

Consolidated balance sheet

3.21 As explained earlier, the consolidated balance sheet will contain an **asset 'Investment in associates'**. The amount at which this asset is stated will be its original cost plus the group's share of any **profits earned since acquisition** which have not been distributed as dividends.

3.22 EXAMPLE: CONSOLIDATED BALANCE SHEET

On 1 January 19X6 the net tangible assets of A Ltd amount to £220,000, financed by 100,000 £1 ordinary shares and revenue reserves of £120,000. H Ltd, a company with subsidiaries, acquires 30,000 of the shares in A Ltd for £75,000. During the year ended 31 December 19X6 A Ltd's profit after tax is £30,000, from which dividends of £12,000 are paid.

Show how H Ltd's investment in A Ltd would appear in the consolidated balance sheet at 31 December 19X6.

3.23 SOLUTION

CONSOLIDATED BALANCE SHEET
AS AT 31 DECEMBER 19X6 (extract)

	£
Fixed assets	
Investment in associate	
Cost	75,000
Group share of post-acquisition retained profits	
(30% × £18,000)	5,400
	80,400

3.24 An important point to note is that this figure of £80,400 can be arrived at in a completely different way. It is the sum of:

(a) the group's share of A Ltd's net assets at 31 December 19X6; and

(b) the premium paid over net book value for the shares acquired.

3.25   This can be shown as follows.

	£	£
(a) A Ltd's net assets at 31 December 19X6		
Net assets at 1 January 19X6	220,000	
Retained profit for year	18,000	
Net assets at 31 December 19X6	238,000	
Group share (30%)		71,400
(b) Premium on acquisition		
Net assets acquired by group on 1 Jan 19X6		
(30% × £220,000)	66,000	
Price paid for shares	75,000	
Premium on acquisition		9,000
Investment in associate per balance sheet		80,400

3.26   The reason why this is important is because FRS 9 requires the investment in associated companies to be analysed in this way, ie:

(a)   Group share of associate's net assets

(b)   Goodwill arising on acquisition of associate less any amortisation or write down is included in (a) but disclosed separately

3.27   **Fair values should be attributed to the associate's underlying assets and liabilities.** These will provide the basis for subsequent depreciation. Both the consideration paid in the acquisition and the goodwill arising should be calculated in the same way as on the acquisition of a subsidiary. The associate's assets should not include any goodwill earned in the balance sheet of the associate.

3.28   The goodwill should be treated in accordance with the provisions of FRS 10 *Goodwill and intangible assets*. The usual treatment would therefore be to capitalise and amortise. (Our example assumes for simplicity that the goodwill has an indefinite life and there is no amortisation.)

Question 2

How should a holding company treat the following items in the financial statements for an associated company, when preparing group accounts:

(a)   turnover;
(b)   inter-company profits;
(c)   goodwill?

Answer

(a)   The holding company should not aggregate the turnover of an associated company with its own turnover.

(b)   Wherever the effect is material, adjustments similar to those adopted for the purpose of presenting consolidated financial statements should be made to exclude from the investing group's consolidated financial statements such items as unrealised profits on stocks transferred to or from associated companies.

(c)   The investing group's balance sheet should disclose 'interest in associated companies'. The amount disclosed under this heading should include both the investing group's share of any goodwill in the associated companies' own financial statements and any premium paid on acquisition of the interests in the associated companies in so far as it has not already been written off or amortised.

Question 3

Corrie plc has a 75% subsidiary, Brookie plc, of which it also owns 25% of the preference shares. Corrie has an associated company, Eastend Ltd, in which it has a 25% interest. Set out below are the balance sheets of the three companies as at 31 December 19X7. (Investment in subsidiary and associate are shown at cost.)

	Corrie plc	Brookie plc	Eastend Ltd
	£m	£m	£m
Fixed assets			
Tangible assets	4,920	4,350	
Investments			1,500
Shares in Brookie	3,960		
Shares in Eastend	900		
	9,780	4,350	1,500
Current assets			
Stock	780	600	
Debtors	610	360	
Cash at bank and in hand	260	30	
	1,650	990	
Creditors: amounts falling due within one year	610	410	
Net current assets	1,040	580	
Total assets less current liabilities	10,820	4,930	
Creditors: amounts falling due after more than one year	1,730	440	
	9,090	4,490	1,500
Capital and reserves			
Ordinary £1 shares	6,000	2,400	1,500
5% preference shares of £1		1,200	
Share premium account	1,490	100	
Profit and loss account	1,600	790	
	9,090	4,490	1,500

You are the new assistant financial controller of Corrie plc and have been asked to prepare a consolidated balance sheet for the Corrie Group. The following further information is available.

(a) Brookie plc was acquired on 1 January 19X7. Corrie plc paid £3,960m for the ordinary and preference shares. On that date Brookie plc's profit and loss account was £898m (credit balance).

(b) The preference shares of Brookie plc are redeemable on 31 December 19Y6 at a premium of 10%. They were originally issued at par on 1 January 19X7. The premium has not yet been accounted for and is to be dealt with using the straight line method for the purposes of FRS 4 *Capital instruments*.

(c) The balance on the share premium account of Brookie plc represents the premium on the issue of the ordinary shares.

(d) It is the policy of Corrie plc to write off goodwill arising on acquisition against the profit and loss account in the year of acquisition. When Brookie plc was acquired the fair value of its net assets was equal to their book value except for some non-material differences.

(e) Eastend Ltd is an investment company. It has no assets other than a portfolio of investments, the market value of which is £2,200m. In the above balance sheet, the investments are shown at their book value of £1,500m. Corrie plc acquired its interest in Eastend Ltd on 31 December 19X7.

(f) Brookie plc paid a dividend for the year of 2p per ordinary £1 share and also paid the 5% preference dividend. There was no dividend proposed at 31 December 19X7. As assistant financial controller, you have advised the directors of Corrie plc that the dividend payment of Brookie plc should be treated as if it were out of pre-acquisition profits, that is as a deduction from the value of the investment.

(g) Brookie plc manufactures and sells industrial machinery. On 1 January 19X7 it sold a machine to Corrie plc which Corrie plc correctly classified as a fixed asset. The item was sold at a mark up of 25% of cost and is shown in the books of Corrie plc at £720m. Of this amount, £20m is still owed to Brookie plc. Corrie plc has charged a year's depreciation on the machine of 25%.

Required

Prepare the consolidated balance sheet for the Corrie Group plc as at 31 December 19X7. Ignore any additional disclosure requirements of FRS 9.

Answer

(b)   CORRIE GROUP PLC
CONSOLIDATED BALANCE SHEET AS AT 31 DECEMBER 19X7

	£m	£m
Fixed assets		
Tangible assets (W4)		9,162
Investment in associate (W6)		550
		9,712
Current assets		
Stocks	1,380	
Debtors (W7)	950	
Cash at bank and in hand	290	
	2,620	
Creditors: amounts falling due within one year (W8)	1,000	
Net current assets		1,620
Total assets less current liabilities		11,332
Creditors: amounts falling due after one year		2,170
		9,162
Capital and reserves		
Share capital		6,000
Share premium		1,490
Profit and loss account (W9)		(21)
		7,469
Minority interest: equity	784	
non-equity	909	
		1,693
		9,162

Workings

1   *Dividends paid*

	Total		Corrie plc
	£m		£m
Ordinary dividend	48	× 75%	36
Preference dividend	60	× 25%	15
	108		51

As these dividends are paid out of pre-acquisition profits, they should be charged against the cost of Corrie plc's investment in Brookie plc.

2   *Goodwill*

	£m	£m
Cost of investment in Brookie plc		3,960
Less dividend from pre-acquisition profits (W1)		51
		3,909
Net assets acquired:		
Share capital	2,400	
Share premium	100	
Profit and loss account	898	
	3,398	
Group share 75%		2,548
		1,361
5% preference shares	1,200	
Group share 25%		300
Goodwill		1,061

3   *Intercompany stock/fixed asset*

	£m	£m
Intercompany profit = $720 \times 25/125$		144
DEBIT Minority interest P&L 25%	36	
DEBIT Group P&L 75%	108	
CREDIT Fixed assets		144

	£m	£m
Depreciation adjustment		
Excess depreciation: 25% of 144 = £36m		
DEBIT Provision for depreciation	36	
CREDIT Group P&L		36

4   *Tangible fixed assets*

	£m
Corrie	4,920
Less intercompany profit	(144)
Add back excess depreciation	36
	4,812
Brookie	4,350
	9,162

5   *Minority interest*

	£m	£m
Equity		784
Share capital	2,400	
Share premium	100	
Profit and loss account (790 − 12)	778	
	3,278	
× 25%		820
Less intercompany profit		36
Non equity		784
Preference shares	1,200	
Premium on redemption	12	
	1,212	
× 75%		909
		1,693

6   *Investment in associate*

	£m
Cost of investment	900
Share of fair value of investments acquired $25\% \times 2,200$	550
Goodwill	350

As the goodwill has been written off, the investment in associate in the consolidated balance sheet will be the share of net assets at fair value, ie £550m.

7   *Debtors*

	£m
Corrie	610
Brookie	360
Less intercompany	(20)
	950

8   *Creditors: amounts falling due within one year*

	£m
Corrie	610
Brookie	410
Less intercompany	(20)
	1,000

9   *Profit and loss account*

	£m
Corrie	1,600
Less: pre-acquisition dividends wrongly accounted for (15 + 36)	(51)
Plus: over depreciation of FA	36
share of deemed dividend/premium	3
Brookie	
75% × (790 − 12 144 − 898)	(198)
Less goodwill: Eastend	(350)
Brookie	(1,061)
	(21)

Minority interests

3.29 FRS 9 dose not specifically address the situation where an investment in an associate is held by a subsidiary. However, the FRS does stipulate that in calculating the amounts to be included in the consolidated financial statements the same principles should be applied as are applied in the consolidation of subsidiaries. This implies that the **group accounts should include the 'gross' share of net assets, operating profit, interest payable and receivable (if any) and tax, accounting for the minority interest separately.** For example, we will suppose that H Ltd owns 60% of S Ltd which owns 25% of A Ltd, an associate of H Ltd. The relevant amounts for inclusion in the consolidated financial statements would be as follows.

CONSOLIDATED PROFIT AND LOSS ACCOUNT
Operating profit (H 100% + S 100%)
Share of operating profit of associate (A 25%)
Interest receivable (group) (H 100% + S 100% + A 25%)
Interest payable (H 100% + S 100% + A 25%)
Exceptional items (H 100% + S 100% + A 25%)
Tax (H 100% + S 100% + A 25%)
Minority interest (S 40% + A 10%)
Retained profits (H 100% + S 60% + A 15%)

CONSOLIDATED BALANCE SHEET
Investment in associated company (figures based on 25% holding)
Minority interest ((40% × shareholders' funds of S) + (10% × post-acquisition reserves of A))
Unrealised reserves (15% × post-acquisition reserves of A)
Group profit and loss account ((100% × H) + (60% × post-acquisition of S))

4   INCORPORATED JOINT VENTURES AND JOINT ARRANGEMENTS

Joint ventures

4.1   Joint ventures are another form of entity which, while not giving the investor control as with a subsidiary, gives it considerable influence.

4.2   There are three important definitions here.

> ### KEY TERMS
>
> • **Joint venture**: an entity in which the reporting entity holds an interest on a long-term basis and is **jointly controlled** by the reporting entity and one or more other venturers under a contractual arrangement.
>
> • **Joint control**: a reporting entity jointly controls a venture with one or more other entities if none of the entities alone can control that entity but all together can do so and decisions on financial and operating policy essential to the activities, economic performance and financial position of that venture require each venturer's consent.
>
> *(FRS 9)*

4.3   **Joint control is exercised by the venturers for their mutual benefit,** each conducting its part of the contractual arrangement with a view to its own advantage. It is possible within the definition for one venturer to manage the joint venture, provided that the venture's principal operating and financial policies are collectively agreed by the venturers and the venturers have the power to ensure that those policies are followed.

4.4   High-level strategic decisions require the consent of each venturer. In effect, each venturer has a veto on such decisions.

Question 4

How is this situation different from that of a minority shareholder in a company? (Think back to your *Legal Framework* studies.)

Answer

A minority shareholder has no veto and is subject to majority rule: *Foss v Harbottle 1843*, except in very limited circumstances.

Accounting aspects: background

4.5   The nature of joint ventures might mean that one line equity accounting is not appropriate. For example, the investor might have a direct interest in certain assets which it has contributed to the venture. Alternatively, it might be considered appropriate to reflect directly in its own financial statements its proportional share of the assets and liabilities of the investee by a form of **proportion consolidation**. This is **a method of accounting where the investor's share of the results, assets and liabilities of its investee is included in its consolidated financial statements on a line-by-line basis.**

4.6   The Companies Act contains provisions which permit proportional consolidation for some joint ventures. This is restricted to unincorporated joint ventures and the joint venture should be managed 'jointly with one or more undertakings not included in the consolidation'.

4.7   FRED 11 *Associates and joint ventures* proposed identifying two classes of joint ventures: those where the venturers shared in common the benefits and risks, which were to be included by the equity method, and those where each venturer had its own separate interest, which were to be included by proportional consolidation.

FRS 9 treatment

4.8   **FRS 9 emphasises the special nature of joint control by identifying joint ventures as a single class of investments wholly separate from associates** to be included by a special method of accounting - the gross equity method.

KEY TERM

Gross equity method: a form of equity method under which the investor's share of the aggregate gross assets and liabilities underlying the net amount included for the investment is shown on the face of the balance sheet and, in the profit and loss account, the investor's share of the investee's turnover is noted.   *(FRS 9)*

4.9   The gross equity method is like the equity method except with regard to the following.

(a)   In the **consolidated profit and loss** account the investor's share of **joint ventures' turnover** is **shown, but not as part of group turnover.** For example:

	£m	£m
Turnover: group and share of joint ventures	560	
Less: share of joint ventures' turnover	130	
Group turnover		430

(b)   In the segmental analysis the investor's share of its joint ventures' turnover should also be distinguished from the turnover of the group.

(c)   In the **consolidated balance sheet, the investor's share of the gross assets and liabilities** underlying the net equity amount included for joint ventures should be shown in amplification of that amount. For example:

	£m	£m	£m
Fixed assets			
Tangible assets			700
Investments			
Investments in joint ventures:			
Share of gross assets	250		
Share of gross liabilities	(120)		
		130	
Investment in associates		80	
			910

(d)   In both the profit and loss account and the balance sheet **any supplemental information given for joint ventures must be shown clearly separate from amounts for the group** and must not be included in the group totals. An exception is made for items below profit before tax in the profit and loss account.

4.10   In the investor's individual financial statements, investments in joint ventures should be treated as fixed asset investments and shown at cost, less any amounts written off, or at valuation.

Further aspects of FRS 9 applying to both joint ventures and associates

Principles of consolidation

4.11 As has been mentioned, when calculating the amounts to be included in the investor's consolidated financial statements, whether using the equity method for associates or the gross equity method for joint ventures, the **same principles should be applied as are applied in the consolidation of subsidiaries**. This has the following implications.

(a) **Fair values** are to be attributed to assets and liabilities on acquisition. Goodwill should be treated as per FRS 10. This point was dealt with in connection with associates in Paragraphs 3.27 and 3.28. The same applies to joint ventures.

(b) In arriving at the amounts to be included by the equity method, the **same accounting policies** as those of the investor should be applied.

(c) The financial statements of the investor and the associate or joint venture should be prepared to the **same accounting date** and for the **same accounting period**; associates/joint ventures can prepare three months before if necessary with appropriate adjustments and disclosure.

(d) **Profits or losses resulting from transactions between the investor and its associate/joint venture** may be included in the carrying amount of assets in either party. Where this is the case, the part relating to the **investor's share should be eliminated**. Any impairment of those or similar assets must be taken into account if evidence of it is given by the transactions in question.

Investor is a group

4.12 **Where the investor is a group, it share of its associate or joint venture is the aggregate of the holdings of the parent and its subsidiaries in that entity.** The holdings of any of the group's **other associates or joint ventures should be ignored** for this purpose. Where an associate or joint venture itself has subsidiaries, associates or joint ventures, the results and net assets to be taken into account by the equity method are those reported in that investee's consolidated financial statements (including the investee's share of the results and net assets of its associates and joint ventures), after any adjustment necessary to give effect to the investor's accounting policies.

Options, convertibles and non-equity shares

4.13 The investor may hold options, convertibles or non-equity shares in its associate or joint venture. In certain circumstances, the conditions attaching to such holdings are such that the investor should take them into account in reflecting its interest in its investee under the equity or gross equity method. In such cases, the costs of exercising the options or converting the convertibles, or future payments in relation to the non-equity shares, should also be taken into account.

Impairment

4.14 In cases where there is impairment in any goodwill attributable to an associate or joint venture the **goodwill should be written down** and the amount written off in the accounting period separately disclosed.

Commencement and cessation of relationship

4.15 The following points apply with regard to commencement or cessation of an associate or joint venture relationship.

(a) An investment **becomes an associate on the date on which the investor begins to:**

    (i)   Hold a **participating interest.**

    (ii)   Exercise **significant influence.**

(b) An investment **ceases to be an associate** on the date **when it ceases to fulfil either of the above.**

(c) An investment **becomes a joint venture on the date on which the investor begins to control it jointly** with other investors, provided it has a long-term interest.

(d) On the date when an investor **ceases to have joint control,** the investment **ceases to be a joint venture.**

(e) The **carrying amount** (percentage of investment retained) should be reviewed and, if necessary, written down to the **recoverable amount.**

Joint arrangements that are not entities

4.16 A reporting entity may operate through a structure that has the appearance of a joint venture but not the reality. It may thus be a separate entity in which the participants hold a long-term interest and exercise joint management, but there may be no common interest because each venturer operates independently of the other venturers within that structure. The framework entity acts merely as an agent for the ventures with each venturer able to identify and control its share of the assets, liabilities and cash flows arising within the entity. **Such arrangements have the form but not the substance of a joint venture.**

The accounting treatment for such joint arrangements required by FRS 9 is that **each venturer should account directly for its share of the assets, liabilities and cash flows held within that structure.** This treatment reflects the substance rather than the form of the arrangement.

Investors that do not prepare consolidated accounts

4.17 A reporting entity may have an associate or joint venture, but **no subsidiaries.** It will thus not prepare group accounts. In such cases it **should present the relevant amounts for associates and joint ventures, as appropriate, by preparing a separate set of financial statements** or by showing the relevant amounts, together with the effects of including them, as additional information to its own financial statements. Investing entities that are exempt from preparing consolidated financial statements, or would be exempt if they had subsidiaries, are exempt from this requirement.

Question 5

Ross plc is a long established business in office supplies. The nature of its business has expanded and diversified to take account of technological changes which have taken place in recent years. Now in addition to stationery and office furniture, it also supplies photocopiers, fax machines and more recently new computer based technologies. The expansion has occurred organically but also through acquisition of existing companies and joint ventures. Ross plc's investments are as follows.

(a) *Joey Ltd.* Ross has a 40% interest in the issued share capital of Joey Ltd and representation on the board. Joey Ltd manufactures office furniture and a large proportion of what it produces is sold to Ross. Ross is therefore actively involved in decisions regarding product ranges, designs and pricing to ensure they get the products they want.

(b) *Rachel NRG.* Rachel NRG is a joint venture company which commenced operations on 1 June 19X7. The joint venturers in Rachel are Ross plc and Monica Inc, a company also in office automation, specialising in computer products. The purpose of the joint venture was to distribute their products to Asia Pacific where the demand for office automation is growing rapidly. Ross and Monica have an equal interest in Rachel.

(c) *Phoebe Ltd*. Phoebe Ltd's principal activities is the supply and fitting of bathroom suites. Its managing director is Mrs Janice Chandler, wife of Mr Paul Chandler, a director of Ross plc. Ross plc has a 25% interest in the share capital of Phoebe and the remaining shares are held by various members of the Chandler family. Mr Chandler is on the board of Phoebe as a non-executive director and this was approved at the last AGM by all the voting members of the Chandler family. The activities of Phoebe and Ross are in totally different markets, the share interest is there for historic reasons and Ross has not exercised its voting rights for several years. During the year Ross plc sold one of the company's executive cars to Phoebe Ltd for an agreed open market value of £30,000.

The following are extracts from the financial statements of Joey, Rachel and Phoebe for the year ended 31 March 19X8.

	Joey	Rachel	Phoebe
	£'000	£'000	£'000
Turnover	4,068	17,720	7,640
Operating costs	3,872	16,834	6,980
Operating profit	196	886	660
Interest payable	-	280	30
Profit before tax	196	606	630
Tax	40	152	200
Profit after tax	156	454	430
Fixed assets	360	1,720	260
Current assets	2,940	2,130	834
Creditors falling due within one year	(2,214)	(710)	(252)
Creditors falling due after one year	(26)	(1,810)	(400)
	1,060	1,330	442
Cost of investment	600	500	400

Sales of office furniture from Joey to Ross amounted to £160,000 during the year. 10% of the goods remain in the closing stock of Ross. These goods had been sold at a mark up of 25% on cost.

Required

Produce extracts from the consolidated profit and loss account and balance sheet of Ross for the year ended 31 March 19X8 indicating clearly the treatments for Joey, Rachel and Phoebe and where each item would appear.

Answer

EXTRACTS FROM THE CONSOLIDATED PROFIT AND LOSS ACCOUNT
FOR THE YEAR ENDED 31 MARCH 19X8

	£'000	£'000
Turnover	X	
Less share of joint ventures' turnover	(8,860)	
Group turnover		X
Group operating profit		X
Share of operating profit in		
Joint ventures	443	
Associates (W1)	77.2	
Interest payable		
Group	X	
Joint ventures	(140)	
Profit before tax		X
Tax (see below)		X
Profit after tax		X
Tax relates to		
Parent and subsidiary		X
Joint ventures		76
Associates		16

EXTRACTS FROM THE CONSOLIDATED BALANCE SHEET AS AT 31 MARCH 19X8

	£'000	£'000
Fixed assets		
Investments		
Investments in joint ventures		
Share of gross assets	1,925	
Share of gross liabilities	1,260	
		665.0
Investments in associates (W2)		422.8
Other investments		400.0

Workings

1   *Share of associate company profit*

	£'000
Profit of Joey per question	196.0
Less PUP $(160,000 \times 10\% \times {}^{25}/_{125})$	3.2
	192.8
Group share (40%) (rounded)	77.2

2   *Investment in associates*

	£'000
Net assets per question	1,060.0
Less PUP (W1)	(3.2)
	1,056.8
Group share (40%) (rounded)	422.8

5   DISCLOSURES FOR ASSOCIATES AND JOINT VENTURES

5.1   The disclosures required by FRS 9 are extensive. Some are required for all associates and joint ventures and other additional disclosures are required if certain thresholds are exceeded. These disclosures are to be made in addition to the amounts required on the face of the financial statements under the equity method or the gross equity method.

5.2 **FRS 9: Summary of disclosure requirements**

All associates and joint ventures	15% threshold*	25% threshold*
• Names of principal associates/joint venture	• Turnover (associates only)	• Turnover
• Proportion of shares held	• Fixed assets	• Profit before tax
• Accounting date if different	• Current assets	• Taxation
• Nature of business	• Liabilities due within one year	• Profit after tax
• Material differences in accounting policies	• Liabilities due after one year or more	• Fixed assets
• Restrictions on distributions		• Current assets
• Intercompany balances		• Liabilities due within one year
• Reason for rebutting 20% presumption of participating interest/ significant influence		• Liabilities due after one year or more

*Threshold refers to investor's aggregate share of gross assets, gross liabilities, turnover or three year average operating result of investee as compared with the corresponding group figure.

Chapter roundup

- **Associates** and **joint ventures** are entities in which an investor holds a **substantial but not controlling interest**.

- They are the subject of an accounting standard: **FRS 9 *Associates and joint ventures.***

- **Associates** are to be included in the investor's consolidated financial statements using the **equity method**.

  o The investor's share of its associates' results should be included immediately after group operating profit.

  o The investor's share of its associates' turnover may be shown as a memorandum item.

- **Joint ventures** are to be included in the venturer's consolidated financial statements by the **gross equity method**.

  o This requires, in addition to the amounts included under the equity method, disclosure of the venturer's share of its joint ventures' turnover, gross assets and gross liabilities.

- Other **joint arrangements**, such as cost-sharing arrangements and one-off construction projects, are to be included in their participants' individual and consolidated financial statements by **each participant including directly** its share of the assets, liabilities and cash flows arising from the arrangements.

Quick quiz

1   Why was SSAP 1, the forerunner of FRS 9, criticised? (see para 1.9)

2   What types of interest does FRS 9 identify? (2.5)

3   How does FRS 9 define associate? (3.2)

4   What is meant by 'participating interest'? (3.3)

5   What is meant by 'exercise of significant influence'? (3.7)

6   How should associates be treated in the consolidated profit and loss account? (3.12)

7   What is a joint venture? (4.2)

8   What is the 'gross equity method'? (4.8)

9   What treatment does FRS 9 prescribe for joint arrangements that are not entities? (4.16)

10 What disclosures are required when the '25% threshold' is exceeded? (5.2)

Question to try	Level	Marks	Time
21	Exam	50	90 mins
22	Full exam	20	36 mins

Part C

The theoretical framework of accounting

Chapter 21

THEORETICAL ASPECTS OF ACCOUNTING

Chapter topic list	Syllabus reference
1 Income and capital	1(a)
2 Entry and exit values	1(a)
3 Current purchasing power (CPP)	1(a)
4 Current cost accounting (CCA)	1(a)
5 Agency theory and the efficient market hypothesis	1(a)
6 Positive and normative accounting concepts	1(a)

Introduction

The topics covered in this chapter fall neatly into three groups.

- Sections 1 and 2 are the first group.
- Sections 3 and 4 are the second group.
- Sections 5 and 6 are the third group.

Ideally, you should study all six topics. However, if you are in a hurry, you would be advised to pick two out of the three groups. We recommend Sections 3 -6. In the unlikely event that you get a question on the topics in Sections 1 and 2 there is a limited amount of choice on the paper which will enable you to avoid it.

1   INCOME AND CAPITAL

Economic income

1.1   'Income' is used here as a term which **means 'profit' to the accountant, and it is not intended to mean 'revenue'.** The term 'income' is used in preference to 'profit' in order to compare economic and accounting theories.

> **KEY TERM**
>
> In accounting, **income** may be measured as a change in the capital value of a business entity between the beginning and end of a period, if we ignore (for the sake of simplicity) new share or loan capital receipts, dividend payments, loan repayments and inflation.

1.2 EXAMPLE: INCOME

Suppose that a company is established on 1 June, with £10,000 in cash financed by ordinary shares (8,000 of £1 each) and £2,000 of 12% loan stock. During the year:

(a) The company buys fixed assets for cash at a cost of £7,000.

(b) On 1 June stocks are bought at a cost of £2,000, also for cash.

(c) During June, all of these stocks are sold for £4,500, £300 of which was unpaid at 30 June.

(d) Depreciation for June amounted to £100.

(e) Other expenses for June amounted to £1,000, of which £150 were unpaid at the month end.

(f) Extra stocks were bought for cash on 30 June, at a cost of £1,500.

1.3 The profit for June would possibly be calculated as follows.

	£	£
Sales	4,500	
Cost of stocks sold	2,000	
Depreciation	100	
Other expenses	1,000	
Loan stock interest ($^1/_{12}$ of 12% of £2,000)	20	
		3,120
Profit in June		1,380

1.4 The balance sheet at 30 June would then be as follows.

	£	£
Fixed assets, net of depreciation		6,900
Current assets		
Stocks	1,500	
Debtors	300	
Cash (note)	2,850	
	4,650	
Current liabilities (accruals, including loan interest)	(170)	
Long-term liability (12% loan stock)	(2,000)	
		2,480
		9,380
Ordinary share capital		8,000
Profit and loss account		1,380
		9,380

Note

Opening cash and revenue	£	Expenditure	£
Sales receipts	4,200	Fixed assets	7,000
Opening cash balance	10,000	Stocks	3,500
	14,200	Other expenses	850
Expenditure	11,350		11,350
Closing cash balance	2,850		

1.5 From this simple example, it can be seen that:

(a) the value of the company's assets at 30 June is partly financed by the profit of £1,380;

(b) since the opening capital of the business on 1 June was £10,000 we can derive the formula:

$$A_1 + P = A_2$$

where A_1 are assets at the beginning of the period

        P is the profit

        A_2 are assets at the end of the period.

Note. New capital receipts, capital repayments and dividend payments are ignored in the formula.

1.6   The formula can be re-stated to include dividend payments, so that $A_1 + P - D = A_2$, where D is the dividend payment.

1.7   This means that income, P, can be expressed as $P = D + (A_2 - A_1)$, so income is the sum of dividend payments plus the increase in capital (asset) values between the beginning and end of the period.

1.8   An important conclusion from this formula is that **income is dependent, not only on the amount of cash paid to the owners of the business entity, but also on changes in asset values between the start and end of the period.**

Economic income theories

1.9   Very little has been written about the definition of accounting income, but in contrast economists have evolved a theory of personal income.

1.10   **Fisher** was one of the earliest economists to **define income** in *The Theory of Interest* 1930.

> He suggested that **income** is not the act of receiving money; income is rather the psychological enjoyment which an individual gets from spending the money on the consumption of goods and services. If an individual increases his savings, he is increasing his stock of future consumption and it is the enjoyment from this future consumption that gives a current stock of wealth (the savings or capital) its value.

1.11   Because psychological enjoyment cannot be measured, Fisher said that 'income = consumption' should be measured in terms of the money value of goods and services consumed; however, 'real' economic income is the 'standard of living' which these goods and services provide.

> '[Money income] is most commonly called income, and [enjoyment income] is the most fundamental. But for accounting purposes, real income, as measured by the cost of living, is the most practical.'   (Fisher)

1.12   Fisher's concept of the value of capital calls for some understanding of the mathematical technique of **discounting** (or discounted cash flow).

1.13   Suppose an individual holds the lease on a property which he rents out for an annual payment of £2,000. The lease has three more years to run.

(a)   The individual's income will be £2,000 per annum for each of the next three years, provided that he spends it all each year and does not save any of it. (If he saves any of the £2,000, these savings will be invested so as to earn more money which in turn will be spent on extra consumption in the future.)

(b)   The **capital value** of the lease:

(i) **Now** will be the present value of £2,000 per annum for 3 years, discounted at the individual's cost of capital.

(ii) **In one years' time** will be the present value of £2,000 per annum for 2 years.

(iii) **In two years' time** will be the present value of £2,000 per annum for 1 year.

(iv) **In three years' time** the capital value of the lease will be nil, because the lease will have expired.

1.14 **Fisher argued that the cost of capital is the prevailing market rate of interest.** Hicks differed from this view, and argued that the cost of capital should be the rate of return which an individual would obtain by investing his capital in the best alternative investment (perhaps in shares, loan stock, a building society).

1.15 **Fisher's theory is rather unsatisfactory, because equating income with consumption is confusing.** Professor Kaldor (*An Expenditure Tax* 1955) wrote that:

> 'if we reserved the term income for consumption we should still need another term for what would otherwise be called income [money receipts] and we should still be left with the problem of how to define the latter.'

1.16 The economic theorist **Sir John Hicks has described the economic concept of income as being the sum of:**

(a) **cash flows realised by the individual** during a period of time; and

(b) **changes in the value of the individual's capital** between the beginning and the end of the period.

FORMULA TO LEARN

As a formula: $I = C + (K_2 - K_1)$

where
C is the cash flows realised by the individual in the period
K_2 is the value of his capital at the end of a period
K_1 is the value of his capital at the start of a period
$K_2 - K_1$ is therefore the value of the individual's saving.

1.17 To this extent, the accounting definition of profit and the economic concept of personal income are similar.

1.18 **The important difference between accounting and economic income relates to the methods of valuing capital.**

(a) To the accountant, capital is valued in terms of net assets, for example with:

(i) Fixed assets at cost less depreciation, or at a revalued amount.

(ii) Stocks at cost or net realisable value.

(iii) Investments at cost or market value.

(iv) Goodwill at the difference between the cost of assets acquired and their net book value.

and so on.

(b) To the economist, capital is a store of wealth which will be used up in future receipts and therefore future consumption. Capital is only valuable in so far as it provides future benefits; if future benefits did not exist, the individual would spend everything now, and would not bother to save any capital at all. To Hicks, capital could be defined as 'welloffness' and this could be valued as the capitalised money value of prospective future receipts. An important feature of this concept is that value is based on *predictions* of future cash receipts, so cash flows are accounted for as soon as they are predicted rather than when they are realised or even reasonably certain to be realised.

Income and capital maintenance

1.19 Hicks defined income (in *Value and Capital* 1946) as follows.

> **HICKS' DEFINITION OF INCOME**
>
> 'the maximum value which (an individual) can consume during a week and still expect to be as well off at the end of the week as he was at the beginning.'

1.20 Thus since $I = C + (K_2 - K_1)$

(a) If $K_2 = K_1$, then $I = C$.

(b) Similarly, if $K_2 > K_1$ (ie if the amount of the individual's capital increases) then $I > C$.

(c) If $K_2 < K_1$, the individual will be consuming an amount which is greater than the value of his income. He would be 'eating into his capital'.

1.21 The Sandilands Committee in its *Report of the Inflation Accounting Committee* 1975 described accounting profit in terms of Hicks' definition as follows.

> 'A company's profit for the year is the maximum value which the company can distribute during the year, and still expect to be as well off at the end of the year as it was at the beginning.'

1.22 As a formula: $P = D + (A_2 - A_1)$.

(a) If $A_2 = A_1$, then $P = D$.

(b) If $A_2 > A_1$, then $P > D$ and some profits are retained in the business to increase its capital 'value'.

(c) If $A_2 < A_1$, then $P < D$ and the company would be paying some dividend out of previous years' profits, so that the company would be 'eating into' its reserves.

1.23 **Income and profit are thus associated with the concept of capital maintenance.** The value of income and the value of capital are inextricably related. Using the concept of capital maintenance:

> 'profit is the sum which may be distributed or withdrawn from a business while maintaining intact the capital which existed at the beginning of the period. In other words, the business's capital at the start of a period is used as a bench-mark to determine the business's profit for a period.'   (*Advanced Financial Accounting* by Lewis, Pendrill and Simon)

The value of capital

1.24 Capital can be valued in a number of ways.

(a) **Economists might value capital as the present value of future receipts** from an asset, discounted at the individual's cost of capital.

(b) **Accountants might value assets at:**

(i)   **Historical cost** (net of depreciation or amounts written off where appropriate).

(ii)   **Market values** (land and buildings, investments).

(iii)   **Replacement costs** (entry values).

(iv)   **Net realisable value** (exit values).

(v)   **Deprival value** or current costs (mixed values).

Each different method of valuing capital must imply a different method of valuing income.

1.25   T A Lee in *Income and Value Measurement: Theory and Practice* made a comparison between the concepts of value and capital maintenance.

> 'The concept of capital maintenance is a vital part of income determination because of the need to incorporate in the income computation a measure of the change in capital during the relevant period. Value, on the other hand, is a necessary ingredient in the computation of capital to which the capital maintenance concept is then applied in determining income. Both are therefore necessary to the income determination process, but neither can of itself measure income.'

1.26   The concepts of valuation and capital maintenance so far described have **ignored the problem of inflation**. It is an axiom of accounting that all assets and liabilities should be measured in money terms, and it is normally assumed that the value of a unit of money (£1) is stable. However, because of inflation, the 'real' value of £1 (the 'purchasing power' of £1) is continually declining.

1.27   This means that if a company has opening capital of £10,000 on 1 January, earns a recorded historical cost profit of £2,000 and pays a dividend of £2,000, it will have closing capital of £10,000, so that:

$$P = D + (A_2 - A_1), \text{ thus}$$
$$2,000 = 2,000 + (10,000 - 10,000)$$

However, in terms of purchasing power A_2 will be less than A_1, and if $A_2 < A_1$, then in 'real' terms P must be less than D; the 'real' profit is less than £2,000.

1.28   It is possible to develop a convention of accounting which **attempts to value profit and capital in terms of a constant money value. This was introduced experimentally in Britain as a provisional statement of standard accounting practice (PSSAP 7) which was subsequently withdrawn.** The accounting convention is known as CPP (current purchasing power) accounting, and is described more fully in Section 3.

Relationship between income measurement and capital measurement

1.29   We have seen that profits or income are related to the concept of capital maintenance, and if we allow for injections of new capital into a business (say a new share issue) then $P = D + (A_2 - A_1) - X$, where X is the amount of new capital introduced during the period.

1.30   A brief study of this formula will suggest that the **measurement of profit depends on the** measurement of A_2 and A_1, the **measurement of capital**. The difference between A_2 and A_1 (the closing and opening balance sheet values) will depend on the methods used to determine how assets in the balance sheet should be valued.

1.31 EXAMPLE: PROFIT AND CAPITAL

For example, suppose that a company has opening stocks of 100 units of finished goods and closing stocks of 200 units. The variable production cost per unit is £5. The increase in capital value over the period in this example would be the difference between opening and closing stock values, and this difference will depend on:

(a)   whether marginal costing or full absorption costing is used; and

(b)   if absorption costing is used, what overhead recovery rate is applied.

1.32   If variable costing is used, the increase in capital value ($A_2 - A_1$) is 100 units $\times$ £5 = £500. If absorption costing is used, and the recovery rate is 100% of variable costs, the increase in capital value would be 100 $\times$ £5 $\times$ 200% = £1,000. If the overhead recovery rate were 125% of variable costs, the increase in capital value would be 100 $\times$ £5 $\times$ 225% = £1,125.

1.33   **Depreciation policy is another example of how capital can be measured in a variety of ways**. For example, if a company buys an asset for £6,000, which has an estimated residual value of nothing, the balance sheet value of the asset will depend on the method of depreciation used (straight line, reducing balance, sum of the digits etc) and also on the number of years over which the asset is depreciated. If the asset is depreciated over 3 years, the loss in capital value in the first year would be £2,000, whereas if it is depreciated over 5 years, the loss in value in the first year would be only £1,200. The choice of 'economic' life would therefore have a direct influence on the reported profit for the year.

1.34   It will have become apparent as you worked through this Study Text that the **choice of accounting policies** for a variety of items **will determine how assets are valued and how much profit can be declared**. These various items include not only stock valuations and depreciation, but also research and development costs, government grants, deferred tax, foreign currency translation and leasing costs.

1.35   There are also several different **conventions** which may be used in accounting **such as historical cost accounting, replacement cost accounting, current cost accounting and current purchasing power accounting**. The choice of convention will help to **determine how assets are valued, and** this in turn will affect **the measurement of profit**. The following sections describe each convention in some detail, but a simple exercise might help to explain the effect of capital measurement on profit measurement.

Question 1

A company has finished goods stocks on 1 January 19X5 which cost £10,000 (using FIFO as a basis for valuation). They were made during 19X4 and at 1 January 19X5 their replacement cost was £12,300. During 19X5 the company produced more goods costing £90,000, and its closing stocks at 31 December (using FIFO) are valued at £8,700. The replacement cost value of the closing stocks is £9,900. Compare the use of historical and replacement cost on the profit and loss account.

Answer

If the historical cost convention is used, and FIFO is the basis of valuation, the cost of sales in 19X5 would be measured as:

		£
Opening stocks		10,000
Production		90,000
		100,000
Less closing stock		8,700
Cost of sales		91,300

If, on the other hand, the 'entry values' or replacement cost convention is used, the cost of sales would be:

		£
Opening stock		12,300
Production		90,000
		102,300
Less closing stock		9,900
Cost of sales		92,400

The difference in the cost of sales (and therefore in profit) by each convention is £(92,400 – 91,300) = £1,100. This difference is due entirely to the method of valuing stocks by each convention.

	Closing stocks (A2)	Opening stocks (A1)	Reduction in stocks
	£	£	£
Historical costs	8,700	10,000	1,300
Replacement costs	9,900	12,300	2,400
Difference			1,100

The entity and proprietary concepts of capital

1.36 Before going on to consider different accounting conventions in the following chapters it may be useful to reconsider two different concepts of business capital, the entity concept and the proprietary concept.

1.37 The **entity concept of capital is that a business consists of assets and liabilities**. The assets are owned and the liabilities are owed by the person or people who finance the business, but the **sources of finance are of secondary importance**.

1.38 As a **formula**, the entity concept can be stated as:

$$A - L = C$$

where   A represents assets
L represents liabilities
C represents the capital of people financing the business.

Re-arranging the formula, we get:

$$A - L - C = 0$$

If we remember that L must be negative and that if A is greater than L, C will also be negative, then this formula could be re-stated as the accounting identity.

$$A + L + C = 0$$

1.39 'This formulation emphasises the fact that the entity has no legal personality - it cannot own assets, or owe liabilities. It is a mere 'shell' containing a set of assets and liabilities which are legally those of one or more persons, either individuals or corporate bodies ... .'

(G A Lee *Modern Financial Accounting*)

1.40 The entity concept of capital suggests that **before a profit can be made, the value of the 'assets minus liabilities' must be maintained,** regardless of the sources of finance of the business, because the entity should be seen primarily as a set of assets and liabilities which combine to make the business operate.

1.41 In comparison, the **proprietary concept of capital, focuses on the equity ownership of the business.** This concept may be expressed by the **formula**:

$$E = A - L - D$$

where   E is the value of equity
                 A is the value of assets
                 L is the value of liabilities (excluding debt capital)
                 D is debt capital

1.42 A business might be partly financed by debt capital, but it can be argued that the **ultimate purpose of a business is to provide profits for its equity owners after paying interest on debt capital and providing for taxation.**

1.43 The distinction between the entity concept, which concentrates on the business as an operating unit, and the proprietary concept, which concentrates on the purposes of a business to make profits for its owners, may be regarded simply as a matter of differing emphasis when the historical cost accounting convention is used. However, when assets are valued by a different convention, the **differing concepts of capital have important implications for capital maintenance and profit.** A simple example might help to illustrate this point.

1.44 Suppose that a new company is formed, financed 50% by equity and 50% by debt capital, so that its balance sheet at the start of operations is as follows.

	£
Cash	8,000
Less debt capital	4,000
	4,000
Equity	4,000

The company buys an asset for £8,000 and pays in cash. It then sells the asset for £11,000 by which time the replacement cost of the asset has risen to £10,000.

1.45 (a) If replacement costing is used to value capital and income, the profit earned by the company, according to the entity concept, would be:

	£
Sale revenue	11,000
Less replacement cost of sale	10,000
Profit	1,000

(b) The balance sheet after the sale might be:

	£
Cash	11,000
Less debt capital	4,000
	7,000
Original equity	4,000
Profit*	1,000
Revaluation reserves (10,000-8,000)	2,000
	7,000

*includes interest payable to debt capital investors, not separately specified here.

1.46 The proprietary concept of capital would be different, because it would take the view that only equity's share of capital needs to be maintained before a profit is made, so that if a company is 50% financed by debt capital, the cost of the sale need only be:

(a) 50% of replacement cost, to protect equity capital; plus

(b) 50% of historical cost, to reflect the share of the asset financed by debt capital.

1.47 Profit would then be:

	£
Sale revenue	11,000
Less cost of sale (50% of £10,000 + 50% of £8,000)	9,000
	2,000

The balance sheet after the sale might be:

	£
Cash	11,000
Less debt capital	4,000
	7,000
Original equity	4,000
Profit (including debt interest as before)	2,000
Revaluation reserve (50% of £10,000 - 8,000)	1,000
	7,000

1.48 The distinction between the entity concept and proprietary concept was apparent in the rules of SSAP 16 on current cost accounting, which distinguished between a current cost operating profit (applying the entity concept of capital maintenance) and a current cost profit attributable to ordinary shareholders (applying the proprietary concept of capital maintenance).

The limitations of economic income models

1.49 There are several disadvantages of these economic theories of income which help to explain perhaps why they do not provide a satisfactory conceptual basis for an accounting theory of profit.

(a) One seeming disadvantage is that **Fisher and Hicks wrote about individuals' income, whereas accountants are concerned with income/profit of a business entity.** It is accepted, however, that Hicks' theory can be applied to business entities without compromising the theory.

(b) A more serious drawback is the **large element of subjective judgement required,** even in the ex post income model. Evaluation of income and capital depends on:

(i) Predictions of the **size** of future cash flows.

(ii) Predictions of the **timing** of future cash flows.

(iii) The choice of an appropriate **discount rate**.

When predictions turn out to be wrong there will be windfall gains or losses, but the very existence of such unexpected gains or losses means that the measurement of income (I) is haphazard and unsatisfactory.

(c) The **assumption** made by Hicks **that C – (I + W) can be reinvested to earn a single, predictable rate of interest is also questionable.** If a company reinvests some of its revenues (C – (I + W)) it is most unlikely that the rate of return from these re-investments can be predicted with certainty.

(d)   If a company plans to achieve capital growth by re-investing some of its income I or windfall profits W, **Hicks' model does not help us to decide how much should be re-invested, and what the largest growth in capital values ought to be.**

Question 2

State and briefly explain Hicks' definition of income and capital.

Answer

Hicks defined income as the maximum amount an individual can consume within a period while remaining as well off at the end of the period as at the beginning. Capital is the discounted present value of the future income stream. Income is thus defined in terms of capital. This contrasts with the accruals model, under which capital is the residue after measuring income. Hicks ignores the distinction made in current financial reporting between realised and unrealised gains.

Hicks' definition of income includes consumption, saving and dis-saving. Sums saved are assumed to be reinvested and to earn interest so as to ensure a constant capital and/or income.

Economic income can be measured only under conditions of certainty. As these normally do not exist, two different models are used as approximations; the ex post model which measures income at the end of the period, and the ex ante model which measures it at the beginning of the period. Both use assumptions about future income streams and capital values and both assume a constant cost of capital. Thus the economic income model is highly subjective and speculative. It is useful as a predictor of future events and for capital investment decisions but not as a method of measuring profit.

Note. This solution extends the Hicks theory a little further than discussed in the text.

2   ENTRY AND EXIT VALUES

2.1   **Current value accounting is an attempt to find an alternative accounting convention which combines the advantages of objective reporting with the use of realistic values for assets.** Compare this with the historical cost approach to valuation and revenue recognition in Chapter 7.

Methods of current value accounting

2.2   There are three types of current value accounting, namely the use of:

(a)   **Replacement costs,** also known as **current entry values.**

(b)   **Realisable values,** also known as **current exit values** (both replacement costs and realisable values are types of market values).

(c)   A mixture of realisable values, replacement costs and economic values, in other words, **mixed values.** This system uses the concept of *deprival value*, and has been brought into accounting practice in the UK as *current cost accounting (CCA)*: see Section 4.

2.3   Each of these methods must be described in some detail, but they share certain **common features.**

(a)   They **use the transactions basis of accounting, and recognise when profits are realised.** However, income (profit) for the period is computed as the sum of realised profits plus some unrealised profits (or holding gains). In this sense, current value accounting attempts to remain objective, and does not include 'windfall profits' arising from changes in expected future cash flows; as distinct from economic income, which accounts for future cash flows as soon as they are predicted.

(b) They **use current values for assets in the balance sheet**. This is a more meaningful concept of value, because it shows the company's situation more realistically than net book values. At the same time, this means that a company will record a profit when an asset is revalued upwards, and a loss when the current value falls.

KEY TERM

A **holding gain** is a revaluation surplus, arising out of the adjustment of an asset's value upwards from historical cost to current value.

2.4   EXAMPLE: HOLDING GAIN

Suppose that an item of stock is manufactured on 1 April at a cost of £20, and at the end of June it has not been sold, although its current value is now £24. The holding gain is £4, because a balance sheet at the end of June would value the item, not at historical cost, but at current cost. The addition of £4 to assets means that £4 must be added to liabilities, to a 'revaluation surplus' reserve. The holding gain is unrealised, because the asset has not yet been sold.

2.5   At the end of September, the asset is still unsold, but its current value is now £26. For the period 1 July to 30 September, there would be an additional unrealised holding gain of £(26 – 24) = £2. The asset would be valued in the balance sheet at £26, and the revaluation surplus would total £6.

2.6   Finally, suppose that the asset is sold on 10 December for £31, when its current value is £28. The profit would now be realised, but would be measured in current value terms as follows.

	£	£	£
Sales value			31
Current value			28
Operating income*			3
Current value at time of sale		28	
Historical cost		20	
Total holding gain		8	
Attributable to the quarter 1 April - 30 June	4		
Attributable to the quarter 1 July - 30 Sept	2		
Attributable to the quarter 1 Oct - 31 Dec (28-26)	2		
			8
Total profit, as per historical cost accounts			11

(*Operating income is measured as sales value minus current value at the time of sale).

2.7   In a system of historical cost accounts, the total profit of £11 would be credited to the final quarter, the period in which the asset was sold.

In current value accounting, the profits would be distributed amongst three different quarterly periods, as follows:

		£
1 April - 30 June	Unrealised holding gain (UHG)	4
1 July - 30 September	Unrealised holding gain (UHG)	2
1 October - 31 December	Realised holding gain (RHG) plus operating profit (OP)(2+3)	5
		11

The holding gain in the final quarter is realised because the asset has now been sold. Indeed, the unrealised holding gains of the previous two quarterly periods also become 'realised' at this time.

2.8 Holding gains, or revaluation surpluses, were referred to as 'realisable cost savings' by Edwards & Bell in *The theory and measurement of business income* 1961 because they represent savings in the cost of sales achieved by obtaining the asset earlier at a lower cost, rather than at current value on the date of sale, and then selling it straight away.

2.9 In our example, the total holding gain of £8 represents the costs saved by making the asset in April for £20 instead of making it in December for £28.

A brief comparison of current value accounting and HCA

2.10 A simple comparison of current value accounting with historical cost accounting can be made with formulae. **In historical cost accounting, the profit for any period is the sum of:**

(a) **Operating profit** (sales minus the current value of items sold).

(b) **Realised holding gains of the current period.**

(c) **Realised holding gains which arose in previous periods, but were not realised until the current period.**

$$\text{HC profit} = \text{OP} + \text{RHG} + \text{RHG}^\star$$

where RHG denotes holding gains in the current period, and RHG* denotes holding gains arising in earlier periods than the current one.

In the numerical analysis above, HCA profit was the sum of:

		£
(a)	Operating profit (OP)	3
(b)	Realised holding gains 1 Oct - 31 Dec (RHG)	2
(c)	Realised holding gains which arose but were unrealised 1 April - 30 Sept (RHG*) (4 + 2)	6
		11

2.11 **In current value accounting, profit is the sum of:**

(a) **Operating profit** (OP).
(b) **Realised holding gains** (RHG).
(c) **Unrealised holding gains** (UHG).

$$\text{Current value profit} = \text{OP} + \text{RHG} + \text{UHG}$$

In our example:

Quarter	OP £	RHG £	UHG £	Total profit £
1 April - 30 June	0	0	4	4
1 July - 30 Sept	0	0	2	2
1 Oct - 31 Dec	3	2	0	5
				11

2.12 Since HCA profit = OP + RHG + RHG*, and
Current value profit = OP + RHG + UHG, then
Current value profit = HCA profit - RHG* + UHG

By making adjustments to the historical cost profit for RHG* and UHG, we can derive the current value profit. This ability to make adjustments is now used to apply current cost accounting in practice.

2.13   In current value accounting, a **distinction** is therefore made between:

(a)   **holding gains** (RHG and UHG); and
(b)   **current operating gains** (OP).

This distinction will be maintained in the descriptions which follow of the different methods of current value accounting.

2.14   We must now go on to consider the different current value accounting systems in more detail, and the advantages and disadvantages of each will be listed separately later on; however, it will be useful at this stage to list the broad **advantages of all current value systems**.

(a)   **They assign a 'true' value to assets** (unfortunately, the 'true' value of assets calls for the subjective judgement of the valuer).

(b)   By separating profit into operating profit, realised holding gains and unrealised holding gains, **they present a more informative account of when and why profit has arisen**, unlike historical cost accounting which assigns all profit (as a single value) to the period when the asset is eventually realised.

(c)   Current value systems are therefore **more helpful to users**, notably shareholders, and long and short-term creditors. They also provide a more useful basis for management to decide whether the capital of the business has been maintained (or increased).

2.15   A numerical example might help to make this clear. Suppose that a trader buys a piece of land on 1 January 19X2 at a cost of £4,000 and sells it on 30 June 19X3. Owing to a sluggish market for land, its market value on 31 December 19X2 was only £4,200 and on 30 June 19X3 £4,500, although the retail price index has risen from 100 on 1 January 19X2 to 115 on 31 December 19X2 and 125 on 30 June 19X3.

	Current value £		Price adjusted value £
1 January 19X2	4,000		4,000
31 December 19X2	4,200	$\left[\times \dfrac{115}{100} \right]$	4,600
30 June 19X3	4,500	$\left[\times \dfrac{125}{100} \right]$	5,000

2.16   The current value at each of the two subsequent dates is higher than historical cost, but it does not allow for the changing value of money, as measured by the retail price index. A collapse in the property market or, in the case of plant and machinery the development of new technology, might cause a *fall* in current values below historical cost, even when there is general price inflation. However, because inflation tends to push most prices up to a greater or lesser degree, it is usual to find that in a period of inflation, current values happen to be higher than historical costs.

2.17   Current value accounting has been given a growing amount of attention from the accountancy profession as a consequence of price-level changes, and the problem of measuring a realistic profit figure in periods of high inflation. This is despite the fact that current value accounting systems are not systems of accounting for inflation. Of the major systems we shall be looking at, **only CPP (current purchasing power accounting) is an inflation accounting system.** It will only be coincidental if current values turn out to be the same as historical costs adjusted for inflation.

Current entry value accounting

2.18   The current entry value of an asset represents the price which would be paid for bringing a similar asset into the business; it **is the replacement cost of the asset**. Two writers who favoured the current entry value system of accounting were Edwards and Bell in *The Theory and Measurement of Business Income* who referred to current entry value 'profit' as 'business income'. Business income, BI, is the sum of:

$$OP + RHG + UHG$$

as described previously in Paragraph 2.12. The calculations are based on the replacement cost of the assets.

2.19   **Holding gains** have already been described in Paragraphs 2.4 - 2.9, but we must now look at them again more closely. Three types of holding gain exist, ie **from**:

(a)   **Inventory**.
(b)   **Depreciable fixed assets**.
(c)   **Fixed assets which do not depreciate** (eg land).

Holding gains from inventory

2.20   A company makes two items of product A in 19X3, at a cost of £35 each, and:

(a)   sells one of them during the year for £44 by which time its replacement cost is £40; and

(b)   has not sold the second unit by the financial year end (31 December) when its replacement cost has risen to £46.

We would identify:

(a)   a realised holding gain of £(40 – 35) = £5 on the first unit;
(b)   an unrealised holding gain of £(46 – 35) = £11 on the second unit.

2.21   Total business income for the year ended 31 December 19X3 in respect of these two units would be as follows.

	£	
Current operating profit (£44 – £40)	4	(OP)
Realised holding gain (first unit)	5	(RHG)
Unrealised holding gain (second unit)	11	(UHG)
Total business income	20	

The closing balance sheet would include a value for the second unit still in stock of £46.

Holding gains from depreciable fixed assets

2.22   Depreciable fixed assets present the **most complicated** aspect of holding gains with replacement costs, and a numerical example might help to explain the principles involved.

2.23   EXAMPLE: HOLDING GAINS FROM DEPRECIABLE FIXED ASSETS

Suppose that a company buys a fixed asset at the beginning of year 1 for £9,000. It has an expected life of 3 years, and nil residual value. Straight line depreciation is used. The replacement cost of the asset is £9,900, £10,500 and £12,000 at the end of years 1, 2 and 3 respectively. These are the replacement costs of a brand new asset.

2.24 In year 1, the current operating profit (OP) is calculated after deducting depreciation as $^1/_3$ of £9,900 = £3,300. Since the asset cost only £9,000, a historical cost depreciation figure would have been only £3,000. This means that in buying the asset one year earlier, the company has made a 'cost saving' or 'holding gain' of £3,300 – £3,000 = £300. This is a realised holding gain (or 'realised cost saving') because the depreciation charge was made against the profits for the current year, year 1.

At the same time, the total holding gain on the asset is £9,900 – £9,000 = £900, of which only £300 has been realised. An additional £600 represents the difference between the written down value of the asset at net replacement cost of £6,600 and net book value, historical cost of £6,000. This saving will be realised in the next two years, but has arisen in year 1; in other words there is an unrealised holding gain (or unrealised cost saving) of £600 in year 1 (which will eventually be 'realised' in year 2 and year 3).

2.25 **Two points must be understood at this stage.**

(a) Depreciation is regarded as a cost which occurs each year, so that a part of the cost of a fixed asset is 'realised' each year.

(b) Replacement cost profit is OP+RHG+UHG, therefore in year 1, both the realised and unrealised holding gains (£300+£600) are added to current operating profit to obtain the total business income for the period (after £3,300 has been deducted in arriving at current operating profit).

2.26 In year 2, the current operating profit (OP) is calculated after deducting depreciation of 2 of £10,500 = £3,500.

By holding the asset between year 1 and 2, there would be a further holding gain. The replacement value of the asset was £9,900 at the end of year 1, and £10,500 at the end of year 2. If we had been dealing with a new asset, the total of RHG and UHG would have been £600. The asset, however, had already had one-third of its life before the start of year 2, and this means that $^1/_3$ of £600 = £200 is irrelevant to the calculation of holding gains, because it relates to depreciation in the first year of the asset's life.

2.27 Holding gains in year 2 would be calculated as follows.

	End of year 1 £	End of year 2 £
Gross replacement cost	9,900	10,500
Assumed (net) replacement cost, based on this value: at end of year 1	6,600	7,000
at end of year 2	3,300	3,500

Total holding gain, year 2 = £(7,000 – 6,600) = £400
Unrealised holding gain, year 2 = £(3,500 – 3,300) = £200 (which will be realised over the remaining life of the asset)

The realised holding gain in year 2 is the difference between the depreciation based on the current year's replacement cost (£3,500) and the depreciation which would have been charged based on the previous year's replacement cost (£3,300): £200.

2.28 In year 3, the same principles apply.

(a) The current operating profit would be calculated after deducting depreciation of $^1/_3$ of £12,000 = £4,000.

(b) By holding the asset between year 2 and year 3, there was a further holding gain, calculated as follows.

	End of year 2 £	End of year 3 £
Gross replacement cost	10,500	12,000
Assumed (net) replacement cost, based		
on this value: at the end of year 2	3,500	4,000
at the end of year 3	0	0

The total holding gain is £(4,000-3,500) = £500, the unrealised holding gain is £0 (which should be expected, since the asset has reached the end of its life and therefore all gains will have been realised).

(c)   The realised holding gain in year 3 is the difference between the depreciation charge based on the current year's replacement cost (£4,000) and the charge which would have been applied using the previous year's replacement cost (£3,500).

2.29   The figures may be summarised in the following two tables.

Table 1

	Year 1 £	Year 2 £	Year 3 £	Total £
Increase in gross replacement				
cost of the asset	900	600	1,500	3,000
Realised holding gain	300	200	500	1,000
	600	400	1,000	2,000
Unrealised holding gain	600	200	0	800
Underprovision of depreciation				
in previous year	0	200 *	1,000 **	1,200

* $1/3$ of £600 (GRC increase)   ** $2/3$ of £1,500 (GRC increase)

Table 2

	Year 1 £	Year 2 £	Year 3 £	Total £
Depreciation charge in arriving				
at current operating profit	(3,300)	(3,500)	(4,000)	(10,800)
Realised holding gain	300	200	500	1,000
Unrealised holding gain	600 *	200 **	0	800
Net charge against business income	(2,400)	(3,100)	(3,500)	9,000
(current entry value a/cs)				

* Realised in years 2 and 3   ** Realised in year 3

Note. The net charge against business income is less in earlier years than in later years, but the total is £9,000 over 3 years. (£9,000 is the historical cost of the asset.)

2.30   The effect of **using replacement costs** as a basis for charging depreciation is that **holding gains are recognised at an earlier stage than in historical cost accounting, and credited to profit before they are realised**. Thus:

	Depreciation Historical cost a/cs £	*Net charge Replacement cost a/cs* £	*Difference* £	
Year 1	3,000	2,400	600	note (a)
Year 2	3,000	3,100	(100)	note (b)
Year 3	3,000	3,500	(500)	note (c)
	9,000	9,000	0	

Notes

(a)   The unrealised holding gain of £600 (eventually realised in years 2 and 3).

(b) The unrealised holding gain of £200 (realised in year 3), less the realised holding gain of £300 from year 1.

(c) The realised holding gains of £300 and £200 from years 1 and 2.

Holding gains of non-depreciating assets

2.31 In replacement cost accounting the calculation of holding gains for assets which do not depreciate is more straightforward, and an example should illustrate the principle. Farrar Termer Ltd bought a piece of land on 8 May 19X0 for £15,200. The replacement cost of the land (which was taken to be its market value) was:

£15,900 on 31 December 19X0
£17,000 on 31 December 19X1
£18,200 on 31 December 19X2
£18,400 on 6 March 19X3, when the land was sold for this amount. The company's accounting year ends on 31 December.

2.32 The total gain £(18,400 – 15,200) = £3,200 is realised when the asset is sold in 19X3, and in historical cost accounting the profit would not be recorded until that year (realisation principle). However, in current entry value accounting, unrealised holding gains (capital gains in the case of non-depreciating assets) would be credited to 'business income' in the year they become apparent.

Year	Unrealised holding gain £	Realised holding gain £	Total addition to business income for the year £
19X0	15,900 – 15,200 = 700	-	700
19X1	17,000 – 15,900 = 1,100	-	1,100
19X2	18,200 – 17,000 = 1,200	-	1,200
19X3	-	18,400 – 18,200 = 200	200
			3,200

2.33 The net effect of using current entry value accounting is that profits on fixed assets are accounted for earlier than under the historical cost convention, which is therefore a more prudent system in this respect.

Business income and holding gains

2.34 In this section so far, it has been stressed that business income is the sum of operating profit plus realised and unrealised holding gains for the period.

To complicate the issue a little further, it should be mentioned that there is some **opposition to the idea that holding gains should be included as a part of business income.** The main reasons for this opposition are as follows.

(a) **Unrealised holding gains** show an increase in the value of assets, but there is **no change in the physical substance of the assets.** To claim a profit when there is no physical change, it can be argued, is unjustifiable.

(b) Realised holding gains are represented by cash or by cost savings in the case of depreciation. For example, if an item costs £15 cash, and is sold for £25 when its replacement cost is £18, the operating profit (£7) plus the realised holding gain (£3) represent the increase in the company's cash position. However, if the company intends to replace the item it has sold, it will need £18 to do it; therefore only £7, the operating profit, is spare cash. It has therefore been **argued that realised holding gains should be excluded from the profit figure, because the revenue** (or cost savings) **from those gains needs to be kept within the business to maintain its substance or operating capability.**

2.35   This point of view was adopted in the accounting standard SSAP 16 *Current cost accounting*, and we shall now assume that in practice replacement costing would be applied in this way. For example, if a company buys a piece of land on 1 January 19X5 for £20,000 and its value on 31 December is £24,000 and on 2 July 19X6 (when it is sold) is £27,500, the:

(a)   Unrealised gain in the year to 31 December 19X5 is £4,000, but the company's physical asset, the land, is still the same.

(b)   Realised holding gain in 19X6 is £3,500, but if the company intends to replace the land sold with a similar piece of land (and we will assume that this is the case) £27,500 will be needed for the purchase, therefore no profit has been made which could safely have been paid out as a dividend to shareholders.

2.36   It is therefore possible to argue against the inclusion of holding gains in the profit figure, and yet still favour replacement cost accounting to measure operating profit. In other words, it is possible to argue:

(a)   profit = current entry value OP;

(b)   holding gains (RHG + UHG) should be credited to a separate reserve account and not treated as profit.

Advantages of replacement costing

2.37   The **advantages of replacement costing** may be summarised as follows.

(a)   It provides management with an **analysis of total profit into operating profit and holding gains**, so that a better assessment can be made about:

(i)   operational decisions in the past;
(ii)   decisions in the past to hold assets rather than defer their purchase.

This division of profit therefore provides a measurement of management efficiency in their control over operations.

(b)   If holding gains are excluded from business income, the business income would be the same as the current operating profit; and this would be an **indication of whether the company has maintained its 'physical substance' or 'operating capability'**, as described in Paragraphs 2.35 to 2.37.

(c)   **Assets** in the balance sheet are **shown at current values**, which **is less misleading** than the historical cost accounting method of showing assets at net book value.

(d)   Replacement cost **provides accounting information** which enables users to assess the stability of the company, its vulnerability to a takeover or liquidation, its operating capability and future prospects.

(e)   It is **consistent with the concepts of going concern and accruals**; and if holding gains are excluded from profit, it is also a more 'prudent' system of accounting than HCA.

(f)   **It can be used within a double entry bookkeeping system,** although not as easily as HCA.

Disadvantages of replacement costing

2.38 There are some important **disadvantages** of replacement costing, which may be summarised as follows.

(a) There are **practical difficulties** in estimating replacement costs, and there is scope for different principles to be applied, as well as scope for the subjective judgement of valuers. If replacement costs are the estimated amounts that would have to be paid to replace the asset 'today' but in fact there is no intention on the part of the company to replace the asset, an estimate of the replacement cost will be difficult unless:

(i) there is an identifiable market (as for property) or available suppliers' list prices;

(ii) the replacement costs of manufactured finished goods are available from the cost accounting system.

The main problems relate to assets for which there is no identifiable market, such as out-of-date equipment, or specially purpose-built premises (such as oil refineries). These problems will be described in more detail in the later chapter on current cost accounting.

(b) There is the **conceptual difficulty** of accepting that replacement costing should be applied to assets which may not be replaced at the end of their life. This problem is also discussed more fully in Section 4 on current cost accounting; it is sufficient to note at this point that if business income is to be a measure of capital maintenance, then some form of current value must be assigned to assets, even if they are either obsolete or unlikely to be replaced.

(c) Some businesses operate with long-life plant and machinery and large stocks of slow-moving inventory. Some companies even make their operating profit out of holding stocks (as do wine merchants and whisky distillers). In such cases, **it is debatable whether holding gains are really gains of an operational nature** which should therefore be included as business income.

(d) Replacement costing is **weak in some areas where historical cost accounting is strong.** Two examples of these areas are:

(i) Assessment of the stewardship of the company by its management.

(ii) Verifiability of raw data by auditors.

It is perhaps partly for this reason that the accounting profession has tended towards the view embodied in SSAP 16 that accounting procedures in practice should remain based on historical costs, with end of year adjustments made to turn the HCA profit and loss account and balance sheet into current value equivalents.

Question 3

The following extract is taken from the historical cost balance sheet of Rochester Enterprises Ltd.

	31 December 19X0	31 December 19X1
	£'000	£'000
Plant and machinery at cost	200	300
Less aggregate depreciation	40	100
Net book value	160	200

The following facts are relevant.

(a) Plant costing £200,000 was acquired on 1 January 19X0. The additional items were acquired on 1 January 19X1.

(b) No plant or machinery was sold or scrapped during 19X0 or 19X1.

(c) Of the year's depreciation written off in the 19X1 accounts, one-third is related to the items acquired on 1 January 19X1.

(d) Price index movements were as follows.

	General price index	Index of plant costs for the type of plant owned by Rochester
1 January 19X0	90	80
31 December 19X0	120	100
31 December 19X1	140	110

You are required to show the entries for plant and machinery in the final accounts of Rochester Enterprises Ltd as at 31 December 19X0 and 19X1, on the assumption that the company used a system of replacement cost accounting.

Answer

CURRENT COST BALANCE SHEETS (EXTRACTS)
AS AT 31 DECEMBER

	19X0 £'000	19X1 £'000
Gross replacement cost	250	385
Accumulated depreciation	50	132
Net replacement cost	200	253

CURRENT COST PROFIT AND LOSS ACCOUNTS
(EXTRACTS) FOR YEAR TO 31 DECEMBER

	19X0 £'000	19X1 £'000
Historical cost depreciation	40	60
Depreciation adjustment (realised holding gain)	10	17
	50	77

(*Note*. In current cost accounts prepared under SSAP 16 the prior year backlog depreciation of £5

(£40 × $\frac{110 - 100}{80}$) would not be identified in the balance sheet.)

Workings

					19X0 £'000				19X1 £'000
1	Gross replacement cost	200 ×	$\frac{100}{80}$	=	250	$\frac{200}{80}$ ×	$\frac{110}{80}$	=	275
						100 ×	$\frac{110}{100}$		$\frac{110}{385}$
2	Accumulated depreciation	40 ×	$\frac{100}{80}$	=	50	80 ×	$\frac{110}{80}$	=	110
						20 ×	$\frac{110}{100}$	=	$\frac{22}{132}$
3	Annual depreciation charge	40 ×	$\frac{100}{80}$	=	50	40 ×	$\frac{110}{80}$	=	55
						20 ×	$\frac{110}{100}$	=	$\frac{22}{77}$

Current exit value accounting

2.39 An alternative to current entry value accounting (replacement costs) is current exit value accounting.

> **KEY TERM**
>
> **Exit values** are **net realisable values for assets.** The net realisable value of an asset is the cash which would be obtained if the asset were realised, so that if a building could be sold for £250,000, less £20,000 in sales expenses, the NRV would be £230,000.

2.40 As a very rough guide for company exit values and entry values, we could probably say that for:

(a) Land and buildings, entry values are likely to be higher than exit values.

(b) Plant and equipment, gross replacement cost may be higher than the net realisable value of an asset, but the net replacement cost may be higher or lower than NRV.

(c) Inventory, net realisable value should normally be higher than replacement cost as the selling price of a product should be higher than the cost of its manufacture.

2.41 Several writers have advocated a system of exit value accounting, including in recent times R J Chambers and R R Sterling. The basic principle is that profit or 'realisable income' should be measured as follows:

$$I = D + (R_t - R_{t-1})$$

where

D   is the amount of distributions made during a period
R_t is the net realisable value of the entity's net assets at the end of the period
R_{t-1} is the net realisable value of the entity's net assets at the beginning of the period.

2.42 Realisable values imply the sale of assets for cash: in other words 'break-up' values. There has been some debate as to whether realisable values should be estimated on the:

(a) Assumption that the entity will be liquidated suddenly, or that the assets could be realised in an 'orderly' manner.

(b) Basis of the existing state of the asset, or on its eventual realisable value minus 'further processing costs'. For example, an item of part-finished work in progress might have a net realisable value of £6 in existing state, but it would eventually have an NRV of £20 when £5 of further processing costs have been spent on it. The exit value could be taken as either £6 or £(20 − 5) = £15.

2.43 It is **generally agreed that exit values should relate to assets in their existing state, on the assumption that assets would be realised in an orderly manner.**

2.44 **Exit values are opportunity costs.**

> **KEY TERM**
>
> An **opportunity cost** could be described as the benefit forgone by holding an asset in its existing form instead of in a next-best-alternative form.

In terms of exit value accounting, the next-best-alternative form of holding an asset is in cash. For example, if an item of machinery has a net realisable value of £500, the opportunity cost of using the machine is the 'sacrifice' of not having the cash from its sale, (£500).

2.45   **Cash** is therefore **a common measure for the opportunity cost of all the net assets of a business entity**. In the theory of exit value accounting, cash provides a common measurement of the alternative goods and services that could be bought if the business entity were liquidated. Chambers wrote that 'realisable income' (ie profit based on the current exit value concept) measures the increase in the potential purchasing power of the owners of the business entity.

2.46   Returning to the formula for realisable income:

$$I = D + (R_t - R_{t-1})$$

you might be able to see that the difference between R_t and R_{t-1} is the increase or decrease in the potential cash value of an entity's assets, therefore total income will conform to Chambers' definition in the previous paragraph.

2.47   Remember that this concept of potential purchasing power, also called 'the entity's ability to command alternative goods and services' by T A Lee, is not related to the separate issue of price inflation and the declining purchase power of money.

2.48   As in the case of entry value accounting, there will be holding gains in exit value accounting. We can again, if required, make a distinction between gains made on assets which are:

(a)   Intended for re-sale (operating gains on inventory).
(b)   Held for use (non-operating gains on fixed assets).

2.49   There may be realised and unrealised gains on both types of asset during an accounting period, so that total profit is the sum of operating gains and non-operating gains as follows:

$$I = (RG + UG) \text{ operating gains, plus } (RG + UG) \text{ non-operating gains.}$$

2.50   **In the current exit value balance sheet, assets are shown at net realisable value.**

Holding gains as profit

2.51   In **current entry value accounting,** it is usually accepted that **profit should exclude holding gains, both realised and unrealised,** so that the operating capability of the business entity can be maintained (Paragraphs 2.35 - 2.37).

2.52   In **current exit value accounting,** the capital maintenance concept relates to the 'potential purchasing power of owners' or the 'command power over resources in general' as measured by the realisable value of net assets. **All holding gains,** whether unrealised or realised, represent an increase in this potential purchasing power, and are therefore legitimately **included** in the profit figure.

2.53   **Current exit value accounting does not conform to the going concern concept** and for this reason it has not received much support from practising accountants.

2.54   **Current entry value accounting is based on the going concern concept, whereas current exit value accounting is based on the assumption of liquidating assets.** This means that whereas current entry value accounting must attempt to allow for the eventual replacement of assets, there is no such theoretical requirement in current exit value accounting. Realisable profit may therefore fail to provide sufficient funds for the replacement of assets at the end of their lives.

Advantages of current exit value accounting

2.55   The **advantages** of current exit value accounting may be summarised as follows.

(a)   It **uses the economic concept of opportunity costs** for the valuation of assets. This acknowledges the current 'sacrifice' which is being made by holding assets instead of converting them into an alternative form.

(b)   **Net realisable values provide a common measure** for the value of assets, cash, which in turn represents the potential capability to purchase different goods and services.

(c)   There is no reason to assume that a business entity will be a going concern for ever, and **exit values recognise that the entity must come to an end some time.** Exit values are therefore more appropriate 'current value' than entry values.

(d)   **It provides an understandable and realistic value for assets.** The 'man in the street' would probably assume that the balance sheet value of an asset is its break-up value, its net realisable value. Creditors would probably find that net realisable values give better information about the security of loans to the entity, and also about the liquidity of the company.

(e)   Although accountants are suspicious of net realisable value because it does not adhere to the going concern concept, Chambers has argued that exit values are **applied to some extent in practice, sometimes by legal requirement.**

(i)   **Monetary assets** (cash, debtors, trade creditors etc) are shown at realisable value.

(ii)   **Stocks** are valued at the lower of cost and net realisable value.

(iii)   It is common practice to revalue **land and buildings** in the balance sheet to a current market value.

(iv)   CA 1985 Sch 7 s 1(2) requires that **directors' reports** should include information about the market value of assets consisting in interests in land (property) where this is held by a company, if it differs from the book amount shown in the balance sheet.

Since realisable values are sometimes used in practice, it could be argued that there are good practical reasons why current exit value accounting is a valid concept, in spite of the prejudice of practising accountants against it.

Disadvantages

2.56   There are many **disadvantages** of current exit value accounting, the most important of which lies in the **practical difficulties of implementing it**. The estimation of net realisable values for stocks and work in progress and plant, machinery, fixtures and fittings and so on, would be highly subjective. Replacement costs are comparatively easier to estimate.

3   CURRENT PURCHASING POWER (CPP)

Capital maintenance in times of inflation

3.1   **Profit** can be measured as the **difference between how wealthy a company is at the beginning and at the end of an accounting period.**

(a)   This wealth can be expressed in terms of the capital of a company as shown in its opening and closing balance sheets.

(b)   A business which maintains its capital unchanged during an accounting period can be said to have broken even.

(c)   **Once capital has been maintained, anything achieved in excess represents profit.**

3.2   For this analysis to be of any use, we must be able to draw up a company's balance sheet at the beginning and at the end of a period, so as to place a value on the opening and closing capital. There are particular difficulties in doing this during a period of rising prices.

3.3   In conventional historical cost accounts, assets are stated in the balance sheet at the amount it cost to acquire them (less any amounts written off in respect of depreciation or diminution in value). Capital is simply the difference between assets and liabilities.

> **IMPORTANT!**
>
> If prices are rising, it is possible for a company to show a profit in its historical cost accounts despite having identical physical assets and owing identical liabilities at the beginning and end of its accounting period.

3.4   For example, consider the following opening and closing balance sheets of a company.

	Opening £	Closing £
Stock (100 items at cost)	500	600
Other net assets	1,000	1,000
Capital	1,500	1,600

Assuming that no new capital has been introduced during the year, and no capital has been distributed as dividends, the profit shown in historical cost accounts would be £100, being the excess of closing capital over opening capital. And yet in physical terms the company is no better off: it still has 100 units of stock (which cost £5 each at the beginning of the period, but £6 each at the end) and its other net assets are identical. The 'profit' earned has merely enabled the company to keep pace with inflation.

3.5   **An alternative to the concept of capital maintenance based on historical costs is to express capital in physical terms.** On this basis, no profit would be recognised in the example above because the physical substance of the company is unchanged over the accounting period. In the UK, a system of accounting (called **current cost accounting** or **CCA**) was introduced in 1980 by SSAP 16 (now withdrawn) and had as its basis a concept of capital maintenance based on 'operating capability'.

> Capital is maintained if at the end of the period the company is in a position to achieve the same physical output as it was at the beginning of the period.

You should bear in mind that financial definitions of capital maintenance are not the only ones possible; in theory at least, there is no reason why profit should not be measured as the increase in a company's *physical* capital over an accounting period.

The unit of measurement

3.6   Another way to tackle the problems of capital maintenance in times of rising prices is to look at the unit of measurement in which accounting values are expressed.

3.7   It is an axiom of **conventional accounting**, as it has developed over the years, that value should be measured in terms of money. It is also **implicitly assumed that money values are stable**, so that £1 at the start of the financial year has the same value as £1 at the end of that year. **But when prices are rising, this assumption is invalid: £1 at the end of the year has less value (less purchasing power) than it had one year previously.**

3.8   This **leads to problems when aggregating amounts which have arisen at different times.** For example, a company's fixed assets may include items bought at different times over a period of many years. They will each have been recorded in £s, but the value of £1 will have varied over the period. In effect the fixed asset figure in a historical cost balance sheet is an aggregate of a number of items expressed in different units. It **could be argued that such a figure is meaningless.**

3.9   Faced with this argument, one possibility would be to re-state all accounts items in terms of a stable monetary unit. There would be difficulties in practice, but in theory there is no reason why a stable unit (£ CPP = £s of current purchasing power) should not be devised. In this section we will look at a system of accounting (current purchasing power accounting, or CPP) based on precisely this idea.

Specific and general price changes

3.10 We can identify two different types of price inflation.

3.11 When prices are rising, it is likely that the current value of assets will also rise, but not necessarily by the general rate of inflation. For example, if the replacement cost of a machine on 1 January 19X2 was £5,000, and the general rate of inflation in 19X2 was 8%, we would not necessarily expect the replacement cost of the machine at 31 December 19X2 to be £5,000 plus 8% = £5,400. The rate of price increase on the machinery might have been less than 8% or more than 8%. (Conceivably, in spite of general inflation, the replacement cost of the machinery might have gone down.)

(a)   There is **specific price inflation**, which **measures price changes over time for a specific asset or group of assets.**

(b)   There is **general price inflation**, which **is the average rate of inflation, which reduces the general purchasing power of money.**

3.12 To counter the problems of specific price inflation some system of current value accounting may be used (for example, the system of current cost accounting described in the following chapter). The capital maintenance concepts underlying current value systems do not attempt to allow for the maintenance of real value in money terms.

3.13 Current purchasing power (CPP) accounting is based on a different concept of capital maintenance.

KEY TERM

CPP measures profits as the increase in the current purchasing power of equity. Profits are therefore stated after allowing for the declining purchasing power of money due to price inflation.

3.14 In Britain attempts to introduce CPP accounting have been in a combination with historical cost accounting, and it is on this aspect that this section will concentrate.

3.15 When applied to historical cost accounting, **CPP is a system of accounting which makes adjustments to income and capital values to allow for the general rate of price inflation.** An attempt to introduce such a system was made in 1974 with the publication of a Provisional Statement of Standard Accounting Practice, PSSAP 7 *Accounting for changes in the purchasing power of money*. Although it was withdrawn after a year, and was then superseded by SSAP 16, it remains a topic of debate and **some knowledge of CPP accounting is necessary to understand the diversity of views currently held on inflation accounting in general.**

The principles and procedures of CPP accounting

3.16 In CPP accounting, profit is measured after allowing for general price changes. It is a fundamental idea of CPP that capital should be maintained in terms of the same monetary purchasing power, so that:

$$P_{CPP} = D_{CPP} + (E_{t(CPP)} - E_{(t-1)CPP})$$

where P_{CPP} is the CPP accounting profit

D_{CPP} is distributions to shareholders, re-stated in current purchasing power terms

E_t the total value of assets attributable to the owners of the business entity at the end of the accounting period, restated in current purchasing power terms

$E_{(t-1)CPP}$ is the total value of the owners' equity at the beginning of the year re-stated in terms of current purchasing power at the end of the year.

A current purchasing power £ relates to the value of money on the last day of the accounting period.

3.17 **Profit in CPP accounting is** therefore **measured after allowing for maintenance of equity capital.** To the extent that a company is financed by loans, there is no requirement to allow for the maintenance of the purchasing power of the loan creditors' capital. Indeed, as we shall see, the equity of a business can profit from the loss in the purchasing power value of loans.

Monetary and non-monetary items

> **KEY TERM**
>
> A **monetary item** is an asset or liability whose amount is fixed by contract or statute in terms of £s, regardless of changes in general price levels and the purchasing power of the pound.

3.18 The main examples of monetary items are cash, debtors, creditors and loan capital.

3.19   These include land and buildings, plant and machinery and stock.

3.20   In CPP accounting, there is an **important difference** between monetary assets and liabilities.

(a)   If a company borrows money in a period of inflation, the amount of the debt will remain fixed (by law) so that when the debt is eventually paid, it will be paid in £s of a lower purchasing power.

For example, if a company borrows £2,000 on 1 January 19X5 and repays the loan on 1 January 19X9, the purchasing power of the £2,000 repaid in 19X9 will be much less than the value of £2,000 in 19X5, because of inflation. Since the company by law must repay only £2,000 of principal, it has gained by having the use of the money from the loan for 4 years. (The lender of the £2,000 will try to protect the value of his loan in a period of inflation by charging a higher rate of interest; however, this does not alter the fact that the loan remains fixed at £2,000 in money value.)

(b)   If a company holds cash in a period of inflation, its value in terms of current purchasing power will decline. The company will 'lose' by holding the cash instead of converting it into a non-monetary asset. Similarly, if goods are sold on credit, the amount of the debt is fixed by contract; and in a period of inflation, the current purchasing power of the money from the sale, when it is eventually received, will be less than the purchasing power of the debt, when it was first incurred.

3.21   In CPP accounting, it is therefore argued that **there are gains from having monetary liabilities and losses from having monetary assets.**

(a)   In the case of monetary assets, there is a need to make a provision against profit for the loss in purchasing power, because there will be a need for extra finance when the monetary asset is eventually used for operational activities. For example, if a company has a cash balance of £200, which is just sufficient to buy 100 new items of raw material stock on 1 January 19X5, and if the rate of inflation during 19X5 is 10%, the company would need £220 to buy the same 100 items on 1 January 19X6 (assuming the items increase in value by the general rate of inflation). By holding the £200 as a monetary asset throughout 19X5, the company would need £20 more to buy the same goods and services on 1 January 19X6 that it could have obtained on 1 January 19X5. £20 would be a CPP loss on holding the monetary asset (cash) for a whole year.

(b)   In the case of monetary liabilities, the argument in favour of including a 'profit' in CPP accounting is not as strong. By incurring a debt, say, on 1 January 19X5, there will not be any eventual cash input to the business. The 'profit' from the monetary liabilities is a 'paper' profit, and T A Lee has argued against including it in the CPP profit and loss account. PSSAP 7, however, noted that

'It has been argued that the gain on long-term borrowing should not be shown as profit in the CPP accounts because it might not be possible to distribute it without raising additional finance. This argument, however, confuses the measurement of profitability with the measurement of liquidity. Even in the absence of inflation, the whole of a company's profit may not be distributable without raising additional finance, for example, because it has been invested in, or earmarked for investment in, non-liquid assets.'

PSSAP 7 therefore concluded that all gains and losses from having monetary liabilities or assets should be included in the calculation of CPP profit. The concept of monetary gains and losses is an important one, and it was introduced into current cost accounting practice in Britain (see next section).

3.22 EXAMPLE: CPP ACCOUNTING

Seep Ltd had the following assets and liabilities at 31 December 19X4.

(a) All fixed assets were purchased on 1 January 19X1 at a cost of £60,000, and they had an estimated life of six years. Straight line depreciation is used.

(b) Closing stocks have a historical cost value of £7,900. They were bought in the period November-December 19X4.

(c) Debtors amounted to £8,000, cash to £2,000 and short-term creditors to £6,000.

(d) There is long-term debt capital of £15,000.

(e) The general price index includes the following information:

Year	Date	Price index
19X1	1 January	100
19X4	30 November	158
19X4	31 December	160
19X5	31 December	180

The historical cost balance sheet of Seep Ltd at 31 December 19X4 was as follows.

	£	£
Fixed assets at cost		60,000
Less depreciation		40,000
		20,000
Stocks	7,900	
Debtors	8,000	
Cash	2,000	
Current assets	17,900	
Less creditors	6,000	
		11,900
		31,900
Financed by:		
Equity		16,900
Loan capital		15,000
		31,900

Required

(a) Prepare a CPP balance sheet as at 31 December 19X4.

(b) What was the depreciation charge against CPP profits in 19X4?

(c) What must be the value of equity at 31 December 19X5 if Seep Ltd is to 'break even' and make neither a profit nor a loss in 19X5?

3.23 SOLUTION

(a)

	£c	£c
Fixed assets, at cost 60,000 × 160/100		96,000
Less depreciation 40,000 × 160/100		64,000
		32,000
Stock* 7,900 × 160/158	8,000	
Debtors**		8,000
Cash**	2,000	
	18,000	
Creditors**	6,000	
		12,000
		44,000
Loan stock**		15,000
Equity ***		29,000
		44,000

Notes

*Stocks purchased between 1 November and 31 December are assumed to have an average index value relating to the mid-point of their purchase period, at 30 November.

**Monetary assets and liabilities are not re-valued, because their CPP value is the face value of the debt or cash amount.

***Equity is a mixture of monetary and non-monetary asset values, and is the balancing figure in this example.

(b) Depreciation in 19X4 would be one sixth of the CPP value of the assets at the end of the year, $1/6$ of £96,000 = £16,000. Alternatively, it is:

$(1/6 \times £60,000) \times 160/100 = £16,000$

(c) To maintain the capital value of equity in CPP terms during 19X5, the CPP value of equity on 31 December 19X5 will need to be:

£29,000 × 180/160 = £32,625

Question 4

Rice and Price set up in business on 1 January 19X5 with no fixed assets, and cash of £5,000. On 1 January they acquired some stocks for the full £5,000 which they sold on 30 June 19X5 for £6,000. On 30 November they obtained a further £2,100 of stock on credit. The index of the general price level gives the following index figures.

Date	Index
1 January 19X5	300
30 June 19X5	330
30 November 19X5	350
31 December 19X5	360

Calculate the CPP profits (or losses) of Rice and Price for the year to 31 December 19X5.

Answer

The approach is to prepare a CPP profit and loss account.

	£c	£c
Sales (6,000 × 360/330)		6,545
Less cost of goods sold (5,000 × 360/300)		6,000
		545
Loss on holding cash for 6 months*	(545)	
Gain by having creditor for 1 month**	60	
		485
CPP profit		60

* (£6,000 × 360/330) - £6,000 = £c 545
**(£2,100 × 360/350) - £2,100 = £c 60

The advantages and disadvantages of CPP accounting

Advantages

3.24 (a) The **restatement of asset values in terms of a stable money value provides a more meaningful basis of comparison** with other companies. Similarly, provided that previous years' profits are re-valued into CPP terms, it is also possible to compare the current year's results with past performance.

(b) Profit is measured in 'real' terms and excludes 'inflationary value increments'. This **enables better forecasts of future prospects to be made.**

(c) CPP **avoids the subjective valuations** of current value accounting, because a single price index is applied to all non-monetary assets.

(d) CPP **provides a stable monetary unit** with which to value profit and capital; ie £c.

(e) Since it is based on historical cost accounting, **raw data is easily verified**, and measurements of value can be readily audited.

Disadvantages

3.25 (a) It is **not clear what £c means**. 'Generalised purchasing power' as measured by the Retail Price Index, or indeed any other general price index, has no obvious practical significance.

> 'Generalised purchasing power has no relevance to any person or entity because no such thing exists in reality, except as a statistician's computation.'   (T A Lee)

(b) The use of indices **inevitably involves approximations** in the measurements of value.

(c) **The value of assets in a CPP balance sheet has less meaning than a current value balance sheet.** It cannot be supposed that the CPP value of net assets reflects:

    (i) the general goods and services that could be bought if the assets were released; nor

    (ii) the consumption of general goods and services that would have to be forgone to replace those assets.

In this respect, a CPP balance sheet has similar drawbacks to an historical cost balance sheet.

4   CURRENT COST ACCOUNTING (CCA)

Value to the business (deprival value)

4.1   The **conceptual basis of CCA is that the value of assets consumed or sold, and the value of assets in the balance sheet, should be stated at their value to the business** (also known as 'deprival value').

4.2   A system of current cost accounting was introduced into the UK by SSAP 16 *Current cost accounting* in March 1980. This was the culmination of a long process of research into the problems of accounting in times of inflation. One result of this process had been the publication of PSSAP 7 on current purchasing power accounting, described previously. SSAP 16 encountered heavy criticism and was finally withdrawn in April 1988.

4.3   **In CCA, a physical rather than financial definition of capital is used: capital maintenance is measured by the ability of the business entity to keep up the same level of operating capability.**

> **KEY TERM**
>
> The **deprival value** of an asset is the loss which a business entity would suffer if it were deprived of the use of the asset.

4.4   **Value to the business**, or deprival value, can be any of the following values.

   (a)   **Replacement cost.** In the case of fixed assets, it is assumed that the replacement cost of an asset would be its net replacement cost (NRC), its gross replacement cost minus an appropriate provision for depreciation to reflect the amount of its life already 'used up'.

   (b)   **Net realisable value** (NRV); what the asset could be sold for, net of any disposal costs.

   (c)   **Economic value** (EV), or utility; what the existing asset will be worth to the company over the rest of its useful life.

4.5   The choice of deprival value from one of the three values listed will depend on circumstances. The decision tree on the next page illustrates the principles involved in the choice, but in simple terms you should remember that in **CCA deprival value is nearly always replacement cost.**

4.6   If the asset is worth replacing, its deprival value will always be net replacement cost. If the asset is not worth replacing, it might be disposed of straight away, or else it might be kept in operation until the end of its useful life.

4.7   You may therefore come across a statement that deprival value is the **lower of**:

   (a)   **net replacement cost**; and
   (b)   the **higher of net realisable value and economic value.**

4.8   We have already seen that if an asset is not worth replacing at the end of its life, the deprival value will be NRV or EV. However, there are many assets which will not be replaced either:

   (a)   because the asset is technologically obsolete, and has been (or will be) superseded by more modern equipment; or

(b) because the business is changing the nature of its operations and will not want to continue in the same line of business once the asset has been used up.

4.9 Such assets, even though there are reasons not to replace them, would still be valued (usually) at net replacement cost, because this 'deprival value' still provides an estimate of the operating capability of the company.

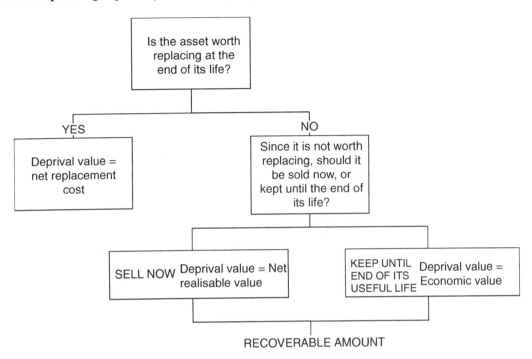

CCA profits and deprival value

4.10 The deprival value of assets is reflected in the CCA profit and loss account by the following means.

(a) **Depreciation** is **charged** on fixed assets **on the basis of gross replacement cost** of the asset (where NRC is the deprival value).

(b) Where **NRV or EV** is the deprival value, the **charge against CCA profits will be the loss in value of the asset during the accounting period**; ie from its previous balance sheet value to its current NRV or EV.

(c) **Goods sold are charged at their replacement cost**. Thus if an item of stock cost £15 to produce, and sells for £20, by which time its replacement cost has risen to £17, the CCA profit would be £3.

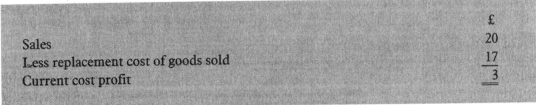

	£
Sales	20
Less replacement cost of goods sold	17
Current cost profit	3

4.11 It is useful to explain the distinction here between CCA and accounting for inflation, and a simple example may help to describe the difference. Suppose that Arthur Smith Ltd buys an asset on 1 January for £10,000. The estimated life of the asset is 5 years, and straight line depreciation is charged. At 31 December the gross replacement cost of the asset is £10,500 (5% higher than on 1 January) but general inflation during the year, as measured by the retail price index, has risen 20%.

(a)   To maintain the value of the business against inflation, the asset should be revalued as follows.

	£
Gross (£10,000 × 120%)	12,000
Depreciation charge for the year (@ 20%)	2,400
Net value in the balance sheet	9,600

(b)   In CCA, the business maintains its operating capability if we revalue the asset as follows.

	£
Gross replacement cost	10,500
Depreciation charge for the year (note)	2,100
NRC; balance sheet value	8,400

Note	£
Historical cost depreciation	2,000
CCA depreciation adjustment (5%)	100
Total CCA depreciation cost	2,100

4.12   **CCA preserves the operating capability of the company but does not necessarily preserve it against the declining value in the purchasing power of money** (against inflation). As mentioned in the previous chapter, CCA is a system which takes account of specific price inflation (changes in the prices of specific assets or groups of assets) but not of general price inflation.

4.13   A strict view of current cost accounting might suggest that a set of CCA accounts should be prepared from the outset on the basis of deprival values. In practice that has not been the procedure adopted in the UK. Instead, current cost accounts have been prepared by starting from historical cost accounts and making appropriate adjustments.

Current cost adjustments to historical cost profit

4.14   In current cost accounting profit is calculated as follows

	£	£
Historical cost profit		X
Less: Cost of sales adjustment (COSA)		X
depreciation adjustment	X	
		(X)
Current cost profit		X

The holding gains, both realised and unrealised, are therefore excluded from current cost profit. The double entry for the debits in the current cost profit and loss account is to credit both COSA and depreciation adjustment to a non-distributable revaluation reserve.

The current cost profit and loss account and balance sheet

4.15   The format of the *current cost profit and loss account* would show the following information, although not necessarily in the order given.

	£	£
Historical cost profit (before interest & taxation)		X
Current cost operating adjustments		
Cost of sales adjustment (COSA)	(X)	
Monetary working capital adjustment (loss or gain) (MWCA)	(X) or X	
Depreciation adjustment	(X)	
		(X)
Current cost operating profit (before interest and taxation)		X
Less interest payable and receivable		(X)
Add gearing adjustment		X
Current cost profit attributable to shareholders		X
Less taxation		(X)
Current cost profit after tax		X
Extraordinary items (loss or gain)		(X) or X
Current cost profit or loss for the financial year		X

Cost of sales adjustment (COSA)

4.16 The COSA is **necessary to eliminate realised holding gains on stock. It represents the difference between the replacement cost and the historical cost of goods sold.** The exclusion of holding gains from CC profit is a necessary consequence of the need to maintain operating capability. The COSA represent that portion of the HC profit which must be consumed in replacing the stock item sold so that trading can continue. Where practical difficulties arise in estimating replacement cost, a simple indexing system can be used.

Depreciation adjustment

4.17 The depreciation adjustment is **the difference between the depreciation charge on the gross replacement cost of the assets and the historical cost depreciation.** This is (as with the COSA) a realised holding gain which is excluded from the CC profit. Where comparison is made with a different asset for the purposes of calculating replacement cost (because of the obsolescence of the old asset), then allowance must be made for different useful lives and different production capabilities.

Monetary working capital adjustment (MWCA)

4.18 Where a company gives or takes credit for the sale or purchase of goods, the goods are paid for at the end of the credit period at the replacement cost as at the beginning of the credit period. If a company measures profit as the excess of revenue over cost:

(a) **creditors protect the company** to some extent **from price changes because the company lags behind current prices in its payment;**

(b) **debtors, in contrast, would be a burden on profits** in a period of rising prices because sales receipts will always relate to previous months' sales at a lower price/cost/profit level.

The MWCA can therefore be either a gain or a loss.

Gearing adjustment

4.19 If a company has **external creditors** who are financing some part of the net assets of the business (stocks, fixed assets and monetary working capital), since the amount owed to these creditors is fixed in monetary terms, and does not rise with inflation, it follows that they are **financing some part of the holding gains represented by COSA, depreciation adjustment and MWCA.** In calculating the amount of current cost profit earned by the shareholders it is **therefore inappropriate to deduct the** *whole* **of these adjustments from historical cost profit.** The deduction **must be abated by the amount of the adjustments** which is **financed by external creditors.**

4.20   In the current cost balance sheet assets will be valued at their 'value to the business' and liabilities at their monetary amount. There will be a current cost reserve to reflect the revaluation surpluses. This has already been described in some detail.

Exam focus point

Although you are not required to produce current cost accounts in your examination, a comprehensive example should help your understanding.

4.21   EXAMPLE: CURRENT COST ACCOUNTS

At the beginning of a period, Arthur Smith Ltd has the following balance sheet.

	£
Fixed assets (newly acquired)	10,000
Stocks (newly acquired)	2,000
	12,000
Financed by	
Equity	8,000
Loan stock (10% interest)	4,000
	12,000

4.22   The company gearing is 33%, in terms of both HC and CCA. During the period, sales of stocks amounted to £15,000, the replacement cost of sales was £13,200 and the historical cost of sales was £12,000. Closing stocks, at replacement cost, were £4,600 and at HC were £4,400. Depreciation is provided for at 10% straight line, and at the end of the period the fixed asset had a gross replacement cost of £11,000. The HC accounts were as follows.

PROFIT AND LOSS ACCOUNT

	£
Sales	15,000
Less cost of sales	12,000
	3,000
Depreciation	1,000
Profit before interest	2,000
Interest	400
Profit	1,600

CLOSING BALANCE SHEET

	£
Fixed asset at cost less depreciation	9,000
Stocks	4,400
Cash	200
	13,600
Equity	9,600
Loan stock	4,000
	13,600

Taxation is ignored.

Prepare workings for the CCA accounts. (Depreciation for the period will be based on the end of year value of the fixed asset.)

4.23 SOLUTION

The COSA is (£13,200 – £12,000)   =   £1,200
The depreciation adjustment is   £100
The MWCA is nil (there are no purchases or sales on credit).

Note. The small cash balance in the closing balance sheet would probably be regarded as necessary for business purposes and therefore taken up in the MWCA as monetary working capital. In this example, we will treat the £200 as a cash surplus.

	£	£
Historical cost profit (before interest)		2,000
Current cost adjustments:		
COSA	1,200	
MWCA	0	
Depreciation	100	
		1,300
Current cost operating profit		700

The gearing adjustment is calculated by multiplying the three current cost adjustments (here £1,300) by the gearing proportion (by the proportion of the gains which is financed by borrowing and which therefore provides additional profits for equity, since the real value of the borrowing is declining in a period of rising prices).

The gearing proportion is the ratio:

$$\frac{\text{Net borrowing}}{\text{Average net operating assets in the year}}$$

Net operating assets consist of fixed assets, stocks and monetary working capital. They are financed partly by net borrowings and partly by equity. The gearing proportion can therefore equally well be expressed as:

$$\frac{\text{Average net borrowing in the period}}{\text{Average equity interests plus average net borrowing in the period}}$$

Equity interests include the current cost reserve, and also any proposed dividends. Average figures are taken as being more representative than end of year figures.

	£
Opening figures	
Net borrowing	4,000
Equity interests	8,000
Equity plus net borrowing	12,000

Closing figures: since cash is here regarded as a surplus amount, the company is losing value during a period of inflation by holding cash - just as it is gaining by having fixed loans. If cash is not included in MWC, it is:

(a)   deducted from net borrowings; and

(b)   excluded from net operating assets.

(Net operating assets consist of fixed assets, long term trade investments, stocks and monetary working capital.)

The closing figures are therefore as follows.

	£	£
Fixed assets (at net replacement cost £11,000-£1,100)		9,900
Stocks (at replacement cost)		4,600
Monetary working capital		0
Net operating assets (equals equity interest plus net borrowings)		14,500
Less: net borrowing	4,000	
cash in hand	(200)	
		3,800
Therefore equity interest		10,700

Average figures	*Opening*	*Closing*	*Average*
Net borrowing	£4,000	£3,800	£3,900
Net operating assets	£12,000	£14,500	£13,250

The gearing proportion is $\dfrac{3,900}{13,250} \times 100\% = 29.43\%$

Question 5

Prepare the CCA accounts based on the above example.

Answer

	£	£
Historical cost profit before interest		2,000
Current cost adjustments:		
COSA	1,200	
MWCA	0	
Depreciation	100	
		(1,300)
Current cost operating profit		700
Interest		(400)
Gearing adjustment (£1,300 × 29.43%)		383
		(17)
Current cost profit attributable to shareholders		683

CCA BALANCE SHEET (end of year)

	£	£
Fixed assets (net replacement cost)		9,900
Stocks (replacement cost)		4,600
Cash		200
		14,700
Financed by		
Equity at start of year		8,000
Addition to P & L reserve during year		683
Current cost reserve		
Excess of net replacement cost over net book value (9,900-9,000)	900	
Depreciation adjustment	100	
COSA	1,200	
MWCA	0	
	2,200	
Less gearing adjustment	(383)	
	1,817	
Add revaluation of year-end stocks	200	
		2,017
		10,700
Loan stock		4,000
		14,700

Summary of double entry: CCA

4.24   It may be useful to summarise the double-entry system in CCA, in which the current cost reserve has a central role.

   (a)   **For fixed assets, there will be an excess of net replacement cost over (historical cost) net book value.** The increase in this excess amount each accounting period will be recorded as:

   DEBIT   net assets (assets account and provision for depreciation account) with the increase in the gross replacement cost minus total extra provision for depreciation;

   CREDIT   current cost reserve account

   (b)   The **various adjustments** will be as follows.

   DEBIT   current cost profit and loss account

   CREDIT   current cost reserve account;

   with the amount of the **COSA**, the depreciation adjustment and the MWCA, if this reduces the current cost profit. If the MWCA increases the current cost profit, the entries would be 'credit P & L account' 'debit current cost reserve'.

   (c)   The **gearing adjustment** is shown as:

   CREDIT   current cost profit and loss account

   DEBIT   current cost reserve;

   (d)   At the end of an accounting period, there may be some **revaluations of closing stocks**:

   DEBIT   stocks

   CREDIT   current cost reserve account

   with the amount of the revaluation.

   On the first day of the next accounting period, this entry is **reversed**; ie

   CREDIT   stocks (to reduce them to historical cost)

   DEBIT   current cost reserve account.

> **Exam focus point**
> In June 1995 a question required candidates to consider the different ratios which would be calculated using historical cost accounting and current cost accounting.

The advantages and disadvantages of current cost accounting

Advantages

4.25   (a)   By excluding holding gains from profit, CCA **can be used to indicate whether** the **dividends** paid to shareholders (which by UK law can exceed the size of the CCA profit) **will reduce the operating capability** of the business.

   (b)   Assets are valued after management has considered the **opportunity cost** of holding them, and the expected benefits from their future use. CCA is therefore **a useful guide for management in deciding whether to hold or sell assets.**

   (c)   It is **relevant to the needs of information users** in:

   (i)   Assessing the stability of the business entity.

(ii)   Assessing the vulnerability of the business (eg to a takeover), or the liquidity of the business.

(iii)   Evaluating the performance of management in maintaining and increasing the business substance.

(iv)   Judging future prospects.

(d)   It can be **implemented fairly easily** in practice, by making simple adjustments to the historical cost accounting profits. A current cost balance sheet can also be prepared with reasonable simplicity.

Disadvantages

4.26   (a)   It is impossible to make valuations of EV or NRV without subjective judgements. The **measurements used are** therefore **not objective.**

(b)   There are **several problems to be overcome in deciding how to provide an estimate of replacement costs for fixed assets.**

(i)   Depreciation based on replacement costs **does not conform to the traditional accounting view** that depreciation can be viewed as a means of spreading the cost of the asset over its estimated life,

(ii)   Depreciation based on replacement costs would appear to be a means of providing that sufficient funds are set aside in the business to ensure that the asset can be replaced at the end of its life. But if it is not certain what technological advances might be in the next few years and how the type of assets required might change between the current time and the estimated time of replacement, it is difficult to argue that depreciation based on today's costs is a valid way of providing for the eventual physical replacement of the asset.

(iii)   It is more correct, however, that **depreciation in CCA does not set aside funds for the physical replacement of fixed assets.**

'CCA aims to maintain no more and no less than the facilities that are available at the accounting date ... despite the fact that the fixed assets which provide those facilities might never be replaced in their existing or currently available form ... In simple language, this means charging depreciation on the basis of the current replacement cost of the assets at the time the facilities are used.'   (Mallinson)

(iv)   It may be argued that depreciation based on **historical cost is more accurate** than replacement cost depreciation, **because the historical cost is known,** whereas replacement cost is simply an estimate. However, replacement costs are re-assessed each year, so that inaccuracies in the estimates in one year can be rectified in the next year.

(c)   The **mixed value approach** to valuation **means** that some assets will be valued at replacement cost, but others will be valued at net realisable value or economic value. It is arguable that the **total assets** will, therefore, have an **aggregate value** which is **not particularly meaningful** because of this mixture of different concepts.

(d)   It can be argued that **'deprival value' is an unrealistic concept, because the business entity has not been deprived of the use of the asset.** This argument is one which would seem to reject the fundamental approach to 'capital maintenance' on which CCA is based.

5 AGENCY THEORY AND THE EFFICIENT MARKET HYPOTHESIS
12/95

5.1 We are now moving on to some more general theories about behaviour within companies and in the stock market.

> **Exam focus point**
> This area may seem obscure, but the examiner has tested it in December 1995.

Agency theory and the 'agency problem'

5.2 **The relationship between management and shareholders is sometimes referred to as an agency relationship,** in which managers act as agents for the shareholders, using delegated powers to run the affairs of the company in the shareholders' best interests.

> **KEY TERM**
>
> **Agency theory** (Fama and Jensen) proposes that, although individual members of the business team act in their own self-interest, the well-being of each individual depends on the well-being of other team members and on the performance of the team in competition with other teams. The firm is seen as constituted by contracts among the different factors of production.

5.3 Agency theory was advanced by two American economists, Jensen and Meckling, in 1976 as a theory to explain relationships within corporations. It has been used to explain management control practices as well as relationships between management and investors: here we are concerned with the latter.

5.4 Jensen and Meckling proposed that corporations be viewed as a set of contracts between management, shareholders and creditors, with management as agents and providers of finance as principals. Financial reports and external audit are two mechanisms by which the agents demonstrate compliance with their obligations to the principals.

5.5 The agency **relationship arising from the separation of ownership from management is sometimes characterised as the 'agency problem'.** For example, if managers hold none or very little of the equity shares of the company they work for, what is to stop them from:

(a) Working inefficiently?
(b) Not bothering to look for profitable new investment opportunities?
(c) Giving themselves high salaries and perks?

5.6 **One power that shareholders possess is the right to remove the directors from office.** But shareholders have to take the initiative to do this, and in many companies, the shareholders lack the energy and organisation to take such a step. Even so, directors will want the company's report and accounts, and the proposed final dividend, to meet with shareholders' approval at the AGM.

5.7 It is the **responsibility of the directors to ensure that management below director level perform well.** Getting the best out of subordinates is one of the functions of management, and directors should be expected to do it as well as they can.

5.8 Another reason why managers might do their best to improve the financial performance of their company is that **managers' pay is often related to the size or profitability of the company**. Managers in very big companies, or in very profitable companies, will normally expect to earn higher salaries than managers in smaller or less successful companies.

5.9 As explained by G Cosserat in an article published in the *Students' Newsletter* (December 1994), **agency theory is based on a number of behavioural and structural assumptions**.

(a) The most important behavioural assumptions are **individual welfare maximisation, individual rationality**, and the assumption that individuals are **risk-averse**.

(b) Structural assumptions include the assumption that **investments are not infinitely divisible**, and that **individuals vary in their access to funds and their entrepreneurial ability**. Some criticisms of the theory have attacked these various assumptions. For example, are individuals satisficers rather than maximisers? And are individuals truly 'rational' or perhaps rather gullible?

5.10 The assumptions of the theory **suggest that investors and entrepreneurs have incentives for sharing risks and rewards of entrepreneurial activity**, for example where the entrepreneur, who may enjoy limited liability, borrows from investors at fixed rates of interest.

5.11 The key feature of **an efficient agency contract**, for example within a company, is that it **allows full delegation of decision-making authority over the use of invested funds to management without excessive risk of abuse** of that authority. In the real world, an 'agency cost' arises, being the difference between the return expected if managers truly maximised shareholder wealth and the actual return, given that managers will actually be seeking to maximise their own wealth.

5.12 **'Bonding' and 'monitoring' procedures** help to **act as safeguards** to minimise the risk of investors incurring agency costs. An example of 'bonding' is a condition attached to a loan (eg security over assets, conditions not to raise further loans). A bank lending money to a business will also expect information to be supplied to enable it to *monitor* compliance with the loan agreement.

5.13 Agency theory suggests that audited accounts of limited companies are an important source of 'post-decision' information minimising investors' agency costs, in contrast to alternative approaches which see financial reports as primarily a source of 'pre-decision' information for equity investors. The theory is advanced as an explanation for the continued use of absorption costing and historic costs in management accounts in spite of their apparent lack of relevance in decision making.

The efficient market hypothesis

5.14 It has been argued that the UK and US stock markets are **efficient capital markets**, that is, markets in which:

(a) The **prices of securities** bought and sold **reflect all the relevant information** which is available to the buyers and sellers. In other words, share prices change quickly to reflect all new information about future prospects.

(b) **No individual dominates** the market.

(c) **Transaction costs** of buying and selling are **not so high** as to discourage trading significantly.

5.15 If the stock market is efficient, **share prices should vary in a rational way.**

   (a) If a company makes a profitable investment, shareholders will get to know about it, and the market price of its shares will rise in anticipation of future dividend increases.

   (b) If a company makes a bad investment shareholders will find out and so the price of its shares will fall.

   (c) If interest rates rise, shareholders will want a higher return from their investments, so market prices will fall.

The definition of efficiency

5.16 The efficiency of a stock market means the ability of a stock market to price stocks and shares fairly and quickly.

> **KEY TERM**
>
> An **efficient market** is one in which the market prices of all the securities traded on it reflect all the available information. There is no possibility of 'speculative bubbles' in which share prices are pushed up or down, by speculative pressure, to unrealistically high or low levels.

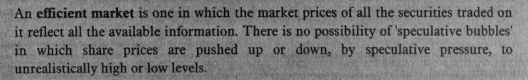

Varying degrees of efficiency

5.17 There are three degrees or 'forms' of efficiency:

   (a) **Weak form.**
   (b) **Semi-strong form.**
   (c) **Strong form.**

5.18 Tests can be carried out on the workings of a stock market to establish whether the market operates with a particular form of efficiency.

Weak form tests and weak form efficiency

5.19 The weak form hypothesis of market efficiency states that **current share prices only reflect all information available from past changes in the price.** Share prices do **not** change **in anticipation** of new information being announced.

5.20 Since new information arrives unexpectedly, changes in share prices should occur in a random fashion: **a weak form test seeks to prove the validity of the random walk theory** of share prices. In addition, if the theory is correct then chartist or technical analysis cannot be based on sound principles.

5.21 Research to prove that the stock market displays weak form efficiency has been based on the principle that:

   (a) if share price changes are random; and

   (b) if there is no connection between past price movements and new share price changes then it should be possible to prove statistically there is no correlation between successive changes in the price of a share, that is, that trends in prices cannot be detected.

Proofs of the absence of trends have been claimed in the work of various writers.

Semi-strong form tests and semi-strong form efficiency

5.22   Semi-strong form tests attempt to show that the stock market displays semi-strong efficiency, by which we mean that **current share prices reflect both**:

(a)   **all relevant information about past price movements and their implications**; and

(b)   **all knowledge** which is **available publicly**.

5.23   **Tests to prove semi-strong efficiency have concentrated on the ability of the market to anticipate share price changes before new information is formally announced**. For example, if two companies plan a merger, share prices of the two companies will inevitably change once the merger plans are formally announced. The market would show semi-strong efficiency, however, if it were able to anticipate such an announcement, so that share prices of the companies concerned would change in advance of the merger plans being confirmed.

5.24   **Research** in both Britain and the USA has suggested that market prices anticipate mergers several months before they are formally announced, and the **conclusion drawn is that the stock market in these countries** *do* **exhibit semi-strong efficiency**.

5.25   It has also been argued that the market displays sufficient efficiency for investors to see through 'window dressing' of accounts by companies which use accounting conventions to overstate profits.

5.26   Suppose that a company is planning a rights issue of shares in order to invest in a new project. A semi-strong form efficient market hypothesis (unlike the weak form hypothesis) would predict that if there is public knowledge before the issue is formally announced, of the issue itself and of the expected returns from the project, then the market price (cum rights) will change to reflect the anticipated profits before the issue is announced.

Strong form tests and strong form efficiency

5.27   A strong form test of market efficiency attempts to prove that the stock market displays a strong form of efficiency, by which we mean that **share prices reflect all information available** from:

(a)   **Past price changes**.

(b)   **Public knowledge or anticipation**.

(c)   **Insider knowledge** available to specialists or experts (such as investment managers).

5.28   It would then follow that in order to maximise the wealth of shareholders, management should concentrate simply on maximising the net present value of its investments and it **need not worry**, for example, **about the effect on share prices of financial results in the published accounts because investors will make allowances for low profits or dividends in the current year if higher profits or dividends are expected in the future.**

5.29   In theory an expert, such as an investment manager, should be able to use his privileged access to additional information about companies to earn a higher rate of return than an ordinary investor. Unit trusts should in theory therefore perform better than the average investor. Research to date has suggested, however, that this expert skill does not exist (or at least, that any higher returns earned by experts are offset by management charges).

How efficient are stock markets?

5.30   **Evidence so far collected suggests that stock markets show efficiency that is at least weak form, but tending more towards a semi-strong form.** In other words, current share prices reflect all or most publicly available information about companies and their securities. However, it is very difficult to assess the market's efficiency in relation to shares which are not usually actively traded.

5.31   Fundamental analysis and technical analysis, which are carried out by analysts and investment managers, play an important role in creating an efficient stock market. This is because an efficient market depends on the widespread availability of cheap information about companies, their shares and market conditions, and this is what the firms of market makers and other financial institutions *do* provide for their clients and for the general investing public.

The implications of the efficient market hypothesis

5.32   If the **strong form** of the efficient market hypothesis is correct, **a company's real financial position will be reflected in its share price.** Its real financial position includes both its current position and its expected future profitability.

5.33   If the management of a company attempt to maximise the net present value of their investments and to make public any relevant information about those investments then current share prices will in turn be maximised.

5.34   The implication for an investor is that **if the market shows strong form or semi-strong form efficiency, he can rarely spot shares at a bargain price that will soon rise sharply in value.** This is because the market will already have anticipated future developments, and will have reflected these in the share price. All an investor can do, instead of looking for share bargains, is to concentrate on building up a good spread of shares (a portfolio) in order to achieve a satisfactory balance between risk and return.

The share price crash of October 1987 and the efficient market hypothesis

5.35   The crash of October 1987, in which share prices fell suddenly by 20% to 40% on the world's stock markets, raised serious questions about the validity of random walk theory, the fundamental theory of share values and the efficient market hypothesis.

5.36   If these theories are correct, how can shares that were valued at one level on one day suddenly be worth 40% less the next day, without any change in expectations of corporate profits and dividends?

5.37   On the other hand, a widely feared crash late in 1989 failed to happen, suggesting that stock markets may not be altogether out of touch with the underlying values of companies.

6   POSITIVE AND NORMATIVE ACCOUNTING CONCEPTS   12/95

6.1   These two types of concepts are directly opposing and recognise two different approaches to accounting theory.

Exam focus point

Like agency theory, this is most likely to come up as part of the third question on the paper.

Positive accounting concepts

KEY TERM

Positive accounting concepts, or descriptive concepts are based on an approach which is essentially concerned with what accountants do in practice.

6.2   Observations are made and general conclusions are made from these observations to develop a theory. In effect, the observer will look for similarity of treatment. Once sufficient instances have occurred, assurance is gained to the extent that a theory can be developed about the practice in question.

6.3   The theory thus developed **allows explanations and predictions to be made about accountants' behaviour,** particularly about how specified items will be treated.

6.4   The **belief which underlies the positive approach is that the objective of financial statements is to report on the stewardship aspect of the management role,** and thus a report of the utilisation of the assets of the business is required by the directors to the shareholders.

6.5   The basic concepts under this approach define assets, **liabilities,** capital, revenue, expenses, income and transactions. The descriptions are very much based on the way each of these items would arise in practice, for example, **liabilities** are the debts of the business.

6.6   **When it comes to choice of accounting policy, positive accounting theory takes a 'real world' approach,** taking into account such factors as the political sensitivity of the enterprise. For example, it is important for such companies as British Gas not to be seen to be making too much profit, hence the accounting policies chosen will be ones which give a low profit figure or low profitability ratios.

Normative accounting concepts

6.7   The normative approach was developed through the concerns of academic accounting theory. The desire to provide a foundation for the 'science' of accounting led to the search for a 'general theory of accounting'. It was argued that, although various theories and systems operated in accounting, there was no coherent thought governing the whole discipline.

6.8   The first argument was that, instead of describing what accountants did, accounting theory should aim to develop *better* accounting practice.

KEY TERM

The **normative theory** is concerned with 'what should be', not 'what is'.

The theory states that it is possible to develop accounting theory independently of current practice. In fact, this is desirable because of the gap between accounting practice and social and economic reality. In particular, lack of compatibility is a great problem. A theory which imposed standards of quality and relevance of information would improve the situation, as alternative accounting rules would no longer be acceptable: the theory would decide which one was correct.

6.9   The normative approach is **based on imperatives: statements of specific objectives which state that types of transactions 'should be' treated in a certain way**. In order to move from these general statements, **deductive reasoning is required** to reach particular statements. This is compared to the positive approach where inductive reasoning is required to produce general principles from individual practical examples.

6.10 **Criticisms** of the normative approach include the fact that **if assumptions are stated broadly enough to obtain general agreement, they will then be accused of being self-evident, whereas if stated too specifically, no general agreement will be reached.**

Chapter roundup

- **Profit** is an important measure in accounting statements.

  o It measures the efficiency of the company's **management** and helps in decision making.

  o It helps **creditors and investors** to decide whether they can safely lend money .

  o The **government** may use profit as a means of imposing direct taxation.

- **Profit** therefore has a variety of uses and users, but its **measurement depends** on the **methods used to value capital** (assets and liabilities) and on the method, if any, of accounting for price level changes.

- Alternative methods of accounting based on **current value concepts** use **exit values, entry values** or **mixed values**. These principles are developed further in current cost accounting.

- **CPP accounting** is a method of accounting for general (not specific) inflation. It does so by expressing asset values in a stable monetary unit, the £c or £ of current purchasing power.

- In the **CPP balance sheet**, **monetary items** are stated at their **face value**. **Non-monetary items** are stated at their **current purchasing power** as at the balance sheet date.

- **CCA** is an alternative to the historical cost convention which attempts to overcome the problems of accounting for **specific price inflation**. Unlike CPP accounting, it does not attempt to cope with general inflation.

- CCA is based on a **physical concept of capital maintenance**. Profit is recognised after the operating capability of the business has been maintained.

- To recognise **holding gains** as part of current cost profit would conflict with the principle of maintaining operating capability.

- The current cost profit and loss account is constructed by taking **historical cost** profit before interest and taxation as a starting point.

  o Current cost **operating adjustments** in respect of **cost of sales, monetary working capital** and **depreciation** are made so as to arrive at **current cost operating profit**.

  o A **gearing adjustment** is then necessary to arrive at a figure of current cost profit attributable to shareholders.

- **Agency/theory** attempts to explain why companies take decisions which **do not necessarily increase shareholders' wealth**.

- **Positive accounting concepts** are based on what accountants do **in practice**.

- **Normative accounting concepts** aim:

  o to develop **better** accounting practice
  o to develop theory **independent** of practice

Quick quiz

1   How did Fisher define income? (see paras 1.10, 1,11))

2   How did Hicks define economic income? (1.19)

3   Distinguish between the entity concept of capital and the proprietary concept of capital. (1.43)

4   What are the three methods of current value accounting? (2.2)

5   What is a holding gain?. (2.3)

6   Can methods of current value accounting be described as systems for accounting for inflation? (2.17)

7   Define the business income of a company which uses the current entry value method of accounting. (2.18)

8   List the advantages and disadvantages of replacement cost accounting. (2.37, 2.38)

9   List the advantages and disadvantages of current exit value accounting. (2.55, 2.56)

10   Distinguish between specific price inflation and general price inflation. (3.11)

11   What constitutes profits in CPP accounting? (3.13)

12   Is plant and machinery an example of a monetary or a non-monetary item? (3.19)

13   List the advantages and disadvantages of CPP as a method of accounting. (3.24, 3.25)

14   What is meant by 'deprival value'? (4.3)

15   What is an asset's deprival value if it is not worth replacing? (4.4(c))

16   Why would it be incorrect to describe current cost accounting as a system of inflation accounting? (4.12)

17   What is the monetary working capital adjustment? (4.18)

18   What is the purpose of the gearing adjustment? (4.19, 4.20)

19   List four advantages and four disadvantages of CCA. (4.25, 4.26)

20   What are the three forms of efficiency according to the EMH? (5.17)

Question to try	Level	Marks	Time
23	Full exam	25	45 mins

Chapter 22

THE ASB'S STATEMENT OF PRINCIPLES

Chapter topic list	Syllabus reference
1 Content of the ASB *Statement of Principles*	1(a), (d)
2 Advantages and disadvantages of the *Statement of Principles*	1(a), (d)

Introduction

By now you should have acquired a thorough grasp of accounting, both for single companies and for groups. You should therefore have little difficulty with this chapter on the ASB's *Statement of Principles*.

It has been said that in the past the standard-setting body took a 'fire-fighting' approach to developing accounting standards. The old SSAPs were not based on a consistent philosophy and this led to the need for a conceptual framework of accounting.

This chapter deals with the ASB's attempt at a conceptual framework, the *Statement of Principles*. In its final form, the *Statement* should provide the basis for all new accounting standards. It is therefore very important and also very topical as you will know from your reading of the financial press.

1   CONTENT OF THE ASB STATEMENT OF PRINCIPLES

1.1   Towards the end of its existence, the ASC recognised the IASC's 1989 *Framework* as a set of guidelines to help it develop proposals for new standards and revisions to existing standards. This represented a significant shift from the previous attitude of developing SSAPs in a haphazard manner as working solutions to practical problems.

1.2   We have already mentioned the IASC's *Framework* in Chapter 1. The IASC believes that further international harmonisation of accounting methods can best be promoted by focusing on the four topics which they believe will lead to producing financial statements that meet the common needs of most users.

1.3   As we will see below, the ASB has gone further than the ASC in that it has already incorporated the IASC's *Framework* into the *Statement of Principles*, as well as the contents of the Solomons report, which was also mentioned in Chapter 1.

ASB *Statement of Principles*

1.4   The ASB published (in November 1995) an exposure draft of its *Statement of Principles for Financial Reporting*.

The *Statement of Principles* will guide the ASB in the formulation of accounting standards by providing a basis for choosing between alternative accounting treatments.

1.5 This is the first time that the full text has appeared in a single document: previously the chapters of the *Statement of Principles* were published for comment separately. The text has been substantially revised with particular attention being given to the clarity of expression. The statement consists of **seven chapters**.

(a) **The objective of financial statements**
(b) **The qualitative characteristics of financial information**
(c) **The elements of financial statements**
(d) **Recognition in financial statements**
(e) **Measurement in financial statements**
(f) **Presentation of financial information**
(g) **The reporting entity**

There are also two appendices. The first reproduces the ASB's *Statement of Aims* and the second is on the *Statement of Principles* and companies legislation.

Exam focus point

The December 1995 examination paper contained a question on accounting theory, part of which related to the *Statement of Principles*. As the Statement of Principles is topical and controversial, you would be advised to familiarise yourself with the material.

Purpose of the *Statement of Principles*

1.6 The main reasons why the ASB developed the *Statement of Principles* were to:

(a) Assist the ASB by providing a basis for **reducing the number of alternative accounting treatments permitted** by accounting standards and company law.

(b) Provide a **framework for the future development** of accounting standards.

(c) **Assist auditors** in forming an opinion as to whether financial statements conform with accounting standards.

(d) **Assist users of accounts** in interpreting the information contained in them.

(e) Provide **guidance in applying accounting standards.**

(f) Give **guidance on areas** which are **not yet covered by accounting standards.**

(g) **Inform interested parties of the approach taken by** the **ASB** in formulating accounting standards.

1.7 The role of the *Statement* can thus be **summed up** as being to provide **consistency, clarity and information.**

Chapter 1 The objective of financial statements

1.8 The main points raised here are:

(a) 'The objective of financial statements is to provide information about the **financial position**, **performance** and **financial adaptability** of an enterprise that is useful to a wide range of users for assessing the stewardship of management and for making economic decisions.'

(b) It is acknowledged that while all not all the information needs of users can be met by financial statements, **there are needs that are common to all users.** Financial statements that meet the needs of providers of risk capital to the enterprise will also meet most of the needs of other users that financial statements can satisfy.

Users of financial statements other than investors include the following, and you should be aware of the individual needs of these users (your previous studies covered these in detail).

(i)   Employees
(ii) Lenders
(iii) Suppliers and other creditors
(iv) Customers
(v)   Government and their agencies
(vi) The public

(c) The limitations of financial statements are emphasised as well as the strengths.

(d) **All of the components of financial statements** (balance sheet, profit and loss account, cash flow statement) **are interrelated** because they reflect different aspects of the same transactions.

(e) The exposure draft emphasises the ways **financial statements provide information about the financial position** of an enterprise. The main elements which affect the position of the company are:

(i)   The economic resources it controls.

(ii) Its financial structure.

(iii) Its liquidity and solvency.

(iv) Its capacity to adapt to changes in the environment in which it operates (called *financial adaptability*).

The exposure draft discusses the importance of each of these elements and how they are disclosed in the financial statements.

Chapter 2 Qualitative characteristics of financial information

1.9   The ED gives a diagrammatic representation of the discussion, shown on page 483.

(a) **Qualitative characteristics that relate to content are relevance and reliability.**

(b) **Qualitative characteristics that relate to presentation are comparability and understanding.**

The diagram shown is reasonably explanatory.

Chapter 3 Elements of financial statements

1.10 The elements of financial statements are listed. Any item that does not fall within one of the definitions of elements should not be included in financial statements.

> **Definitions**
>
> (a) **Assets** are rights or other access to future economic benefits controlled by an entity as a result of past transactions or events.
>
> (b) **Liabilities** are obligations of an entity to transfer economic benefits as a result of past transactions or events.
>
> (c) **Ownership interest** is the residual amount found by deducting all of the entity's liabilities from all of the entity's assets.
>
> (d) **Gains** are increases in ownership interest, other than those relating to contributions from owners.
>
> (e) **Losses** are decreases in ownership interest, other than those relating to distributions to owners.
>
> (f) **Contributions from owners** are increases in ownership interest resulting from investments made by owners in their capacity as owners.
>
> (g) **Distributions to owners** are decreases in ownership interest resulting from transfers made to owners in their capacity as owners.

Chapter 4 Recognition in financial statements   12/97

1.11 This chapter explains what is meant by recognition. It discusses the three stages of recognition of assets and liabilities and then goes on to describe the criteria which determine each of these stages.

   (a) **Initial recognition.** An element should be recognised **if there is sufficient evidence that the change in assets or liabilities inherent in the element has occurred,** including, where appropriate, evidence that a future inflow or outflow of benefit will occur, and it can be measured at a monetary amount with sufficient reliability.

   (b) **Subsequent remeasurement.** A change in the amount at which an asset or liability is recorded should be recognised **if** there is sufficient evidence that **the amount of an asset or liability has changed and the new amount of the asset or liability can be measured with sufficient reliability.**

   (c) **Derecognition.** An asset or liability should cease to be recognised **if there is no longer sufficient evidence** that the entity has access to future economic benefits or an obligation to transfer economic benefit (including, where appropriate, evidence that a future inflow or outflow of benefit will occur).

1.12 The chapter goes on to state the criterion for recognition of gains and losses; this clearly derives from the treatment of assets and liabilities defined above.

   'At any stage in the recognition process, where a change in total assets is not offset by an equal change in total liabilities or a transaction with owners, a gain or loss will arise.'

   'The recognition of gains involves consideration of whether there is sufficient evidence that an increase in net assets (ie in ownership interest) had occurred before the end of the reporting period.'

   'The recognition of losses involves consideration of whether there is sufficient evidence that a decrease in ownership interest had occurred before the end of the reporting period. Prudence has the effect that less evidence of occurrence and reliability of measurement is required for the recognition of a loss than for a gain.'

THE QUALITATIVE CHARACTERISTICS OF FINANCIAL INFORMATION

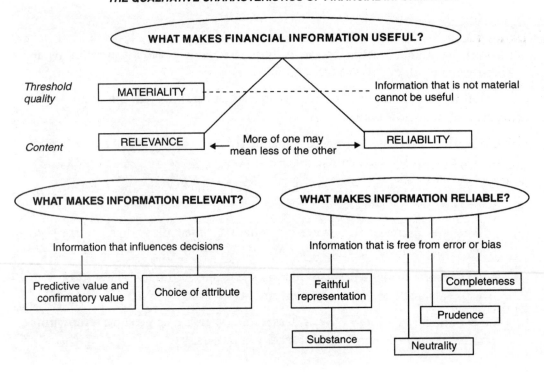

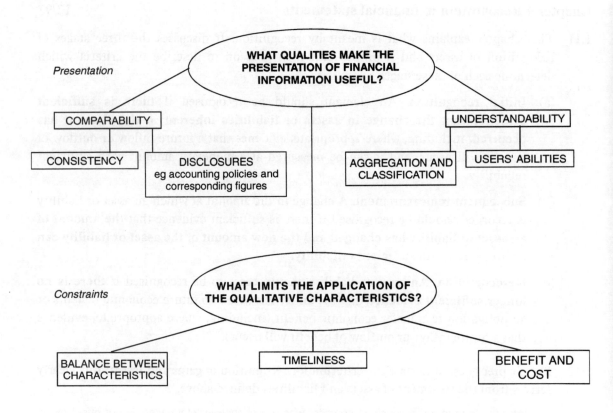

The numbers indicate the paragraphs in which the qualitative characteristics are discussed

Question 1

Consider the following situations. In each case, do we have an asset or liability within the definitions given by the *Statement of Principles?* Give reasons for your answer.

(a) Pat Ltd has purchased a patent for £20,000. The patent gives the company sole use of a particular manufacturing process which will save £3,000 a year for the next five years.

(b) Baldwin Ltd paid Don Brennan £10,000 to set up a car repair shop, on condition that priority treatment is given to cars from the company's fleet.

(c) Deals on Wheels Ltd provides a warranty with every car sold.

Answer

(a) This is an asset, albeit an intangible one. There is a past event, control and future economic benefit (through cost savings).

(b) This cannot be classified as an asset. Baldwin Ltd has no control over the car repair shop and it is difficult to argue that there are 'future economic benefits'.

(c) This is a liability; the business has taken on an obligation. It would be recognised when the warranty is issued rather than when a claim is made.

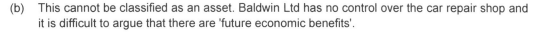

Chapter 5 Measurement in financial statements

1.13 As will be made clear below this chapter, with its emphasis on current values, is fairly radical and controversial. The following approach is taken.

(a) **Initially,** when an asset is purchased or a liability incurred, the asset/liability is **recorded at the transaction cost,** that is historical cost, which at that time is equal to current replacement cost.

(b) An asset/liability **may subsequently be 'remeasured'.** When the recognition criteria for a change are met, the monetary amount at which an asset or liability is recorded is changed. In a historical cost system, this can involve writing down an asset to its recoverable amount. For a liability, the corresponding treatment would be 'amendment of the monetary amount ... to the amount ultimately expected to be paid'.

(c) A **current value system is recommended.**

'Practice should develop by evolving in the direction of greater use of current values to the extent that this is consistent with the constraints of reliability and cost.'

This is justified, the chapter argues, on the following grounds.

(i) Current value is relevant to users who wish to assess the current state or recent performance of the business.

(ii) Assets and liabilities are re-measured regularly so that changes in value are recorded as they occur rather than simply when they are realised.

(iii) Both holding gains and current operating margins are shown, so that 'users of real terms financial statements are able to select the particular information they require'.

(d) The **appropriate current value to be used for assets is 'value to the business'**. This is the lower of replacement cost and recoverable amount. Recoverable amount is the higher of net realisable value and value in use. For liabilities, market values may be used as an effective measure of value to the business.

(e) The statement notes, however, that **historical cost has the merit of familiarity and (to some extent) objectivity.**

1.14 An appendix to Chapter 5 illustrates the effect of real terms measures on the profit and loss account and the statement of total recognised gains and losses.

Chapter 6 Presentation of financial information

1.15 Aspects of this chapter have also given rise to some controversy, as will be discussed below. The chapter begins by making the general point that financial information is presented in the form of a structured set of financial statements comprising **primary statements and supporting notes and, in some cases, supplementary information.**

Features of financial statements

1.16 The chapter goes on to look at the **factors which affect the 'arrangement of information** in financial reporting' as follows.

(a) **Aggregation:** how transactions are condensed and simplified.

(b) **Classification:** facilitates analysis by grouping items by nature or function into reasonably homogeneous groups.

(c) **Structure:** proper structuring will mean that items are given the correct prominence in the financial statements.

(d) **Articulation:** or interrelating, reflects the way that different aspects of the same transaction will be shown in different primary statements (for example, sales and debtors).

Components of financial statements

1.17 The **primary financial statements** are as follows.

(a) **Profit and loss account**
(b) **Statement of total recognised gains and losses**
(c) **Balance sheet**
(d) **Cash flow statement**

1.18 The **notes** to the financial statements **'amplify and explore'** the primary statements; together they form an 'integrated whole'. Disclosure in the notes does not correct or justify non-disclosure or misrepresentation in the primary financial statements.

1.19 'Supplementary information' embraces voluntary disclosures and information which is too subjective for disclosure in the primary financial statement and the notes.

Statements of financial performance

1.20 These are:

(a) the **profit and loss account**; and
(b) the **statement of total recognised gains and losses**

All gains and losses must be considered in assessing the overall financial performance of an entity during a period, and only those gains and losses arising in the period.

1.21 The chapter then stipulates that **the only gains and losses to be reported** in the statement of total recognised gains and losses **are those that relate to assets and liabilities whose primary function is to enable the entity's operations to be carried out,** for example (by implication) fixed assets. All other gains and losses are to be reported in the profit and loss account. In other words, it is not proposed that the **distinction between these two primary financial statements should rest on whether or not a profit is realised.**

1.22 Chapter 6 also makes it clear that:

> 'A particular item should be reported separately if its disclosure is likely to be significant for appraising the stewardship of management or as a factor in assessing or reassessing future performance and cash flows.'

Balance sheet

1.23 The chapter states:

> 'The balance sheet (together with related notes) provides information about an entity's assets and liabilities and its ownership interest and shows their relationships to each other at a point of time. The balance sheet delineates the entity's resource structure (major classes and amounts of assets) and its financial structure (major classes and amounts of liabilities and ownership interest).'

> 'The financial position of an entity is determined by the economic resources it controls, its financial structure, its liquidity and solvency, and its capacity to adapt to changes in the environment in which it operates.'

1.24 The chapter goes on to discuss the usefulness of the various attributes of the balance sheet, but recognises that fundamentally **'a balance sheet does not purport to show the value of a business enterprise'.** The assets minus the liabilities shown in the balance sheet will never show the value of a company. However, the information within a balance sheet may help users to make their own assessment of the value of the company.

Cash flow statement

1.25 A cash flow statement 'reflects an entity's cash inflows and outflows during a period, distinguishing those that are the result of operations and those that result from other activities'.

1.26 A cash flow statement provides useful information about the ways in which an entity's activities generate and use cash, thus helping users to assess factors such as risk, the entity's liquidity, solvency, financial adaptability and the relationship between profits and cash flow. **A cash flow statement does *not*, however, provide a complete basis for judging future possible cash flows.**

Financial adaptability

1.27 The exposure draft places a great deal of stress on this concept.

> **KEY TERM**
>
> **Financial adaptability** is: 'the ability of an entity to take effective action to alter the amounts and timing of cash flows so that it can respond to unexpected needs or opportunities.'

Financial adaptability is thus the ability to meet unexpected problems with sufficient resources, particularly cash, to ensure the survival of the company. Obviously this is important in view of the recent collapse of various large companies and groups.

1.28 Financial adaptability **comes from the ability to:**

   (a) **Raise new capital**, perhaps by issuing debt securities at short notice.

   (b) **Obtain cash by selling assets** without disrupting continuing operations.

   (c) Achieve a **rapid improvement in the net cash inflows** generated by operations.

Each of the primary statements gives information which helps to assess financial adaptability.

Supplementary information

1.29 The chapter finishes in a discussion of the use of highlights and summary indicators, and the different kinds of supplementary information which might be published alongside the primary statements. These are:

   (a) An **operating and financial review**.

   (b) **Information prepared from a different perspective** from that adopted in the financial statements.

   (c) **Statistical information**.

   (d) **Highlights and summary indicators**.

1.30 The chapter also notes that summary indicators may be useful as general indicators of the amount of investment or overall past performance. But in a complex business enterprise, summary amounts cannot, on their own, adequately describe an enterprise's financial position, performance or financial adaptability.

Chapter 7 The reporting entity

1.31 The reporting entity is 'the entity that is the subject of a given set of financial statements'. This chapter discusses different kinds of investments, and changes in the reporting entity.

Different kinds of investments

1.32   'The classification of investments needs to reflect the way in which they are used to further the business of the investor and the consequent effect on the investor's financial position, performance and financial adaptability. The two key factors for this purpose are the degree of influence of the investor and the nature of the investor's interest in the results, assets and liabilities of its investee.'

1.33 **Control is the highest degree of influence** that an investor can have over its investee. Control is the power to direct. There are **two aspects to control:**

(a) The **ability to deploy the economic resources,** or **direct the entities.**

(b) The ability to **ensure that any resulting benefits accrue to itself** (with corresponding exposure to losses) and to restrict the access of others to those benefits.

Parent and subsidiary

1.34 Parent entities prepare consolidated financial statements to provide financial information about the group as a single reporting entity. Consolidation is a process that aggregates the total assets, liabilities and results of the parent and its subsidiaries.

1.35 In determining which investments should be consolidated, the **principle of control should predominate. However, consolidated financial statements should also:**

'**reflect the extent of outside ownership interests** because they are important factors in considering the parent's access and exposure to the results of its subsidiaries.'

Changes in the reporting entity

1.36 Two aspects are dealt with.

(a) **Mergers.** A merger is a business combination where no party is dominant or obtains control over any other. In merger accounting, the assets and liabilities of the individual merging entities and are pooled at 'existing recognised values', thus reflecting the uniting of interests. Mergers are rare.

(b) **Acquisitions and goodwill.** Change in the reporting entity is also brought about by the parent entity acquiring or disposing of ownership interests. Assets and liabilities of the acquired entity are brought in at their fair value. The balance of the purchase consideration not recognised as an identifiable asset or liability in the post acquisition fair value exercise is recognised as 'goodwill'.

Associates and joint ventures

1.37 This part of the chapter makes the point that associates and joint ventures are media through which the investor conducts part of its activities, but which, unlike subsidiaries, are not 'extensions to the investor's business' because the investor does not control them.

1.38 An **associate** is defined as:

'an investment where the investor has a long-term beneficial interest, participating in its investment's operating and financial policies and exercising significant influence over them.'

Such investments should be accounted for under the equity method.

1.39 A **joint venture** is defined as:

'an entity jointly controlled with other venturers under a contractual agreement with a view to benefit.'

Two kinds of joint ventures are identified.

(a) The **venturers share in common the risks and rewards of their joint venture as a separate business.** The venturer's interest in its joint venture relates to its share of the business as a whole and not to its share of the individual assets, liabilities and cash flows of the joint venture, and should be included in the **consolidated** financial statements **using the equity method.**

(b) **Each venturer has its own separate interest in the risks and rewards** that derive either from its particular share of the fixed assets of the venture or by its having a distinct share of the output or service of the joint venture or its financing. This type of joint venture is less common. **Proportional consolidation is the appropriate accounting treatment** because the venturer's interests relate directly to its share of the underlying assets and liabilities rather than its share in the joint venture itself as an entity.

1.40 This is the approach taken in FRS 9 *Associates and joint ventures,* covered in Chapter 20.

2   ADVANTAGES AND DISADVANTAGES OF THE STATEMENT OF PRINCIPLES   12/95

Exam focus point

Because the basic aspects of the *Statement* are covered in Paper 1, Paper 10 is more likely to examine some of the more controversial aspects.

Advantages

2.1 The advantages of having a coherent conceptual framework for financial reporting in the form of a set of principles have been very well summarised by Andrew Lennard, technical director at the Accounting Standards Board.

> 'Principles are powerful. A single principle, consistently applied, can suggest solutions to many issues. A principled approach to different issues not only ensures solutions are consistent with each other; if the principle is soundly framed, the solutions will be the right ones.'
> (*Accountancy Age,* November 1995)

2.2 To illustrate this general advantage, in the same article Mr Lennard gives examples of the ways in which **the ASB has been using the ideas in the *Statement of Principles* as it develops accounting standards.**

   (a) The desirability of a cash flow statement, which was introduced by FRS 1, follows naturally from the objective of financial statements.

   (b) The demand that accounts contain relevant information, and that this cannot always be achieved by strict adherence to legal form, forms much of the reasoning behind FRS 5 *Reporting the substance of transactions.*

   (c) The definition of a liability is central to FRS 4 *Capital instruments.*

   (d) That same definition of a liability is also the key to the most controversial aspect of FRS 7 *Fair values in acquisition accounting.*

2.3 The principles have also been applied in the development of standards on business combinations, as follows.

   (a) The distinction between mergers and acquisitions is consistent with FRS 6 *Acquisitions and mergers.*

   (b) The recommended treatment of associates and the two kinds of joint venture is consistent with FRS 9 *Associates and joint ventures.*

2.4 Further advantages which could be claimed for the *Statement of Principles* are as follows.

   (a) The *Statement* **helps reduce scope for individual judgement** and the potential subjectivity that this implies.

   (b) **Financial statements should be more comparable** because although alternative treatments will still be available, there will be a consistent and coherent framework on which to base one's choice of a particular alternative.

(c)   The *Statement* **puts forward a consistent terminology and consistent objectives,** for example in the definitions and the qualitative characteristics.

(d)   If a particular procedure is not the subject of an accounting standard, then the *Statement* **can provide guidelines and produce consistency of treatment between companies.**

2.5   While the advantages outlined in Paragraph 3.42 could apply to *any* coherent and well formulated statement of principles, the content and approach of the ASB's version has elicited praise, for example in the way in which it **places proper emphasis on the balance sheet.**

> 'A review of accounting standards will demonstrate that in may areas the standard setting process has been profit driven, designed to ensure reported earnings reflect the activities during the period. This has, however, often been at the expense of the balance sheet.
>
> Has not the time come for the standard setters to ensure that the quality of the information in the balance sheet is of the same standard as that in the profit and loss?'
>
> (John Morley, *Accountancy Age*, 15 May 1996)

This view is not universally shared, however, as will be seen.

Disadvantages

2.6   The publication of the *Statement of Principles* marks a watershed in the development of UK accounting. The *Statement* has drawn criticism from several sources, by far the most vocal being Ernst & Young, with the publication in February 1996 of their paper *The ASB's Framework - Time to Decide*.

The Ernst & Young paper

2.7   The Ernst & Young publication launched a strong attack on the ASB's conceptual framework and called on UK businesses to follow its lead before 'some version of current cost accounting is with us once again'! **In general terms, the framework is criticised for being an academic diversion and its proposals unprompted by user demand.**

2.8   Three areas of particular concern are singled out.

(a)   The *Statement* **places an 'unwarranted faith in current values',** when such values have proved to be inconsistent and subjective. There is no demand from the business community for current cost accounting. Furthermore, no distinction is made in the framework between the valuation of investments (which should be marked to market in order to measure properly the effects of investment decisions taken in the year) and operational assets.

(b)   There is **undue emphasis on the statement of total recognised gains and losses,** which would become 'a dumping ground for miscellaneous accounting entries'. The profit and loss account is thereby undermined.

(c)   The **building up of the financial statements from balance sheet values, is the 'wrong starting point'.** Examples of ways in which accounting practice would change under a strict reading of the framework, include the abolition of deferred tax, since it does not meet the *Statement's* definition a liability.

The firm concludes that the framework 'leads to **unnecessarily complicated rules,** founded on unclear principles and logic'.

2.9   Accounting Standards Board chairman, Sir David Tweedie put up a spirited defence of the framework and dismissed concerns that the Board has a 'hidden agenda' to revert to current cost accounting. He stated that he had never concealed the Board's preference for current values, but that it never had plans to go in that direction faster than the business community will allow.

2.10   The debate continues, sometimes on a rather personal level. Whatever the outcome, or the firm's motives for their attack, the Ernst & Young paper raised the profile of what might otherwise have been a rather obscure document.

Other criticisms and views

2.11   The views expressed in the Ernst & Young paper have found widespread support. For example, Michael Davies of the London Institute, writing in *Accountancy* in April 1996 voiced concern about the emphasis on current cost accounting which has 'been tried and found wanting', and criticised the *Statement's* **'muddled' treatment of the fundamental accounting concept of prudence.**

2.12   From the point of view of the employee user group, John Sittle, writing in *Accountancy Age* in November 1995 said that **although the *Statement* identifies employees as a user group, it does nothing to address their needs.**

Question 2

The Ernst & Young paper argues against the idea of a conceptual framework of accounting. True or False?

Answer

False. The paper is opposed to the framework proposed in the ASB's Exposure Draft, not to the principle of a conceptual framework of accounting.

The way forward

2.13   In July 1996, in response to the many articles and letters on the subject of the *Statement of Principles*, the ASB issued a 'progress paper' entitled *Statement of Principles for Financial Reporting - the Way Ahead.*

2.14   The progress paper stated that there had been some **'key points of misunderstanding'** which were as follows.

'(a)   The statement is not and was never intended to be a mandatory accounting standard.

(b)   Bedrock notions such as true and fair, accruals, and going concern are and will remain part of the framework.

(c)   A system of current cost accounting (CCA) has never been on our agenda, it is not on our agenda now nor do we have any plans to put it on the agenda - even though some were led to believe otherwise.'

2.15   The ASB accepts that the draft was 'not as clear on some issues as it might have been', and, at the time of writing (June 1998), is continuing work on a revised exposure draft. The text is being largely rewritten with the aim of making it clearer and easier to understand.

2.16   The ASB argues much of the criticism of the previous exposure draft resulted from confusion and misunderstandings about what the *Statement* was trying to achieve. However, technical aspects were also criticised. The most vocal critic was again Ernst & Young. In March 1998 the firm published a further discussion paper: *The ASB's*

Framework - Time for Action, in which it criticised the ASB for producing new accounting standards based on the original exposure draft when the latter had not found acceptance. The paper argues that those new standards, particularly those on impairment and provisions were flawed in a way that reflects flaws in the original exposure draft.

2.17   The ASB is expected to make detailed changes to the exposure draft in the light of some of the criticisms and a revised exposure draft is expected in the second half of 1998.

Exam focus point

Chapter 7 of the *Statement* was covered in a *Current Accounting and Auditing Issues* column in the September 1997 *Students' Newsletter*. The *Statement* could come up as the subject of question , or part of a question.

Chapter roundup

- The ASB's *Statement of Principles,* now in exposure draft form, should provide the **backbone of the conceptual framework** in the UK.

- **Key elements** in the *Statement* are as follows.

  o   Financial statements should give **financial information** useful for **assessing stewardship** of management and for **making economic decisions**.

  o   Financial information should be **relevant, reliable, comparable and understandable**.

  o   **Assets and liabilities** have conceptual **priority over the profit and loss account**.

  o   Accounts should move towards **current cost valuations**.

  o   **Statement of total recognised gains and losses** is for assets held for the business to continue trading.

- The *Statement* has been **criticised** and will probably have to be revised extensively before it appears in its final form. Key areas which have attracted criticism include the following.

  o   Too much faith in current value accounting

  o   Not enough emphasis on prudence

  o   Balance sheet emphasised at the expense of the profit and loss account

  o   The framework proposed is not helpful to management accountants or relevant to employees

  o   Role of the statement of total recognised gains and losses is confusing.

  o   The *Statement* is too theoretical and lacks the support of the business community

Quick quiz

1   What are the seven chapters of the *Statement of Principles?* (see para 1.5)

2   How does the *Statement* define 'gains' and 'losses'? (1.10)

3   On what grounds does the *Statement* recommend current value accounting? (1.13)

4   What gains and losses should be reported in the statement of total recognised gains and losses? (1.21)

5   Which accounting standards could be said to be based on ideas in the *Statement of Principles*? (2.2)

6   What aspect of the *Statement* did the firm Ernst & Young single out for criticism? (2.8)

Question to try	Level	Marks	Time
24	Full exam	20	36 mins

Part D

Analysing and appraising financial and related information

Chapter 23

INTERPRETATION OF FINANCIAL STATEMENTS

Chapter topic list	Syllabus reference
1 The broad categories of ratios	3, 4
2 Profitability and return on capital	3, 4
3 Liquidity, gearing and working capital	3, 4
4 Shareholders' investment ratios	3, 4
5 Accounting policies and the limitations of ratio analysis	3, 4
6 Reports on financial performance	3, 4

Introduction

You may remember some of the basic interpretation of accounts you studied for Paper 1. This chapter recaps and develops the calculation of ratios and covers more complex accounting relationships. More importantly, perhaps, this chapter looks at how ratios can be analysed, interpreted and how the results should be presented to management.

Wide reading is encouraged in this area. If you want to look at real sets of accounts you could try the Financial Times Free Annual Reports Service - look in the FT at the London Share Service page. In any case, you should read regularly the *Students' Newsletter* and the *Financial Times* at least.

1   THE BROAD CATEGORIES OF RATIOS

1.1   So far in this text we have looked at how financial statements are prepared, and have described their features and contents. What we begin to do in this chapter is to think about the significance of the figures they contain.

- If you were to look at a balance sheet or P & L account, how would you decide whether the company was doing well or badly?

- Or whether it was financially strong or financially vulnerable?

- And what would you be looking at in the figures to help you to make your judgement?

Exam focus point
Your syllabus requires you to be able to interpret a set of accounts, in particular by the use of ratio analysis, and to present your analysis in the form of a report. You will already have some knowledge of the basic ratios from your earlier studies.

1.2 Ratio analysis involves **comparing one figure against another** to produce a ratio, and assessing whether the ratio indicates a weakness or strength in the company's affairs.

The broad categories of ratios

1.3 Broadly speaking, basic ratios can be grouped into five categories:

- **Profitability and return**
- **Long-term solvency and stability**
- **Short-term solvency and liquidity**
- **Efficiency (turnover ratios)**
- **Shareholders' investment ratios.**

1.4 Within each heading we will identify a number of standard measures or ratios that are normally calculated and generally accepted as meaningful indicators. However, each individual business must be considered separately, and a ratio that is meaningful for a manufacturing company may be completely meaningless for a financial institution. **Try not to be too mechanical when working out ratios and constantly think about what you are trying to achieve.**

1.5 **The key to obtaining meaningful information from ratio analysis is comparison.** This may involve comparing ratios over time within the same business to establish whether things are improving or declining, and comparing ratios between similar businesses to see whether the company you are analysing is better or worse than average within its specific business sector.

1.6 Ratio analysis on its own is not sufficient for interpreting company accounts, and that there are **other items of information** which should be looked at, for example:

(a) Comments in the **Chairman's report** and directors' report.

(b) The **age and nature of the company's assets**.

(c) **Current and future developments** in the company's markets, at home and overseas, recent acquisitions or disposals of a subsidiary by the company.

(d) **Exceptional items** in the P&L account.

(e) **Any other noticeable features** of the report and accounts, such as post balance sheet events, contingent liabilities, a qualified auditors' report, the company's taxation position, and so on.

1.7 EXAMPLE: CALCULATING RATIOS

To illustrate the calculation of ratios, the following balance sheet and P & L account figures will be used.

FURLONG PLC PROFIT AND LOSS ACCOUNT
FOR THE YEAR ENDED 31 DECEMBER 19X8

	Notes	19X8 £	19X7 £
Turnover	1	3,095,576	1,909,051
Operating profit	1	359,501	244,229
Interest	2	17,371	19,127
Profit on ordinary activities before taxation		342,130	225,102
Taxation on ordinary activities		74,200	31,272
Profit on ordinary activities after taxation		267,930	193,830
Dividend		41,000	16,800
Retained profit for the year		226,930	177,030
Earnings per share		12.8p	9.3p

FURLONG PLC BALANCE SHEET
AS AT 31 DECEMBER 19X8

	Notes	19X8 £	19X7 £
Fixed assets			
Tangible fixed assets		802,180	656,071
Current assets			
Stocks and work in progress		64,422	86,550
Debtors	3	1,002,701	853,441
Cash at bank and in hand		1,327	68,363
		1,068,450	1,008,354
Creditors: amounts falling due within one year	4	881,731	912,456
Net current assets		186,719	95,898
Total assets less current liabilities		988,899	751,969
Creditors: amounts falling due after more than one year			
10% first mortgage debenture stock 19Y4/19Y9		(100,000)	(100,000)
Provision for liabilities and charges			
Deferred taxation		(20,000)	(10,000)
		868,899	641,969
Capital and reserves			
Called up share capital	5	210,000	210,000
Share premium account		48,178	48,178
Profit and loss account		610,721	383,791
		868,899	641,969

NOTES TO THE ACCOUNTS

			19X8 £	19X7 £
1	*Turnover and profit*			
	(i)	Turnover	3,095,576	1,909,051
		Cost of sales	2,402,609	1,441,950
		Gross profit	692,967	467,101
		Administration expenses	333,466	222,872
		Operating profit	359,501	244,229
	(ii)	Operating profit is stated after charging:		
		Depreciation	151,107	120,147
		Auditors' remuneration	6,500	5,000
		Leasing charges	47,636	46,336
		Directors' emoluments	94,945	66,675

2   *Interest*

	8,115	11,909
Payable on bank overdrafts and other loans	8,115	11,909
Payable on debenture stock	10,000	10,000
	18,115	21,909
Receivable on short-term deposits	744	2,782
Net payable	17,371	19,127

3   *Debtors*

Amounts falling due within one year

Trade debtors	884,559	760,252
Prepayments and accrued income	89,822	45,729
Advance corporation tax recoverable	7,200	-
	981,581	805,981

Amounts falling due after more than one year

Advance corporation tax recoverable	9,000	7,200
Trade debtors	12,120	40,260
	21,120	47,460
Total debtors	1,002,701	853,441

	19X8	*19X7*
	£	£

4   *Creditors: amounts falling due within one year*

Trade creditors	627,018	545,340
Accruals and deferred income	81,279	280,464
Corporation tax	108,000	37,200
Other taxes and social security costs	44,434	32,652
Dividend	21,000	16,800
	881,731	912,456

5   *Called up share capital*

Authorised ordinary shares of 10p each	1,000,000	1,000,000
Issued and fully paid ordinary shares of 10p each	210,000	210,00

2   PROFITABILITY AND RETURN ON CAPITAL

2.1   In our example, the company made a profit in both 19X8 and 19X7, and there was an increase in profit on ordinary activities between one year and the next:

(a)   of 52% before taxation;
(b)   of 39% after taxation.

2.2   **Profit on ordinary activities before taxation is generally thought to be a better figure to use than profit after taxation,** because there might be unusual variations in the tax charge from year to year which would not affect the underlying profitability of the company's operations.

2.3   **Another profit figure that should be calculated is PBIT, profit before interest and tax.** This is the amount of profit which the company earned before having to pay interest to the providers of loan capital. By providers of loan capital, we usually mean longer-term loan capital, such as debentures and medium-term bank loans, which will be shown in the balance sheet as 'creditors: amounts falling due after more than one year'.

> **FORMULA TO LEARN**
>
> **Profit before interest and tax** is therefore:
>
> (a)   the profit on ordinary activities before taxation; plus
> (b)   interest charges on long-term loan capital.

2.4   Published accounts do not always give sufficient detail on interest payable to determine how much is interest on long-term finance. We will assume in our example that the whole of the interest payable (£18,115, note 2) relates to long-term finance.

2.5   PBIT in our example is therefore:

	19X8	*19X7*
	£	£
Profit on ordinary activities before tax	342,130	225,102
Interest payable	18,115	21,909
PBIT	360,245	247,011

This shows a 46% growth between 19X7 and 19X8.

Return on capital employed (ROCE)

2.6   It is impossible to assess profits or profit growth properly without relating them to the amount of funds (capital) that were employed in making the profits. The most important profitability ratio is therefore return on capital employed (ROCE), which states the profit as a percentage of the amount of capital employed.

> **FORMULA TO LEARN**
>
> $$\text{ROCE} = \frac{\text{Profit on ordinary activities before intereest and taxation}}{\text{Capital employed}}$$
>
> **Capital** = Shareholders' funds plus 'creditors: amounts falling due after more
> **employed**   than one year' plus any long-term provision for liabilities and charges
>   (*or* total assets less current liabilities).

2.7   The underlying principle is that we must compare like with like, and so if capital means share capital and reserves plus long-term liabilities and debt capital, profit must mean the profit earned by all this capital together. This is PBIT, since interest is the return for loan capital.

2.8   In our example, capital employed =   19X8 868,899 + 100,000 + 20,000 = £988,899
                                                19X7 641,969 + 100,000 + 10,000 = £751,969

These total figures are the total assets less current liabilities figures for 19X8 and 19X7 in the balance sheet.

		19X8	*19X7*
ROCE	=	$\dfrac{360,245}{988,899}$	$\dfrac{247,011}{751,969}$
	=	36.4%	32.8%

2.9   **What does a company's ROCE tell us?** What should we be looking for? There are **three comparisons** that **can be made.**

(a)   The **change in ROCE from one year to the next** can be examined. In this example, there has been an increase in ROCE by about 10% or 11% from its 19X7 level.

(b)   The **ROCE being earned by other companies**, if this information is available, can be compared with the ROCE of this company. Here the information is not available.

(c)   A **comparison of the ROCE with current market borrowing rates** may be made.

   (i)   What would be the cost of extra borrowing to the company if it needed more loans, and is it earning a ROCE that suggests it could make profits to make such borrowing worthwhile?

   (ii)   Is the company making a ROCE which suggests that it is getting value for money from its current borrowing?

   (iii) Companies are in a risk business and commercial borrowing rates are a good independent yardstick against which company performance can be judged.

2.10   In this example, if we suppose that current market interest rates, say, for medium-term borrowing from banks, is around 10%, then the company's actual ROCE of 36% in 19X8 would not seem low. On the contrary, it might seem high.

2.11   However, **it is easier to spot a low ROCE than a high one,** because there is always a chance that the company's fixed assets, especially property, are undervalued in its balance sheet, and so the capital employed figure might be unrealistically low. If the company had earned a ROCE, not of 36%, but of, say only 6%, then its return would have been below current borrowing rates and so disappointingly low.

Return on shareholders' capital (ROSC)

2.12   Another measure of profitability and return is the return on shareholders' capital which is calculated as follows.

FORMULA TO LEARN

$$ROSC = \frac{\text{Profit on ordinary activities before tax}}{\text{Share capital and reserves}}$$

2.13   It is intended to focus on the return being made by the company for the benefit of its shareholders, and in our example, the figures are:

<table>
<tr><td>19X8</td><td>19X7</td></tr>
<tr><td>$\dfrac{342,130}{868,899} = 39.4\%$</td><td>$\dfrac{225,102}{641,969} = 35.1\%$</td></tr>
</table>

These figures show an improvement between 19X7 and 19X8, and a return which is clearly in excess of current borrowing rates.

2.14   ROSC is not a widely-used ratio, however, because there are more useful ratios that give an indication of the return to shareholders, such as earnings per share, dividend per share, dividend yield and earnings yield, which are described later.

Analysing profitability and return in more detail: the secondary ratios

2.15 We often sub-analyse ROCE, to find out more about why the ROCE is high or low, or better or worse than last year. There are **two factors** that **contribute towards a return on capital employed, both related to sales turnover.**

(a) **Profit margin.** A company might make a high or low profit margin on its sales. For example, a company that makes a profit of 25p per £1 of sales is making a bigger return on its turnover than another company making a profit of only 10p per £1 of sales.

(b) **Asset turnover.** Asset turnover is a measure of how well the assets of a business are being used to generate sales. For example, if two companies each have capital employed of £100,000 and Company A makes sales of £400,000 per annum whereas Company B makes sales of only £200,000 per annum, Company A is making a higher turnover from the same amount of assets (twice as much asset turnover as Company B) and this will help A to make a higher return on capital employed than B. Asset turnover is expressed as 'x times' so that assets generate x times their value in annual turnover. Here, Company A's asset turnover is 4 times and B's is 2 times.

2.16 Profit margin and asset turnover together explain the ROCE and if the ROCE is the primary profitability ratio, these other two are the secondary ratios. **The relationship between the three ratios can be shown mathematically.**

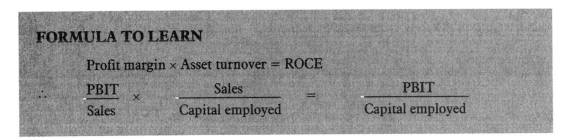

FORMULA TO LEARN

Profit margin × Asset turnover = ROCE

$$\therefore \quad \frac{PBIT}{Sales} \times \frac{Sales}{Capital\ employed} = \frac{PBIT}{Capital\ employed}$$

2.17 In our example:

		Profit margin		Asset turnover		ROCE
(a)	19X8	$\dfrac{360,245}{3,095,576}$	×	$\dfrac{3,095,576}{988,899}$	=	$\dfrac{360,245}{988,899}$
		11.64%	×	3.13 times	=	36.4%
(b)	19X7	$\dfrac{247,011}{1,909,051}$	×	$\dfrac{1,909,051}{751,969}$	=	$\dfrac{247,011}{751,969}$
		12.94%	×	2.54 times	=	32.8%

2.18 In this example, the company's improvement in ROCE between 19X7 and 19X8 is attributable to a higher asset turnover. Indeed the profit margin has fallen a little, but the higher asset turnover has more than compensated for this.

2.19 It is also worth commenting on the change in sales turnover from one year to the next. You may already have noticed that Furlong plc achieved sales growth of over 60% from £1.9 million to £3.1 million between 19X7 and 19X8. This is very strong growth, and this is certainly one of the most significant items in the P & L account and balance sheet.

A warning about comments on profit margin and asset turnover

2.20   It might be tempting to think that a high profit margin is good, and a low asset turnover means sluggish trading. In broad terms, this is so. But **there is a trade-off between profit margin and asset turnover, and you cannot look at one without allowing for the other.**

(a)   A high profit margin means a high profit per £1 of sales, but if this also means that sales prices are high, there is a strong possibility that sales turnover will be depressed, and so asset turnover lower.

(b)   A high asset turnover means that the company is generating a lot of sales, but to do this it might have to keep its prices down and so accept a low profit margin per £1 of sales.

2.21   Consider the following.

Company A		*Company B*	
Sales	£1,000,000	Sales	£4,000,000
Capital employed	£1,000,000	Capital employed	£1,000,000
PBIT	£200,000	PBIT	£200,000

These figures would give the following ratios.

$$\text{ROCE} = \frac{200,000}{1,000,000} = 20\% \qquad \text{ROCE} = \frac{200,000}{1,000,000} = 20\%$$

$$\text{Profit margin} = \frac{200,000}{1,000,000} = 20\% \qquad \text{Profit margin} = \frac{200,000}{4,000,000} = 5\%$$

$$\text{Asset turnover} = \frac{1,000,000}{1,000,000} = 1 \qquad \text{Asset turnover} = \frac{4,000,000}{1,000,000} = 4$$

2.22   The companies have the same ROCE, but it is arrived at in a very different fashion. Company A operates with a low asset turnover and a comparatively high profit margin whereas company B carries out much more business, but on a lower profit margin. Company A could be operating at the luxury end of the market, whilst company B is operating at the popular end of the market (Fortnum and Masons v Sainsbury's).

Gross profit margin, net profit margin and profit analysis

2.23   Depending on the format of the P & L account, you may be able to calculate the gross profit margin as well as the net profit margin. Looking at the two together can be quite informative.

2.24   For example, suppose that a company has the following summarised profit and loss accounts for two consecutive years.

	Year 1	Year 2
	£	£
Turnover	70,000	100,000
Cost of sales	42,000	55,000
Gross profit	28,000	45,000
Expenses	21,000	35,000
Net profit	7,000	10,000

Although the net profit margin is the same for both years at 10%, the gross profit margin is not.

In year 1 it is:

$$\frac{28,000}{70,000} = 40\%$$

and in year 2 it is:

$$\frac{45,000}{100,000} = 45\%$$

The improved gross profit margin has not led to an improvement in the net profit margin. This is because expenses as a percentage of sales have risen from 30% in year 1 to 35% in year 2.

3   LIQUIDITY, GEARING AND WORKING CAPITAL   6/95

Long-term solvency: debt and gearing ratios

3.1   Debt ratios are concerned with how much the company owes in relation to its size, whether it is getting into heavier debt or improving its situation, and whether its debt burden seems heavy or light.

(a)   **When a company is heavily in debt banks and other potential lenders may be unwilling to advance further funds.**

(b)   **When a company is earning only a modest profit before interest and tax, and has a heavy debt burden, there will be very little profit left over for shareholders after the interest charges have been paid.** And so if interest rates were to go up (on bank overdrafts and so on) or the company were to borrow even more, it might soon be incurring interest charges in excess of PBIT. This might eventually lead to the liquidation of the company.

These are two big reasons why companies should keep their debt burden under control. There are four ratios that are particularly worth looking at, the debt ratio, gearing ratio, interest cover and cash flow ratio.

Debt ratio

> **FORMULA TO LEARN**
>
> The **debt ratio** is the ratio of a company's total debts to its total assets.

3.2   (a)   Assets consist of fixed assets at their balance sheet value, plus current assets.

(b)   Debts consist of all creditors, whether amounts falling due within one year or after more than one year.

You can **ignore long-term provisions and liabilities, such as deferred taxation.**

3.3   There is no absolute guide to the maximum safe debt ratio, but as a very general guide, you might regard 50% as a safe limit to debt. In practice, many companies operate successfully with a higher debt ratio than this, but 50% is nonetheless a helpful benchmark. In addition, if the debt ratio is over 50% and getting worse, the company's debt position will be worth looking at more carefully.

3.4   In the case of Furlong plc the debt ratio is as follows.

		19X8	*19X7*
$\dfrac{\text{Total debts}}{\text{Total assets}}$	=	$\dfrac{(881,731 + 100,000)}{(802,180 + 1,068,450)}$	$\dfrac{(912,456 + 100,000)}{(656,071 + 1,008,354)}$
		= 52%	= 61%

3.5 In this case, the debt ratio is quite high, mainly because of the large amount of current liabilities. However, the debt ratio has fallen from 61% to 52% between 19X7 and 19X8, and so the company appears to be improving its debt position.

Gearing ratio

3.6 **Capital gearing is concerned with a company's long-term capital structure**. We can think of a company as consisting of fixed assets and net current assets (ie working capital, which is current assets minus current liabilities). These assets must be financed by long-term capital of the company, which is either:

(a) share capital and reserves (shareholders' funds) which can be divided into:

(i) ordinary shares plus reserves; and
(ii) preference shares; or

(b) long-term debt capital: 'creditors: amounts falling due after more than one year'.

3.7 **Preference share capital is not debt**. It would certainly not be included as debt in the debt ratio. However, like loan capital, preference share capital has a prior claim over profits before interest and tax, ahead of ordinary shareholders. Preference dividends must be paid out of profits before ordinary shareholders are entitled to an ordinary dividend, and so we refer to preference share capital and loan capital as prior charge capital.

3.8 **The capital gearing ratio is a measure of the proportion of a company's capital that is prior charge capital**. It is measured as follows.

> **FORMULA TO LEARN**
>
> $$\text{Capital gearing} = \frac{\text{prior charge capital}}{\text{total capital}}$$

(a) **Prior charge capital is capital carrying a right to a fixed return**. It will include preference shares and debentures.

(b) **Total capital is ordinary share capital and reserves plus prior charge capital plus any long-term liabilities or provisions.** In group accounts we would also include minority interests. It is easier to identify the same figure for total capital as total assets less current liabilities, which you will find given to you in the balance sheet.

3.9 As with the debt ratio, there is no absolute limit to what a gearing ratio ought to be. A company with a gearing ratio of more than 50% is said to be high-geared (whereas low gearing means a gearing ratio of less than 50%). Many companies are high geared, but if a high geared company is becoming increasingly high geared, it is likely to have difficulty in the future when it wants to borrow even more, unless it can also boost its shareholders' capital, either with retained profits or by a new share issue.

3.10 A similar ratio to the gearing ratio is the debt/equity ratio, which is calculated as follows.

> **FORMULA TO LEARN**
>
> $$\text{Debt/equity ratio} = \frac{\text{prior charge capital}}{\text{ordinary share capital and reserves}}$$

This gives us the same sort of information as the gearing ratio, and a ratio of 100% or more would indicate high gearing.

3.11 In the example of Furlong plc, we find that the company, although having a high debt ratio because of its current liabilities, has a low gearing ratio. It has no preference share capital and its only long-term debt is the 10% debenture stock.

	19X8	*19X7*
Gearing ratio	$\dfrac{100,000}{988,899}$	$\dfrac{100,000}{751,969}$
	= 10%	= 13%
Debt/equity ratio	$\dfrac{100,000}{868,899}$	$\dfrac{100,000}{641,969}$
	= 12%	= 16%

The implications of high or low gearing

3.12 We mentioned earlier that **gearing is, amongst other things, an attempt to quantify the degree of risk involved in holding equity shares in a company**, risk both in terms of the company's ability to remain in business and in terms of expected ordinary dividends from the company. The problem with a high geared company is that by definition there is a lot of debt. Debt generally carries a fixed rate of interest (or fixed rate of dividend if in the form of preference shares), hence there is a given (and large) amount to be paid out from profits to holders of debt before arriving at a residue available for distribution to the holders of equity. The riskiness will perhaps become clearer with the aid of an example.

	Company A £'000	*Company B* £'000	*Company C* £'000
Ordinary share capital	600	400	300
Profit and loss account	200	200	200
Revaluation reserve	100	100	100
	900	700	600
6% preference shares	-	-	100
10% loan stock	100	300	300
Capital employed	1,000	1,000	1,000
Gearing ratio	10%	30%	40%

3.13 Now suppose that each company makes a profit before interest and tax of £50,000, and the rate of corporation tax is 30%. Amounts available for distribution to equity shareholders will be as follows:

	Company A £'000	*Company B* £'000	*Company C* £'000
Profit before interest and tax	50	50	50
Interest	10	30	30
Profit before tax	40	20	20
Taxation at 30%	12	6	6
Profit after tax	28	14	14
Preference dividend	-	-	6
Available for ordinary shareholders	28	14	8

3.14 If in the subsequent year profit before interest and tax falls to £40,000, the amounts available to ordinary shareholders will become:

	Company A £'000	Company B £'000	Company C £'000
Profit before interest and tax	40	40	40
Interest	10	30	30
Profit before tax	30	10	10
Taxation at 30%	9	3	3
Profit after tax	21	7	7
Preference dividend	-	-	6
Available for ordinary shareholders	21	7	1

Note the following.

Gearing ratio	10%	30%	40%
Change in PBIT	– 20%	– 20%	– 20%
Change in profit available for ordinary shareholders	– 20%	– 50%	– 87.5%

3.15 **The more highly geared the company, the greater the risk that little (if anything) will be available to distribute by way of dividend to the ordinary shareholders.**

(a) The example clearly displays this fact in so far as the more highly geared the company, the greater the percentage change in profit available for ordinary shareholders for any given percentage change in profit before interest and tax.

(b) The relationship similarly holds when profits increase, and if PBIT had risen by 20% rather than fallen, you would find that once again the largest percentage change in profit available for ordinary shareholders (this means an increase) will be for the highly geared company.

(c) This means that there will be greater volatility of amounts available for ordinary shareholders, and presumably therefore greater volatility in dividends paid to those shareholders, where a company is highly geared.

(d) That is the risk: you may do extremely well or extremely badly without a particularly large movement in the PBIT of the company.

3.16 The risk of a company's ability to remain in business was referred to earlier. Gearing is relevant to this. A high geared company has a large amount of interest to pay annually (assuming that the debt is external borrowing rather than preference shares). If those borrowings are '**secured**' in any way (and debentures in particular are secured), then the **holders of the debt are perfectly entitled to force the company to realise assets** to pay their interest **if funds are not available from other sources**. Clearly the more highly geared a company the more likely this is to occur when and if profits fall. Individual items to consider when looking at gearing include convertible loan stock, preference shares, deferred loans and a revaluation reserve.

Interest cover

3.17 The interest cover ratio shows whether a company is earning enough profits before interest and tax to pay its interest costs comfortably, or whether its interest costs are high in relation to the size of its profits, so that a fall in PBIT would then have a significant effect on profits available for ordinary shareholders.

FORMULA TO LEARN

$$\text{Interest cover} = \frac{\text{profit before interest and tax}}{\text{interest charges}}$$

3.18 An interest cover of 2 times or less would be low, and should really exceed 3 times before the company's interest costs are to be considered within acceptable limits.

3.19 Returning first to the example of Companies A, B and C, the interest cover was as follows.

		Company A	Company B	Company C
(a)	When PBIT was £50,000 =	$\dfrac{50,000}{10,000}$	$\dfrac{50,000}{30,000}$	$\dfrac{50,000}{30,000}$
		5 times	1.67 times	1.67 times
(b)	When PBIT was £40,000 =	$\dfrac{40,000}{10,000}$	$\dfrac{40,000}{30,000}$	$\dfrac{40,000}{30,000}$
		4 times	1.33 times	1.33 times

Note. Although preference share capital is included as prior charge capital for the gearing ratio, **it is usual to exclude preference dividends from 'interest' charges.** We also look at all interest payments, even interest charges on short-term debt, and so interest cover and gearing do not quite look at the same thing.

3.20 Both B and C have a low interest cover, which is a warning to ordinary shareholders that their profits are highly vulnerable, in percentage terms, to even small changes in PBIT.

Question 1

Returning to the example of Furlong plc in Paragraph 1.8, what is the company's interest cover?

Answer

Interest payments should be taken gross, from the note to the accounts, and not net of interest receipts as shown in the P & L account.

	19X8	19X7
PBIT	360,245	247,011
Interest payable	18,115	21,909
	= 20 times	= 11 times

Furlong plc has more than sufficient interest cover. In view of the company's low gearing, this is not too surprising and so we finally obtain a picture of Furlong plc as a company that does not seem to have a debt problem, in spite of its high (although declining) debt ratio.

Cash flow ratio

3.21 The cash flow ratio is **the ratio of a company's net cash inflow to its total debts.**

   (a) Net cash inflow is the amount of cash which the company has coming into the business from its operations. A suitable figure for net cash inflow can be obtained from the statement of source and application of funds.

   (b) Total debts are short-term and long-term creditors, together with provisions for liabilities and charges. A distinction can be made between debts payable within one year and other debts and provisions.

3.22 Obviously, a company needs to be earning enough cash from operations to be able to meet its foreseeable debts and future commitments, and the cash flow ratio, and changes in the cash flow ratio from one year to the next, provide a useful indicator of a company's cash position.

Short-term solvency and liquidity

3.23 Profitability is of course an important aspect of a company's performance and debt or gearing is another. Neither, however, addresses directly the key issue of **liquidity**.

> **KEY TERM**
>
> **Liquidity** is the amount of cash a company can put its hands on quickly to settle its debts (and possibly to meet other unforeseen demands for cash payments too).

3.24 Liquid funds consist of:

(a) Cash.

(b) Short-term investments for which there is a ready market, (short-term investments are distinct from investments in shares in subsidiaries or associated companies).

(c) Fixed-term deposits with a bank or building society, for example, a six month high-interest deposit with a bank.

(d) Trade debtors (because they will pay what they owe within a reasonably short period of time).

(e) Bills of exchange receivable (because like ordinary trade debtors, these represent amounts of cash due to be received within a relatively short period of time).

3.25 In summary, **liquid assets are current asset items that will or could soon be converted into cash, and cash itself.** Two common definitions of liquid assets are:

(a) All current assets without exception.
(b) All current assets with the exception of stocks.

3.26 A company can obtain liquid assets from sources other than sales, such as the issue of shares for cash, a new loan or the sale of fixed assets. But a company cannot rely on these at all times, and in general, obtaining liquid funds depends on making sales and profits. Even so, **profits do not always lead to increases in liquidity.** This is mainly because funds generated from trading may be immediately invested in fixed assets or paid out as dividends. You should refer back to the chapter on cash flow statements to examine this issue.

3.27 The reason why a company needs liquid assets is so that it can meet its debts when they fall due. Payments are continually made for operating expenses and other costs, and so there is a cash cycle from trading activities of cash coming in from sales and cash going out for expenses. This is illustrated by the diagram overleaf.

The cash cycle

3.28 To help you to understand liquidity ratios, it is useful to begin with a brief explanation of the cash cycle. The cash cycle **describes the flow of cash out of a business and back into it again as a result of normal trading operations.**

3.29 Cash goes out to pay for supplies, wages and salaries and other expenses, although payments can be delayed by taking some credit. A business might hold stock for a while and then sell it. Cash will come back into the business from the sales, although customers might delay payment by themselves taking some credit.

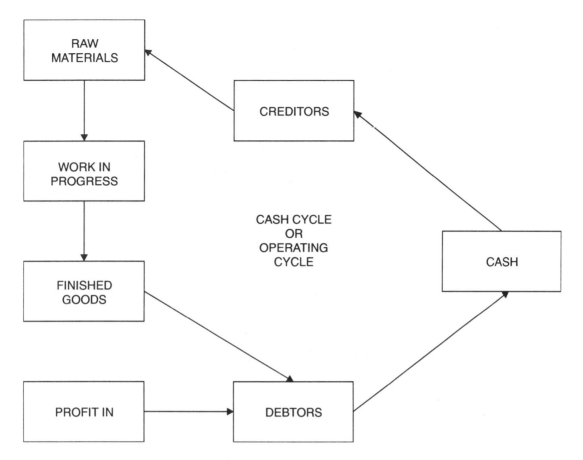

RAW MATERIALS

WORK IN PROGRESS

FINISHED GOODS

PROFIT IN

DEBTORS

CREDITORS

CASH

CASH CYCLE OR OPERATING CYCLE

3.30   The main points about the cash cycle are as follows.

(a)   The timing of cash flows in and out of a business does not coincide with the time when sales and costs of sales occur. **Cash flows out can be postponed by taking credit. Cash flows in can be delayed by having debtors.**

(b)   The **time between making a purchase and making a sale also affects cash flows**. If stocks are held for a long time, the delay between the cash payment for stocks and cash receipts from selling them will also be a long one.

(c)   **Holding stocks and having debtors** can therefore be seen as **two reasons why cash receipts are delayed**. Another way of saying this is that if a company invests in working capital, its cash position will show a corresponding decrease.

(d)   Similarly, **taking credit** from creditors can be seen as a reason why **cash payments are delayed**. The company's liquidity position will worsen when it has to pay the creditors, unless it can get more cash in from sales and debtors in the meantime.

3.31   The liquidity ratios and working capital turnover ratios are used to test a company's liquidity, length of cash cycle, and investment in working capital.

Liquidity ratios: current ratio and quick ratio

3.32   The 'standard' test of liquidity is the current ratio. It can be obtained from the balance sheet.

> **FORMULA TO LEARN**
>
> Current ratio: $\dfrac{\text{Current assets}}{\text{Current liabilities}}$

The idea behind this is that a company should have enough current assets that give a promise of 'cash to come' to meet its future commitments to pay off its current liabilities. Obviously, a **ratio in excess of 1 should be expected**. Otherwise, there would be the prospect that the company might be unable to pay its debts on time. In practice, a ratio comfortably in excess of 1 should be expected, but what is 'comfortable' varies between different types of businesses.

3.33 Companies are not able to convert all their current assets into cash very quickly. In particular, some manufacturing companies might hold large quantities of raw material stocks, which must be used in production to create finished goods stocks. Finished goods stocks might be warehoused for a long time, or sold on lengthy credit. In such businesses, where stock turnover is slow, most stocks are not very 'liquid' assets, because the cash cycle is so long. For these reasons, we calculate an additional liquidity ratio, known as the quick ratio or acid test ratio.

FORMULA TO LEARN

The quick ratio, or acid test ratio is:

$$\frac{\text{Current assets less stocks}}{\text{Current liabilities}}$$

3.34 **This ratio should ideally be at least 1 for companies with a slow stock turnover**. For companies with a fast stock turnover, a quick ratio can be comfortably less than 1 without suggesting that the company should be in cash flow trouble.

Case examples

(a) Both the current ratio and the quick ratio offer an indication of the company's liquidity position, but the absolute figures should not be interpreted too literally. It is often theorised that an acceptable current ratio is 1.5 and an acceptable quick ratio is 0.8, but these should only be used as a guide. Different businesses operate in very different ways. Budgens (the supermarket group) for example had (as at 30 April 1993) a current ratio of 0.52 and a quick ratio of 0.17. Budgens has low debtors (people do not buy groceries on credit), low cash (good cash management), medium stocks (high stocks but quick turnover, particularly in view of perishability) and very high creditors (Budgens buys its supplies of groceries on credit).

(b) Compare the Budgens ratios with the Tomkins group which had a current ratio of 1.44 and a quick ratio of 1.03 (as at 1 May 1993). Tomkins is a manufacturing and retail organisation and operates with liquidity ratios closer to the standard. At 25 September 1993, Tate & Lyle's figures gave a current ratio of 1.18 and a quick ratio of 0.80.

3.35 **What is important is the trend of these ratios.** From this, one can easily ascertain whether liquidity is improving or deteriorating. If Budgens has traded for the last 10 years (very successfully) with current ratios of 0.52 and quick ratios of 0.17 then it should be supposed that the company can continue in business with those levels of liquidity. If in the following year the current ratio were to fall to 0.38 and the quick ratio to 0.09, then further investigation into the liquidity situation would be appropriate. It is the relative position that is far more important than the absolute figures.

3.36 **Don't forget the other side of the coin either. A current ratio and a quick ratio can get bigger than they need to be.** A company that has large volumes of stocks and debtors might be over-investing in working capital, and so tying up more funds in the business than it needs to. This **would suggest poor management** of debtors (credit) or stocks by the company.

Efficiency ratios: control of debtors and stock

3.37   A rough measure of the average length of time it takes for a company's debtors to pay what they owe is the 'debtor days' ratio, or average debtors' payment period.

> **FORMULA TO LEARN**
>
> The estimated average **debtors' payment period** is calculated as:
>
> $$\frac{\text{trade debtors}}{\text{sales}} \times 365 \text{ days}$$

3.38   The figure for sales should be taken as the turnover figure in the P & L account. The trade debtors are not the total figure for debtors in the balance sheet, which includes prepayments and non-trade debtors. The trade debtors figure will be itemised in an analysis of the debtors total, in a note to the accounts.

3.39   The estimate of debtor days is **only approximate**.

   (a)   The balance sheet value of debtors might be abnormally high or low compared with the 'normal' level the company usually has.

   (b)   Turnover in the P & L account is exclusive of VAT, but debtors in the balance sheet are inclusive of VAT. We are not strictly comparing like with like. (Some companies show turnover inclusive of VAT as well as turnover exclusive of VAT, and the 'inclusive' figure should be used in these cases.)

3.40   Sales are usually made on 'normal credit terms' of payment within 30 days. Debtor days significantly in excess of this might be representative of poor management of funds of a business. However, some companies must allow generous credit terms to win customers. Exporting companies in particular may have to carry large amounts of debtors, and so their average collection period might be well in excess of 30 days.

3.41   The **trend of the collection period (debtor days) over time is probably the best guide.** If debtor days are increasing year on year, this is indicative of a poorly managed credit control function (and potentially therefore a poorly managed company).

3.42   DEBTOR DAYS: EXAMPLES

Using the same examples as before, the debtor days of those companies were as follows.

Company	Date	Trade debtors turnover	Debtor days (× 365)	Previous year	Debtor days (× 365)
Budgens	30.4.93	$\dfrac{£5,016K}{£284,986K} =$	6.4 days	$\dfrac{£3,977K}{£290,668K} =$	5.0 days
Tomkins	1.5.93	$\dfrac{£458.3m}{£2,059.5m} =$	81.2 days	$\dfrac{£272.4m}{£1,274.2m} =$	78.0 days
Tate & Lyle	25.9.93	$\dfrac{£304.4m}{£3,817.3m} =$	29.3 days	$\dfrac{£287.0m}{£3,366.3m} =$	31.1 days

3.43   The differences in debtor days reflect the differences between the types of business. Budgen's has hardly any trade debtors at all, whereas the manufacturing companies have far more. The debtor days are fairly constant from the previous year for all three companies.

Stock turnover period

3.44 Another ratio worth calculating is the stock turnover period, or stock days. This is **another estimated figure**, obtainable from published accounts, which indicates the average number of days that items of stock are held for. As with the average debt collection period, however, it is only an approximate estimated figure, but one which should be **reliable enough for comparing changes year on year.**

FORMULA TO LEARN

The number of **stock days** is calculated as:

$$\frac{\text{stock}}{\text{cost of sales}} \times 365$$

FORMULA TO LEARN

The reciprocal of the fraction:

$$\frac{\text{cost of sales}}{\text{stock}}$$

is termed the **stock turnover.**

3.45 This is **another measure of how vigorously a business is trading.** A lengthening stock turnover period from one year to the next could indicate a slowdown in trading or a build-up in stock levels, perhaps suggesting that the investment in stocks is becoming excessive.

3.46 **Generally the higher the stock turnover is the better,** but several aspects of stockholding policy have to balanced.

    (a) Lead times.
    (b) Seasonal fluctuations in orders.
    (c) Alternative uses of warehouse space.
    (d) Bulk buying discounts.
    (e) Likelihood of stock perishing or becoming obsolete.

3.47 Presumably if we add together the stock days and the debtor days, this should give us an indication of how soon stock is convertible into cash. **Both debtor days and stock days** therefore **give us a further indication of the company's liquidity.**

3.48 STOCK TURNOVER: EXAMPLES

Returning once more to our first example, the estimated stock turnover periods for Budgens were as follows.

Company	Date	$\dfrac{\text{Stock}}{\text{Cost of sales}}$	Stock turnover period (days × 365)	Previous year		
Budgens	30.4.92	$\dfrac{£15,554K}{£254,571K}$	22.3 days	$\dfrac{£14,094K}{£261,368K}$	× 365 =	19.7 days

3.49 The figures for cost of sales were not shown in the accounts of either Tate & Lyle or Tomkins.

Question 2

Calculate liquidity and working capital ratios from the accounts of the BET Group, a business which provides service support (cleaning etc) to customers worldwide.

	1993	1992
Turnover	2,176.2	2,344.8
Cost of sales	1,659.0	1,731.5
Gross profit	517.2	613.3
Current assets		
Stocks	42.7	78.0
Debtors (note 1)	378.9	431.4
Short-term deposits and cash	205.2	145.0
	626.8	654.4
Creditors: amounts falling due within one year		
Loans and overdrafts	32.4	81.1
Corporation taxes	67.8	76.7
Dividend	11.7	17.2
Creditors (note 2)	487.2	467.2
	599.1	642.2
Net current assets	27.7	12.2

Notes

1	Trade debtors	295.2	335.5
2	Trade creditors	190.8	188.1

Answer

		1993			1992
Current ratio	$\dfrac{626.8}{599.1}$ =	1.05	$\dfrac{654.4}{642.2}$ =		1.02
Quick ratio	$\dfrac{584.1}{599.1}$ =	0.97	$\dfrac{576.4}{642.2}$ =		0.90
Debtors' payment period	$\dfrac{295.2}{2,176.2}$ × 365 =	49.5 days	$\dfrac{335.5}{2,344.8}$	× 365 =	52.2 days
Stock turnover period	$\dfrac{42.7}{1,659.0}$ × 365 =	9.4 days	$\dfrac{78.0}{1,731.5}$	× 365 =	16.4 days
Creditors' turnover period	$\dfrac{190.8}{1,659.0}$ × 365 =	42.0 days	$\dfrac{188.1}{1,731.5}$	× 365 =	40.0 days

3.50 BET Group is a service company and hence it would be expected to have very low stock and a very short stock turnover period. The similarity of debtors' and creditors' turnover periods means that the group is passing on most of the delay in receiving payment to its suppliers.

FORMULA TO LEARN

Creditors' turnover is ideally calculated by the formula:

$$\frac{\text{Creditors}}{\text{Purchases}} \times 365$$

3.51   However, **it is rare to find purchases disclosed in published accounts and so cost of sales serves as an approximation.** The creditors' turnover ratio often helps to assess a company's liquidity; an increase in creditor days is often a sign of lack of long-term finance or poor management of current assets, resulting in the use of extended credit from suppliers, increased bank overdraft and so on.

3.52   BET's current ratio is a little lower than average but its quick ratio is better than average and very little less than the current ratio. This suggests that stock levels are strictly controlled, which is reinforced by the low stock turnover period. It would seem that working capital is tightly managed, to avoid the poor liquidity which could be caused by a high debtors' turnover period and comparatively high creditors.

4   SHAREHOLDERS' INVESTMENT RATIOS

4.1   These are the ratios which **help equity shareholders and other investors to assess the value and quality of an investment in the ordinary shares of a company.** The value of an investment in ordinary shares in a listed company is its market value, and so investment ratios must have regard not only to information in the company's published accounts, but also to the current price, and some of these ratios involve using the share price.

4.2   Earnings per share is a valuable indicator of an ordinary share's performance and is the subject of SSAP 3. This was discussed in Chapter 13.

Dividend per share and dividend cover

4.3   The dividend per share in pence is self-explanatory, and clearly an item of some interest to shareholders.

FORMULA TO LEARN

Dividend cover is a ratio of: $\dfrac{\text{Earnings per share}}{\text{Net dividend per (ordinary) share}}$

4.4   **It shows what proportion of profit on ordinary activities for the year that is available for distribution to shareholders has been paid (or proposed) and what proportion will be retained in the business to finance future growth.** A dividend cover of 2 times would indicate that, ignoring extraordinary items, the company had paid 50% of its distributable profits as dividends, and retained 50% in the business to help to finance future operations. Retained profits are an important source of funds for most companies, and so the dividend cover can in some cases be quite high.

4.5   A **significant change** in the dividend cover from one year to the next **would be worth looking at closely**. For example, if a company's dividend cover were to fall sharply between one year and the next, it could be that its profits had fallen, but the directors wished to pay at least the same amount of dividends as in the previous year, so as to keep shareholder expectations satisfied.

P/E ratio

> **FORMULA TO LEARN**
>
> The **P/E ratio** is the ratio of a company's current share price to the earnings per share.

4.6   A high P/E ratio indicates strong shareholder confidence in the company and its future, eg in profit growth, and a lower P/E ratio indicates lower confidence.

4.7   The P/E ratio of one company can be compared with the P/E ratios of:

(a)   Other companies in the same business sector.

(b)   Other companies generally.

Dividend yield

4.8   Dividend yield is **the return a shareholder is currently expecting on the shares of a company.**

> **FORMULA TO LEARN**
>
> $$\text{Dividend yield} = \frac{\text{Dividend on the share for the year } (grossed\ up)}{\text{Current market value of the share (ex div)}} \times 100\%$$

(a)   The dividend per share is taken as the dividend for the previous year.

(b)   The dividend is inclusive of the tax credit. The net dividend is the amount paid out of the P & L account, and the gross dividend is found by multiplying the net dividend by a factor of:

$$\frac{100}{(100 - IT)}$$

IT used to be the basic rate of income tax. Thus, given a basic rate of income tax of 25%, the gross dividend was the net dividend multiplied by a factor of $^{100}/_{75}$ (or $^4/_3$). This percentage is now 20% as specified by the 1993 Finance Act, therefore the factor is $^{100}/_{80}$ or $^5/_4$.

4.9   **Shareholders look for both dividend yield and capital growth. Obviously, dividend yield is therefore an important aspect of a share's performance.**

Question 3

In the year to 30 September 19X4, Plumb plc declared an interim ordinary dividend of 7.4p per share and a final ordinary dividend of 8.6p per share. Assuming an ex div share price of 315 pence, what is the dividend yield, given an ACT rate of 20%?

Answer

The net dividend per share is (7.4 + 8.6) = 16 pence

$$\frac{16 \times \frac{100}{80}}{315} \times 100 = 6.3\%$$

Earnings yield

4.10   Earnings yield is **a performance indicator** that is not given the same publicity as EPS, P/E ratio, dividend cover and dividend yield. It is **measured as earnings per share, grossed up, as a percentage of the current share price**. It therefore, indicates what the dividend yield could be if:

(a)   The company paid out all its profits as dividend and retained nothing in the business.

(b)   There were no extraordinary items in the P & L account.

4.11   Some companies retain a bigger proportion of their profits than others, and so the dividend yield between companies can vary for this reason. **Earnings yield overcomes the problem of comparison by assuming that all earnings are paid out as dividends**. *Note.* The earnings yield is equal to the dividend yield multiplied by the dividend cover.

5   ACCOUNTING POLICIES AND THE LIMITATIONS OF RATIO ANALYSIS   6/95

5.1   We discussed the disclosure of accounting policies in our examination of SSAP 2. The choice of accounting policy and the effect of its implementation are almost as important as its disclosure in that the results of a company can be altered significantly by the choice of accounting policy.

The effect of choice of accounting policies

5.2   Where accounting standards allow alternative treatment of items in the accounts, then the accounting policy note should declare which policy has been chosen. It should then be applied consistently.

5.3   Consider, though, the **radically different effects produced by the different treatment of some items**. An example is the treatment of development expenditure under SSAP 13. Although the criteria for capitalising development expenditure are very strict, the choice of whether to capitalise and amortise or write off such costs can have a significant impact on profit. Consider the size of the R & D expenditure of the large drugs companies and you can see how important such an accounting policy could be.

5.4   You should be able to think of other examples of how the choice of accounting policy can affect the financial statements.

Changes in accounting policy

5.5   The effect of a change of accounting policy is **treated as a prior year adjustment** according to FRS 3 *Reporting financial performance* (see Chapter 13). This just means that the comparative figures are adjusted for the change in accounting policy for comparative purposes and an adjustment is put through reserves.

5.6   FRS 3 states that, as consistency is a fundamental accounting concept, any change in policy may:

'only be made if it can be justified on the grounds that the new policy is preferable to the one it replaces because it will give a fairer presentation of the result and of the financial position of a reporting entity.'

5.7   The problem with this situation is that the directors may be able to manipulate the results through change(s) of accounting policies. This would be done to avoid the effect of an old accounting policy or gain the effect of a new one. It is likely to be done in a sensitive period, perhaps when the company's profits are low or the company is about to announce a rights issue. The management would have to convince the auditors that the new policy was much better, but it is not difficult to produce reasons in such cases.

5.8   The effect of such a change is very short-term. Most analysts and sophisticated users will discount its effect immediately, except to the extent that it will affect any dividend (because of the effect on distributable profits). It may help to avoid breaches of banking covenants because of the effect on certain ratios.

5.9   Obviously, **the accounting policy for any item in the accounts could only be changed once in quite a long period of time.** Auditors would not allow another change, even back to the old policy, unless there was a wholly exceptional reason.

5.10 The managers of a company can choose accounting policies *initially* to suit the company or the type of results they want to get. **Any changes in accounting policy must be justified, but some managers might try to change accounting policies just to manipulate the results.**

Limitations of ratio analysis

5.11 The consideration of how accounting policies may be used to manipulate company results leads us to some of the other limitations of ratio analysis. These can be summarised as follows.

(a) **Availability of comparable information.**
(b) **Use of historical/out of date information.**
(c) **Ratios are not definitive - they are only a guide.**
(d) **Interpretation needs careful analysis and should not be considered in isolation.**
(e) **It is a subjective exercise.**
(f) **It can be subject to manipulation.**
(g) **Ratios are not defined in standard form.**

> **Exam focus point**
> In the exam, always bear these points in mind; you may even be asked to discuss such limitations, but in any case they should have an impact on your analysis of a set of results.
>
> In June 1995 you were asked to discuss the limitations of certain ratios.

Operating and Financial Review (OFR)

5.12 The ASB document *Operating and Financial Review* is mentioned in the examinable documents for Paper 10. It introduces a statement which is **voluntary rather than mandatory**. It applies mainly to listed companies, but also those large corporations where there is a legitimate public interest. Such companies would be called on to produce an Operating and Financial Review (OFR) in their financial statements.

5.13   The purpose of the OFR is to provide:

> 'a framework for the directors to discuss and analyse the business's performance and the factors underlying its results and financial position, in order to assist users to assess for themselves the future potential of the business.'

5.14   The OFR should be developed in format and content to suit each organisation, but there would be some **essential features** of an OFR. It should:

(a)   **Be written in a clear style and as succinctly as possible**, to be readily understandable by the general reader of annual reports, and should include only matters that are likely to be significant to investors.

(b)   **Be balanced and objective**, dealing even-handedly with both good and bad aspects.

(c)   **Refer to comments** made **in previous statements** where these have **not** been **borne out by events.**

(d)   **Contain analytical discussion** rather than merely numerical analysis.

(e)   **Follow a 'top-down' structure**, discussing individual aspects of the business in the context of a discussion of the business as a whole.

(f)   Explain the reason for, and effect of any **changes in accounting policies**.

(g)   **Make it clear how any ratios or other numerical information given relate to the financial statements.**

(h)   **Include discussion of:**

(i)   **trends and factors** underlying the business that have affected the results but are not expected to continue in the future; and

(ii)   **known events, trends and uncertainties** that are expected to have an impact on the business in the future.

5.15   The OFR is in two sections.

(a)   **Operating review**

(i)   Operating results for the period
(ii)   Dynamics of the business
(iii)   Investments for the future
(iv)   Profit for the year, recognised gains/losses etc
(v)   Dividends, EPS
(vi)   Accounting policies

(b)   **Financial review**

(i)   Capital structure and treasury policy
(ii)   Funds
(iii)   Current liquidity
(iv)   Going concern
(v)   Balance sheet values

5.16   A statement of compliance with the OFR statement is not required, although it might be helpful to the users of the accounts. You can see that the OFR should be of great benefit to less sophisticated users of accounts as it should carry out the analysis of a company's performance on the user's behalf. It should thus highlight the important items in the current year annual report, as well as drawing out 'those aspects of the year under review that are relevant to an assessment of future prospects'.

6   REPORTS ON FINANCIAL PERFORMANCE

6.1   You may have experience already in writing reports within your organisation. Accountants are called upon to write reports for many different purposes. These range from very formal reports, such as those addressed to the board of directors or the audit committee, to one-off reports of a more informal nature. You should appreciate the following general points about report writing.

Checklist for report writing

6.2   The following checklist for report writing indicates many of the factors that should be considered.

(a)   **Purpose or terms of reference**

   (i)   What is the report being written about?

   (ii)   Why is it needed?

   (iii)   What effect might the report have if its findings or recommendations are acted upon?

   (iv)   Who are the report users? How much do they know already?

   (v)   What is wanted, a definite recommendation or less specific advice?

   (vi)   What previous reports have there been on the subject, what did they find or recommend, and what action was taken on these findings, or recommendations?

(b)   **Information in the report**

   (i)   What is the source of each item of information in the report?

   (ii)   How old is the information?

   (iii)   What period does the report cover - a month, a year?

   (iv)   How can the accuracy of the information be checked and verified? To what extent might it be subject to error?

(c)   **Preparing the report**

   (i)   Who is responsible for preparing the report?

   (ii)   How long will it take to prepare?

   (iii)   How is the information in the report put together (for numerical information, what computations are carried out on the source data to arrive at the figures in the report)?

   (iv)   How many copies of the report should be prepared and to whom should they be sent?

(d)   **Usefulness of the report**

   (i)   What use will the report be in its present form? What action is it intended to trigger?

   (ii)   How will each recipient of the report use it for his or her own purposes?

   (iii)   Does the report meet the requirements of the terms of reference?

Format of reports in the examination

Exam focus point

In an examination your time is limited and you are under pressure. To make life a little easier, we suggest that you adopt the following format for any report you are requested to write.

REPORT (OR MEMORANDUM)

To: Board of Directors (or Chief Accountant, etc)

From: Financial Controller   **Date:**

Subject: Report format

Body of report

Signed: Accountant

6.3   If you adopt this style in your practice questions, you should end up producing it automatically. This should ensure that you do not lose any presentation marks.

6.4   Now you have considered the problems and difficulties of report writing, attempt the following question.

Question 4

The following information has been extracted from the recently published accounts of DG plc.

EXTRACTS FROM THE PROFIT AND LOSS ACCOUNT

	£'000	£'000
Sales	11,200	9,750
Cost of sales	8,460	6,825
Net profit before tax	465	320
This is after charging:		
Depreciation	360	280
Debenture interest	80	60
Interest on bank overdraft	15	9
Audit fees	12	10

BALANCE SHEET AS AT 30 APRIL

	19X9 £'000	19X8 £'000
Fixed assets	1,850	1,430
Current assets		
Stock	640	490
Debtors	1,230	1,080
Cash	80	120
	1,950	1,690
Current liabilities		
Bank overdraft	110	80
Creditors	750	690
Taxation	30	20
Dividends	65	55
	955	845
Total assets less current liabilities	2,845	2,275
Long-term capital and reserves		
Ordinary share capital	800	800
Reserves	1,245	875
	2,045	1,675
10% debentures	800	600
	2,845	2,275

The following ratios are those calculated for DG plc, based on its published accounts for the previous year, and also the latest industry average ratios:

	DG plc 30 April 19X8	Industry average
ROCE (capital employed = equity and debentures)	16.70%	18.50%
Profit/sales	3.90%	4.73%
Asset turnover	4.29	3.91
Current ratio	2.00	1.90
Quick ratio	1.42	1.27
Gross profit margin	30.00%	35.23%
Debtors control	40 days	52 days
Creditors control	37 days	49 days
Stock turnover	13.90	18.30
Gearing	26.37%	32.71%

Required

(a)   Calculate comparable ratios (to two decimal places where appropriate) for DG plc for the year ended 30 April 19X9. All calculations must be clearly shown.

(b)   Write a report to your board of directors analysing the performance of DG plc, comparing the results against the previous year and against the industry average.

Answer

(a)

	19X8	19X9	Industry average
ROCE	$\frac{320+60}{2,275} = 16.70\%$	$\frac{465+80}{2,845} = 19.16\%$	18.50%
Profit/sales	$\frac{320+60}{9,750} = 3.90\%$	$\frac{465+80}{11,200} = 4.87\%$	4.73%
Asset turnover	$\frac{9,750}{2,275} = 4.29\text{x}$	$\frac{11,200}{2,845} = 3.94\text{x}$	3.91x
Current ratio	$\frac{1,690}{845} = 2.00$	$\frac{1,950}{955} = 2.04$	1.90
Quick ratio	$\frac{1,080+120}{845} = 1.42$	$\frac{1,230+80}{955} = 1.37$	1.27
Gross profit margin	$\frac{9,750-6,825}{9,750} = 30.00\%$	$\frac{11,200-8,460}{11,200} = 24.46\%$	35.23%

		19X8	19X9	Industry average
Debtors turnover		$\dfrac{1,080}{9,750} \times 365 = 40\text{days}$	$\dfrac{1,230}{11,200} \times 365 = 40\text{days}$	52 days
Creditors turnover		$\dfrac{690}{6,825} \times 365 = 37\text{days}$	$\dfrac{750}{8,460} \times 365 = 32\text{days}$	49 days
Stock turnover		$\dfrac{6,825}{490} = 13.9\text{x}$	$\dfrac{8,460}{640} = 13.2\text{x}$	18.30x
Gearing		$\dfrac{600}{2,275} = 26.37\%$	$\dfrac{800}{2,845} = 28.12\%$	32.71%

(b) (i)

REPORT

To:	Board of Directors	
From:	Management accountant	Date: *xx/xx/xx*
Subject:	Analysis of performance of DG plc	

This report should be read in conjunction with the appendix attached which shows the relevant ratios (from part (a)).

Trading and profitability

Return on capital employed has improved considerably between 19X8 and 19X9 and is now higher than the industry average.

Net income as a proportion of sales has also improved noticeably between the years and is also now marginally ahead of the industry average. Gross margin, however, is considerably lower than in the previous year and is only some 70% of the industry average. This suggests either that there has been a change in the cost structure of DG plc or that there has been a change in the method of cost allocation between the periods. Either way, this is a marked change that requires investigation. The company may be in a period of transition as sales have increased by nearly 15% over the year and it would appear that new fixed assets have been purchased.

Asset turnover has declined between the periods although the 19X9 figure is in line with the industry average. This reduction might indicate that the efficiency with which assets are used has deteriorated or it might indicate that the assets acquired in 19X9 have not yet fully contributed to the business. A longer term trend would clarify the picture.

(ii) *Liquidity and working capital management*

The current ratio has improved slightly over the year and is marginally higher than the industry average. It is also in line with what is generally regarded as satisfactory (2:1).

The quick ratio has declined marginally but is still better than the industry average. This suggests that DG plc has no short term liquidity problems and should have no difficulty in paying its debts as they become due.

Debtors as a proportion of sales is unchanged from 19X8 and are considerably lower than the industry average. Consequently, there is probably little opportunity to reduce this further and there may be pressure in the future from customers to increase the period of credit given. The period of credit taken from suppliers has fallen from 37 days' purchases to 32 days' and is much lower than the industry average; thus, it may be possible to finance any additional debtors by negotiating better credit terms from suppliers.

Stock turnover has fallen slightly and is much slower than the industry average and this may partly reflect stocking up ahead of a significant increase in sales. Alternatively, there is some danger that the stock could contain certain obsolete items that may require writing off. The relative increase in the level of stock has been financed by an increased overdraft which may reduce if the stock levels can be brought down.

The high levels of stock, overdraft and debtors compared to that of creditors suggests a labour intensive company or one where considerable value is added to bought-in products.

(iii) *Gearing*

The level of gearing has increased only slightly over the year and is below the industry average. Since the return on capital employed is nearly twice the rate of interest on the debentures, profitability is likely to be increased by a modest increase in the level of gearing.

Signed: Accountant

Chapter roundup

- This lengthy chapter has gone into quite a lot of detail about basic ratio analysis. The ratios you should be able to calculate and/or comment on are as follows.

  o **Profitability ratios**

  - Return on capital employed
  - Net profit as a percentage of sales
  - Asset turnover ratio
  - Gross profit as a percentage of sales

  o **Debt and gearing ratios**

  - Debt ratio
  - Gearing ratio
  - Interest cover
  - Cash flow ratio

  o **Liquidity and working capital ratios**

  - Current ratio
  - Quick ratio (acid test ratio)
  - Debtor days (average debt collection period)
  - Average stock turnover period

  o **Ordinary shareholders' investment ratios**

  - Earnings per share
  - Dividend cover
  - P/E ratio
  - Dividend yield
  - Earnings yield

- With the exception of the last three ratios, where the share's market price is required, all of these ratios **can be calculated from information in a company's published accounts.**

- Ratios provide **information through comparison**:

  o **trends** in a company's ratios from **one year to the next**, indicating an improving or worsening position;

  o in some cases, **against a 'norm' or 'standard'**;

  o in some cases, **against the ratios of other companies**, although differences between one company and another should often be expected.

- You must realise that, however many ratios you can find to calculate, **numbers alone will not answer a question**. You *must* interpret all the information available to you and support your interpretation with ratio calculations.

Quick quiz

1 Apart from ratio analysis, what other information might be helpful in interpreting a company's accounts? (see para 1.6)

2 What is the usual formula for ROCE? (2.6)

3 ROCE can be calculated as the product of two other ratios. What are they? (2.16)

4 Define the 'debt ratio'. (3.2)

5 Give two formulae for calculating gearing. (3.8, 3.10)

6 What is a company's cash flow ratio? (3.21)

7 What are the formulae for:

(a) the current ratio? (3.32)
(b) the quick ratio? (3.33)
(c) the debtors payment period? (3.37)
(d) the stock turnover period? (3.44)

8 What is the relationship between the dividend yield and the earnings yield? (4.11)

9 What are the main limitations of ratio analysis? (5.11)

10 What are the suggested contents for each part of an Operating and Financial Review? (5.15)

Question to try	Level	Marks	Time
25	Full exam	25	45 mins

Appendix
Examination questions on published accounts

Introduction

(a)   Before attempting these questions, you should be familiar with the requirements both of statute and of accounting standards (SSAPs and FRSs) in respect of the presentation and content of published accounts.

(b)   Provided that you know the legal and accounting regulations, published accounts questions are not difficult to answer. They are, however, very time consuming and almost certainly you will not have time in the examination unless you adopt a clear and systematic approach. In this appendix we suggest an approach which should provide you with a useful guide. However, it is not the only approach, and you might develop your own method and means of answering such questions. Never be put off by the volume of detail given; it provides you with all the information necessary to produce a clear and detailed solution.

(c)   Your aim in answering these questions should be to disclose the minimum information required by statute, SSAPs and FRSs. To disclose more than this might suggest to the examiner that you are unclear about what information is *required* to be disclosed and what information is sometimes *voluntarily* disclosed in practice.

(d)   In the time available in the examination it is virtually impossible to provide the examiner with all the information normally given in an actual set of accounts, and indeed, the examiner does not expect you to do so. It is only necessary to comply with the statutory and quasi-statutory requirements so far as you are able from the information given. There is generally no need to embellish your solution with made-up information.

Suggested approach

(e)   Read the question carefully to ensure you do not do more than the examiner wants. For example, questions often end with a statement that you may ignore the requirement to disclose accounting policies.

(f)   It is likely that the examiner will ask you to prepare accounts for presentation to the members (ie the 'full' accounts rather than the modified versions for small and medium-sized companies) and it is suggested that you adopt the 'operational format' profit and loss account (unless otherwise requested) and the vertical balance sheet in your solutions. As far as possible, use the words given in the CA 1985 formats, but remember that certain alternative or additional headings are allowable and may be used in the examination.

(g)   Head up a sheet of paper for the profit and loss account, a second sheet for the balance sheet and a third for the notes to the accounts. Keep a fourth sheet ready for your workings. Begin by writing a statement of accounting policies as note 1 to the accounts, unless the question has instructed you to ignore this requirement.

(h)   Now, keeping in mind the 1985 Act pro-formas and the FRS 3 requirements, write out the profit and loss account, beginning with turnover and working line by line through the pro-forma. Search through the question for the information relevant to each line as you come to it and mark the question paper to indicate which bits of information have been used.

(i)   While you are writing out the profit and loss account you should be building up the notes to the accounts, writing out each in conjunction with the profit and loss caption to which it refers and, of course, entering the cross reference on the face of the profit and loss account. The process of writing out the relevant note will often remove the need to prepare a working and thus save valuable time.

(j)   Don't forget to disclose the EPS at the foot of the profit and loss account for a public company, if the figure is given. (You should assume that the company is listed unless told to the contrary.)

(k)   Once the profit and loss account and related notes are complete, follow the same procedure to construct the balance sheet, again working line by line through the pro-forma and writing out the relevant notes at the same time as entering the figures on the balance sheet.

(l)   Complete the notes to the accounts by considering whether any notes are necessary other than those arising directly from the profit and loss account and balance sheet. Common examples include:

     (i)   post balance sheet events; and
     (ii)   contingent liabilities.

(m)   If you *are* asked to produce financial statements which comply with FRS 3, you may be asked to produce:

(i)   a statement of total recognised gains and losses;

(ii)   a profit and loss account which shows the turnover and operating profit from continuing activities, acquisitions and discontinued activities;

(iii)   a note of historical cost profits and losses, reconciling P & L retained profit to historical cost profit;

(iv)   a reconciliation of movements in shareholders' funds; and

(v)   a reserves note.

We have ignored the requirements of FRS 3 in the two questions given here, partly because practice is given in those areas elsewhere in the text, but also to avoid distracting you from the main focus of the preparation of the standard CA 1985 pro-formas. Any FRS 3 requirements will be an 'extra' to your questions. Refer back to Chapter 3 to refresh your memory of these formats and notes.

(n)   Finally, do not forget that SSAP 17 requires that the balance sheet should be dated. Indicate at the foot of the balance sheet where the date and director's signature are to appear.

(o)   You should now attempt to apply this approach to the illustrative questions which follow. Do not set yourself any time limit in answering these questions. Published accounts can only be mastered by absorbing the mass of detail required by statute and professional practice.

1   KITCHENTECH

The following list of balances was extracted from the books of Kitchentech Ltd on 31 December 19X1. The company is involved in the retailing of hardware through four shops which it owns in various parts of the country.

	£
Sales	1,875,893
Cost of sales	1,597,777
Administrative expenses	124,723
Directors' salaries	43,352
Debenture interest to 30.6.X1	3,000
Freehold premises at cost (land £100,000)	215,000
Motor vehicles, at cost	37,581
Accumulated depreciation on motor vehicles to 31.12.X0	16,581
Fixtures and fittings at cost	26,550
Accumulated depreciation on fixtures & fittings to 31.12.X0	8,200
Stock	88,452
ACT recoverable	4,000
Debtors	14,550
Creditors and accruals	47,609
Bank overdraft	11,433
Cash in hand	386
Provision for bad debts at 31.12.X0	1,200
Share capital	100,000
Profit and loss account at 31.12.X0	18,455
General reserve	16,000
10% debentures 19X8/X9 (secured on the freehold buildings)	60,000

The following adjustments are to be made.

(a)   Directors' remuneration is divided amongst the three directors as follows.

	£
Mr Ames - Chairman	4,000
Mr Bird - Marketing director	20,000
Mr Crown - Finance director	19,352
	43,352

Fees of £2,000 each are to be provided for the directors.

A pension of £1,900 paid to Mr Jones, a former director, is included in the administration expenses.

The salary of Mr James, the company secretary, is £18,000 and is also included in the administrative expenses.

(b)   Depreciation is to be provided in the accounts for the year as follows.

Buildings 2% on cost
Motor vehicles 25% on written down value
Fixtures and fittings 10% on cost

(c)   Messrs Checkit and See, the company's auditors, rendered an account in early March 19X2 as follows.

	£
Assistance in preparation of taxation computation for the year ended 31.12.X0	500
Audit of accounts for the year ended 31.12.X0	1,000
	1,500

This bill was the subject of an accrual of £1,200 on 31 December 19X0. A similar bill for £1,500 is expected for the 19X1 accounts in due course.

(d)   The debtors include a balance of £400 owing from Catering Supplies Ltd. This is to be written off as it has proved irrecoverable. The provision for bad debts is to be adjusted to 10% of debtors.

(e)   Corporation tax based upon the profits for the year at the rate of 35% amounting to £40,000 is to be provided.

(f)   A dividend of 14% is to be provided on the ordinary share capital. The authorised ordinary share capital is £200,000 divided into £1 shares. All issued shares are fully paid.

(g)   £30,000 is to be transferred to general reserve.

(h)   The basic rate of income tax should be taken as 25% and the ACT rate as ¼. ACT recoverable concerns a dividend paid during 19X1 out of the profit for 19X0.

Required

Within the limits of the information given, prepare a profit and loss account and balance sheet for the year ended 31 December 19X1 for submission to the members of the company in accordance with statutory requirements and best professional practice.

2   ALPINE

Alpine Athletic Training plc is a manufacturer of sports equipment. Set out below is a trial balance extracted from the books of the company as at 31 December 19X3.

	£	£
Sales		2,925,900
Cost of sales	1,785,897	
Selling expenses	120,000	
Administrative expenses	649,296	
Debtors/creditors	469,332	371,022
Provision for doubtful debts		22,500
Directors' remuneration	181,500	
Audit fee	3,000	
Debenture interest	7,500	
Half year preference dividend paid on 30.6.X3	2,100	
ACT paid on 14.7.X3	700	
Premises at cost	600,000	
Plant and machinery at cost	135,000	
Provision for depreciation on plant and machinery at 1.1.X3		60,000
Motor vehicles at cost (salesmen's cars)	54,000	
Provision for depreciation on motor vehicles at 1.1.X3		24,000
Stock in trade and work in progress	282,728	
Trade investment at cost	72,000	
Bank overdraft		354,528
Profit and loss account balance at 1.1.X3		65,103
General reserve		30,000
Ordinary share capital		300,000
7% preference share capital		60,000
10% debentures 19X9 secured on premises		150,000
	4,363,053	4,363,053

The following information is also related to the accounts for the year to 31 December 19X3.

(a)   The bad debt provision is to be increased to an amount which is equal to 1% of the turnover for the year.

(b)   The directors' remuneration is divided amongst the four directors of the company as follows.

	£
Chairman	24,000
Managing director	60,000
Finance director	49,500
Sales director	48,000
	181,500

In addition provision must be made for directors' fees of £5,000 to each of the above directors.

(c)   Depreciation is to be provided for the year as follows.

Buildings	2% on cost
Plant and machinery	10% on cost
Motor vehicles	25% on written down value

The only changes in fixed assets during the year were an addition to plant and machinery in early January 19X3 costing £30,000 and the purchase of premises for £600,000 comprising £150,000 for buildings and £450,000 for land.

(d)   A provision of £60,000 is to be made for corporation tax at 35% based upon the profits for the year. This will be payable on 30 September 19X4.

(e)   The half year preference dividend to 31 December 19X3 and a final dividend of 6.5 pence a share on the ordinary share capital, are to be provided in the accounts.

(f)   The sum of £15,000 is to be transferred to general reserve.

(g)   The authorised preference share capital is £60,000 in £1 shares.

(h)   The authorised ordinary share capital is £600,000 in 50p shares. All shares in issue are fully paid.

(i)   Assume the basic rate of income tax to be 25% and the ACT rate ¼.

(j)   Administrative expenses include £5,244 interest on the overdraft.

(k)   The directors consider the value of the trade investment to be £75,000. It consists of 10,000 20p ordinary shares in Crampon Ltd, a company with an issued share capital of 200,000 ordinary shares.

Required

Within the limits of the above information, prepare the final accounts of Alpine Athletic Training plc for the year ended 31 December 19X3 in a form suitable for presentation to the members and which complies with the requirements of the Companies Act 1985.

The required information should be shown as part of the accounting statements or by way of note, whichever is considered most appropriate.

1   **KITCHENTECH**

PROFIT AND LOSS ACCOUNT FOR THE YEAR ENDED 31 DECEMBER 19X1

	Notes	£	£
Turnover	1		1,875,893
Cost of sales			(1,597,777)
Gross profit			278,116
Distribution costs (W1)		30,520	
Administrative expenses (W1)		156,175	
			(186,695)
Operating profit	2		91,421
Interest payable	3		(6,000)
Profit on ordinary activities before taxation			85,421
Tax on profit on ordinary activities	4		(40,000)
Profit on ordinary activities after taxation			45,421
Dividend: proposed ordinary dividend		14,000	
Transfer to general reserve		30,000	
			44,000
Retained profit for the year			1,421
Earnings per share	5		45.4p

STATEMENT OF RETAINED PROFITS

	£
Retained profit for the year	1,421
Retained profits brought forward	18,455
Retained profits carried forward	19,876

BALANCE SHEET AS AT 31 DECEMBER 19X1

	Notes	£	£
Fixed assets			
Tangible assets	6		244,145
Current assets			
Stock		88,452	
ACT recoverable	7	3,500	
Debtors £(14,550 - 400 - 1,415)		12,735	
Cash in hand		386	
		105,073	
Creditors: amounts falling due within one year			
Bank overdraft		11,433	
Creditors and accruals (W2)		58,409	
Other creditors including taxation	8	53,500	
		123,342	
Net current liabilities			(18,269)
Total assets less current liabilities			225,876
Creditors: amounts falling due after more than one year			
10% debentures 19X8/X9			(60,000)
			165,876
Capital and reserves			
Called up share capital			
£1 ordinary shares fully paid (authorised: £200,000)			100,000
Reserves			
General reserve		46,000	
Profit and loss account		19,876	
			65,876
			165,876

Approved by the Board of Directors on....................

...............................Director

NOTES TO THE ACCOUNTS

1   *Turnover*

Turnover is the value, net of VAT, of goods sold during the year in a single class of business in the UK.

2   *Operating profit*

	£	£
Operating profit is stated after charging:		
Directors' remuneration		
Salaries	43,352	
Fees	6,000	
Pension to former director	1,900	
		51,252
Depreciation		10,205
Auditors' remuneration		1,000

(*Tutorial note*. No further details are required of directors' remuneration, since in total it is less than £200,000. Note that Mr James is *not* a director and so his salary is not included in the above total.)

3   *Interest payable*

Interest on 10% debentures 19X8/X9	£6,000

4   *Tax on profit on ordinary activities*

UK corporation tax at 35% on the profit of the year	£40,000

5   *Earnings per share*

Earnings per share is based on earnings of £45,421 and 100,000 ordinary shares in issue during the year

6   *Fixed assets*

	Land and buildings £	Motor vehicles £	Fixtures & fittings £	Total £
Cost				
At 1 January and 31 December 19X1	215,000	37,581	26,550	279,131
Depreciation				
At 1 January 19X1	-	16,581	8,200	24,781
Charge for year	2,300	5,250	2,655	10,205
At 31 December 19X1	2,300	21,831	10,855	34,986
Net book value				
At 1 January 19X1	215,000	21,000	18,350	254,350
At 31 December 19X1	212,700	15,750	15,695	244,145

7   *Deferred asset*

ACT recoverable: ACT on proposed final dividend (£14,000 × ¼)	3,500

8   *Other creditors including taxation*

	£
Corporation tax £(40,000 − 4,000)	36,000
ACT on proposed dividend	3,500
	39,500
Proposed dividend	14,000
	53,500

Workings

1   *Allocation of costs*

	Distribution costs £	Administrative expenses £
Per list of balances		124,723
Directors' salaries	20,000	23,352
Directors' fees	2,000	4,000
Depreciation:		
Buildings (2% × £115,000)		2,300
Motor vehicles 25% × £(37,581 – 16,581)	5,250	
Fixtures (10% × £26,550)	2,655	
Audit and tax advice		1,800
(includes £300 under-provided in previous year)		
Bad debt	400	
Provision for doubtful debts		
10% × £(14,550 – 400) – £1,200	215	
	30,520	156,175

(*Note*. The allocation above is somewhat arbitrary, especially as regards the depreciation costs. Other allocations would be acceptable.)

2   *Creditors and accruals*

	£
Per list of balances	47,609
Directors' fees	6,000
Half-year's debenture interest	3,000
19X1 audit and tax fee	1,500
Increase in accrual for 19X0 and audit tax fee	300
	58,409

2   ALPINE

PROFIT AND LOSS ACCOUNT FOR THE YEAR ENDED 31 DECEMBER 19X3

	Note	£	£
Turnover (continuing operations)	1		2,925,900
Cost of sales (W1)			(1,799,397)
Gross profit			1,126,503
Distribution costs (W2)		187,259	
Administrative expenses (W3)		798,552	
			(985,811)
Operating profit	2		140,692
Interest payable	3		(20,244)
Profit on ordinary activities before taxation			120,448
Tax on profit on ordinary activities	4		(60,000)
Profit on ordinary activities after taxation			60,448
Dividends	5	43,200	
Transfer to general reserve		15,000	
			(58,200)
Retained profit for the financial year			2,248
Earnings per share	6		10.7p

STATEMENT OF RETAINED PROFITS

	£
Retained profit for the financial year	10,248
Retained profits brought forward	65,103
Retained profits carried forward	75,351

BALANCE SHEET AS AT 31 DECEMBER 19X3

	Note	£	£
Fixed assets			
Tangible assets	7		681,000
Investments (directors' valuation: £75,000)			72,000
			753,000
Deferred asset	8		10,275
Current assets			
Stocks and work in progress		282,728	
Debtors £(469,332 – 29,259)		440,073	
		722,801	
Creditors: amounts falling due within one year			
Bank overdraft		354,528	
Trade creditors		371,022	
Other creditors including taxation	9	110,675	
Accruals (£7,500 deb int + £20,000 dir rem)		27,500	
		863,725	
Net current liabilities			(140,924)
Total assets less current liabilities			622,351
Creditors: amounts falling due after more than one year			
10% debentures 19X9			(150,000)
			472,351
Capital and reserves			
Called up share capital			
50p ordinary shares fully paid (authorised: £600,000)		300,000	
£1 7% preference shares fully paid (authorised:£60,000)		60,000	
			360,000
Reserves			
General reserve		45,000	
Profit and loss account (£65,103 + £2,248)		67,351	
			120,351
			472,351

Approved by the Board of Directors on ....

....................Director

NOTES TO THE ACCOUNTS

1   *Turnover*

Turnover represents amounts invoiced, net of VAT, for goods and services supplied during the year in a single class of business in the UK.

2   *Operating profit*

Operating profit is stated after charging:

	£
Depreciation	24,000
Directors' emoluments	201,500
Auditors' remuneration	3,000

Directors' emoluments comprise fees of £20,000 and remuneration of £181,500.

The emoluments of the highest paid director were £63,000. (This information is required because the total of directors' emoluments is over £200,000.)

3   *Interest payable*

	£
On debentures repayable in more than five years	15,000
On bank overdraft	5,244
	20,244

4   *Taxation*

	£
UK corporation tax at 35% on the profits for the year	£60,000

5   *Dividends*

		£
Preference:	interim paid	2,100
	final proposed	2,100
		4,200
Ordinary: final proposed (600,000 × 6.5p)		39,000
		43,200

6   *Earnings per share*

Earnings per share is based on earnings of £(68,448 - 4,200) = £64,248 and 600,000 ordinary shares in issue during the year.

7   *Fixed assets*

	Premises £	Plant and machinery £	Motor vehicles £	Total £
Cost				
At 1 January 19X3	-	105,000	54,000	159,000
Additions in year	600,000	30,000		630,000
At 31 December 19X3	600,000	135,000	54,000	789,000
Depreciation				
At 1 January 19X3	-	60,000	24,000	84,000
Charge for the year	3,000	13,500	7,500	24,000
At 31 December 19X3	3,000	73,500	31,500	108,000
Net book value				
At 1 January 19X3	-	45,000	30,000	75,000
At 31 December 19X3	597,000	61,500	22,500	681,000

8   *Deferred asset*

The deferred asset is ACT on the proposed dividends which is expected to be recoverable against the 19X4 liability to corporation tax.

9   *Other creditors including taxation*

	£
Corporation tax £(60,000 – 700)	59,300
Dividends proposed	41,100
ACT on proposed dividends £(41,100 × 20/80)	10,275
	110,675

Workings

1   *Cost of sales*

	£
Per TB	1,785,897
Add depreciation on plant (10% × £135,000)	13,500
	1,799,397

2	*Distribution costs*	£	£
	Selling expenses		120,000
	Sales director's remuneration £(48,000 + 5,000)		53,000
	Provision for doubtful debts:		
	Provision required (1% × £2,925,900)	29,259	
	Less existing provision	22,500	
	Increase in provision		6,759
	Depreciation on motor vehicles (25% × £30,000)		7,500
			187,259

3	*Administrative expenses*	£
	Per TB	649,296
	Directors' remuneration £(24,000 + 60,000 + 49,500 + 15,000)	148,500
	Audit fee	3,000
	Depreciation on buildings (2% × £150,000)	3,000
		803,796
	Less overdraft interest	5,244
		798,552

Exam question bank

Examination standard questions are indicated by the mark and time allocations.

1   REGULATORS   *27 mins*

State three different regulatory influences on the preparation of the published accounts of quoted companies and briefly explain the role of each one. Comment briefly on the effectiveness of this regulatory system.

2   TOM AND GERRY   *36 mins*

Tom and Gerry were trading in partnership sharing profits in the ratio of 2 to 1. Butch was trading as a sole trader in the same class of business. Both businesses made up their accounts to 31 December in each year.

It was agreed that with effect from 1 January 19X3 the two businesses should be merged with Gerry and Butch sharing profits equally and Tom retiring. For the purpose of the merger and retirement, goodwill was to be valued at 2 years purchase of the average adjusted profits of the last three years but was not to be brought in as an asset in the new firm.

The summarised balance sheet of the businesses at 31 December 19X2 were as follows.

	Tom and Gerry £	Butch £
Capital accounts		
Tom	30,000	
Gerry	15,000	
Butch		25,000
Current accounts		
Tom	4,500	
Gerry	9,600	
Creditors	42,000	36,000
	101,100	61,500

	Tom and Gerry £	Butch £
Fixed assets		
Freehold premises at cost	36,000	9,000
Furniture, fixtures and fittings at cost, less depreciation to date	10,500	3,600
Current assets		
Stock at cost	27,000	18,000
Debtors	9,600	8,400
Balance at bank	18,000	22,500
	101,100	61,500

You ascertain the following.

(a) In valuing goodwill, the profits were to be adjusted for the following:

   (i)   the surplus or deficiency arising on the valuation of the furniture, fixtures and fittings was to be adjusted over the life of the assets to date, on a straight line basis;

   (ii) the salary of £1,500 pa paid to Butch's wife was to be added back; and

   (iii) obsolete stock and bad debts were to be eliminated.

(b) Premises and furniture, fixtures and fittings were to be taken into the new firm at the value placed on them by an independent valuer.

(c) Stocks were to be taken in at cost less £900 in respect of obsolete stock held by Tom and Gerry.

(d) Creditors, debtors and bank balances were to be taken in at book value less bad debts amounting to £450 in the case of Tom and Gerry and £300 in the case of Butch.

(e) The new firm was to take over the liability to Tom for his share in Tom and Gerry.

(f)   The valuations by the independent valuer were:

	Tom and Gerry £	Butch £
Freehold premises	54,000	30,000
Furniture, fixtures and fittings:		
all purchased 10 years ago		3,000
all purchased 3 years ago	11,400	

(g)   The profits of the business for the last three years were:

	Tom and Gerry £	Butch £
Year to 31 December 19X0	21,900	9,900
Year to 31 December 19X1	18,300	11,400
Year to 31 December 19X2	22,530	11,700

You are required to prepare in columnar form:

(a)   the partners' account in each of the business showing the closing of the businesses, and the opening of the new business; and

(b)   the balance sheet of the new firm Gerry and Butch on 1 January 19X3.

3   HOMER AND BART (20 marks)   *36 mins*

On 1 July 19X6, Homer and Bart formed a partnership. The details of the partnership agreement were as follows.

(a)   The profit sharing ratio was Homer 7/10 : Bart 3/10.
(b)   Neither partner was to be paid a salary.
(c)   There was to be no interest paid on the capital accounts.

Neither partner made any drawings during the period that the partnership was in operation.

Bart and Homer decided that they would be better off trading as a limited company. Accordingly, on 1 January 19X7 Simpson Ltd was formed.

Shortly after 31 December 19X7, Simpson Ltd's accounting year end, the company employed Lisa, an ACCA, to prepare the year end accounts. She was told that during the eighteen months to 31 December 19X7 only one set of accounting records was kept; the records of the company were not kept separate from those of the partnership. No capital adjustments had been made on conversion to a limited company, but Homer and Bart did employ a temporary bookkeeper who managed to calculate the profit for the periods 1.7.X6 to 31.12.X6 and 1.1.X7 to 31.12.X7. The bookkeeper had also drawn up the following trial balance.

	Dr £	Cr £
Ordinary shares of £1 each (note 1)		28,000
Purchase consideration: Simpson Ltd	38,000	
Building: cost	12,000	
provision for depreciation		400
Plant and equipment: cost	12,000	
provision for depreciation		1,200
Motor vehicles: cost	7,200	
provision for depreciation		1,800
Loss on revaluation of net assets on 31 December 19X6 (note 2)	800	
Net profit before tax 1.7.X6 to 31.12.X6		6,600
Net profit before tax and interest 1.1.X7 to 31.12.X7		22,400
Stock	14,800	
Debtors subject to financing arrangements (note 5)	2,000	
Debtors (including ACT recoverable)	18,200	
Cash at bank and in hand	5,400	
Creditors		20,400
Dividends paid 1.7.X7 (note 6)	4,000	
5% debentures (redeemable 1.1.Y7) (note 7)		6,000
Issue costs of debentures	400	
Capital accounts at 1 July 19X6		
Homer		20,000
Bart		8,000
	114,800	114,800

Notes

1 The purchase consideration on formation of Simpson Ltd was agreed at £38,000, to be satisfied as follows.

> 28,000 ordinary shares of £1 each issued at par
> £6,000 5% debenture stock issued at par
> The balance paid in cash

Homer paid £1,200 dissolution expenses out of his own money. The shares and debentures were divided between the partners in their profit sharing ratio.

2 At 31 December 19X6, the net assets of the partnership had the following fair values, which were incorporated in the books at 31 December 19X7.

	Fair value £
Building	12,000
Plant and equipment	12,000
Motor vehicles	7,200
Stock	6,400
Debtors	19,600
Cash at bank and in hand	10,000
Creditors	(33,400)
	33,800

These values were used to determine the purchase consideration.

3 Any goodwill arising must be amortised on a straight-line basis over five years.

4 Depreciation has been charged in the accounts for the period 1.1.X7 to 31.12.X7.

5 On 31 December 19X7 Simpson Ltd entered into an agreement with Factory Finance Ltd. Factory Finance was to take over Simpson Ltd's debtors of £13,200 on which there is a provision for doubtful debts of £400. Factory Finance paid £10,800 for these debtors. Of this amount, £1,600 is returnable depending on the collectability of the debtors, and £9,200 is non-returnable. There is no obligation on Simpson Ltd to repurchase any of these debts. The company will recognise the finance charges on this transaction in the next accounting period.

The figure in the trial balance for debtors subject to financing arrangements is made up as follows.

	£
Amount of debtors factored	13,200
Cash received	(10,800)
Provision for doubtful debts	(400)
	2,000

6   The company has proposed a dividend of 5p per share.

7   The 5% debentures were issued on 1 January 19X7. Issue costs were £400 and are to be dealt with on a straight-line basis. No interest on the debentures has been paid or accrued for the year ended 31 December 19X7. The debentures are redeemable on 1 January 19Y7.

8   Simpson Ltd is to provide £6,800 for corporation tax. The ACT fraction is $^{20}/_{80}$.

Required

(a)   Record the cessation of the partnership of Homer and Bart at 31 December 19X6 in the realisation and capital accounts. (6 marks)

(b)   Prepare the balance sheet of Simpson Ltd:

(i)   as at 1 January 19X7;
(ii)   as at 31 December 19X7.

(*Note*. You must show in your workings how the adjusted profit for the year to 31 December 19X7 is calculated.) (14 marks)

---

4   **DAY AND KNIGHT (25 marks)** *45 mins*

The following trial balance was extracted from the books of Day and Knight Ltd as on 31 December 19X6.

	£	£
Capital accounts: Day		125,000
Knight		85,000
Current accounts: Day	12,000	
Knight	10,000	
Debtors (including pre 1 January 19X6 £17,500)	130,000	
Creditors		53,250
Purchases	304,000	
Sales		360,000
Stock on 1 January 19X6	46,000	
Discounts allowed (pre 1 January 19X6 £500)	6,500	
Bad debts (pre 1 January 19X6 £1,500)	6,900	
Rent and rates	7,000	
Salaries	20,000	
Advertising (all after 1 April 19X6)	5,200	
Sundry expenses	3,400	
Fixtures, balance on 1 January 19X6	20,000	
Motor vehicles: balance on 1 January 19X6	16,000	
cost on October 19X6	8,000	
Bank balance	28,250	
	623,250	623,250

You ascertain that Day and Knight were equal partners carrying on business until 31 December 19X5. On 1 April 19X6 Day and Knight Ltd was incorporated with a capital of £300,000 in ordinary shares of £1 each. It acquired the partnership business as from 1 January 19X6.

(a)   The vending agreement contained the following provisions.

(i)   The company took over all the partnership assets, excluding debtors, at book value.

(ii)   The creditors (£41,000) and the bank overdraft (£10,000) were not taken over, but were discharged by the company out of money collected from debtors outstanding on 1 January 19X6 (total outstanding £70,500).

(iii) The purchase consideration was £100,000 satisfied by the allotment of shares at par.

(iv)   On 1 April 19X6 Day and Knight were appointed directors at annual salaries of £15,000 each, which salaries were undrawn on 31 December 19X6.

(b) Knight paid Day £20,000 during 19X6, but no entry has been made in the books.

(c) In March 19X6 Knight collected one debtor (£2,500) outstanding at 1 January 19X6, and retained the cash. No entry has been made in the books.

(d) Day and Knight each subscribed £50,000 for shares to be allotted at par. The consideration payable is to be debited to directors' current accounts.

(e) Stock on 31 December 19X6 was £62,000.

(f) Although the gross profit margin was uniform throughout the year, trade was seasonal. Average monthly sales for the period April to September inclusive was double the average monthly sales for the preceding and succeeding quarters.

(g) Fixtures are to be depreciated at the rate of 10% per annum and motor vehicles at 25% per annum.

(h) Except where indicated, expenses should be apportioned on a time basis.

The books of the business had been carried on without a break and no entries concerning the company formation had been made.

Required

(a) Prepare the realisation account and the partners' personal accounts showing the effects of the partnership dissolution.

(b) Prepare the directors' current accounts in the books of the company.

(c) Prepare, in columnar form, the trading and profit and loss accounts of the business:

     (i)   for the three months ended 31 March 19X6;
     (ii)   for the nine months ended 31 December 19X6;
     (iii)   for the twelve months ended 31 December 19X6.

(d) Prepare the balance sheet of Day and Knight Ltd as at 31 December 19X6.

5   BLUNT AND SHARP (20 marks)   *36 mins*

Blunt and Sharp Ltd operate retail stores in Edinburgh, which is the head office, and Glasgow. A trial balance prepared as of 31 May 19X5 revealed the following position.

	Head Office		Branch	
	Debit	Credit	Debit	Credit
	£	£	£	£
Share capital - authorised issued and fully paid in ordinary shares of £1 each		260,000		
Share premium account		40,000		
General reserve		30,000		
Profit and loss account		55,000		
Debtors/creditors	47,500	35,000	14,700	7,200
Head office current account				51,500
Land and buildings at cost	250,000		50,000	
Fixtures and fitting at cost	50,000		20,000	
Motor vehicles at cost	45,000			
Accumulated depreciation:				
Fixtures		10,100		6,400
Motors		3,600		
Stock at cost or mark-up on 31 May 19X4	48,500		15,400	
Bank	14,900		2,600	
Cash	1,000		500	
Purchases/sales	255,000	229,700	148,500	199,700
Administration expenses	31,000		10,500	
Selling and distribution expenses	10,500		2,100	
Provision for unrealised profit on stocks		1,400		
Branch current account	60,000			
Financial, legal and professional expenses	5,400		500	
Goods sent to branch		154,000		
	818,800	818,800	264,800	264,800

Additional information

(a)   All goods sold by the branch are supplied from head office at cost plus 10%. At 31 May 19X5 goods to the value of £5,500 were in transit to the branch.

(b)   The branch deposited £3,000 on behalf of head office in the local branch of the company's bank on 31 May 19X5. No record of this transaction had been made in head office books.

(c)   Stocks at 31 May 19X5, excluding the goods in transit, were valued as follows.

	£
Head office at cost	54,500
Branch at mark-up	17,600

Required

From the information given show the results for (i) head office, (ii) branch and (iii) combined, in columnar form by means of:

(a)   draft trading and profit and loss accounts for the year ended 31 May 19X5; and
(b)   draft balance sheets as at that date.

6   **BULWELL (20 marks)**   *36 mins*

Bulwell Aggregates Ltd wish to expand their transport fleet and purchased three heavy lorries with a list price of £18,000 each. Robert Bulwell has negotiated hire purchase finance to fund this expansion, and the company has entered into a hire purchase agreement with Granby Garages plc on 1 January 19X1. The agreement states that Bulwell Aggregates will pay a deposit of £9,000 on 1 January 19X1, and two annual instalments of £24,000 on 31 December 19X1, 19X2 and a final instalment of £20,391 on 31 December 19X3.

Interest is to be calculated at 25% on the balance outstanding on 1 January each year and paid on 31 December each year.

The depreciation policy of Bulwell Aggregates Ltd is to write off the vehicles over a four year period using the straight line method and assuming a scrap value of £1,333 for each vehicle at the end of its useful life.

The cost of the vehicles to Granby Garages is £14,400 each.

Required

(a)   Account for the above transactions in the books of Granby Garages plc, showing the entries in the hire purchase trading account for the years 19X1, 19X2 and 19X3. This is the only hire purchase transaction undertaken by this company.

(b)   Account for the above transactions in the books of Bulwell Aggregates Ltd showing the entries in the profit and loss account and balance sheet for the years 19X1, 19X2, 19X3. This is the only hire purchase transaction undertaken by this company.

Calculations to the nearest £.

7   **DIVIDEND DISTRIBUTION (20 marks)**   *36 mins*

(a)   What do you understand by the statement that dividends must not be paid out of the capital of a company?

(b)   What would be the effect on the maximum distributable profits of Donor plc, a public company, of the following transactions:

(i)   an upward revaluation of a fixed asset by £20,000 on 1 January, and a consequential increase in the depreciation charge of £4,000 in the year to 31 December;

(ii)   the sale of some land for £500,000, which had a historical cost of £150,000 but which was valued in the balance sheet at £440,000.

8   **STANDARD SETTERS (20 marks)**   *36 mins*

There are those who suggest that any standard setting body is redundant because accounting standards are unnecessary. Other people feel that such standards should be produced, but by the government, so they are legislated.

The old Accounting Standards Committee (ASC) was said by many critics to have failed in its primary objective of achieving greater uniformity and therefore comparability between the financial statements of different entities. Various problems were cited.

(i)   Nearly all the members of the ASC were drawn from the accountancy profession rather than from academia, user groups or other independent bodies.

(ii) The ASC was not able to react immediately to new problems or controversies.

(iii) The ASC succumbed to political pressures from interested parties on a number of occasions.

(iv) The ASC adopted a 'fire-fighting' approach, introducing standards as the need arose, rather than adopting an underlying 'conceptual framework' which directly addressed the needs of users.

(v)   The ASC's only method of enforcing accounting standards was to require qualification of the audit report, which many felt was insufficient as deterrent or enforcement.

The dissolution of the ASC and its replacement by the ASB, along with the implementation of all the other Dearing Committee recommendations, was designed to address these criticisms.

Required

(a)   Discuss the statement that accounting standards are unnecessary for the purpose of regulating financial statements.

(b)   Has the ASB (and the other new bodies) remedied all the failings of the ASC listed above? Discuss to what extent the criticisms have been addressed by the new regime.

9   PUBLISHED ACCOUNTS (25 marks)   *45 mins*

(a)   Why is the disclosure of accounting policies required by the Companies Act 1985?

(b)   The Companies Act 1985 regulates the concept of small and medium-sized companies and allows certain 'accounting exemptions' for such entities.

    Required

    (i)   State the criteria which are taken into account to determine whether a company is 'small' or 'medium-sized'.

    (ii) With regard to small companies only, list the exemptions which are allowed.

(c)   List the contents of the directors' report.

10   D'URBERVILLE (25 marks)   *45 mins*

The financial controller of D'Urberville plc is preparing forecast balance sheets as at 31 December 19X4, 19X5, 19X6 and 19X7.

The 19X4 forecast has been prepared and shows the following figure in respect of motor vehicles.

	£'000
Cost	540
Accumulated depreciation	130
Net book value	410

Depreciation on motor vehicles is charged at 25% on the reducing balance. A full year's depreciation is charged in the year of purchase and none in the year of sale.

The following information has been collated by the assistant accountant in order to help the financial controller prepare his forecast.

FORECAST PURCHASES OF MOTOR VEHICLES
FOR THE YEAR ENDED 31 DECEMBER

	19X5 £'000	19X6 £'000	19X7 £'000
List price			
Cash purchase	180	300	450
Hire purchase	-	400	-
Trade discount (20%)			
Cash purchase	36	60	90
Hire purchase	-	80	-
Cash discount (5% of net price)	7	12	18
Delivery costs (paid to supplier)	10	12	15
Costs of valeting old vehicles to prepare them for sale	2	3	4
Trade-in allowances on old vehicles to be set off against hire purchase deposit or finance lease first year rental		25	20
Hire-purchase deposit	-	85 (110 – 25)	-
Finance lease first year rental			90 (110 – 20)
Total cash to be paid to the suppliers of the new vehicles in the year of purchase	147 (180 – 36 – 7 + 10)	97 (85 + 12)	105 (90 + 15)

FORECAST DISPOSALS OF MOTOR VEHICLES (AT COST)
IN THE YEARS ENDED 31 DECEMBER

	19X5 £'000	19X6 £'000	19X7 £'000
Vehicle			
Originally acquired in year ended 31 December			
19X0	30		
19X1	40		
19X2		45	
19X3		65	
19X4			75

The following methods of purchase will be used to acquire the vehicles.

Year ended 31 December 19X5: cash purchase.

Year ended 31 December 19X6: hire purchase. The agreement in question requires an initial deposit of £110,000, then in each of the three years following an instalment of £70,000.

Year ended 31 December 19X7: finance lease agreement. A rental of £110,000 will be payable in arrears for six years.

Required

For the asset motor vehicles in the forecast balance sheets of D'Urberville plc as at 31 December 19X5, 19X6, 19X7, produce a schedule showing cost, accumulated depreciation and net book value. You should show all your workings and make all calculations to the nearest £000.

11   **BLECO (30 marks)**   *54 mins*

The following information relates to the R & D activities of Bleco plc. All projects are given designatory prefixes to indicate their nature.

        PR = pure research
        AR = applied research
        D = development

At 1 September 19X0, the balance brought forward as development costs consisted of:

	£
Project: D363	198,300
D367	242,700
D368	nil

During the year ended 31 August 19X1 the following took place.

(a) Project D368 satisfied the SSAP 13 deferment criteria. In previous years, a total of £47,830 expended on this project had been written off to the profit and loss account. The directors have resolved to defer, by capitalisation, the aggregate of the current year's expenditure together with the reinstated figure from previous years.

(b) An applied research project, AR204, was converted into a development project and redesignated D369, but all expenditure up to this point is to be written off.

(c) Two more development projects were instituted, D370 and D371. This latter project was commissioned by Lytax Ltd under a contract for full reimbursement of expenditure; to date, £24,000 has been received from Lytax Ltd.

(d) It has become apparent that the technical feasibility and commercial viability of Project D370 are doubtful.

(e) All other development projects satisfy the SSAP 13 deferment criteria.

(f) (See below)

(g) Project D363 entered full commercial production and is to be amortised on a straight line basis over six years.

Bleco plc depreciates fixed assets on a straight line basis, assuming no residual value, at the following rates.

	% per annum on cost
Laboratory buildings	10
Laboratory equipment	20

A full year's depreciation is charged in the year of acquisition.

Expenditure was incurred as follows.

	PR119 £	AR187 £	AR204 £	D367 £	D368 £	D369 £	D370 £	D371 £	Unallocated £
Wages, salaries and related charges	35,100	27,300	15,260	2,090	16,480	34,070	29,800	27,500	3,300
Materials	810	520	290	340	410	1,560	2,650	3,400	4,070
Direct expenses (other)	250	210	180	170	230	640	690	710	2,240
Production overheads	1,240	3,600	2,950	3,540	4,650	6,980	6,010	6,420	7,070
Fixed assets: Experimental laboratory buildings		200,000							
Testing laboratory buildings						310,000			
Laboratory equipment		170,000				472,000			
Related selling and administrative overheads									76,200
Market research									55,600

Required

Prepare extracts from the profit and loss account of Bleco plc for year ended 31 August 19X1 and from the company's balance sheet at that date, to incorporate the financial effects of the research and development expenditure.

Your answer should comply with the requirements of SSAP 13 *Accounting for research and development.*

Detailed workings for each item must be shown.

12   SOAP (30 marks)   *54 mins*

Soap plc is working on a number of short-term and long-term contracts. Its policy with regard to attributable profit on the long term contracts is to calculate it as follows.

Degree of completion (%) × total estimated profit (adjusted for known variations in costs accruing in the period)

The directors are sure that their cost calculations for the contracts are accurate, and the auditors concur with them in their belief that the degree of completion is sufficient to accrue profit. It is 31 December 19X7, the company's accounting year end. Further details of the contracts are as follows.

(a)   The short term contracts are 7 to 9 months in duration. Some of them will not be completed until 31 March 19X8. It is the directors' policy to accrue profit earned to date on these contracts in the accounts as at 31 December 19X7.

(b)   On 1 April 19X7 Soap plc commenced work on a contract with Emmerdale plc. The total contract price was £9 million and the total contract costs were expected to be £7.5 million. The contract is expected to run for two years.

During the year to 31 December 19X7, Soap plc incurred unforeseen additional costs of £500,000 on the contract in the light of which it revised its estimate of the total expected costs to £8 million. The following details are relevant to the position as at 31 December 19X7.

(i)   Costs incurred to date: £4m
(ii)   Payments on account: £3m
(iii)   Percentage complete per independent surveyor: 45%.

(c)   On 1 July 19X7 Soap plc entered into a contract with Archers plc. The details of the contract were as follows.

(i)   Duration of contract: 2 years

(ii)   Total contract price: £150,000

(iii)   Estimated total cost: £120,000

(iv)   Percentage of completion (directors' estimate): 20%

(The terms of the contract did not require an independent valuation by a surveyor.)

(v)   Costs incurred up to 31 December 19X7: £47,500

(vi)   Payments on account received: £40,000

A special machine had been purchased for the purposes of the contract and was being depreciated over the two year period on a straight line basis. The cost of the machine was £20,000, and the depreciation charge to date had been included in the costs incurred figure (v). On 31 December 19X7 it was decided that this machine should be written off. (Assume no residual value.)

(d)   On 1 August 19X7, Soap plc entered into a contract with Neighbours Ltd. The details of the contract were as follows.

(i)   Duration: 1½ years
(ii)   Total contract price: £6.4 million
(iii)   Estimated total costs: £5 million
(iv)   Payments on account: £2.5 million
(v)   Costs incurred up to 31 December 19X7: £1.8 million
(vi)   Percentage of completion (independent surveyor's estimate): 25%

Neighbours Ltd was a new customer, so as a precaution, Soap plc had asked for a large deposit.

Required

(a)   State whether you think it is good accounting practice to accrue profit on the short term contracts. Give reasons for your view.   (4 marks)

(b)   For the year ended 31 December 19X7, show the relevant extracts from the profit and loss account and balance sheet of Soap plc as regards the contracts with Emmerdale plc, Archers plc and Neighbours Ltd. You do not need to show the cash and bank balances.   (11 marks)

(c)   An independent surveyor is used on some contracts but not on others. As auditor, would you consider this to be acceptable? Give reasons for your answer.   (5 marks)

(d)   What audit procedures would you use to verify long term contract balances?

(10 marks)

---

13   CORAX (20 marks)   *36 mins*

Corax plc has an allotted capital of £350,000 in fully paid 50p ordinary shares. At 31 December 19X6 the following balances were included in the company's balance sheet.

	£
Agreed corporation tax liability on 19X5 profits	16,300
Estimated corporation tax liability on 19X6 profits	5,000
Deferred taxation account	29,400
Profit and loss account (credit)	43,000

(No dividends had been paid or proposed in respect of 19X6)

The following information relates to the year ended 31 December 19X7.

(a)   Corporation tax liability for 19X5 profits was settled (January).

(b)   Interim dividend of 3p per share was paid (August).

(c)   ACT on the interim dividend was paid (October).

(d)   Corporation tax liability for 19X6 was agreed at £3,800 (December), paid January 19X8.

(e)   Profit for 19X7 (before tax) on ordinary activities was calculated at £100,000.

(f)   Corporation tax based on the 19X7 profits was estimated at £36,000.

(g)   Directors proposed a final dividend of 4.5p per share.

(h)   A transfer to the deferred taxation account of £7,000 for 19X7 is to be made in respect of capital allowances in excess of depreciation charges (the entire balance on the deferred tax account being of a similar nature).

Required

(a)   Make all relevant entries in the ledger accounts (except bank and share capital).

(b)   Complete the profit and loss account for 19X7 and show how the final balances would be included the balance sheet at 31 December 19X7. Show the details given in the notes to the accounts.

Assume income tax at 25% and ACT at $^1/_4$ of the net dividend.

---

14   CHER (25 marks)   *45 mins*

Note. To answers parts (b) to (d) of this question, you will need to refer to the profit and loss accounts in the appendix at the end of the question.

(a)   'Reported earnings per share is a very important indicator of performance for a quoted company.'

Why do you think that this is, and do you agree?   (5 marks)

(b)   Cher (Holdings) plc was formed fifteen years ago. As at 1 July 19X3, the issued share capital of the group was as follows, all shares being issued at par.

Ordinary £1 shares fully paid	800,000
Ordinary £1 shares 60p paid	200,000
	1,000,000

On 1 October 19X3, Cher (Holdings) plc received the monies due on the partly paid shares.

Required

Calculate the earnings per share figure for the year ended 30 June 19X4, as it would appear in the financial statements of the group.   (3 marks)

(c) On 28 February 19X5 Cher (Holdings) plc made a 1 for 4 rights issue at £1.30 per share. The actual *cum rights* price was £1.90 per share on the last day of quotation *cum rights*.

Required

(i) Calculate earnings per share for the year ended 30 June 19X5. Show the comparative figure for 19X4. (5 marks)

(ii) Explain the reasoning behind your calculation in part (c)(i). (7 marks)

(d) On 1 January 19X6, a new group Sonny (Holdings) plc was formed. Its purpose was to take over the business of Cher (Holdings) plc, and the need to do so arose from the fact that Cher (Holdings) plc was becoming linked in the mind of the public with an unconnected, somewhat disreputable group, Sheer Moldings plc. Sonny (Holdings) plc was to issue 2 shares for every 1 share in Cher (Holdings) plc. In preparing the financial statements of Sonny (Holdings) plc, which is essentially a continuation of Cher (Holdings) plc, merger accounting principles were adopted.

Required

Calculate earnings per share for the year ended 30 June 19X6. Show the comparative figure for 19X5. (5 marks)

APPENDIX: PROFIT AND LOSS ACCOUNTS

	Cher (Holdings) plc		Sonny (Holdings) plc
Year ended 30 June	*19X4*	*19X5*	*19X6*
	£'000	£'000	£'000
Turnover	2,000	3,400	4,500
Cost of sales	900	800	1,500
Gross profit	1,100	2,600	3,000
Distribution costs	150	240	310
Administrative expenses	260	410	420
Profit on ordinary activities before tax	690	1,950	2,270
Taxation	230	640	750
Profit on ordinary activities after tax	460	1,310	1,520
Dividends	100	200	250
Profit for the financial year	360	1,110	1,270

15   SPICE (25 marks)   *45 mins*

The following financial statements relate to Spice plc.

PROFIT AND LOSS ACCOUNT FOR THE YEAR TO 31 MARCH 19X6

	£m	£m
Turnover		710
Cost of sales		(314)
Gross profit		396
Distribution costs	(62)	
Administrative costs	(54)	
		(116)
Operating profit		280
Interest payable	(14)	
Interest receivable	6	
		(8)
Profit before tax		272
Taxation		(64)
Profit for the financial year		208
Dividends		(40)
Retained profit for the year		168

SUMMARISED BALANCE SHEETS

	31 March 19X6		31 March 19X5	
	£m	£m	£m	£m
Tangible fixed assets		550		400
Current assets				
Stock	280		310	
Debtors	260		220	
Interest receivable	2		4	
Short term investments	190		-	
Cash	12		42	
	744		576	
Creditors: amounts falling due within one year	(498)		(344)	
Net current assets		246		232
Total assets less current liabilities		796		632
Creditors: amounts falling due after more than one year		(140)		(164)
Provisions for liabilities and charges - deferred tax		(24)		(16)
Net assets		632		452
Capital and reserves				
Ordinary shares £1 each		220		180
10% £1 preference shares		-		40
		220		220
Reserves				
Share premium account	88		70	
Capital redemption reserve	20		-	
Revaluation reserve	14		-	
Profit and loss account	290		162	
		412		232
		632		452

The following information is relevant.

(a) During the year Spice plc issued 20 million £1 ordinary shares at a premium of 100%, incurring issue costs of £2 million. Subsequent to this a bonus issue of 1 for 10 shares held was made. On 1 September 19X5 Spice plc decided to purchase and cancel all of its preference shares at a premium of 20p per share. The premium has been charged to the profit and loss account as an administrative cost.

(b) Tangible fixed assets include certain properties which were revalued during the year giving a surplus of £14 million. Assets capitalised under finance lease agreements during the year amounted to £56 million. Disposals of assets having a net book value of £38 million realised £42 million. Depreciation for the year was £76 million.

(c) Short term investments of £160 million fall within the definition of 'liquid resources' in FRS 1 (revised). The remainder of the investments is a loan note to a major public company which is repayable on demand. The plc meets the definition of a 'qualifying financial institution' for cash purposes.

(d) *Analysis of creditors as at:*

	31 March 19X6	31 March 19X5
	£m	£m
Repayable within one year:		
Bank overdraft	16	40
Obligations under finance leases	10	6
Trade creditors	424	254
Corporation tax	32	20
Advance corporation tax	2	4
Dividends	8	16
Interest payable	6	4
	498	344
Repayable after more than one year:		
Obligations under finance leases	100	84
6% debentures 19X6/19Y1	40	80
	140	164

(e) Some of the debentures were redeemed at par on 31 March 19X6.

(f) Advance corporation tax recoverable at each year end has been offset against deferred tax.

(g) Interest on finance leases of £6 million is included in the interest charge in the profit and loss account.

Required

(a) Prepare a cash flow statement for Spice plc for the year ended 31 March 19X6 in compliance with FRS 1 (revised) *Cash flow statements* (indirect method) together with the accompanying notes. (16 marks)

(b) Prepare an analysis of the movement on share capital and reserves during the year.(5 marks)

(c) The Accounting Standards Board (ASB) would prefer to use the 'direct' (gross) method of presenting cash flow information, yet almost all companies use the 'indirect' (net) method of presentation. Why do the ASB and most listed companies appear to differ on this issue? (4 marks)

16 PENSION COSTS (25 marks) *45 mins*

(a) (i) Curtis Ltd runs a pension scheme for its employees, who have an estimated remaining service life of 10 years. The scheme is over-funded by £4m.

(ii) The same situation applies as in part (i) except that the scheme is under-funded by £4m.

Required

For (i) and (ii) above calculate the necessary profit and loss account and balance sheet figures for the next 10 years for pension contributions.

(b) SSAP 24 has been criticised for ignoring the balance sheet aspects of the pension cost problem. Discuss these criticisms and potential solutions to the problem.

17 GROUP ACCOUNTS (20 marks) *36 mins*

For many years, under UK law, companies with subsidiaries have been required to publish group accounts, usually in the form of consolidated accounts. You are required to state why you feel the preparation of group accounts is necessary and to outline their limitations, if any.

18 ARLENE AND AMANDA *36 mins*

Arlene plc acquired 135,000 shares in Amanda Ltd in 19X3. The reserves of Amanda Ltd at the date of acquisition comprised: revenue reserve £20,000; capital reserve £10,000. The draft balance sheets of both companies are given below as at 31 December 19X5.

	Arlene plc		Amanda Ltd	
	£	£	£	£
Fixed assets				
Tangible assets		350,000		210,000
Investments				
Shares in Amanda Ltd at cost		190,000		
		540,000		
Current assets				
Stocks	83,000		42,000	
Debtors	102,000		48,000	
Current account with Amanda Ltd	5,000		-	
Bank and cash	40,000		12,000	
	230,000		102,000	
Current liabilities				
Trade creditors	90,000		37,000	
Current account with Arlene Ltd	-		1,000	
Proposed dividend	30,000		10,000	
	120,000		48,000	
Net current assets		110,000		54,000
Total assets less current liabilities		650,000		264,000

	Arlene plc		Amanda Ltd	
	£	£	£	£
Share capital and reserves				
Ordinary shares of £1 each		400,000		150,000
Revenue reserve		190,000		99,000
Capital reserve		60,000		15,000
		650,000		264,000

Arlene plc has not yet accounted for its share of the dividend proposed by Amanda Ltd.

On 29 December 19X5 Amanda Ltd sent a cheque for £4,000 to Arlene Ltd, which was not received until 3 January 19X6.

You are required to prepare the consolidated balance sheet of Arlene plc as at 31 December 19X5. (Goodwill arising on consolidation is deemed to have an indefinite useful life and is therefore to remain in the balance sheet.)

19   HAND (25 marks)   45 mins

The following are the draft balance sheets as at 31 December 19X1 of Hand Ltd and its subsidiary Finger Ltd.

	Hand Limited		Finger Limited	
	£	£	£	£
Fixed assets				
Tangible assets		100,000		76,000
Investment in Finger Ltd at cost				
40,000 £1 ordinary shares		50,000		-
		150,000		76,000
Current assets				
Sundry	195,000		62,000	
Current account with Finger Ltd	8,000		-	
	203,000		62,000	
Current liabilities				
Sundry	163,000		36,000	
Current account with Hand Ltd	-		6,000	
	163,000		42,000	
Net current assets		40,000		20,000
		190,000		96,000

	Hand Limited	Finger Limited
	£	£
Capital and reserves		
Ordinary shares of £1 each	100,000	60,000
Revenue reserves	90,000	36,000
	190,000	96,000

You ascertain the following information.

(a)   Hand Ltd purchased its shareholding in Finger Ltd on 30 June 19X1.

(b)   The revenue reserves of Finger Ltd consist of the following.

	£
Balance at 31 December 19X0	18,000
Profit for the year	18,000
	36,000

(c)   On 30 June 19X1 the fair value of Finger Ltd's tangible fixed assets exceeded their book value by £3,000. It is group policy to depreciate such assets over five years.

(d)   In July 19X1 Finger Ltd paid an ordinary dividend for 19X0 of £6,000. The dividend had been provided for in Finger Ltd's balance sheet at 31 December 19X0. Hand Ltd has credited its share of the dividend received to profit and loss account.

(e)   The difference in the current account balances represents cash in transit.

Required

Prepare Hand's consolidated balance sheet as at 31 December 19X1.

Note. All goodwill is to be treated in accordance with the provisions of FRS 10.

20   WAR (25 marks)   *45 mins*

(a)   When an acquisition takes place, the purchase consideration may be in the form of share capital. Where no suitable market price exists (for example, shares in an unquoted company) how may the fair value of the purchase consideration be estimated?   (4 marks)

(b)   On 1 May 19X7, War plc acquired 70% of the ordinary share capital of Peace Ltd by issuing 500,000 ordinary £1 shares at a premium of 60p per share. The costs associated with the share issue were £50,000.

As at 30 June 19X7, the following financial statements for War plc and Peace Ltd were available.

PROFIT AND LOSS ACCOUNTS
FOR THE YEAR ENDED 30 JUNE 19X7

	War plc	Peace Ltd
	£'000	£'000
Turnover	3,150	1,770
Cost of sales	(1,610)	(1,065)
Gross profit	1,540	705
Distribution costs	(620)	(105)
Administrative expenses	(325)*	(210)
Operating profit	595	390
Interest payable	(70)	(30)
Dividends from Peace plc	42	-
Profit on ordinary activities before taxation	567	360
Tax on profit	(283)	(135)
Profit after tax	284	225
Dividends paid	(38)	(60)
Retained profit for the year	246	165

Note. The issue costs of £50,000 on the issue of ordinary share capital are included in this figure.

BALANCE SHEETS AS AT 30 JUNE 19X7

	War plc	Peace Ltd
	£'000	£'000
Fixed assets		
Tangible fixed assets	1,750	350
Investment in Peace Ltd	800	-
	2,550	350
Current assets		
Stock	150	450
Debtors	238	213
Cash	187	112
	575	775
Creditors: amounts falling due within one year	(400)	(250)
Net current assets	175	525
Total assets less current liabilities	2,725	875
Creditors: amounts falling due after one year	(1,050)	(175)
	1,675	700
Capital and reserves		
Ordinary shares of £1 each	750	100
Share premium	300	150
Profit and loss account	625	450
	1,675	700

You have been asked to prepare the consolidated financial statements, taking account of the following further information.

(i)   Any goodwill arising on acquisition is to be amortised over 5 years on a straight line basis, with a full year's amortisation charged in the year of acquisition. The charge is to be included in administrative expenses.

(ii)   War plc accounts for pre-acquisition dividends by treating them as a deduction from the cost of the investment. Peace Ltd paid an ordinary dividend of 10p per share on 1 June 19X7. No dividends were proposed as at 30 June 19X7. War plc and Peace Ltd had both accounted for ACT on the dividends.

(iii)   The profit of Peace Ltd may be assumed to accrue evenly over the year.

(iv)   The tangible fixed assets of Peace Ltd had a net realisable value of £400,000 at the date of acquisition. Their open market value was £500,000. It has been decided that, as Peace Ltd was acquired so close to the year end, no depreciation adjustment will be made in the group accounts; the year end value will be taken as the carrying value of the tangible fixed assets in the accounts of Peace Ltd. The remaining assets and liabilities of Peace Ltd were all stated at their fair value as at 1 May 19X7.

(v)   Peace Ltd did not issue any shares between the date of acquisition and the year end.

(vi)   There were no intercompany transactions during the year.

Required

Prepare the consolidated balance sheet and the consolidated profit and loss account of the War Group plc for the year ended 30 June 19X7. You should work to the nearest £'000. You do not need to prepare notes to the accounts.   (21 marks)

21   CHIGWELL (50 marks)   *90 mins*

During the year to 31 December 19X2, before the publication of FRS 6 *Acquisitions and mergers*, Chigwell plc acquired two subsidiaries as follows.

(a)   Chigwell plc had an associated company, Tracy Ltd, of which it owned 25% of the share capital. On 1 September 19X2 it acquired the remainder of the share capital, the consideration being the issue of 200,000 £1 ordinary shares in Chigwell plc. The value of the consideration was £280,000. Goodwill arising on consolidation was £95,000 and should be written off against profit for the year.

The transaction qualified as a merger under the old SSAP 23 because it was effected by a sale of 20% of the original holding to Fiddlers Bank and a subsequent repurchase, all of which was part of the same offer.

(b)   On 1 April 19X2, Chigwell plc offered a share exchange in order to acquire the remainder of Sharon plc's issued share capital. The offer became unconditional on 1 May 19X2. Previous shareholdings of the company had been acquired at a cost of £960,000. The total cost of the acquisition, including the £960,000 previously paid, was £4,425,000.

The difference between the nominal value of the shares issued and their value at the date of issue was £573,000. Goodwill on consolidation amounted to £986,000, and should be written off in full against profit for the year.

Summarised profit and loss accounts for the three companies for the year ended 31 December 19X2 are shown below.

	Chigwell plc	Sharon plc	Tracy Ltd
	£'000	£'000	£'000
Turnover	80,946	17,194	3,420
Cost of sales and expenses	62,184	13,592	2,560
Operating profit	18,762	3,602	860
Dividends receivable*	45	-	-
Interest receivable	120	50	-
Profit before tax	18,927	3,652	860
Taxation	6,740	1,525	390
Profit after tax	12,187	2,127	470
Ordinary dividends			
Interim	550	**24	12
Final	50	12	6
Preference dividends	12	-	-
Retained profit for the year	11,575	2,091	452

Notes

* Chigwell plc has credited all dividends, whether pre- or post-acquisition, to the profit and loss account.

** Interim dividends were paid on 1 July 19X2.

Required

(a) Prepare the consolidated profit and loss account for the Chigwell group for the year ended 31 December 19X2 under the acquisition method. Goodwill written off should be shown separately. (14 marks)

(b) Prepare a note showing the amount of the group retained profit for the year (from part (a)) which has been retained by each of the three companies. (3 marks)

(c) Prepare the consolidated profit and loss account for the Chigwell group for the year ended 31 December 19X2 using merger accounting. (10 marks)

(d) Show in a note the amount of group retained profit (from part (c)) which has been retained by each of the three companies. (3 marks)

(e) Prepare a schedule reconciling the retained profit for the year as calculated under the acquisition method with the retained profit for the year as calculated under the merger method. (5 marks)

(f) Prepare a schedule showing how the amount shown for investment in subsidiaries under the merger method is calculated. (5 marks)

(g) Explain why, under FRS 6 *Acquisitions and mergers*, the purchase of the share capital of Tracy would not qualify as a merger. (10 marks)

22   ENTERPRISE AND VULCAN

Enterprise plc purchased 30% of Vulcan Ltd on 1 July 19X4. At all times, Enterprise participates fully in Vulcan's financial and operating policy decisions. Goodwill is to be capitalised and amortised over five years.

EXTRACT FROM VULCAN LTD'S BALANCE SHEET AT ACQUISITION

	£'000
Share capital	2,000
Revaluation reserve	200
Profit and loss reserve	900
	3,100

BALANCE SHEETS AS AT 30 JUNE 19X8

	Enterprise plc group £'000	£'000	Vulcan Ltd £'000	£'000
Fixed assets				
Tangible fixed assets		8,000		7,000
Investment in therapy		2,000		-
		10,000		7,000
Current assets				
Stock	1,340		860	
Debtors	1,000		790	
Cash	260		430	
	2,600		2,080	
Creditors (due within one year)	(1,500)		(1,140)	
		1,100		940
		11,100		7,940
Capital and reserves				
Equity share capital		4,000		2,000
Revaluation reserve		2,000		1,000
Profit and loss reserve		5,100		4,940
		11,100		7,940

PROFIT AND LOSS ACCOUNTS FOR THE YEAR ENDING 30 JUNE 19X8

	Enterprise plc group £'000	Vulcan Ltd £'000
Turnover	10,000	6,0000
Cost of sales	(6,000)	(3,000)
Gross profit	4,000	3,000
Expenses	(1,500)	(880)
Operating profit	2,500	2,120
Interest	(100)	(20)
Profit on ordinary activities before tax	2,400	2,100
Tax on ordinary activities	(800)	(700)
Profit on ordinary activities after tax	1,600	1,400
Dividends	(600)	(100)
Retained profit	1,000	1,300

Required

Prepare the consolidated balance sheet and P&L account for the year ended 30 June 19X8. Ignore any additional disclosure requirements of FRS 9. (20 marks)

23 **CPP AND CCA (25 marks)** *45 mins*

(a) 'It is important that managements and other users of financial accounts should be in a position to appreciate the effects of inflation on the business with which they are concerned.' (PSSAP 7)

Required

Explain how inflation obscures the meaning of accounts prepared by the traditional historical cost convention, and discuss the contribution which CPP accounting could make to providing a more satisfactory system of accounting for inflation.

(b) Compare the general principles underlying CPP and CCA accounting.

(c) Define the term 'realised holding gain'.

(d) Explain briefly the use in CCA accounting of:

(i) the cost of sales adjustment;
(ii) the monetary working capital adjustment;
(iii) the depreciation adjustment;
(iv) the gearing adjustment.

24 STATEMENT OF PRINCIPLES (20 marks)   *36 mins*

'A major achievement of the ASB was the development of its *Statement of Principles*. However, it is too theoretical to be applied to accounting standards.'

What are the merits of the *Statement of Principles* and do you agree with the criticism that it is too theoretical?

25 XYZ GROUP (25 marks)   *45 mins*

A new managing director will soon be taking over the management of the XYZ Group which consists of three companies carrying on similar businesses in the same trade. The group accountant has produced a summary and comparison of the balance sheets, sales and profits for the most recent years to help the new managing director to familiarise himself with the main figures. These are reproduced below.

As the new managing director is essentially a production and marketing expert rather than being from a financial background, he has not had too much experience in reading accounting and financial statements for a group of companies and would find some additional information helpful for use in preliminary discussion with the managers of each of the group companies. However, he has specifically asked that the extra information should not be another extensive statement showing long lists of ratios and percentages which would need yet another statement to interpret the figures. Further, he has managed to obtain a checklist which suggests some 'Criteria for a healthy company' against which the group companies could be compared.

He thinks this checklist could be helpful to the person preparing the report giving the extra information. It suggest the following criteria.

(a)   There should be a strong asset base.

(b)   There should be adequate control of working capital such as stocks and debtors.

(c)   There should be adequate liquidity to ensure that debts can be paid as they arise.

(d)   If new funds are likely to be required for any reasons, there should be sufficient borrowing capacity available, or a potential shareholder should be able to invest with confidence.

(e)   The operating performance of any individual group company should generally be as good as any other group company, unless there are special reasons otherwise.

(f)   A fair commercial return should be earned for the shareholders which covers the risk taken in running the business.

(g)   The figures in the accounts should represent accurate valuations of assets and liabilities. Any item of concern should be the subject of further investigations in the context of good account practices.

One immediate problem that the new managing director has to face, when he visits company Y for the first time, is to advise the directors about this year's ordinary dividend. The directors are anxious to keep up good relations with one of the minority shareholders who happens to be a director of their main materials supplier. They therefore wish to pay a dividend of £60,000 as usual, even though a loss was made this particular year. They wish to use the capital redemption reserve to make up any balance not available in general reserve.

SUMMARY AND COMPARISON OF THE BALANCE SHEETS,
SALES AND PROFIT OF THE XYZ GROUP
FOR THE YEAR 19X5/X6

	Company X		Company Y		Company Z		Group	
	£'000	£'000	£'000	£'000	£'000	£'000	£'000	£'000
Fixed assets								
Intangible assets								
Goodwill		-		-		200		866
Research/development		180		-		-		180
Licences/trade marks		140		-		-		140
		320		-		200		1,186
Tangible assets								
Freehold at cost or								
revaluation		300		-		800		1,100
Leasehold at cost	-		-		600		600	
Less amortisation	-		-		580		580	
		-		-		20		20
Plant at cost	1,200		900		1,000		3,100	
Less depreciation	600		400		200		1,200	
		600		500		800		1,900
		1,220		500		1,820		4,206
Investments								
In group companies		2,000		-		-		-
Current assets								
Stock and work in progress	516		250		198		964	
Debtors	468		418		312		1,198	
Bank	100		-		36		136	
	1,084		668		546		2,298	
Liabilities due within one year								
Bank overdraft	-		172		-		172	
Trade creditors	442		330		86		858	
Customers prepayments	-		106		-		106	
		642		60		460		1,162
		3,862		560		2,280		5,368
Liabilities due after one year								
Debentures (19Y7)		1,000		-		-		1,000
Loan capital		724		-		-		724
Minority interest		-		-		-		620
		2,138		560		2,280		3,024

	Company X		Company Y		Company Z		Group	
	£'000	£'000	£'000	£'000	£'000	£'000	£'000	£'000
Capital and reserves								
Share capital		1,300		340		1,500		1,300
Reserves								
Revaluation	-		-		300		300	
Capital redemption	-		200		-		200	
General	838		20		480		1,224	
		838		220		780		1,724
		2,138		560		2,280		3,024
Sales		1,752		1,136		2,316		5,204
Cost of sales		1,488		1,182		1,890		4,560
Net profit (before interest)		264		(46)		426		644
Interest on loans and								
debentures	108		-		-		108	
Taxation	50		-		98		148	
		158		-		98		256
		106		(46)		328		388
Less minority interest		-		-		-		45
Earnings (loss) after tax		106		(46)		328		343
Extraordinary item		-		-		73		73
Net earnings (loss)								
available for shareholders		106		(46)		255		270

Required

(a) Prepare a report for the use of the new managing director which highlights any major weaknesses, or other special features, of each of the group companies in the light of the suggested criteria for a healthy company as mentioned above. Use may be made of any appropriate accounting ratios to illustrate specific points.

(b) Identify any items in the summary which you think may require some 'further investigation in the context of good accounting practices' giving reasons for specifying each of these items for special examination and quoting the particular accounting assumption, precept, rule or standard under which it should be examined.

(c) Advise the new managing director as to whether any dividend can be paid by Company Y this year.

Exam answer bank

1   REGULATORS

A listed company is a public limited company whose shares are bought and sold on The Stock Exchange. This involves the signing of a listing agreement which requires compliance with the 'Listing Rules' (formerly known as the Yellow Book). This contains amongst other things The Stock Exchange's detailed rules on the information to be disclosed in listed companies' accounts. This, then, is one regulatory influence on a listed company's accounts. The Stock Exchange enforces compliance by monitoring accounts and reserving the right to withdraw a company's shares from The Stock Exchange List: ie the company's shares would no longer be traded through The Stock Exchange. There is, however, no statutory requirement to obey these rules.

All companies in the UK have to comply with the Companies Acts, which lay down detailed requirements on the preparation of accounts. Company law is becoming more and more detailed, partly because of EU Directives. Another reason to increase statutory regulation is that listed companies are under great pressure to show profit growth and an obvious way to achieve this is to manipulate accounting policies. If this involves breaking the law, as opposed to ignoring professional guidance, company directors may think twice before bending the rules - or, at least, this is the government's hope.

Professional guidance is given by the Accounting Standards Board (ASB), overseen by the Financial Reporting Council. Prescriptive guidance is given in Statements of Standard Accounting Practice (SSAPs) and Financial Reporting Standards (FRSs) which must be applied in all accounts required to show a 'true and fair view' (ie all companies). SSAPs and FRSs are issued after extensive consultation and are revised as required to reflect economic or legal changes. Until fairly recently, companies have been able to disguise non-compliance if their auditors did not qualify the audit report. However, the Companies Act 1989 requires details of non-compliance to be disclosed in the accounts. 'Defective' accounts will in future be revised under court order if necessary and directors signing such accounts can be prosecuted and fined (or even imprisoned). This sanction applies to breach of both accounting standards and company law.

2   TOM AND GERRY

(a)   PARTNERS' CAPITAL ACCOUNTS - OLD FIRMS

	Tom & Gerry				*Tom & Gerry*		
	Tom	*Gerry*	*Butch*		*Tom*	*Gerry*	*Butch*
	£	£	£		£	£	£
Loan account - Tom	69,380			Balances b/f	30,000	15,000	25,500
Balances to new firm -				Current a/c		9,600	
Gerry & Butch		44,290	70,280	Goodwill a/c	27,680	13,840	24,680
				Revaluation a/c:			
				surplus	11,700	5,850	20,100
	69,380	44,290	70,280		69,380	44,290	70,280

(b)   BALANCE SHEET AS AT 1 JANUARY 19X3

	£	£
Fixed assets		
Freehold premises		84,000
Furniture, fixtures and fittings		14,400
		98,400
Current assets		
Stock	44,100	
Debtors	17,250	
Bank balances	40,500	
	101,850	
Creditors: amounts falling due within one year		
Creditors	78,000	
Loan account - Tom	73,880	
	151,880	
Net current liabilities		(50,030)
		48,370

Partners' capital accounts   £

	£
Gerry	11,190
Butch	37,180
	48,370

Note. It is assumed that Tom's loan is repayable within 12 months of the merger.

CURRENT ACCOUNTS - OLD FIRM

	Tom £	Gerry £		Tom £	Gerry £
Loan account - Tom	4,500		Balances b/f	4,500	9,600
Capital account		9,600			
	4,500	9,600		4,500	9,600

PARTNERS' ACCOUNTS - NEW FIRM

	Gerry £	Butch £		Gerry £	Butch £
Goodwill a/c	33,100	33,100	Balances from old firms		
			Tom and Gerry	44,290	
Balances c/d	11,190	37,180	Butch		70,280
	44,290	70,280		44,290	70,280
			Balances b/d	11,190	37,180

Workings

1   *Goodwill computation*

		Tom & Gerry		Butch
	£	£		£
Profits: 19X2		22,530		11,700
Less: obsolete stock	900			
bad debts	450			300
	1,350			
		21,180		11,400
19X1		18,300		11,400
19X0		21,900		9,900
		61,380		32,700
Average of three years profits		20,460		10,900
Add wife's annual salary				1,500
Adjustment on revaluation of furniture				
Tom and Gerry - surplus £900/3		300		
Butch - deficiency £600/10				(60)
Adjusted average profit		20,760		12,340
Goodwill - two years' purchase		41,520		24,680

Note. It is assumed that the stock obsolescence and the bad debts occurred in 19X2.

2   ### GOODWILL ACCOUNT

	£	£		£
Capital accounts (old firms)			Capital accounts (new firm)	
Tom ($^2/_3$)	27,680		Gerry ($^1/_2$)	33,100
Gerry ($^1/_3$)	13,840		Butch ($^1/_2$)	33,100
		41,520		
Butch		24,680		
		66,200		66,200

REVALUATION ACCOUNTS

	Tom & Gerry		Butch		Tom & Gerry	Butch
	£	£	£		£	£
Deficiencies						
Furniture			600			
Obsolete stock		900		Surpluses		
Bad debts		450	300	Freehold premises	18,000	21,000
Surplus to capital a/cs				Furniture	900	
Tom (²/₃)	11,700					
Gerry (¹/₃)	5,850	17,550				
Butch			20,100			
		18,900	21,000		18,900	21,000

3 HOMER AND BART

> *Tutorial note.* This question may have made you panic at first sight. However, it is actually fairly straightforward when approached methodically. Tricky points are the factored debts and the treatment of the issue costs of the debentures.

(a)

REALISATION ACCOUNT

	£		£
Sundry net assets		Purchase consideration	38,000
(33,800 + 800)	34,600		
Expenses	1,200		
Profit (bal): Homer 70%	1,540		
Bart 30%	660		
	38,000		38,000

CAPITAL ACCOUNTS

	Homer	Bart		Homer	Bart
	£	£		£	£
Ordinary shares	19,600	8,400	Balance b/f	20,000	8,000
Debentures	4,200	1,800	Expenses	1,200	
Cash (bal fig - see W2)	3,560	440	Profit for period (W1)	4,620	1,980
			Profit on realisation	1,540	660
	27,360	10,640			10,640
				27,360	

Workings

1 *Net profit for six months to 31 December 19X6*

	£	£
Per trial balance		6,600
Homer 70%	4,620	
Bart 30%	1,980	
		6,600

2 *Cash*

	£	£
Cash from Simpson Ltd: 38,000 − (28,000 + 6,000)		4,000
To Homer	3,560	
To Bart	440	
		4,000

(b)   (i)   SIMPSON LIMITED
BALANCE SHEET AS AT 1 JANUARY 19X7

	£	£
Fixed assets		
Tangible assets		
Buildings		12,000
Plant and equipment		12,000
Motor vehicles		7,200
		31,200
Intangible asset: goodwill (W1)		4,200
		35,400
Current assets		
Stock	6,400	
Debtors	19,600	
Cash at bank and in hand (W2)	5,600	
	31,600	
Creditors: amounts falling due within one year	(33,400)	
Net current liabilities		(1,800)
Total assets less current liabilities		33,600
Creditors: amounts falling due after one year		
5% debentures (6,000 – 400)		(5,600)
		28,000

	£
Capital and reserves	
£1 ordinary shares	28,000

Workings

1   *Goodwill*

	£
Purchase consideration	38,000
Fair value of net assets	33,800
Goodwill	4,200

2   *Cash*

	£	£
Balance from partnership		10,000
Included in purchase consideration (part (a))	4,000	
Issue costs*	400	
		(4,400)
		5,600

Note. The debentures are shown on the balance sheet net of issue costs.

(ii) SIMPSON LIMITED
BALANCE SHEET AS AT 31 DECEMBER 19X7

	Cost	Depreciation	NBV
	£	£	£
Fixed assets			
Tangible assets			
Buildings	12,000	400	11,600
Plant and equipment	12,000	1,200	10,800
Motor vehicles	7,200	1,800	5,400
	31,200	3,400	27,800
Intangible asset: goodwill	4,200	840	3,360
			31,160
Current assets			
Stock		14,800	
Debtors (W2)		17,550	
Debtors subject to financing			
arrangements (W3)		3,600	
Cash at bank and in hand		5,400	
		41,350	
Creditors: amounts falling due within			
one year (W4)		(29,850)	
Net current assets			11,500
Total assets less current liabilities			42,660
Creditors: amounts falling due after one year			
5% debentures (W5)			5,640
			37,020
Capital and reserves			
£1 ordinary shares			28,000
Profit and loss account (W1)			9,020
			37,020

Workings

1   *Profit and loss account*

	£
Net profit per trial balance	22,400
Goodwill written off	(840)
Interest payable (5% × 6,000)	(300)
Issue costs $400/10$	(40)
Corporation tax	(6,800)
Dividends paid and proposed 4,000 + (28,000 × 5p)	(5,400)
	9,020

2   *Debtors*

	£
Per trial balance	18,200
Less ACT recoverable $20/80 × 4,000$	(1,000)
Plus ACT recoverable on proposed dividend $20/80 × 1,400$	350
	17,550

3   *Debtors subject to financing arrangements*

	£
Gross amount (13,200 – 400)	12,800
Less non-returnable proceeds	9,200
	3,600

4   Creditors: amounts falling due within one year

	£	£
Creditors per trial balance		20,400
Corporation tax	6,800	
Less ACT recoverable	(1,000)	
		5,800
ACT payable		350
Cash returnable to Factory Finance Ltd		1,600
Interest payable		300
Proposed dividend		1,400
		29,850

5   5% debentures

	£
As at 1 January 19X7	5,600
Issue costs spread over ten years $^{400}/_{10}$	40
	5,640

4   DAY AND KNIGHT

(a)

REALISATION ACCOUNT

	£		£
Stock	46,000	Day and Knight Ltd	
Fixtures	20,000	purchase consideration	100,000
Motor vehicles	16,000		
Profit on realisation			
Day	9,000		
Knight	9,000		
	100,000		100,000

PARTNERS' ACCOUNTS

	Day £	Knight £		Day £	Knight £
Debtor		2,500	Therefore:		
Bad debts	750	750	Balances b/f *	69,500	32,000
Discount	250	250	Profit on realisation	9,000	9,000
Debtors	7,500	7,500			
Cash	20,000		Cash		20,000
Consideration:					
Day & Knight Ltd	50,000	50,000			
	78,500	61,000		78,500	61,000

* *Day's and Knight's balances b/f*

(i)   In the trial balance, Day's and Knight's balance stand:

	Capital	Current	Net
Day	£125,000 Cr	£12,000 Dr	£113,000 Cr
Knight	£85,000 Cr	£10,000 Dr	£75,000 Cr

However, no indication is given that these are balances at 1.1.X6 (indeed they are not dated at all).

Therefore their 1.1.X6 balances must be deduced as above.

(ii)   However, their sum could have been predicted.

TRIAL BALANCE AT 1.1.X6 (final trial balance of partnership)

	Debit £	Credit £
Creditors		41,000
Bank overdraft		10,000
Debtors	70,500	
Stock	46,000	
Fixtures	20,000	
Motor vehicle	16,000	
	152,500	51,000
Therefore - Capital		101,500
	152,500	152,500

Notice that the opening balances on the partners' accounts do indeed total £101,500:

	£
Knight	69,500
Day	32,000
	101,500

Workings

1

CREDITORS

	£		£
Bank	41,000	Balance at 1.1.X6	41,000

2

BANK

	£		£
∴ Debtors	51,000	Balance at 1.1.X6	10,000
		Creditors	41,000
	51,000		51,000

3

DEBTORS

	£		£
Balance at 1.1.X6	70,500	Knight - debt collected	2,500
		Discount allowed	500
		Bad debts	1,500
		Balance at 31.12.X6	15,000
		Bank	51,000
	70,500		70,500

4

DAY AND KNIGHT LIMITED

	£		£
Realisation account:		Partners' accounts:	
purchase consideration	100,000	shares in limited company	100,000
	100,000		100,000

(b)

DIRECTORS' CURRENT ACCOUNTS

	Day £	Knight £		Day £	Knight £
Consideration	50,000	50,000	Cash (W)	43,500	43,000
Balance c/d	4,750	4,250	Salaries	11,250	11,250
	54,750	54,250		54,750	54,250

Cash introduced

To account for the movements on their personal accounts during the year, Day and Knight must have introduced further cash.

	Balance at 1.1.X6 (part (a))	Balance at 31.12.X6 (net)	Therefore cash introduced
Day	£69,500 Cr	£113,000 Cr	£43,500
Knight	£32,000 Cr	£75,000 Cr	£43,000

(c) TRADING AND PROFIT AND LOSS ACCOUNTS
FOR THE YEAR ENDED 31 DECEMBER 19X6

	£	£
Sales		360,000
Cost of sales		
Stock at 1.1.19X6	46,000	
Purchases	304,000	
	350,000	
Less stock at 31.13.19X6	62,000	
		288,000
Gross profit		72,000

	1.1.X6 - 31.3.X6		1.4.X6 - 31.12.X6		Whole year	
	£	£	£	£	£	£
Gross profit (W)		12,000		60,000		72,000
Expenses (W)						
Rent and rates	1,750		5,250		7,000	
Salaries: directors	-		22,500		22,500	
others	5,000		15,000		20,000	
General expenses	850		2,550		3,400	
Advertising	-		5,200		5,200	
Bad debts	900		4,500		5,400	
Discounts	1,000		5,000		6,000	
Deprecation						
Fixtures	500		1,500		2,000	
Motor vehicles	1,000		3,500		4,500	
		11,000		65,000		76,000
						(4,000)
Pre-incorporation profit applied						
in reducing cost of goodwill		1,000				1,000
Net loss for the period				(5,000)		(5,000)
						(4,000)

Working

Apportionment of gross profit and expenses

		3 months to 31.3.X6	9 months to 31.12.X6	Total
Sales weighting				
Jan to Mar	3 × 1	3		3
Apr to Sep	6 × 2		12	12
Oct to Dec	3 × 1		3	3
		3	15	18

		3/18	15/18	
Proportion		£	£	£
Applied to:				
(i) gross profit		12,000	60,000	72,000
(ii) bad debts		900	4,500	5,400
(iii) discounts		1,000	5,000	6,000
(iv) depreciation (apportioned on time basis)				
Fixtures (10% of £20,000)		500	1,500	2,000
Motor vehicles:				
25% of £16,000		1,000	3,000	4,000
25% of £8,000 for 3 months			500	500
		1,000	3,500	4,500

(v) directors' salaries commence from date of incorporation

(vii) all other items except advertising have been apportioned on a time basis

(d)   BALANCE SHEET AS AT 31 DECEMBER 19X6

	Cost £	Accumulated Depreciation £	£
Fixed assets			
Goodwill	17,000	-	17,000
Motor vehicles	24,000	4,500	19,500
Fixtures	20,000	2,000	18,000
	61,000	6,500	54,500
Current assets			
Stock		62,000	
Debtors		112,500	
Cash at bank		28,250	
		202,750	
Creditors: amounts falling due within one year			
Creditors		53,250	
Directors' current accounts		9,000	
		62,250	
			140,500
			195,000
Capital and reserves			
Share capital			
Authorised: 300,000 ordinary shares of £1 each		300,000	
Issued and fully paid: 200,000 ordinary shares of £1 each			200,000
Profit and loss account			(5,000)
			195,000

5   BLUNT AND SHARP

(a)   DRAFT TRADING AND PROFIT AND LOSS ACCOUNTS
FOR THE YEAR ENDED 31 MAY 19X5

	Head office £	Branch £	Combined £
Sales	229,700	199,700	429,400
Goods sent to branch	154,000	-	-
	383,700	199,700	429,400
Opening stock	48,500	15,400	62,500
Purchases	255,000	-	255,000
Goods received from head office	-	148,500	-
	303,500	163,900	317,500
Closing stock (W1)	54,500	17,600	75,500
Cost of sales	249,000	146,300	242,000
Gross profit	134,700	53,400	187,400
Administration expenses	31,000	10,500	41,500
Selling and distribution expenses	10,500	2,100	12,600
Financial, legal and professional expenses	5,400	500	5,900
Provision for unrealised profit (W2)	700	-	-
	47,600	13,100	60,000
Net profit for the year	87,100	40,300	127,400
Transfer between current accounts	40,300	(40,300)	
Profits brought forward	55,000		55,000
Profit carried forward	182,400	-	182,400

Workings

1   *Combined closing stocks*

	£	£
HO stock		54,500
Branch stock	17,600	
Goods in transit	5,500	
	23,100	
Less provision of unrealised profit (W2)	2,100	
		21,000
		75,500

2   *Provision for unrealised profit*

Price structure	Units
Cost to HO	100
Mark-up	10
Cost to branch	110

The provision for unrealised profit is **therefore as follows**.

	£
On branch closing stock - £17,600 × 10/110	
(deducted from goods in transit in HO **balance sheet**)	1,600
On goods in transit - £5,500 × 10/10	
(deducted from goods in transit in HO **balance sheet**)	500
	2,100
Provision b/f	1,400
Additional provision required (Dr P & L a/c)	700

(b)   DRAFT BALANCE SHEETS AS AT 31 MAY 19X5

	Head office £	Branch £	Combined £
Tangible fixed assets			
Land and buildings	250,000	50,000	300,000
Fixtures and fittings	39,900	13,600	53,500
Motor vehicles	41,400		41,400
	331,300	63,600	394,900
Current assets			
Goods in transit	*5,000		
Stock	54,500	17,600	75,500
Debtors	47,500	14,700	62,200
Branch current account	**90,200		
Bank	14,900	2,600	17,500
Cash in transit	3,000		3,000
Cash	1,000	500	1,500
	216,100	35,400	159,700
Total assets	547,400	99,000	554,600
Creditors: amounts falling due within one year			
Trade creditors	35,000	7,200	42,200
Head office current account (W)	-	91,800	
	35,000	99,000	42,200
Total assets less current liabilities	512,400	-	512,400
Capital and reserves			
Called up share capital	260,000		260,000
Reserves			
Share premium account	40,000		40,000
General reserve	30,000		30,000
Profit and loss account	182,400		182,400
	512,400		512,400

* £(5,500 – 500)
**£(91,800 – 1,600)

Working

HO BOOKS: BRANCH CURRENT ACCOUNT

	£		£
Balance b/f	60,000	Cash in transit c/d	3,000
Profit and loss account		Goods in transit c/d	5,500
- branch profit	40,300	Balance c/d	91,800
	100,300		100,300
Cash in transit b/d	3,000		
Goods in transit b/d	5,500		
Balance b/d	91,800		

6   BULWELL

(a)   BOOKS OF BULWELL AGGREGATES LIMITED

LORRIES ACCOUNT

19X1		£		£
1 Jan	Granby Garages	54,000		

PROVISION FOR DEPRECIATION ON LORRIES

19X1		£	19X1		£
			31 Dec	P & L account: ¼ ×	
31 Dec	Balance c/d	12,500		£(54,000 − (3 × 1,333))	12,500
19X2			19X2		
31 Dec	Balance c/d	25,000	1 Jan	Balance b/d	12,500
			31 Dec	P & L account	12,500
		25,000			25,000
19X3			19X3		
31 Dec	Balance c/d	37,500	1 Jan	Balance b/d	25,000
			31 Dec	P & L account	12,500
		37,500			37,500
19X4			19X4		
31 Dec	Balance c/d	50,000	1 Jan	Balance b/d	37,500
			31 Dec	P & L account	12,500
		50,000			50,000
			19X5		
			1 Jan	Balance b/d	50,000

HP INTEREST PAYABLE

19X1		£	19X1		£
31 Dec	Bank (W)	11,250	31 Dec	P & L account	11,250
19X2			19X2		
31 Dec	Bank (W)	8,063	31 Dec	P & L account	8,063
19X3			19X3		
31 Dec	Bank (W)	4,078	31 Dec	P & L account	4,078

GRANBY GARAGES PLC

19X1		£	19X1		£
1 Jan	Bank - deposit	9,000	1 Jan	Lorries a/c	54,000
31 Dec	Bank (W)	12,750			
	Balance c/d	32,250			
		54,000			54,000
19X2			19X2		
31 Dec	Bank (W)	15,937	1 Jan	Balance b/d	32,250
	Balance c/d	16,313			
		32,250			32,250
19X3			19X3		
31 Dec	Bank (W)	16,313	1 Jan	Balance b/d	16,313

PROFIT AND LOSS ACCOUNTS (EXTRACTS)

	19X1	19X2	19X3	19X4
	£	£	£	£
HP interest	11,250	8,063	4,078	
Depreciation on lorries	12,500	12,500	12,500	12,500

BALANCE SHEETS AT 31 DECEMBER (EXTRACTS)

	19X1	19X2	19X3	19X4
	£	£	£	£
Fixed assets				
Lorries: at cost	54,000	54,000	54,000	54,000
depreciation	12,500	25,000	37,500	50,000
	41,500	29,000	16,500	4,000
Current liabilities				
HP obligations	15,937	16,313	-	-
Long-term liabilities				
HP obligations	16,313	-	-	-

(b)   BOOKS OF GRANBY GARAGES PLC

BULWELL AGGREGATES LIMITED

19X1		£	19X1		£
1 Jan	Sales	54,000	1 Jan	Bank	9,000
			31 Dec	Bank	12,750
				Balance c/d	32,250
		54,000			54,000
19X2			19X2		
1 Jan	Balance b/d	32,250	31 Dec	Bank	15,937
				Balance c/d	16,313
		32,250			32,250
19X3			19X3		
1 Jan	Balance b/d	16,313	31 Dec	Bank	16,313

HP INTEREST RECEIVABLE

19X1		£	19X1		£
31 Dec	P & L account	11,250	31 Dec	Bank	11,250
19X2			19X2		
31 Dec	P & L account	8,063	31 Dec	Bank	8,063
19X3			19X3		
31 Dec	P & L account	4,078	31 Dec	Bank	4,078

TRADING AND PROFIT AND LOSS ACCOUNTS (EXTRACTS)

	£	19X1 £	19X2 £	19X3 £
Sales	54,000		-	-
Cost of sales on HP	43,200		-	-
Gross profit on HP sales		10,800	-	-
HP interest receivable		11,250	8,063	4,078

Working

Apportionment of HP instalments between interest and capital repayment.

	19X1 £	19X2 £	19X3 £
Opening liability (after deposit)	45,000	32,250	16,313
Add interest at 25%	11,250	8,063	4,078
	56,250	40,313	20,391
Less instalment	24,000	24,000	20,391
Closing liability	32,250	16,313	Nil
Interest element as above	11,250	8,063	4,078
∴Capital repayment	12,750	15,937	16,313
Total instalment	24,000	24,000	20,391

7 DIVIDEND DISTRIBUTION

(a) (i) This statement of principle is now expressed in a statutory rule (s 263 CA 1985) that a distribution (a dividend) may only by made out of profits available for that purpose, namely, accumulated realised profits less accumulated realised losses (so far as the losses have not already been written off). However, 'realised' profits have been defined by the Act only in rather obscure terms, and this leaves a query over such items as profits on long-term contract work in progress.

(ii) A public company is subject to the additional requirement that it may only distribute a surplus of its net assets over the aggregate of its called-up share capital and undistributable reserves (s 264 CA 1985). The statement that profits shall be 'accumulated' requires a company to make good losses of past years out of profits. In effect, this means that any surplus of unrealised losses over unrealised profits must be deducted from realised profits less realised losses in determining the maximum amount available for distribution.

(iii) The requirement that profits shall be realised prevents a company from distributing a revaluation surplus on retained assets.

(iv) Provisions made in the accounts, for example for depreciation, are generally treated as realised losses which must be deducted in computing profits available for dividend: s 275(2), but this rule does not apply to an increased provision for depreciation made necessary by revaluation of fixed assets.

(v) There is no objection to payment of dividends out of capital profits (that is, surplus over book value of fixed assets) but such profits must have been realised by sale. An unrealised capital profit arising from revaluation of retained fixed assets may only be distributed by a bonus issue of shares, not as a dividend: s 263 (2) CA 1985.

(vi) The amount of profit available for distribution is determined by the 'relevant accounts' which are in a typical case the latest audited accounts (provided that the auditor has not qualified his report).

(b) (i) The revaluation represents an unrealised holding gain of £20,000. The net difference between unrealised profits and unrealised losses would thus improve, thereby providing a greater 'safety margin' for a public company under s 264 CA 1985. Depreciation is usually regarded as a realised loss, but this does not apply to additional depreciation arising as a consequence of an asset revaluation, therefore the extra depreciation charge would not be treated as a realised loss in computing the maximum amount available for distribution.

(ii)   The company had an unrealised gain of £(440,000 − 150,000) = £290,000 prior to the sale. This would have been included in the 'safety margin' under s 264, as described in (a) above, but it disappears when the sale occurs, because a realised profit of £350,000 is now made, and this is a distributable capital profit.

8   STANDARD SETTERS

(a)   The users of financial information - creditors, management, employees, business contacts, financial specialists, government and the general public - are entitled to this information about a business entity to a greater or lesser degree. However, the needs and expectations of these groups will vary.

The preparers of the financial information often find themselves in the position of having to reconcile the interests of different groups in the best way for the business entity. For example whilst shareholders are looking for increased profits to support higher dividends, employees will expect higher wage increases; and yet higher profits without corresponding higher tax allowances (increased capital allowances for example) will result in a larger corporation tax bill.

Without accounting standards to prescribe how certain transactions should be treated, preparers would be tempted to produce financial information which meets the expectations of the favoured user group. For example creative accounting method, such as off balance sheet finance were used to enhance a company's balance sheet to make it more attractive to investors/lenders.

The aim of accounting standards is that they should regulate financial information in order that it shows the following characteristics.

    (i)   Objectivity
    (ii)   Comparability
    (iii)   Completeness
    (iv)   Consistency

(b)   (i)   *Composition of the ASC*

The ASB membership is still drawn from the accounting profession who act on a voluntary part-time basis, but the Board now has a full-time chairman and technical director. This, it could be argued, shows very little change from the ASC. Unlike the ASC, however, which was controlled by the CCAB and hence the accounting profession, the ASB is controlled by the Financial Reporting Council (FRC) which has 25 members drawn from a wider sphere and includes users, preparers and auditors of accounts.

   (ii)   *Emerging issues*

The ASC could only react to emerging issues by going through the long- drawn out process of producing an exposure draft which in due course and after some amendment would become an accounting standard. The effective date of the standard coming in to force was usually some months after its publication.

Under the new regime the Urgent Issues Task Force has been set up as an offshoot of the ASB. It deals with urgent issues not covered by existing standards. Its pronouncements, called abstracts, are intended to come into effect quickly, usually within one month of publication. They may later become incorporated into accounting standards, but in some cases a standard will not be necessary.

   (iii)   *ASC too open to pressure*

The ASC was open to political pressure in two ways. Firstly, its members, all being from the accounting profession, were reluctant to produce standards that would act to the detriment of their clients. Secondly, the ASC was pressurised via the government, which was subject to lobbying by large companies with vested interests.

   (iv)   *Failure to develop an agreed conceptual framework and to specify user needs*

The need for a conceptual framework is demonstrated by the way UK standards have developed over recent years, haphazardly and in response to perceived problems. The lack of a conceptual framework also meant that fundamental principles were tackled more than once in different standards, thereby producing contradictions and inconsistencies in basic concepts such as those of prudence and matching. Towards the end of its life the ASC realised the need for a conceptual framework and recognised the IASC's *Framework* as a set of guidelines.

In contrast, the ASB identified a need for a conceptual framework at an early stage in its work. In its *Statement of Aims* issued in July 1991 it states that it intends to achieve its aims by 'developing principles to guide it in establishing standards and to provide a framework within which others can exercise judgement in resolving accounting issues'. The framework is being formulated within the *Statement of Principles*, which consists of seven chapters which cover the fundamental principles of accounting and the content of accounts. The ASB is using the IASC *Framework* to a large extent as the basis for the *Statement of Principles*, adding material where necessary.

With regard to users, they were not consulted directly under the ASC regime, merely asked to comment on exposure drafts. A variety of user groups are now represented on the FRC which controls the work of the ASB.

(v)   *Inadequate enforcement of standards*

The enforcement of accounting standards, particularly for the large public companies has been enhanced in two ways.

(1)   The CA 1989 requirement that financial statements must state that they have been prepared in accordance with accounting standards. Where there are any significant departures these must be explained and justified.

(2)   The setting up of a Review Panel under the control of the FRC. Its brief is to examine the accounts of large companies and question the departure from accounting standards. The Panel has the power, as its ultimate weapon, to apply to the court for revision of the accounts. The experience to date however is that most companies prefer to resolve any issues by discussion.

9   PUBLISHED ACCOUNTS

(a)   Before the development of accounting standards it was argued that a 'credibility gap' had developed in financial reporting. Some companies were producing accounts based on the principle of prudence; others were selecting from the range of accounting bases available in such a way as to achieve the most favourable profit figure. Users of accounts could not tell which were which.

The range of profit figures which a single enterprise can present by choosing different accounting policies in respect of, say, depreciation, research and development expenditure and deferred taxation is very wide. Investors are unable to take rational decisions if the information presented to them may be interpreted with such latitude. Loan creditors and potential loan creditors cannot decide on the security of their investment unless they are aware of the basis adopted in valuing the assets of the enterprise.

These problems are more serious in the case of quoted companies because of the far greater number of people who have an interest in the activities of such companies. People who may in some degree rely on the accounts of quoted companies, apart from investors and loan creditors, include the companies' employees and business contacts, all kinds of investment analysts and advisers, and the government. Many (particularly investors and employees) will be interested primarily in the future prospects of the company, but others (particularly loan creditors and the government) will be more concerned about the degree of reliance they can place on reported figures.

There are several ways in which disclosure of accounting policies can help to achieve these aims.

(i)   It enables a comparison to be made between companies with different policies. This is useful not only for investment and lending decisions, but also for the purpose of collecting statistics, for example, by government agencies.

(ii)   It prevents possible abuse of the range of accounting bases available so as to distort a company's results and financial position.

(iii)   It enables a proper computation to be made of certain figures important for legal reasons (for example, the amount of corporation tax due; the amount which may be distributed by way of dividend).

(b)   (i)   A company which qualifies to be treated as a *small or medium-sized company* is exempted from delivering its full accounts to the registrar of companies. Full accounts must still be presented to and approved by the members of the company, but the exemptions allow for a reduction in the information which must be published and available (through the registrar) to the general public.

A company cannot benefit from the relevant exemptions for individual accounts in respect of any accounting reference period if it is (or was at any time within the financial year to which the accounts relate):

(1)   a public company;

(2)   a banking company or insurance company;

(3)   an authorised person under the Financial Services Act 1986;

(4)   a member of an ineligible group (which is one in which any of its members is a public company, banking company, insurance company or authorised under the Financial Services Act 1986).

An eligible company or group will qualify for treatment as a small or medium sized company (or group) if it satisfies any two or more of the qualifying conditions for both the current and the previous year. (*Note*. Once qualified, a company will not cease to be so, unless the conditions are not satisfied for two successive years.)

The conditions (which relate to company size) in respect of each company category may be summarised in tabular form.

Category	Turnover	Gross assets	Average employees per week
Small company	Up to £2.8m	Up to £1.4m	Up to 50
Medium company	Up to £11.2m	Up to £5.6m	Up to 250

(ii)   The directors of a company which is entitled to the benefit of a small company exemption (for individual accounts in respect of any accounting reference period) may file, with the registrar of companies, 'abbreviated accounts' (formerly 'modified accounts') as follows:

(1)   a summarised balance sheet;

(2)   notes only on accounting policies, fixed assets (aggregate movements for tangible and intangible fixed assets and fixed asset investments), share capital, allotments, debts, foreign currency translation and corresponding amounts;

(3)   no profit and loss account;

(4)   no information on directors' emoluments or auditors' remuneration;

(5)   no directors' report.

(c)   The directors' report is expected to contain the following information.

(i)   A fair review of the development of the business of the company and its subsidiary undertakings during that year and of their position at the end of it. No guidance is given on the form of the review, nor the amount of detail it should go into.

(ii)   The amount, if any, recommended for dividend.

(iii)   The principal activities of the company and its subsidiaries in the course of the financial year, and any significant changes in those activities during the year.

(iv)   Where significant, an estimate should be provided of the difference between the book value of land held as fixed assets and its realistic market value.

(v)   Information about the company's policy for the employment for disabled persons.

(vi)   The names of persons who were directors at any time during the financial year.

(vii)   For those persons who were directors at the year end, the interests of each (or of their spouse or infant children) in shares or debentures of the company or subsidiaries:

(1)   at the beginning of the year, or at the date of appointment as director, if this occurred during the year; and

(2)   at the end of the year.

If a director has no such interests at either date, this fact must be disclosed. (The information in (e) may be shown as a note to the accounts instead of in the directors' report.)

(viii)   Political and charitable contributions made, if these together exceeded more than £200 in the year, giving:

(1)   separate totals for political contributions and charitable contributions; and

   (2)   the amount of each separate political contribution exceeding £200, and the name of the recipient.

Wholly owned British subsidiaries are exempt from requirement (g) because the information will be disclosed in the directors' report of the holding company.

   (ix)   Particulars of any important events affecting the company or any of its subsidiaries which have occurred since the end of the financial year (significant 'post-balance sheet events').

   (x)   An indication of likely future developments in the business of the company and of its subsidiaries.

   (xi)   An indication of the activities (if any) of the company and its subsidiaries in the field of research and development.

   (xii)   Particulars of purchases (if any) of its own shares by the company during the year, including reasons for the purchase.

   (xiii)   Particulars of other acquisitions of its own shares during the year (perhaps because shares were forfeited or surrendered, or because its shares were acquired by the company's nominee or with its financial assistance).

   (xiv)   Details of any measures taken by the company directed at increasing employee participation and information.

   (xv)   Details of the company's creditor payment policy.

10   D'URBERVILLE

SCHEDULE OF MOTOR VEHICLES
FOR THE YEARS ENDED 31 DECEMBER 19X5, 19X6, 19X7

		£'000
19X5		
Cost:	At 1 January 19X5	540
	Additions	147
	Disposals	70
	At 31 December 19X5	617
Accumulated depreciation:	At 1 January 19X5	130
	Disposals (W1)	50
	Charge for year 25% × (617 − (130 − 50))	134
	At 31 December 19X5	214
Net book value at 31 December 19X5		403

		£'000
19X6		
Cost:	At 1 January 19X6	617
	Additions*	252
	Disposals	110
	At 31 December 19X6	759
Accumulated depreciation:	At 1 January 19X6	214
	Disposals (W2)	68
	Charge for year 25% (759 − (214 − 68))	153
	At 31 December 19X6	299
Net book value at 31 December 19X6		460

Note. The acquisitions in 19X6 are capitalised at cash price less trade discount (for cash purchases), plus delivery costs £(300 − 60 + 12) = £252,000.

		£'000
19X7		
Cost:	At 1 January 19X7	759
	Additions**	375
	Disposals	75
	At 31 December 19X7	1,059

19X7		£'000
Accumulated depreciation:	At 1 January 19X7	299
	Disposals (W3) (1,059 – (299 – 43)) × 25%	43
	Charge for year 25%	201
	At 31 December 19X7	457
Net book value at 31 December 19X5		602

** *Note.* The acquisitions in 19X7 are capitalised at cash price less trade discount (for cash purchase) plus delivery cost: £(450 – 90 + 15) = £375.

Workings

1   *Accumulated depreciation on 19X5 disposals*

Vehicles acquired in 19X0:

		£
19X0	25% × £30,000	7,500
19X1	25% × £(30,000 – 7,500)	5,625
19X2	25% × £(30,000 – (7,500 + 5,625))	4,219
19X3	25% × £(30,000 – (7,500 + 5,625 + 4,219))	3,164
19X4	25% × £(30,000 – (7,500 + 5,625 + 4,219 + 3,164))	2,373
Total		22,881

Vehicles acquired in 19X1:

		£
19X1	25% × £40,000	10,000
19X2	25% × £(40,000 – 10,000)	7,500
19X3	25% × £(40,000 – (10,000 + 7,500))	5,625
19X4	25% × £(40,000 – (10,000 + 8,500 + 5,625))	4,219
Total		27,344

Total accumulated depreciation on disposals: £(22,881 + 27,344) = £50,225.

2   *Accumulated depreciation on 19X6 disposals*

Vehicles acquired in 19X2:

		£
19X2	25% × £45,000	11,250
19X3	25% × £(45,000 – 11,250)	8,438
19X4	25% × £(45,000 – (11,250 + 8,438))	6,328
19X5	25% × £(45,000 – (11,250 + 8,438 + 6,328))	4,746
Total		30,762

Vehicles acquired in 19X3:

		£
19X3	25% × £65,000	16,250
19X4	25% × £(65,000 – 16,250)	12,188
19X5	25% × £(65,000 – (16,250 + 12,188))	9,141
Total		37,579

Total accumulated depreciation on 19X6 disposals £(30,762 + 37,579) = £68,341

3   *Accumulated depreciation on 19X7 disposals*

Vehicles acquired in 19X2:

		£
19X4	25% × £75,000	18,750
19X5	25% × £(75,000 – 18,750)	14,063
19X6	25% × £(75,000 – (18,750 + 14,063))	10,547
Total		43,360

11 **BLECO**

Notes

(a) Under the original SSAP 13, development expenditure written off could not be reinstated if it subsequently met the SSAP's criteria for capitalisation. The revised SSAP permits such expenditure to be reinstated.

(b) Project D371 is contract WIP, not a development project, because costs are being reimbursed in full and so Bleco is taking no risk itself.

(c) SSAP 13 requires that depreciation on assets used in R & D should be included in the expenditure on R & D to be disclosed and it should also be disclosed separately in accordance with SSAP 12.

(d) It is possible (but not obligatory) to capitalise depreciation, just like the other expenses deferred.

(e) Common errors in this question include capitalisation of pure and applied research projects, omission of opening balances, treating the contract WIP as an intangible asset and taking individual expenses to P & L rather than a global figure for R & D written off.

BLECO PLC
PROFIT AND LOSS ACCOUNT
FOR THE YEAR ENDED 31 AUGUST 19X1 (EXTRACT)

	£
Included in cost of sales (or other appropriate category):	
Research and development costs written off (W2)	329,340
Amortisation of development costs (W1)	33,050
	362,390

BLECO PLC
BALANCE SHEET AS AT 31 AUGUST 19X1 (EXTRACTS)

	£
Fixed assets	
Intangible assets	
Deferred development expenditure	652,340
Current assets	
Stocks	
Contract work in progress	14,030
Profit and loss account	
At 1 September 19X0:	
As previously reported	X
Development expenditure previously written off,	
now reinstated	47,830
As restated	X + 47,830

Workings

1   *Deferred development expenditure/long-term contract*

	D369 £	D368 £	D363 £	D367 £	Total £	D371 £
Brought forward	-		198,300	242,700	488,830	-
Reinstated		47,830				
Current year expenditure						
Staff costs	34,070	16,480	-	2,090	52,640	27,500
Materials	1,560	410	-	340	2,310	3,400
Other direct expenses	640	230	-	170	1,040	710
Production overheads	6,980	4,650	-	3,540	15,170	6,420
Depreciation (W3):						
buildings	31,000	-	-	-	31,000	
equipment	94,400	-	-	-	94,400	-
	168,650	21,770	-	6,140	196,560	
Reimbursed						(24,000)
Contract WIP						14,030
Amortisation ($^1/_6$)	-		33,050	-	33,050	
Carried forward	168,650	69,600	165,250	248,840	652,340	

2   *Expenditure to be written off*

	Total £	PR119 £	AR187 £	AR204 £	D370 £	Unallocated £
Staff costs	110,760	35,100	27,300	15,260	29,800	3,300
Materials	8,340	810	520	290	2,650	4,070
Direct expenses	3,570	250	210	180	690	2,240
Production overheads	20,870	1,240	3,600	2,950	6,010	7,070
	143,540	37,400	31,630	18,680	39,150	16,680
Sales/admin o'hds	76,200					76,200
Market research	55,600					55,600
Depreciation:						
buildings (W3)	20,000		20,000		-	
equipment (W3)	34,000		34,000		-	
	329,340	37,400	85,630	18,680	39,150	148,480

3   *Depreciation*

	AR187 £	D369 £
Buildings		
£200,000 × 10%	20,000	
£310,000 × 10%		31,000
Equipment		
£170,000 × 20%	34,000	
£472,000 × 20%		94,400

12   SOAP

> *Tutorial note.* The key to avoiding getting muddled in part (b) of this question is to set out the proformas (including those for workings) and present your workings logically. Remember, only 11 out of a total of 30 marks are available for the computational aspects of this question.

(a)   The definition of a long term contract in SSAP 9 *Stocks and long term contracts* generally applies to contracts which last for more than one year, but does not exclude contracts of less than one year which fall into different accounting periods. The relevant wording of the definition is as follows.

> '(A long term contract is) one where the time taken substantially to complete the contract is such that the contract activity falls into different accounting periods. A contract that is required to be accounted for as long term . . . will usually extend for a period exceeding one year . . . Some contracts with a shorter duration than one year

should be accounted for as long term contracts if they are sufficiently material . . . that not to record turnover and attributable profit would lead to distortion'.

The accounting treatment adopted by Soap plc for the shorter contracts would appear to be consistent with this SSAP 9 definition. It is also consistent with the treatment of the other contracts. It is important, however, that the same accounting treatment is used every year, even if the results are not as favourable, unless there are good reasons for changing it.

(b)   SOAP PLC
      PROFIT AND LOSS ACCOUNT
      FOR THE YEAR ENDED 31 DECEMBER 19X7 (EXTRACT)

	£'000
Turnover	5,680
Cost of sales	(5,165)
Gross profit on long term contracts	515

SOAP PLC
BALANCE SHEET AS AT 31 DECEMBER 19X7

	£'000
Current assets	
Stock	
Long term contract balances	137.5
Debtors	
Amounts recoverable on contracts	1,050
Current liabilities	
Payments on account	(350)

Workings

1   *Archers plc*

	£
Costs incurred to date	47,500
Machine write-off (20,000 – ($^6/_{12}$ × 10,000))	15,000
	62,500
Less cost of sales (W4)	(40,000)
Long term contract balance	22,500
Excess of payments on account over turnover (40 – 30)	(10,000)
	12,500

2   *Neighbours Ltd*

	£'000
Costs incurred to date	1,800
Cost of sales (W4)	(1,250)
Long term contract balance	550
Less excess of payments on account over turnover (2,500 – 1,600)	(900)
Current liability	(350)

3   *Emmerdale plc*

	£'000
Costs incurred to date	4,000
Cost of sales (W4)	(3,875)
Long term contract balance	125
Turnover (W4)	4,050
Payments on account	3,000
Amounts recoverable on contracts	1,050

4   *Profit and loss account*

	Emmerdale £'000		Archers £'000		Neighbours £'000	Total £'000
Turnover						
(45% × 9)	4,050	(20% × 150)	30	(25% × 6.4)	1,600	5,680
Cost of sales						
(45% × 7.5)	3,375	(20% × 120 – 20*)	20	(25% × 5)	1,250	4,645
Additional costs						
(8 – 7.5)	500		20			520
	(3,875)		(40)		(1,250)	
						(5,165)
Profit (loss) on						
long term contracts	175		(10)		350	515

* Note. Because the machine is being written off in one year, its total cost, rather than a percentage, is allocated to that year.

5   *Balance sheet*

	Emmerdale £'000	Archers £'000	Neighbours £'000	Total £'000
Current assets				
Stocks				
Long term contract				
balances	125 (W3)	12.5 (W1)		137.5
Debtors				
Amounts recoverable				
on contracts	1,050 (W3)			1,050
Current liabilities				
Payments on account			(350) (W2)	(350)

(c)   The objectivity of the valuer of a long-term contract is one of the factors that has to be considered under SAS 520 *Using the work of an expert.* However SAS 520 does not prohibit valuation by directors and thus in theory auditors could accept valuation of some contracts by the independent surveyor, some contracts by the directors.

In deciding whether or not to accept director valuation the auditor should consider the following factors.

(i)   The directors could use the certification as a means of profit manipulation. The auditor should therefore consider the results of their inherent risk assessment, particularly whether the directors might be particularly motivated to distort profits.

(ii)   The basis used by the directors and the independent surveyor should be consistent. The following principles should be followed.

(1)   The basis of valuation should be in accordance with industry practice.

(2)   The basis should be used consistently over time, and should be consistent over different contracts.

(3)   The basis should be reasonable having regard to Soap's business and the nature of the contract.

It may be easier for the auditor to accept the directors' valuation if the directors certified the smaller contracts, and the independent valuer certified the more material ones.

(d)   The audit work that be carried out would be as follows.

(i)   *Details*

The auditor should have details of all material long-term contracts on file, including type of contract, price, terms of payment, other relevant terms and details to date.

(ii)   *Completeness*

Check whether previous years' long-term work in progress has been brought forward, and is either still in progress or has been completed.

(iii)   *Completed contracts*

Confirm the contracts have been completed, invoices have been correctly posted and all remaining costs have been transferred to cost of sales.

(iv)   *Valuation*

(1)   Verify direct costs with invoices and check that elements of direct costs are included consistently.

(2)   Review overhead allocations, checking they are based on actual activity and are in accordance with SSAP 9.

(3)   Consider whether the valuations made can be relied on, considering:

- independence and experience of valuer(s);
- information used;
- basis used; and
- assumptions made.

(4)   Consider whether calculation of attributable profit is reasonable, taking account of:

- terms of contract;
- valuation used;
- carrying value; and
- whether the outcome of the contract can be assessed with reasonable certainty and whether the policy appears to be prudent.

(5)   Consider whether provisions for long-term losses are reasonable, taking account of:

- likely future costs; and
- penalties.

(6)   Consider the likelihood of future claims or liabilities on contracts.

(v)   *Existence*

Verify contracts in progress by physical inspection.

(vi)   *Cut-off*

Compare costs in contract records around the year-end with invoices to ascertain whether costs are included in the correct period.

(vii)   *Receipts*

Check all amounts that should have been billed have been billed. Confirm receipts of monies to cash records.

(viii)   *Analytical review*

Consider previous year's contracts, particularly profits taken and whether in retrospect amounts taken were reasonable.

(ix)   *Presentation*

(1)   Ensure that disclosures of stock and debtors are in accordance with SSAP 9.

(2)   Confirm that contract payments have treated in accordance with SSAP 9.

(3)   Ascertain whether long-term contract balances equal costs incurred less amounts transferred to cost of sales less foreseeable losses less contract receipts not matched with turnover.

13   CORAX

(a)

CORPORATION TAX (19X5) ACCOUNT

	£		£
Bank	16,300	Balance b/f	16,300

CORPORATION TAX (19X6) ACCOUNT

	£		£
Profit and loss a/c over provision	1,200	Balance b/f	5,000
Balance c/d	3,800		
	5,000		5,000

CORPORATION TAX (19X7) ACCOUNT

	£		£
ACT a/c	5,250	Profit and loss a/c	36,000
Balance c/d	30,750		
	36,000		36,000

ACT ACCOUNT

	£		£
Bank ($1/4 \times 700,000 \times £0.03$)	5,250	Corporation tax 19X7	7,000
		Deferred taxation - ACT on	
		proposed dividend	
Balance c/d	9,625	($1/4 \times 700,000 \times £0.045$)	7,875
	14,875		14,875

DEFERRED TAXATION ACCOUNT

	£		£
ACT on proposed dividend	7,875	Balance b/f	29,400
		Profit and loss a/c	
Balance c/d	28,525	(increase in provision)	7,000
	36,400		36,400

(b) PROFIT AND LOSS ACCOUNT
FOR THE YEAR ENDED 31 DECEMBER 19X7 (EXTRACT)

Note		£
	Profit for the year on ordinary activities	100,000
1	Tax on profit for the year	(41,800)
	Profit for the financial year	58,200
2	Dividends paid and proposed	(52,500)
	Retained profit for the year	5,700
	Unappropriated profits brought forward*	43,000
	Unappropriated profits carried forward	48,700

* Movements on the profit and loss account may be shown separately in a note to the accounts.

BALANCE SHEET AS AT 31 DECEMBER 19X7 (EXTRACT)

Note		£
	Creditors: amounts falling due within one year	
3	Other creditors including taxation	
	(£3,800 + £30,750 + £7,875 + £31,500)	73,925
	Provisions for liabilities and charges	
4	Taxation, including deferred taxation	28,525
	Capital and reserves	
	Called up share capital - 700,000 ordinary shares of 50p each,	
	allotted and fully paid	350,000
	Profit and loss account	48,700

The notes referred to in the left margin form an integral part of these accounts.

NOTES ON THE ACCOUNTS (EXTRACTS)

		£
1	The tax on profit for the year comprises:	
	UK corporation tax (provided at X% on taxable profits for the year)	36,000
	Less over provision on profits of previous year	1,200
		34,800
	Transfer to deferred taxation account	7,000
		41,800

2	Dividends for the year on the allotted ordinary share capital are:	£
	Paid: 3p on 700,000 shares	21,000
	Proposed: 4.5p on 700,000 shares	31,500
		52,500

3   The figure for creditors includes a proposed dividend of £31,500 payable on the ordinary shares.

4	Deferred tax balance at 31 December 19X6	£ 29,400
	Charge for the year	7,000
		36,400
	Less ACT on proposed dividend	7,875
	Balance at 31 December 19X7	28,525

14   CHER

> *Tutorial note.* The calculations involved in this question are not particularly complicated. However, a large number of marks are available for explanations and understanding. Part (d), particularly requires you to think very carefully about the implications of merger accounting for EPS.

(a)   Earnings per share (EPS) is one of the most frequently quoted statistics in financial analysis. Because of the widespread use of the price earnings (P/E) ratio as a yardstick for investment decisions, it became increasingly important.

It seems that reported and forecast EPS can, through the P/E ratio, have a significant effect on a company's share price. Thus, a share price might fall if it looks as if EPS is going to be low. This is not very rational, as EPS can depend on many, often subjective, assumptions used in preparing a historical statement, namely the profit and loss account. It does not necessarily bear any relation to the value of a company, and of its shares. Nevertheless, the market is sensitive to EPS.

EPS has also served as a means of assessing the stewardship and management role performed by company directors and managers. Remuneration packages might be linked to EPS growth, thereby increasing the pressure on management to improve EPS. The danger of this, however, is that management effort goes into distorting results to produce a favourable EPS.

The ASB believed that undue emphasis was being placed on EPS, and that this led to simplistic interpretations of financial performance. Consequently, in issuing FRS 3 *Reporting financial performance*, the ASB attempted to de-emphasise EPS by requiring it to be calculated after extraordinary items. Because of this, and other changes, EPS is now very volatile and, arguably less useful for analysis; many companies are providing additional EPS figures, prepared on what they see as a more meaningful basis.

(b)   CHER (HOLDINGS) PLC
EARNINGS PER SHARE FOR THE YEAR ENDED 30 JUNE 19X4

Earnings		£460,000
Number of shares		
In issue for full year		800,000
In issue 1.7.X3 - 30.9.X3		
$200,000 \times {}^{3}/_{12} \times 60\%$	30,000	
In issue 1.10.X3 - 30.6.X4		
$200,000 \times {}^{9}/_{12} \times 100\%$	150,000	
		180,000
		980,000

Earnings per share $= \dfrac{460,000}{980,000} = 46.9\text{p}$

(c)   (i)   *Theoretical ex rights price per share*

	£
Value of 4 shares before rights issue (4 × 1.90)	7.60
Value of 1 rights issue share	1.30
Value of 5 shares after rights issue	8.90

Theoretical ex rights price $\dfrac{8.90}{5}$ = £1.78

Earnings

£1,310,000

Number of shares in issue
1.7.X4 - 28.2.X5

$1,000,000 \times \dfrac{8}{12} \times \dfrac{1.90}{1.78}$ 711,610

1.3.X5 - 30.6.X5
$1,250,000 \times {}^{4}/_{12}$ 416,667

1,128,277

EPS $\dfrac{1,310,000}{1,128,277}$ = 116.1p

Revised EPS calculation for 19X4

$46.9p \times \dfrac{1.78}{1.90}$ = 43.9p

CHER (HOLDINGS) PLC
EARNINGS PER SHARE FOR THE YEAR ENDED 30 JUNE

	19X5	19X4
	116.1p	43.9p

(ii)   A rights issue is a popular method through which public companies are able to access the stock market for further capital. Under the terms of such an issue, existing shareholders are given the opportunity to acquire further shares in the company on a pro-rata basis to their existing shareholdings.

The 'rights' shares will usually be offered at a discount to the market price. In such cases, the issue is equivalent to a bonus issue combined with an issue at full market price. Bonus issues are treated as though they have been in issue for the whole year and are also taken into account in the previous year's EPS calculation to give a comparable result. Appendix 1 to SSAP 3 states that it is necessary to adjust the number of shares in issue before the rights issue to reflect the bonus element inherent in the issue. The notes to the financial statements should preferably refer to the adjustments made to the comparative EPS figure to reflect the bonus element of the rights issue.

The bonus element of the rights issue is given by the following fraction, sometimes referred to as the *bonus fraction*.

$$\frac{\text{Actual cum rights price on last day of quotation cum rights}}{\text{Theoretical ex rights price}}$$

The 'cum rights price' is the *actual* price at which the shares are quoted inclusive of the right to take up the future shares under the rights issue.

The 'ex rights price' is the *theoretical* price at which the shares would be quoted, other stock market factors apart, after the rights issue shares have been issued.

In order to calculate earnings per share with a rights issue, the shares are time apportioned before and after the date of the rights issue. The number of shares is calculated in two stages as follows.

Before rights issue

Number of shares before rights issue	× Bonus fraction ×	Fraction of year before rights issue

After rights issue

Number of shares after rights issue × Fraction of year after rights issue

The two figures produced by the above calculations are added together to give the denominator for the fraction required in calculating earnings per share.

When calculating the revised earnings per share for the previous year, the latter has to be adjusted to take account of the bonus element by multiplying it by the following

$$\frac{\text{Theoretical ex rights price}}{\text{Actual cum rights}}$$

This makes the previous year's figure comparable with that of the current year.

(d) *Current year*

Earnings	£1,520,000

Number of shares		
As at 1 July 19X5	1,250,000	
2 Sonny for 1 Cher	× 2	2,500,000

$$\text{EPS} = \frac{1,520,000}{2,500,000} = 60.8\text{p}$$

Note. We are told in the question that the principles of merger accounting have been adopted. This means that the shares in issue at the end of the year are assumed to have been in issue for the whole of the year. There is therefore no need to time apportion as we had to with the rights issue. The previous year's EPS figure will have to be adjusted to reflect the number of shares deemed to have been in issue in that year, ie twice as many as were in fact in issue.

Previous year

EPS = 116.1p × ½ = 58.05p

SONNY (HOLDINGS) PLC
EARNINGS PER SHARE FOR THE YEAR ENDED 30 JUNE

	19X6	*19X5*
	60.8p	58.05p

15   SPICE

(a) SPICE PLC
CASH FLOW STATEMENT
FOR THE YEAR ENDED 31 MARCH 19X6

Reconciliation of operating profit to net cash inflow from operating activities

	£m
Operating profit	280
Depreciation	76
Profit on sale of fixed asset (42 − 38)	(4)
Decrease in stocks	30
Increase in debtors	(40)
Increase in creditors (424 − 254)	170
Premium on cancellation of preference shares 40 × 20p	
to be included in finance costs	8
	520

CASH FLOW STATEMENT

	£m
Net cash inflow from operating activities	520
Returns on investments and servicing of finance (note 1)	(4)
Taxation (W1)	(46)
Capital expenditure (note 1)	(152)
	318
Equity dividends paid (W3)	(48)
	270
Management of liquid resources (note 1)	(160)
	110
Financing (note 1)	(86)
Increase in cash	24

Reconciliation of cash flow to movement in net debt (note 2)

	£m	£m
Increase in cash in the period	24	
Cash inflow from increase in finance lease	36	
Cash used to repurchase debentures	40	
Cash used to increase liquid resources	160	
Change in net debt resulting from cash flows		260
New finance lease		(56)
Movement in net debt in the period		204
Net debt at 1 April 19X5		(168)
Net funds at 31 March 19X6		36

NOTES TO THE CASH FLOW STATEMENT

1   *Gross cash flows*

	£m	£m
Returns on investments and servicing of finance		
Interest received (6 + 4 – 2)	8	
Interest paid (14 + 4 – 6 – 6)	(6)	
Interest element of finance lease	(6)	
		(4)
Capital expenditure		
Purchase of tangible fixed assets (W2)	(194)	
Sale of tangible fixed assets	42	
		(152)
Management of liquid resources		
Purchase of short term investments	(160)	
		(160)
Financing		
Issue of share capital	20	
Share premium	20	
Cost of share capital issue	(2)	
Cancellation of preference shares	(40)	
Premium on cancellation of preference shares	(8)	
Repurchase of debentures	(40)	
Capital element of finance lease (W4)	(36)	
		(86)

2   *Analysis of changes in net debt*

	At 1 April 19X5	Cash flows	Other changes	At 31 March 19X6
	£m	£m	£m	£m
Loan notes repayable on demand (190 – 160)	-	30		30
Cash	42	(30)		12
Bank overdraft	(40)	24		(16)
		24		
Debt due within one year	-	-	-	-
Debt due after one year				
Debentures	(80)	40	-	(40)
Obligations under finance leases	(90)	36	(56)	(110)
Current asset investments	-	160	-	160
	(168)	260	(56)	36

Workings

1 *Taxation*

TAX

	£m		£m
Cash paid (bal fig)	46	B/d 1.4.X5	
C/d 31.3.X6		Corporation tax	20
Corporation tax	32	ACT	4
ACT	2	Deferred tax	16
Deferred tax	24	P&L charge	64
	104		104

2 *Purchase of tangible fixed assets*

TANGIBLE FIXED ASSETS

	£m		£m
Bal b/d 1.4.X5	400	Depreciation	76
Finance leases	56	Disposals at NBV	38
Revaluations	14	Bal c/d 31.3.X6	550
Cash purchases (bal fig)	194		
	664		664

3 *Dividends*

DIVIDENDS

	£m		£m
Cash paid (bal fig)	48	Balance b/d 1.4.X5	16
Bal c/d 31.3.X6	8	P&L charge	40
	56		56

4 *Capital element of finance lease*

OBLIGATIONS UNDER FINANCE LEASES

	£m		£m
Capital repayment (bal fig)	36	Bal b/d 1.4.X5 (3 + 42)	90
Bal c/d 31.3.X6 (5 + 50)	110	Additions	56
	146		146

(b) *Movement on share capital and reserves*

	Ordinary £m	Preference £m	Share premium £m	Capital redemption reserve £m	Revaluation reserve £m	Profit and loss account £m
Balance at 1.4.X5	180	40	70	-	-	162
Issues of shares for cash	20		18			
Bonus issue	20			(20)		
Redemption		(40)				
Transfer to CRR				40		(40)
Revaluation					14	
Profit for year						208
Dividends						(40)
Balance at 31.4.X6	220	-	88	20	14	290

(c) Under the direct method, the operating element of the cash flow statement is shown as follows.

	£m
Operating activities	
Cash received from customers	X
Cash payments to suppliers	(X)
Cash paid to and on behalf of employees	(X)
Other cash payments	(X)
Net cash flow from operating activities	X

The direct method is, in effect, an analysis of the cash book. The information it shows is not found elsewhere in the financial statements and it may be useful in assessing future cash flows relating to the items in question. It can also be argued in favour of the direct method that the indirect method does not provide new information and is not a significant improvement on the old source and applications of funds statement required under SSAP 10.

There are problems with the direct method, however. Many companies might find it difficult to collect the required information. The cash book may need to be re-analysed to collate results from different cash sources. A further problem is that the figures in the cash book generally include VAT. The indirect method is easier as it draws on figures which can be obtained from the financial statements fairly easily.

FRS 1 (revised) does not require the direct method, and in practice it is rarely used. Marks & Spencer is an example of a company which has opted for the direct method, possibly because the nature of its business is such that its information systems collect the information in any event. It could be argued that *all* companies ought to monitor their cash flows carefully enough on an ongoing basis to be able to use the direct method at minimal extra cost.

16   PENSION COSTS

(a)   (i)

Year	Funding £m	Profit & loss charge £m	∴ Balance sheet provision £m
1	-	0.6	0.6
2	-	0.6	1.2
3	-	0.6	1.8
4	-	0.6	2.4
5	1	0.6	2.0
6	1	0.6	1.6
7	1	0.6	1.2
8	1	0.6	0.8
9	1	0.6	0.4
10	1	0.6	-
	6	6.0	

Funding = cash paid into the scheme.
The profit and loss charge is the £6 million spread evenly over 10 years.
The balance sheet accruals is the balancing figure.

In other words, the profit and loss charge is as follows.

	£m
Normal contribution	1.0
Less the experience variation spread over the life of the employees	(0.4)
	0.6

(ii)

Year	Funding £m	Profit & loss charge £m	∴ Balance sheet prepayment £m
1	5	1.4	3.6
2	1	1.4	3.2
3	1	1.4	2.8
4	1	1.4	2.4
5	1	1.4	2.0
6	1	1.4	1.6
7	1	1.4	1.2
8	1	1.4	0.8
9	1	1.4	0.4
10	1	1.4	-
	14	14.0	

Profit and loss charge is £14 million spread over 10 years.

OR

	£m
Normal contribution	1.0
Plus variation $\dfrac{£4m}{10}$	(0.4)
	$\overline{1.4}$

(b) In (i) above, at the end of year 1 the company still has an over-funded pension scheme but the balance sheet is showing a £0.6m provision.

Unsophisticated readers of the financial statements might think the contributions are in arrears. A suggestion is that it is reclassified out of provisions and into deferred income.

The ASB has been urged to review this aspect of the SSAP.

If we look at an example of an under-funded scheme (as in (ii) above), the same principle emerges. In this example a company which has an under-funded scheme ends up with a balance sheet asset. This could be reclassified as a deferred cost.

17   GROUP ACCOUNTS

The object of annual accounts is to help shareholders exercise control over their company by providing information about how its affairs have been conducted. The shareholders of a holding company would not be given sufficient information from the accounts of the holding company on its own, because not enough would be known about the nature of the assets, income and profits of all the subsidiary companies in which the holding company has invested. The primary purpose of group accounts is to provide a true and fair view of the position and earnings of the holding company group as a whole, from the standpoint of the shareholders in the holding company.

A number of arguments have been put forward, however, which argue that group accounts have certain limitations.

(a) Group accounts may be misleading.

    (i)   The solvency (liquidity) of one company may hide the insolvency of another.

    (ii)   The profit of one company may conceal the losses of another.

    (iii)   They imply that group companies will meet each others' debts (this is certainly not true: a parent company may watch creditors of an insolvent subsidiary go unpaid without having to step in).

(b) There may be some difficulties in defining the group or 'entity' of companies, although the Companies Act 1989 has removed many of the grey areas here.

(c) Where a group consists of widely diverse companies in different lines of business, a set of group accounts may obscure much important detail unless supplementary information about each part of the group's business is provided.

18   ARLENE AND AMANDA

Stage 1. Amanda Ltd has accounted for a proposed dividend of £10,000, but Arlene plc has not yet accounted for its share of the dividend receivable. Arlene's draft balance sheet is therefore adjusted as follows.

		£	£
DEBIT	Dividends receivable (90% × £10,000)	9,000	
CREDIT	Revenue reserve		9,000

The adjusted balance on Arlene's revenue reserve is £199,000.

Stage 2. There are no current accounts to be agreed.

Stage 3. There are two part-cancelling items: Amanda Ltd's share capital and the dividend receivable/payable.

Stage 4. Minority interests

	£
Ordinary share capital (10% × 150,000)	15,000
Revenue reserves (10% × 99,000)	9,900
Capital reserves (10% × 15,000)	1,500
	26,400

Stage 5

Goodwill

	£	£
Cost of investment		190,000
Share of net assets acquired as represented by:		
Ordinary share capital	150,000	
Revenue reserves on acquisition	20,000	
Capital reserves on acquisition	10,000	
	180,000	
Group share 90%		162,000
Goodwill		28,000

Consolidated revenue reserve

	£
Arlene plc (adjusted balance)	199,000
Share of Amanda Ltd's post acquisition reserves	
(99,000 – 20,000) × 90%	71,100
	270,100

Consolidated capital reserve

	£
Arlene plc	60,000
Share of Amanda's post-acquisition reserve	
(15,000 – 10,000) × 90%	4,500
	64,500

ARLENE PLC
CONSOLIDATED BALANCE SHEET AS AT 31 DECEMBER 19X5

	£	£
Intangible fixed assets: goodwill		28,000
Tangible fixed assets		560,000
Current assets		
Stocks	125,000	
Debtors	150,000	
Bank and cash	56,000	
	331,000	
Current liabilities		
Trade creditors	127,000	
Proposed dividend to members of Arlene plc	30,000	
Minority proposed dividend (10% × £10,000)	1,000	
	158,000	
Net current assets		173,000
Total assets less current liabilities		761,000
Capital and reserves		
Ordinary shares of £1 each		400,000
Reserves		
Revenue reserves	270,100	
Capital reserves	64,500	
		334,600
		734,600
Minority interest		26,400
		761,000

19 HAND

Note. This is quite a complex question which brings together a number of complications. It is important in dealing with such questions to be methodical in following the recommended five-stage approach.

Stage 1. All dividends have been accounted for by both companies, but Hand Ltd has treated its share of Finger Ltd's 19X0 dividend incorrectly. The dividend comes from pre-acquisition profits of Finger Ltd and should be credited not to profit and loss account, but to the 'investment in subsidiary' account. The following adjustment is therefore necessary to Hand Ltd's draft balance sheet.

DEBIT	Revenue reserves (40/60 × £6,000)	£4,000
CREDIT	Investment in Finger Ltd	£4,000

Hand Ltd now has a balance of £(90,000 - 4,000) = £86,000 on revenue reserve, while its investment in Finger Ltd is stated at cost less amounts written down £(50,000 - 4,000) = £46,000.

Stage 2. The current accounts differ by £2,000, being cash in transit from Finger Ltd to Hand Ltd. £2,000 cash in transit will appear in the consolidated balance sheet as an asset.

Stage 3. The only cancelling items, apart from the current accounts, are Hand Ltd's investment in subsidiary and Finger Ltd's share capital. These will be dealt with in the goodwill calculation.

Stage 4

	£
Share capital ($^1/_3$ × £60,000)	20,000
Reserves ($^1/_3$ × £38,700)	12,900
Minority interest	32,900

Goodwill	£	£
Cost of investment		50,000
Less dividend from pre-acquisition profits		4,000
		46,000
Share of net assets acquired, as represented by		
Share capital	60,000	
Reserves (W)	30,000	
	90,000	
Group share ($^2/_3$)		60,000
Capital reserve		14,000

Reserves	£
Hand Ltd (see stage 1)	86,000
Share of Finger Ltd's post acquisition retained reserves	
£(38,700 –30,000) × $^2/_3$	5,800
Revenue reserve	91,800

Working: reserves of Finger Ltd

	£	£
Pre-acquisition		
Balance at 31.12.X0	18,000	
Profit for 6 months to 30.6.X1 ($^6/_{12}$ × £18,000)	9,000	
Consolidation adjustment: revaluation surplus *	3,000	
		30,000
Post-acquisition		
Profit for 6 months to 31.12.X1 ($^6/_{12}$ × £18,000)	9,000	
Consolidation adjustment: increase in dep'n charge		
($^1/_5$ × £3,000 × $^6/_{12}$)*	(300)	
		8,700
		38,700

* These consolidation adjustments are necessary so that the assets of Finger Ltd are revalued to their fair value on acquisition.

HAND LIMITED
CONSOLIDATED BALANCE SHEET AS AT 31 DECEMBER 19X1

	£	£
Intangible fixed assets: goodwill		(14,000)
Tangible fixed assets		178,700
Current assets		
Sundry	257,000	
Cash in transit	2,000	
	259,000	
Current liabilities	199,000	
Net current assets		60,000
		224,700
Capital and reserves		
Ordinary shares of £1 each		100,000
Revenue reserve		91,800
		191,800
Minority interest		32,900
		224,700

20   WAR

> *Tutorial note.* This question may look intimidating because it involves an acquisition part of the way through the year, some FRS 7 issues and both the consolidated profit and loss account and balance sheet. It is, however, fairly straightforward. You should not have overlooked FRS 3 aspects in the consolidated profit and loss account.

(a)   FRS 7 *Fair values in acquisition accounting* states that quoted shares should be valued at market price on the date of acquisition. However, the standard acknowledges that the market price may be difficult to determine if it is unreliable because of an inactive market. In particular, where the shares are not quoted, there may be no suitable market. In such cases the value must be estimated using:

(i)   the value of similar quoted securities; or
(ii)   the present value of the cash flows of the shares; or
(iii)   any cash alternative which was offered; or
(iv)   the value of any underlying security into which there is an option to convert.

It may be necessary to undertake a valuation of the company in question should none of the above methods prove feasible.

(b)   WAR GROUP PLC
CONSOLIDATED BALANCE SHEET AS AT 30 JUNE 19X7

	£'000	£'000
Fixed assets		
Tangible assets (1,750 + 500)		2,250
Goodwill (W3)		151
		2,401
Current assets		
Stocks	600	
Debtors	451	
Cash at bank and in hand	299	
	1,350	
Creditors: amounts falling due within one year	(650)	
Net current assets		700
Total assets less current liabilities		3,101
Creditors: amounts falling due after one year		(1,225)
		1,876
Capital and reserves		
Ordinary share capital		750
Share premium (W6)		250
Profit and loss account (W5)		621
		1,621
Minority interests (equity) (W4)		255
		1,876

WAR GROUP PLC
CONSOLIDATED PROFIT AND LOSS ACCOUNT
FOR THE YEAR ENDED 30 JUNE 19X7

	£'000	£'000
Turnover		
Continuing operations	3,150	
Acquisitions ($^2/_{12}$) × 1,770)	295	
		3,445
Cost of sales		(1,788)
Gross profit		1,657
Distribution costs	638	
Administrative expenses (W7)	348	
		(986)
Operating profit		
Continuing operations	606	
Acquisitions	65	
		671
Interest payable		(75)
Profit on ordinary activities before taxation		596
Tax on profit on ordinary activities		(306)
Profit after tax		290
Minority interests (equity) (W8)		(11)
		279
Dividends paid		(38)
Retained profit for the financial year attributable to the group		241

Workings

1   *Revaluation surplus*

	£'000
Peace Ltd: tangible fixed assets at market value	500
Carrying value	350
Revaluation surplus	150

FRS 7 *Fair values in acquisition accounting* states that open market values should be used to value tangible fixed assets, and it is this figure which is compared with the carrying value here, rather than the net realisable value. The latter is lower because the costs of realisation are deducted. However, as the group does not intend to dispose of the asset, the market value is more appropriate.

2   *Pre-acquisition dividend*

Dividend paid by Peace to War: £42,000
Pre-acquisition element $^{10}/_{12}$ × £42,000 = £35,000

3   *Goodwill*

	£'000	£'000
Cost of investment		800
Less pre-acquisition dividend (W2)		(35)
		765
Share capital	100	
Share premium	150	
Revaluation surplus	150	
Profit and loss account		
Prior year: 450 – 165	285	
Current year: $^{10}/_{12}$ × 165	138	
	823	
Group share: 70%		576
Goodwill		189

4   *Minority interests (balance sheet)*

	£'000
Share capital	100
Share premium	150
Revaluation surplus	150
Profit and loss account	450
	850

MI = £850,000 × 30% = £255,000.

5   *Profit and loss account*

	£'000	£'000
War plc		625
Less goodwill written off ($189 \times {}^1/_5$)	38	
Less pre-acquisition dividend	35	
		(73)
		552
Add back issue costs		50
		602
Peace Ltd $165 \times {}^2/_{12} \times 70\%$		19
		621

6   *Share premium account*

	£'000
War plc	300
Less issue costs	(50)
	250

7   *Administrative expenses*

	£'000
War plc	325
Peace Ltd (${}^2/_{12} \times 210$)	35
Goodwill written off	38
	398
Less issue costs	(50)
	348

8   *Minority interests (p & l)*

$225 \times {}^2/_{12} \times 30\% = £11,250$

21   CHIGWELL

> *Tutorial note*. This question tested in detail your understanding of the differences between acquisition and merger accounting.
>
> The question does not, therefore, contain as many of the complications such as unrealised profit or intercompany sales, usually associated with consolidation questions. You would not have scored highly if you ignored some of the fundamental differences such as the treatment of goodwill.

(a)   CHIGWELL PLC
CONSOLIDATED PROFIT AND LOSS ACCOUNT
FOR THE YEAR ENDED 31 DECEMBER 19X2

	£'000
Group turnover ($80,946 + (17,194 \times {}^8/_{12}) + (3,420 \times {}^4/_{12})$)	93,549
Cost of sales and expenses ($62,184 + (13,592 \times {}^8/_{12}) + (2,560 \times {}^4/_{12})$)	72,099
Group operating profit	21,450
Share of operating profit in associate	143
Interest receivable ($120 + (50 \times {}^8/_{12})$)	153
Goodwill written off (W3)	(1,063)
Profit before tax	20,683
Taxation ($6,740 + (1,525 \times {}^8/_{12}) + (390 \times {}^4/_{12}) + (390 \times 25\% \times {}^8/_{12})$)	7,952
Profit after tax	12,731
Ordinary dividends	
Interim	550
Final	50
Preference dividend	12
Retained profit for the year	12,119

(b)   Of the group retained profit of £12,119,000

	£'000
Retained by Chigwell plc (W4)	10,495
Retained by Sharon plc (W4)	1,398
Retained by Tracy Ltd (W4)	226
	12,119

(c) CHIGWELL PLC
CONSOLIDATED PROFIT AND LOSS ACCOUNT
FOR THE YEAR ENDED 30 DECEMBER 19X2

	£
Turnover (80,946 + 17,194 + 3,420)	101,560
Cost of sales and expenses (62,184 + 13,592 + 2,560)	78,336
Operating profit	23,224
Interest receivable (120 + 50)	170
Profit in ordinary activities before taxation	23,394
Taxation (6,740 + 1,525 + 390)	8,655
Profit after tax	14,739
Interim dividend to outside interests (75% × 12)	9
Profit for the year	14,730
Ordinary dividends: interim	550
final	50
Preference dividend	12
Retained profit for the year	14,118

(d) Of the group retained profit of £14,118,000

	£'000
Retained by Chigwell plc	11,575
Retained by Sharon plc	2,091
Retained by Tracy Ltd	452
	14,118

(e) RECONCILIATION OF RETAINED PROFIT FIGURES

	£'000	£'000
Retained profit under acquisition method		12,119
Add goodwill		1,063
		13,182
Pre-acquisition profits to be included under merger accounting		
Sharon		
$^{4}/_{12} \times 2,127$	709	
Less pre-acquisition dividend (W2)	16	
		693
Tracy		
$^{8}/_{12} \times 75\% \times 452$		226
Add pre-acquisition dividend		17
		14,118

(f) INVESTMENT IN SUBSIDIARIES UNDER THE MERGER METHOD

	£'000	£'000
Investment using acquisition method		
Sharon	960	
Less pre-acquisition dividend	(16)	
		944
Tracy	280	
Cost of previous holding 280 × $^{25}/_{75}$	93	
Less pre-acquisition dividend	(1.5)	
		372
Add back pre-acquisition dividend		18
		1,334
Reserve (excess of market value of shares over nominal value)		
Sharon	573	
Tracy	80	
		(653)
Investment using merger method		681

Workings

1 *Group structure*

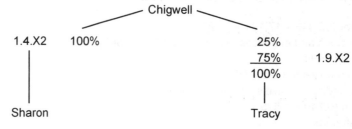

	Chigwell	
1.4.X2 100%		25%
		75% 1.9.X2
		100%
Sharon		Tracy

Subsidiary for $^8/_{12}$ months

Associate for $^8/_{12}$ months
Subsidiary for $^4/_{12}$ months

2 *Dividends receivable*

	Associated Co £'000	Subsidiary pre-acquisition £'000	Subsidiary post-acquisition £'000	Total £'000
From Sharon				
Interim				
$24 \times 100\% \times {}^4/_6$		16.0		16.0
$24 \times 100\% \times {}^2/_6$			8.0	8.0
Final				
$12 \times 100\% \times {}^6/_6$			12.0	12.0
	-	16.0	20.0	36.0
From Tracy				
Interim				
$12 \times 25\% \times {}^6/_6$	3.0			3.0
Final				
$6 \times 25\% \times {}^2/_6$	0.5			0.5
$6 \times 75\% \times {}^2/_6$		1.5		1.5
$6 \times 100\% \times {}^4/_6$			4.0	4.0
	3.5	1.5	4.0	9.0
Total	3.5	17.5	24.0	45.0

3 *Goodwill*

	£'000
Sharon	
Per question	986
Pre-acquisition dividends	
to be deducted from cost of investment (W2)	16
	970
Written off to P & L	(970)
	0

	£'000
Tracy	
Per question	95.0
Pre-acquisition dividends (W2)	1.5
	93.5
Written off to P & L	93.5
	0.0

∴ Total to be written off to P & L = £(970,000 + 93,500) = £1,063,500

4   *Profit retained by each company*

	£'000	£'000
Sharon		
Profit after tax ($^8/_{12} \times 2,127$)	1,418	
Less post acquisition dividends (W2)	20	
		1,398.0
Chigwell		
Retained profit	11,575.0	
Less pre-acquisition dividends	(17.5)	
Less goodwill	(1,063.0)	
		10,494.5
Retained by Tracy (bal. fig.)		226.0
		12,118.5

(g)   FRS 6 *Acquisitions and mergers* is more strict than the old SSAP 23 *Accounting for acquisitions and mergers*. The new FRS has heightened the requirements for merger accounting by concentrating on the *spirit* of the transactions, rather than on mechanical aspects such as levels of shareholding. The following criteria are set out in FRS 6 to determine whether a transaction is a merger.

Criterion 1

Neither party is portrayed, by either its management or any other party, as either acquirer or acquired.

Criterion 2

All parties take part in setting up a management structure and selecting personnel for the combined entity on the basis of consensus rather than purely by exercise of voting rights.

Criterion 3

The relative sizes of the parties are not so disparate that one party dominates the combined entity by virtue of its relative size.

Criterion 4

A substantial part of the consideration for equity shareholdings in each party will comprise equity shares; conversely, non-equity shares or equity shares with reduced voting rights will comprise only an 'immaterial' part of the consideration. This criterion also covers existing shareholdings.

> 'Where one of the combining entities has, within the period of two years before the combination acquired shares in another of the combining entities, the consideration for this acquisition should be taken into account in determining whether this criterion has been met.

Note that this criterion states in general terms what is laid out in the Companies Act 1985 in terms of specific shareholdings.

Criterion 5

No equity shareholders of any of the combining entities retains any material interest in the future performance of only part of the combined equity.

Note that, for the purpose of Criterion 4, the consideration should not include:

'(a)   an interest in a peripheral part of the business of the entity in which they were shareholders and which does not form part of the combined entity; or

(b)   the proceeds of the sale of such a business, or loan stock representing such proceeds.

A peripheral part of the business is one that can be disposed of without having a material effect on the nature and focus of the entity's operations.'

It should be apparent that Chigwell's purchase of the remainder of Tracy's share capital obeys the letter of the Companies Act and SSAP 23 rules, but is against the spirit of merger accounting. It is not clear when Chigwell acquired its original 25% holding in Tracy. If it was within the last two years and was for cash rather than equity shares, the combination would fail on criterion 4. The sale to a merchant bank and subsequent re-purchase of 20% of the original holding is clearly an attempt to circumvent the old rule on the minimum shareholding to be acquired (90%).

Criteria 1, 2 and 3 are concerned with whether the combination is in the spirit of an acquisition or a merger. The transaction would certainly fail on criterion 3 and probably on 1 and 2. Criterion 5 is less relevant.

It is apparent from the above that the combination of Chigwell and Tracy would not qualify as a merger; in fact it is exactly the kind of transaction that FRS 6 was intended to outlaw.

22   ENTERPRISE AND VULCAN

Step 1

Calculate the goodwill in the investment in Vulcan Ltd. This will be needed in order to calculate the 'Investment in associated undertakings' line on the balance sheet since goodwill is being amortised, and is not yet fully amortised.

Goodwill

	£'000	£'000
Cost of investment		2,000
Share capital	2,000	
Revaluation reserve	200	
Profit and loss reserve	900	
	3,100	
× 30%		(930)
		1,070

£1,070,000 ÷ 5 = 214,000 amortised per year
3 years amortised already £214,000 × = 642,000

Add this year's amortisation of £214,000:

£	
856,000	amortised to date
214,000	unamortised
1,070,000	total goodwill

Step 2

Complete the top half of the balance sheet including the 'Investments in associates' line as below, and insert the share capital of Enterprise plc.

	£'000
Investment in associate's net assets	
(30% × 7,940,000)	2,382
Unamortised goodwill (see Step 1))	214
	2,596

Step 3

Calculate the balance sheet reserves.

1   *Revaluation reserve*

		£'000	£'000
Enterprise plc			2,000
Vulcan Ltd:	at balance sheet	1,000	
	at acquisition	(200)	
		800	
	× 30%		240
			2,240

2   *Profit and loss reserve*

	£	£
Enterprise plc		5,100
Vulcan Ltd: at balance sheet	4,940	
at acquisition	(900)	
	4,040	
	× 30%	1,212
Less goodwill amortised to date (see Step 1)		(856)
		5,456

Step 4

Complete the consolidated P&L account up to the group operating profit line, and calculate the share of operating profit in the associate. Any adjustments to the P&L account for the amortisation of goodwill should be charged now to reduce this figure.

Share of operating profit in associate

	£'000
Operating profit × 30% (£2,120,000 × 30%)	636
Amortisation for the year (see task one)	(214)
	422

Step 5

Complete the balance sheet and profit and loss account.

ENTERPRISE PLC
CONSOLIDATED BALANCE SHEET AS AT 30 JUNE 19X8

	£'000	£'000
Fixed assets		
Tangible assets		8,000
Investments:		
Investments in associates		2,596
		10,596
Current assets		
Stock	1,340	
Debtors	1,000	
Cash	260	
	2,600	
Creditors (due within one year)	(1,500)	
Net current assets		1,100
		11,696

ENTERPRISE PLC GROUP
CONSOLIDATED PROFIT AND LOSS ACCOUNT
FOR THE YEAR ENDING 30 JUNE 19X8

	£'000	£'000
Group turnover		10,000
Cost of sales		(6,000)
Gross profit		4,000
Expenses		(1,500)
Group operating profit		2,500
Share of operating profit in associates	636	
Amortisation in associate	(214)	
		422
		2,922
Interest payable:		
Group		(100)
Associates (30% × 20,000)		(6)
Profit on ordinary activities before tax		2,816
*Tax on profit on ordinary activities**		(1,010)
Profit on ordinary activities after tax		1,806
Equity dividends		(600)
Retained profit for the group and its share of associates		1,206

* Tax relates to the following:

Parent and subsidiaries	£800,000
Associates (30% × £700,000)	£210,000

Note: As the share in the associates is equal to more than 25% of the group figure (before associates) for operating profit, additional disclosures required under FRS 9 would need to be given, if not specifically excluded from the question requirements.

23   CPP AND CCA

(a)   In accounting, the value of income and capital is measured in terms of money. In simple terms, profit is the difference between the closing and opening balance sheet values (after adjustment for new sources of funds and applications such as dividend distribution). If, because of inflation, the value of assets in the closing balance sheet is shown at a higher monetary amount than assets in the opening balance sheet, a profit has been made. In traditional accounting, it is assumed that a monetary unit of £1 is a stable measurement; inflation removes this stability.

CPP accounting attempts to provide a more satisfactory methods of valuing profit and capital by establishing a stable unit of monetary measurement, £1 of current purchasing power, as at the end of the accounting period under review.

A distinction is made between monetary items, and non-monetary items. In a period of inflation, keeping a monetary asset (eg debtors) results in a loss of purchasing power as the value of money erodes over time. Non-monetary assets, however, are assumed to maintain 'real' value over time, and these are converted into monetary units of current purchasing power as at the year end, by means of a suitable price index. The equity interest in the balance sheet can be determined as a balancing item.

The profit or deficit for the year in CPP terms is found by converting sales, opening and closing stock, purchases and other expenses into year-end units of £CPP. In addition, a profit on holding net monetary liabilities (or a loss on holding net monetary assets) is computed in arriving at the profit or deficit figure.

CPP arguably provides a more satisfactory system of accounting since transactions are expressed in terms of 'today's money' and similarly, the balance sheet values are adjusted for inflation, so as to give users of financial information a set of figures with which they can:

(i)   decide whether operating profits are satisfactory (profits due to inflation are eliminated); and

(ii)   obtain a better appreciation of the size and 'value' of the entity's assets.

(b)   CPP and CCA accounting are different concepts, in that CCP accounting makes adjustments for general inflationary price changes, whereas CCA makes adjustments to allow for specific price movements (changes in the deprival value of assets). Specific price changes (in CCA) enable a company to determine whether the operating capability of a company has been maintained; it is not a restatement of price levels in terms of a common unit of money measurement. The two conventions use different concepts of capital maintenance (namely operating capability with CCA, and general purchasing power with CPP).

In addition CPP is based on the use of a general price index. In contrast, CCA only makes use of a specific price index where it is not possible to obtain the current value of an asset by other means (eg direct valuation).

(c)   In CCA, holding gains represent the difference between the historical cost of an asset and its current cost. If the asset is unsold, and appears in the balance sheet of a company at current cost, there will be an 'unrealised' holding gain, which must be included in a current cost reserve. When the asset is eventually sold, the profit (equal to the sale price minus the historical cost) may be divided into:

(i)   an operating profit which would have been made if the cost of the asset were its current value; and

(ii)   a *realised* holding gain which has arisen because of the appreciation in value of the asset between the date of its acquisition and the date of its sale.

The handbook's method of CCA excludes realised holding gains from the calculation of current cost operating profit, and the implication is that realised holding gains should not be made available for distribution as a dividend, because to do so would result in a loss of 'business substance' or 'operating capability' by the business.

(d)   (i)   The cost of sales adjustment is the difference between the historical cost of goods sold and their current cost. In a CCA statement, the COSA is therefore used to adjust 'historical cost profit' towards 'current cost profit' by, in effect, changing the cost of sales from an historical cost to a current cost basis.

      (ii)   The COSA does not allow for the fact that purchased goods are acquired on credit and finished goods are likewise sold on credit. In a period of inflation, a company benefits from creditors (because payments are made at 'yesterday's prices') but loses with debtors, because a delay in the receipt of cash means that more money is required to purchase replacement assets (at 'tomorrow's prices') in order to maintain the operating capability of the business. The MWCA is therefore a charge, if the company has positive, rather than negative, monetary working capital (MWC defined roughly as debtors minus creditors) which takes account of the effect of deferred payments on business substance in arriving at the current cost operating profit.

      (iii)   The depreciation adjustment is the difference between the depreciation share based on the historical cost of fixed assets and the charge based on their current cost. In a CCA statement, the depreciation adjustment is therefore used to adjust 'historical cost profit' towards 'current cost operating profit' in order to reflect the current value of fixed assets 'consumed'.

      (iv)   The gearing adjustment is calculated after the current cost operating profit has been determined. A company is financed not only by share capital, but also by debt capital, which falls in 'real' value over time in a period of inflation. There is no need to maintain the operating capability of the business with respect to assets financed by debt capital. The more usual 'type 1' gearing adjustment is the amount of holding gains (ie a proportion of the three adjustments described in (i) to (iii) above) which is attributable to assets financed by debt capital rather than equity. These gains, because they will never be paid to the holders of debt capital, are 'free' to the equity shareholders, and the gearing adjustment is therefore added to the current cost operating profit in order to arrive at a value for 'current cost profit attributable to shareholders' of the company.

24   STATEMENT OF PRINCIPLES

The merits of the ASB's *Statement of Principles* should, ideally, be summarised in its objective, which is given in the *Foreword to Accounting Standards*:

> 'to provide a framework for the consistent and logical formulation of individual accounting standards (and to provide) a basis on which others can exercise judgement in resolving accounting issues.'

The following points may be made in favour of the *Statement of Principles.*

(a)   The principles have in fact been used in the formulation of standards, for example its definitions of assets and liabilities have been used in FRS 5 *Reporting the substance of transactions*.

(b)   The *Statement* helps reduce scope for individual judgement and the potential subjectivity that this implies.

(c)   Financial statements should be more comparable because, although alternative treatments will still be available, there will be a consistent and coherent framework on which to base one's choice of a particular alternative.

(d)   The *Statement* puts forward a consistent terminology and consistent objectives, for example in the definitions and the qualitative characteristics.

It could be argued that the *Statement of Principles* is too theoretical. It is certainly general rather than particular. However, as has been seen with FRS 5, the general principles can be applied to very specific issues in accounting standards. Moreover, in areas not at present covered by accounting standards, the statement can give general guidance. Nevertheless, in the short term, the principles in the *Statement* may conflict with some accounting standards which had already been issued before it was written.

25   XYZ

(a)   To: Managing director
       From: Company Secretary
       Date: 3 June 19X6
       Subject: *XYZ Group performance 19X5/X6*

In accordance with your instructions, I have prepared a report on the XYZ Group. The report is presented under the 'criteria for a healthy company' suggested by you. Appropriate ratios are listed in the appendix.

Asset base

The fixed assets are in each case covered by the shareholders' funds. The asset base of company X appears adequate, although substantial investments in intangible assets appear in the balance sheet. The freehold property is reported at cost and is therefore likely to be undervalued. Plant is on average half-way through its useful life. Company Y does not own its own property and rental agreements should be examined to check on security of tenure. Again plant is approximately half-way through its useful life. Company Z has a substantial asset base and its plant has been purchased fairly recently. However, the term of the lease appears to have almost expired and details of arrangement for renewal or replacement need to be investigated.

Control of working capital

There are unexpectedly large variations in the stock holding period, in view of the fact that all three companies are engaged in the same trade. The reason why Y and X, respectively, carry stocks for twice and three times the period of Z needs to be examined. Similarly the debt collection periods of X (14 weeks) and Y (19 weeks) appear excessive. Systems of stock and debtor control in companies X and Y require investigation.

Liquidity

All three companies are engaged in manufacturing. The current and liquid ratios of X appear adequate for this type of operation. The liquidity position of Y is weak, which may be the reason why it takes 14½ weeks to pay suppliers. Also the company has a large bank overdraft in relation to its scale of operations. The solvency ratios of Z appear excessive and, with suppliers representing 2½ weeks purchases, it does not seem as if maximum credit is being taken. The possibility of transferring resources from Z to Y should be explored.

Borrowing capacity

The gearing of both X and Y is high. At X, the amounts due to suppliers and providers of loan finance (£2,166,000) exceed the equity interest; at Y, there is a substantial balance of liabilities due within one year. In neither of these cases is a great deal of borrowing capacity apparent. Z has no borrowings, low creditors and cash at the bank; its borrowing capacity is therefore more promising.

Operating performance

Again there are substantial unexplained variations in performance. The net profit ratio of Z (18.4%) is well above the average for the group (10.3%). The negative net margin of Y requires careful investigation.

Commercial return for shareholders

The return on shareholders' funds earned by Z appears adequate, that of X is low while Y produces a negative return on the shareholders' investment.

Appendix: accounting ratios

Ratio	Calculation	X	Y	Z	Group
Stock turnover *	$\dfrac{\text{Closing stock}}{\text{Cost of goods sold}} \times 52$ (weeks)	18	11	$5^{1}/_{2}$	11
Debt collection *	$\dfrac{\text{Closing debtors}}{\text{Sales}} \times 52$ (weeks)	14	19	7	12
Payment of creditors	$\dfrac{\text{Creditors}}{\text{Cost of sales} **} \times 52$ (weeks)	$15^{1}/_{2}$	$14^{1}/_{2}$	$2^{1}/_{2}$	$9^{3}/_{4}$
Current ratio	$\dfrac{\text{Current assets}}{\text{Current liabilities}}$:1	2.5:1	1.1:1	6.4:1	2:1
Liquid ratio	$\dfrac{\text{Debtors + bank}}{\text{Current liabilities}}$:1	1.3:1	0.7:1	4:1	1.2:1
Gearing ratio	$\dfrac{\text{External finance}}{\text{Total finance}} \times 100$	50%	52%	4%	44%
Net profit ratio	$\dfrac{\text{Net profit } ***}{\text{Sales}} \times 100$	8.9%	(4%)	18.4%	10.3%
Return on capital employed	$\dfrac{\text{Net profit } **}{\text{Shareholders equity}} \times 100$	7.3%	(8.2%)	18.7%	14.7%

*   Closing balances used as insufficient data provided to calculate averages.

**   Cost of goods sold used as an approximation of purchases.

***   Net profit after interest and before tax.

(b)   *Items requiring further investigation*

Company X. Research and development of £180,000 needs to be investigated to check that the requirements of SSAP 13 are satisfied. According to this standard, and the Companies Act, research expenditure should be written off immediately it is incurred. Development expenditure may only be capitalised where stringent conditions are met, including the requirement for a clearly defined project where commercial viability is reasonably certain.

Freehold property, £300,000. SSAP 12 and the Companies Act require fixed assets to be written off either immediately or over its useful economic life. There is no evidence that this is being done.

Company Y. Customer prepayments of £106,000. The nature of this item should be investigated. Is the company able to supply the goods at the agreed price?

Company Z. Goodwill £200,000. SSAP 22 and the Companies Act require purchased goodwill to be written off either immediately or over its useful economic life. Non-purchased goodwill should not appear in the accounts. The accounting policy followed should be investigated to ensure compliance with these regulation.

Freehold property at valuation £800,000. Again a check needs to be made to ensure that the asset is being depreciated over its estimated useful life.

Extraordinary item £73,000. FRS 3 contains regulations regarding the treatment of rare, unusual items. Only extraordinary items may be reported 'below the line' and evidence must be produced to prove that this item has been properly classified.

(c)   A company may, legally, pay a dividend out of accumulated realised profits less accumulated realised losses. The available balance is £20,000 and so the company is clearly unable to make the proposed payment of £60,000. The capital redemption reserve is, for all purposes, to be treated as share capital, and is therefore not available to back the proposed payment. Apart from legal regulations, cash availability is the crucial practical constraint on proposals to pay a dividend. The company's bank overdraft of £172,000 suggest that even a dividend payment of £20,000 would be ill-advised at this stage.

Lecturers' question bank

Examination standard questions are indicated by the mark and time allocations.

1   HYDE, TANNING AND SKINNER (20 marks)   *36 mins*

Hyde, Tanning and Skinner had traded for a number of years as leather goods manufacturers in Clapham. The partnership agreement provided that profits and losses should be shared in the ratio 2:3:3. Furthermore, the rule in *Garner v Murray* was excluded. On 31 December 19X7 it was agreed that the partnership should be dissolved. A summary of the balance sheet at that date showed the following.

	£
Assets	
Furniture and fittings	1,000
Trade debtors	8,000
Stocks	35,000
Balance at bank	6,000
	50,000
Liabilities	
Trade creditors	10,000
	40,000

	£	£
Capital accounts		
Hyde	10,000	
Tanning	14,000	
Skinner	14,000	
		38,000
Current accounts		
Hyde	1,500	
Tanning	(1,500)	
Skinner	2,000	
		2,000
		40,000

Transactions during dissolution comprised the following.

		£
3 January 19X8	Purchase of annuity for retiring employee (cost to be borne by Skinner)	3,000
6 January 19X8	Furniture and fittings sold by auction for	400
7 January 19X8	Stocks with book value of £10,000 sold to In-Skin for cash	8,000
31 January 19X8	Paid trade creditors	10,000
	Trade debtors taken over by Hyde for an agreed sum of	6,000
	Paid realisation expenses	600
	Cash on hand distributed to partners in a manner whereby no partner would be required to repay any part of the distribution received.	

On 31 March 19X8 Tanning and Skinner took over the remaining assets of the partnership, including goodwill not yet raised in the books, merging with Teeter and Yodel of Kings Road to form a new partnership trading under the name of Cattlewash. The partners in the Kings Road firm had shared equally in capital profits and losses. The assets taken over by the new partnership were valued at amounts acceptable to all concerned, both for dissolution and amalgamation purposed as follows.

	Clapham business £	Kings Road business £
Stock	20,000	60,000
Furniture	-	3,000
Motor van	-	1,000
Goodwill	4,800	20,000

The partnership agreement of Cattlewash directs that profits and losses should be shared as to: Tanning 10%; Skinner 15%, Teeter 35% and Yodel 40%. Capital was to be contributed in the same proportions, and was to amount in aggregate to assure sufficient to reflect the values attributable to the acquired assets and, in addition, to provide £8,000 for working capital. Goodwill was not to appear in the books of the firm.

Required

(a)   Prepare:

    (i)   the realisation account;
    (ii)   the bank account;
    (iii)   the capital accounts;

    in sufficient detail to show the piecemeal dissolution of the Clapham firm (balancing on 31 January 19X8).   (10 marks)

(b)   Prepare the capital accounts and a summary balance sheet of Cattlewash as at 31 March 19X8.   (10 marks)

Ignore taxation.

2   ALAMEIN (30 marks) *54 mins*

Alamein plc has decided to reorganise its capital structure. The company's summarised draft balance sheet as at 31 December 19X5 is as follows.

	£	£	£
Fixed assets			
Freehold property, at cost		81,000	
Less depreciation		16,000	
			65,000
Plant and machinery at cost		550,000	
Less depreciation		290,000	
			260,000
			325,000
Current assets			
Stocks		360,000	
Debtors		245,000	
Cash at bank		20,000	
		625,000	
Creditors: amounts falling due within one year			
Trade creditors		146,000	
Taxation		104,000	
Proposed dividend		40,000	
		290,000	
Net current assets			335,000
			660,000
Capital and reserves			
Called up share capital			
Authorised, allotted and fully paid			
800,000 ordinary shares of £0.25 each			200,000
150,000 9% redeemable preference shares			
(redeemable at a premium of £0.10 per share)			150,000
			350,000
Reserves			
Share premium		20,000	
Retained profits			
Balance at 31 December 19X4	220,000		
Transfer from profit and loss account	70,000		
Balance at 31 December 19X5		290,000	
			310,000
			660,000

There was no change in the share premium account during the year.

On 31 December 19X5 various resolutions were passed.

(a)   A bonus issue of one ordinary share for every two ordinary shares held by the existing shareholders is to be made from retained profits (these bonus shares will not rank for dividend out of the 19X5 profits).

(b)   A rights issue of one ordinary share for every three shares held (after the bonus issue) is to be made at a price of £0.31 a share. These shares will rank for the 20% dividend out of the 19X5 profits. The purpose of the rights issue is to provide part of the finance for the redemption of the preference shares.

(c)   The preference shares, which had originally been issued at a premium of 4p each are to be redeemed.

(d)   An £80,000 12% debenture will be issued at a price of 95 (ie £95 per £100 nominal value).

These transactions (including payments and receipts) were duly carried into effect and completed on 31 December 19X5.

From the information given you are required to prepare:

(a)   the ledger accounts necessary to record the closing transactions and adjustments set out above, making the maximum use of existing reserves;

(b)   the balance sheet immediately after giving effect to these adjustments;

(c)   a schedule showing the movement on reserves.

Taxation is to be ignored.

---

3   FARGO (25 marks)   *45 mins*

(a)   Fargo Ltd makes sausages. It makes up its financial statements to 30 June each year, and its policy is to revalue its fixed assets every other year. It does not charge depreciation in the year of sale of an asset. The company wishes to maximise distributable profit and to comply with the requirements of FRS 3 *Reporting financial performance*.

The following details relate to a sausage machine purchased on 1 July 19X2 for £64,000.

(i)   The machine is depreciated using the reducing balance method at 25% per annum.

(ii)   The machine was revalued on 30 June 19X4 to £45,000. Its remaining useful economic life was revised to five years. In addition, the method of depreciation was changed to the straight line method.

(iii)   On 30 June 19X6 the asset was revalued to £15,000. This was believed to be a permanent diminution in value. The method of depreciation and the useful economic life remained the same.

(iv)   The asset was sold for £17,000 on 1 October 19X6.

Required

Show, where appropriate, how the events described above would affect the following items in the financial statements for the five accounting periods from 1 July 19X2 to 30 June 19X7.

(i)   The profit and loss account for the year
(ii)   The brought forward profit and loss reserve in the balance sheet
(iv)   The revaluation reserve
(v)   The statement of total recognised gains and losses   (9 marks)

(b)   'FRS 3 *Reporting financial performance* changed the character of financial reporting.'

What were the five important changes introduced by FRS 3?   (5 marks)

(c)   'For an item to be recognised in the financial statements, certain criteria must apply. Once an item is recognised various factors must be considered in determining whether the item appears in the profit and loss account or the statement of total recognised gains and losses.'

Discuss.   (8 marks)

(d)   What rules are laid down in FRS 3 for calculating the profit or loss on the disposal of a fixed asset? Why does FRS 3 specify this method?   (3 marks)

---

4   LA GROUP (30 marks)   *54 mins*

(a)   On 1 October 19X1 LA plc acquired 60% of the issued share capital of TS plc, at a cost of £2.90 per share.

The trial balances of the two companies at 30 September 19X2 (their accounting year end) are as follows.

	LA plc	TS plc
	£	£
Debit balances		
Fixed assets at cost	450,000	100,000
Debtors	126,000	110,000
Shares in TS plc at cost	62,640	-
Stock and work in progress	96,000	57,000
Cost of sales	988,000	500,000
Current account with TS plc	28,400	-
Distribution costs	108,000	47,000
Administration expenses	72,000	33,000
Cash in hand	2,360	2,400
Cash at bank	42,000	26,000
	1,975,400	875,400
Credit balances		
Ordinary shares of £1 each, fully paid	180,000	36,000
General reserve balance at 1 October 19X1	234,000	54,700
Profit and loss balance at 1 October 19X1	68,400	23,400
Current account with LA plc	-	27,200
Sales	1,318,000	659,000
Provision for depreciation at 1 October 19X1	67,000	32,400
Creditors	108,000	42,700
	1,975,400	875,400

(i)   TS plc's purchases include £36,000 of goods which were brought from LA plc. This stock was transferred at cost plus a mark-up of 20%. On 30 September 19X2 the stock of TS plc included £6,000 of these goods, at transfer price.

(ii)   On 29 September 19X2 TS plc had sent a cheque for £1,200 to LA plc; this was not received by LA plc until 3 October 19X2.

(iii) Depreciation for the year is to be charged as follows.

LA plc	£23,000
TS plc	£10,000

(iv)   Dividends proposed are as follows.

LA plc	£18,000
TS plc	£13,000

(v)   Corporation tax on profits for the year are to be provided as follows.

LA plc	£55,000
TS plc	£35,000

(vi)   LA plc and TS plc have not made any issues or redemptions of shares during the year.

(vii) LA plc has not yet made any necessary adjustment for goodwill or capital reserve on acquisition arising from its acquisition of shares in TS plc. This goodwill is deemed to have an indefinite useful life and therefore is to remain on the balance sheet.

Note. ACT is to be ignored.

You are required to prepare for the LA Group the consolidated profit and loss account for the year ended 30 September 19X2 and a balance sheet at that date.   (24 marks)

(b)   In (a) above the shares in the subsidiary were acquired at the beginning of the financial year. If the acquisition had taken place part way through the year it would have affected the preparation of the consolidated profit and loss account and balance sheet.

You are required to state how the final accounts which you have prepared in answer to (a) above would have been different. Give reasons for the differences.

Note. Figures are not required.   (6 marks)

5   **STRIDER (25 marks)**   *45 mins*

From the information given below you are required to interpret the results of Strider Ltd. Your comments should, where possible, be supported by ratios and grouped under suitable 'user' groups (eg management, shareholders, creditors and employees).

Information extracted from the accounts of Strider Ltd (not in CA 1985 format)

Year	19X6	19X7	19X8	19X9
	£'000	£'000	£'000	£'000
Sales	374,000	408,000	442,000	476,000
Profit before tax	47,600	55,400	55,000	65,360
After charging:				
Directors' emoluments	950	950	1,000	1,100
Depreciation	29,100	23,980	19,984	16,607
After crediting:				
Gross dividends	3,400	7,100	9,500	13,600
Profit on sale of plant	-	-	-	10,000
Taxation on profits	22,000	26,000	28,000	30,000
Taxation on dividends received	1,020	2,130	2,850	4,080
Profit after tax	24,580	27,270	24,150	31,280
Purchases of materials and services	239,992	283,190	309,342	327,499
Employees' remuneration	93,500	104,800	116,200	123,000
Number of employees	27,200	30,600	34,000	37,000

	19X6	19X7	19X8	19X9
	£'000	£'000	£'000	£'000
Assets employed				
Leasehold premises at cost	35,000	35,000	35,000	35,000
Depreciation	(7,000)	(10,500)	(14,000)	(17,500)
Plant and machinery at cost	160,000	160,000	160,000	120,000
Depreciation	(57,600)	(78,080)	(94,464)	(80,678)
Investments at cost	34,000	70,000	80,000	115,000
Total fixed assets	164,400	176,420	166,536	171,822
Current assets				
Stock	81,940	94,860	111,500	125,200
Debtors	62,330	76,120	91,540	106,900
Cash	31,790	26,000	17,800	2,000
Total	176,060	196,980	220,840	234,100
Current liabilities				
Trade creditors	48,460	65,930	77,956	85,222
Current tax	17,000	25,200	27,000	31,000
Proposed dividends	20,000	24,000	24,000	30,000
Total	85,460	115,130	128,956	146,222
Net current assets	90,600	81,850	91,884	87,878
Net assets employed	255,000	258,270	258,420	259,700
Capital				
Ordinary share capital	200,000	200,000	200,000	220,000
Reserves	55,000	58,270	58,420	39,700
Equity capital employed	255,000	258,270	258,420	259,700

You may assume that prices have remained stable over the four year period; advance corporation tax on the proposed dividends has been ignored. All sales are zero rated for value added tax. Stock at the end of 19X5 may be taken as equal to that at the end of 19X6.

List of key terms
and index

622

These are the terms which we have identified throughout the text as being KEY TERMS. You should make sure that you can define what these terms mean; go back to the pages highlighted here if you need to check.

List of key terms

Recoverable amount, 366
Residual value, 169

Useful economic life, 169

Value in use, 366

ORDER FORM

To order your ACCA books, you can phone us on 0181 740 2211, email us at publishing@bpp.co.uk, fax this form to 0181 740 1184 or cut this form out and post it to the address below.

To: BPP Publishing Ltd, Aldine House, Aldine Place,
London W12 8AW

Tel: 0181-740 2211
Fax: 0181-740 1184

Forenames (Mr / Ms): _____   Surname:_____

Daytime delivery address: _____

_____

Post code: _____   Date of exam (month/year):_____

Please send me the following books:

	Price 6/98 Text £	Price 1/98 Kit £	Price 1/98 Passcards £	Quantity Text	Quantity Kit	Quantity Passcards	Total £
Foundation							
The Accounting Framework	18.95	8.95	4.95	....	....	....	....
The Accounting Framework (Int'l)	18.95	8.95★		....	....		....
The Legal Framework	18.95	8.95	4.95	....	....	....	....
Management Information	18.95	8.95	4.95	....	....	....	....
The Organisational Framework	18.95	8.95	4.95	....	....	....	....
Certificate							
Information Analysis	18.95	8.95	4.95	....	....	....	....
The Audit Framework	18.95	8.95	4.95	....	....	....	....
The Audit Framework (Int'l)	18.95	8.95★		....	....		....
The Tax Framework FA 98 (7/98 Text, 8/98 P/c, 8/98 Kit)	18.95	8.95	4.95	....	....	....	....
Managerial Finance	18.95	8.95	4.95	....	....	....	....
Professional							
Information for Control and Decision Making	19.95	9.95	5.95	....	....	....	....
Accounting and Audit Practice A: Accounting	15.95	9.95	5.95	....	....	....	....
Accounting and Audit Practice A: Accounting (Int'l)	15.95	9.95★		....	....		....
Accounting and Audit Practice B: Auditing	13.95			....			....
Accounting and Audit Practice B: Auditing (Int'l)	13.95			....			....
(Kit and Passcards cover both accounting and auditing)							
Tax Planning FA 98 (7/98 Text, 8/98 P/c, 8/98 Kit)	19.95	9.95	5.95	....	....	....	....
Management and Strategy	19.95	9.95	5.95	....	....	....	....
Financial Reporting Environment	19.95	9.95	5.95	....	....	....	....
Financial Reporting Environment (Int'l)	19.95	9.95★		....	....		....
Financial Strategy	19.95	9.95	5.95	....	....	....	....

Postage and packaging:

		Text	Kit	Passcards	£
UK:	Texts £3.00 for first plus £2.00 for each extra	....	....	....	....
	Kits and Passcards £2.00 for first plus £1.00 for each extra	....	....	....	....
Europe (inc ROI & CI):	Texts £5.00 for first plus £4.00 for each extra	....	....	....	....
	Kits and Passcards £2.50 for first plus £1.00 for each extra	....	....	....	....
Rest of the World:	Texts £20.00 for first plus £10.00 for each extra	....	....	....	....
	Kits and Passcards £15.00 for first plus £8.00 for each extra	....	....	....	....

(Single Kits/Passcards are airmailed. All other parcels are sent by courier and should arrive in not more than six days.)

★ International Stream Kits will be published in Autumn 1998   Total _____

I enclose a cheque for £ _____ or charge to Access/Visa/Switch

Card number [ ][ ][ ][ ][ ][ ][ ][ ][ ][ ][ ][ ][ ][ ][ ][ ][ ][ ][ ]

Start date (Switch only) _____   **Expiry date** _____   **Issue no. (Switch only)**___

Signature _____

REVIEW FORM & FREE PRIZE DRAW

All original review forms from the entire BPP range, completed with genuine comments, will be entered into one of two draws on 31 January 1999 and 31 July 1999. The names on the first four forms picked out on each occasion will be sent a cheque for £50.

Name: _____   Address: _____

_____

_____

How have you used this Text?
(Tick one box only)

☐ Home study (book only)

☐ On a course: college _____

☐ With 'correspondence' package

☐ Other _____

Why did you decide to purchase this Text?
(Tick one box only)

☐ Have used BPP Texts in the past

☐ Recommendation by friend/colleague

☐ Recommendation by a lecturer at college

☐ Saw advertising

☐ Other _____

During the past six months do you recall seeing/receiving any of the following?
(Tick as many boxes as are relevant)

☐ Our advertisement in *Students' Newsletter*

☐ Our advertisement in *Pass*

☐ Our brochure with a letter through the post

Which (if any) aspects of our advertising do you find useful?
(Tick as many boxes as are relevant)

☐ Prices and publication dates of new editions

☐ Information on Text content

☐ Facility to order books off-the-page

☐ None of the above

Your ratings, comments and suggestions would be appreciated on the following areas

	Very useful	Useful	Not useful
Introductory section (Key study steps, personal study plan etc)	☐	☐	☐
Chapter introductions	☐	☐	☐
Key terms	☐	☐	☐
Explanations	☐	☐	☐
Case examples and examples	☐	☐	☐
Questions and answers	☐	☐	☐
Chapter roundups	☐	☐	☐
Quick quizzes	☐	☐	☐
Exam focus points	☐	☐	☐
Exam question bank	☐	☐	☐
Exam answer bank	☐	☐	☐
List of key terms and index	☐	☐	☐
Icons	☐	☐	☐

	Excellent	Good	Adequate	Poor
Overall opinion of this Text	☐	☐	☐	☐

Do you intend to continue using BPP Study Texts/Kits?   ☐ Yes   ☐ No

Please note any further comments and suggestions/errors on the reverse of this page.

Please return to: Edmund Hewson, BPP Publishing Ltd, FREEPOST, London, W12 8BR

REVIEW FORM & FREE PRIZE DRAW (continued)

Please note any further comments and suggestions/errors below

FREE PRIZE DRAW RULES

1   Closing date for 31 January 1999 draw is 31 December 1998. Closing date for 31 July 1999 draw is 30 June 1999.

2   Restricted to entries with UK and Eire addresses only. BPP employees, their families and business associates are excluded.

3   No purchase necessary. Entry forms are available upon request from BPP Publishing. No more than one entry per title, per person. Draw restricted to persons aged 16 and over.

4   Winners will be notified by post and receive their cheques not later than 6 weeks after the relevant draw date. Lists of winners will be published in BPP's *focus* newsletter following the relevant draw.

5   The decision of the promoter in all matters is final and binding. No correspondence will be entered into.